HOW TO cheat IN Motion

HOW TO cheat IN Motion

Patrick Sheffield

AMSTERDAM • BOSTON • HEIDELBERG • LONDON
NEW YORK • OXFORD • PARIS • SAN DIEGO
SAN FRANCISCO • SINGAPORE • SYDNEY • TOKYO
Focal Press is an imprint of Elsevier

Focal Press is an imprint of Elsevier
30 Corporate Drive, Suite 400, Burlington, MA 01803, USA
Linacre House, Jordan Hill, Oxford OX2 8DP, UK

Library of Congress Cataloging-in-Publication Data
Sheffield, Patrick.
How to cheat in Motion / Patrick Sheffield.
p. cm.
Includes index.
ISBN 978-0-240-81097-3 (pbk.: alk. paper) 1. Computer animation. 2. Computer graphics. 3. Motion (Electronic resource) 4. Macintosh (Computer)–Programming. I. Title.
TR897.7.S3897 2010
006.6'96–dc22

2009038370

British Library Cataloguing-in-Publication Data
A catalogue record for this book is available from the British Library.

ISBN: 978-0-240-81097-3

For information on all Focal Press publications
visit our website at www.elsevierdirect.com

09 10 11 12 13 5 4 3 2 1

Printed in the United States of America

Contents

Contents

What is this book?

The goal of *How to Cheat in Motion* is to provide a "cookbook" style of learning, presenting the user with specific recipes to achieve desirable outcomes. A cookbook is essentially "How to Cheat at Cooking". You don't have to be a master chef, just follow the recipe and you'll come out with a great result.

Much like a cookbook doesn't seek to educate the reader on the complex chemistries involved in making a meringue, this book doesn't delve into a lot of theory. That is not to say that it is strictly paint by number, but that explanations are provided in a manner that allows the reader to ignore them and still come out with a working project.

I concentrate on the projects which are, like recipes, essentially a listing of ingredients, order of combination, how long to bake, etc. I don't spend a lot of time hand holding–I'll tell you to grab something from Library/Generators, I'm not going to tell you where to find the Library. In other words, I'll tell you to add 2½ cups of flour–I won't tell you what flour is or how to open the bag.

This book is structured around projects which are presented here as small "bite-sized" undertakings covering a few pages. They are single dishes, not meals. However, they may be used as "snap-together" concepts, allowing the reader to build them into more complex projects to suit their needs.

And just as your average home cook will, upon becoming familiar with their recipes, add to and expand them, it is hoped that the Motion user, after doing the projects in this book, will come to a better understanding of Motion and make these projects their own.

One way this book differs from a cookbook is that the Motion user interface is far more complex than any given pile of cooking ingredients. Multiple groups/layers/filters/behaviors/etc. are much more difficult to describe than "Add 2 eggs." I have attempted to evolve a standard, albeit of necessity terse, nomenclature to reduce the chance of errors. If there are any questions as to what is being referred to in the text, consult the accompanying picture. As a friend used to say when editing a scene, “This ain’t radio.” In other words, the images and their framing have been chosen to aid the reader. Don’t try to go it on the written instructions alone.

I should note that unless otherwise specified, all the projects in this book are 720×486, standard definition NTSC dimensions. If you are using different project sizes, you may need to alter the values for some of the parameters specified.

Also, while the bullk of the projects in this book were designed in Motion 3, some are specific to Motion 4. This is noted in the project introduction. You will find final versions of all projects that have a disc icon in the right-hand sidebar on the companion disc. Sometimes additional variations on the project are included on the disc.

All images and clips included on the companion disc are only licensed for inclusion on the disc. They may not be re-distributed or re-used.

By no means is this book an alpha and omega of Motion instruction. While it has been over a year in the making (much to my publisher’s chagrin), there are projects that I’ve had to leave out for lack of time. I’m reminded of my days as a software engineer.

Management, driven by market forces, had a tendency to want to release a project as soon as it was anywhere past the concept stage, untested, lacking features, and full of bugs. This meant that, left to themselves, they’d release perfect junk.

Engineers, on the other hand, would work forever, refining, removing bugs, adding features, not wanting to let go until the project was finished and free of flaws. This meant they would release perfect nothing. It was this tug-of-war between perfect junk and perfect nothing that always led to an imperfect but usable *something* that was released.

I’ve done my best to ensure that this book you now hold in your hands is that healthy compromise—that *usable something*—that enlightens, entertains, and advances your knowledge and abilities.

Now get started!

Patrick Sheffield
North Hollywood, 2009

Acknowledgments

This book is dedicated to my father, Daniel Sheffield, who taught me this basic truth: *Complexity is merely Simplicity put together.* It may sound a bit silly, but I assure you it's been the basis for my learning ever since. Whenever a problem or a task or a concept seemed too complex to comprehend or complete, I would fall back on this. Break it down. Once the pieces are small enough to understand or master, march through all the pieces and you'll arrive at a solution.

I'd also like to thank my family: my wife, Chris; son, Reilly; and daughter, Parker, for putting up with the many many hours it's taken me to complete this book. Most of those hours were borrowed from time at home when I probably should have been doing something else.

Thank you too, to Matt Mahurin, best friend from high school onward. Without him I'd never have gotten started in this crazy business. He's helped me pull off a few other stunts as well.

And thanks to my friends from the online community at the Apple pro-video discussions: Travis Ballstadt, Peter Barrett, David Bogie, Nelson Brann, Jon Chappell, Brian Conner, Jim Cookman, Neil Ghoshal, Doug Gilmore, Michael Grenadier, David Harbsmeier, Michael Hoffman, Jerry Hofmann, Randy Holder, Nick Holmes, Tom Meegan, Andy Mees, Mike Mench, Shane Ross, David Saraceno, Adam Scoffield, David Slater, Craig Somerer, specialcase, Mark Spencer, and others too numerous to mention. I hope your heads aren't dented from my bouncing ideas off them.

Thanks also to Apple and their great group of engineers and tech-heads who make the fantastic software and hardware that make my job possible. Especially thouse in the Motion group.

Finally, thanks Mom! If it weren't for you, I wouldn't be anywhere.

Between the content bundled with Final Cut Studio and what you can easily build on your own, you should never want for a unique stylish backdrop, text fill, lower third, or animated graphics overlay.

1

Background Activity

BACKGROUNDS AND FILLS ARE IN CONSTANT DEMAND in any motion graphics production environment.

This chapter will tell you how to take advantage of the power of Motion to fashion new and stylish backdrops.

1 Background Activity

Simple Animated Grid

WHETHER FOR A BACKGROUND, a fill, or an overlay, this simple animated grid is a handy graphic element to add to your palette. Above, I've combined it with the World Back background from LiveType.

Recently, I used this to add some "sizzle" to mundane presentation graphics.

We'll be getting our animation from the a customized Cellular generator fed through the pixilate filter and overlaid with the Grid generator.

I should mention that most of the projects in this book, unless otherwise mentioned, are standard def—720x486.

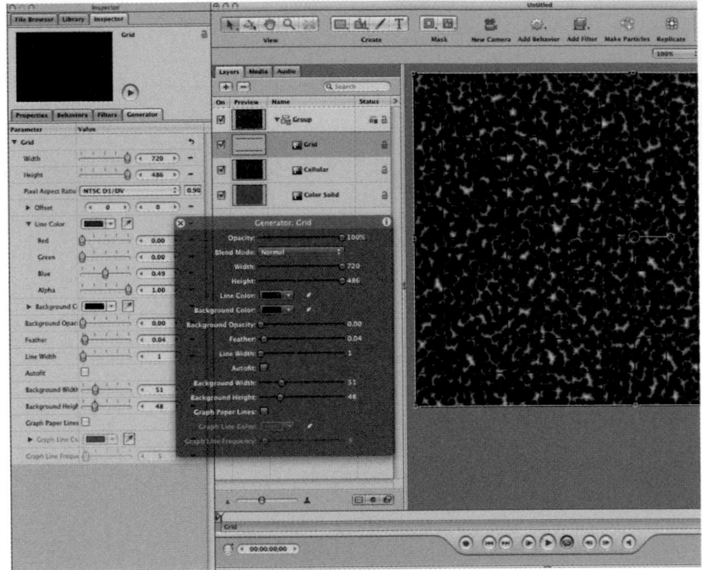

1 In a new project, name the default group **Generators**. Add the **Color Solid** generator. On top of that, add the **Cellular** generator and the **Grid** generator. Set the **Grid's Background Opacity** to **0**, the **Line Color** to a dark blue, the **Feather** to **.04**, the **Line Width** to **1**, the **Background Width** to **51**, and the **Background Height** to **48**.

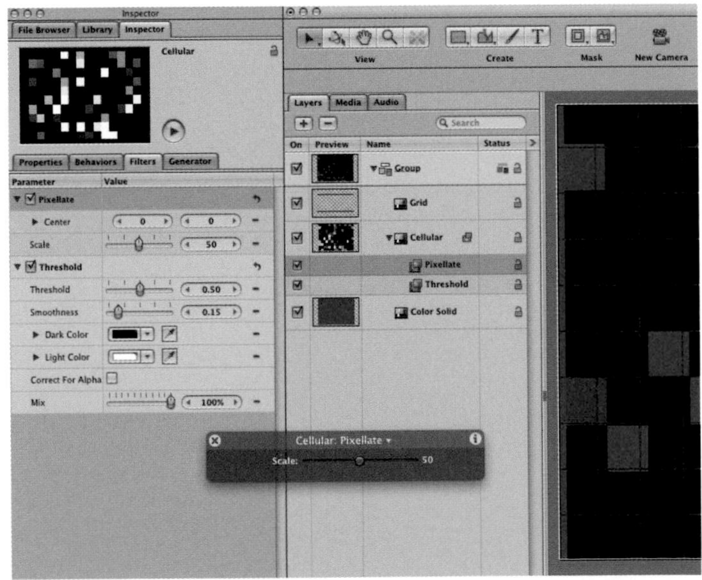

3 **Add Filter/Color Correction/Threshold**, then **Add Filter/Stylize/Pixilate**, set the **Scale** to **50**. You'll notice the squares almost line up with the grid. We'll fix that with the next step.

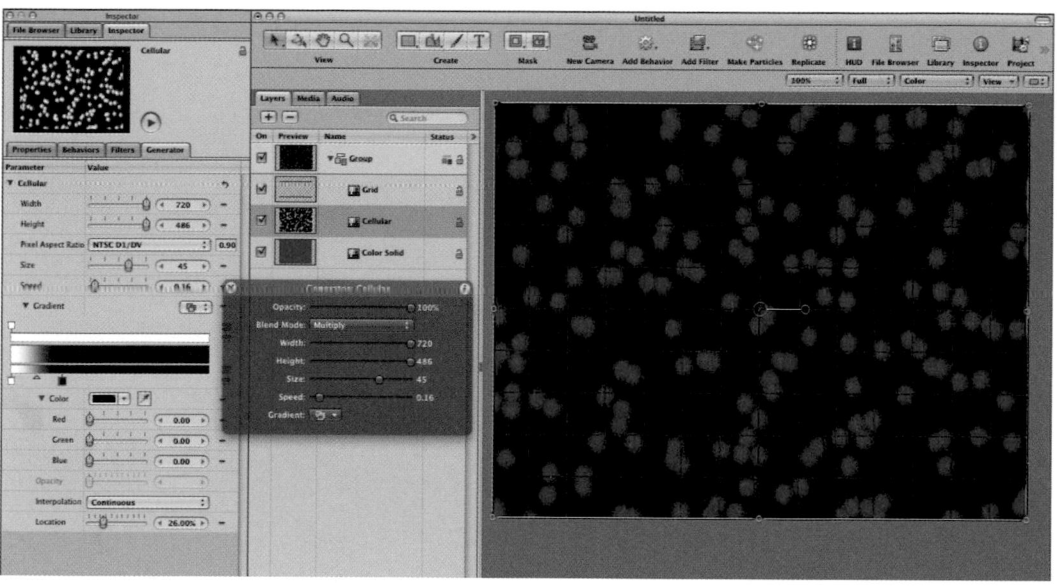

2 Now set the **Cellular** generator's **Size** to **45**, Speed to **0.16**, and invert the gradient; then slide the black of the gradient down to about **26**. Set the **Blend Mode to Multiply**. You should see a bunch of small blue dots.

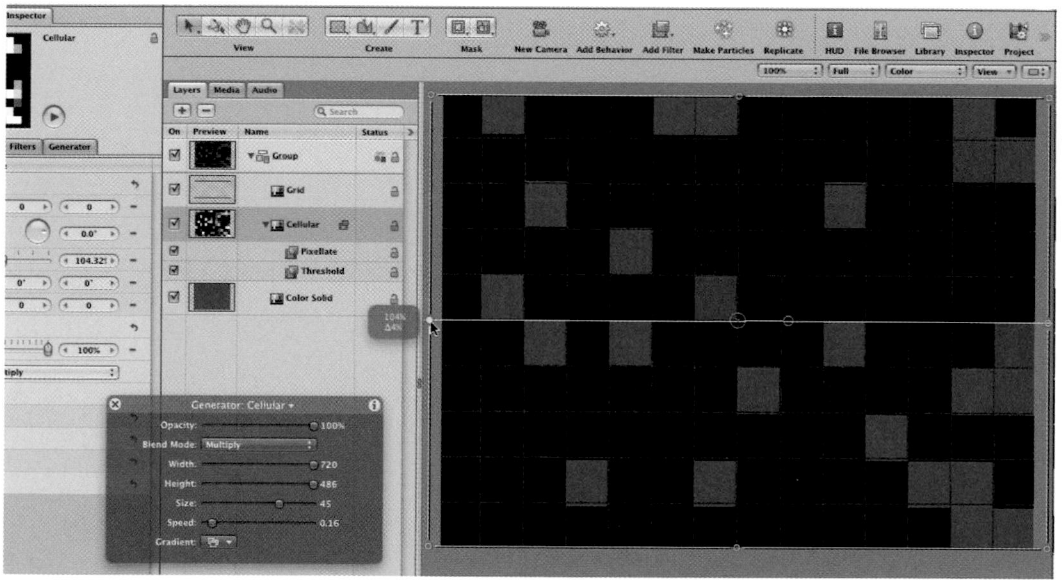

4 Click on the **Cellular** generator (make sure the *Show Overlays* is turned on, ⌘/). Grab the side handle and hold down the option key ⌥ (this will cause the size change to happen on both sides). Pull out until the squares line up horizontally, about **104%**. Do the same for the top handle: squeeze it down to about **98%**.

HOT TIP

The ⌘ key temporarily turns off snappng.

Free Fun Stuff!

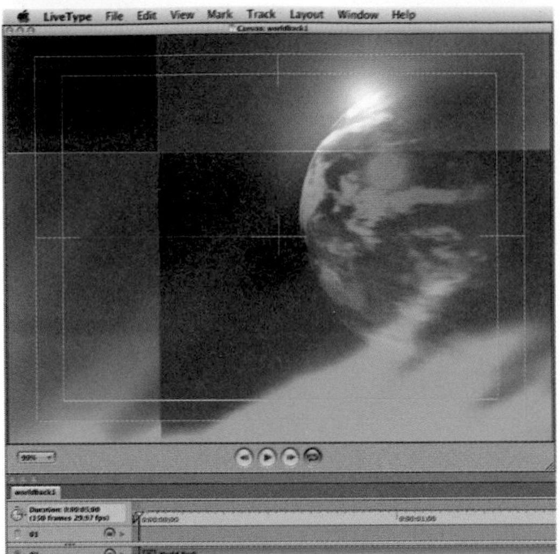

I USED TO USE LiveType a lot before Motion came along. It's a very powerful yet simple program. After I started using Motion, LiveType fell into disuse. A friend recently told me how much fun he was having using LiveType doing the menus and backgrounds for his DVDs and I thought I'd take a look again at LiveType—especially now that it's 2.0—and I realized something.

LiveType is a great enhancer to Motion. Just open LiveType (if you've got Final Cut Studio 1 or 2, you've got it—Apple dropped LiveType for FCS 3). Now go to the Textures tab of the media browser. There are hundreds of fantastic, professionally designed textures that make great backgrounds, lower thirds, font/graphic fills, right there—ripe for the plucking. And they're looping.

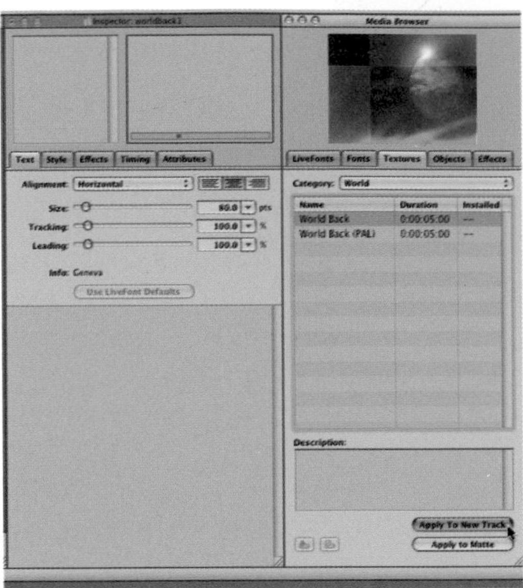

1 Open LiveType, click on the Textures tab. Pick a backdrop—say, **World Back** from the **World Category.** Click on **Apply to New Track.**

4 Save your project to your new My LiveType Textures directory (or wherever you want). And because these are just pointers into the LiveType media, they only take up 4k on disk. While you're at it, save a bunch. When you're done you'll have a whole directory full of cool .ipr files.

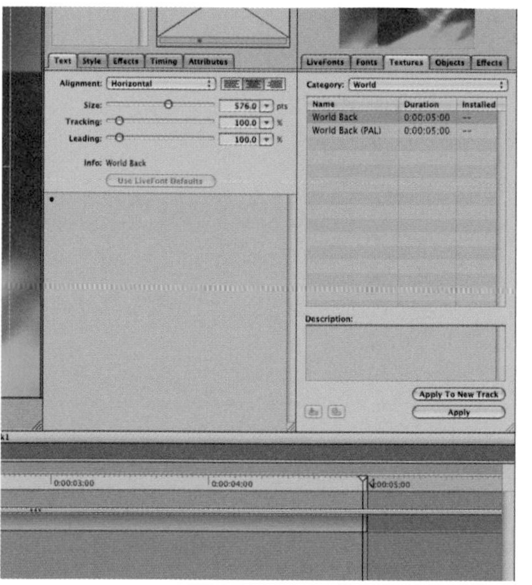

2 Set your outpoint to the duration of the texture (in this case **5:00**).

3 Now the crucial bit. Use the **Edit/Project Properties** menu or ⌘O. Go to the "Background" section, set the opacity to 100, and click the Render Background.

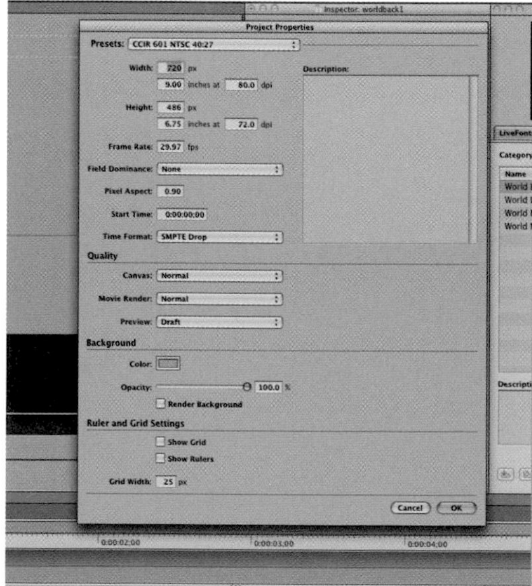

5 Objects are a little different. Because they have alpha channels, you shouldn't set the Render Background setting.

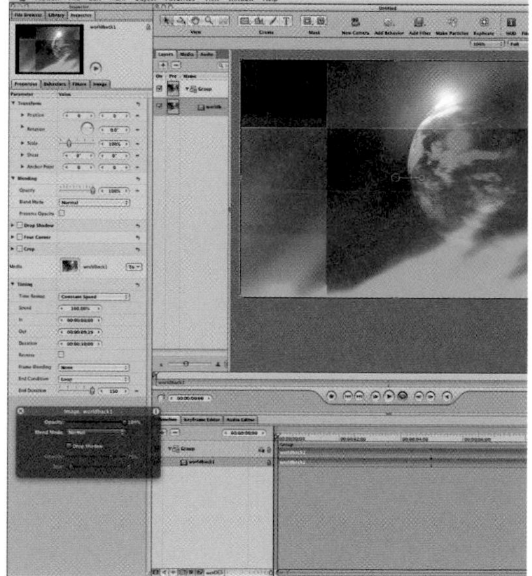

6 Because of the wonderful ProApp integration, they just load into Motion like Quicktime files. And because they're like media, you can set their end condition flag to be loop (in their Properties tab under Timing) and stretch them to be however long you need in Motion.

Light Grid

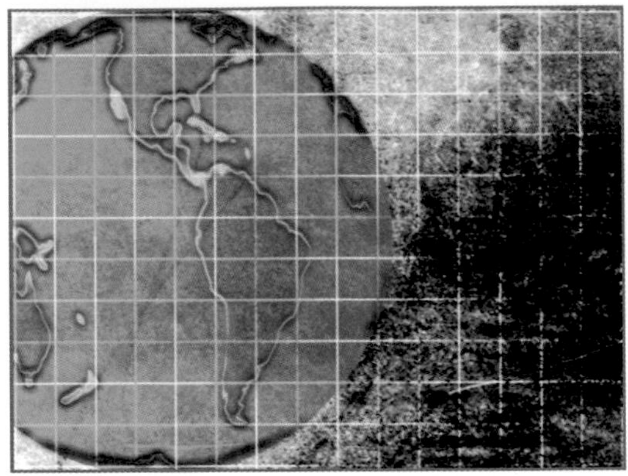

COMBINED WITH SOME ELEMENTS from the Contents folder, you can make a pretty snazzy animated backdrop.

In this, we'll be using the color cycle animation technique (see the Animation chapter for more details), a clone layer, and a pair of replicators to construct an animated grid.

The Color Cycle animation technique is a handy, low overhead way to add animation to your project—it scales well and thus lends itself to be used with replication.

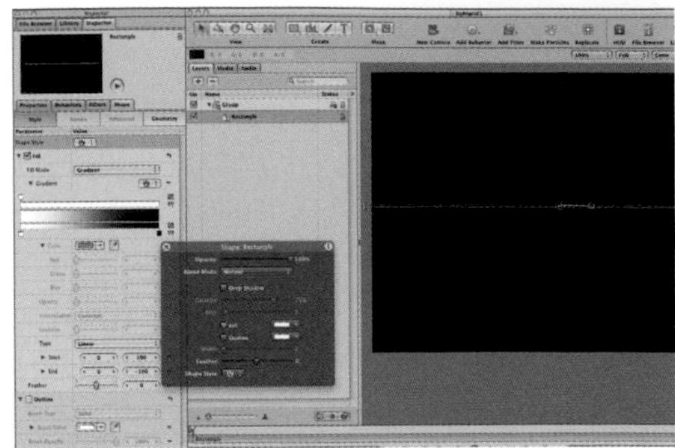

1 First, press **R** to select the **Rectangle** tool. Use it to create a thin rectangle, a little bit wider than the screen. Set the fill type to be **Gradient** and the gradient to be Grayscale.

4 Now set the wave shape to **Sawtooth**, the **Amplitude** to **360**, and the **Speed** to **24**. Click on the Keyframe Editor to see what's going on.

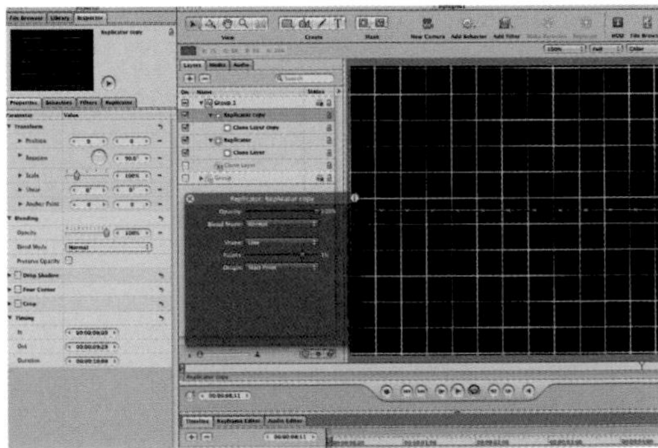

7 Duplicate your replicator (⌘D) and set it at 90 degrees to the first replicator. Then change the points to 16 (4:3 aspect ratio). Using the **Adjust Item** tool, drag the replicator to the full width of the screen. You can use this light grid just the way it is, or continue on for extra credit.

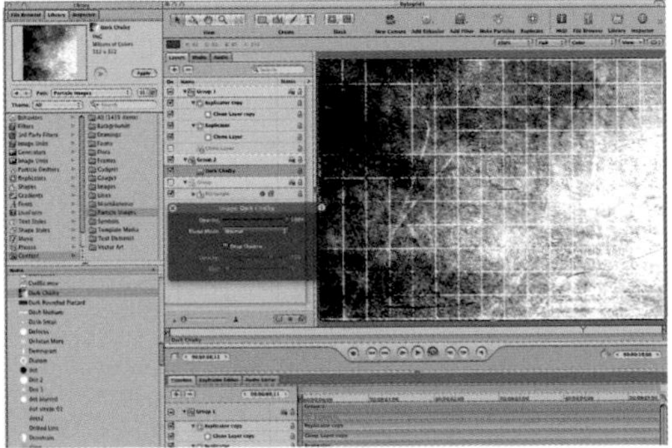

8 Change the blend mode of our grid (**Group 1**) to **Color Dodge** and add another group below it. Dip into the **Library/Content/Particle Images/** folder and pull out **Dark Chalky.** Put in our new layer. Grab the side handle, and holding the ⌥ key, pull it out full width (about 128% on X scale).

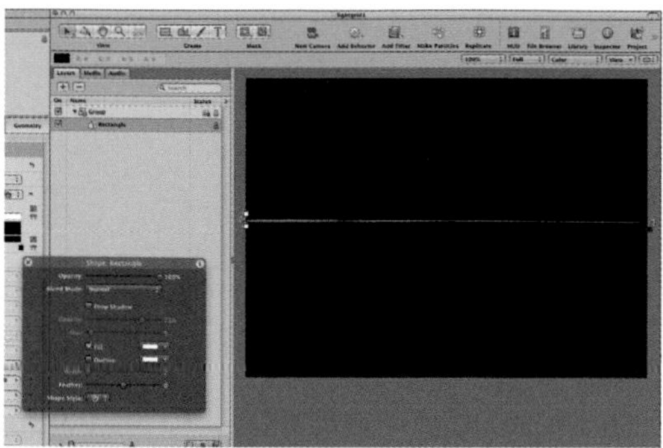

2 Select the **Adjust Item** tool to edit the gradient. Turn it so the black is on one end of our narrow rectangle and white is on the other.

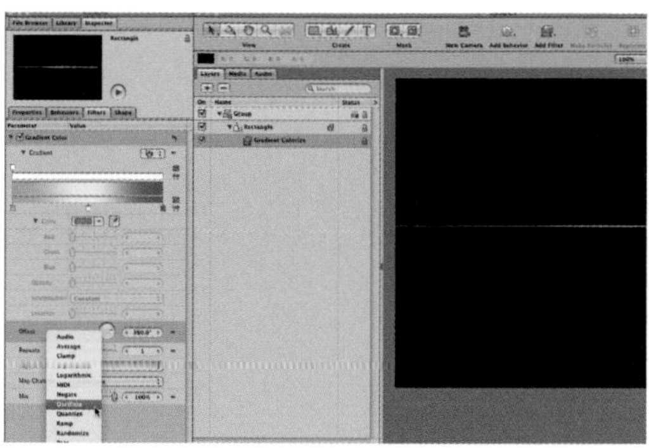

3 Add **Filter/Color Correction/Gradient Colorize** and Set the Filter's Gradient to **Blue Chrome**. Set the **Offset** to **360**, then Right/ctrl-click on the **Offset** and add an **Oscillate** behavior.

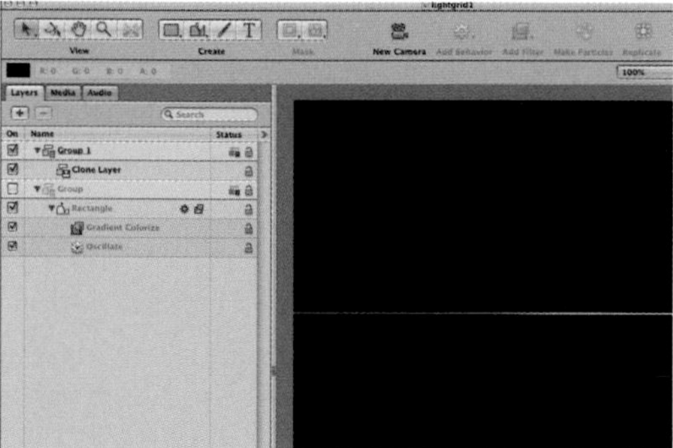

5 Press play and you should see the yellow color slide across your narrow rectangle. Press stop and position the playhead at the beginning of the timeline. Click on Group and press K to create a clone layer, and then turn off Group.

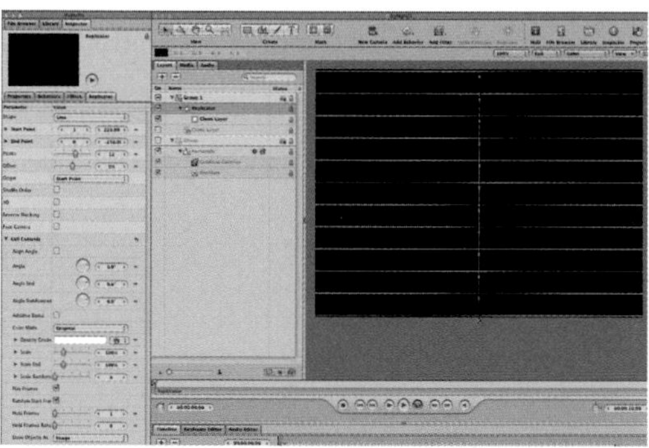

6 Click on the **Clone Layer** and press L or the *Replicate* button. Change the **Type** from **Rectangle** to a **Line** replicator. Set the **Points** to **12**. Click on the **Random Start Frame** checkbox.

HOT TIP

Hit the Generate button to change the Random Seed in the Replicator tab until you get a light/dark pattern you like.

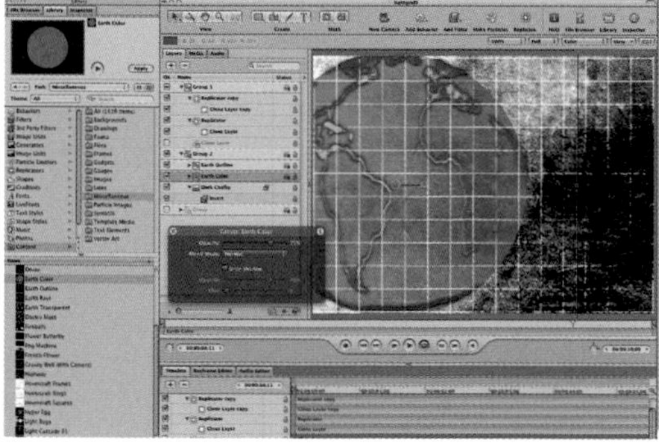

9 Add **Filter/Color Correction/Invert** to **Dark Chalky**. Now go to the **Content/Miscellaneous/** and grab **Earth Color** and throw it over **Dark Chalky**. Set its opacity to 75%. From the same place, grab **Earth Outline** and place it directly over **Earth Color** on the canvas.

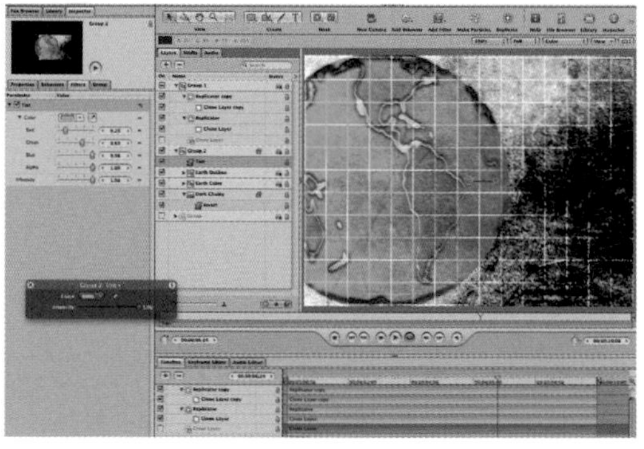

10 Finally, **add Filter/Color Correction/Tint** to Group 2. Set the color to your liking. I set mine to **Red 0.20**, **Green 0.69**, and **Blue 0.98**.

1 Background Activity

Starfields

STARFIELDS ARE ALWAYS useful. In this exercise, we'll learn how to create two Starfields—one 2D and one 3D.

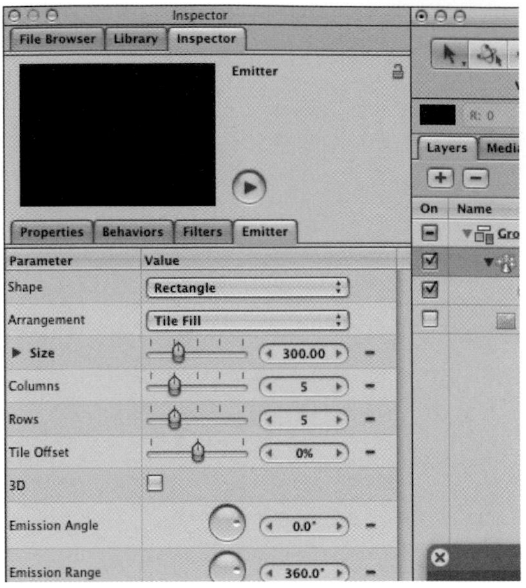

1 Grab **Content/Particle Images/Blur01**. Plop it on your Canvas. Click **Make Particles.** Change the Shape from Point to Rectangle.

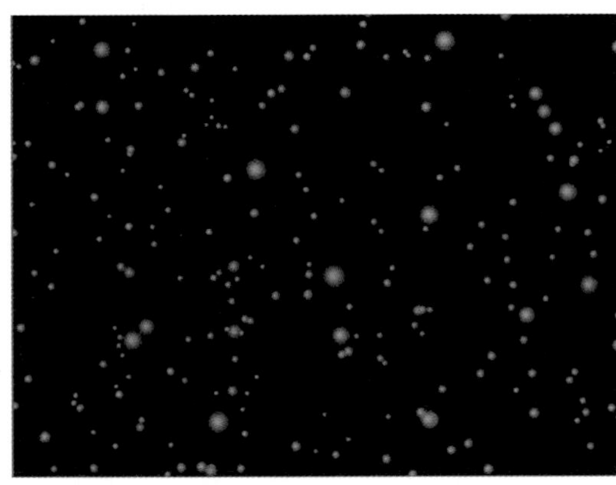

To convert to a 3D Starfield, follow steps 4-6.

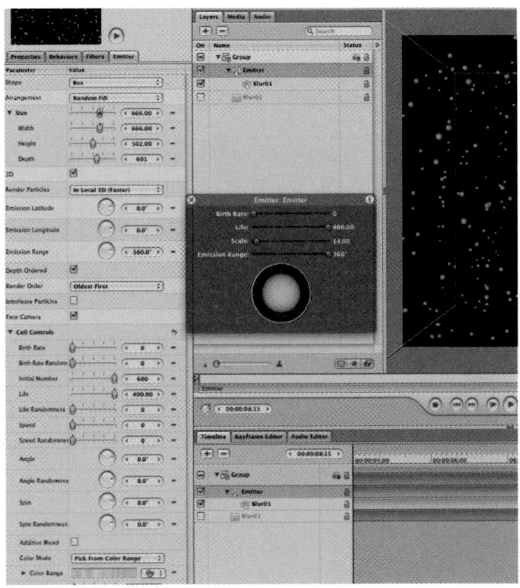

4 Click the **3D** box in the **Emitter**. Change the **Shape** to **Box**. Set the **Depth** to **600** or so. Up the **Initial Number** to **600**.

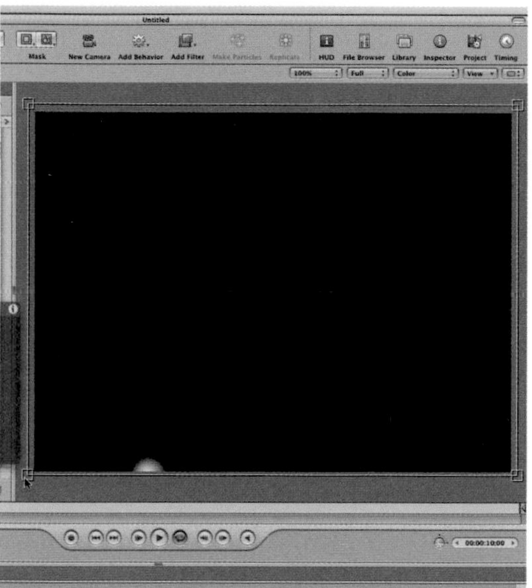

2 Set your tool to **Adjust Item** and drag the handles to the corners of the frame.

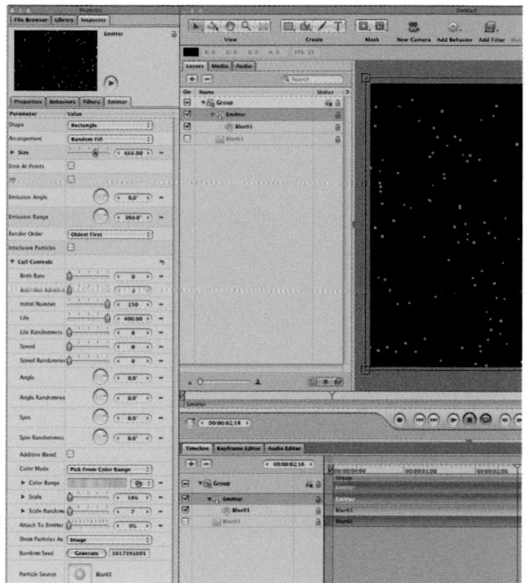

3 Now set the **Arrangement** to **Random Fill**, the **Birth Rate** to 0, **Init number** to 240, **Life** to 400, **Speed** to 0, **Color Mode** to **Pick From Color Range**. Set the **Color Range** gradient to the **Light Metal** preset. Set the **Scale** to 13%, and the **Scale Randomness** to 7. Click the **Random Seed** a few times to get a sky you like.

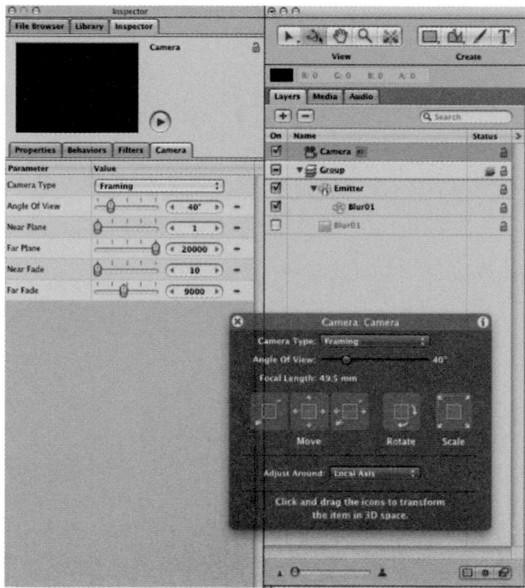

5 Now click *New Camera* in your toolbar. Agree to changing your project to 3D. Set the **Angle of View** to **40. Far Fade 9000**.

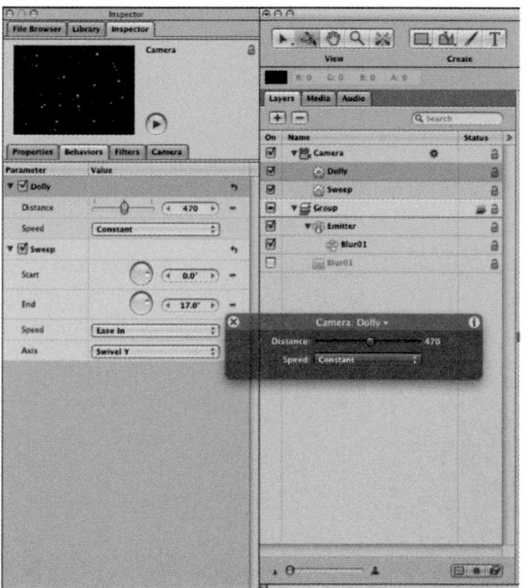

6 Now **Add Behavior/Camera/Sweep** and **Add Behavior/ Camera/Dolly**. Set the **Dolly Distance** to **470**. Set the **Sweep End** to **17** and the **Speed** to **Ease In**.

The Oscars

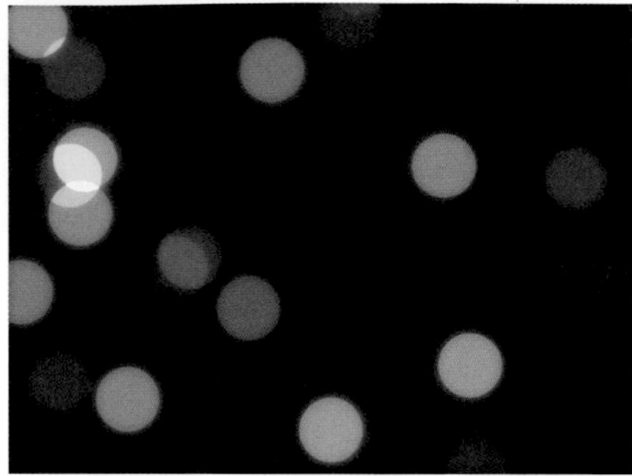

I WAS WATCHING THE 2006 Academy Awards and I really liked the elegant black and white motion graphics—way better than flying chromium sparkles. I thought they might have actually been created in Motion, so I gave it a go. This is only from memory, but it looks pretty good and is at least similar.

I started with a circle and did Make Particles. I used a Line emitter and a Select from Range for coloring, with additive blend and a slight ramp at beginning and end for transparency. I also added a Compound Blur filter. I inverted the map so that the lighter circles were sharper and the darker ones were more blurrier.

Finally, I remembered there being a muted out of focus background, so I used the Light Dots2 particle emitter preset, took off the grid, tweaked a bit, and put that behind all the circles.

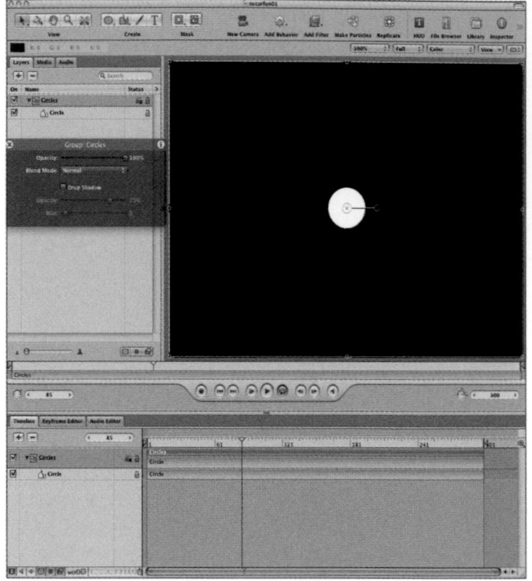

1 Start with a new project. Name the default group **Circles**. Click the **Fixed Resolution** checkbox. Press **C** to activate the **Circle** tool. Draw a small circle about one tenth of a screen width in the center of the Canvas.

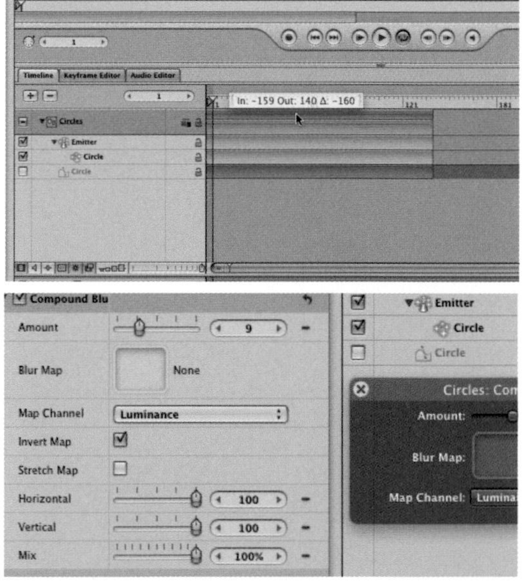

4 We want to start with the circles already onscreen, so grab your **Circles** group and slide it back 160 frames. Go the the end and press **O** to bring the duration back to the full project length. Return to frame 1. **Add Filter/Blur/Compound Blur**. Set the **Amount** to **9**. Click the **Invert Map** checkbox.

2 Select the Circle shape. Press **E** to create a Particle generator. Change **Shape** to **Line**. Set **Start Point** to **-325, 338; 325, 338**. You want it to be just off screen (see inset). Set **Emission Range** to **5.7**. Check the **Interleave Particles** box. Set **Birth Rate** to **5**, **Life** to **6**, **Speed** to **122**, **Speed Randomness** to **122**. Click the **Additive Blend** checkbox.

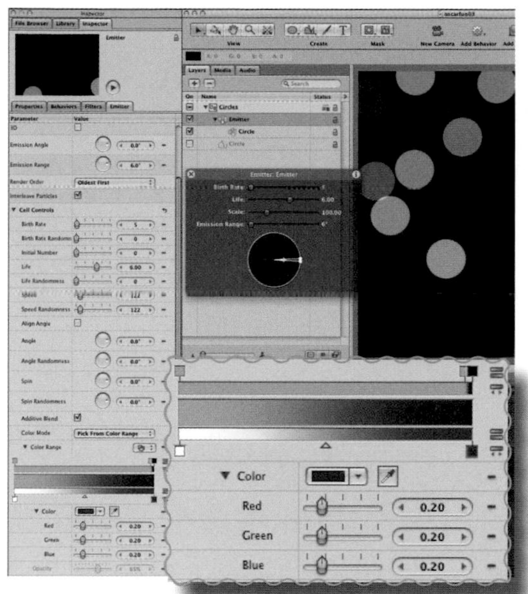

3 Change the **Color Mode** to **Pick From Color Range.** Set the **Gradient** to Grayscale. Change the end color from Black to 20% gray (Red 0.20, Green 0.20, Blue 0.20). Set the **Opacity** to **65**. To make the particles fade out at the end of their life, add a small ramp at the end of the opacity gradient (see inset).

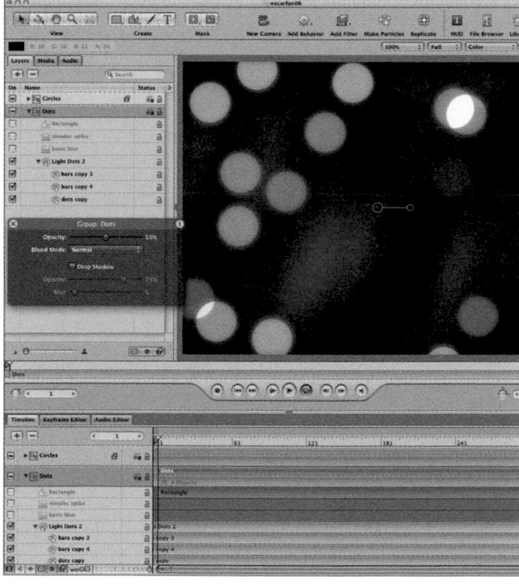

5 Go into the Library and grab **Particle Emitters/Abstract/ Light Dots 02**. Place it underneath your Circles group. Name its group **Dots**. Set the **Opacity** to **50%**. Drag it back 15 frames like we did with Circles to lose the startup delay and trim the end to add what we lost at the head.

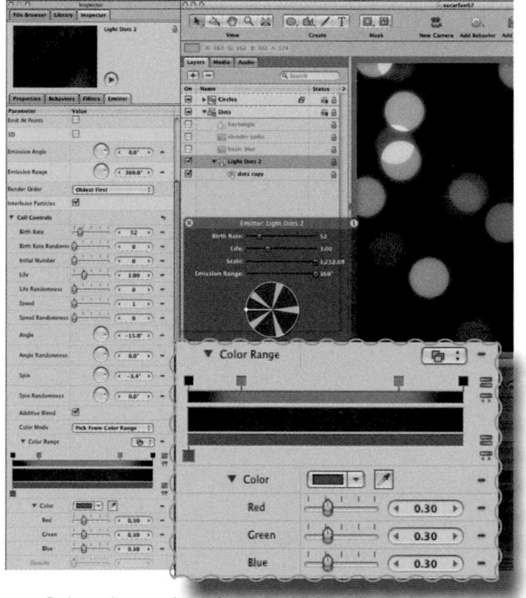

6 Delete the two bars from the **Light Dots** emitter. Change the **Birthrate** to **52**, **Life** to **3**, **Speed** to **1**. Change the color to dark gray (r 0.30, g 0.30, b 0.30) (see inset). Now you've got a classy backdrop for your own awards show.

Holiday Mosaics

IMAGE COURTESY PARKER AND REILLY SHEFFIELD

OKAY—HERE'S SOMETHING I thought up to give more interest to photographs, but could just as well be used on moving bits or as background.

We'll start with our base image and clone it. We'll use a particle emitter to generate a matte of moving boxes for the clone and use the particles to color the clone.

1 Start with a new project. Place your photograph or clip in the base group and name that group **Image**. Add a new group above your picture. Call it **Mask**. Press R to activate the rectangle tool. Draw a small rectangle in the center of the screen. Click the **Drop Shadow** button.

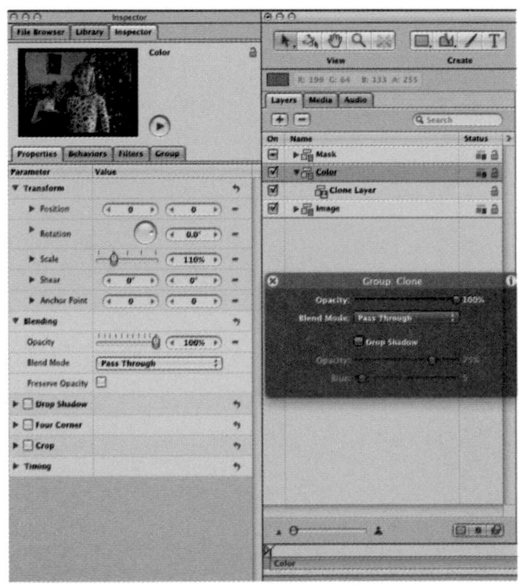

4 Trim the emitter back to the end of the project. Click on the Image group. With the playhead on Frame 1, press K to create a clone layer. Name that group **Color** and place it between the **Mask** and **Image** groups. Set its **Scale** to 110%.

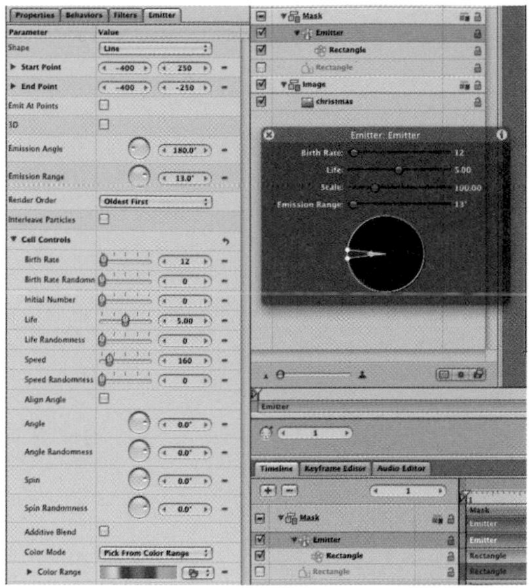

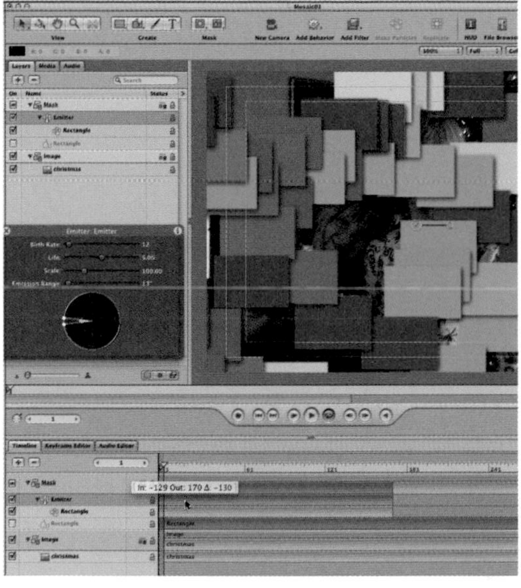

2 With the rectangle still selected, press E or click the *Make Particles* button in the toolbar. Set **Shape** to **Line**. **Start Point** to **-400, 250**. **End Point** to **-400 -250**. **Emission Angle** to **180**. **Emission Range** to **13**. **Birthrate** to **12**, **Life** to **5.0**, **Speed** to **160**. **Color Mode** to **Pick From Color Range**. Set the **Color Range** gradient to **Rainbow**.

3 Now, because we want to start with a screen full of boxes, with the playhead parked on frame 1, drag the Emitter to the left until the boxes fill the screen (about -130 frames in my case).

HOT TIP

You can vary the color scheme by changing the gradient in the Replicator.

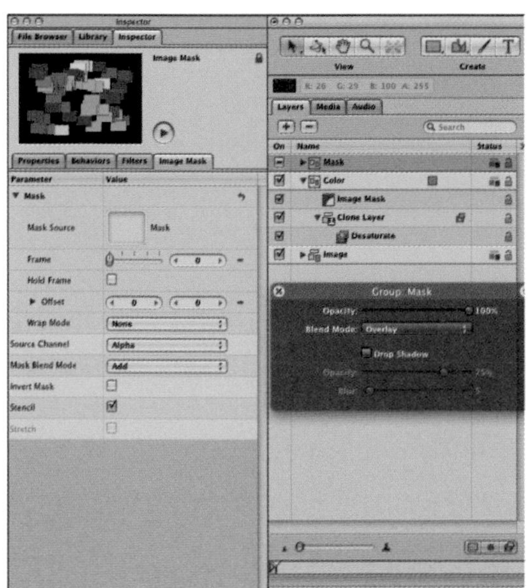

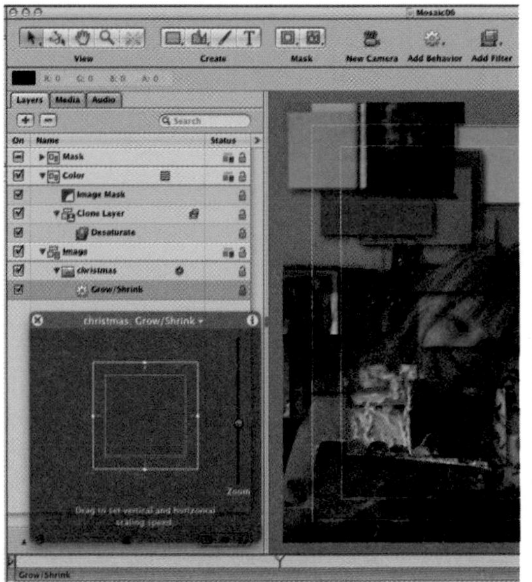

5 Click on the **Clone** layer. **Add Filter/Color Correction/ Desaturate.** Click on the **Color** group. Add a mask with ⌘ Shift M. Drag the **Mask** group into the image well. Turn back on the **Mask** group (placing it in the image well de-activated it) and set its **Blend Mode** to **Overlay**.

6 Finally, select your original image and **Add Behavior/ Basic Motion/GrowShrink** and set it appropriate to your image. Now save your project as **Mosaic1**.

More Holiday Mosaics

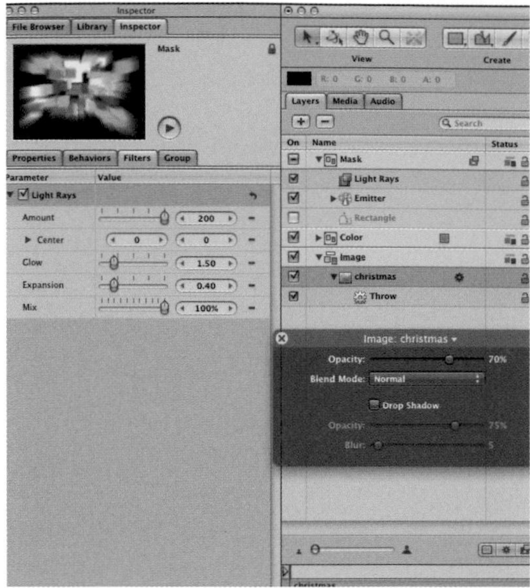

1 Start with the holiday **Mosaic1** project from the previous page. Save it as **Mosaic2**. Click on the **Mask** group. **Add Filter/Glow/Light Rays.** Change **Glow** to **1.5**. Click on your image, set the **Opacity** to **70%**. You might want to change the **Grow/Shrink** on your image to a **Throw**. Adjust size and position as appropriate.

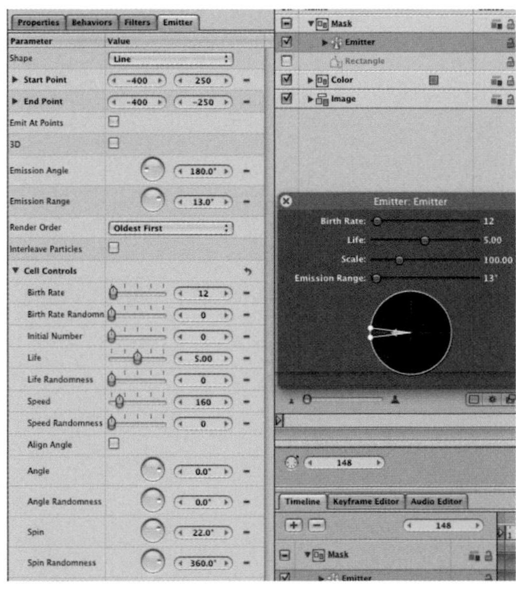

3 Start with the **Mosaic3** project. Save it as **Mosaic4**. Click on the **Emitter**. Change the **Spin** to **22.0**, **Spin Randomness** to **360**, **Scale Randomness** to **75**.

IMAGE COURTESY REILLY AND PARKER SHEFFIELD

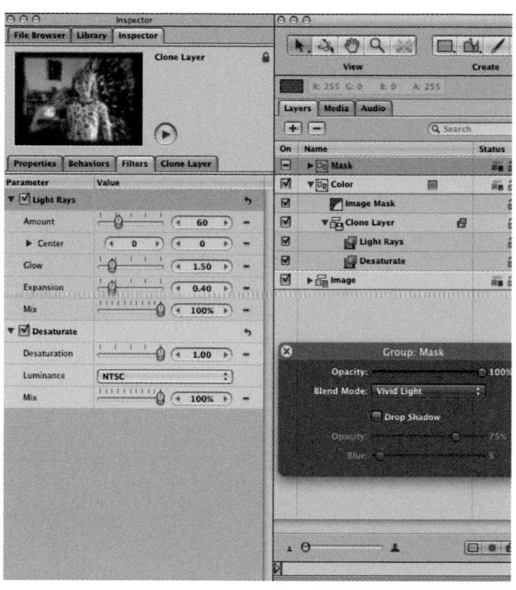

2 Start with **Mosaic1** from the previous page. Save it as **Mosaic3**. Click on the **Clone Layer**. **Add Filter/Glow/ Light Rays**. Change the **Amount** to 60 and the **Glow** to **1.50**. Click on the **Mask** group. Change the **Blend Mode** to **Vivid Light**. Try changing the **Grow/Shrink** from **Grow** to **Shrink**.

HOT TIP

To mix things up a bit, hit the Generate button in the Random Seed under the particle emitter.

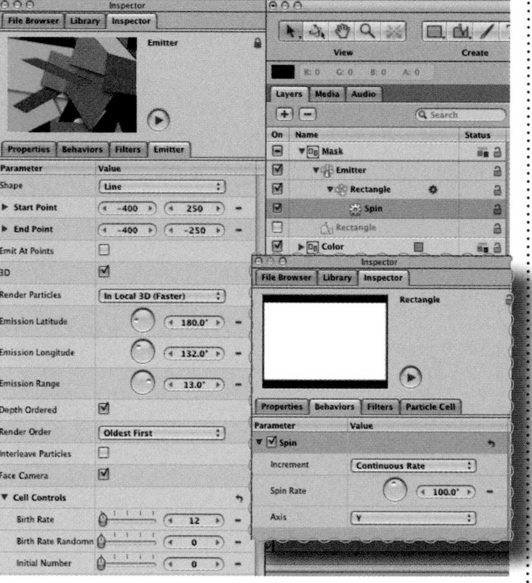

4 Start with the **Mosaic4** project. Save it as **Mosaic5**. Click on the **3D** checkbox in the **Emitter**. Set the **Emission Latitude** to **180**, **Emission Longitude** to **132**. Select the **Emitter/Rectangle**. **Add Behavior/Basic Motion/Spin**. Set the **Spin Rate to 100**. Set the **Axis** to **Y** (see inset).

Roll Your Own

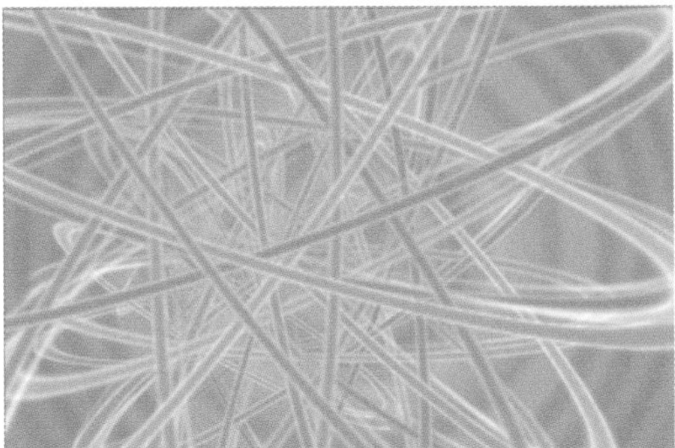

USING THE CONTENT PROVIDED with Motion and replicators, you can create an infinite variety of your own backdrops to place behind text, talking heads, as lower third fills, etc.

In this case, we'll be using the Atom 01 and a replicator, but feel free to try it with other content.

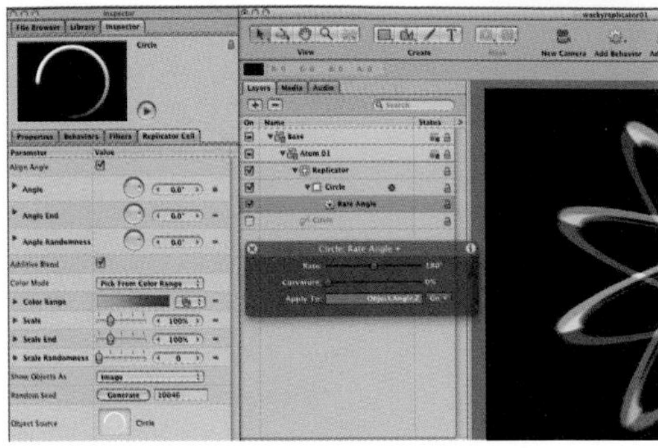

1 Start with a new project. Rename the default group **Base**. Select **Atom 01** from Library/Content. Place it in **Base**. Select the **Atom Replicator** and change the **Color Mode** to **Pick From Color Range**. Set the **Color Range** to **Sundown**. Change the **Rate** to **180°**.

4 Right/ctrl-click on **Offset**, and then select **Ramp**. Set the **End Value** to 200%. Set the **Curvature** to 50%.

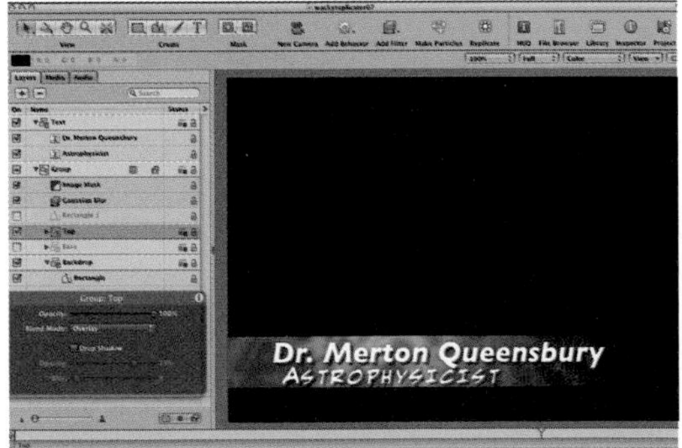

7 You can group everything, and then add a Mask and a blur to use this a a fill for a lower third.

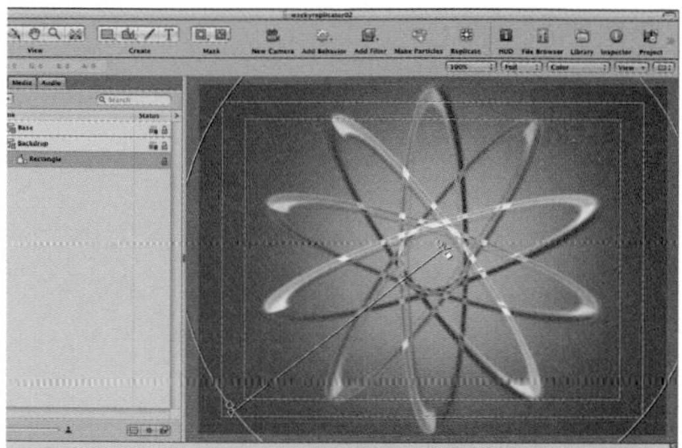

2 Add a new group, call it **Backdrop**. Place it behind the **Base** group. Draw a rectangle that fills your screen. Change the **Fill Mode** to **Gradient**. Change the gradient to **Sundown**. Change the **Type** to **Radial**. Press ⇥ until you get the **Adjust Item** tool, and then edit the gradient to your liking.

3 Click on the **Base** group and press L or the Replicate button. Name the new group **Top**. Change the **Shape** to **Circle**. Set the **Arrangement** to **Outline**, the **Radius** to **80**. Set the **Angle End** to **-140**. Click the **Additive Blend** checkbox. Change the **Scale** to **200** and the **Scale End** to **0**. Move your replicator a little off center.

HOT TIP

Adding an oscillator to the radius of the replicator can add even more variety.

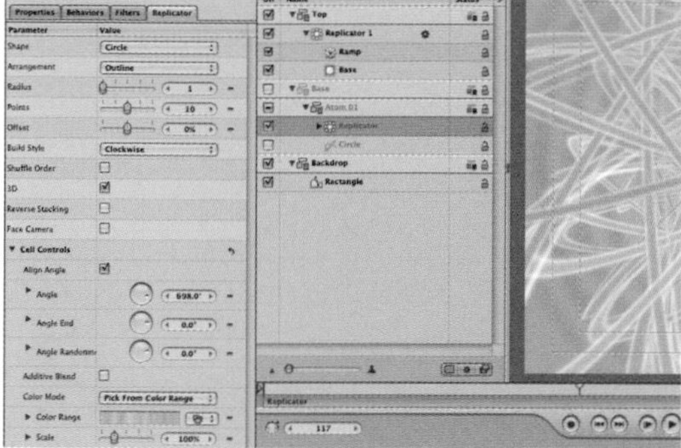

5 You can vary the look by changing the **Color Range** gradient, turning off the **Additive Blend**, **Reverse Stacking**, etc.

6 Or changing the **Blend Mode** of the **Top** group. A **Blend Mode** of **Screen** is seen above.

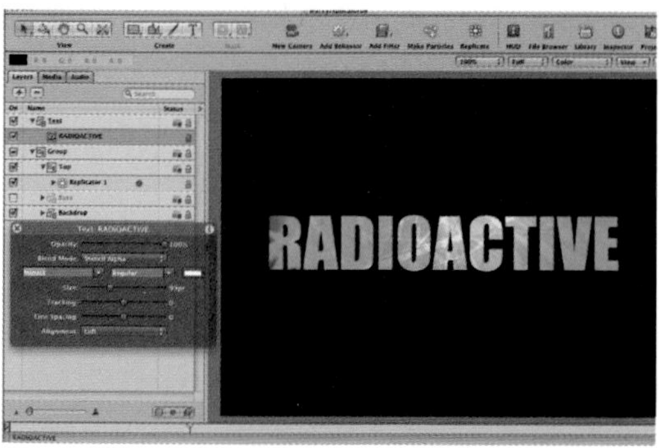

8 Or use it as a fill for text.

9 Or change the element in the **Base** group.

Perspective Reflection

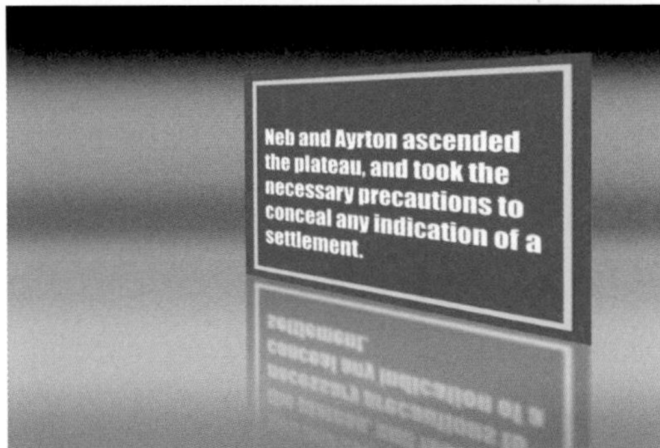

THE REFLECTION EFFECT, made popular by Apple, is easy to achieve in Motion.

Anything we place in our Billboard group will be reflected—including moving material.

To do this, we'll clone our source and flip it to create the reflection. Then we'll vary the opacity of the reflection with a gradient and put a slight blur on it.

IMAGE COURTESY TIKIBAR TV

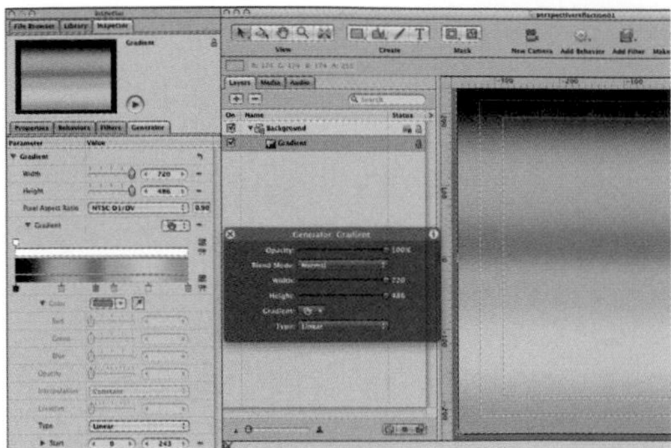

1 Start with a new project. Name the default group **Background**. Place a gradient generator in it and set the gradient to look like the screenshot. Gray in the foreground, fading up to a lighter horizon, quickly followed by a darker area, fading up to a lighter sky, then fading down to very dark at the top of the screen.

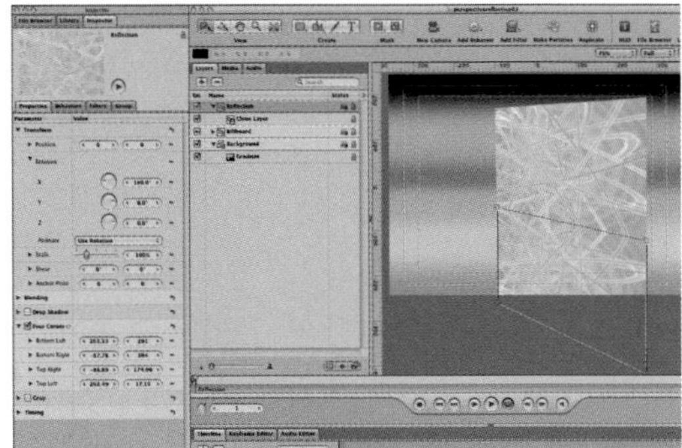

4 If it's on, turn off the **Four Corner** properties of the Clone Layer. Use corner pinning to adjust the perspective of the **Reflection** group until it precisely mirrors the **Billboard** group.

7 Notice the reflection is just barely visible. This is because the mask is used without being affected by the **Four Corner** properties of the **Reflection** group. Let's fix that.

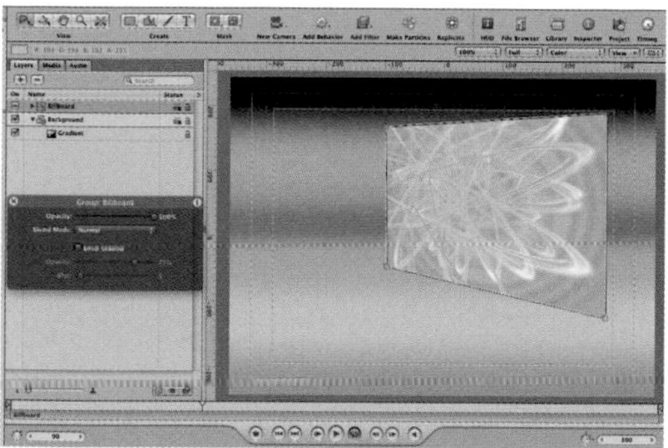

2 Create a new group. Call it **Billboard**. Set it to **Fixed Resolution**. Place whatever you want into it (text, graphics, movie, etc.). I'm using one of the **Roll Your Own** background projects from the previous project. Use **Corner Pinning** to position it in the frame with perspective.

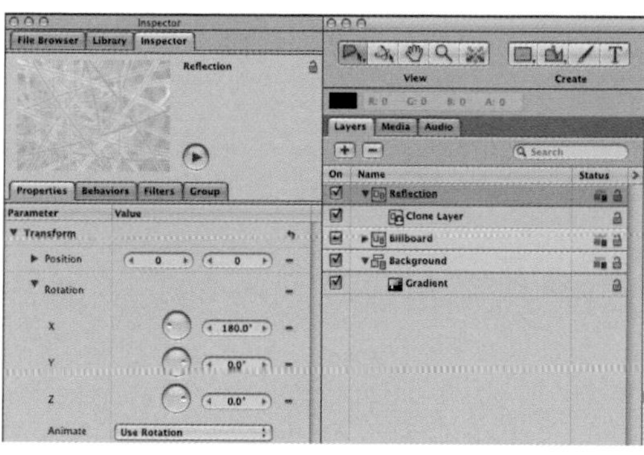

3 Select the **Billboard** group. Press **K** to create a clone layer. Name the new group **Reflection**. Set the **X** rotation to **180**. Turn on **Fixed Resolution**.

5 Temporarily turn off the **Four Corner** properties of the **Reflection** group. Create a full-screen **Gradient**-filled rectangle in the reflection group.

6 Select the **Reflection** group. Type **⌘ Shift M** to add a mask to it. Set the **Source Channel** to **Luminance**. Drag the rectangle into the mask well. Turn back on the **Four Corner** properties.

HOT TIP

Motion 4 lets you turn any surface into a reflector.

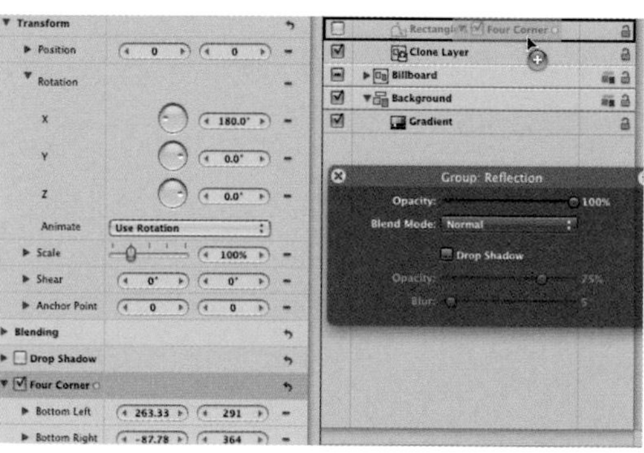

8 Select the **Reflection** group. Drag its **Four Corner** properties to the **Rectangle 1** layer.

9 There we go. Select the **Reflection** group. **Add Filter Blur/Gaussian Blur**. Adjust the **Reflection** group's **Opacity** until it looks good.

Underwater Basket Weaving

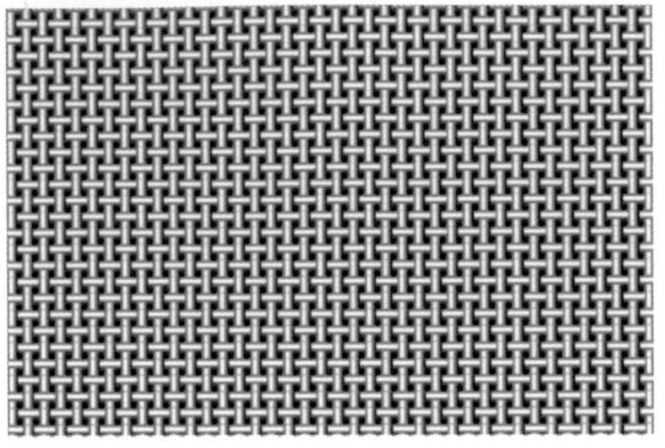

TO CREATE A SEEMINGLY interwoven background, first I created a replicator for the vertical stripes, followed by one for the horizontal. When combined, it produces an image like this.

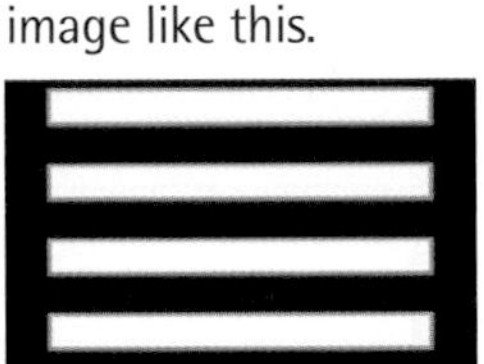

To make them appear interwoven, I needed to make every other intersection transparent.

By using a replicator with the Color Mode of Over Pattern adjusting the color repetitions, I could get a pattern of alternating black and white squares to make a mask for weaving.

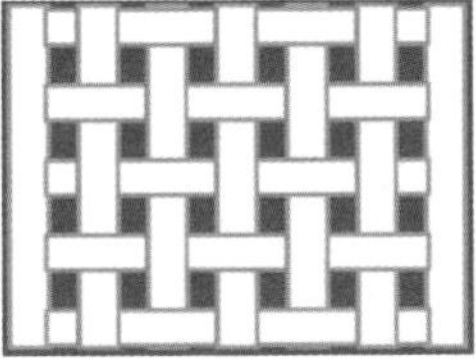

It has been pointed out to me that this project can be frustrating, trying to get the squares aligned. You might try first with larger "strips."

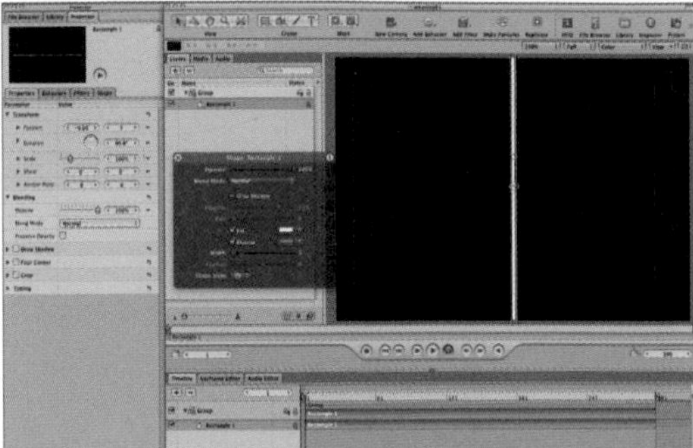

1 Start with a new project. Draw a horizontal bar the full width of the screen. Make it white fill and outlined in blue. Rotate it 90 degrees.

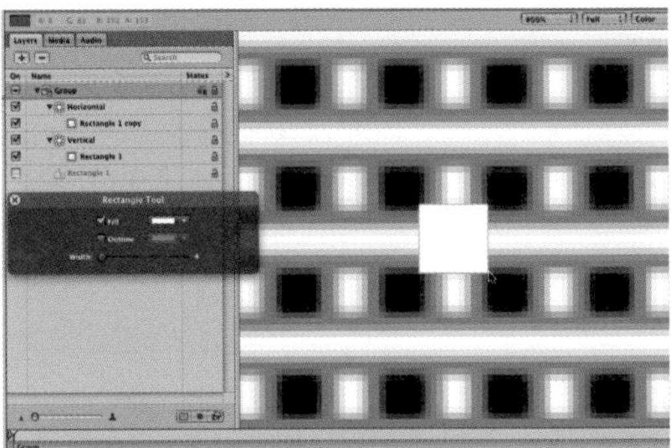

4 Zoom in on your canvas to 800%. Draw a rectangle that is big enough to cover an intersection in your grid.

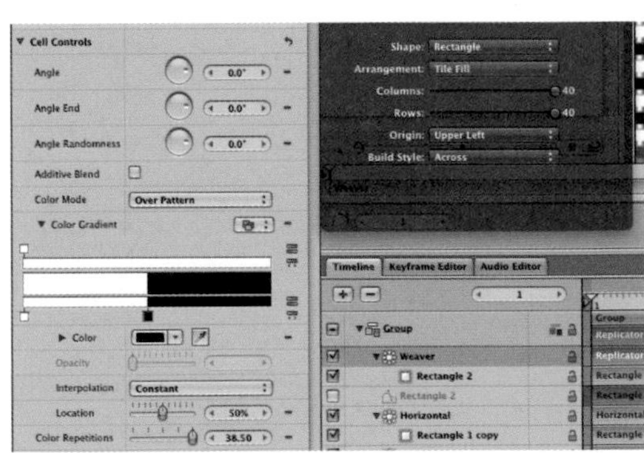

7 Change the **Origin** to **Upper Left**. Change the **Color Mode** to **Over Pattern**. Set the **Gradient** to **Grayscale**. Click on the white color box in the gradient editor. Set the **Interpolation** to be **Constant**. Click on the black color box. Set the **Location** to be **50%**, **Color Repetitions** to **38.5**.

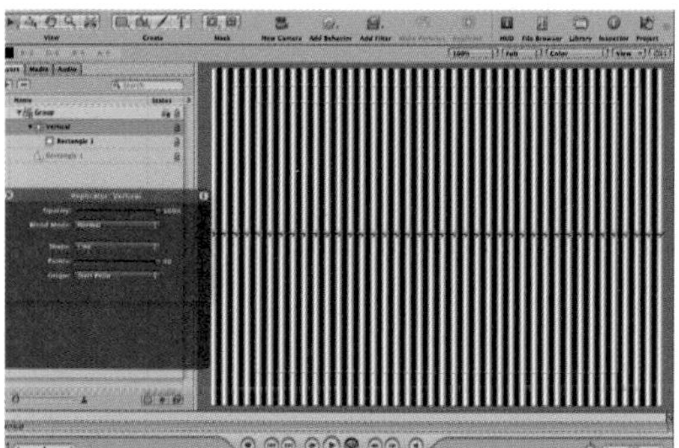

2 Press L or click the *Replicate* button in the toolbar. Change the **Shape** to Line. Name the new replicator **Vertical**. Set the Points to 40. Stretch it out so it creates a pattern of vertical stripes.

3 Click on the **Vertical** replicator. Type ⌘D to duplicate it. Name the copy **Horizontal**. Rotate it 90 degrees.

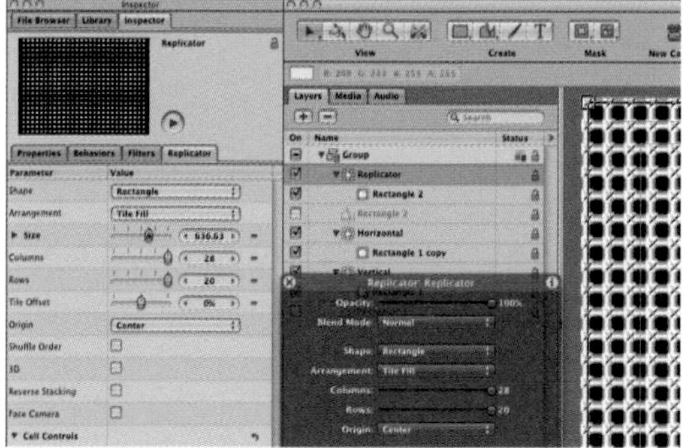

5 With that rectangle selected, Press L or click the *Replicate* button in the toolbar. Name this replicator **Weaver**. Set the **Columns** to 40, the **Rows** to 40.

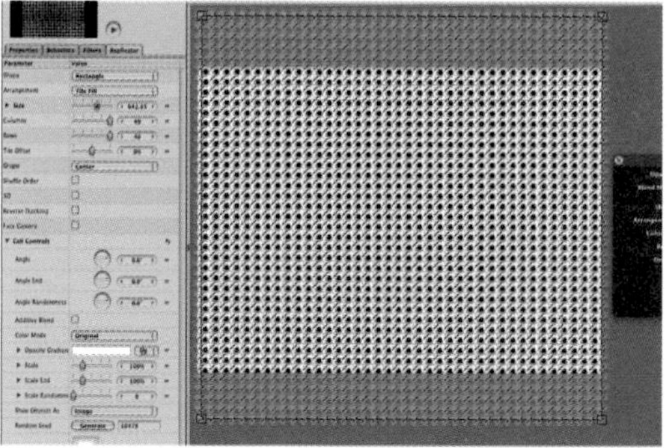

6 With the *Adjust Item* tool selected, adjust the size of the replicator until the squares fall on each intersection of the horizontal and vertical bars. It can be a little finicky. Pressing Shift V to see the offscreen portions of the grid can help.

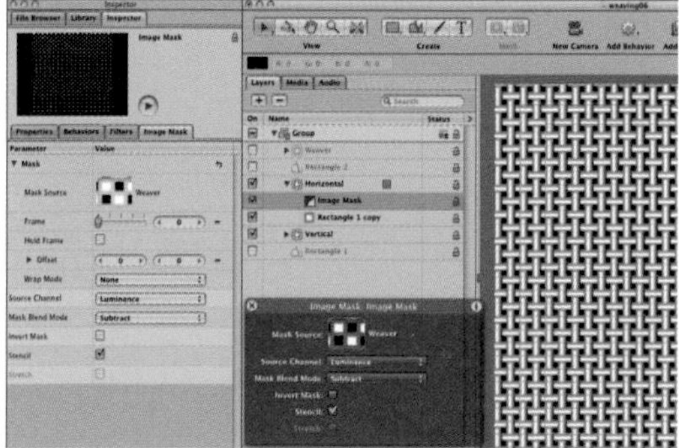

8 Click on the **Horizontal** replicator. Type ⌘Shift M to add a mask layer. Set the **Channel** to **Luminance**, the **Mask Blend** mode to **Subtract**. Then drag the **Weaver** replicator into the **Mask Source** well.

9 Now with every other intersection transparent, you have the appearance of a weave.

HOT TIP

Hold down the Shift key during rotation to have it stop in 45 degree increments.

Situational Maps

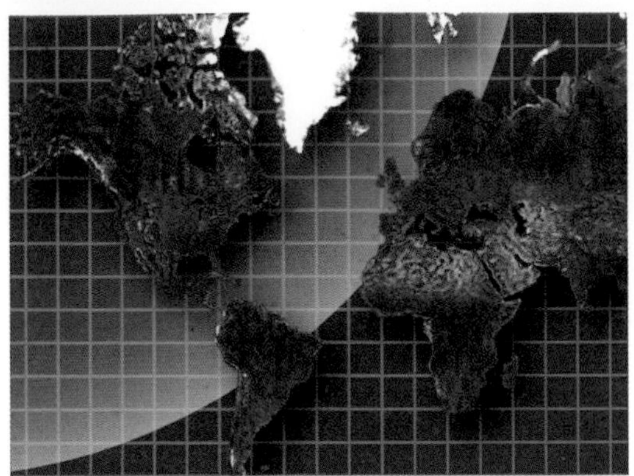

I SAW A BACKGROUND on the Situation Room on CNN and thought, "Hey you could do that in Motion."

We'll create the backdrop with a rectangle filled with a radial gradient and use the "color cycling" method (see Color Cycling in the Animation chapter) to shift around the colors.

We'll lay the Grid Generator over that. Then we will chroma key a map with drop shadows over the background.

Finally, we'll chop up some circles to make the "radar pulses."

If you're working for Wolf Blitzer, this could come in handy.

1 Lets start with a fresh project. Grab a Gradient generator and throw it into the default **Group**. Name the group **Background**. Change the **Gradient Type** to **Radial**. Set the **Gradient** to **Grayscale**. Using the **Adjust Item** tool, make your gradient look something like the picture.

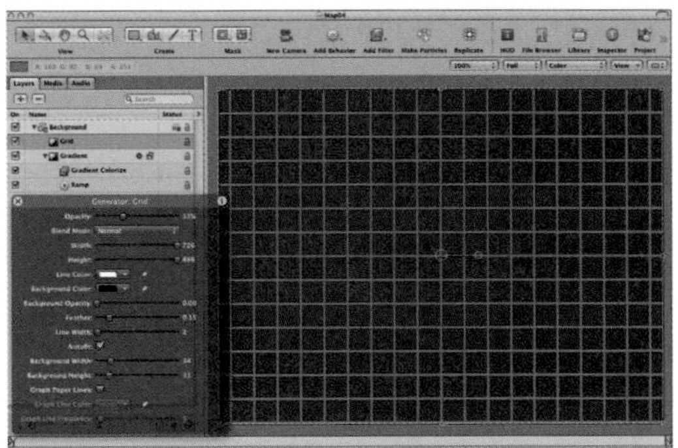

4 Above the **Gradient**, add a **Grid generator**. Set the **Background Opacity** to 0, **Feather 0.15**, **Line Width 2**. Click the **Autofit** checkbox. Set the **Background Width** to 34, **Background Height** to 31. Set the grid **Opacity** to 33%.

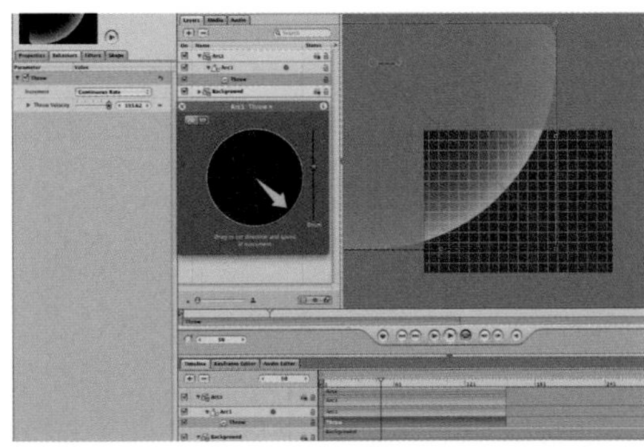

7 Now, move **Arc1** offscreen and use a **Throw** behavior to cause it to travel across our background in about 150 frames.

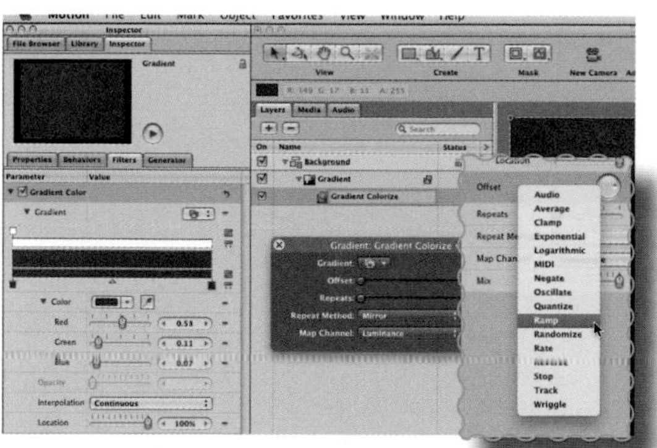

2 Add **Filter/Color Correction/Gradient Colorize** to the **Gradient** layer. Set the colors to some nice close-in-value earth tones. I used **.68, 0, 0** and **.53, .11, .07**. Right/ctrl-click on the **Offset** parameter and select **Ramp** (see inset).

3 Change the **End Value** to **1440**. This will cause the background gradient to subtly converge on the centerpoint as the animation plays. 1440 is just 360 (one complete cycle) times 4, so the color cycle animation will complete 4 times in 10 seconds.

5 Add a new group above the **Background** group. Call it **Arcs**. Press C to select the **Circle** tool. Draw a large circle that will spread across your background. Change the fill to **Gradient**, change the **Type** to **Radial**. Edit the gradient to produce a light edge and a transparent, bluish interior. Shift V will help you see the full circle.

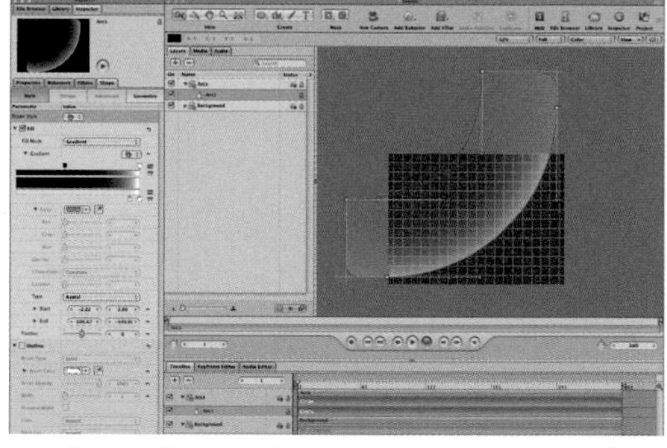

6 The complete circle is much larger than we need, so let's cut it down. Select the **Adjust Control Points** tool and edit the circle to produce an arc. Name it **Arc1**.

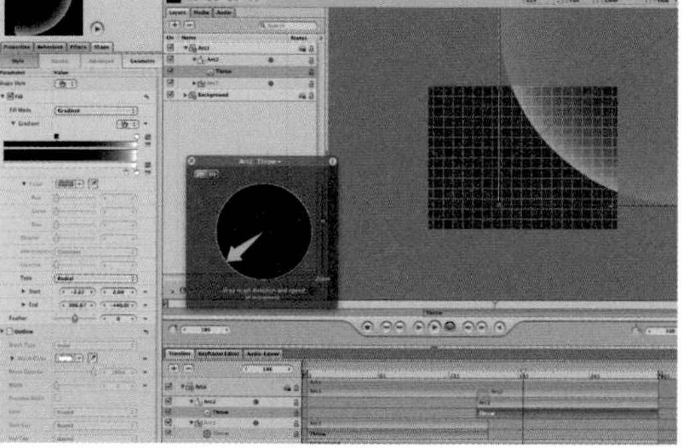

8 Duplicate **Arc1** and call it **Arc2**. Adjust it to come from the upper right corner over the second half of our project.

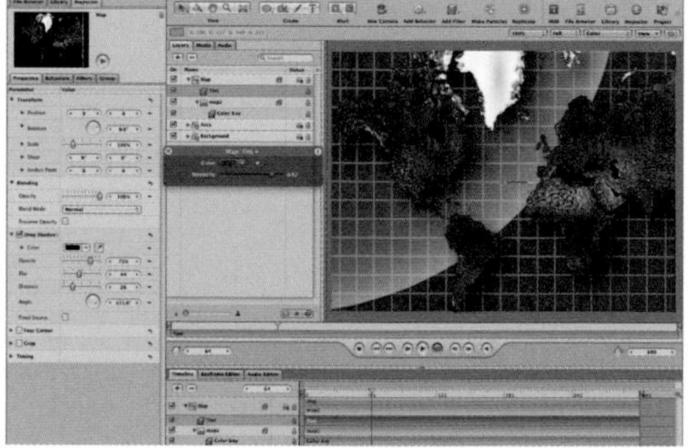

9 Add a new group above the **Arcs** group. Name it **Map**. Take your map image and place it in this group. Use the color key to remove the oceans if necessary. Add **Filter/Color Correction/Tint** to the **Map** group. Set it to a complementary earth tone. Turn on drop shadow and adjust.

HOT TIP

A map image may be found on the disc.

Spiral Background

IN THIS PROJECT WE'RE GOING to create a simple moving background using the Spirals generator (new to Motion 4) and for some additional fun we'll also use the Link behavior (also new with Motion 4). The Link behavior is very powerful for animation and lets you link multiple parameters to build complex animations that respond to a single change.

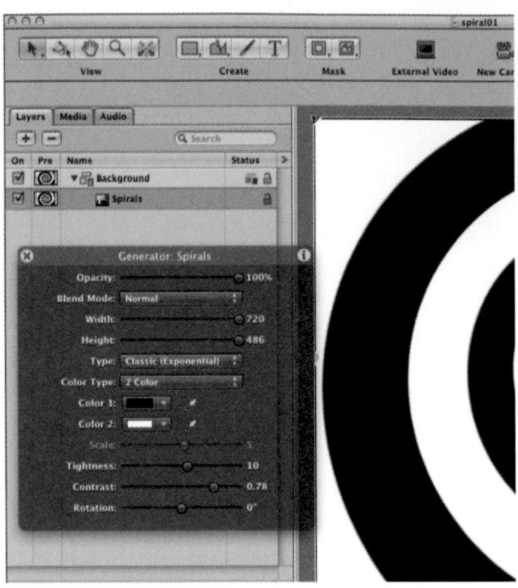

1 Start by renaming the default group **Background**. In **Library/Generators**, click on the **Spirals** generator and press the **Apply** button.

4 Go back to **Library/Generators**, click on the **Spirals** generator, and again press the **Apply** button. Make sure the second **Spirals** is above the first one. Set the **Blend Mode** to **Difference**.

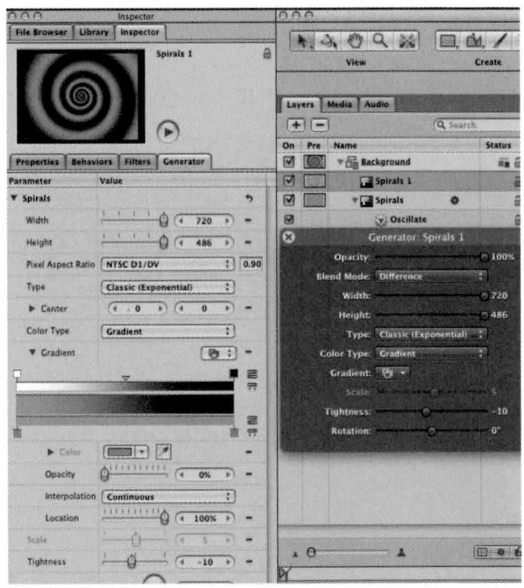

5 Set the **Color Type** to **Gradient**. Set both colors to middle gray. Set the left side of the opacity gradient to 100%, the right side to 0%. Set **Tightness** to **-10**.

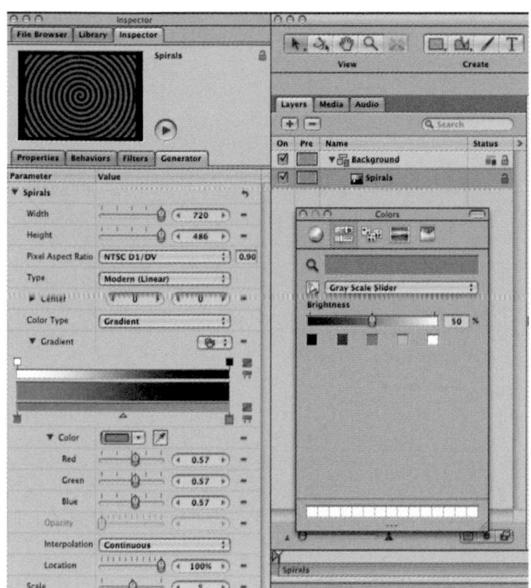

2 Set the **Type** to **Modern (Linear)**, **Color Type** to **Gradient.** Set the left side to a nice Teal color. Set the right side to middle gray. Add a tag to the right side of the **Opacity** gradient and set it to **0**.

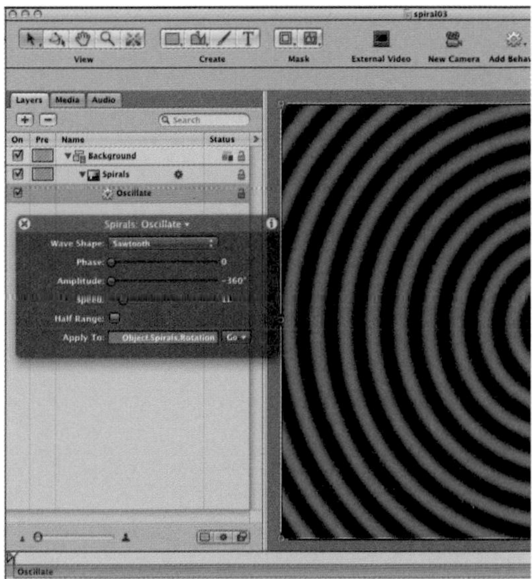

3 Right/ctrl-click on **Rotation**. Select **Oscillate**. Change the **Wave Shape** to **Sawtooth**, **Amplitude** to **-360°**, **Speed** to **12**.

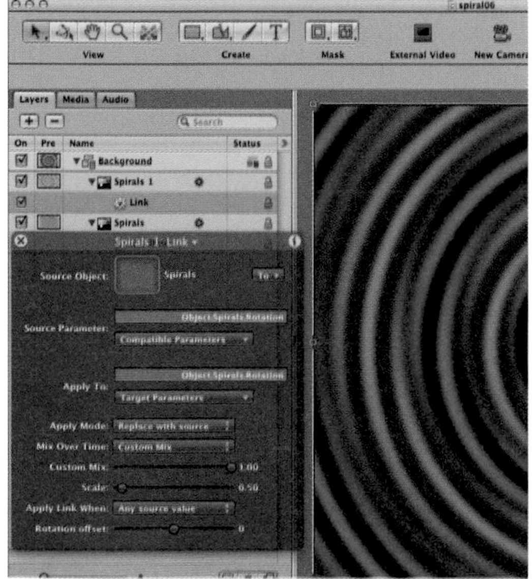

6 Right/ctrl-click on **Rotation**. Select **Link**. Drag the first **Spirals** into the **Source Object** well. The **Source Parameter** should already be set to **Object/Spirals/Rotation**. Set **Scale** to **.5**

7 Select the **Background Group**. **Add Filter/Stylize/Indent**. Set **Depth** to **2**. Now you can add a new group above your **Background** group and place your text there.

HOT TIP

Some Motion 4 projects can be opened in Motion 3 by editing the project in a text editor and changing the version from 4.0 to 3.0.

Any 4.0 only effects etc. will be missing, however.

Random Numbers

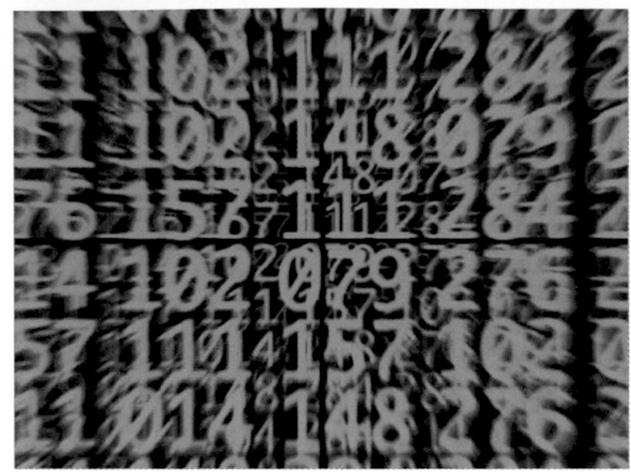

A CONSTANTLY CHANGING FIELD of numbers can be a useful background to present financial data, or change it to ones and zeros for a binary "computer data" backdrop.

This takes advantage of the Numbers generator, new to Motion 4. We'll build a single "sheet" of changing numbers with a Replicator. An Offset filter will help us to scroll the numbers past the screen, and then we'll carry them into the distance with a second Replicator. A replicator of a replicator—hope that's not like "crossing the streams" in *Ghostbusters*.

Finally, to add some texture to our background, we'll use a Light Rays filter.

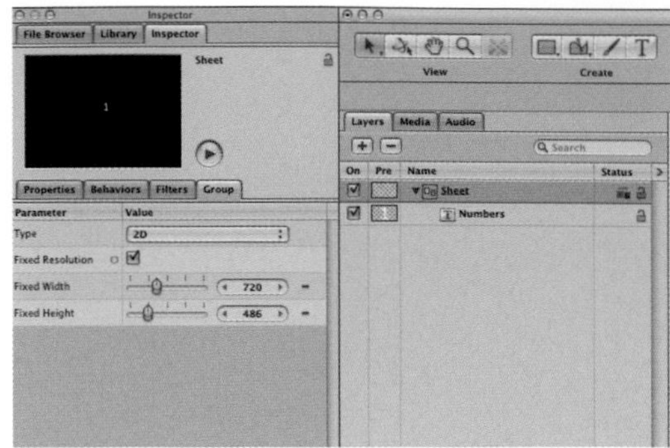

1 Begin by renaming the default group to **Sheet**. Set its **Fixed Resolution** checkbox. Reach into the **Library/ Generators/Text Generators** and grab the **Number** generator and place it in the middle of the screen.

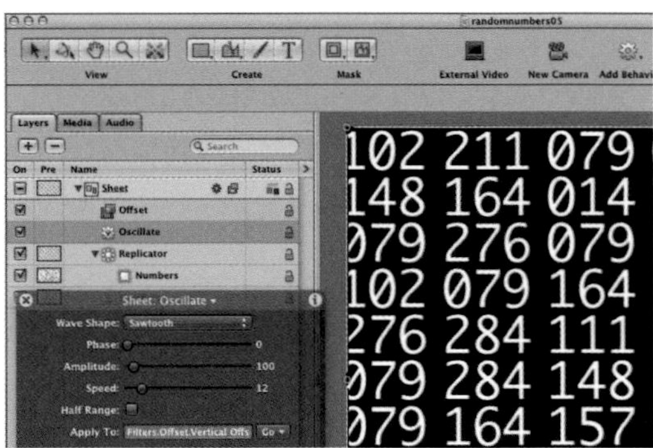

4 Select your **Sheet** group. **Add Filter/Tiling/Offset.** Right click on **Vertical Offset** and select **Oscillate.** Set the **Wave Shape** to **Sawtooth, Speed** to **12.** Press Play, and you should get a sheet of changing numbers scrolling by your screen.

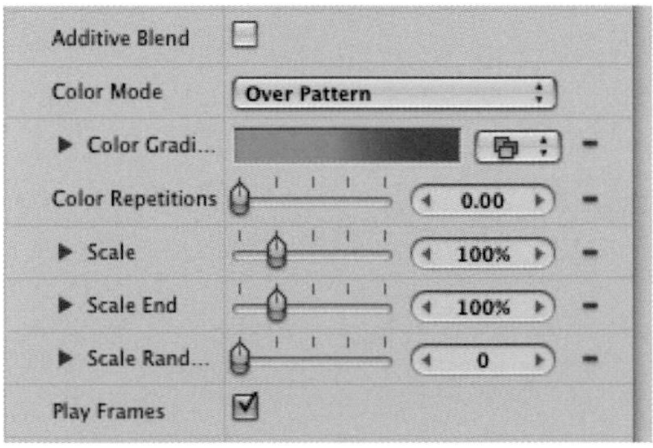

7 I set **Color Mode** to be **Over Pattern** and used a light green to dark green gradient—this means the layers get darker as they recede.

2 Select the **Text Generator/Generator** tab. Set **Minimum Digits** to 3. Click **Random**. Set **Random Hold** to **30**. In the **Format** tab, select your font. I chose **Monaco, 48** pt.

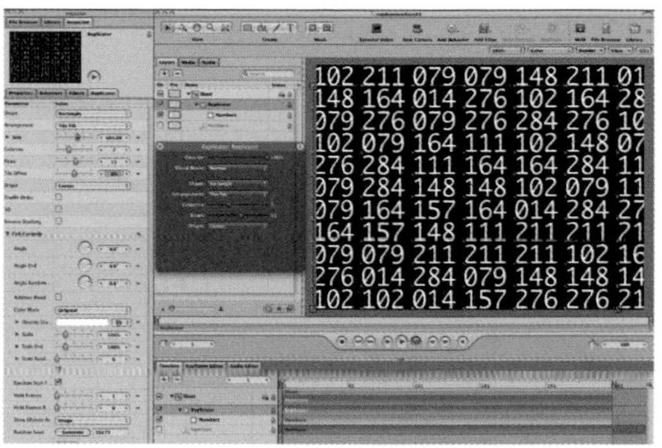

3 With **Numbers** selected, press **L** or click the **Replicate** button in the toolbar. Set **Columns** to **7**, rows to **11**. Click the **Random Start Frame** button. Drag the size out until you fill the screen.

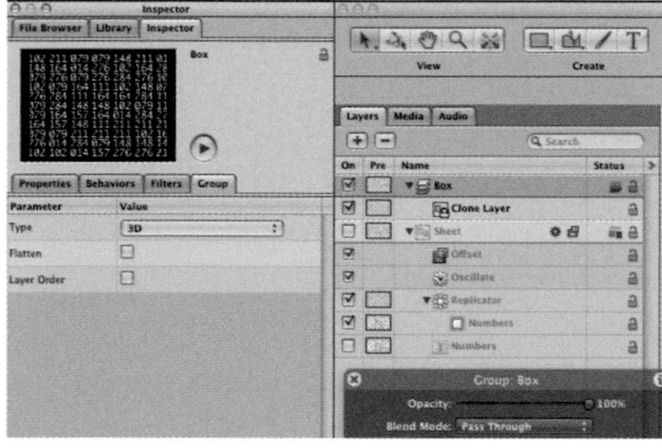

5 Pause playback and go back to frame 1. With **Sheet** selected press **K** to create a **Clone Layer**. Name the new group **Box**. Change the layer type to **3D**. Turn off the **Sheet** group.

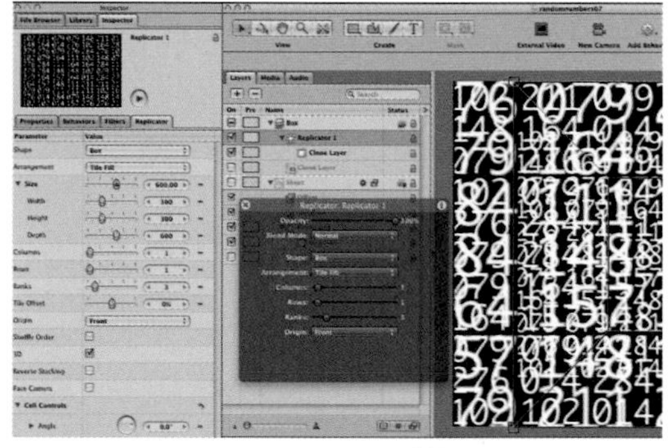

6 With **Clone Layer** selected, press **L** or click the Replicate button in the toolbar. Click the **3D** checkbox. Set the **Shape** to **Box**. Open **Size**. Set **Depth** to **600**. Set **Columns** to **1**, **Rows** to **1**, **Ranks** to **3**. **Origin** to **Front**.

▶ Scale	100%
▶ Scale End	100%
▶ Scale Rand...	0
Play Frames	☑
Random Start F...	☐
Source Start Fr...	45
Source Frame ...	0
Hold Frames	1

8 Set **Source Start Frame** to **45**. This offsets each layer so they are not repeats of each other.

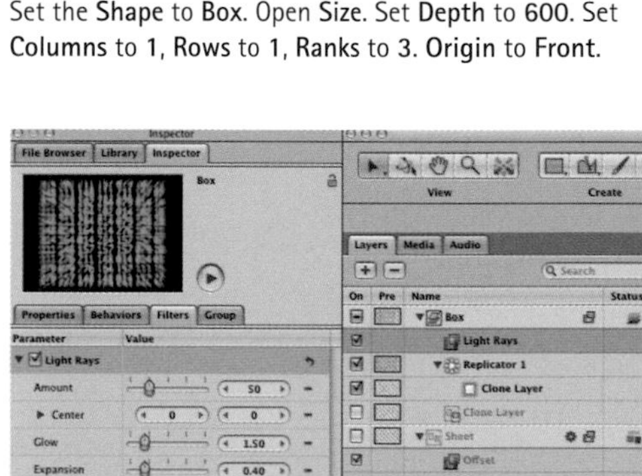

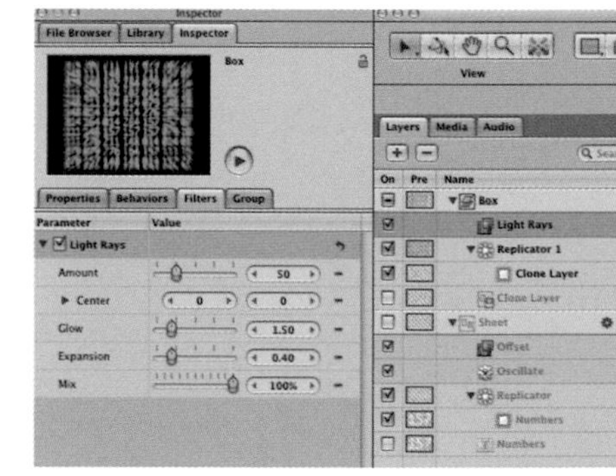

9 Finally, select the **Box** group. **Add Filter/Glow/Light Rays**.

HOT TIP

You can add a Camera and use Depth of Field to make layers of numbers drop in and out of focus.

Or make more layers and fly the camera through them.

Who am I and how'd I get here?

I HAVE BEEN A WORKING BROADCAST professional for nearly 20 years now. There's a good chance you've seen my work. At least one of those pesky commercials you tried to fast forward through on your TiVo, or used as an opportunity to run to the kitchen while watching your favorite TV show was likely one I worked on. If not that, maybe one of the hundreds of music videos I've edited for artists such as REM, Madonna, or Radiohead among others is one you're familiar with.

I didn't start out to become what I am. So my journey can hardly be used as a roadmap for those seeking to get into this business. However, I'll present it as an example. There is no one right way to proceed down your career path. Or, to put it another way, there are many roads to Rome.

When I left high school, I was sure I wanted to be a motorcycle mechanic, and eventually own my own shop. I went to college with that goal in mind. After 2 years, I had my AS degree in motorcycle mechanics. After 3 years, I was certain I didn't want to spend the rest of my life doing it.

Following a brief side trip as a sewing machine repairman, I did a 3-year stint as a graphic artist. This was back when cut and paste meant breaking out your exacto knife and rubber cement. I learned a lot, but I knew I had yet to find my calling.

While unemployed after that, surviving largely on cup-o-noodles, I taught myself programming and worked my way into a job as a software engineer. I did that for a decade, eventually working up to leading a team of engineers on large projects.

Then came that fateful lunch meeting with my best friend since high school. He is a very successful artist (he did the cover for this book) and photographer and had just started doing music videos, being pulled into it by a band whose album cover he'd photographed. Over pasta at a local Italian eatery, he told me he thought that software engineering was too esoteric an art form for me. He thought I'd be a good editor, saying it was a just the right mixture of technical know-how and esthetic judgment.

He also said that while he couldn't give me enough work to make ends meet, he could get me started. I didn't decide at that moment—no heavenly choir gave voice, no scales fell from my eyes, but I was intrigued. After giving it a few months, thought, in 1990, I quit my day job to join the circus.

My friend was just as successful at directing music videos as he had been at his other pursuits, so I had the good fortune to be involved in some high end projects early on in my new career. But while he got me started, the rest was up to me. I was aided in this by one simple fact. I loved editing. And I had come into the profession as a music video editor at precisely the right time. I think of it as the golden age of music videos—after the spandex and smoke, but before the formula had set in.

I could tell lots of stories from this period, but this is not the place for them. If we ever meet for a beer, I'd be happy to regale you with some. Eventually, I made my way into commercials where I spend the bulk of my time these days.

The industry has changed a lot since I first got into it. At that time, all the final work was done at large facilities with VERY expensive and temperamental equipment with entire staffs of experts employed just to keep them running. Now, more likely than not, I'll finish a spot in my own edit bay, renting a deck for final layoff at the end of a project. Or increasingly, I just compress and upload to the distributer.

This means that my responsibilities have changed as well. When I started, my chief role was creative. The task of ensuring the legality of signals, providing effects, doing motion graphics, etc. fell on the shoulders of others. Now, in this era of shrinking budgets, if I want to keep working, I have to do a lot of them. This is neither all good nor all bad. It just is the way things work these days. I certainly miss the opportunity to collaborate with others in producing a final piece, but I can often get more done (and often have to) on my own.

Which, I guess, is the point of this book. Motion graphics used to be a realm of high expertise, those skilled in the esoteric ins and outs of After Effects, etc. Now it falls to the editor as often as not. And rapid turnaround is constantly of the essence. Motion is an excellent tool for this job.

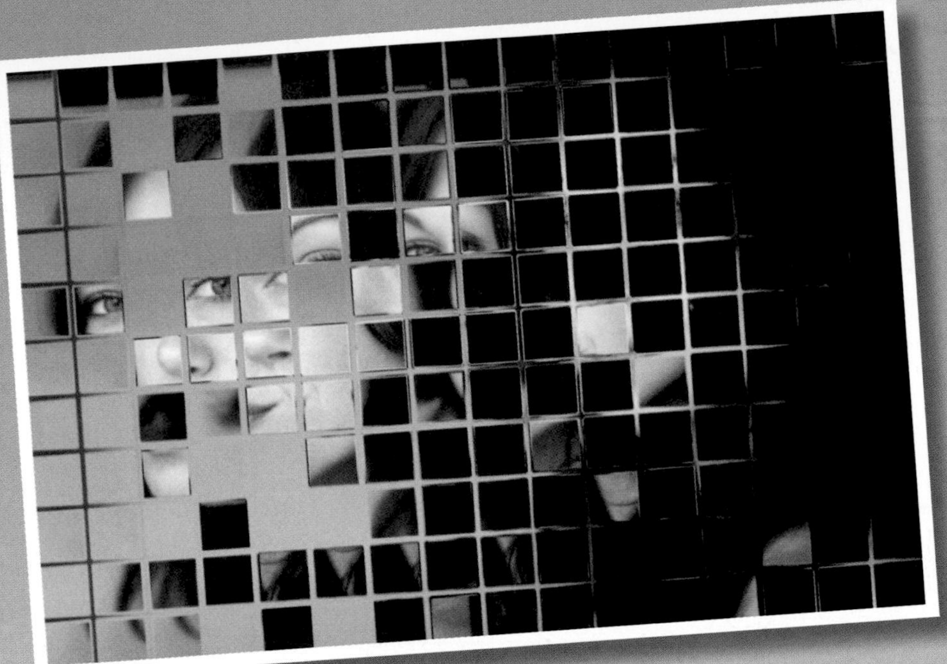

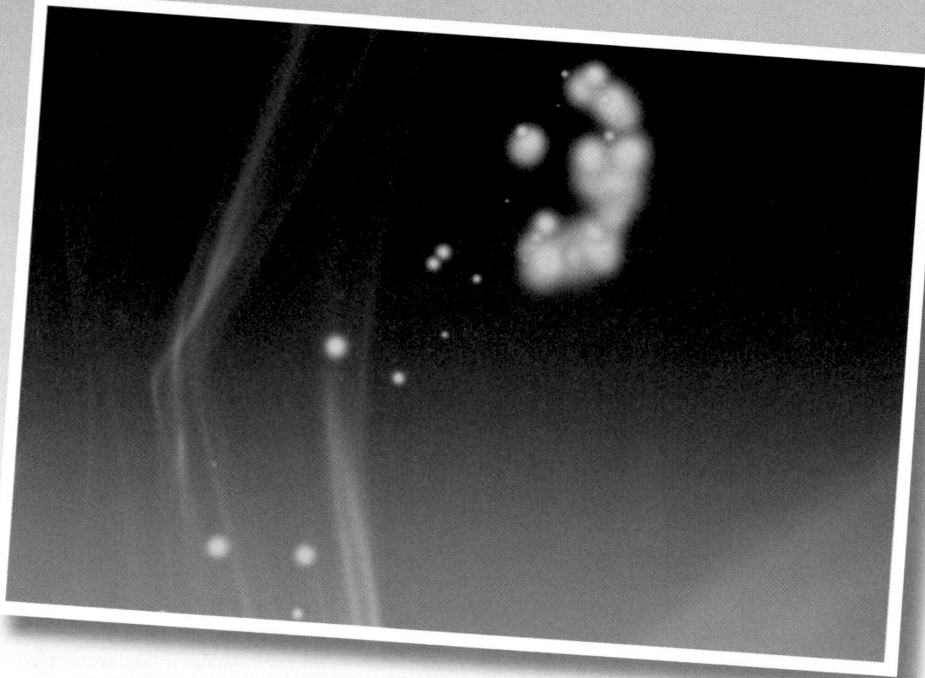

Replicators, Emitters, Filters, Behaviors—all can be used to enhance the movement of your Motion project.

2 Animation

THE HEART OF MOTION is movement. There are many ways to enhance your Motion project through animation.

And if we're clever, it won't take a lot of horsepower to do it. In this chapter, we'll explore techniques like Color Cycle animation, Simulation Behaviors, Displacement Maps, and more to get maximum animation at minimal cost.

Color Cycle Animation

SOMETIMES A PROJECT NEEDS a little extra "spice," something to give it a little more "oomph." I had a project to put some arrows on a graph and it occurred to me that if I showed some movement along the arrows as the text typed on it would really add the extra polish my project needed.

The definition of Color Cycling is *a technique that simulates animation by continuously changing colors rather than moving the objects.*

The technique was used extensively in early video games because it was easier for the processor to shift around a color table than it was to keep multiple frames in memory and swap them to screen. You can utilize the same advantages. This technique requires very little of the graphics processor or much memory and allows you to add animation to your projects with a minimum of effort.

1 First select the **Shape** tool and create your shape. In this case, I've created a simple arrow.

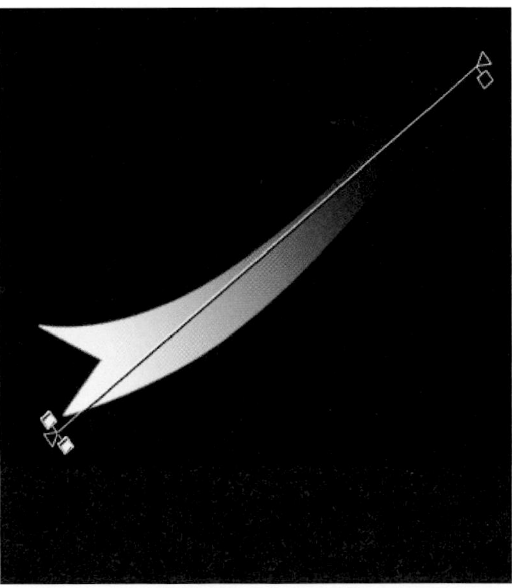

4 Adjust it to make the gradient follow the arrow.

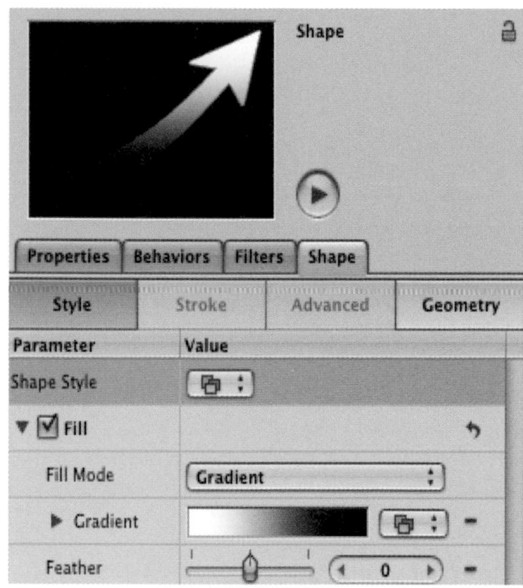

2 Select the Shape tab and set the **Fill Mode** to **Gradient** and choose grayscale as the gradient.

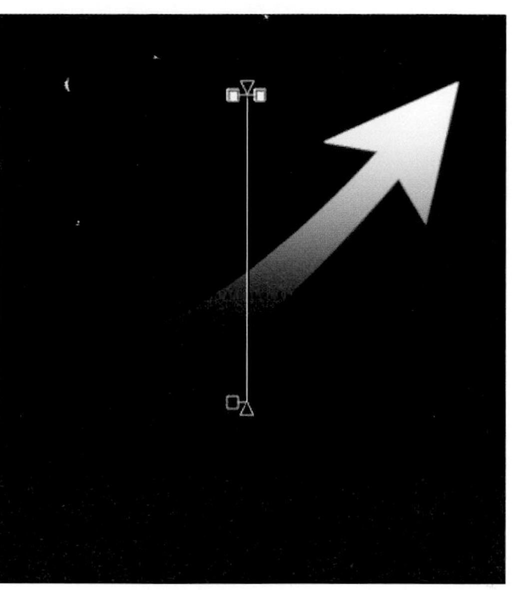

3 Now activate the **Adjust Item** tool by pressing and holding the tool selection button or repeatedly pressing ⇥ (tab) to bring up the gradient editor.

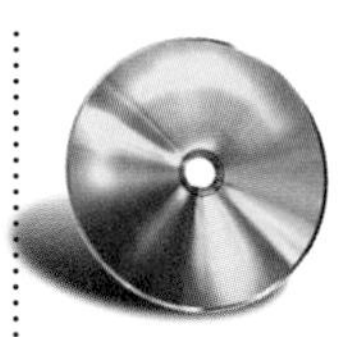

HOT TIP

For fun, try altering the repeats in the Gradient Colorize filter, change the Repeat Method from Mirror to Wrap, and play with the gradient.

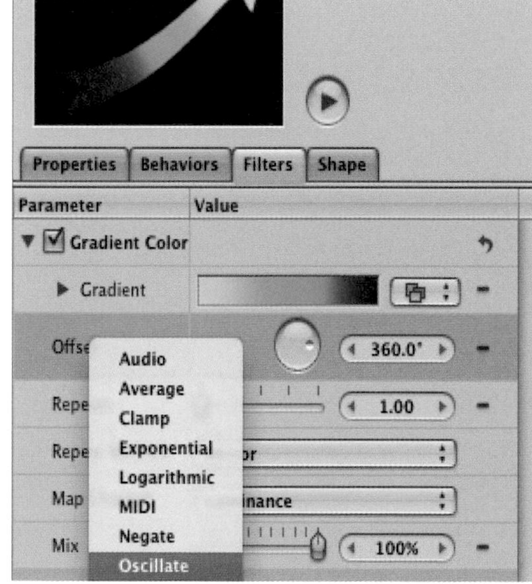

5 Add **Filter/Color Correction/Gradient Colorize** and set the **Gradient** to, say, **Radioactive** for now, leave the **Repeats** at 1, set the **Offset** to **360**, and right/ctrl-click on the **Offset** and select **Oscillate**.

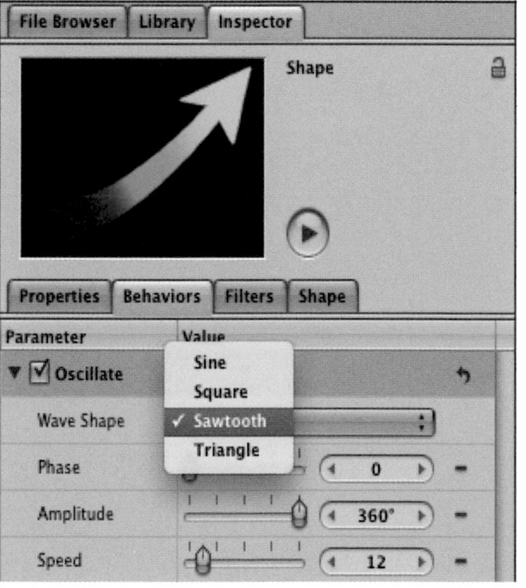

6 In the Behaviors tab, select **Oscillate**, change the **Wave Shape** to **Sawtooth**, the **Amplitude** to **360**, and the **Speed** to **12**. Press Play and you'll see the bright color at the head shift down the arrow.

Flag Waving

THERE IS AN EXCELLENT PLUG-IN for Motion that produces a very realistic waving banner or flag. Or one might use a luminance map from an actual flag to drive a displace filter to get a realistic effect. However, I thought it might be fun to try a stylized look.

This project uses a radial gradient and the color cycling effect (with repeats) to create a "displacer" that is used both to wave our flag and to shade it.

1 Start with a new project. Name the default group **Flag Waving.** Create a group within it and call it **flag**. Place your flag image there. The creation of the flag is left to the reader. I used a white rectangle, a blue rectangle, replicators for the stars, and a replicator for the red stripes. A photo or artwork could be used instead.

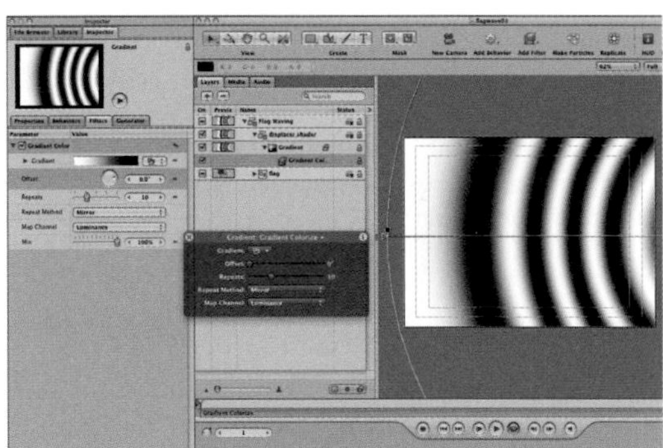

4 Now we're going use the same trick as the **Color Cycling** animation from earlier in this chapter. **Add Filter/Color Correction/Gradient Colorize** to the **Gradient** generator and set the **Repeats** to 10

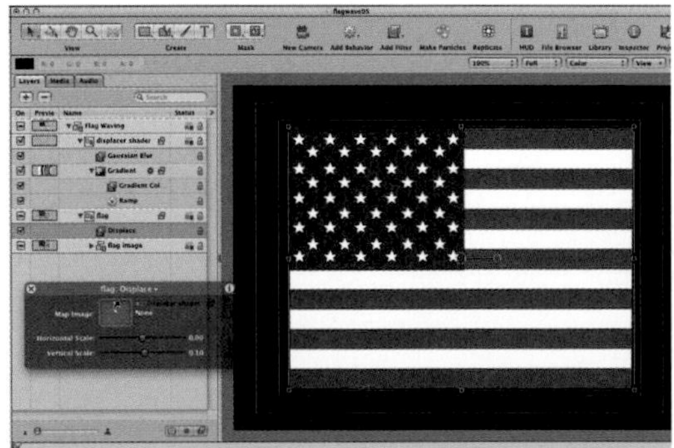

7 Let's set the **Opacity** of the **displacer shader** group to zero while we concentrate for a bit on the **flag** group. Select the **flag** group. **Add Filter/Distortion/Displace.** Drag the **Displacer Shader** layer to the **Map Image** well and set the **Horizontal Scale** to **0** and the **Vertical Scale** to **0.10.**

2 However you get your flag (the project on disc has one), collect it up and stick it in a new group within **flag** called **flag image**.

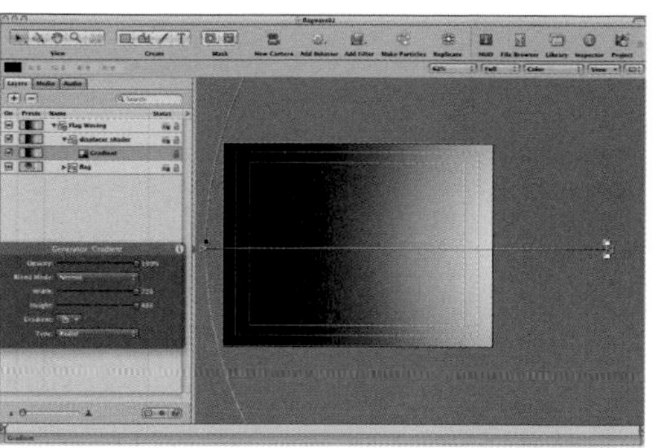

3 Next build the displacement generator. First add a new group above your flag. Call it **Displacer Shader**. Add a **Gradient** generator and set the gradient to Grayscale; then change the **Gradient Type** to **Radial**. Select the Adjust Item tool and set your gradient to look like the picture above.

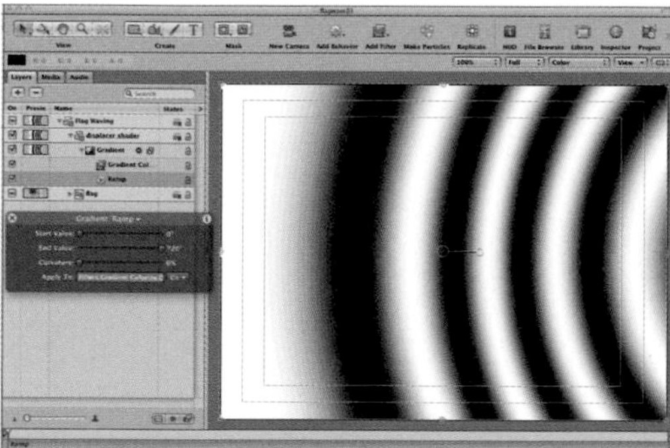

5 Right/ctrl-click on **Offset**, select **Ramp**, and set the **Ramp End** value to **720°** (even multiples of 360° will allow looping). Now if you press play you should see a series of concentric lines slowly move from left to right across the screen.

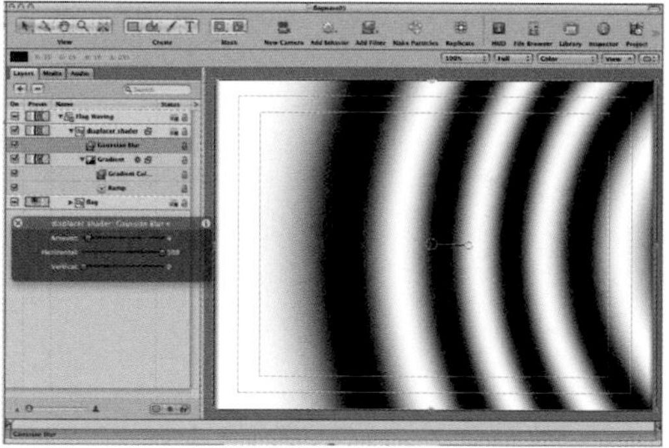

6 You'll also notice some banding. Let's fix that. **Add Filter/Blur/Gaussian Blur.** Set the **Vertical** value to zero. This will cause only horizontal blurring.

8 Hmmm... Seems that Motion is truncating the bottom of the flag. Press R to activate the **Rectangle** tool. Draw a large black rectangle bigger than the screen and place it behind the **Flag Image** group (but still in the **Flag** group).

9 Now to add the shading. Click on the **Displacer Shader** group and set the **Opacity** to 50% and the **Blend Mode** to **Multiply**. That'll give us the shading we're looking for.

HOT TIP

For variation, try a linear gradient in the displacer.

LiteBrite on Crack

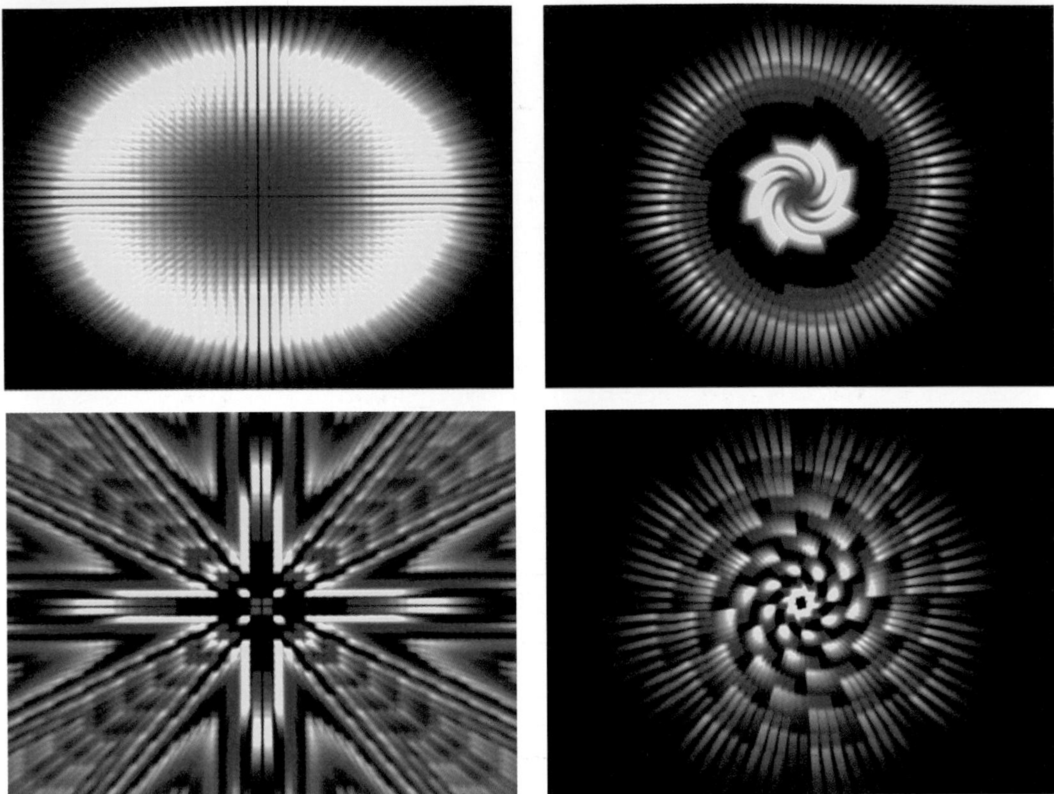

WHILE WORKING ON THE MASK for the Weaving project (from the last chapter) I noticed that by playing with the color repetitions slider, I got some wild patterns, so I threw a ramp on it and showed it to specialcase from the Apple Discussions forum. He added Extrude and Light Rays (everything looks better with Extrude and Light Rays!) and sent it back to me and thus was born LiteBrite on Crack.

I thought Why limit ourselves to a rectangle?, so I modified the Replicator and got the second example above.

All of this animation is achieved by modifying a single slider. Pretty cool, eh?

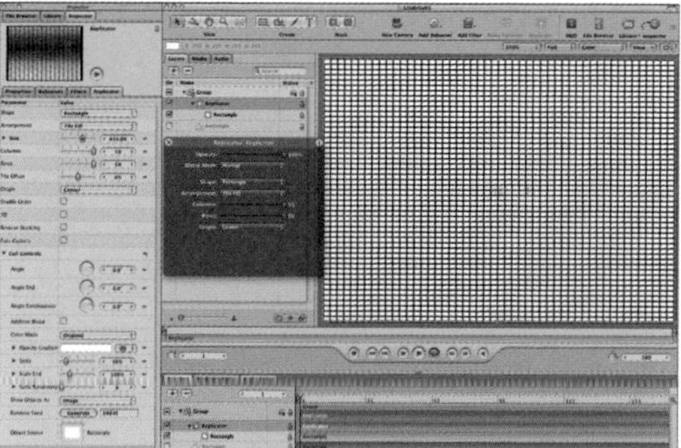

1 Start with a new project. Draw a small rectangle in the middle of the screen. With it selected, press L or click the Replicate button on the toolbar. Set your columns and rows to 50. Adjust your scale and sizing until the Replicator fits neatly on the screen with just a thin line between all the rectangles.

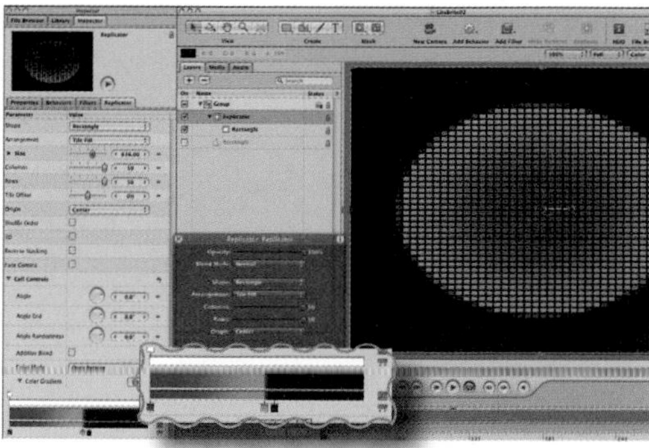

2 Now change the **Color Mode** to be **Over Pattern** and edit the gradient to look like the picture (see inset). Essentially, make the lower value Red, the middle value Orange, and everything above that Black.

3 Right/ctrl-click on the **Color Repetitions** slider and select **Ramp**. Set the **End Value** to be **115**.

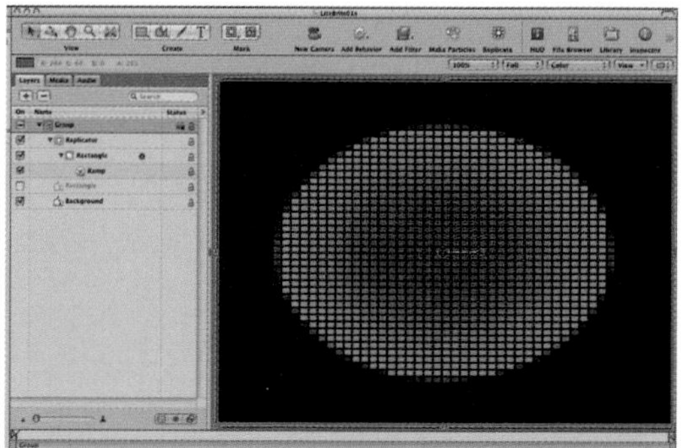

4 Add a black-filled rectangle behind the Replicator. Name it **Background**.

HOT TIP

The gradient used in the Color Mode is what determines the look of this animation.

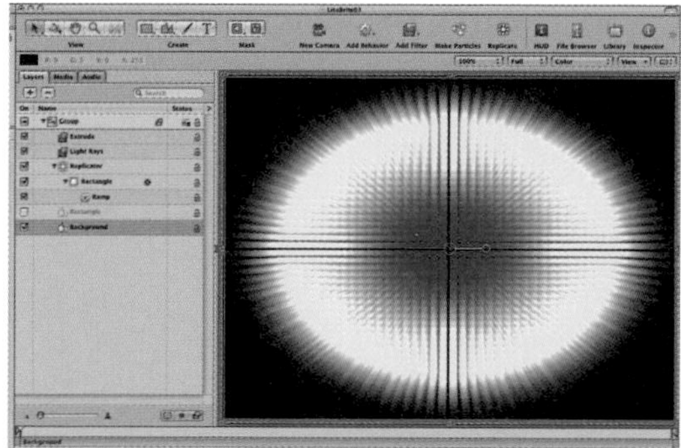

5 Select **Group**. Add **Filter/Glow/Light Rays**. Set **Amount** to **169**. Set **Glow** to **3.64**. Add **Filter/Stylize/Extrude**. Set the **Distance** to 0. **Back Size** to 0.61. **Face Brightness** to 1.30.

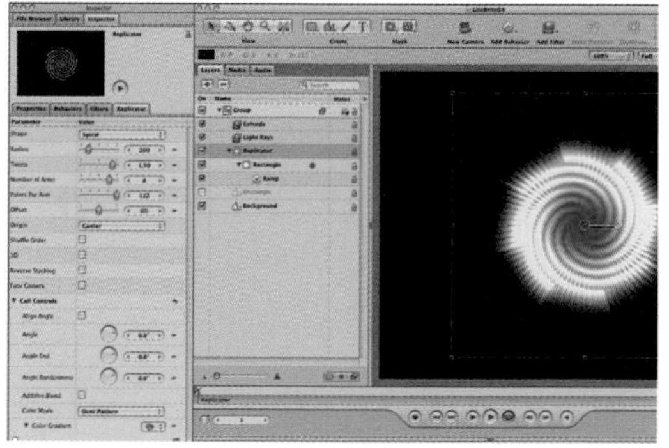

6 For a cool variation, select the **Replicator**, change the **Shape** to **Spiral**. Set the **Twists** to **1.50**, **Number of Arms** to **8**, **Points per Arm** to **122**.

Mirror Tiles

I WAS TRYING TO DO SOMETHING WITH THE DISPLACE filter to make an image look like it bubbled away, but it just didn't work quite right, but while I was playing, I came up with this idea. It looked like the reflections you get when looking into those mirror tile walls.

I used a replicator to create a screen of random shades of gray and used them to drive the Displace filter. I put a couple of Oscillate behaviors on the X and Y displacement. Then, for good measure, I used a gradient colorize with a ramp on the offset to vary the grays over time and put fade in/out on the replicator so the displacement would eventually go to zero (and have the picture resolve).

I can imagine some fun titles that could be designed around this—maybe have the tiles quite small and the displacement only in the vertical direction, so pieces would look like they fell into place. Use your imagination:

IMAGE COURTESY LARA DOUCHETTE

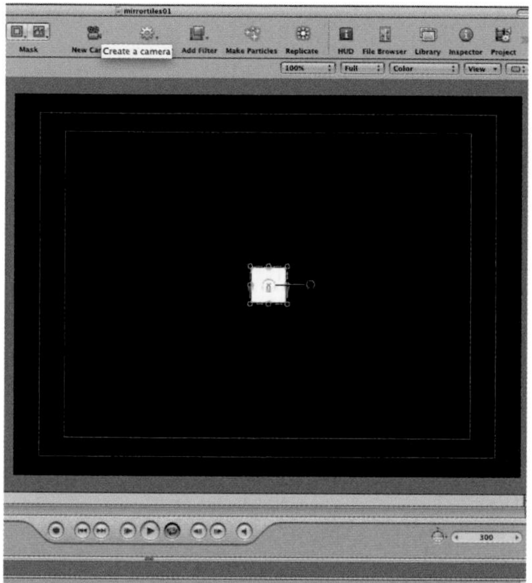

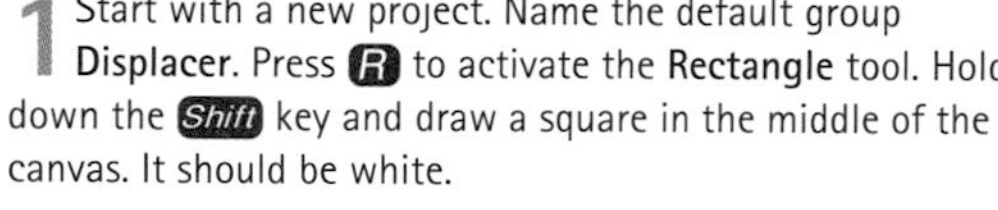

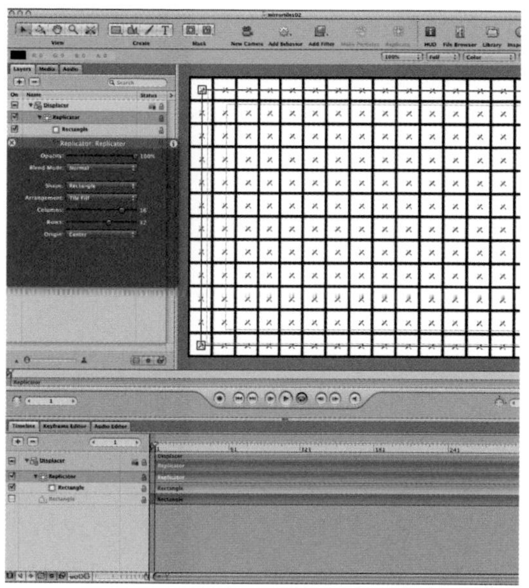

1 Start with a new project. Name the default group **Displacer**. Press R to activate the **Rectangle** tool. Hold down the Shift key and draw a square in the middle of the canvas. It should be white.

2 With the square selected, press L or click on the Replicate button in the toolbar. Adjust the **Scale** and **Rows** and **Columns** to create a grid of squares filling the screen.

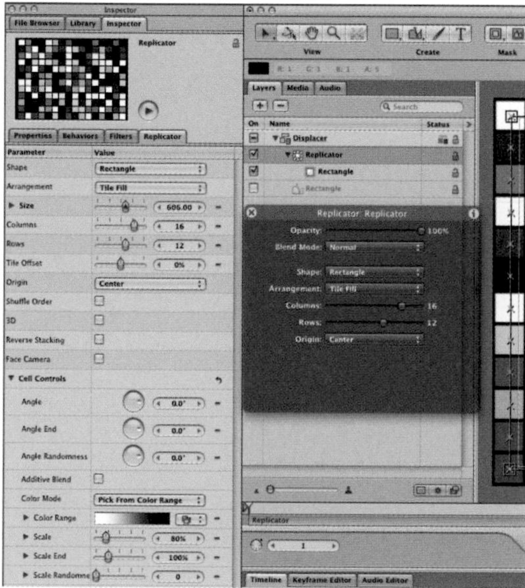

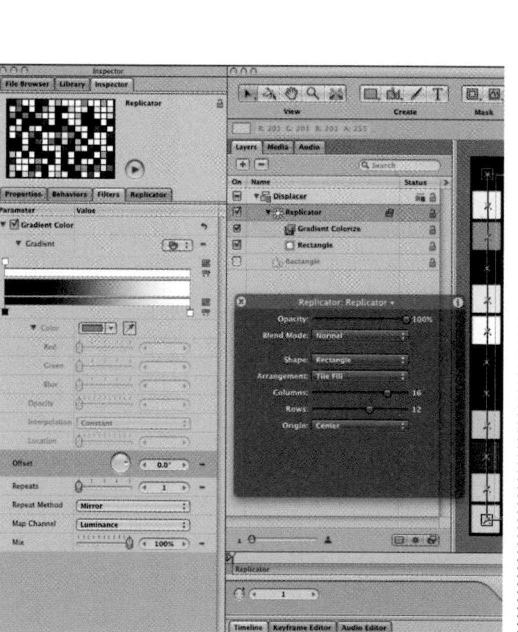

3 Set the **Color Mode** to **Pick From Color Range**. Set the Color Range **Gradient** to **Grayscale**.

4 With the **Replicator** selected, **Add Filter/Color Correction/Gradient Colorize**. Invert the gradient.

HOT TIP

Use the button to the right of the gradient editor that looks like an equal sign ("=") to invert the gradient.

continued...

Mirror Tiles (continued)

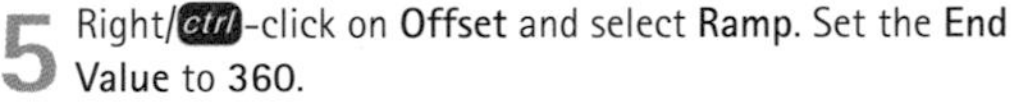

5 Right/ctrl-click on **Offset** and select **Ramp**. Set the **End Value** to 360.

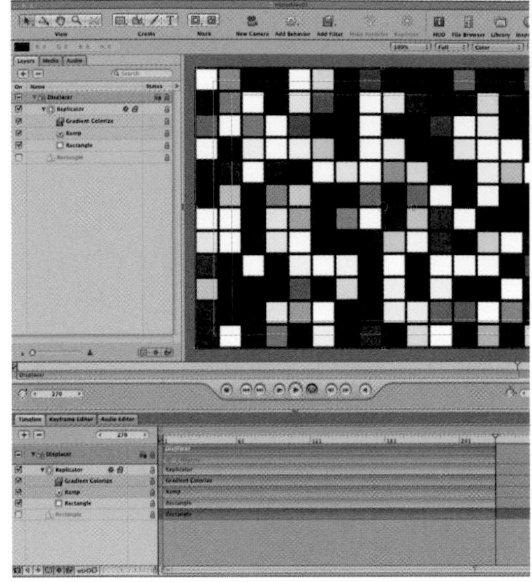

6 Position to frame 270. Select the **Displacer** Group. Press O to truncate the **Displacer** group there.

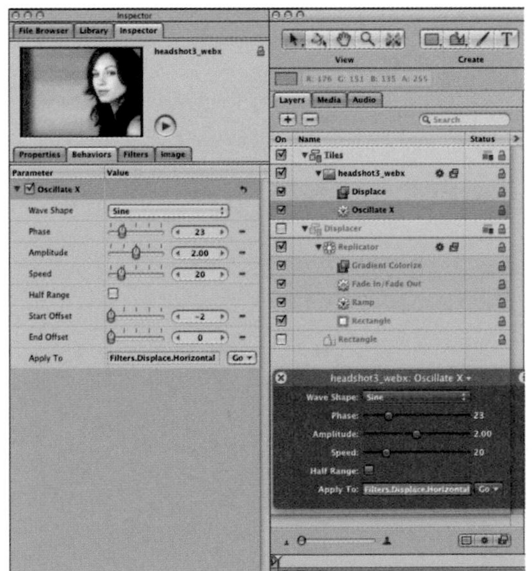

9 Turn off the **Displacer** group. Select the Displace filter. Right/ctrl-click on the **Horizontal Scale**, select **Oscillate**. Name that behavior **Oscillate X**. Set the **Phase** to 23, the **Amplitude** to **2.00**, the **Speed** to 20, and the **Start Offset** to **-2**.

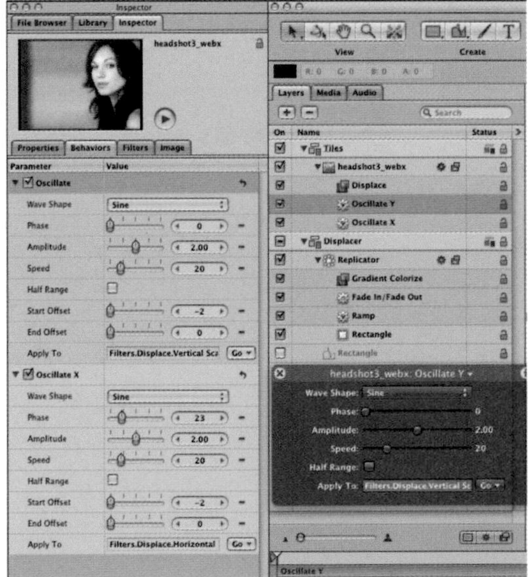

10 Select the **Displace** filter. Right/ctrl-click on the **Vertical Scale**, select **Oscillate**. Name that behavior **Oscillate Y**. Set the **Amplitude** to **2.00**, the **Speed** to **20**, and the **Start Offset** to **-2**.

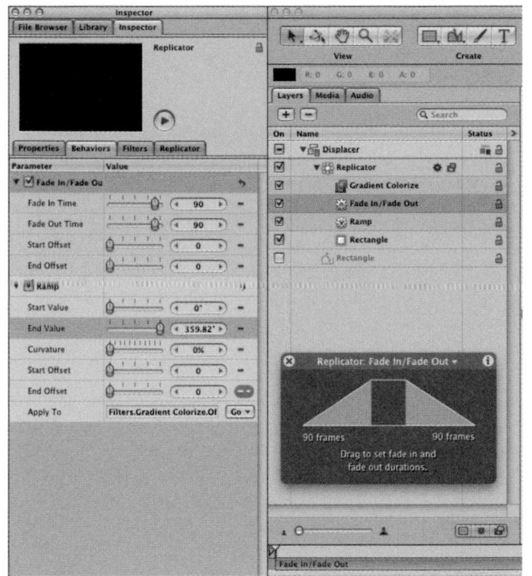

7 Position back to frame 1. Select the **Replicator** (not the Displacer group). **Add Behavior/Basic Motion/Fade In/ Fade Out**. Set the **Fade In** and the **Fade Out** to **90** frames.

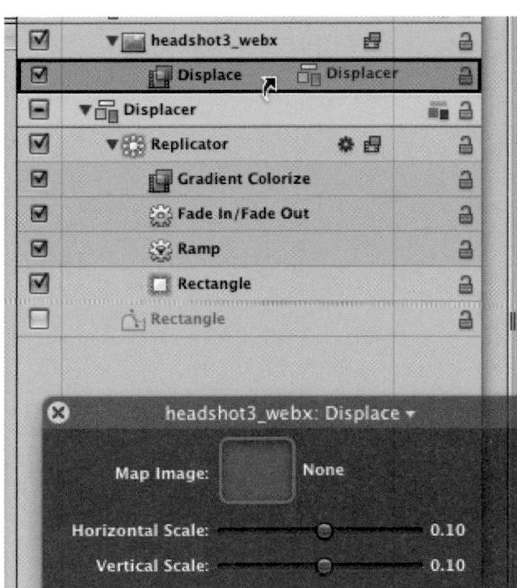

8 Create a new group above the **Displacer** group. Call it **Tiles**. Place your image there. **Add Filter/Distortion/ Displace**. Drag the **Displacer** group into the **Displace Map** image well.

HOT TIP

If a layer has an object well, you can drag an object onto that layer to place it in the object well.

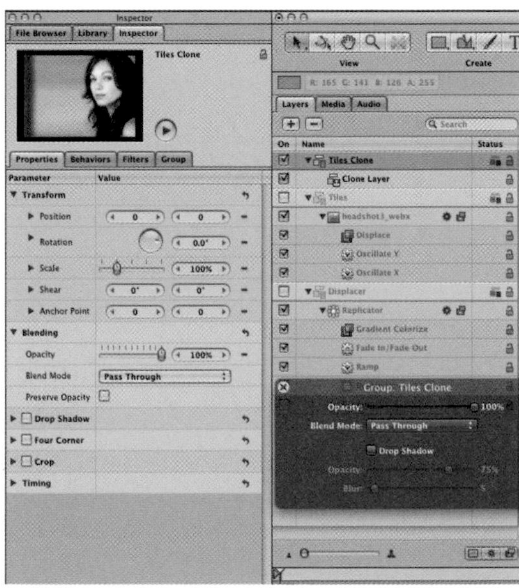

11 That works, the image starts out clear, then distorts, then comes back to clear and holds. But let's add a twist. Let's have it start out distorted, resolve, hold, and then distort again. Select the Tiles group. Press **K** to create a clone layer. Name the new group Tiles Clone. Turn off the Tiles group.

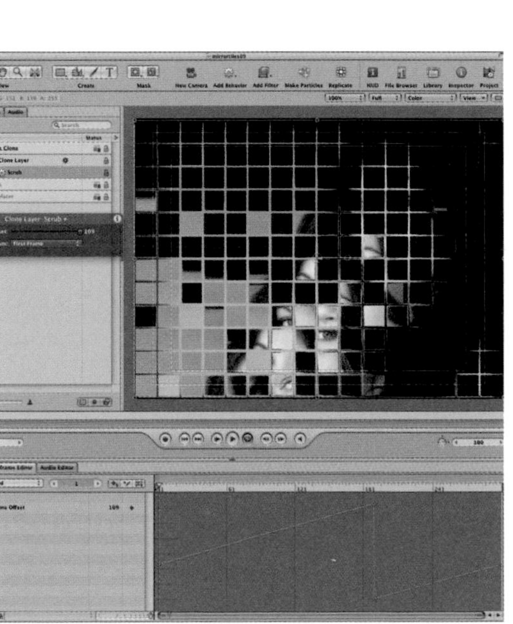

12 Select the **Clone** Layer. **Add Behavior/Retiming/ Scrub**. Set **Offset From** to **First Frame**. Press **A** to turn on record. On frame 1, set the **Offset** to **109**. On frame 290, set the **Offset** to **298**. On frame 291, set the **Offset** to **0**. On frame 300, set the **Offset** to 108. Press **A** to turn off record. You're done!

QuickSilver

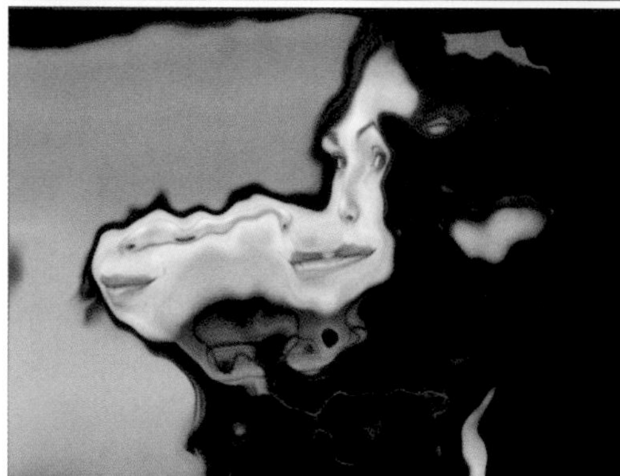

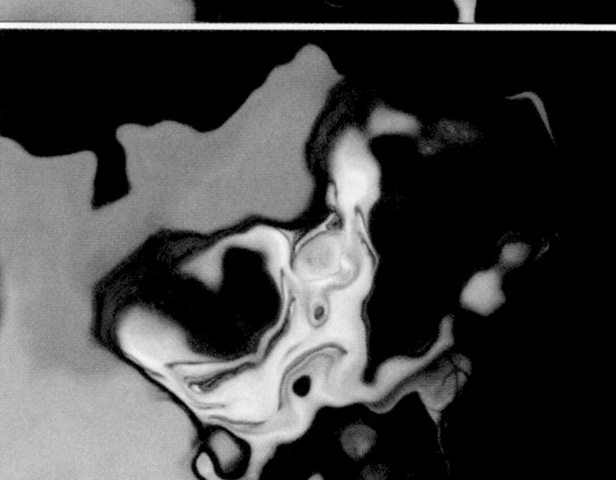

WHEN PLAYING with the Fun with Mirror Tiles project, I decided to try the same displace kind of thing using the Clouds generator.

I called it Quick Silver because it looks like a reflection in mercury.

IMAGE COURTESY LARA DOUCHETTE

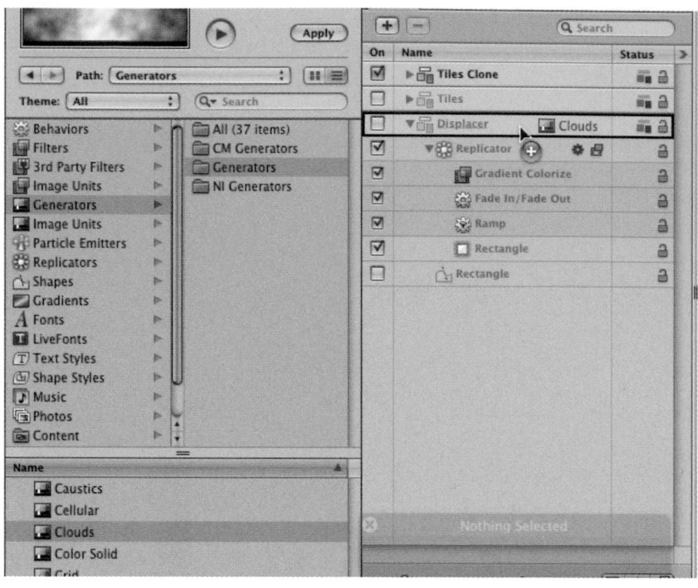

1 Start with the **Mirror Tiles** project from the previous page. Position to frame 1. From **Library/Generators**, add the **Clouds** generator to the **Displacer** group.

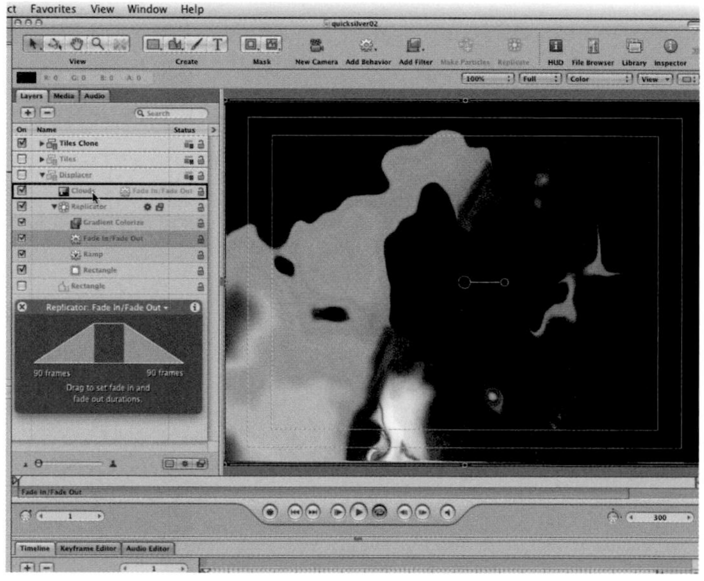

3 Back to frame 1. Drag the **Fade In/Fade Out** from the **Replicator** to the **Clouds** generator.

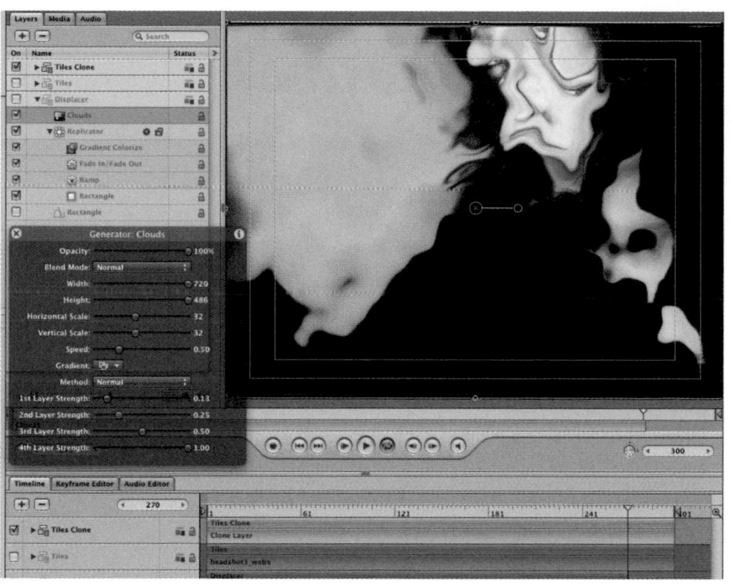

2 Position to frame 270. Press O to truncate the **Clouds** generator there.

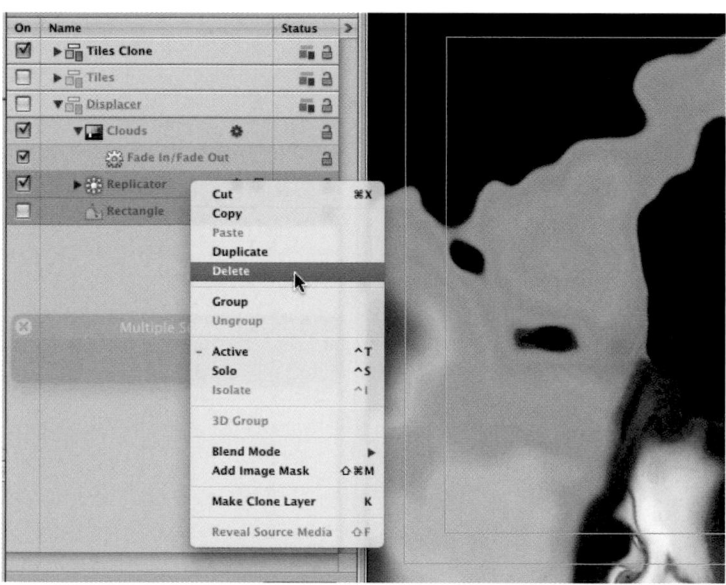

4 Now delete the **Replicator** and **Rectangle** and you're done!

Shuffle

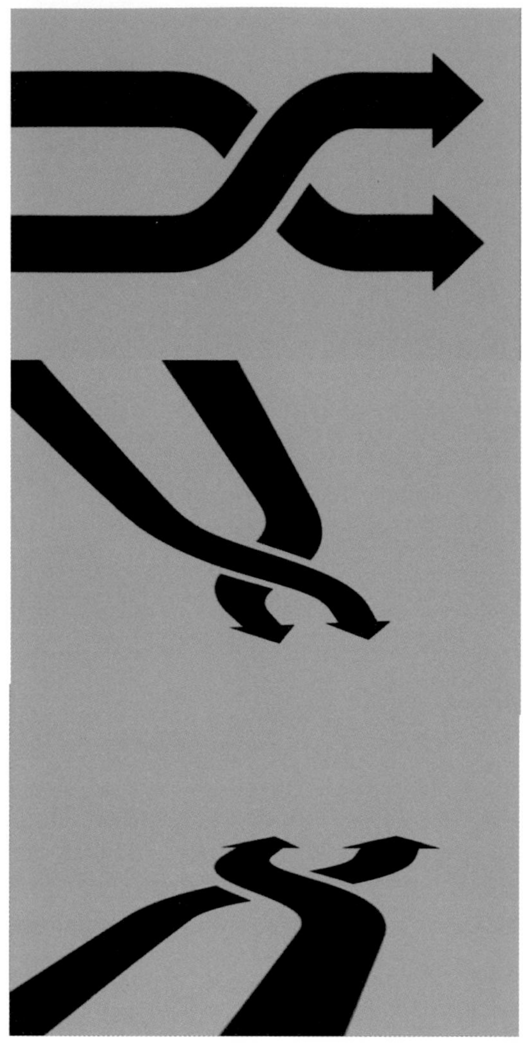

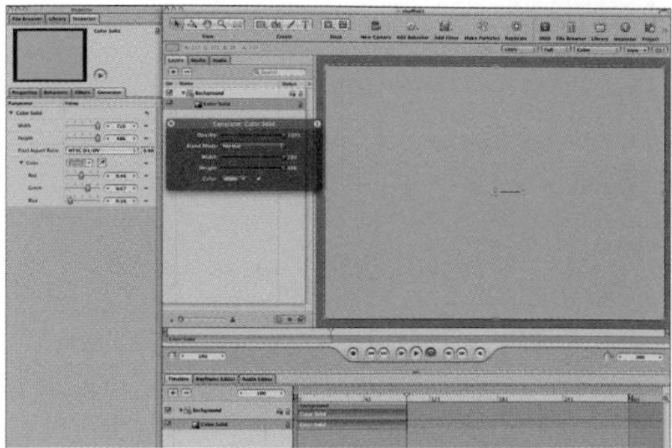

1 Start with a new project. Name the default group **Background**. Put a **Color Solid** generator in it, set the color to **Red 0.46**, **Green 0.67**, and **Blue 0.10**. Position to frame 100. Press O to truncate the background layer there.

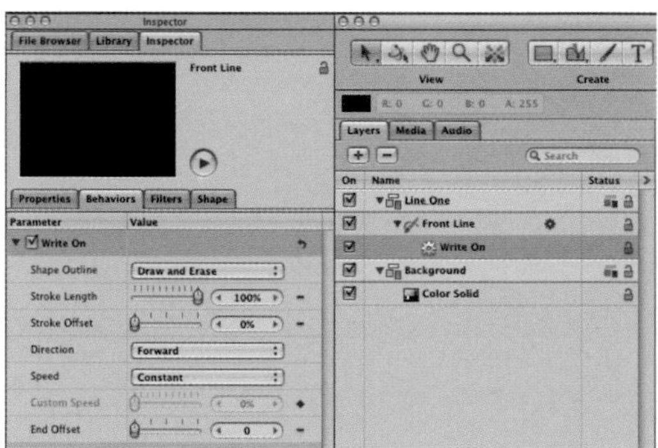

4 Add **Behavior/Shape/Write On**. Change the **Shape Outline** to **Draw and Erase**.

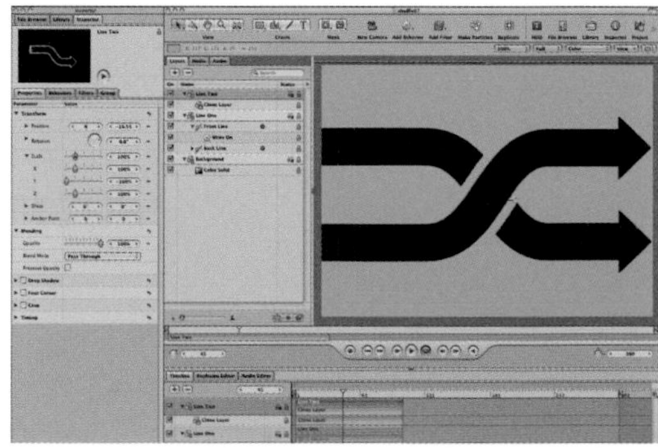

7 Turn back on the Background group. Position to Frame 1. Select the Line One group. Press K to create a Clone Layer. Name the new group **Line Two**. Set the Properties **Y** scale to -100%. Position to frame 45—you may need to adjust the y position slightly to get the arrows to line up.

WHEN THE iPOD SHUFFLE first came out, Apple produced a commercial with dancing people and advancing lines with arrows and everyone wanted to know how to do it.

I first did this in Motion 1 and it took over 90 layers to complete. Not terribly difficult, just moving masks, etc. Now in Motion 3, it takes only 13 layers. And it looks better.

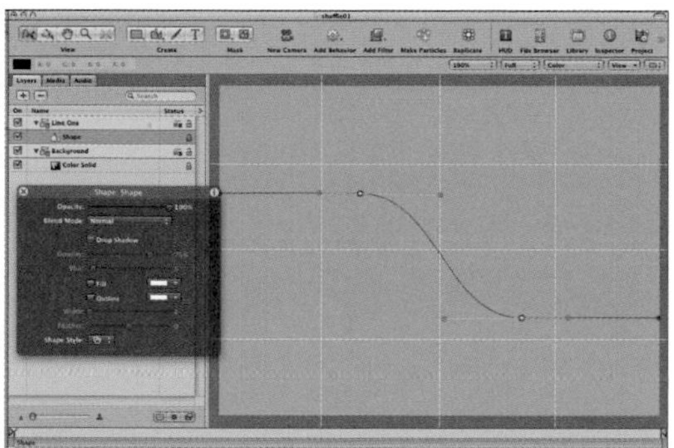

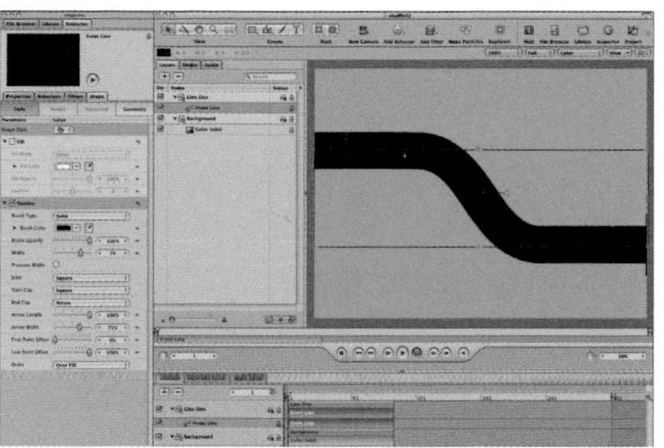

2 Go back to frame 1. Add a new group above **Background**. Name it **Line One**. Press **B** to activate the **Bezier** tool. Draw a 4-point open shape like the picture above (press tab when you're done drawing). Select the **Adjust Control Points** tool to edit the shape to get it to look right. Add guides to assist. Accuracy is critical to achieving a good outcome.

3 Name the new shape **Front Line**. Turn on **Outline**. Set the **Brush Color** to **Black**. Set **Brush Width** to **74**, **Joint** to **Square**, **Start Cap** to **Square**, **End Cap** to **Arrow**. Set the **Arrow Width** to **71%**. Position to frame 100 and press **O** to truncate the **Line One** group.

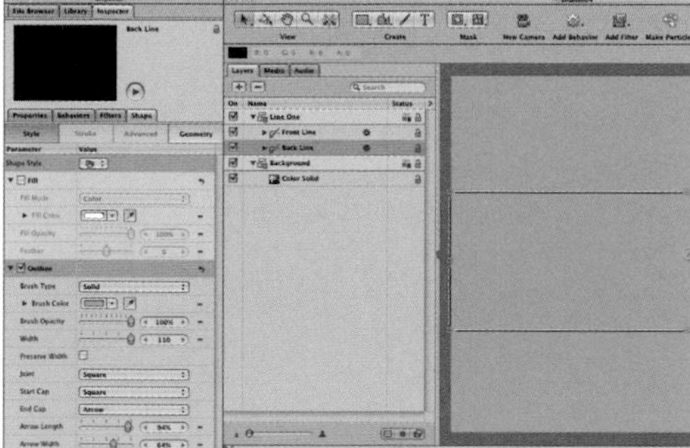

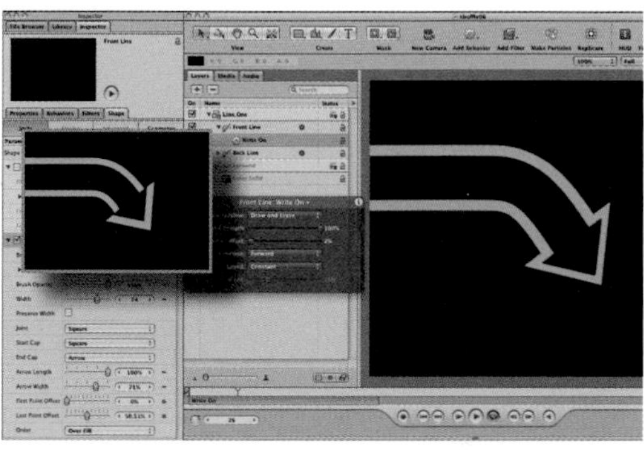

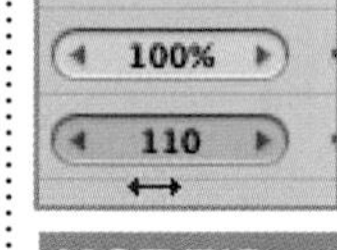

HOT TIP

When sliders reach their limits, often the virtual slider of clicking and dragging over the numerical value will allow you to set values outside the range allowed by the slider.

5 Select **Front Line**. Type **⌘D** to duplicate the **Front Line** shape. Name the duplicate **Back Line**. Place it under the **Front Line** in the Layer Palette. Set the **Brush Color** to be the same as the **Background**. Set the **Width** to **110**. **Arrow Length** to **94%**. **Arrow Width** to **64%**.

6 Turn off the **Background** and you can see that the arrowhead is not centered within its border (inset). To fix this, we'll advance the **Front Line** a small amount. In **Front Line**'s **Write On** behavior set the **Stroke Offset** to **2%**, and see how that centers it within the **Back Line**'s border.

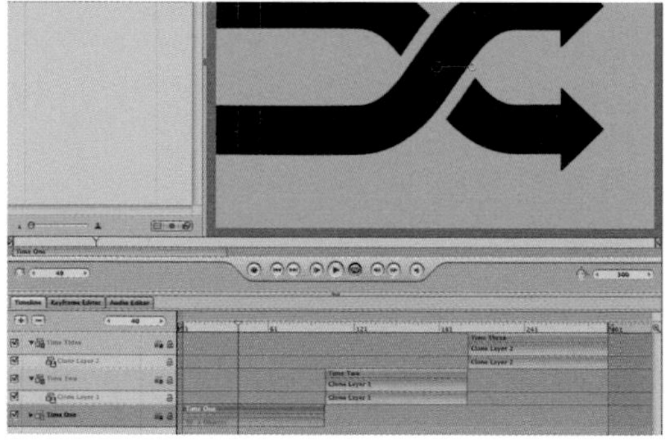

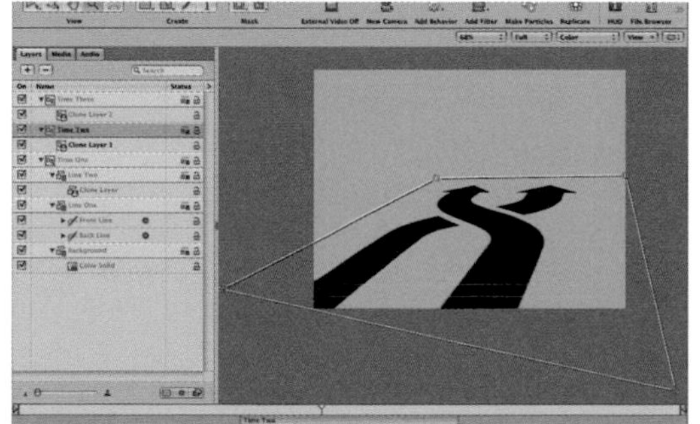

8 Go back to frame 1. **⌘**-select **Line One**, **Line Two**, and **Background**. Press **⌘ Shift G** to group them all. Name this **Time One**. Then press **K** to create a clone layer. Call this **Time Two**. Select **Time One** again and press **K**. Name the new clone layer group **Time Three**. Slide **Time Two** to start at frame 101. Slide **Time Three** to start at frame 201.

9 Now take the newly created clones and use Corner Pinning to skew them into different perspectives. And there it is, your own iPod Shuffle commercial. For extra credit, you can set the background color to the same green color.

Lava Lamp

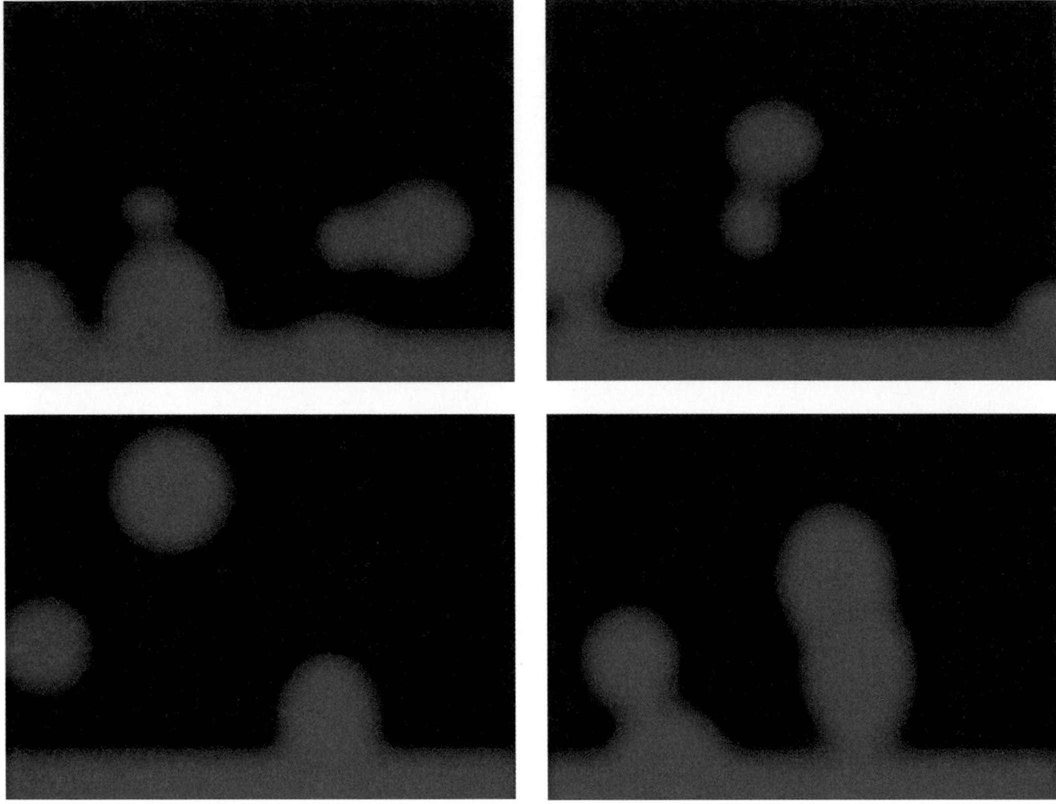

I WAS TRYING TO SIMULATE the filling of a glass of milk and the first attempt ended up looking like a lava lamp. Which was a lot more interesting than a glass filling with liquid, so here it is.

I animated a circle to make it look "jiggly" and used a particle emitter to send copies of it flying toward the top of the screen. An attractor at the bottom of the screen provides the "gravity." Then to tie it together, a vectorize color filter makes the circles stick togeher when they get close to each other.

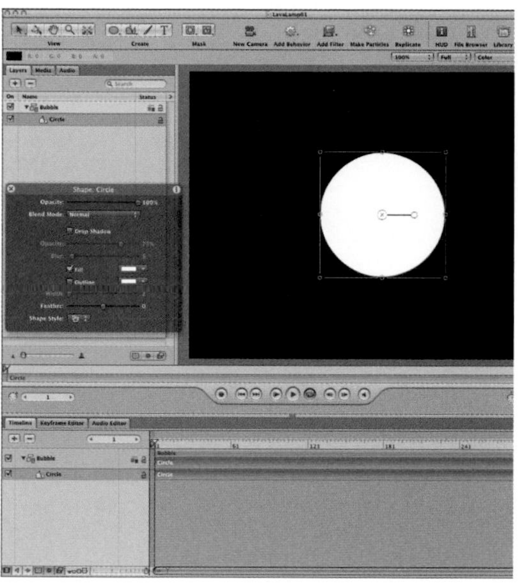

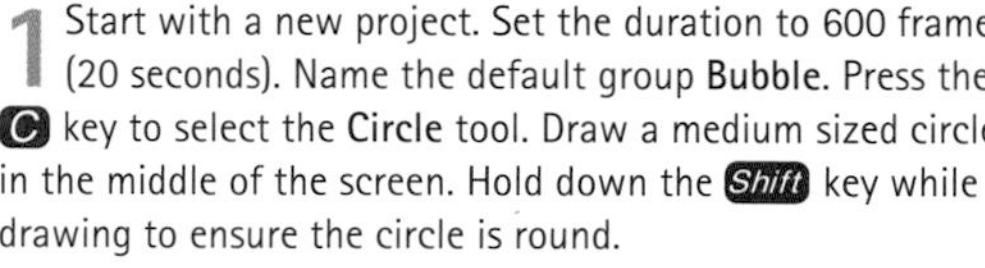

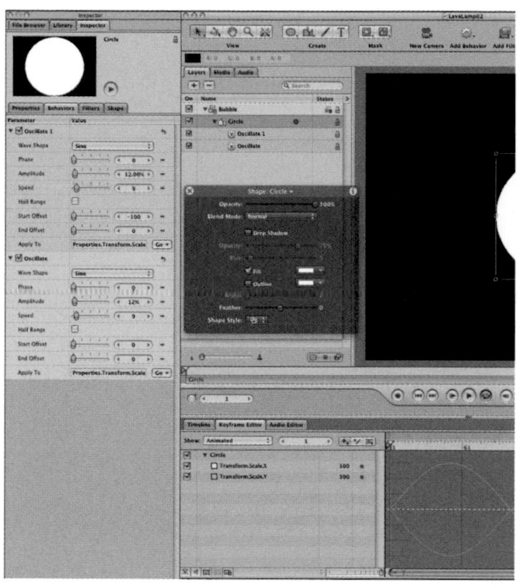

1 Start with a new project. Set the duration to 600 frames (20 seconds). Name the default group **Bubble**. Press the **C** key to select the **Circle** tool. Draw a medium sized circle in the middle of the screen. Hold down the **Shift** key while drawing to ensure the circle is round.

2 In the **Circle's** Properties pane, right/**ctrl**-click on the **X Scale** and select **Oscillate**. Set the **Amplitude** to 12%, **Speed** to 9. Repeat for the **Y Scale**—again, in the **Properties** pane, right/**ctrl**-click on the **Y Scale** and select **Oscillate**. Set the **Amplitude** to 12%, **Speed** to 9, and the **Start Offset** to -100.

HOT TIP

Clone layers can allow groups to be treated as movie clips.

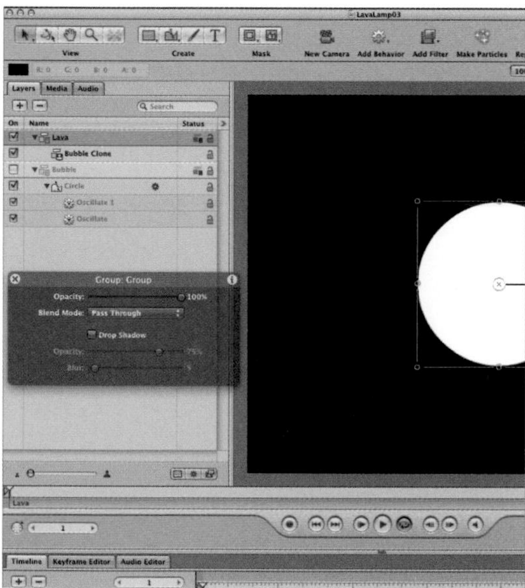

3 If you press play, you'll see your circle "jiggle." Back on Frame 1, click on the **Bubble** group. Press **K** to get a clone layer. Rename the new group **Lava**. Rename the **Clone Layer** to **Bubble Clone**. Turn off the **Bubble** group.

4 With **Bubble Clone** selected, press **E** or the **Make Particles** button. Change the **Shape** to **Line**. Set the **Start Point** to -325, -300 and the **End Point** to 325, -300. Set the **Emission Angle** to 180, **Emission Range** to 5.0, **Birth Rate** to 1, Life to 8, **Speed** to 280, **Speed Randomness** to 188, **Spin Randomness** to 7, **Scale** to 51%, **Scale Randomness X** to 49, **Scale Randomness Y** to 54.

continued...

Lava Lamp (continued)

5 Press **R** to activate the **Rectangle** tool. Draw a rectangle just off the bottom of the screen. Name it **Gravity**.

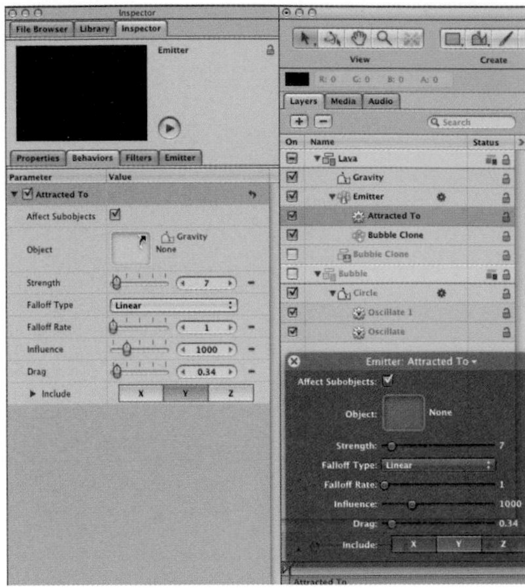

6 Click on the **Emitter**. Add **Behavior/Simulations/Attracted To**. Set the **Strength** to **7** and the **Drag** to **0.34**. Turn off the **Include X**, so only the **Y** is turned on. Drag the **Gravity** rectangle into the **Object** well.

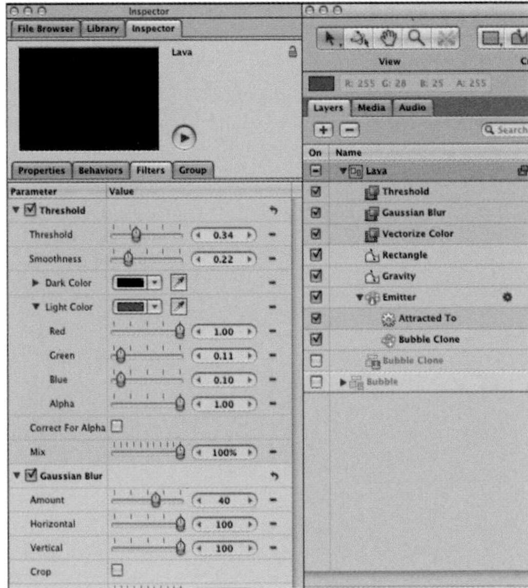

9 Add **Filter/Blur/Gaussian Blur**. Set the **Amount** to 40. Add **Filter/Color Correction/Threshold**. Set the **Threshold** to **0.34**, the **Smoothness** to **0.22**. Leave the **Dark Color Black**, set the **Light Color** to a bright **Red**.

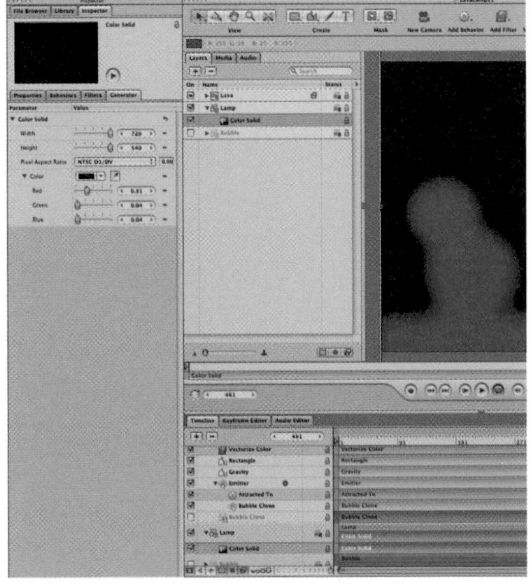

10 Finally, let's add some background liquid for the bubbles to float in. Create a new group below the Lava group. Call it Lamp. Place a color solid in it. Set the color to a deep red.

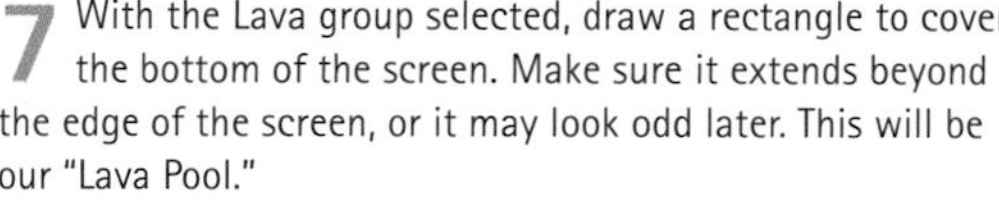

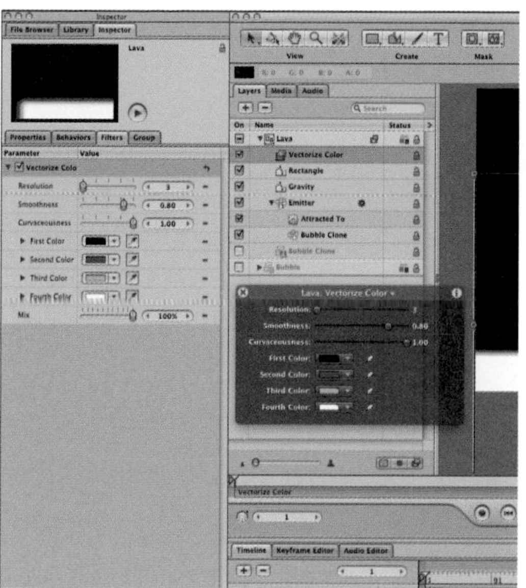

7 With the Lava group selected, draw a rectangle to cover the bottom of the screen. Make sure it extends beyond the edge of the screen, or it may look odd later. This will be our "Lava Pool."

8 Now to create the effect. Select the Lava group. **Add Filter/Stylize/Vectorize Color**. Set the **Resolution** to 3, the **Smoothness** to **0.80**, the **Curvaceousness** to **1.00**. Set the First color to black, the Fourth color to white, and the colors inbetween to middle grays.

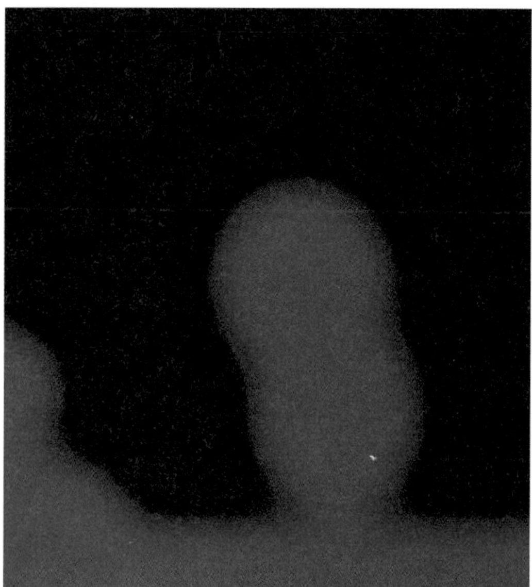

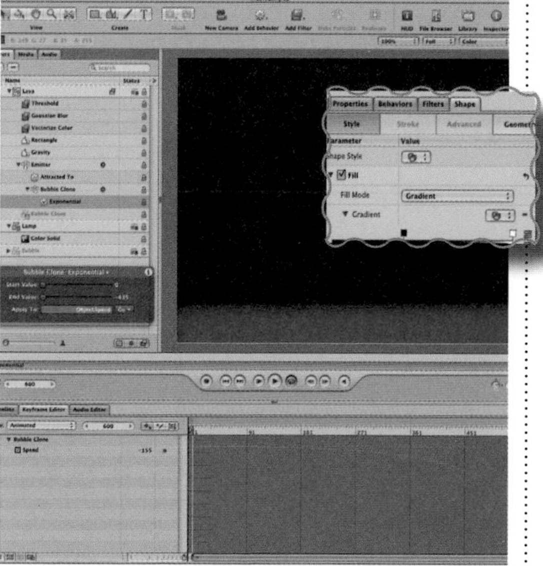

11 Now for some extra credit—let's make the animation looping. To do that, we'll drop the speed near the end using an **Exponential** behavior on the speed. That will stop the bubbles from jumping up at the end of the timeline and allow us to seamlessly loop back to the beginning.

12 Select the **Emitter/Bubble Clone**. Right/ctrl-click on **Speed**. Select **Exponential**. Set the **End Value** to **-425**, the **Start Offset** to **-1000**. Position to frame 600—alter the **Start Offset** until you have no more bubbles in the "air."

Newton's Pendulum

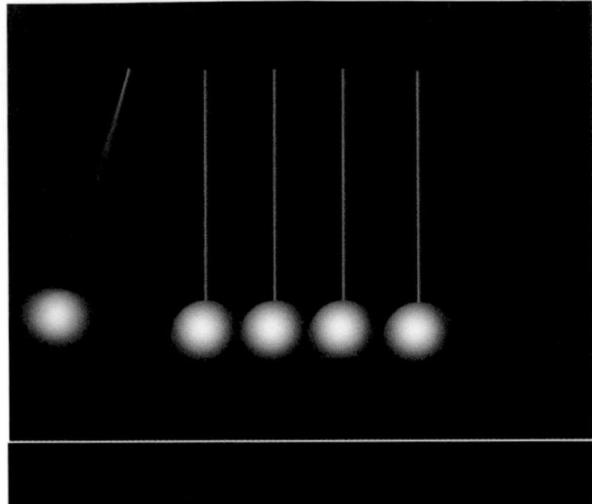

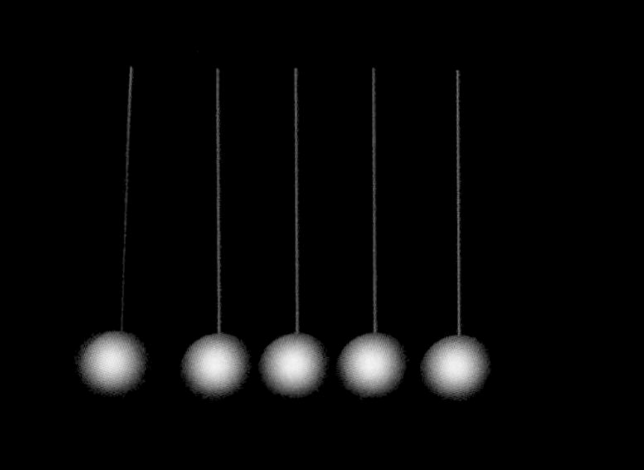

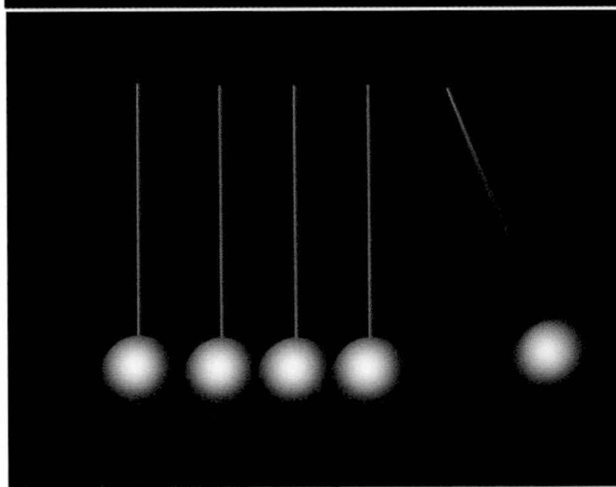

THIS PROJECT STARTED AS A CHALLENGE—how to make a realistic portrayal of one of those desktop knick-knacks—the Newton Pendulum.

Properly timed behaviors give it the realism it needs.

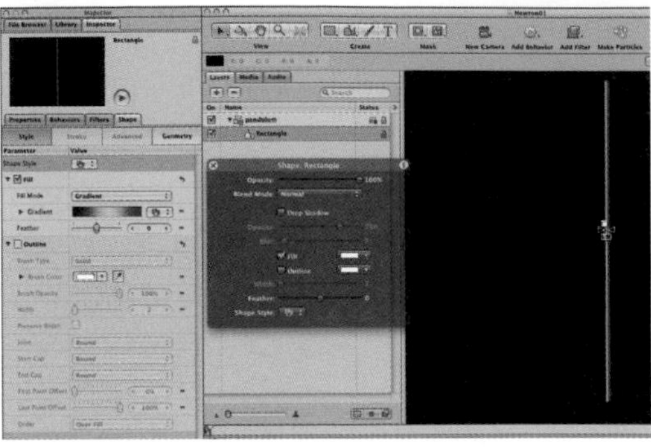

1 Start with a new project. Name the default group **Pendulum**. Set the project duration to 50 frames. Press **R** to activate the Rectangle tool. Draw a thin rectangle. For extra credit, use a gradient fill to make it seem round.

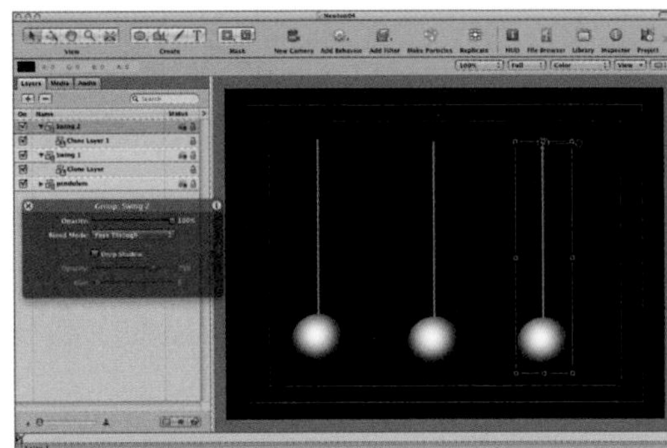

4 With the **Pendulum** group selected, press **K** to create a clone layer. Name the new group **Swing 1**. Repeat and name the second new group **Swing 2**. Spread them out a bit as seen above with **Swing 1** on the left and **Swing 2** on the right. Accurate positioning will take place in Step 7.

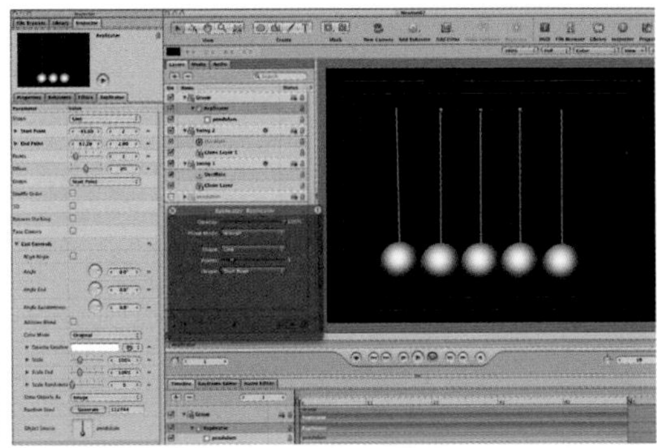

7 Now go back to frame 1 and select the **Pendulum** group. Press **L** to replicate. Change the **Shape** to **Line, Points** to 3. Position the replicator between two outside "Swing" pendulums. Tighten everything up so all the balls are just touching each other.

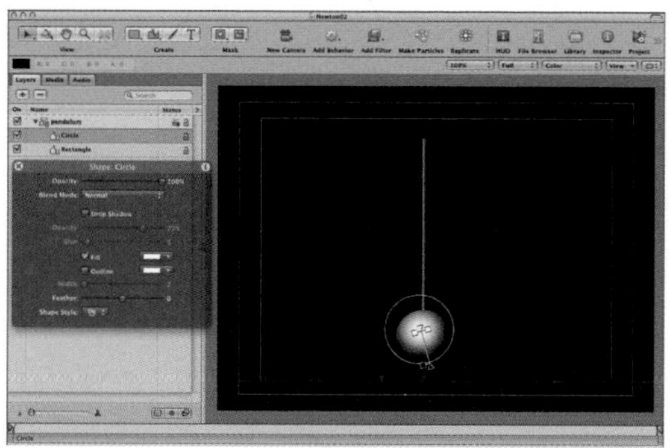

2 Now press **C** to activate the **Circle** tool and make a ball for the end of it, also using a gradient fill (radial) to make it seem round too.

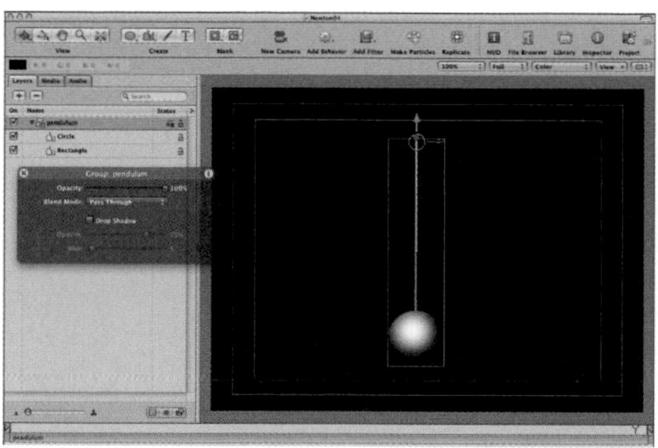

3 Select the **Pendulum** group. Move the Anchor Point using the **Adjust Anchor Point** tool to the tip of the rectangle like the picture above.

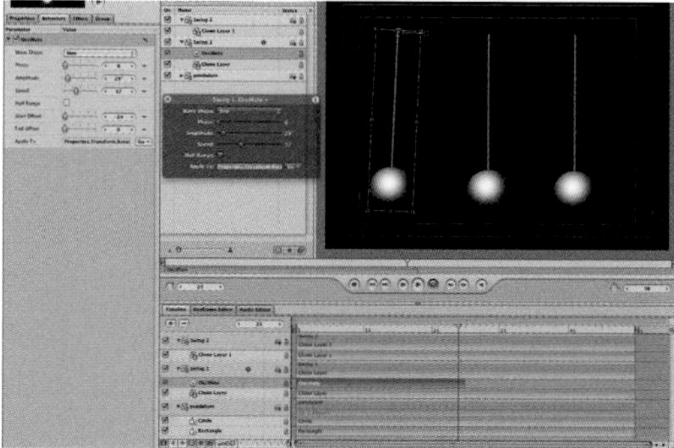

5 Select **Swing 1**. Right/ctrl-click on **Rotation**. Choose **Oscillate**. Set **Amplitude** to **29**, **Speed** to **37**, and **Start Offset** to **-24**. Go to frame **25**, Press **O** to truncate the **Oscillate** behavior there.

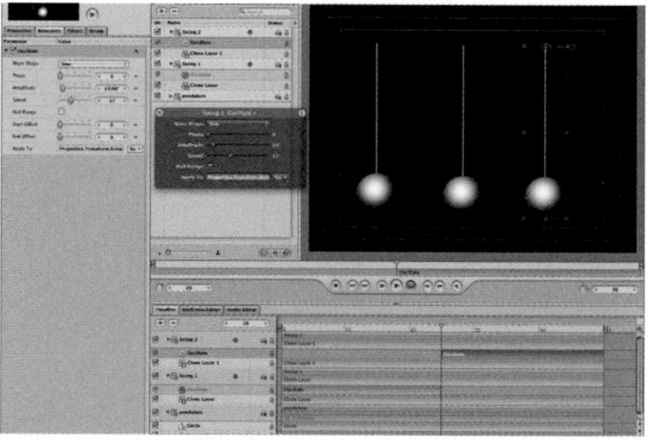

6 Select **Swing 2**. Right/ctrl-click on **Rotation**. Choose **Oscillate**. Set **Amplitude** to **29** and **Speed** to **37**. Go to frame **26**. Press **I** to begin the **Oscillate** behavior there.

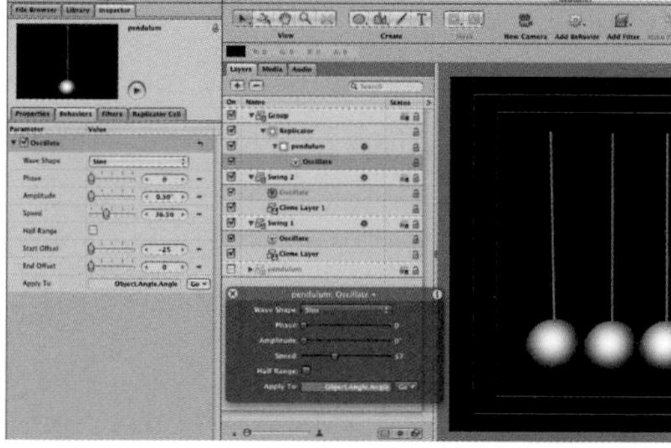

8 Let's add a little life to the inner pendulums. With the replicator cell (pendulum) selected, right/ctrl-click on the **Angle**. Select **Oscillate**. Set the **Phase** to **-0.29**, the **Amplitude** to **0.30**, the **Speed** to **36.5**, **Start Offset** to **-25**.

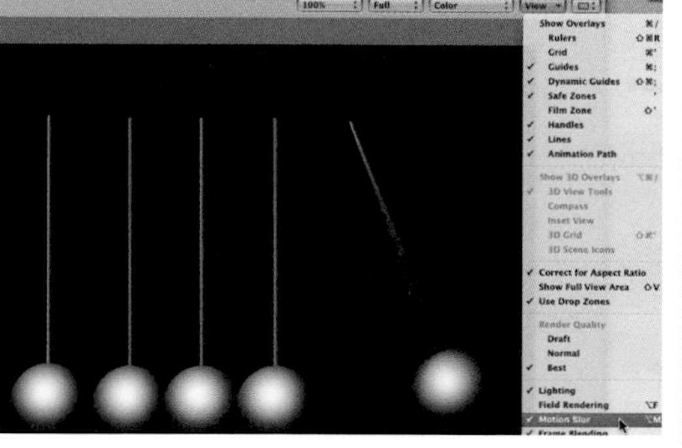

9 For extra realism, turn on Motion Blur.

HOT TIP

Effects like Motion Blur are best enabled last as their overhead can severly impact Motion's interactive performance.

Motion Welcome

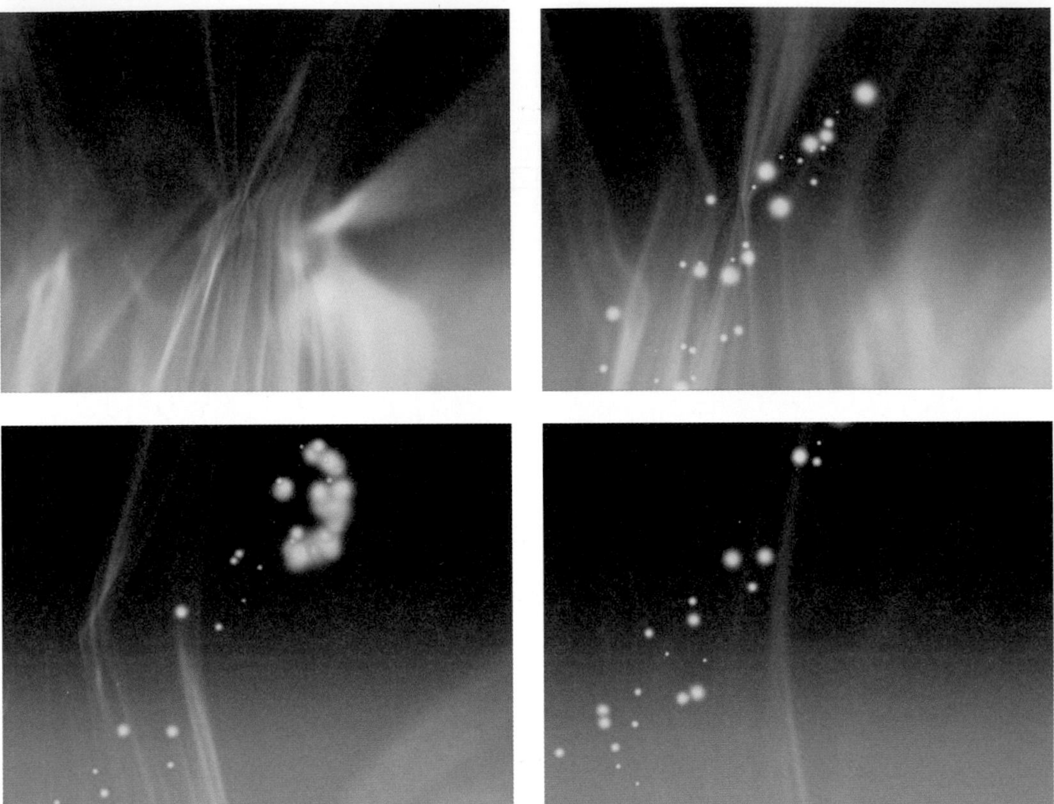

AFTER MOTION 1 CAME out, the "Welcome" animation was a popular inspiration—discussed in online circles and fora. When Motion 2 came out, it used the same animation and still no one had posted a successful recreation. After consulting a number of online sources and some friends, I came up with this version. I believe this successfully recreates the feel and gross details of that animation without being a slavish copy.

This project has three elements that make it match the Motion opening animation: (1) The light blue to dark blue backdrop; (2) the spray of "bubbles" that swirl around the screen, stirred by an unseen oscillation; and (3) the wisps, which are distorted smoke tendrils.

It seems like a complicated build, but it takes longer to explain than to do. Just follow the steps precisely and you'll be rewarded with your own Motion Welcome animation.

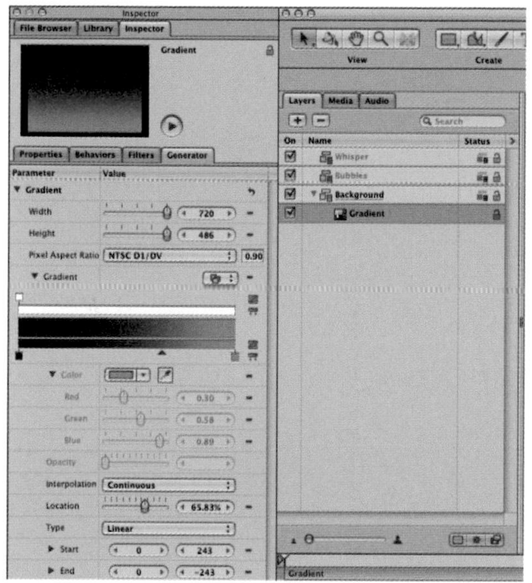

1 Start with a new project with 3 groups: **Background**, **Bubbles**, and **Whisper**. Set **Fixed Resolution** on all of them. Add a gradient generator to the **Background** layer and set the colors to **Red** 0.00, **Green** 0.04, **Blue** 0.13 at one end and **Red** 0.30, **Green** 0.58, **Blue** 0.89 at the other end. Adjust the center triangle a little toward the light blue.

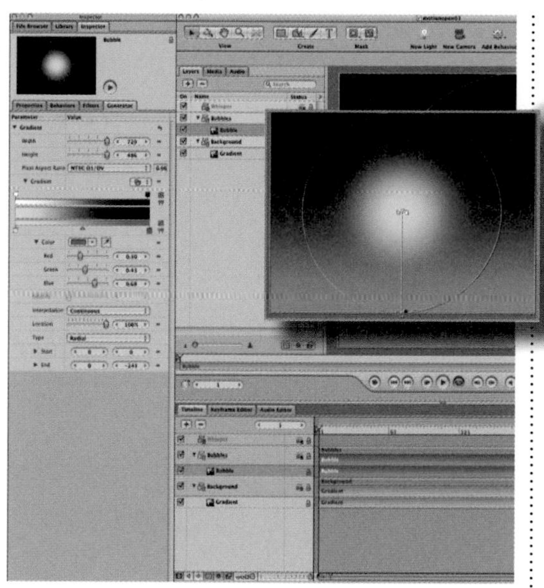

2 Add a new gradient generator to the **Bubbles** group. Name it **Bubble**. Change **Type** to **Radial**. Set the left tag color to **Red** 0.64, **Green** 0.89, **Blue** 1.00. Set the right tag color to **Red** 0.30, **Green** 0.43, **Blue** 0.68. Set the **Opacity** at the darker blue end to 0. Adjust the gradient as above to place it in the center of the screen.

3 In the **Properties** tab, set the **Scale** of **Bubble** to 25%. With **Bubble** selected, press E or click on the **Make Particles** button in the toolbar. Change the name of the Emitter to **Bubbles Rising**; **Shape** to **Line**; **Start Point** -100, -600; **End Point 100, -600** (which, you can see above, places the emitter offscreen).

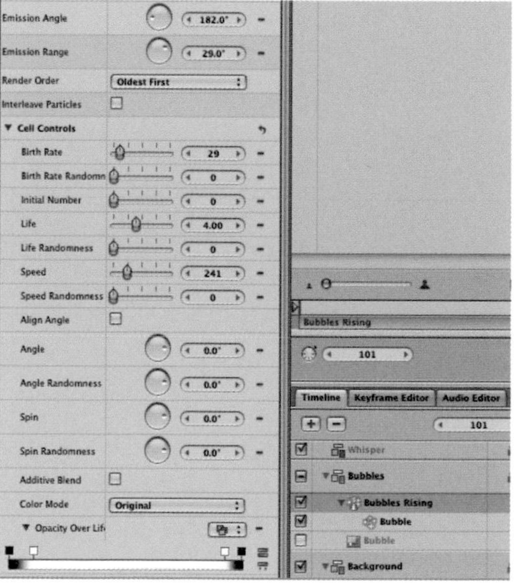

4 Set the **Emission Angle** to 182, **Emission Range** to 98, **Birth Rate** to 29, **Life** to 4, **Speed** to 241, **Speed Randomness** to 525. Set the **Opacity Over Life** to have small ramps at the beginning and end. **Scale** = 30%, **Scale Randomness** 100 (not shown above).

HOT TIP

An object need not be visible to be used in simulations.

continued...

Motion Welcome (continued)

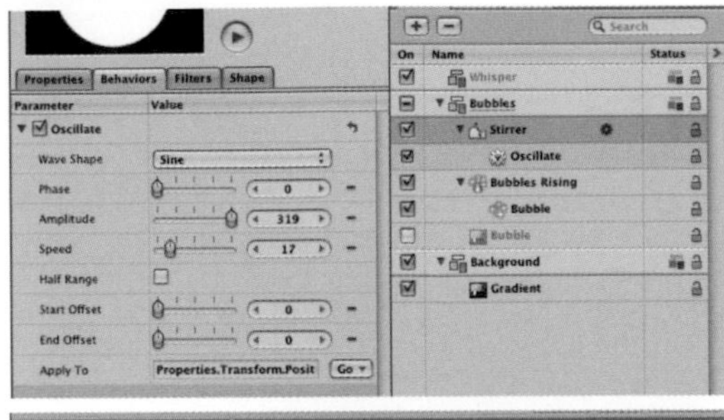

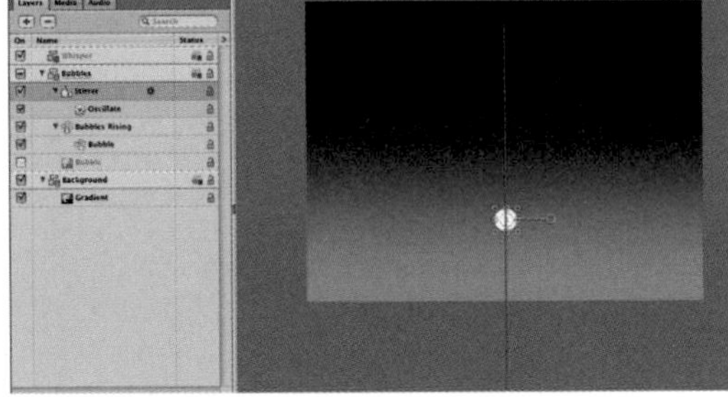

5 Press C to activate the **Circle** tool. Draw a small circle about 1/3 from the bottom of the screen. Name it **Stirrer**. Right/ctrl-click on the **Y** position and select **Oscillate**. Set the **Amplitude** to 320 and the **Speed** to 17.

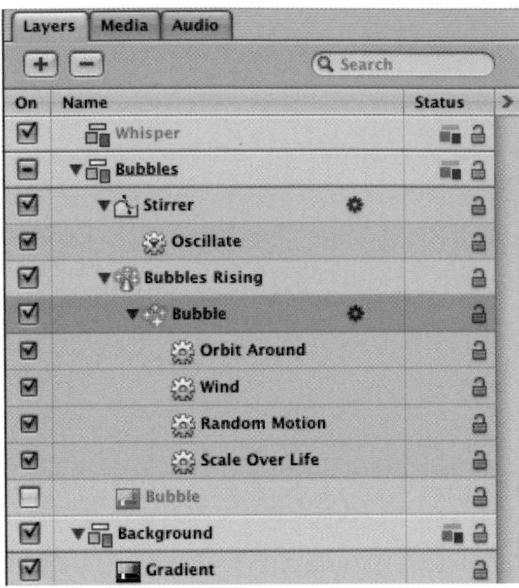

6 Select **Bubbles Rising/Bubble**. Add **Behavior/Particles/Scale Over Life**, **Add Behavior/Simulation/Random Motion**, **Add Behavior/Simulation/Wind**, **Add Behavior/Simulation/Orbit Around**.

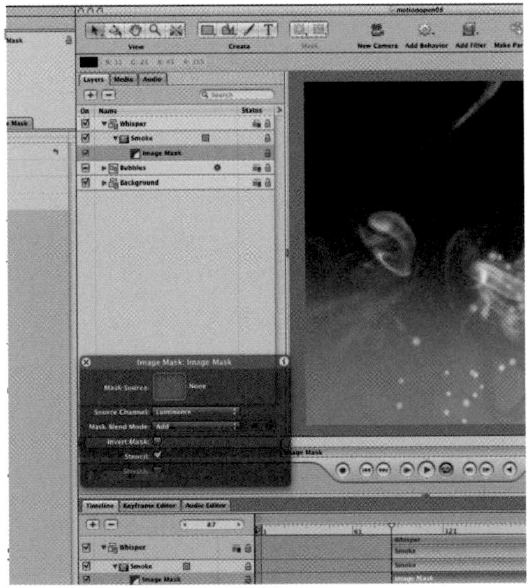

9 Go to your **Contents** folder and find the **Smoke** movie. Place it in the **Whisper** group. Position to frame 87. Press I to truncate the head of the **Smoke** clip. Type ⌘ Shift M. Set the **Channel** to **Luminance**. In the absence of anything in the **Mask Source** well, the clip itself is used.

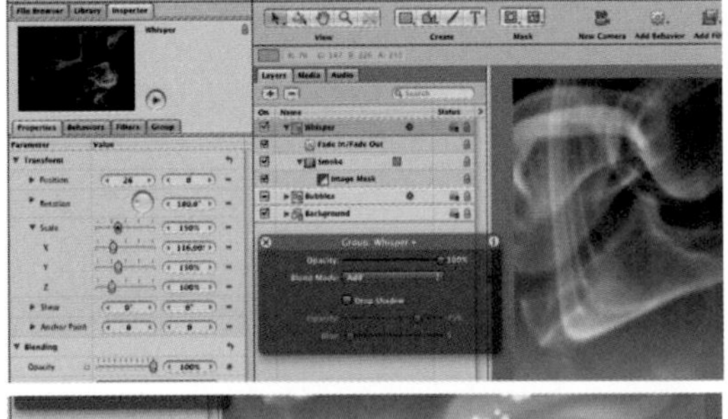

10 Drag the **Whisper** layer back to frame 1 (drag, not trim). Set the **Blend Mode** to **Add**. Set the Position to **26.0**, **Rotation** to **180**, **Scale X** to **116**, **Scale Y** to **150**, **Add Behavior/Basic Motion/Fade In/Fade Out**. Position to frame 300. Press O to truncate the **Whisper** group there.

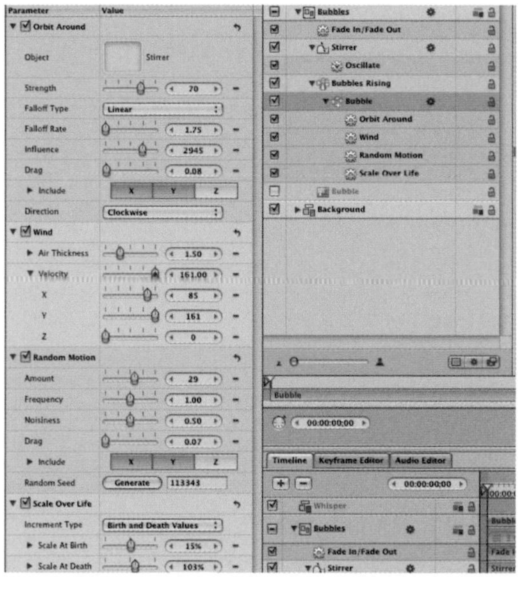

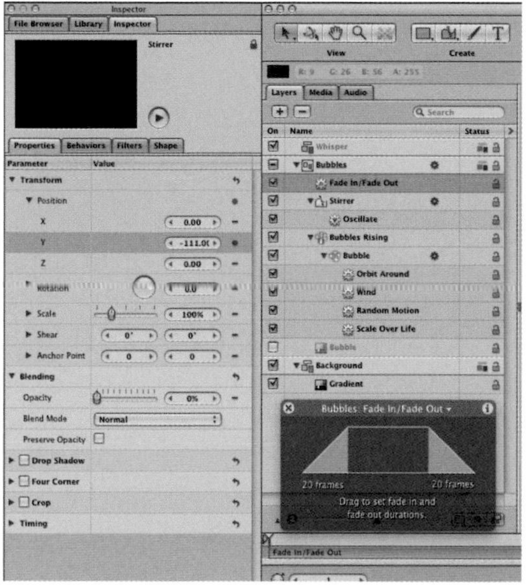

7 Drag **Stirrer** into the **Orbit Around Object** well. Set **Strength** to **70**, **Falloff Rate** to **1.75**, **Influence** to **2945**, **Drag** to **0.08**, **Wind Air Thickness 1.5**, **Velocity X 85**, **Y 161**, **Random Motion Amount 29**, **Drag 0.07**, **Scale Over Life Increment Type** to **Birth and Death Values**, **Scale at Birth 15%**, **Scale at Death 103%**.

8 Before moving on to the **Whisper** group, set the **Opacity** of **Stirrer** to **0%**. Select **Bubbles** and **Add Behavior/ Basic Motion/Fade In/Fade Out**.

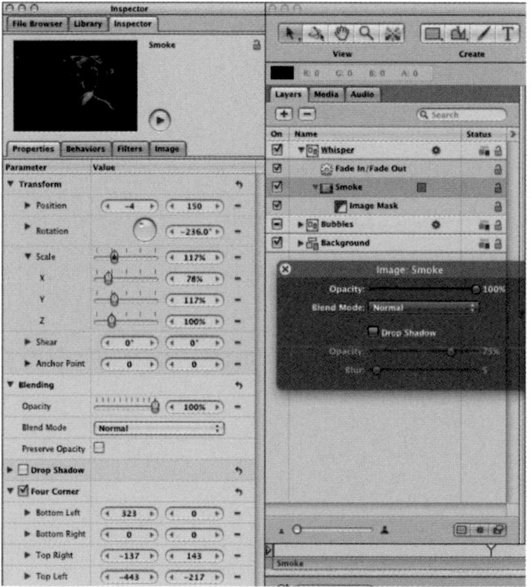

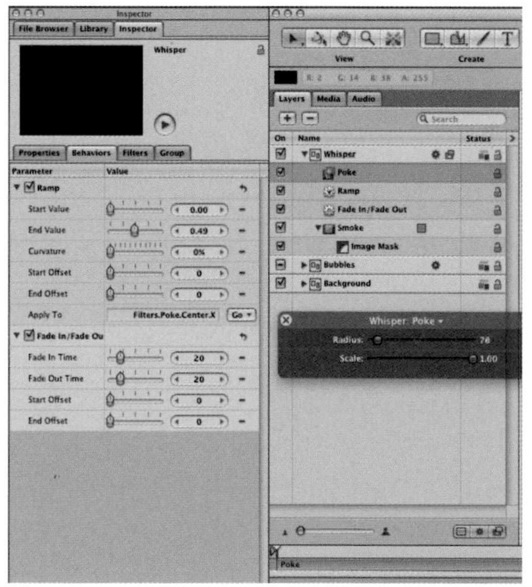

11 Select **Smoke**. Set **Position** to **-4,150**, **Rotation** to **-236**, **X Scale** to **78**, **Y Scale** to **117**. Turn on **Four Corner**. Set **Bottom Left** to **323,0**; **Top Right** to **-137, 143**; **Top Left** to **-443, -217**.

12 Select the **Whisper** group. **Add Filter/Distortion/ Poke**. Set **Radius** to **78** and **Scale** to **1.00**. **Right/ ctrl-click** on **Center X** and select **Ramp**. Set **End Value** to **0.49**. That's it—complex build, but you've done it!

HOT TIP

Movies of elements like smoke or flames can lend organic qualities to your projects that are difficult to achieve any other way.

2 Animation

Gearhead

IN THIS PROJECT, WE'LL BE TAKING some basic shape primitives (square, circle) and turning them into 3D-looking gears that rotate. They're not actually 3D—we'll be using the Extrude filter and angling our image to make it appear 3D.

If you have Motion 4, you'll be able to link all the gears to each other so that when you turn one, they all rotate appropriately. If you don't have Motion 4, you'll have to set each gear's spin as needed.

I should also note that we'll be linking all gears to a master "drive" gear. A perhaps more accurate method would be to link each gear to the one that is driving it and use the Scale parameter as appropriate to the gear ratio. I just felt this method was easier to describe.

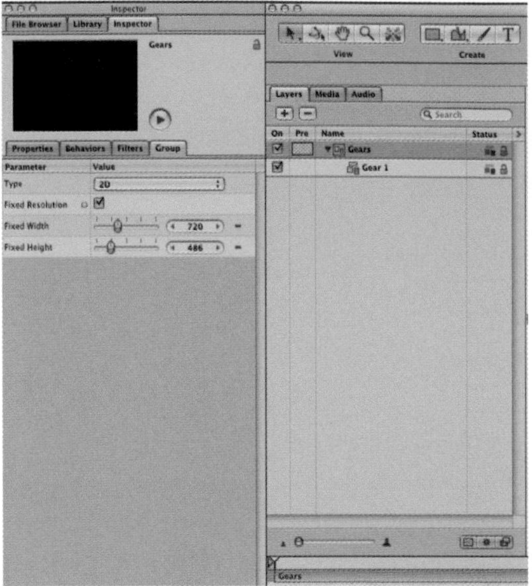

1 Start with a new project. Name the default group **Gears**. Click **Fixed Resolution**. Add a new group and call it **Gear 1**. Drag **Gear 1** to be inside **Gears**.

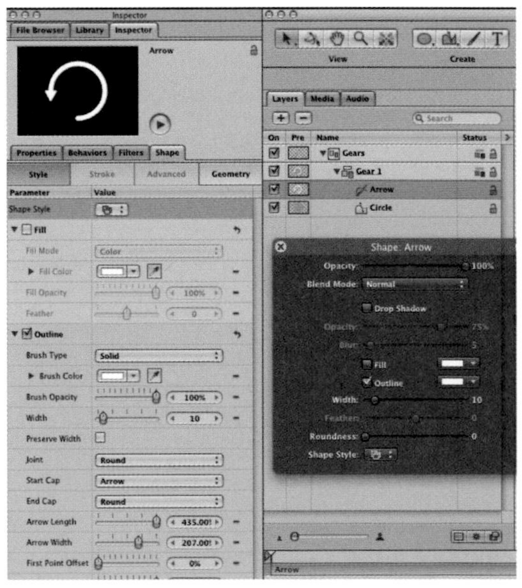

4 Under the **Shape/Style** tab, set the **Start Cap** to be **Arrow**. Adjust the **Arrow Length** and **Width** to suit. Ensure **Arrow** is concentric with **Circle**.

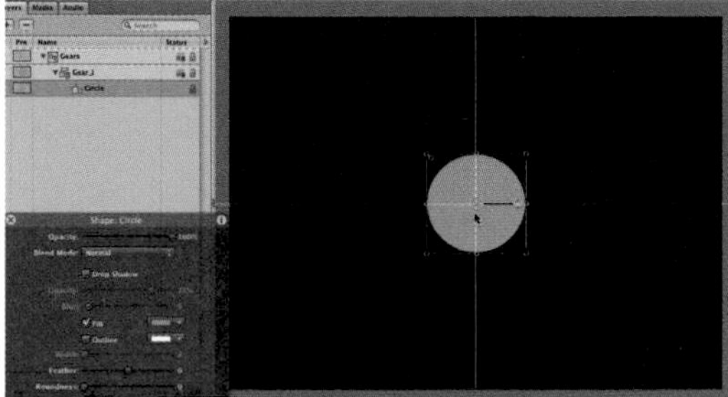

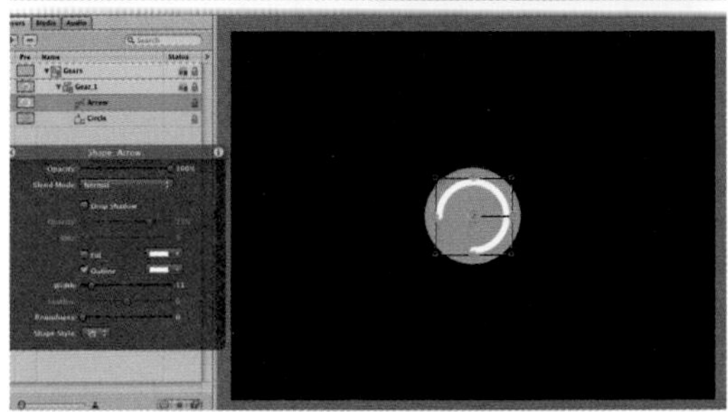

2 With **Gear 1** selected, Press C and draw a medium-sized circle (hold down the Shift key). Set the **Fill** to light gray. Position the circle using the dynamic guides in the exact center of the screen—this is important. If it isn't in the exact center, the gear's "axle" will be off center and the gear will wobble.

3 Draw another circle, about two thirds the size of the original and name it **Arrow**. Turn off its **Fill**. Set the **Outline Width** to about **10**. In the **Shape/Geometry** tab, unselect the **Closed** checkbox.

HOT TIP

Press N to toggle the dynamic guides to aid in positioning.

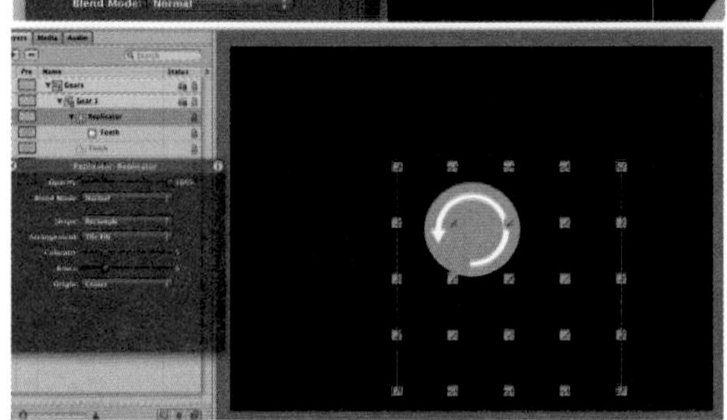

5 Press R to activate the rectangle tool. Draw a small box that we'll use for our gear teeth. Name it **Tooth**. Set its color to light gray. With **Tooth** selected, press L or click the Replicate button in the toolbar.

6 Set **Shape** to **Circle** and **Arrangement** to **Outline**. Click **Align Angle**. Position the Replicator and adjust its **Radius** until the teeth are sticking out around Circle's circumference. Adjust the **Points** until it looks like the picture above.

continued...

Gearhead (continued)

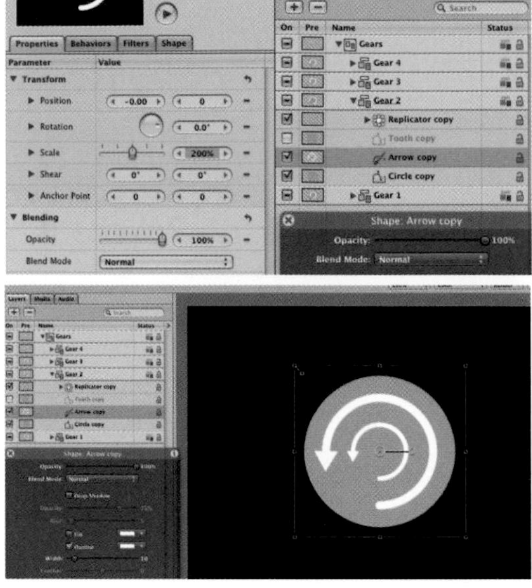

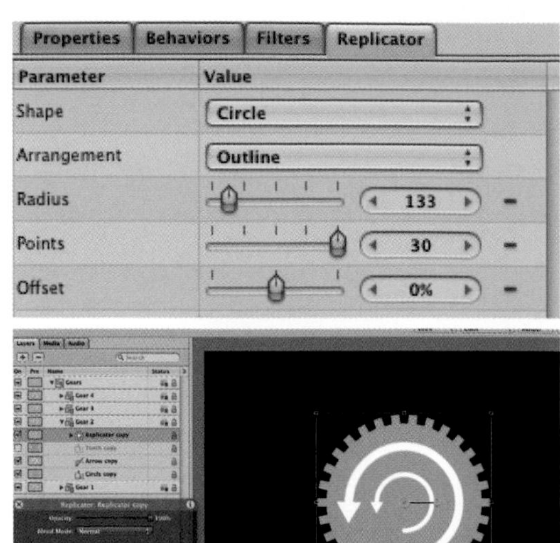

7 With the **Gear 1** group selected, press ⌘D three times to make three copies. Name them **Gear 2**, **Gear 3**, and **Gear 4**. Select the **Circle copy** in **Gear 2**. Under the Properties Tab, set **Scale** to be **200%**. Do the same to **Arrow copy**.

8 Now set the **Replicator copy**'s **Radius** to about twice as big and the number of **Points** to twice as many (so you now have a gear that's twice as big).

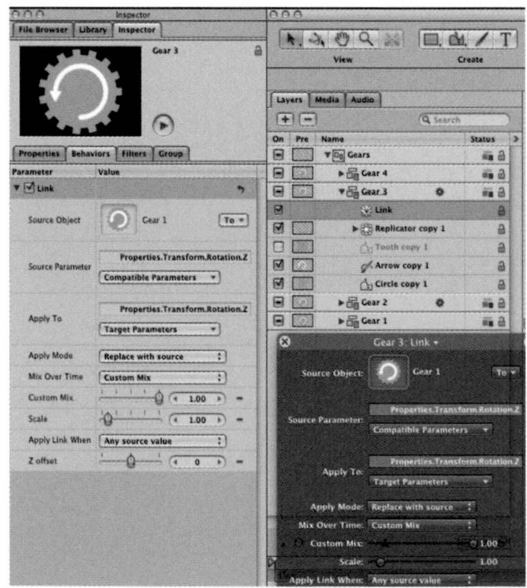

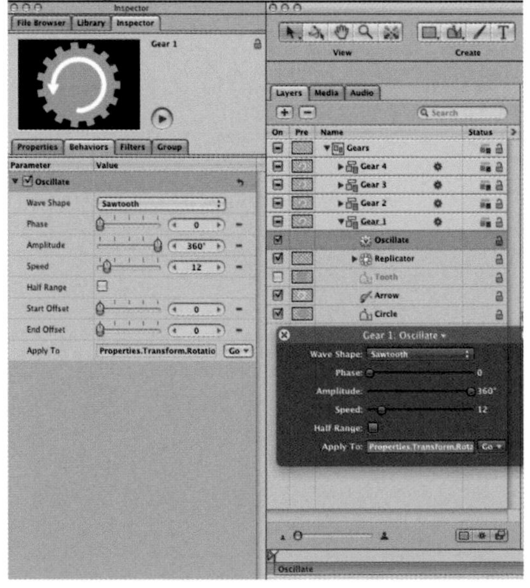

11 Select the **Gear 4** group. In the Properties tab, Right/ctrl-click on the **Z Rotation**. Select **Link**. Drag the **Gear 1** group into the **Source Object** well. Set the **Scale** to **-1.0**.

12 Select the **Gear 1** group. In the Properties tab, Right/ctrl-click on the **Z Rotation**. Select **Oscillate**. Set the **Wave Shape** to **Sawtooth**. Set the **Amplitude** to **360** and **Speed** to **12**.

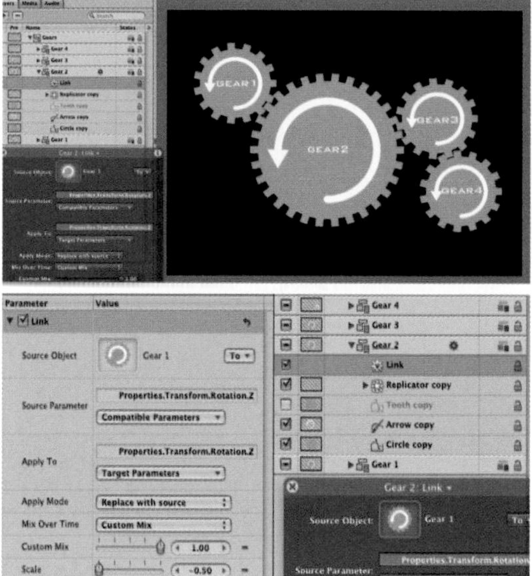

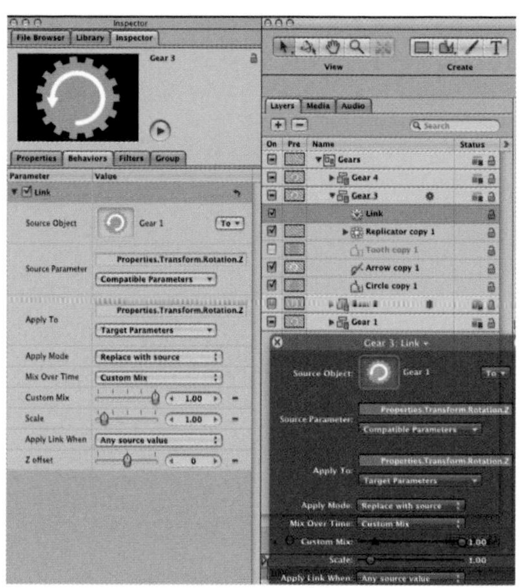

9 Position the gears so they mesh as above. Select the **Gear 2** group. In the properties tab, Right/ctrl-click on the **Z Rotation**. Select **Link**. Drag the **Gear 1** group into the **Source Object** well. Set the **Scale** to **-0.5**.

10 Select the **Gear 3** group. In the Properties tab, Right/ctrl-click on the **Z Rotation**. Select **Link**. Drag the **Gear 1** group into the **Source Object** well.

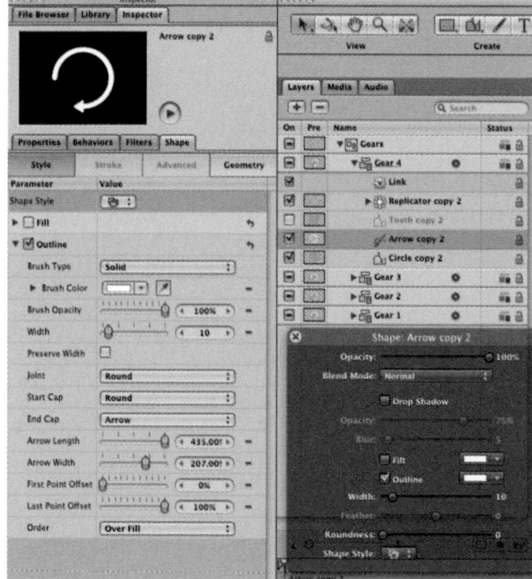

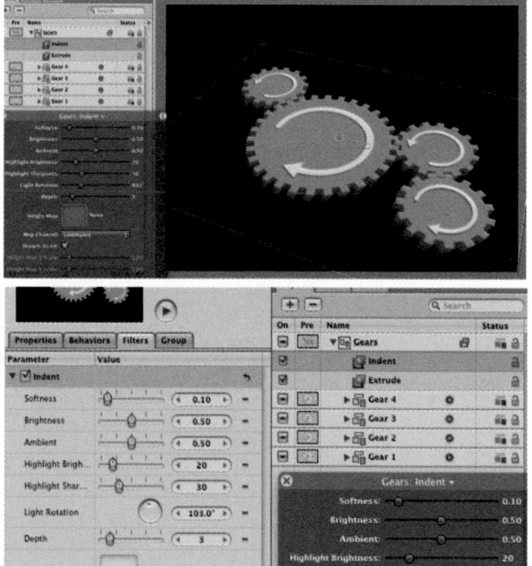

13 Now when you press Play, all the gears turn, but two of them have their **Arrow** pointing the wrong way. Select each of them and in their **Shape/Style** tab, change the **Start Cap** to be **Round** and the **End Cap** to be **Arrow**.

14 Select the **Gears** group. In the **Properties** tab, set the **X Rotation** to **-50°** and **Z Rotation** to **-23°**. Add **Filter/Stylize/Extrude**. Set **Angle** to **276°**, **Distance** to **26**, **Back Size** to **.95**. Add **Filter/Stylize/Indent**. Set **Softness** to **0.10**, **Light Rotation** to **103°**, **Depth** to **3**.

What do I use Motion for?

I HADN'T REALLY GIVEN THIS MUCH THOUGHT, but then I was invited to give a presentation to Apple's Motion engineers about how I use Motion so they could see how the product that they work so hard on is actually incorporated into a post environment.

When I first started using Motion, I thought—wow—this is like LiveType on steroids. I used it largely for text. In fact, my first real project was incorporating a music video's lyrics into visuals in interesting ways. It was a good way to become acquainted with Motion's type capabilities.

It took me a while, in fact, to latch onto the full range of Motion's power. Behaviors, particle generators, replicators, image processing, masking/rotoscoping, keying (though the current chroma keying capabilities of Motion leave a lot to be desired), templates, motion tracking, painting, image stabilization, optical flow retiming, 3D, lights, shadows, parameter linking, audio.

No—Motion is not hyper-LiveType. And while I think Shake-Lite is a misnomer, in my day-to-day workflows, I increasingly reach for Motion in many areas where I used to incorporate Shake.

I use it for titling, graphic overlays, transitions, image processing, tracking, speed changes, compositing, creating backdrops, slide shows, animations, credit sequences, mock screen graphics, tutorials, etc. Heck, as you'll see in the Grab Bag chapter, I've even used it for desktop publishing.

I've used it to create an animated cartoon dream sequence from single frame drawings for a feature film. I've used it to build an endless stream of dump trucks winding into the distant desert for a commercial. I've used it to billow fake steam from a boiling over radiator for a music video, and added the smoke of battle to a documentary.

I've cloned a girl, created a flock of birds, set off an atomic blast, discovered a unicorn, altered the flow of time, and visited the depths of outer space. All with Motion. It also does some nice things with type.

In the years since Motion was added to Final Cut Studio, I've used it in hundreds of projects. And while Final Cut Pro remains the hub of my workflow, some projects are built entirely in Motion. Some portion of nearly every project I work on has been affected by Motion.

Motion has become my postproduction Swiss army knife.

Movement is not the only way to bring your text to life.

The techniques, like most in this book, are easy to alter and adapt. The HEAT image above, for example, was built using the **Ice Nine** exercise in this chapter.

Whether carved from ice, or constructed of bubbles, text in Motion will enhance your project.

3

Text Effects

TEXT IN MOTION CAN BE WAY MORE THAN than plain. This chapter takes you beyond basics to explore some interesting ways to use text as a graphic element itself.

This is one of the longest chapters in the book and it could've been even longer. Playing with text in Motion is just plain fun.

Animated Fill

ADDING AN ANIMATED fill to your text brings a whole new level of life to your presentation.

We'll be using content from your library to illustrate the principle—you should be able to easily adapt the technique to your own material.

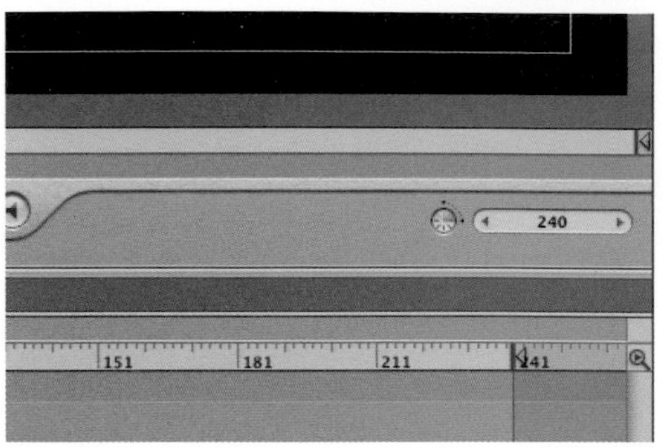

1 Start with a new project. Let's set it to 240 frames long (just because we're going to be using a background that's only that long).

4 Now, with **Fire Wall** selected, type ⌘ Shift M to add a mask. Then drag the **Fire** text into the **Image Mask** well.

7 So, let's nest **Fire Wall** in a group and work with that. Select **Fire Wall** and type ⌘ Shift G. Call the new group **HotText**.

8 Go to the properties tab and click the **Drop Shadow** checkbox. You'll notice the text jumps. Click on the **FIRE** layer and reposition the text until we're centered again.

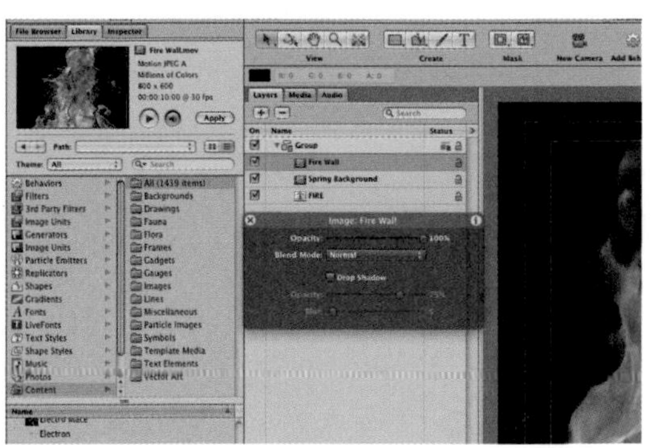

2 Now press T to activate the Text tool and click on the screen. Choose a nice fat font—I'm using **Impact**. Set the size to something large, 200 pt. Then type in the word **FIRE**. Press the esc key to end and position the word in the center of the screen.

3 Now go to **Library/Content** and find **Fire Wall**. Select it and click the **Apply** button. Then find the **Spring Background** and click **Apply**. Arrange your layers as above, if necessary, so that **Fire Wall** is above **Spring Background**.

5 Now you may notice some interlace artifacting on the **Fire Wall** movie—let's fix that. Select the **Fire Wall** clip. **Add Filter/Video/De-Interlace**. And while we're at it, let's position it up a little higher to get less black in our fill. Notice that when we move our fill, the word FIRE doesn't move.

6 Notice if you add dropshadow or any of the other effects to the text, they don't behave as you'd expect because the text is supplying the mask. You can add it to the Fire Wall clip, but it acts more like a dark glow.

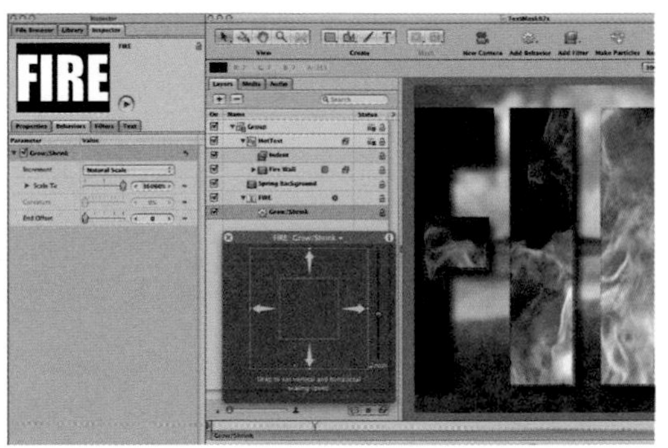

9 Now as a final touch, select **HotText**. **Add Filter/Stylize/Indent**. Notice the interesting effect you get. Then change the **Map Channel** to **Alpha** for a nice beveled edge. Change the **Brightness** to **0.80**.

10 Oh, one more. Select **FIRE**. **Add Behavior/Basic Motion/Grow/Shrink**. Leave the increment at **Natural Scale**. Set the **Scale** to to **36000** and press Play to watch our text expand and we fly through it into the fire.

Realistic Text Shadows

SOMETIMES YOU NEED REALISM beyond what you get by simply clicking the Drop Shadow button.

In this project we'll spend some time constructing a realistic-looking shadow to some 3D-looking text—we won't actually use 3D or lighting or incur the overhead associated with those.

1 Start with a new project. Add a **Gradient** generator to it. Make the gradient go from white to light gray and adjust it to look like the screenshot above.

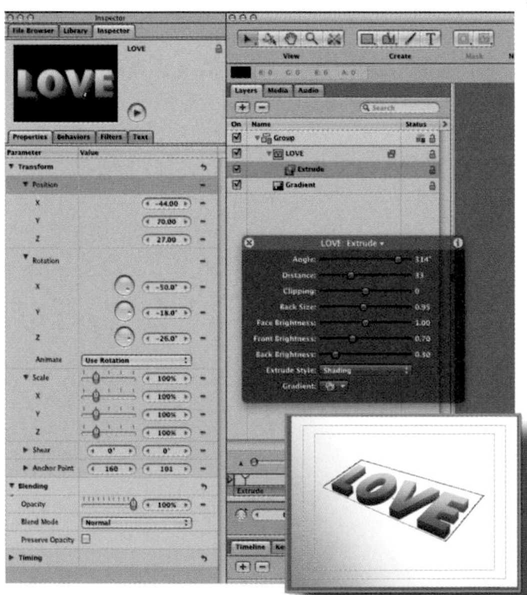

4 Go to **Properties**. Set **Position** to **-44, 99, 27**; **Rotation** to **-50, -18, -26**; **Anchor Point** to **160, 101**. Add **Filter/Stylize/Extrude**. Set **Angle** to **314**, **Distance** to **33**, **BackSize** to **0.95**. Turn back on the **Gradient** background.

5 Type **T** for the **Text** tool. Click on the screen. Type the word **HATE**. Set the **Font Size** to **160**. Place that layer between **LOVE** and **Gradient**. Click on the Style tab. Set the **Face Fill** to **Gradient**.

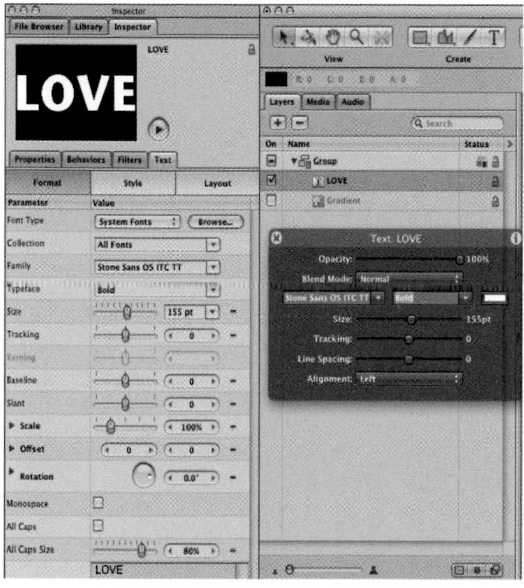

2 Turn off the **Gradient** temporarily so we can see what we're doing. Press **T** to select the **Text** tool. Click on the canvas. Set your **Font** to **155** point **Stone Sans**. Type **LOVE**.

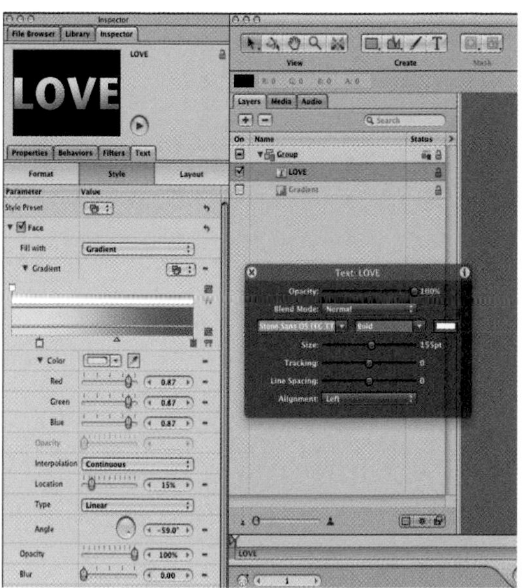

3 Go to the Style tab. Set the **Face** to **Fill with Gradient**. Select the left tag and set RGB each to 0.87. Set the **Location** to 15%. Select the right tag and set RGB each to 0.38. Set the **Angle** to **-59 degrees**.

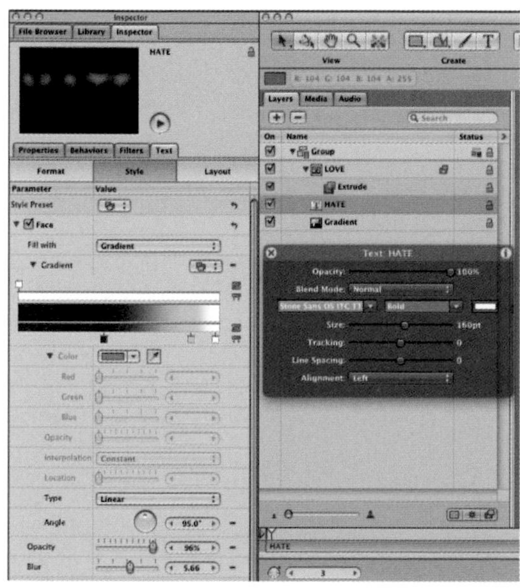

6 Edit the **Gradient** as follows. At 42%, set the color to **Red 0.15**, **Green 0.11**, **Blue 0.08**. At 86% set **Red**, **Green**, and **Blue** to 0.79. At 98%, set the **R**, **G**, **B** to **1.0**. Change the **Angle** to 95. Set the **Opacity** to 86%. Set the **Blur** to 5.66.

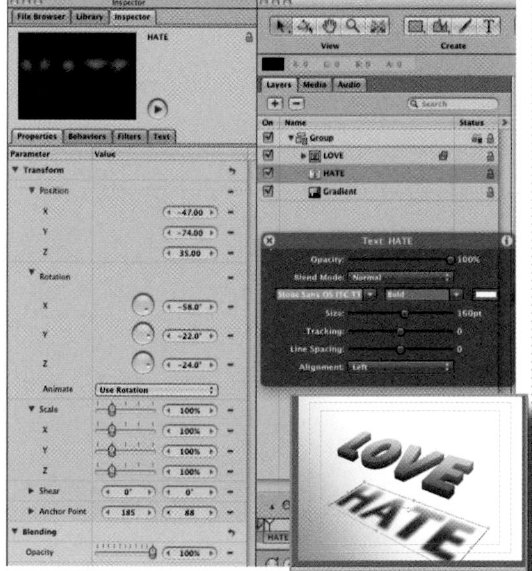

7 Go to the **Properties** tab of **HATE**. Set **Position** to **-47**, **-74**, **35**. Set **Rotation** to **-58**, **-22**, **-24**. Set **Anchor Point** to **185**, **88**. And we're done.

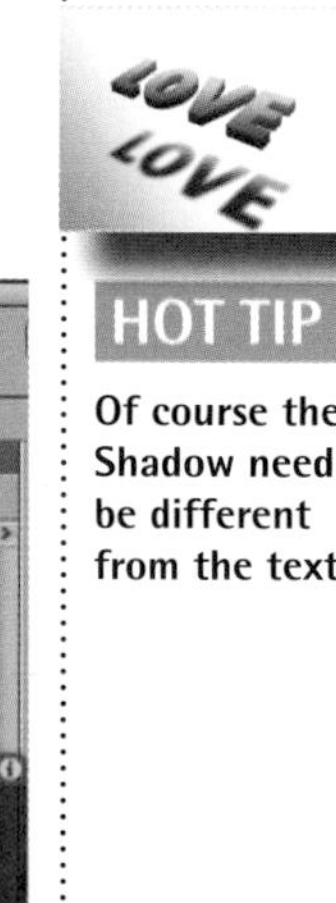

HOT TIP

Of course the Shadow needn't be different from the text.

Bubbles

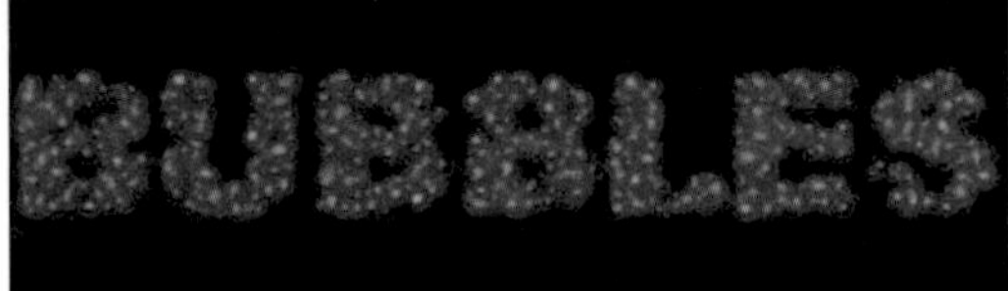

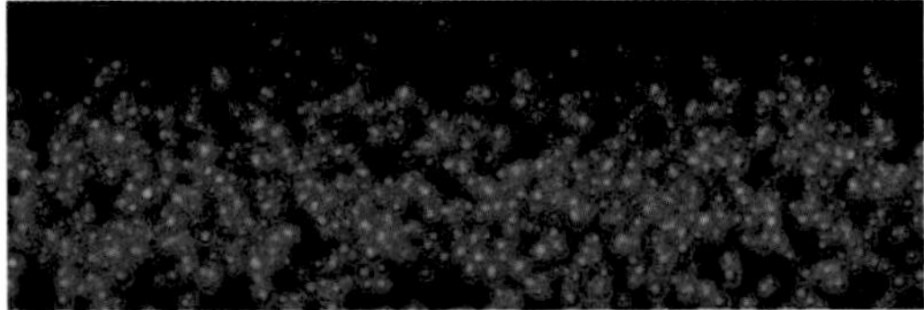

BIT'O THE BUBBLY, my dear? We'll be doing a few interesting things with this project. First, we're using a particle emitter to fill out the letters and then Random Motion and negative Gravity to cause it to drift up.

Second, we'll be using a clone layer to reverse the effect and have our bubbles assemble the word.

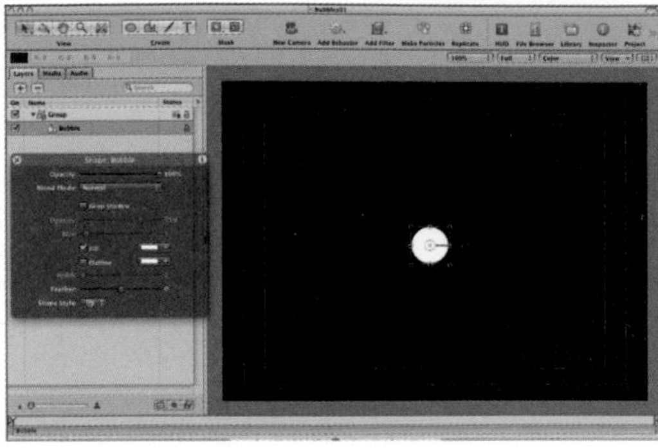

1 Start with a new project. Press the **C** key to activate the **Circle** tool. Draw a small circle in the middle of the screen. Name it **Bubble.**

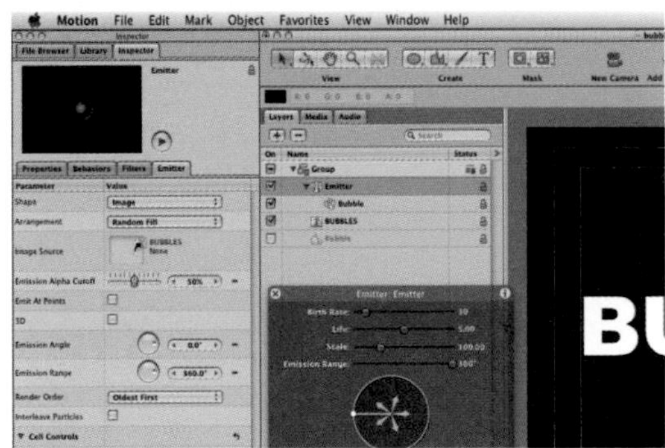

4 Select Bubble. Press **E** or click on the **Make Particles** button in the toolbar. Change the **Shape** to **Image** and the **Arrangement** to **Random Fill**. Drag the **BUBBLES** text layer into the **Image Source** well. Do not try the shortcut of dropping it on the **Emitter** layer itself; that will just add it to the particles emitted.

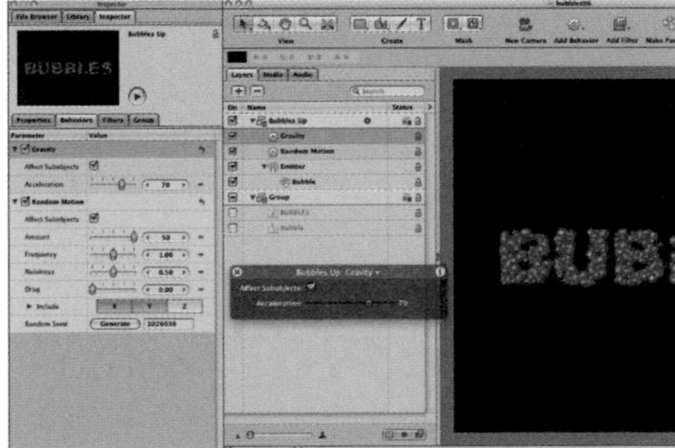

7 Set the **Affect Sub Objects** in both **Gravity** and **Random Motion**. Set **Gravity Acceleration** to 70. Set **Random Motion Amount** to 50.

8 Position to frame **151**. Hold down the **⌥** (option) key. In the Layers palette, grab **Bubbles Up** and drag it down to the clear area below the layers until the pointer turns to a plus sign, and then release it to create a copy.

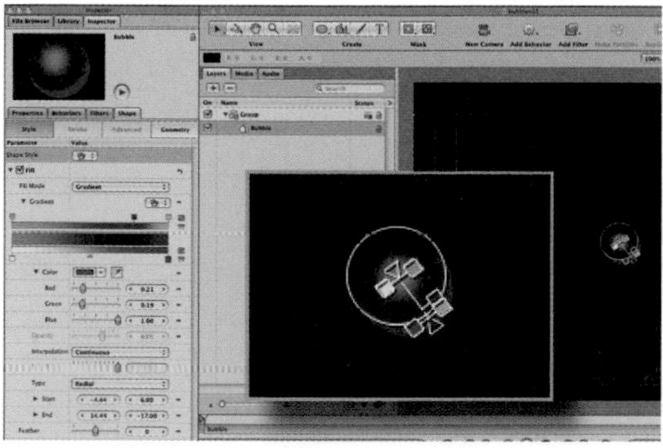

2 In the **Style** tab, set the **Fill Mode** to **Gradient**. For the **Opacity Gradient**, set **58%** opacity at **Location 0%**, **20%** at location **78%**, and **65%** at location **100%**. For the **Color gradient**, set the left color to **R 0.70**, **G 0.87**; **B 0.91** and the right color to **0.21**, **0.19**, **1.00**. **Type** to **Radial**. Adjust as on the bubble above.

3 Activate the Text tool (press **T**). Click on the screen and type **BUBBLES**. Set the **Font** to 100 point Arial Black. Center the word on the screen.

5 Turn off the **BUBBLES** text. Set **Birth Rate** to **0**, **Initial Number** to **2000**, **Angle Randomness** to **7.0**. **Scale** is going to depend on how big your initial circle was. I set mine to **17%**. Set **Scale Randomness** to something less than that. Mine is **12**.

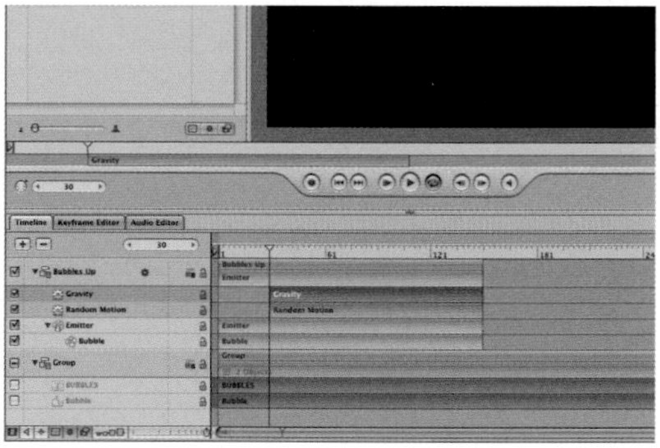

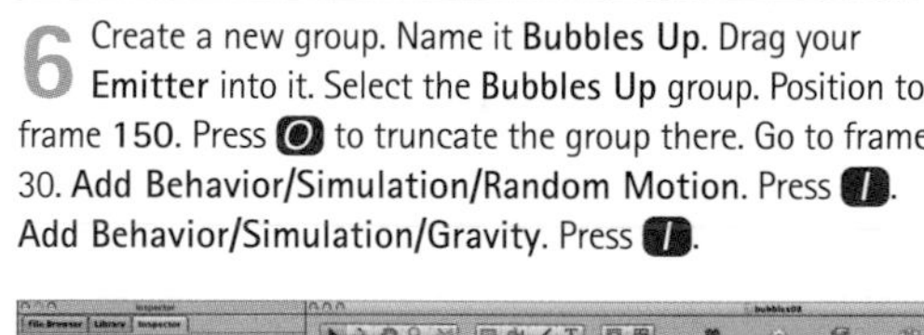

6 Create a new group. Name it **Bubbles Up**. Drag your **Emitter** into it. Select the **Bubbles Up** group. Position to frame **150**. Press **O** to truncate the group there. Go to frame 30. **Add Behavior/Simulation/Random Motion**. Press **I**. **Add Behavior/Simulation/Gravity**. Press **I**.

HOT TIP

The same technique can be used with smoke or dust particles.

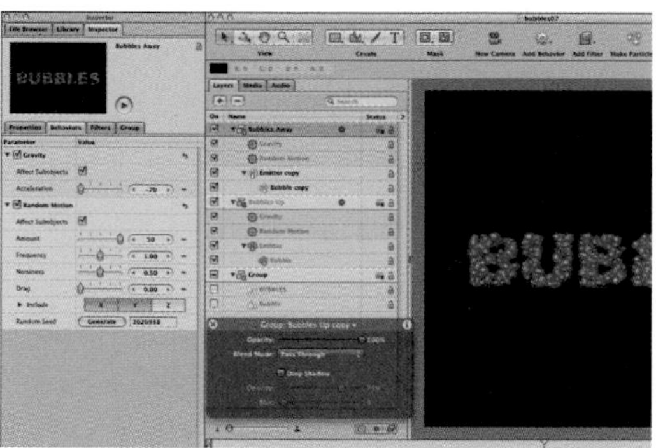

9 Rename **Bubbles Up copy** to **Bubbles Away**. Click on the **Gravity** layer. Set the **Acceleration** to **-70**.

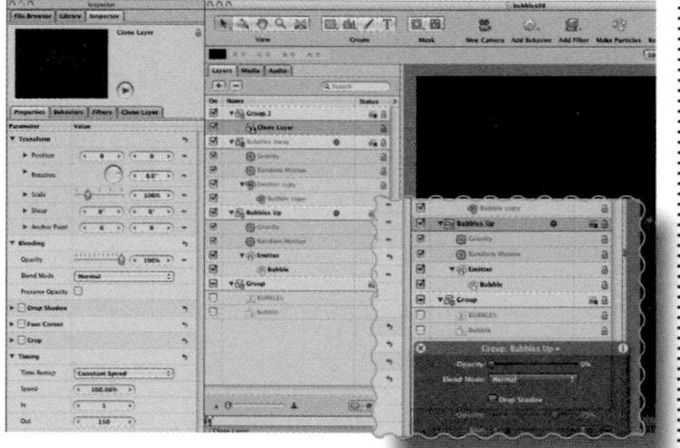

10 Go back to frame 1. Select **Bubbles Up**. Press **K** to create a clone layer. Go to **Properties** and click the **Reverse** checkbox under **Timing**. Finally, select **Bubbles Up**. Set the **Opacity** to **0** (see inset).

Magnify Text

THIS MAGNIFICENT LIST displayer can be used to convey information, as a chapter indicator, DVD animation, etc. The project *seems* complicated, but it's really quite simple.

We're just going to make three clones of our list and mask them for the top, middle, and bottom of our display.

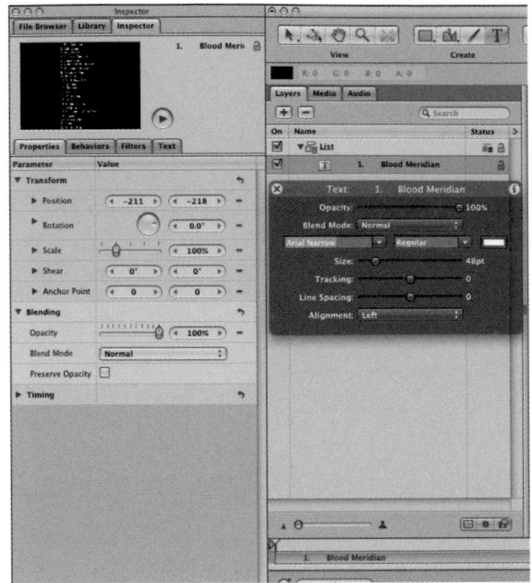

1 Start with a new project. Name the default group **List**. Select the Text tool and click on the canvas. Set your text font and sizing as you'd like the magnified text to appear. I'm using 48 point **Arial Narrow**. Paste or type in your list. In the Properties tab, set **Position** to **-211 -218**.

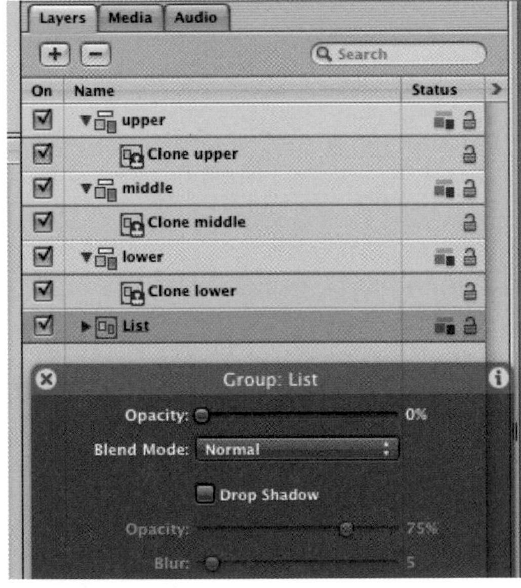

4 Click on the **List** group. Set its **Opacity** to 0%.

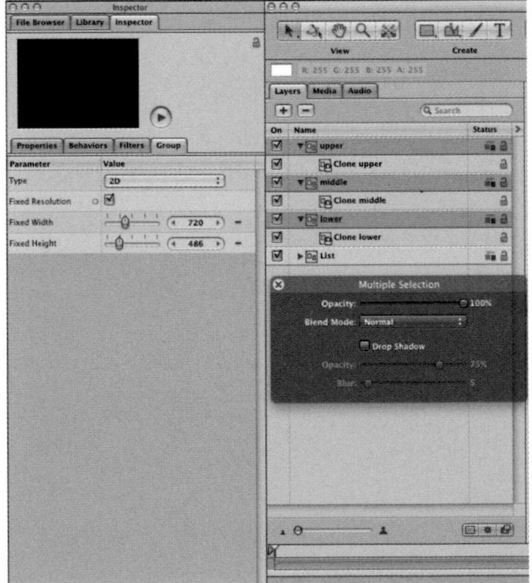

5 ⌘-Select **upper, middle,** and **lower**. Click the **Fixed Resolution** checkbox.

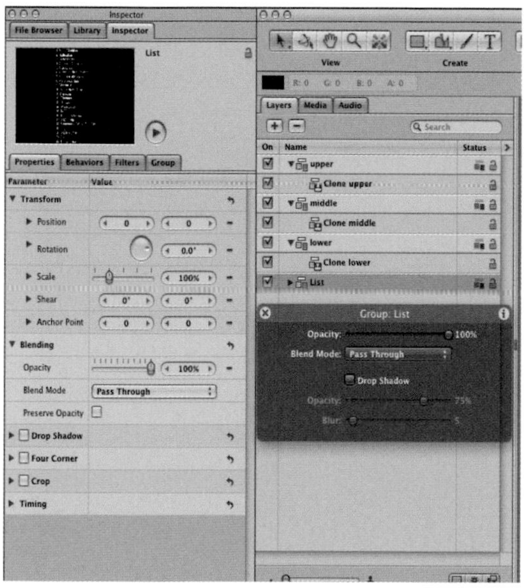

2 Select the **List** group. Press **K** to create a clone layer. Name the new group **lower**. Rename **Clone Layer** to **Clone lower**. Select the **List** group. Press **K** again. Name the new group **middle**, the clone layer **Clone middle**. Select the **List** group. Press **K**. Name the new group **upper**, the clone layer **Clone upper**.

3 Set the **Properties/Scale** of **Clone lower** and **Clone upper** to 50%.

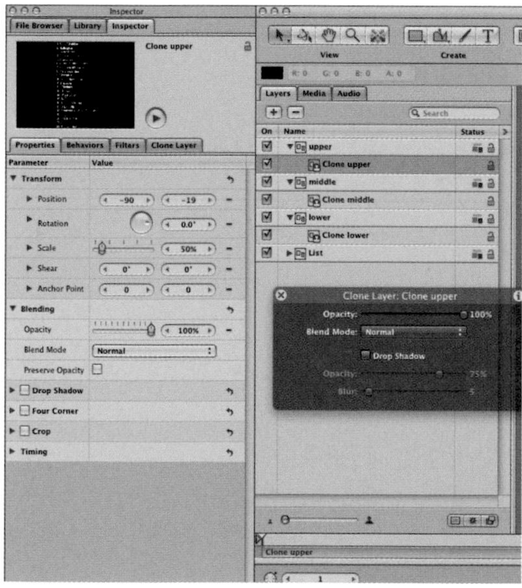

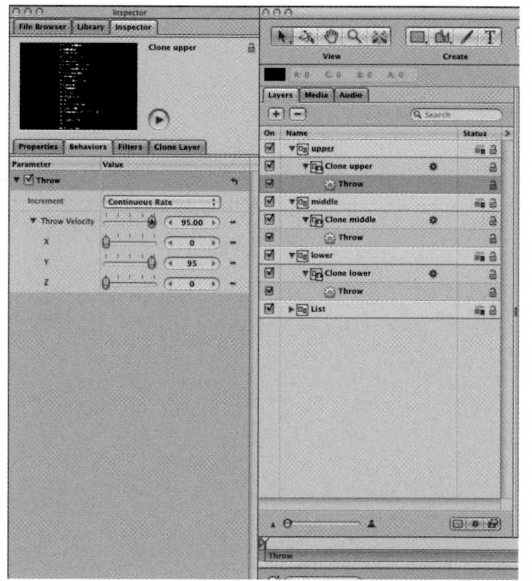

6 Select **Clone lower**. Set its Position to **-90, -65**. Select **Clone upper**. Set its **Position** to **-90, -19**.

7 **⌘**-Select Clone upper, **Clone middle,** and **Clone lower**. Add Behavior/Basic Motion/Throw. Set **Clone lower**'s Throw Velocity to 0, 95, 0. Set **Clone middle**'s Throw Velocity to 0, 180, 0. Set **Clone upper**'s Throw Velocity to 0, 95, 0.

continued...

Magnify Text (continued)

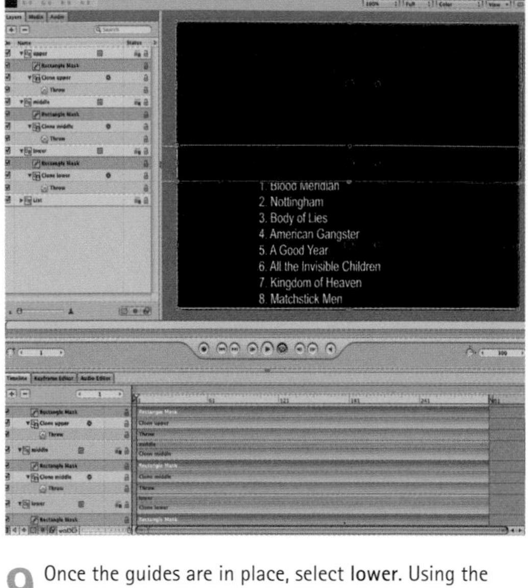

8 To help us judge this, position in the timeline so that one of the lines from **Clone middle** is in the middle of the screen. Place horizontal guides above and below it as in the picture above.

9 Once the guides are in place, select **lower**. Using the rectangular mask tool, draw a mask that covers the lower portion of the screen upto the guide. Then select the **middle** group and draw a mask for the middle between the guides. Finally, select **upper** and draw a mask that extends from the upper guide to the top of the screen.

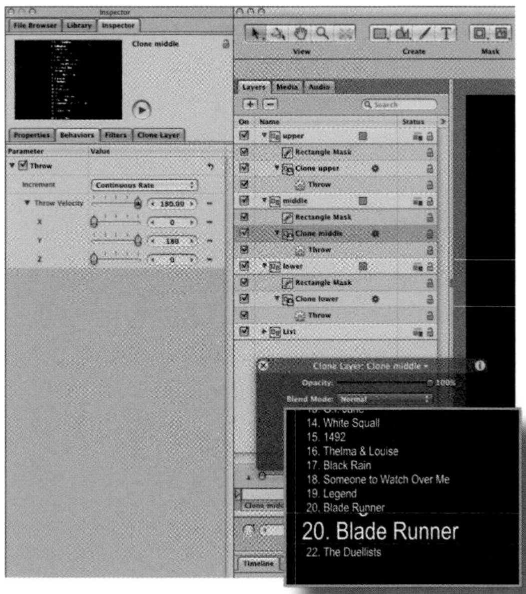

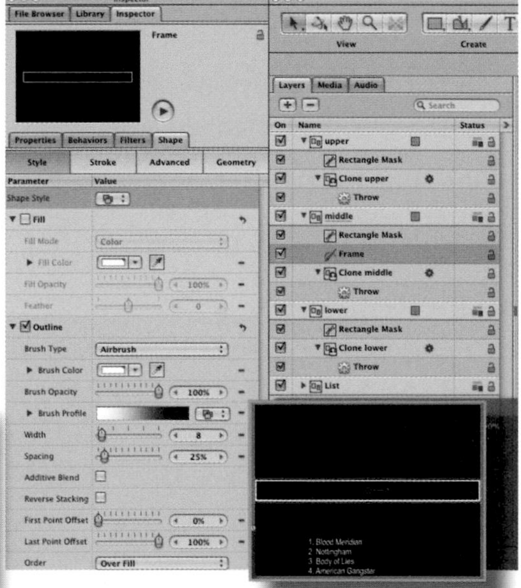

12 Now go to about frame **215** so that the last item in your list is just before the bottom. Since the upper and lower have the same scroll rate, they should be okay. However, if your middle item is not the right one, you'll have to adjust its throw velocity slightly until you get the proper item showing.

13 Now let's construct our "magnifying glass." Go back to frame 1. Select the **middle** group and draw a full screenwidth rectangle between the two guides. Name it **Frame**. Turn off the **Fill**, turn on **Outline**, set **Brush Type** to **Airbrush**. Set the width to **8**.

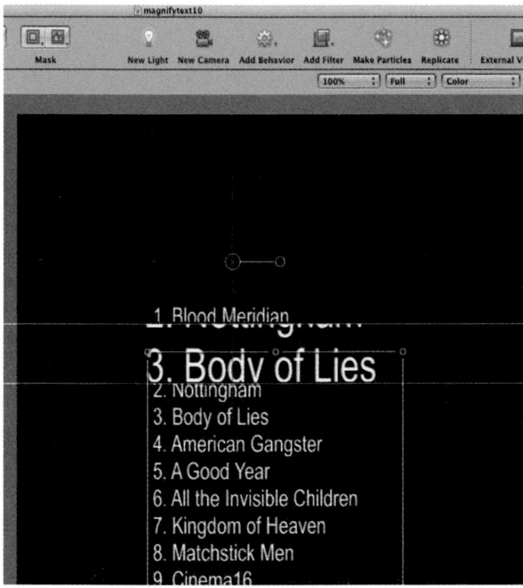

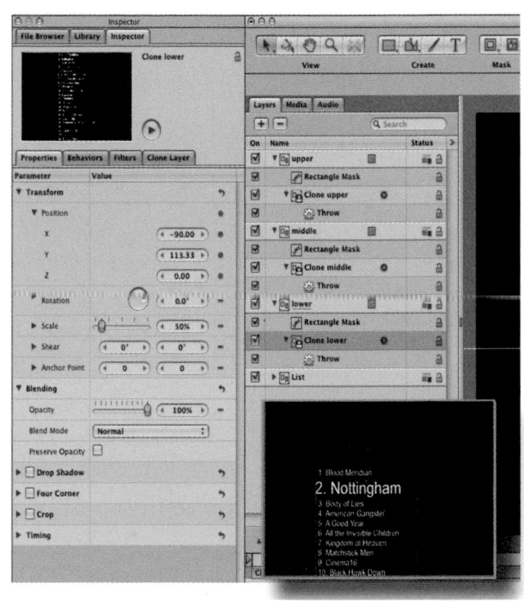

10 Now that the guides are in place, let's adjust the spacing and timing to allow for differences in font height, etc. Drag through the timeline until list item 1 is in the top region, Item 2 is in the middle region (larger), and Item 3 tops the lower region. As you can see, some tweakage is required.

11 Select **Clone upper** and adjust its **Y** position until it is just above the middle region. Then select **Clone middle** and adjust the **Y** position so it falls on list item 2. Finally select **Clone lower** and adjust so list item 3 is just below the middle region.

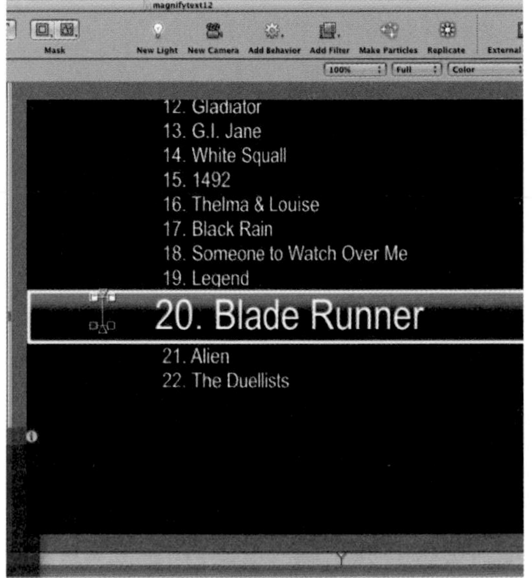

14 You can now clear out the guides. While on frame 1, select **Frame**. Press ⌘D to duplicate it. Name the copy **Highlight**. Set its **Fill** to gradient, its **Gradient** to **Grayscale**, its **Blend Mode** to **Screen**, and its **Opacity** to **50%**.

15 Adjust it as above to give a nice highlight.

Text Reflected

THE MOTION TEAM HAVE provided an enormous amount of free and useful content. In this project, we'll make it appear as though some colossal text is resting on a thin pool of rippling water.

To make our lives easier, we'll nab a pre-built stage from the handy Library.

1 Begin with a new project. Name the default group Text. Select a nice fat font like Arial Black. Set **Alignment** to **Center**. Type **REFLECTIONS** and center it on the screen. Set the fill color to a middle gray. Set your size so the word fills the screen horizontally (within title safe if for broadcast).

4 This will place **Gradient Stage 12** above your **Text** group. Reorder them so **Text** is on top.

7 Click on **Text Reflection**. **Add Filter/Distortion/ Underwater**. Set **Size** to **0.85**, **Speed** to **0.17**, **Refraction** to **17**. Set the **Opacity** of the group to **39%**.

8 Expand **Text Reflection**. Click on the **Clone Layer**. ⌘ Shift M to add an Image Mask. Set the channel to Luminance. This will use our image's own luminance as a mask.

2 Click on your **REFLECTIONS** layer. **Add Filter/Stylize/Extrude.** Set **Angle** to **360°**, **Distance** to **1**, **Back Size** to **0.90**.

3 Grab **Gradient Stage 12** from the **Content** folder and drag it to your Layers palette.

5 Click on your **Text** group. Press **K** to create a clone layer. Name the new group containing the clone layer **Text Reflection**. Move it below the **Text** group in the Layers palette. Set the **Y Scale** to **-100%**. That will flip the clone layer upside down.

6 Slide the **Y Position** of **Text Reflection** until it is just below the Text on screen (about -55 in my case).

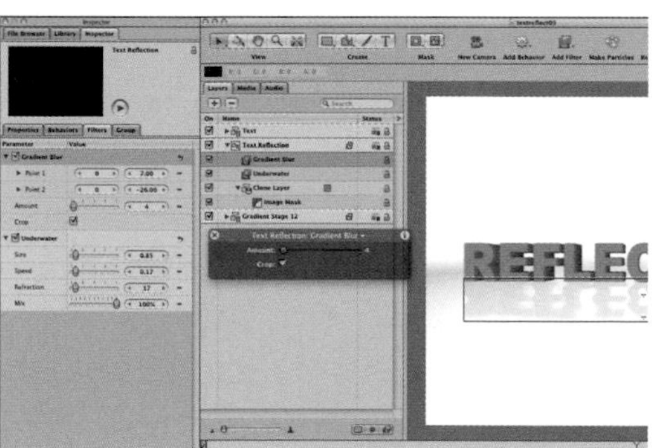

9 Select the **Text Reflection** group. **Add Filter/Blur/ Gradient Blur.** Set the points to **0, 7** and **0, -26**. Set the **Amount** to **3**.

10 Select **Gradient Stage 12. Add Filter/Distortion/ Underwater.** Set **Size** to **0.09**, **Speed** to **0.17**, **Refraction** to **17**. And we're done!

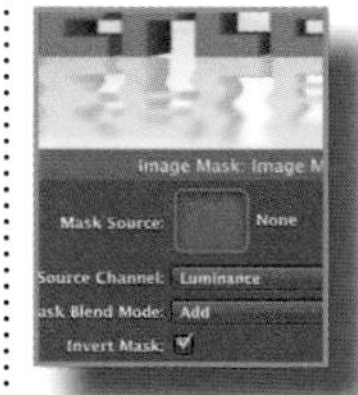

HOT TIP

You can strengthen the reflection by clicking Invert Mask on the Text Reflection clone layer.

Materials Science

TURNING YOUR TEXT INTO different substances requires only your imagination and the basic tools provided in Motion.

We'll explore four examples in the folowing pages: ice, water, jello, and pockmarked metal.

That doesn't mean you should stop there. Fire, dirt, smoke, glass are all options open to the crafty Motioneer.

We'll be using a combination of Indent and Displace filters to distort our text, driven by Cloud and Cellular generators. We'll be controlling the animation of our text by altering the speed and other characteristics of those generators.

To begin, we'll create ICE. Subsequent projects are modifications of the basics we'll set down in the ICE project.

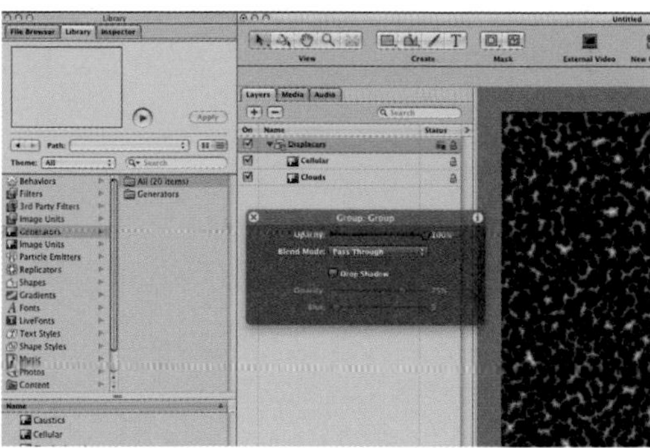

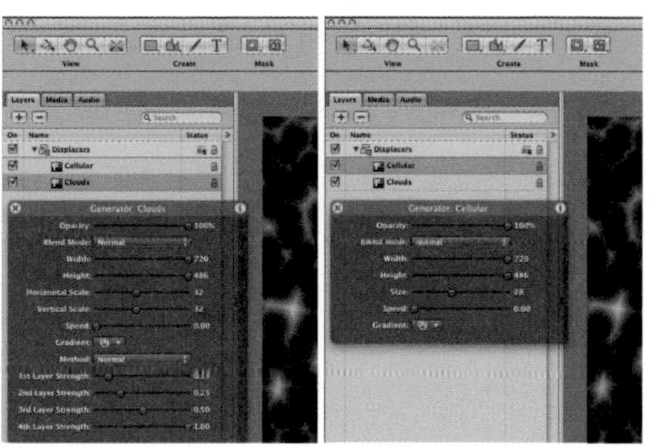

1 Start with a new project. Name the default layer **Displacers**. From the library, add a **Clouds** generator and top that with a **Cellular** generator.

2 Click on the **Clouds** generator. Change the **Speed** to 0. Click on the **Cellular** generator. Set the **Size** to **28**. Set the **Speed** to 0.

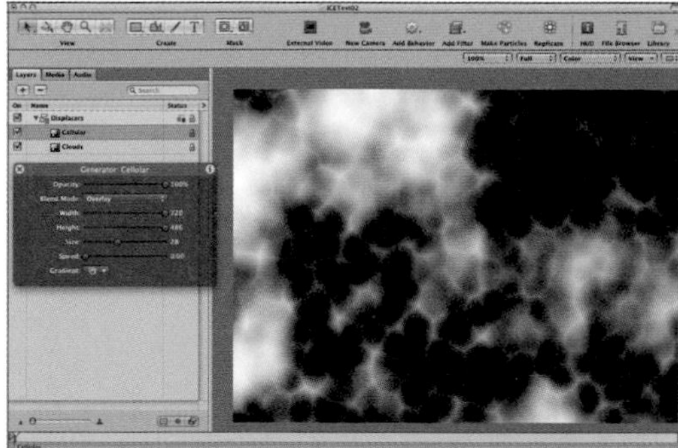

3 Just for fun, set the blend mode of the **Cellular** generator to **Overlay** to see an interesting effect (we won't be doing anything with that in this project, but it is kinda cool). Set it back to **Normal**.

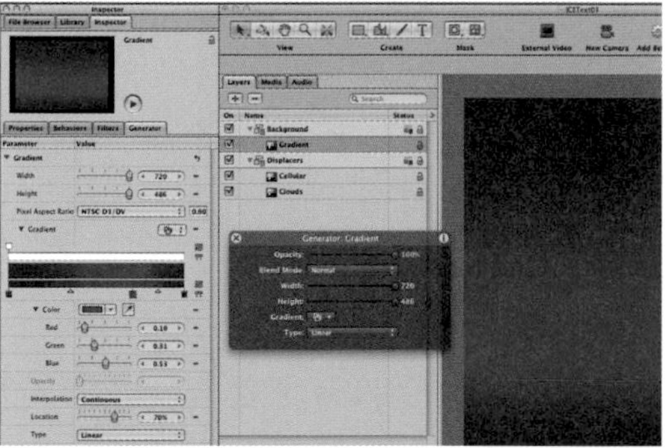

4 Add a new group and call it **Background**. Add a **Gradient** generator from the library. Set it to look like the picture above. Set the tag at 0% to R **0.05**, G **0.15**, B **0.35**. Set the tag at 100% the same. Set the middle tag to R **0.10**, G **0.31**, B **0.53**. Move the middle tag's **Location** to **70%**.

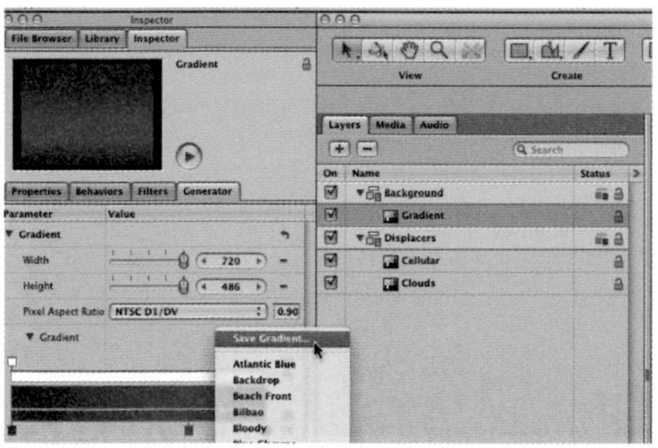

5 We're gonna use that gradient later, so let's save it. Call it **ICY**.

6 Add another group, call it **Text**. Set its blend mode to **Screen**. Press **T** to activate the **Text** tool. Click on the center of the screen. Choose **Arial Black** as the font. Set the size to **160** (or larger). Set the alignment to **Center**. Type the word **ICE**.

continued...

Materials Science (continued)

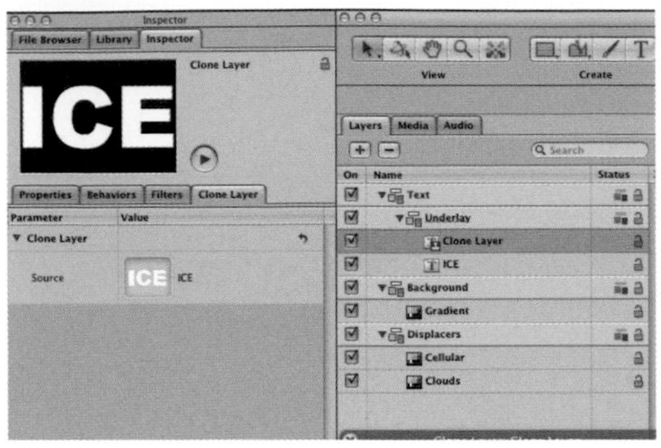

7 Click on the **ICE** text layer and type ⌘ Shift G to place it in its own group. Name the new group **Underlay**. Click on the **ICE** text layer again and press K to create a clone layer.

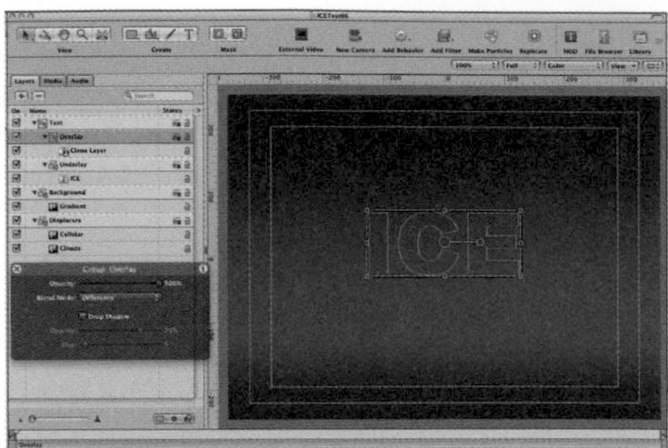

8 Type ⌘ Shift G and name the new group **Overlay**. Move it above the **Underlay** group. Change its blend mode to **Difference**. Move the **Overlay** group to align with the **Underlay** group. If you're not getting the outline effect, check that your **Text** group blend mode is set to **Screen**.

11 With the **Overlay** group selected, **Add Filter/Stylize/ Extrude**. Set the **Angle** to **226**, the **Distance** to **3**, and the **Back Size** to **0.90**.

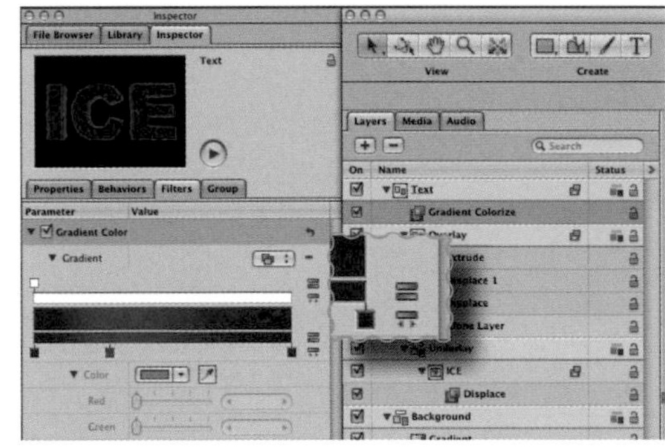

12 Click on the **Text** group. **Add Filter/Color Correction/Gradient Colorize**. Remember when we saved that gradient in step 5? Let's set our gradient to that, only click the little "=" next to the gradient to invert it (see inset).

15 If you slide the **Reflection** group down until it's just under the **ICE** text, it looks just like two "ICE" lines stacked on top of each other. Let's fix that. Click on the **Reflection** group and type ⌘ Shift M to add a mask layer. Set the **Source Channel** to **Blue**.

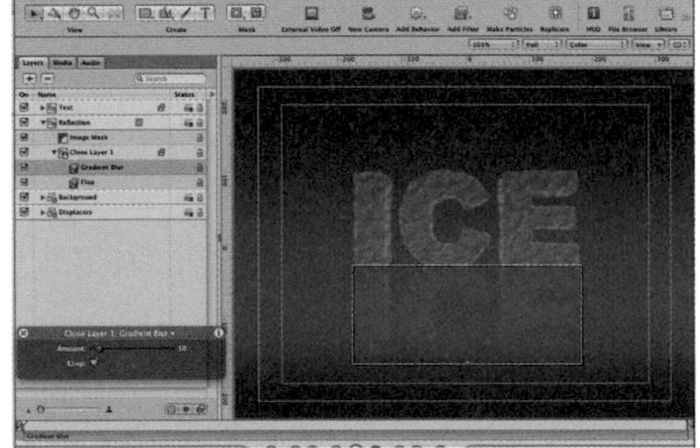

16 Okay—one last step. Click on the **Clone Layer 1** within the **Reflection** group. **Add Filter/Blur/Gradient Blur**. Adjust the two points as you see above—one just at the top of our reflection and one just at the bottom. Save your project as ICE Text. We'll use it as a starting point for the rest of our Materials looks.

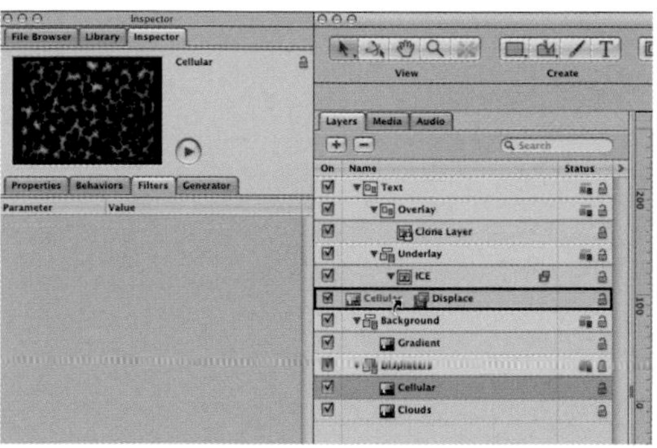

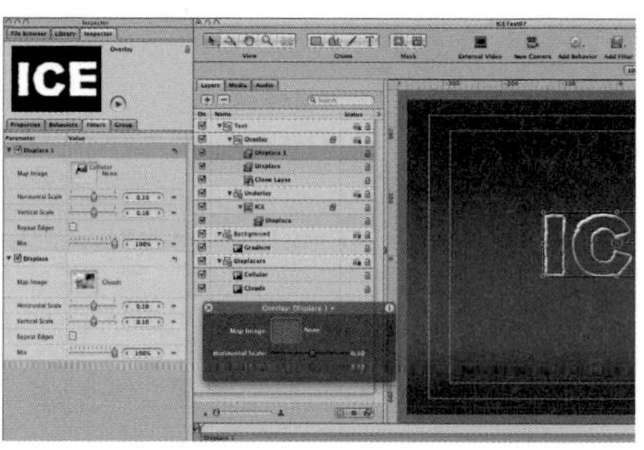

9 Click on the **ICE** text layer. **Add Filter/Distort/Displace.** Drag the **Cellular** displacer into the image well.

10 Next, click on the **Overlay** group. **Add Filter/Distortion/Displace.** Drag the **Clouds** displacer into the image well. **Add Filter/Distortion/Displace.** Add the **Cellular** displacer into its image well.

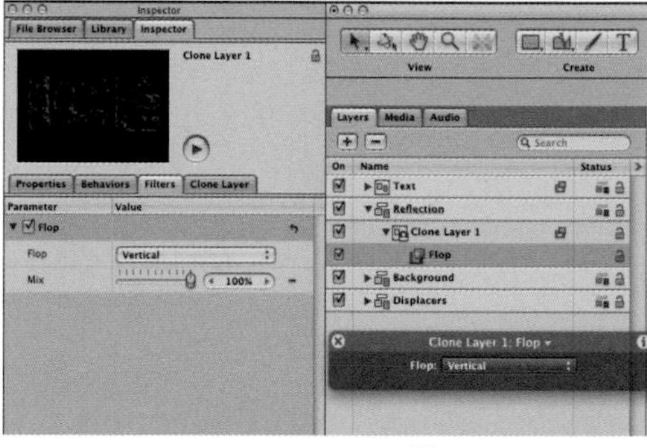

13 Now **Add Filter/Stylize/Indent.** Drag the **Cellular** displacer into its well. *Now* we're looking icy! All that's left is to create the reflection. Collapse all the groups to make our project easier to work with.

14 Click on the **Text** group. Press K to create a clone layer. Name the Clone Layer group **Reflection**. Set its blend mode to **Screen**. Drag it below the **Text** group in the Layers palette. Click on **Clone Layer 1. Add Filter/Distort/Flop.** Set it to **Vertical.**

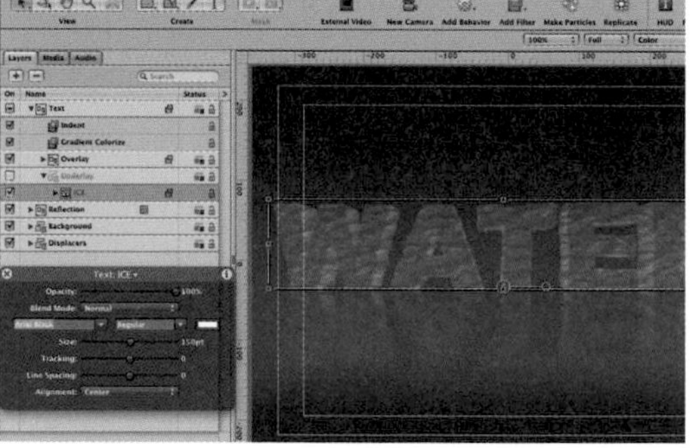

17 Now let's "melt" our ice and change it to water by animating it and altering the texture slightly.

18 Start with your **ICE Text** project. Change the text to **WATER**. You might have to change the font size down to 150. Then turn off the **Underlay** group.

continued...

Materials Science (continued)

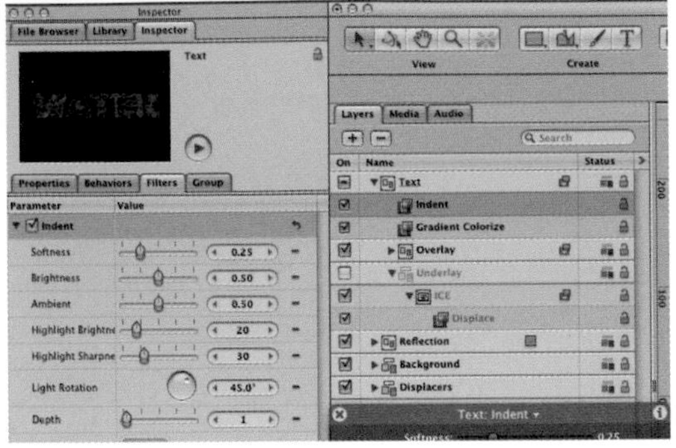

19 Open the **Text** group and click on the **Indent** filter. Change the **Depth** to **1**.

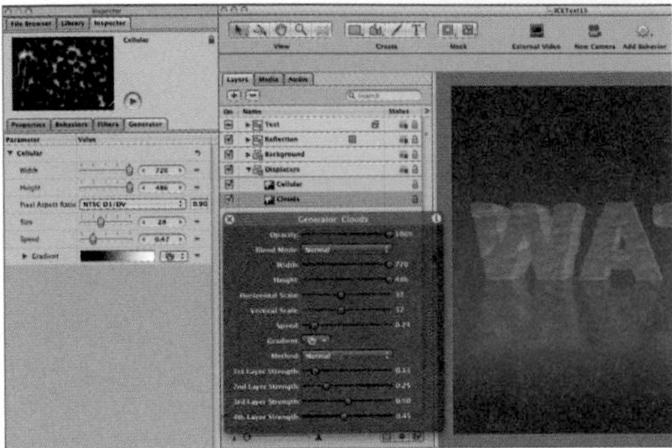

20 Finally, click on the **Cellular** displacer. Change the **Speed** to **0.47**. Select the **Clouds** displacer. Set the **Speed** to **0.24**. Change the **4th Layer Strength** to **0.45**. Now your water text will slosh around. Save your project as **WATER Text**.

23 Next, change the gradient in the **Gradient Colorize** filter to green by swapping the G and B values for each of the tags. Also change the source channel for the Reflection image mask to Green.

24 Now we'll alter the setting for the **Indent** filter so it's not so "wavy." First adjust the **Highlight Brightness** to **8**. Then drag the **Clouds** displacer into the image well. Save your project as **JELLO Text**.

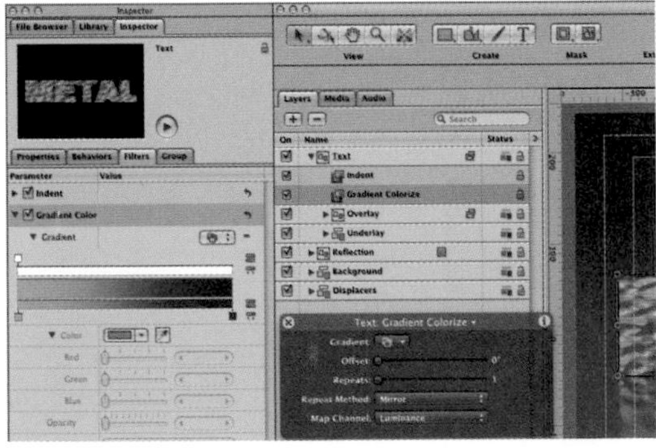

27 Change the blend mode of the **Overlay** group to **Normal**. Change the **Gradient Colorize** gradient to **Gray Scale**, and change the white tag to be light blue-gray and the black tag to be dark blue-gray.

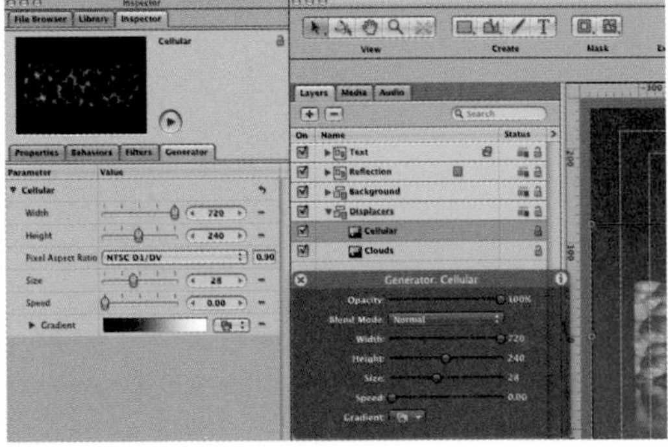

28 Click on your **Cellular** displacer—change the **Height** to **240**.

21 Jiggling gelatine is our goal now. Start with the **WATER Text** project.

22 First change the Text to read JELLO, and then change the blend modes of both the **Text** and **Reflection** groups to **Normal**.

25 To create text that looks like pockmarked metal, start with the ICE Text project.

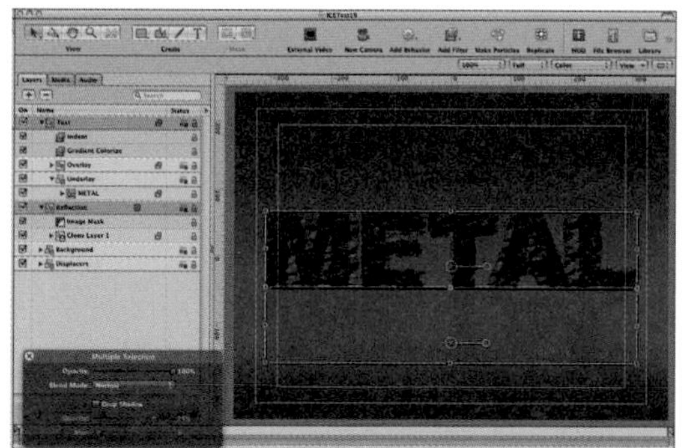

26 Change the blend modes of both the **Text** and **Reflection** groups to **Normal**. Change your text to **METAL** (you might have to size it down some and readjust the reflection).

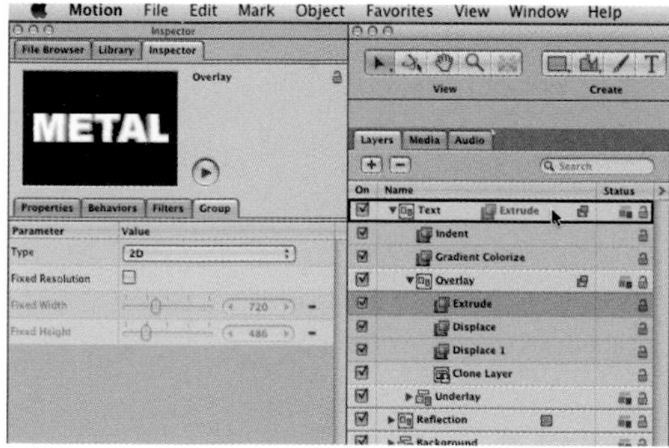

29 Finally open the **Text** group and drag the **Extrude** filter from the **Overlay** group to the **Text** group.

30 This last example is left as an exercise to the reader. (hint–start with Jello).

Electric Text

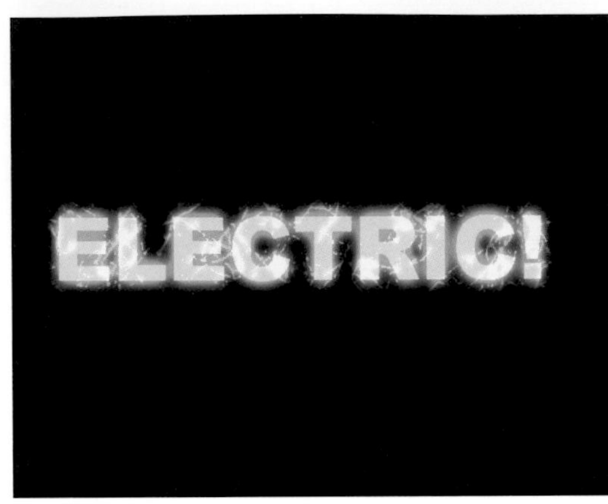

ISING THE TEXT ELECTRIC ... or something like that. In this project, we'll be using a generator from the Library and a filter to create text that will shock you.

Okay, seriously—it's simple to spark up your project with these easy steps.

1 Start with a new project. Add a group (by clicking the + on the Layers tab). Name the new group **Text** and place it inside the default **Group**. Select it. Press **T** to activate the **Text** tool. Click in the middle of your screen. Select **Arial Black**, **90** point, Alignment: **Center**. Type the word **ELECTRIC!**

4 We want to expand **Masker** and we'll use a Bloom to do so. **Add Filter/Glow/Bloom**. Set the **Amount** to **12**.

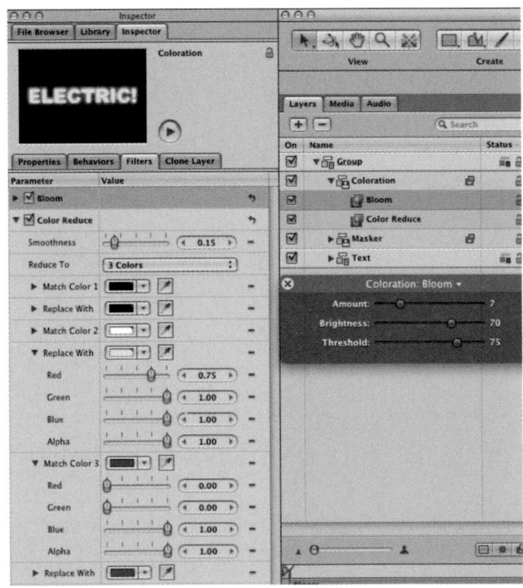

5 Select the **Coloration** layer. **Add Filter/Color Correction/Color Reduce**. Set **Reduce** to **3 Colors**. Set **Match Color 1** and **Replace With** to Black. Set **Match Color 2 to White**. Set the **Replace With** to R **0.75**, G **1.0**, B **1.0**. Set **Match Color 3** and the **Replace With** to R 0, G 0, B **1**. **Add Filter/Glow/Bloom**.

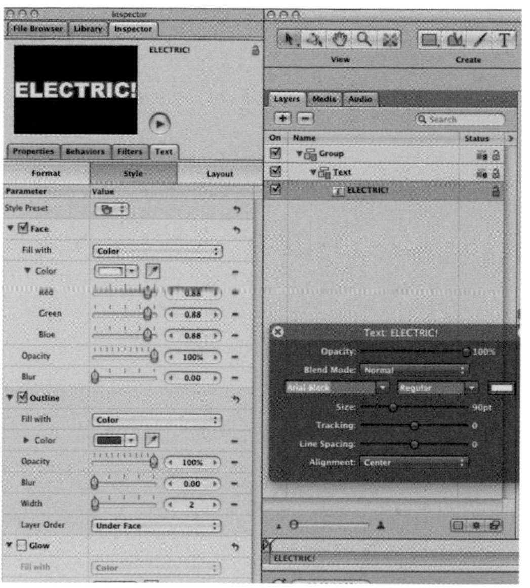

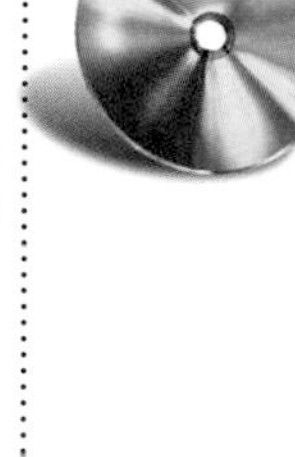

2 Click on the **ELECTRIC!** layer. Select the **Text/Style** tab. Set the **Face** color to 88% gray. Activate the **Outline**, Set its color to deep blue, set the **Width** of the outline to **2**.

3 Click on the **Text** group. Press **K** to create a clone layer. Name the clone layer **Coloration**. Click on the **Text** group and press **K** again. Name the new clone layer **Masker**.

6 In **Library/Generators**, click on the **Caustics** generator. Click the **Apply** button. Set **Blend Mode** to **Add**, **Size** to **.06**, **Speed** to **.93**, **Refraction** to **200**, **Brightness** to **50**. Add **Filter/Stylize/Edge Work**. Set **Radius** to **1**, **Blur 1.04**, **Amount 13**, Add **Filter/Glow/Bloom**. Set **Amount** to **2**, **Brightness 60**.

7 Now select **Caustics** and type **⌘ Shift M** to add an **Image Mask**. Set the **Source Channel** to **Luminance**. Drag the **Masker** layer into the **Mask Source** well.

Germs!

WASH YOUR HANDS after building this project. While working up the Electric Text project, I stumbled across this disgusting effect.

Just goes to show you that your mom was right—always look out for germs.

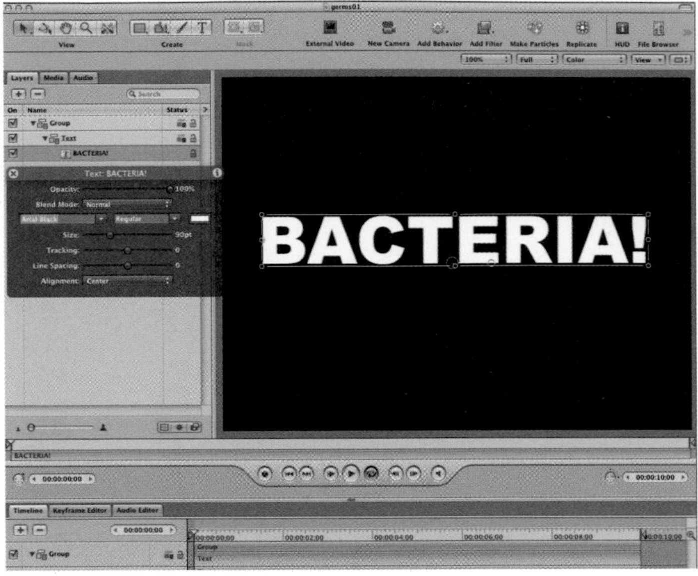

1 Start with a new project. Add a group (by clicking the + on the **Layers** tab). Name the new group **Text** and place it inside the default **Group**. Select it. Press **T** to activate the text tool. Click in the middle of your screen. Select **Arial Black, 90 point, Alignment: Center**. Type the word **BACTERIA!**

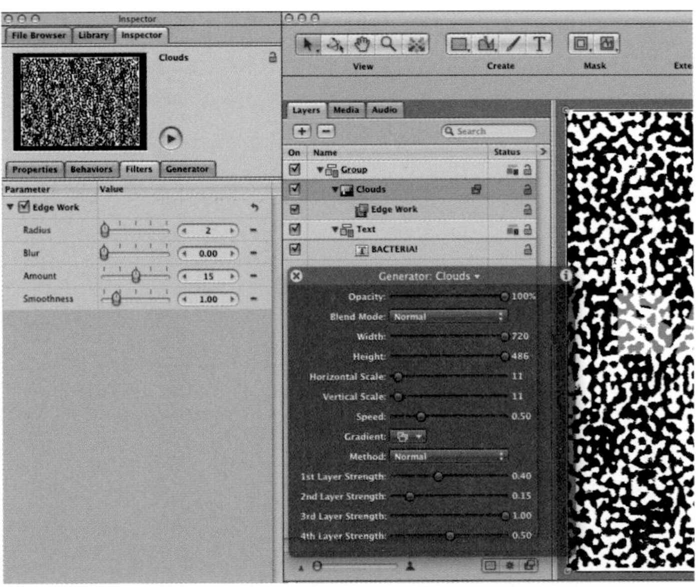

3 Select **Group**. In the **Library/Generators**, select **Clouds** and click **Apply**. Set the **Horizontal** and **Vertical Scales** to **11**, the **Method** to **Turbulent**, **1st Layer Strength** to **0.40**, **2nd Layer Strength** to **0.15**, **3rd Layer Strength** to **1.00**, and **4th Layer Strength** to **0.50**. Add **Filter/Stylize/Edge Work**. Set **Blur** to **0.00**.

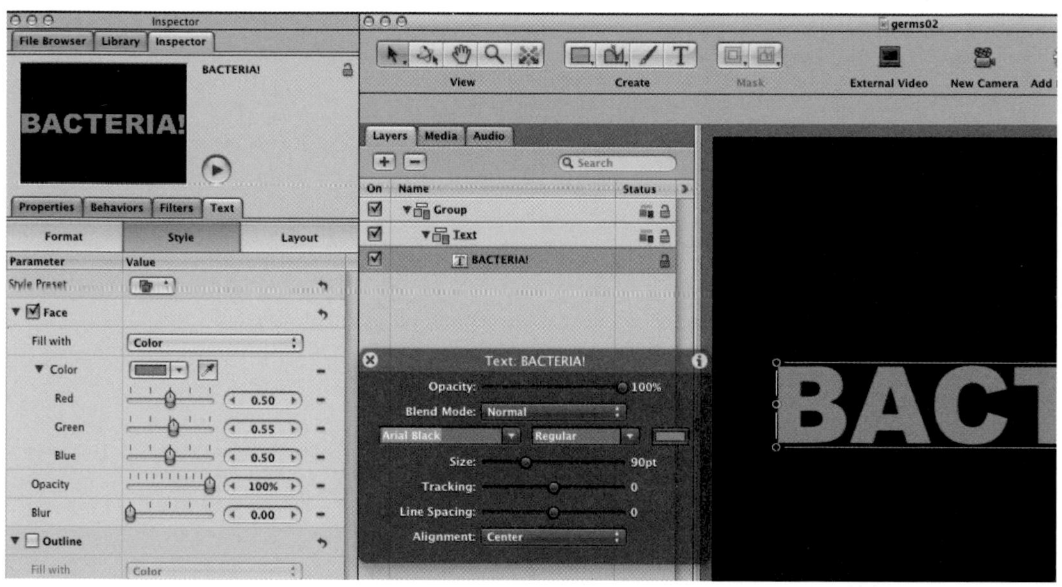

2 Click on the **BACTERIA!** layer. Select the **Text/Style** tab. Set the **Face** color to R **0.50**, G **0.55**, B **0.50**.

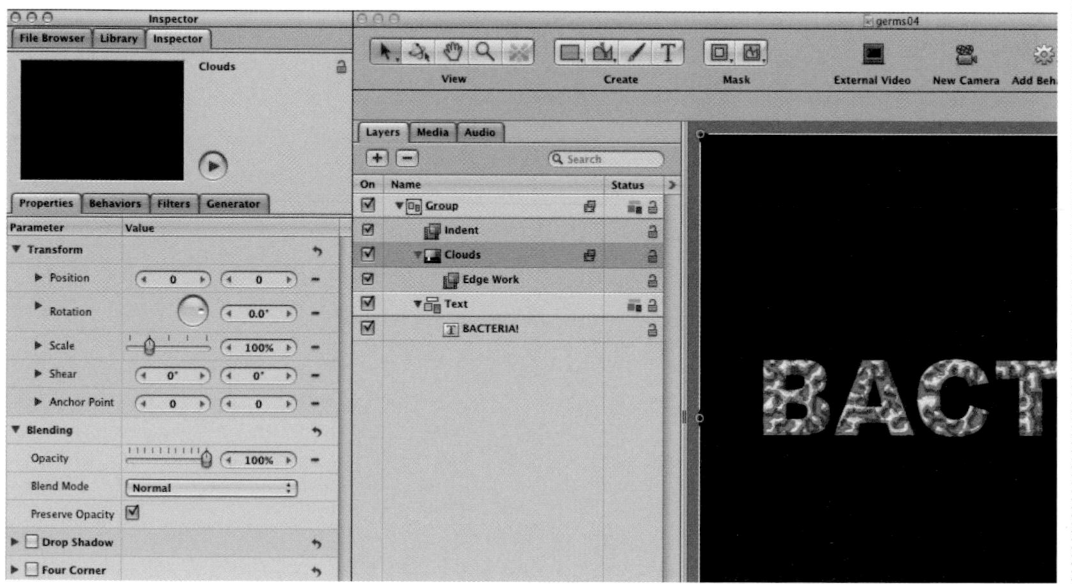

4 Go to the **Properties** tab of the **Clouds** layer. Select **Preserve Opacity**. Select **Group**. Add **Filter/Stylize/Indent**. Bingo—we're done!

HOT TIP

Using the Preserve Opacity checkbox is quicker and simpler than adding an image mask to an object. Basically it makes the object transparent in all areas where there is not something immediately below it.

Chocolate Text

MMMMMM... CHOCOLATE. Just like the Electric Text project led to Germs, Germs brought me to this sweet effect.

Playing in Motion can be its own reward. Indulge yourself.

1 Start with a new project. Press **T** to activate the **Text** tool. Click in the middle of your screen. Select **Arial Black**, **140 point**, **Alignment: Center**. Type the word **CHOCOLATE!** The word will be too wide, so in **Text/Format** tab, set the **X scale** to **50%**.

3 Add **Filter/Stylize/Indent**. Set the **Softness** to **0.96**, **Brightness** to **0.77**, **Ambient** to **0.65**, **Highlight Brightness** to **100**, **Highlight Sharpness** to **24**.

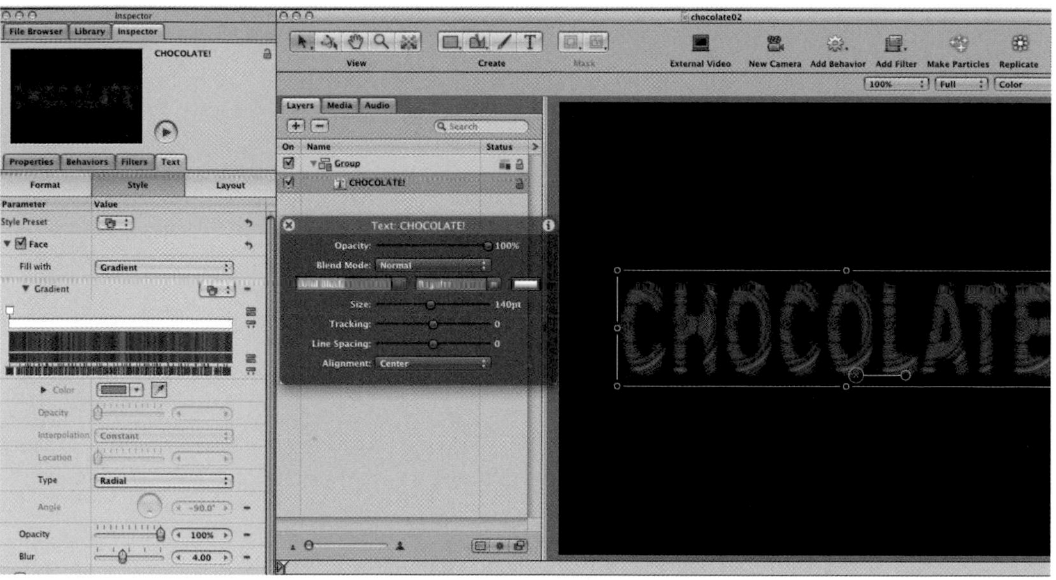

2 Click on the **Style** tab. Set the **Fill With** to **Gradient**. Set the **Gradient** to **Walnut**. Set the **Type** to **Radial**. Set the **Blur** to 4.0.

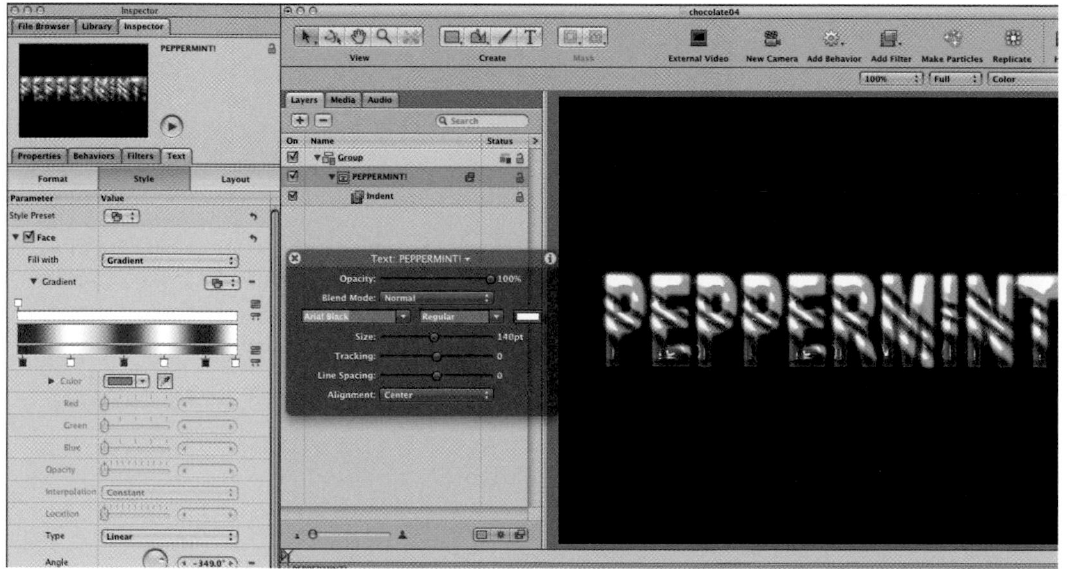

4 Change the **Gradient**, change the material. Peppermint anyone?

HOT TIP

The Indent filter is very useful for creating shiny wet or plasticy textures.

Sludge Text

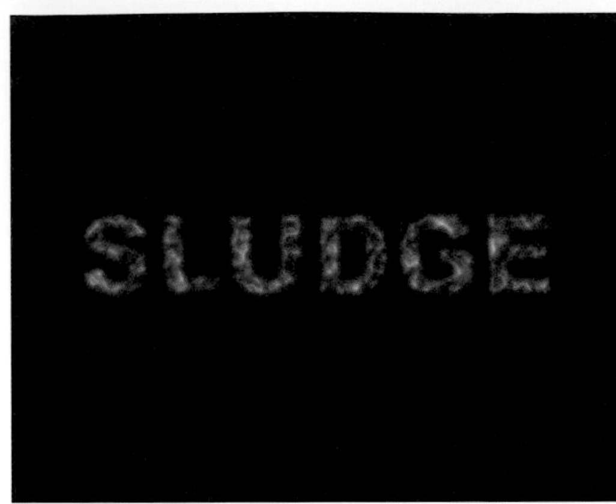

DISGUSTING IS THE WORD for this animated project. Use the effect sparingly—your viewers will be suitably nauseated.

We're going to use a couple of generators and the ever handy Indent filter.

1 Start with a new project. In this case I was using **Presentation Large**. Press **T** to activate the text tool. Click in the middle of your screen. Select **Arial Black, 176** point, **Alignment: Center**. Type **SLUDGE**.

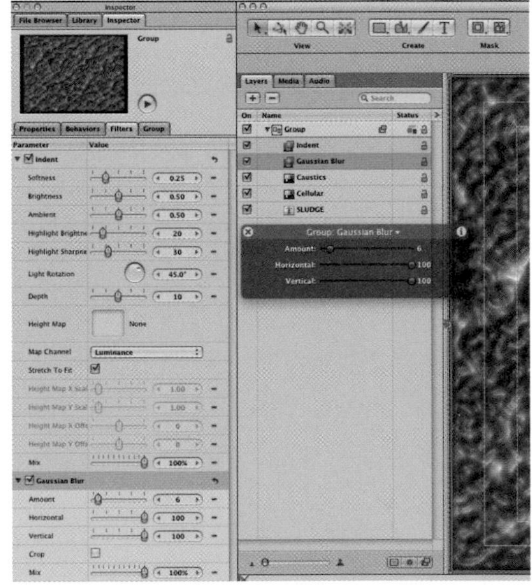

4 Select the default **Group**. Add **Filter/Blur/Gaussian Blur**. Set **Amount** to 6. Add **Filter/Stylize/Indent**.

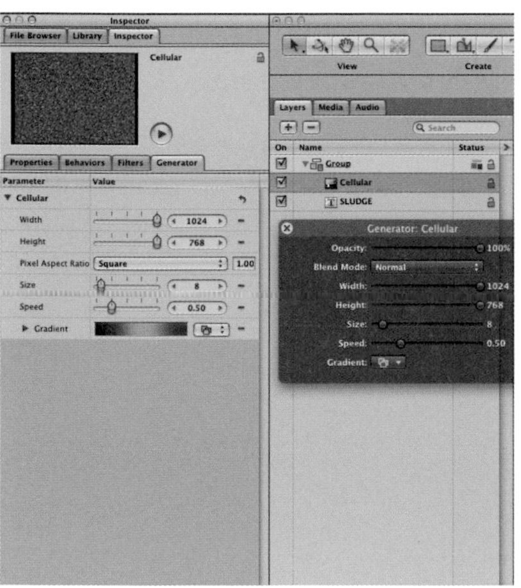

2 In the Library/Generators, select Cellular. Click Apply. Set the Gradient to Charcoal.

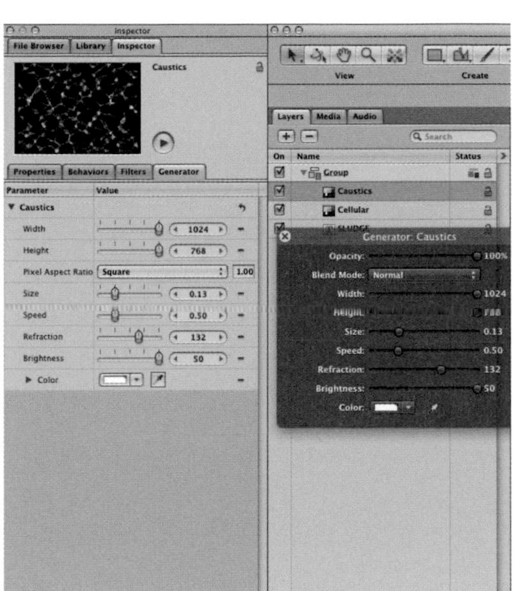

3 In the Library/Generators, select Caustics. Click Apply. Set Size to 0.13. Set Refraction to 132. Set Brightness to 50.

HOT TIP

When the image well is left empty, most effects use the image the effect is applied to as a default.

For instance, the height map for the Indent filter is provided by the luminance of the layer we're applying the filter to.

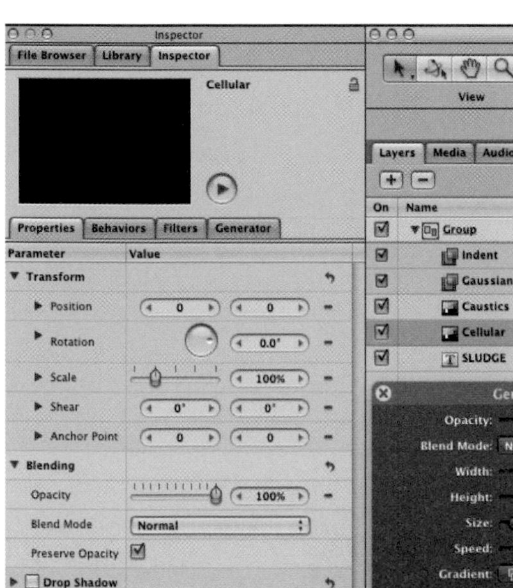

5 Click on Caustics. In the Properties tab, select Preserve Opacity. Click on Cellular. In the Properties tab, select Preserve Opacity. This avoids the need to apply a Matte layer to both generators by using the text's opacity.

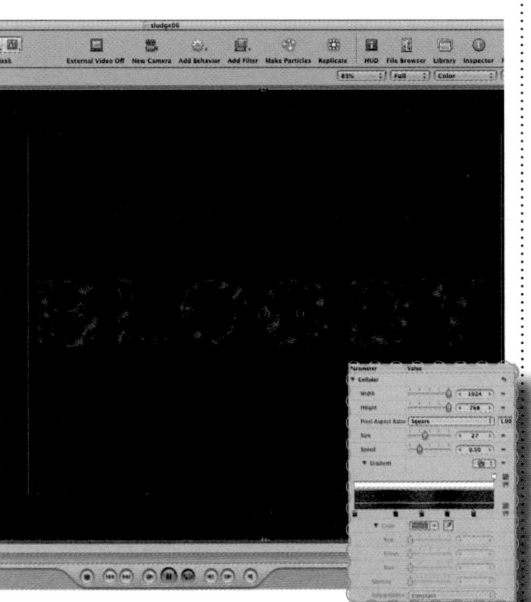

6 Extra credit–change the Gradient in the Cellular generator, fiddle with the sizes, change the blend mode of Caustics (to Subtract), and get something equally disgusting.

Plastic Text

ANDY WARHOL ONCE SAID, "I love plastic. I want to *be* plastic." Now the text in your project can be just like Andy. There are so many variations on this effect. Experiment and you'll see.

We'll be using some shading and the Indent filter for this effect.

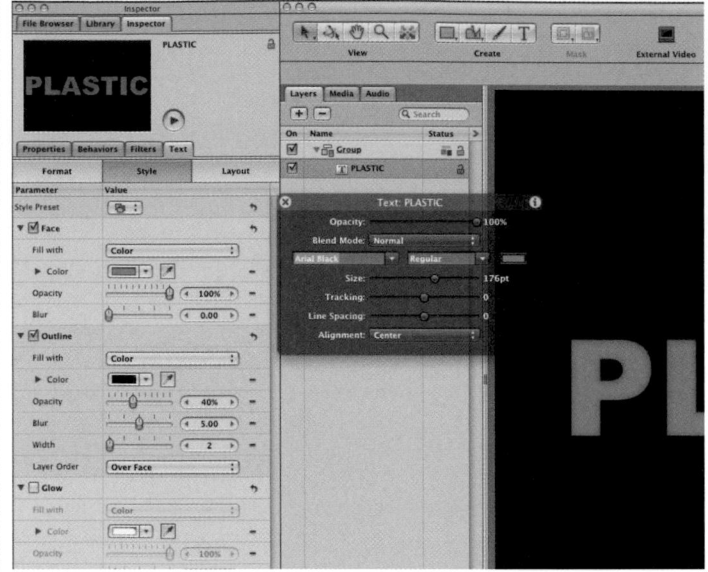

1 Start with a new project. I'm using **Presentation Large**. Press **T** to activate the **Text** tool. Click in the middle of your screen. Select **Arial Black**, **176** point, **Alignment: Center**. Type the word **PLASTIC**. In the **Text/Style** tab, set the **Color** to a nice blue. Activate **Outline**. Set the **Color** to Black, **Opacity** to **40%**, **Blur** to **6**, **Width** to **2**, and **Layer Order** to **Over Face**.

3 That doesn't look bad, but let's enhance it. Click on **PLASTIC.** Type **⌘D**. Align the duplicate exactly with the original. In **Text/Style**, turn off the **Face.** Set the **Outline** to **Gradient** fill. Set the color in the left tab to the same blue as your **Face** in Step 1 above. Set the right-hand tab to **Black.** Set the Type to **Radial**, the **Opacity** to **100**, the **Blur** to **0.0**, and the **Width** to **2.**

2 Add **Filter/Blur/Gaussian Blur**. Add **Filter/Stylize/Indent**. Set the **Highlight Brightness** to **32**. Set the **Highlight Sharpness** to **22**. Set **Depth** to **6**.

4 Just some fine tuning remaining. Click on **Indent**. Set **Softness** to **0.19**, **Highlight Brightness** to **29**, **Highlight Sharpness** to **23**.

HOT TIP

The Indent filter has similar effects to the "Plastic Wrap" filter in Photoshop.

Erosion

OFTEN YOU DON'T WANT PERFECT pristine text; you need it to show some wear and tear. You need it to have character.

To get nice battle-scarred text, we'll use the Caustics generator and a filter or two to supply some corrosion.

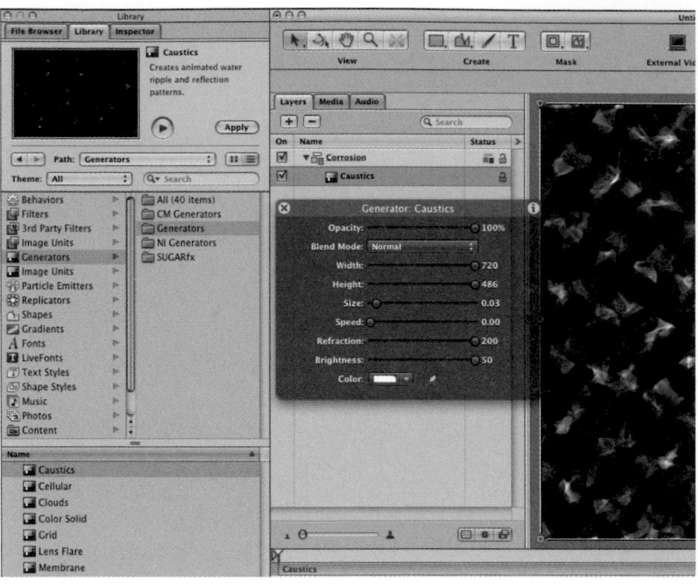

1 Start with a new project. Rename the default group to **Corrosion**. In **Library/ Generators**, select **Caustics**. Click Apply. Set the **Size** to **.03**, **Speed** to 0, **Refraction** to **200**, **Brightness** to **50**.

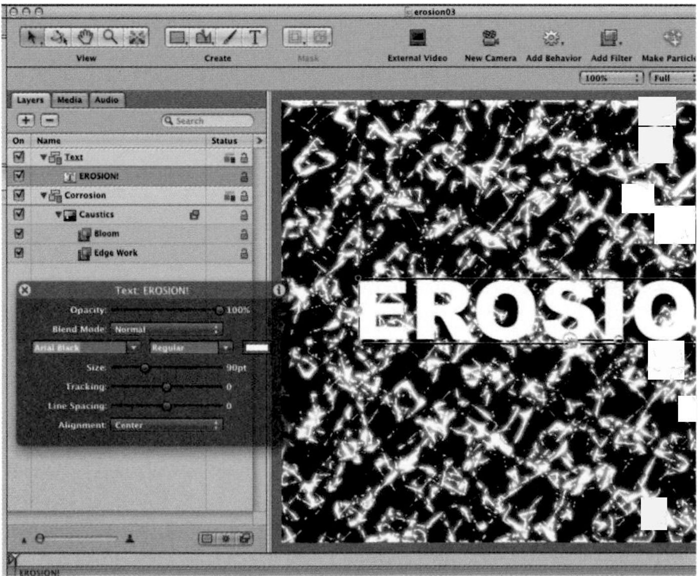

3 Add a new group. Name it **Text**. Press T to activate the Text tool. Click in the center of the screen. Set the **Font** to **Arial Black**, the **Size** to **90 pt**, the **Alignment** to **Center**. Type the word **EROSION!** and then press the esc key.

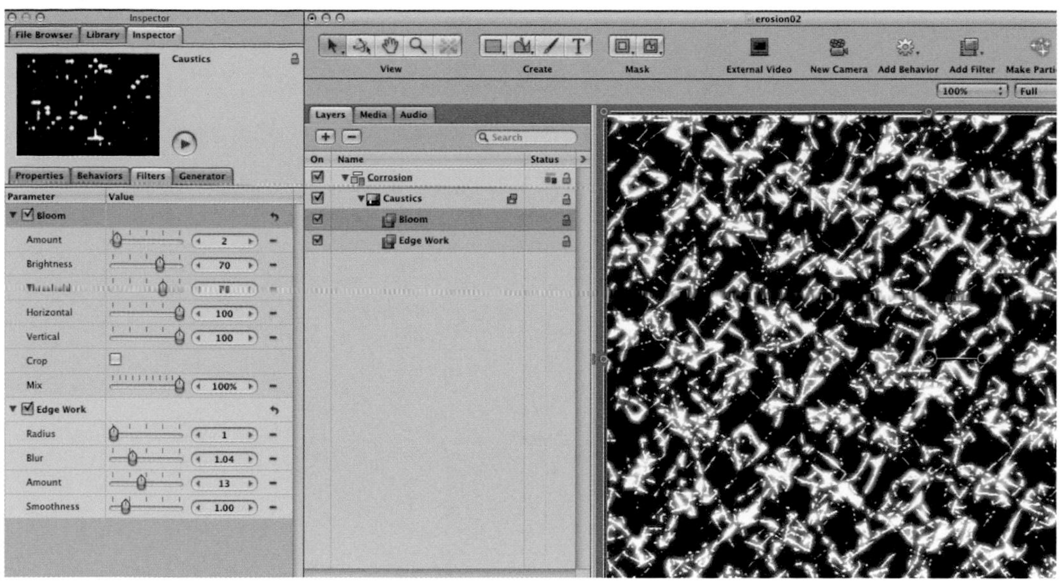

2 Add Filter/Stylize/Edge Work. Set Radius to 1, Blur to 1.04, Amount to 13. Add Filter/Glow/Bloom. Set Amount to 2.

HOT TIP

The techniques in this chapter can be combined to produce even more effects.

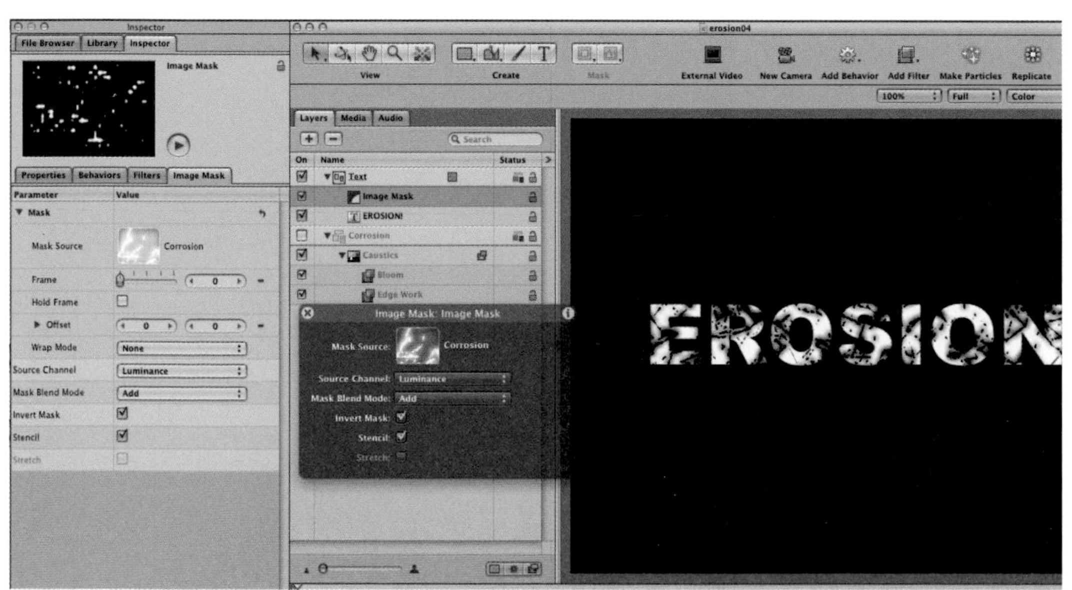

4 With the Text group selected, press ⌘ Shift M to add an Image Mask. Change the Source Channel to Luminance. Click the Invert Mask button. Drag the Corrosion group into the Mask Source well and you're done.

Super Easy Chrome Text

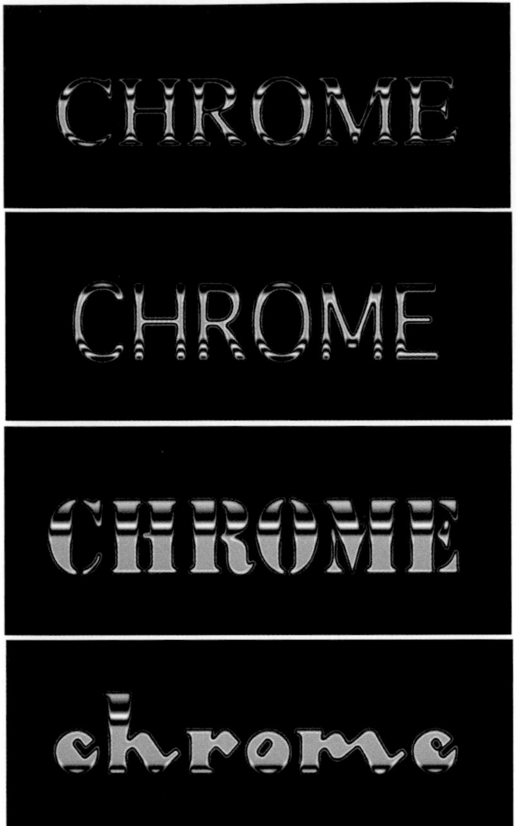

THIS IS THE CHROME like we see on logo and text badges on cars. And as you can see, it holds up pretty well on a variety of fonts.

We'll be using the Indent filter and the Gradient Colorize filter.

1 Start with a new project. Press T to activate the **Text** tool. Click in the middle of your screen. Choose **Times** (for now) as the font and then select **Alignment: Center**. Type the word **CHROME**. Adjust the size so that the word fills the screen.

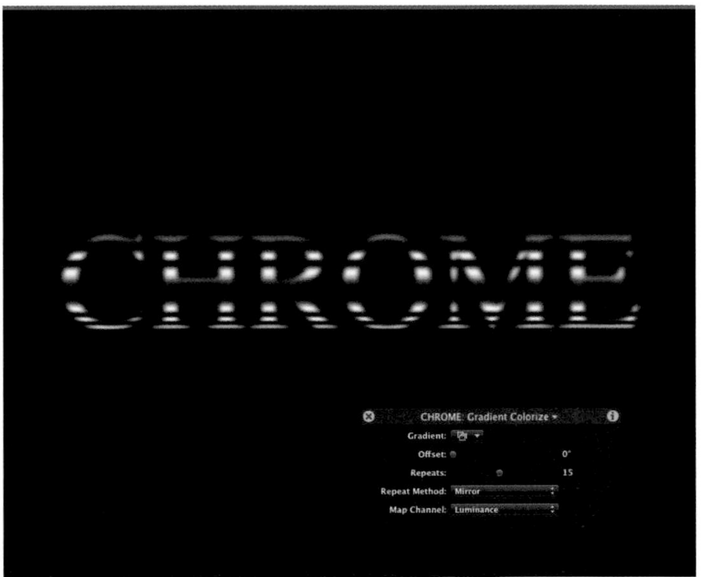

3 Now Add Filter/Color Correction/Gradient Colorize. Set the Repeats to about 15. That doesn't look right—but wait—we're almost there.

2 Click on the **Text** tab. Select **Style**. Change the **Face Fill** with to **Gradient**. Change the **Gradient** to (interestingly enough) **Blue Chrome**. Set **Blur** to 3.75.

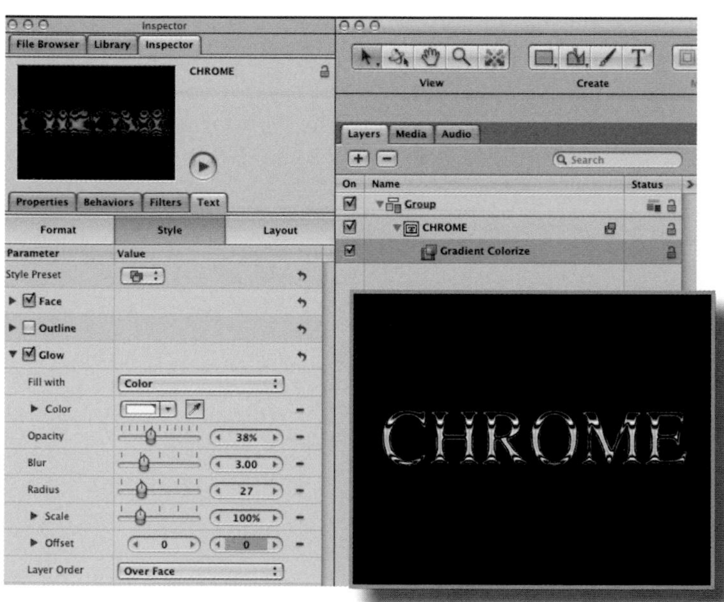

4 Go back to the **Text/Style** tab and go down to the **Glow** pane and activate it. Set the **Blur** to **3**, the radius to **27**, and the **Layer Order** to **Over Face**. Now adjust the **Opacity** of the **Glow** to around **38%**. You can play with the all of these parameters to enhance your effect.

Burl Wood

BURL WOOD IS USED BY artists to create sculptures and inlays. It is highly prized because of its unique shapes and ring patterns cased by abnormal growth of the tree.

Burl wood is relatively rare in nature but easy for us to produce in Motion.

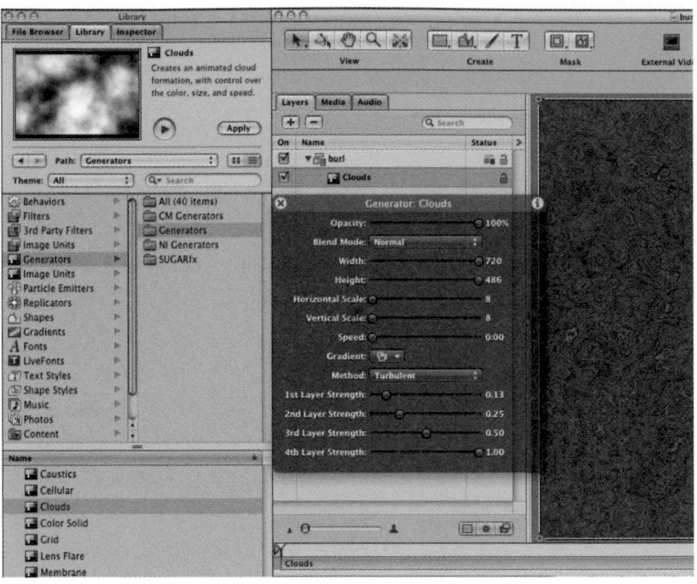

1 Start with a new project. Name the default group **Burl**. Select **Library/ Generators/Cloud**. Press **Apply**. Set the **Horizontal** and **Vertical Scales** to 8. Set the **Speed** to 0. Set the **Gradient** to **Walnut**. Set the **Method** to **Turbulent**.

3 With the **BurlWood** group selected, press ⌘ Shift M to add an **Image Mask**. Drag the **Text** group into the **Mask Source** well and you're done.

2 Add a new group. Name it **Text**. Press T to activate the **Text** tool. Click in the center of the screen. Set the **Font** to **Arial Black**, the **Size** to **125 pt**, the **Line Spacing** to **-50** or so, **Alignment** to **Center**. Type the word **BURL**, press *Return*, and type **WOOD**. Then press the *esc* key.

4 You can alter the **Horizontal Scale** and **Vertical Scale** and **Offset** and **Method** in the **Clouds** generator to achieve different results.

Underground

THIS LOOKS LIKE ONE OF those museum presentations of what's happening in the loamy shadows just beneath the surface of our front lawn: stringy bits of root pump fluid up to the plants above, worms glide slickly through the soil, bacteria and fungi glisten wetly.

This starts much the same way as the Burl Wood project and uses the always handy Indent filter.

1 Start with a new project. Press **T** to activate the Text tool. Click in the center of the screen. Set the **Font** to **Arial Black**, the **Size** to **116 pt**, the **Line Spacing** to **-51**, **Alignment** to **Center**. Type the word **UNDER**, press *Return*, type **GROUND**, and then press the *esc* key.

3 Press **K** to create a clone layer. Set the **Blend Mode** to **Overlay**. **Add Filter/ Stylize/Indent**. Set **Ambient** to **.79**, **Highlight Brightness** to **100**. Now, press play to see the underground world come to life.

2 Select **Library/Generators/Clouds**. Press **Apply**. Set the **Horizontal** and **Vertical Scales** to **8**. Set the **Speed** to **.07**. Set the **Gradient** to **Walnut**. In the **Properties** tab, click the **Preserve Opacity** checkbox.

4 For a fun variation, click on the **Clouds** generator and change the **Horizontal** scale to **40**, the speed to **.54**, the **Gradient** to **Beach Front**, and the **Method** to **Turbulent**.

Golden Text

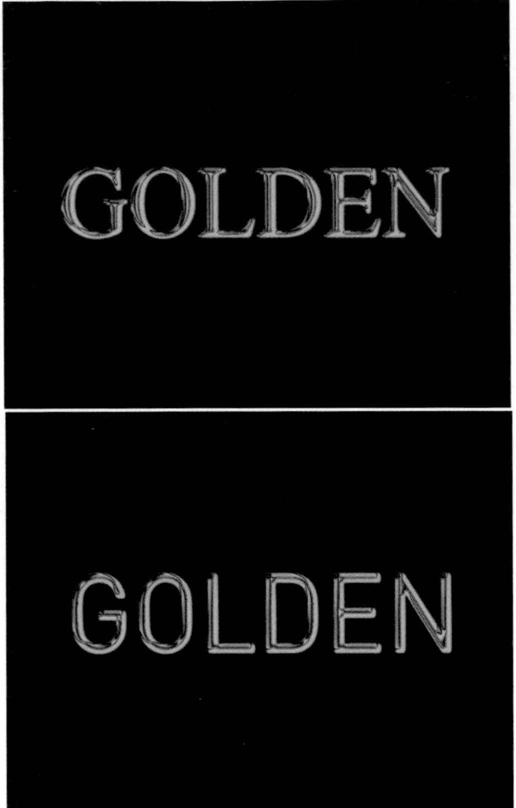

I SAY GOLDEN TEXT, but you can really make it whatever color you need. This works best with thinner fonts.

Similar to the Super Easy Chrome text project, we'll be using the Indent filter and the Gradient Colorize filter.

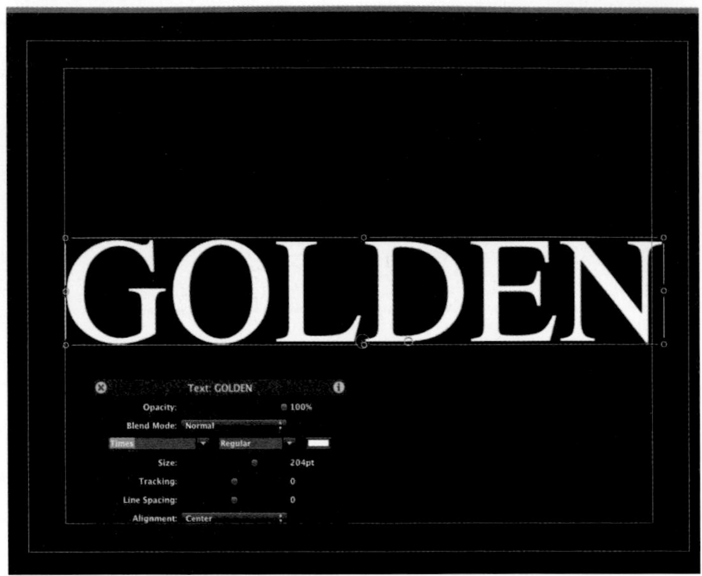

1 Start with a new project. Press T to activate the **Text** tool. Click in the middle of your screen. Choose **Times** (for now) as the font and then select **Alignment: Center**. Type the word **GOLDEN.** Adjust the size so that the word fills the screen.

3 Add Filter/Stylize/Indent. Set Softness to .82, Highlight Brightness to 0, Depth to 20, Add Filter/Blur/Gaussian Blur. Set Amount to 1.

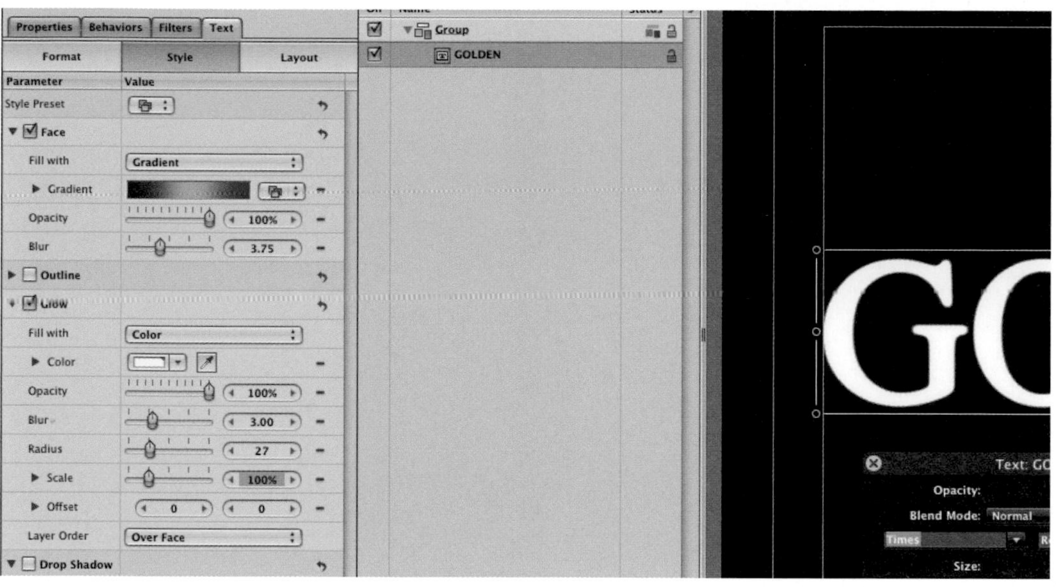

2 Click on the **Text** tab. Select **Style**. Change the **Face Fill** with to **Gradient**. Change the **Gradient** to **Charcoal**. Set **Blur** to **3.75**. Activate **Glow**. Set the **Blur** to **3**, the **Radius** to **27**, and the **Layer Order** to **Over Face**.

4 Now **Add Filter/Color Correction/Gradient Colorize**. Set **Offset** to **110**. Set the **Repeats** to about **10**. But that looks like Silver! Okay edit the gradient. Change the White color to **Red .95**, **Green .78**, and **Blue .14**. Now you're golden!

Rubber Stamp

TO ACHIEVE THE IMPERFECT look of a rubber stamp, we're going to use a technique very similar to the earlier Burl Wood project.

This shows how a simple variation can produce entirely different results.

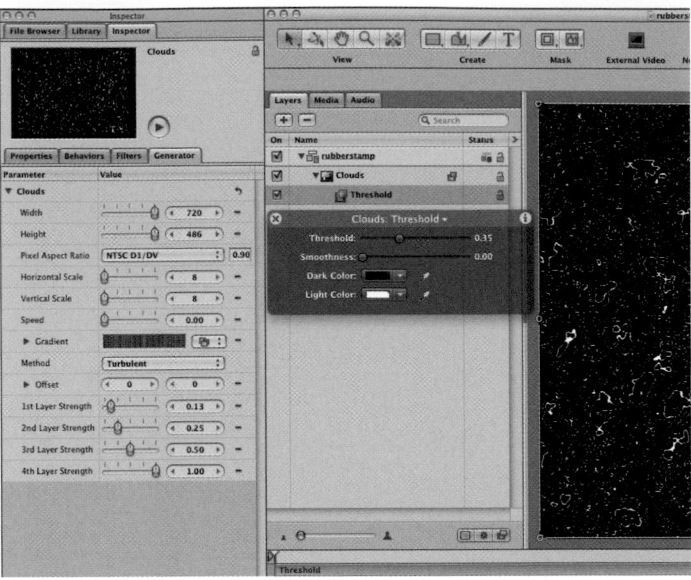

1 Start with a new project. Name the default group **Rubberstamp**. Select **Library/Generators/Cloud**. Press **Apply.** Set the **Horizontal** and **Vertical Scales** to **8**. Set the **Speed** to **0**. Set the **Gradient** to **Walnut**. Set the **Method** to **Turbulent**. Add **Filter/Color Correction/Threshold**. Set the **Threshold** to **.35**, **Smoothness** to 0.

3 With the **Text** group selected, press **⌘ Shift M** to add an **Image Mask**. Change the **Source Channel** to **Luminance**. Click the **Invert Mask** button. Drag the **Rubberstamp** group into the **Mask Source** well. In keeping with our rubber stamp look, rotate your text layer about 30 degrees.

2 Add a new group. Name it **Text**. Press **T** to activate the **Text** tool. Click in the center of the screen. Set the **Font** to **Arial Black**, the **Color** to **red**, the **Size** to **125 pt**, the **Line Spacing** to **-50** or so, **Alignment to Center**. Type the word **RUBBER**, press *Return*, and type **STAMP**. Then press the *esc* key.

4 Finally, add a new group below our **Text** group. Call it **Background**. In **Library/Generators**, select **Color Solid**. Click **Apply**. Change the **Color** to white. Adjust the color of your stamp text as you see fit (I made mine a bit darker).

Ice Nine

NODS TO KURT V. for the project name Inspired by a Photoshop tutorial in the NAPP magazine, but since we don't have a Chrome filter or a Plastic Wrap, we'll just have to make do. This one's a bit more complicated, but we'll get there.

In this project we'll build on techniques used in the Chrome and Golden Text projects.

1 Begin with a new project. I'm using **Presentation Large.** Name the default group **Base.** From the **Library,** grab the **Clouds** generator and place it in **Base.** Set **Horizontal** and **Vertical** scales to **20.** Set **Speed** to **0** (you can play with animating it later). Set **2nd Layer Strength** to **.34** and **4th Layer Strength** to **.50.**

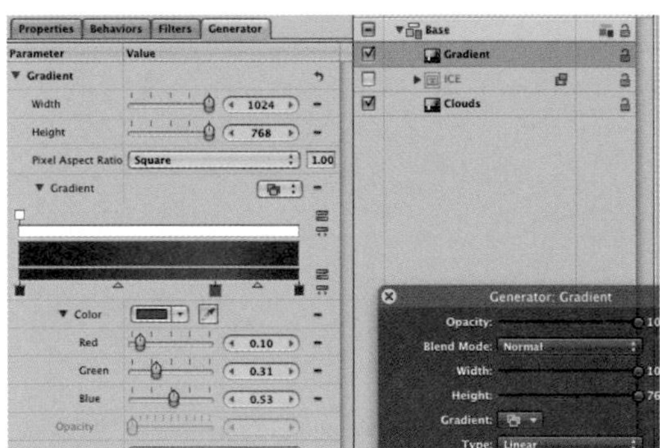

4 Go to the **Library,** grab a **Gradient** generator, and slap it in the **Base** group over **ICE.** Match the **Gradient** in the picture above. Set the left tag's RGB to **.05, .15, .35.** Set the right tag the same. At **70%** add a third tag, set it to **.10, .31, .53.**

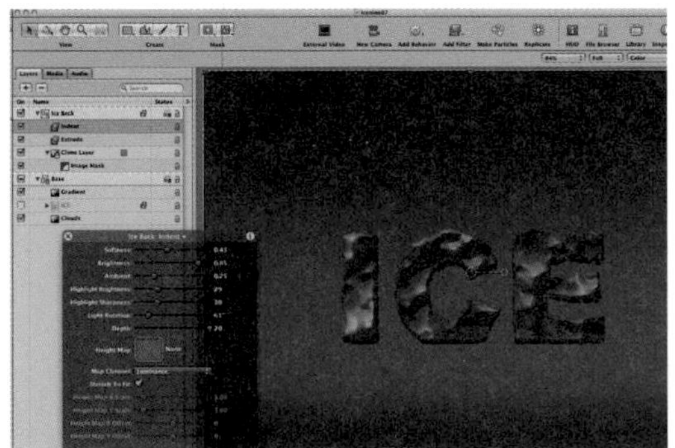

7 **Add Filter/Stylize/Indent.** Set **Softness** to **.43, Brightness** to **.85, Ambient** to **.25, Highlight Brightness** to **29, Light Rotation** to **61,** and **Depth** to **20.**

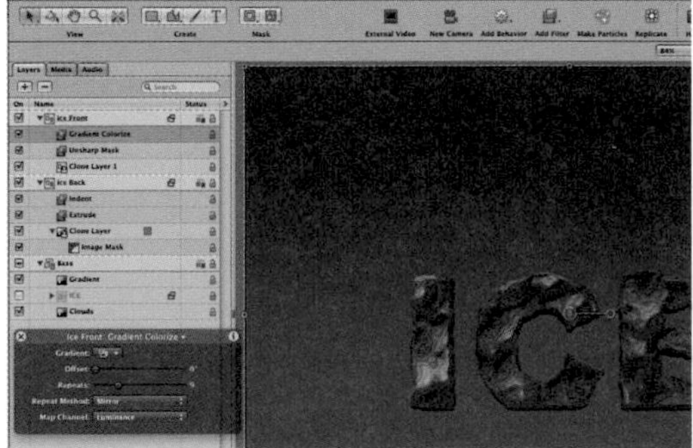

8 Select **Ice Back.** Press **K** to create a clone layer. Name the new group **Ice Front.** Set the **Blend Mode** to **Overlay.** Set the **Opacity** to **40%. Add Filter/Sharpen/ Unsharp Mask. Add Filter/Color Correction/Gradient Colorize.** Set the **Repeats** to **9.**

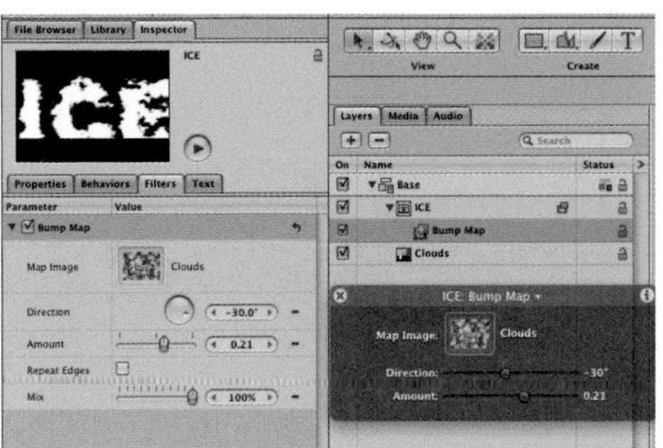

2 Press T to activate the **Text** tool. Click in the lower middle of your screen. Choose a thick font like **Arial Black**. Set **Alignment** to **Center**. Type the word **ICE.** Size it to be large on screen.

3 Add **Filter/Distortion/Bump Map**. Set the **Direction** to **-30** and the **Amount** to **.21**. Drag the **Clouds** generator into the **Map Image** well.

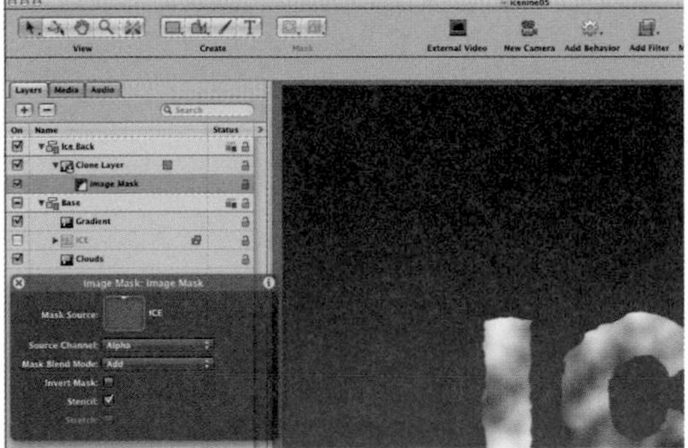

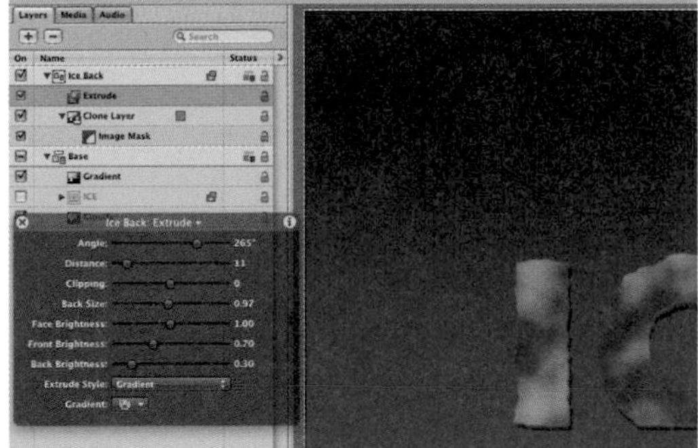

HOT TIP

You can vary the cloud pattern by changing the Offset values in the Cloud generator.

5 Add a new group at the top level. Rename it **Ice Back**. Click on the **Clouds** layer. Press K to create a clone layer. Drag it into **Ice Back**. While the **Clone Layer** is selected, type ⌘ Shift M to add a mask layer. Drag the **ICE** text layer into the **Mask Source** well.

6 Select **Ice Back**. Set the **Blend Mode** to **Hard Light**. Set the **Opacity** to **50%**. Add **Filter/Stylize/Extrude**. Set **Angle** to **265**, **Distance** to **11**, **Back Size** to **.97**, and **Extrude Style** to **Gradient**.

9 Now for the reflection. ⌘-Select **Ice Front** and **Ice Back**. Type ⌘ Shift G to **Group** them. Name the new group **Ice Main**. Press K to create a clone layer. Name the new group **Reflection**. Set the **Blend Mode to Overlay**. Drag it below the **Ice Main** group.

10 Select **Clone Layer 2**. In the **Properties** pane, set the **Y** and **Z** rotations to **180°**. Then position it just below the **Ice Main** image onscreen. Select the **Reflection** group. **Add Filter/Blur/Gradient Blur**. Set **Point 1** just at the top of the reflection. Set **Point 2** near the bottom of it.

Shiny Happy Text

THIS ONE FELL out of the methods developed for the Ice Nine project and we'll be using similar techniques.

It's all about the gradients you choose. Different gradients, different feelings. Try the Sundown gradient for a new effect.

1 Start with a new project. I'm using **Presentation Large**. Name the default group **Base**. From the **Library**, grab the **Clouds** generator and place it in **Base**. Set **Horizontal** and **Vertical** scale to **60**. Set **Speed** to **0** (you can play with animating it later). Set the **Gradient** to **Thundercloud**. Set **X Offset** to about **150**.

4 Add a new group at the top level. Rename it **Shiny Back**. Click on the **Clouds** layer. Press K to create a clone layer. Drag it into **Shiny Back**. While the **Clone Layer** is selected, type ⌘ Shift M to add a mask layer. Drag the **Shiny** text layer into the **Mask Source** well.

7 Select **Shiny Back**. Press K to create a clone layer. Name the new group **Shiny Front**. Set the **Blend Mode** to **Overlay**. Set the **Opacity** to **65%**. **Add Filter/Color Correction/Gradient Colorize**. Set the **Repeats** to **12**.

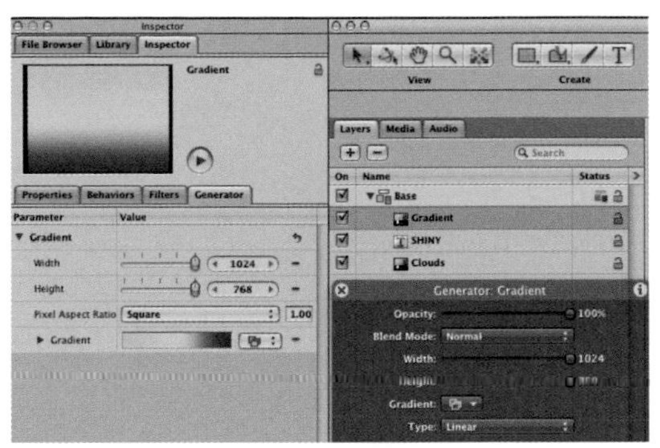

2 Press **T** to activate the **Text** tool. Click in the lower middle of your screen. Choose a thick font like **Arial Black**. Set **Alignment** to **Center**. Type the word **SHINY**. Size it to be large on screen. Lets make it a bit taller—set **Y Scale** to **150%**.

3 Go to the **Library** and grab a **Gradient** generator and slap it in the **Base** group over **SHINY**. Select the **Thundercloud** gradient

5 Select **Shiny Back**. Set the **Blend Mode** to **Hard Light**. Set the **Opacity** to **75%**. **Add Filter/Stylize/Extrude**. Set **Angle** to **265**, **Distance** to **11**, and **Back Size** to **.97**.

6 **Add Filter/Stylize/Indent**. Set **Softness** to **.67** and **Highlight Sharpness** to 23.

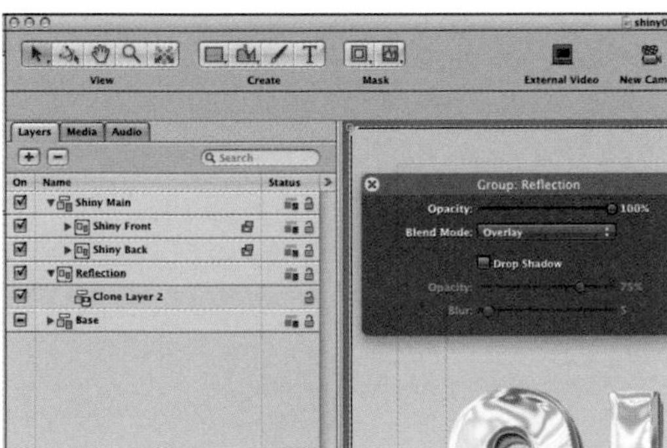

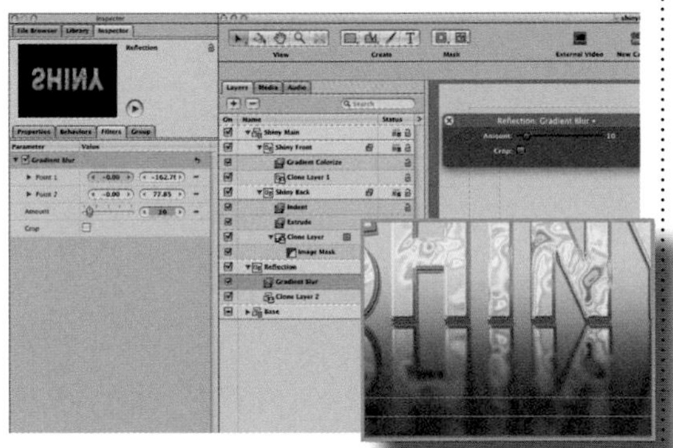

8 Now for the reflection. **⌘**-Select **Shiny Front** and **Shiny Back**. Type **⌘ Shift G** to group them. Name the new group **Shiny Main**. Press **K** to create a clone layer. Name the new group **Reflection**. Set the **Blend Mode** to **Overlay**. Drag it below the **Ice Main** group.

9 Select **Clone Layer 2**. In the **Properties** pane, set the **Y** and **Z** rotations to **180°**. Then position it just below the **Ice Main** image onscreen. Select the **Reflection** group. **Add Filter/Blur/Gradient Blur**. Set **Point 1** just at the top of the reflection. Set **Point 2** near the bottom of it.

Award-Winning Text

INSPIRED BY THE AWARDS SHOW SEASON graphics, I decided to create some "dazzling" text.

We will be using the Edge Work filter on a clone of our text layer to create a "sparkle map." We'll animate it with the ever handy Cellular generator and turn it into sparkles with the Dazzle filter.

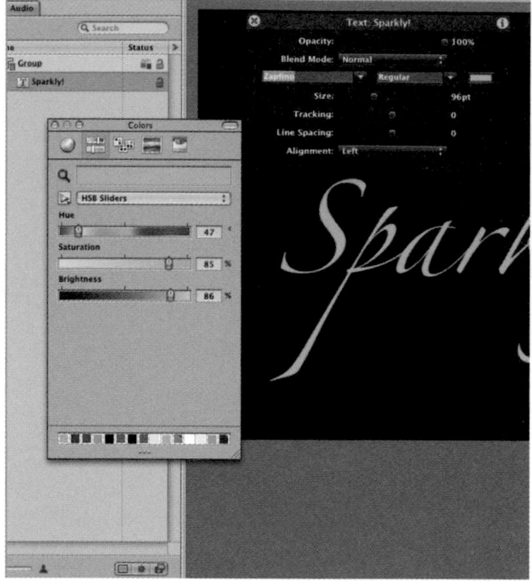

1 First, let's create some text. Hit the **T** key for the **Text** tool. Set your font to **Zapfino** for now, size **96**, color a nice golden yellow. Type the word **Sparkly**. Now select the group your text is in and press the **K** key to clone it.

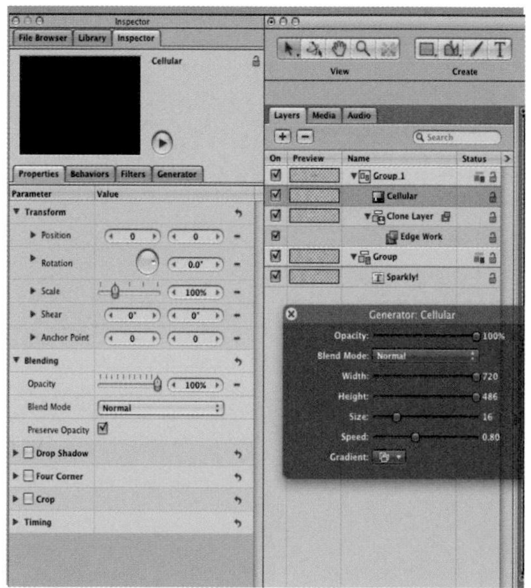

4 In the **Library** tab, under **Generators**, grab the **Cellular** generator and place it above our clone layer. Set the **Size** to **16** and the **Speed** to **0.80**. In the **Inspector/Properties** tab, click on the **Preserve Opacity** check box. This makes the layer transparent unless something is directly below it.

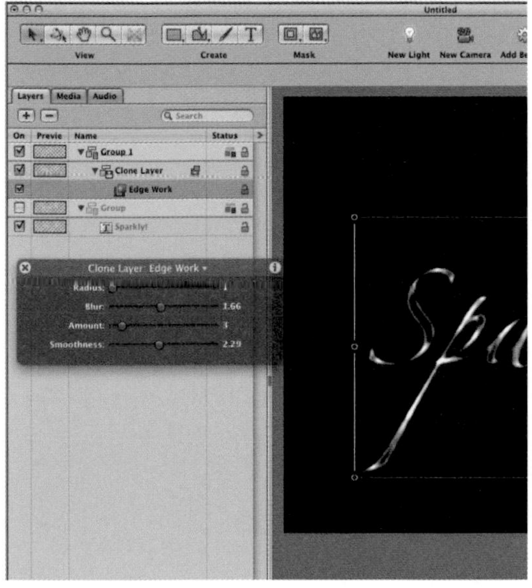

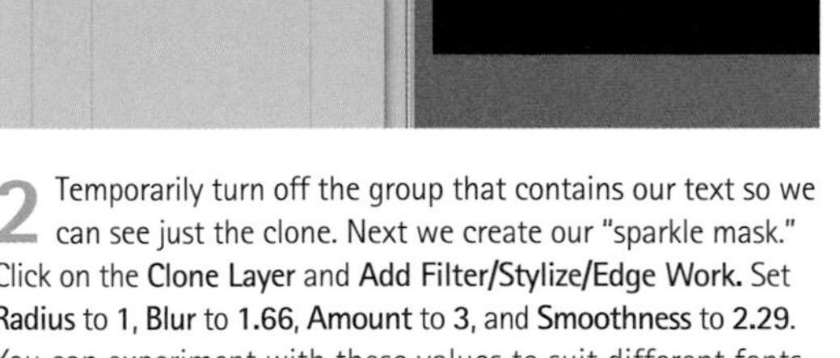

2 Temporarily turn off the group that contains our text so we can see just the clone. Next we create our "sparkle mask." Click on the **Clone Layer** and **Add Filter/Stylize/Edge Work.** Set **Radius** to **1**, **Blur** to **1.66**, **Amount** to **3**, and **Smoothness** to **2.29**. You can experiment with these values to suit different fonts.

3 Turn your text group back on. If you set your **Group 1** layer's **Blend** mode to **Add** and its **Opacity** to about 50%, you'll get a nice metallic gold ribbon letter effect. Okay, turn **Group 1's Opacity** back up to **100%.**

5 Now you should see some nice shiny highlights on our letters. Click on **Group 1, Add Filter/Glow/Dazzle.** Set the **Amount** to 37, the **Brightness** to 65, and **Threshold** to 19.

6 For an extra bit of fun, right/ctrl-click on the **Angle** setting in the **Dazzle** filter and select **Wriggle.** Set the amount to **20, Apply Mode** to **Add and Subtract,** and **Noisiness** to **0.00**—now press Play and watch your sparkles rotate.

HOT TIP

If you turn off the Dazzle filter and change the Blend mode of the Group 1 layer to Color Burn, you get a very different effect.

3 INTERLUDE

Blend modes

IF YOU ALREADY UNDERSTAND BLEND modes—those settings you can play with to alter how different layers interact with each other—skip on ahead.

When I first considered writing this essay, I poked around online for a while, thinking—surely someone has written a good explanation already. And I'm still sure someone has, I just didn't find it. All the ones I found (including the one in the Motion user manual) I felt were in some way a bit confusing.

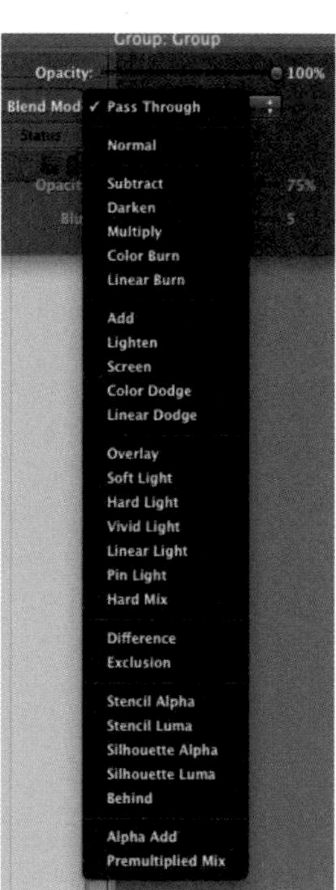

Let's start with some basics. All the pixels in your layers are really just numbers. Most likely you think of them as values from 0-255 in colors Red, Green, and Blue. For our purposes, think of them instead as a range from 0 for black to 1 for full brightness. Pixel values of 0.5, 0.5, 0.5 for RGB, for instance, yield middle gray.

If you get that, the rest is easy. Blend modes are simply mathematical ways of combining the image with the image from the layer below it.

All of the Blend modes are affected by the percentage that Opacity is set to. Basically, it takes the result of the blend and mixes it back into the original image. If Opacity is set to 50%, the result will be a mixture of half of the original image and half of the blended image.

Within Motion, the different Blend modes are grouped by function—whether they darken or lighten or affect contrast, etc. To make it easier to follow, we'll group our descriptions by simple to complex. Further, let's establish a naming convention. We'll call the lower image the "Base," and the upper image with the Blend mode we'll call the "Blend."

Normal simply takes Blend.

Final = Blend

Subtract takes the Blend and subtracts it from the Base.

Final = Base – Blend

Add is Blend added to the Base.

Final = Blend + Base

Multiply is the Blend multiplied by the Base.

Final = Blend * Base

Screen inverts Blend, multiplies it by the inverse of Base, and then inverts the result.

Final = invert (invert (Blend) * invert (Base))

Darken compares Blend and Base and chooses the darkest value.

Final = minimum (Base, Blend)

Lighten compares Blend and Base and chooses the lightest value.

Final = maximum (Base, Blend)

continued...

Blend-modes (continued)

Now we get a little more complicated.

Color Burn takes the inverse of Base and divides it by the Blend, and then inverts the result.

Final = invert (invert (Base)/Blend)

Color Dodge is Base divided by the inverse of Blend.

Final = Base/inverse (Blend)

Linear Burn is Blend added to Base and then 1 is subtracted from the total.

Final = Blend + Base – 1

Linear Dodge is the same as **Add**. The Blend and Base are added together.

Final = Blend + Base

The next ones are somewhat complicated.

Overlay takes each pixel from the Base and if it is brighter than .5, it performs a Screen operation; otherwise it performs a Multiply.

Final = Base > .5 ? Screen (Base) else Multiply (Base)

Softlight is like **Overlay**, just less harsh. Rather than switching sharply at .5, it seems to gradually use a mix of Multiply and Screen and the ratio depends on the brightness of the pixel.

Final = Blend(Screen (Base), Multiply (Base), Base)

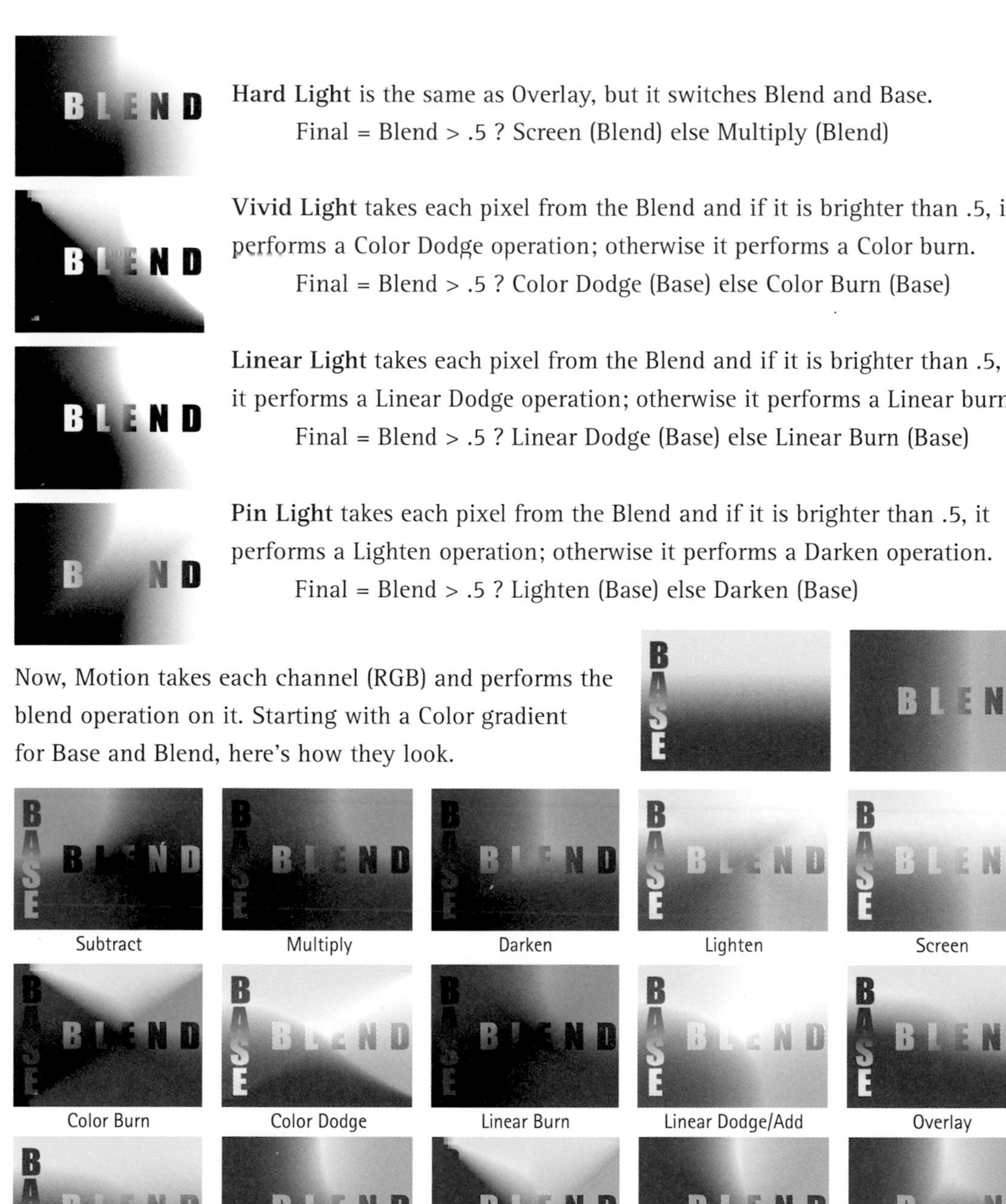

Hard Light is the same as Overlay, but it switches Blend and Base.

Final = Blend > .5 ? Screen (Blend) else Multiply (Blend)

Vivid Light takes each pixel from the Blend and if it is brighter than .5, it performs a Color Dodge operation; otherwise it performs a Color burn.

Final = Blend > .5 ? Color Dodge (Base) else Color Burn (Base)

Linear Light takes each pixel from the Blend and if it is brighter than .5, it performs a Linear Dodge operation; otherwise it performs a Linear burn.

Final = Blend > .5 ? Linear Dodge (Base) else Linear Burn (Base)

Pin Light takes each pixel from the Blend and if it is brighter than .5, it performs a Lighten operation; otherwise it performs a Darken operation.

Final = Blend > .5 ? Lighten (Base) else Darken (Base)

Now, Motion takes each channel (RGB) and performs the blend operation on it. Starting with a Color gradient for Base and Blend, here's how they look.

Subtract | Multiply | Darken | Lighten | Screen

Color Burn | Color Dodge | Linear Burn | Linear Dodge/Add | Overlay

Softlight | Hard Light | Vivid Light | Linear Light | Pin Light

Finally, Pass Through is only available for groups. When used, each layer in the group is blended with all objects and groups that are below it. If Pass Through is not used, the layers within a group are blended with each other. Then the final result is processed using the group's blend mode with the lower groups.

■ From Line Drawings to Cartoons to Comic books to complicated color effects, Motion can do amazing things to your still and moving images.

4 Image Effects

OFTEN MOTION IS CONSIDERED SIMPLY A fancy text toy. However, with the basic tools provided, elaborate graphic effects can be achieved.

I prefer to think of Motion as Photoshop for moving images. It's like the ultimate plugin for Final Cut Pro.

Photocopy

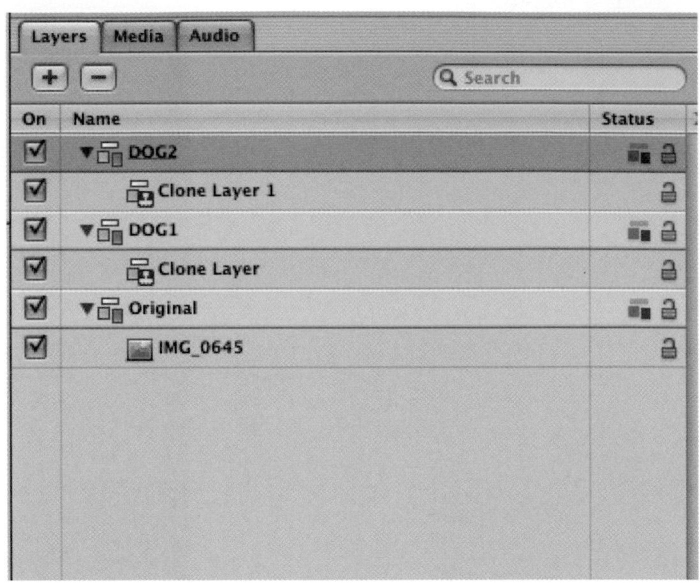

PHOTOSHOP HAS A FILTER called Photocopy. It simulates the look of old electrostatic photocopiers where large areas of "toner" fade out. It's also called a Difference of Gaussians (or DOG) edge detection.

An image added to the inverse of the same image results in a white screen. This is because every pixel is matched by its exact inverse. If we slightly blur our inverse image, every pixel is no longer precisely matched and we get dark areas. Because detailed areas are affected more by blurring than featureless regions, we get dark lines around the details.

1 Start with a new project. Name the default group **Original**. Take an image or clip and place it on your canvas, in the **Original** group. Click on the **Original** group and press K to create a clone group. Name the new group **DOG1**. Again, select your Original group. Press K to create a clone group. Name the new group **DOG2**.

3 ⌘-Select **DOG1** and **DOG2**. Press ⌘ Shift G to group them both. Name the new group **Photocopy**. **Add Filter/Sharpen/Unsharp Mask**. Drag **Amount** to **2.0**.

IMAGE COURTESY REILLY SHEFFIELD

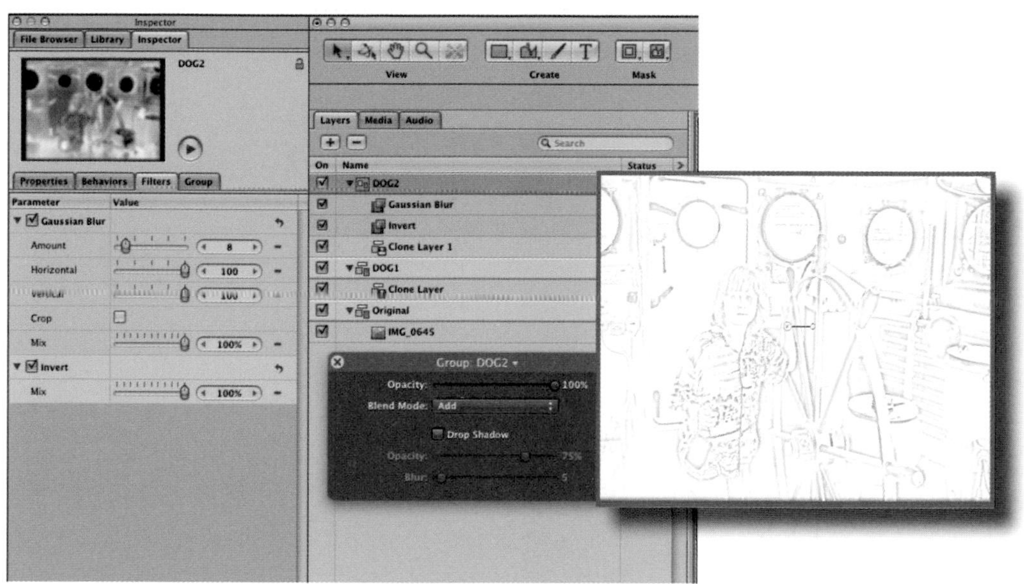

2 Select the **DOG2** group. **Add Filter/Color Correction/Invert. Add Filter/Blur/Gaussian Blur**. Change the Blend Mode of **DOG2** to **Add**. If you've done everything right, you should see a white screen with a faint outline of your image. Adjust the **Gaussian Blur Amount** up to about **8**.

HOT TIP

For an interesting effect, after Step 3, change the Blend mode of the Photocopy group to Color Burn.

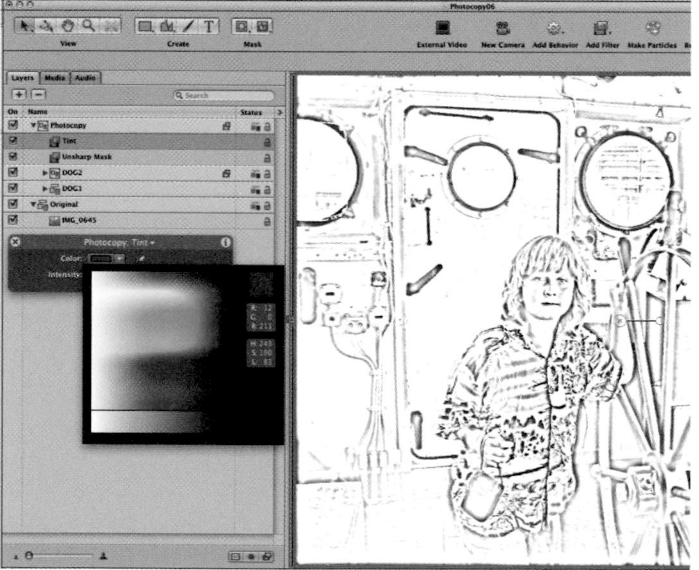

4 **Add Filter/Color Correction/Tint**. Choose a color.

Photo Illustration

GIVE YOUR CLIP AN "ARTSY," illustration-like quality using this simple project.

Adjusting the image color with the High Pass filter and adding the Edge Work filter along with the Line Art filter is all it takes.

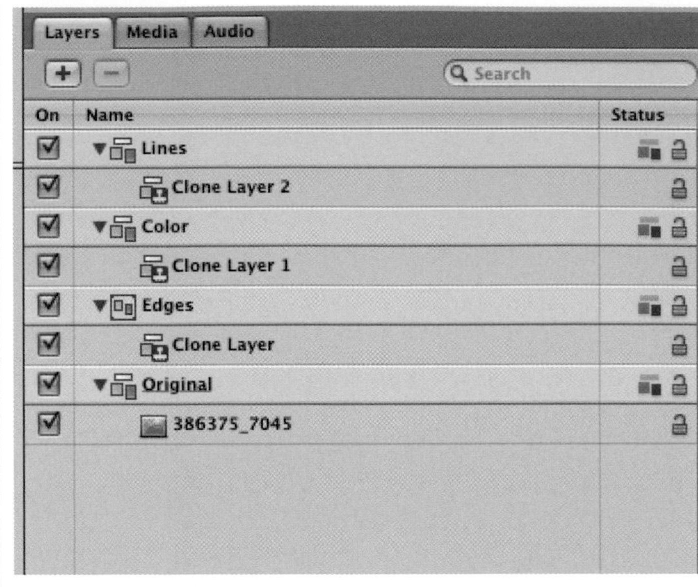

1 Start with a new project. Name the default group **Original**. Take an image or clip and place it in the **Original** group. Click on the **Original** group and press **K** to create a clone group. Name the new group **Edges**. Again, select your **Original** group. Press **K** to create a clone group. Name the new group **Color**. Once more, click on the **Original** group and press **K**. Name the new group **Lines**.

3 Collapse the **Edges** group, and then activate and expand the **Color** group. **Add Filter/Stylize/High Pass**. Adjust the **Radius** to **21**. Set the **Amount** to **8**. Set the **Color** group's **Blend Mode** to **Color Burn**. Set the **Opacity** to **36**.

IMAGE COURTESY PETR KURECKA

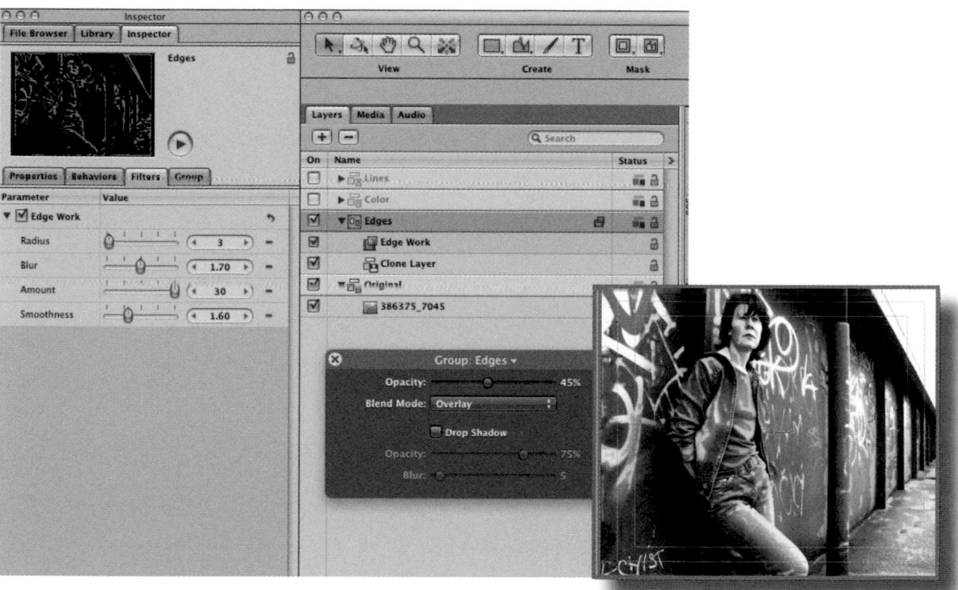

2 Collapse and disable the **Lines** and **Color** groups for now. Click on the **Edges** group. Add **Filter/Stylize/Edge Work**. Set the **Radius** to **3**, the **Blur** to **1.7**, the **Amount** to **30**, and the **Smoothness** to **1.6**. Set the **Blend Mode** of **Edges** group to **Overlay** and its **Opacity** to **45**.

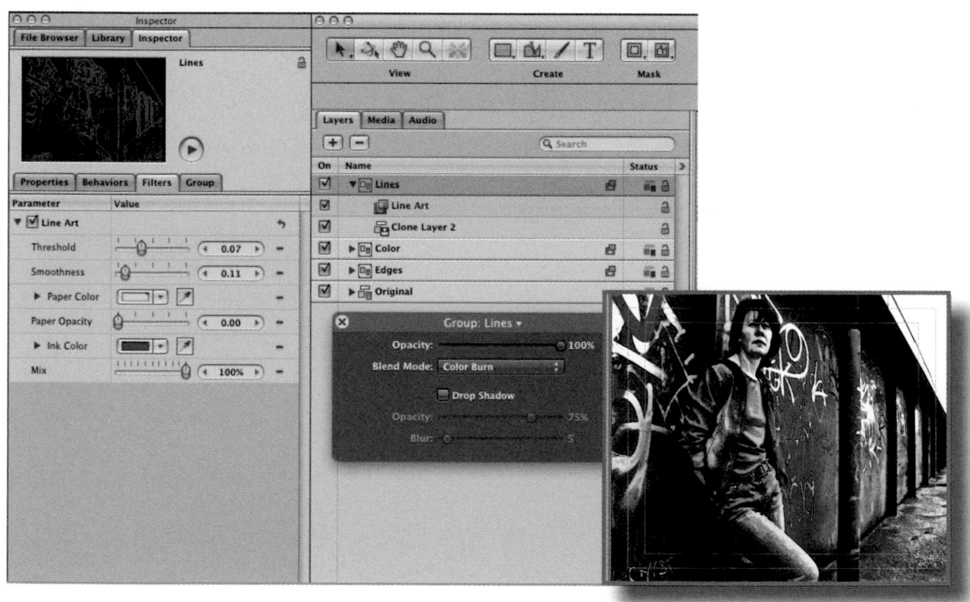

4 Collapse the **Color** group, and then activate and expand the **Lines** group. **Add Filter/Stylize/Line Art**. Set the **Paper Opacity** to 0% and choose an **Ink Color** that complements your image—in this case, I chose a deep blue I sampled from the image. Optionally, set the **Blend Mode** to **Color Burn**.

Line Drawing

IMAGES COURTESY NICOLE KOCHMAN, MAREK BERNAT, FRANCIS VALADJ

THE LINE ART FILTER PRODUCES some nice results, but it's not exactly a line drawing. Let's explore what it takes to make your clip into a black and white line drawing.

We need to add back in the dark fill. A threshold filter will help there and let's get rid of those nasty outlines around highlights.

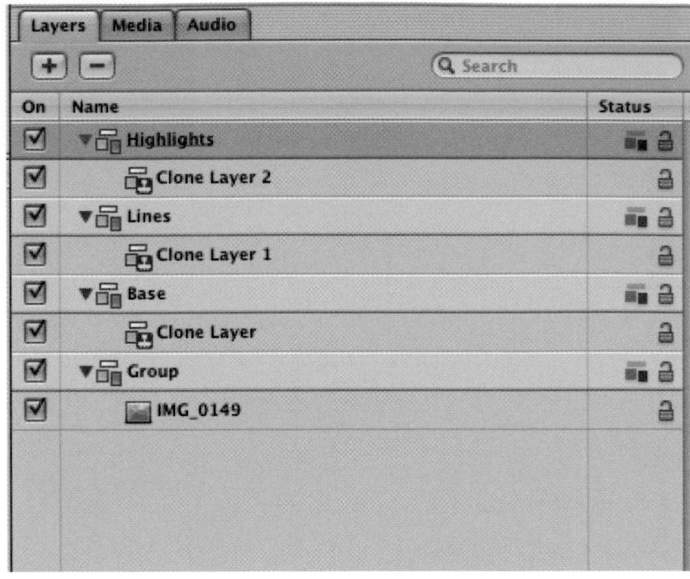

1 Start with a new project. Name the default group **Original.** Take an image or clip and place it on your canvas in the **Original** group. Click on the **Original** group and press **K** to create a **Clone** group. Name the new group **Base.** Again, select your **Original** group. Press **K** to create a Clone group. Name the new group **Lines.** Once more, click on the **Original** group and press **K**. Name the new group **Highlights.**

3 Select the **Line Art Filter**. Set the **Paper Opacity** to 0. Select **Base. Add Filter/ Color Correction/Threshold.** Adjust so that you bring back the dark areas of your image. Set **Smoothing** to a minimum. The goal is minimal gray.

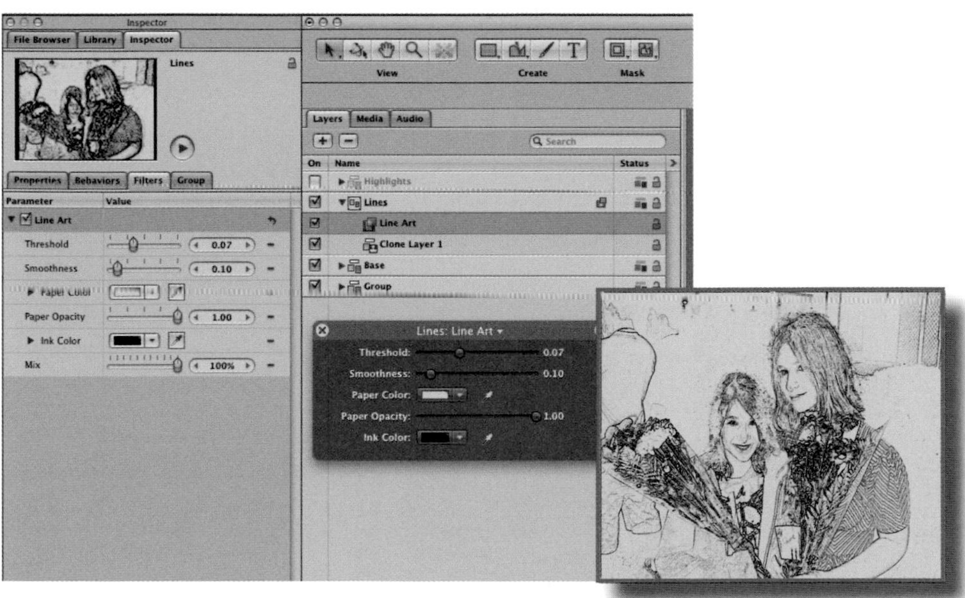

2 Collapse and disable the Highlights group. Select the **Lines** group. **Add Filter/Stylize/Line Art.** Adjust the values to get an effect you like. Looks good, but we need to replace the dark areas.

4 Now, notice that we get these unattractive artifacts involving lines around highlights. In this instance it makes Parker look like she's got a wart on the end of her nose. Activate the **Highlights** layer and select it. Change the **Blend Mode** to **Add. Add Filter/Color Correction/Threshold.** Now adjust it to minimize these artifacts.

HOT TIP

Another way to combat artifacts around highlights is to add a Gamma filter and raise the levels so that the highlights blend in with their surroundings.

Wobble Vision

TRADITIONAL ANIMATION is a very labor intensive process that required new hand-drawn images for each frame of animation. With the advent of the computer, alternative methods that require less work have been developed. One of these, popularized by the show *Dr. Katz, Professional Therapist*, is called Squigglevision™. With Squigglevision™, a random perturbation was added to the outline layer of the animation which caused them to wiggle and undulate. The constant "squiggling" keeps the scene feeling dynamic without the need for constant redraws.

Our rendition of the technique, which I'm calling *Wobble Vision*, uses a different method. We use the outline layer as a mask for the random motion of the Cellular generator. We blur that outcome to blend the dots together, and then use a threshold filter to merge it into a wiggling outline .

1 Create three layers in a new project: **Image**, **Inking**, and **Color**. Begin with the **Image** layer. Create your black and white line drawing image any way you like. I made this quick sketch in Photoshop, and then added the thought bubble and text inside Motion. The lines should not be too thin.

4 Click on **Cellular**. Type ⌘ Shift G to create a new group for it. **Add Filter/Blur/Gaussian Blur**. Set **Amount** to **5**.

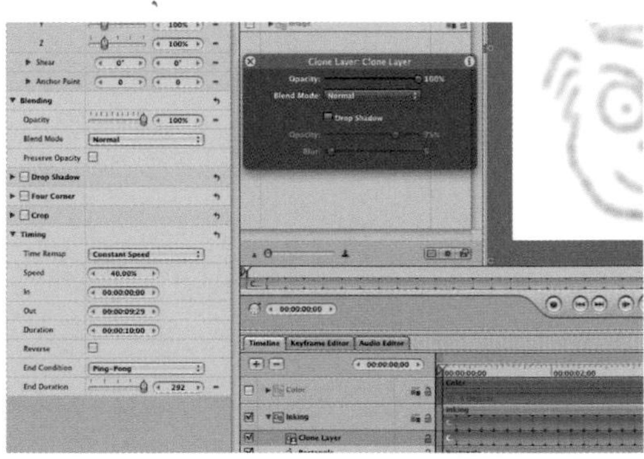

7 Select **Clone Layer**. Under **Properties/Timing**, change the **Speed** to **40%** and the **End Condition** to **Ping-Pong**. Then drag the **Clone Layer** out the full length of the project.

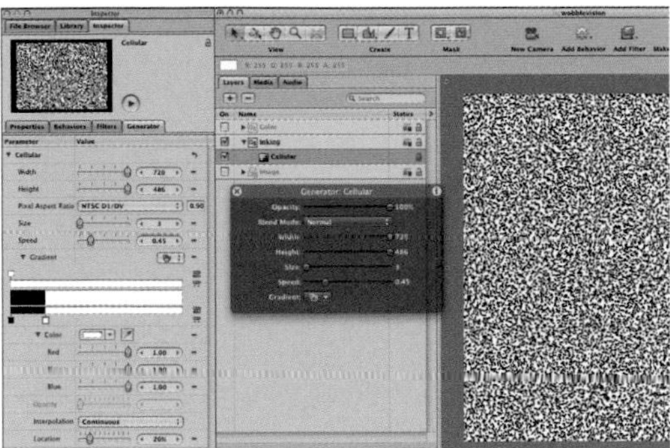

2 Add the **Cellular** generator to the **Inking** group. Set **Size** to 3, **Speed** to 0.45. Twirl down the **Gradient** disclosure triangle. Click on the black tag to the left of the **Gradient** editor. Set the **Interpolation** to **Constant**. Then click on the white tag to the left and drag it down until the **Location** is 20%.

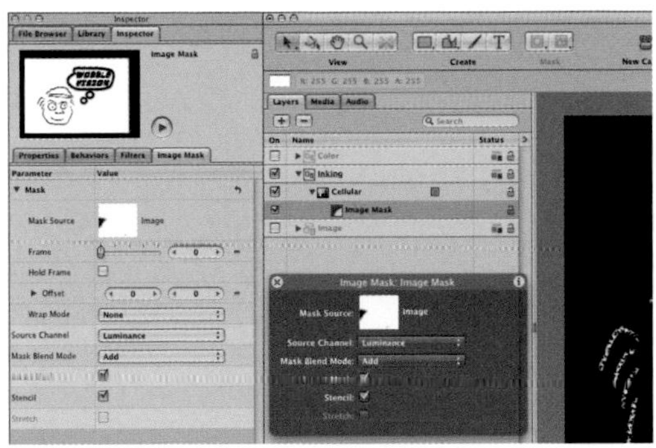

3 Click on **Cellular**. Type ⌘ Shift M to add an Image Mask, set its **Source Channel** to **Luminance**, and then click the **Invert Mask** checkbox. Drag the **Image** group into the **Mask Source** well.

5 Trim the duration of the group holding the **Cellular** generator to a 3 frame duration. Then add a plain white rectangle to the **Inking** group to cover our entire canvas.

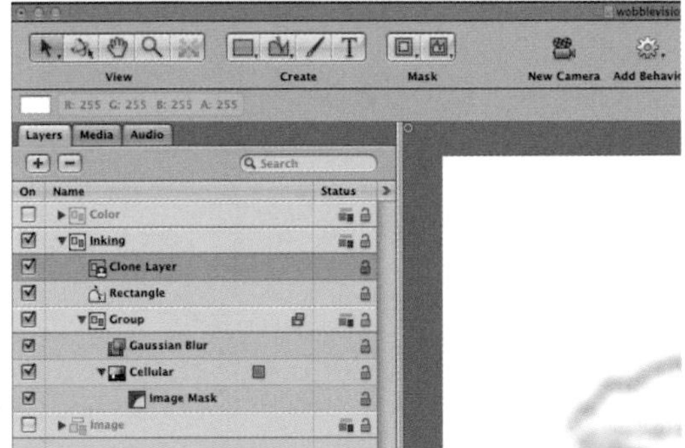

6 Click on the **Group** containing **Cellular**. Press K to create a clone layer. Move it above **Rectangle**.

8 Click on **Inking**. **Add Filter/Color Correction/Threshold**. Set the **Threshold** to 0.90 and the **Smoothness** to 0.02.

9 Finally, for your **Color** group, set the **Blend Mode** to **Multiply**. Then add colored shapes to finish your masterpiece.

Graphic Novel Look

THIS IS A KIND OF GRAPHIC NOVEL look with high contrast, saturated colors, and inked outlines providing detail.

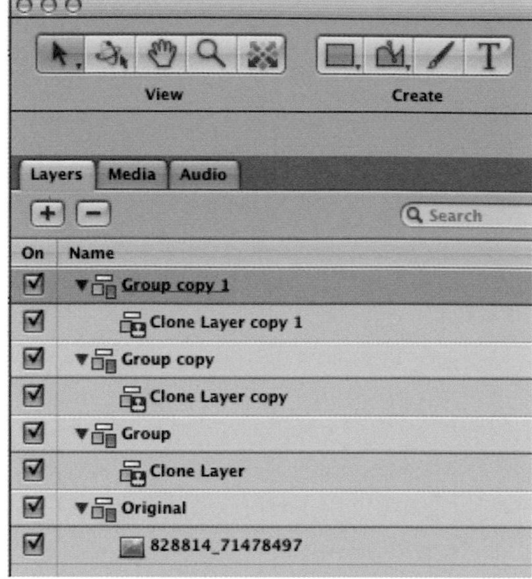

1 Start with a new project—name the default group **Original**. Put your clip in it. Press K to create a clone layer. Click on the new group. Press ⌘D to duplicate it. Press ⌘D again.

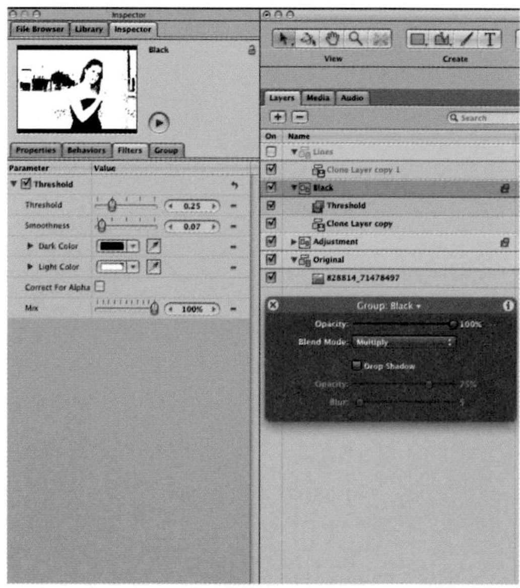

4 Enable the **Black** group. Set **Blend Mode** to **Multiply**. **Add Filter/Color Correction/Threshold**. Set **Threshold** to about **0.25** and **Smoothness** to about **0.07**.

IMAGE COURTESY SCOTT SNYDER

2 Name the bottom **Clone Layer** group **Adjustment**. Name the middle **Clone Layer** group **Black**. Name the top **Clone Layer** group **Lines**. Disable both **Lines** and **Black**.

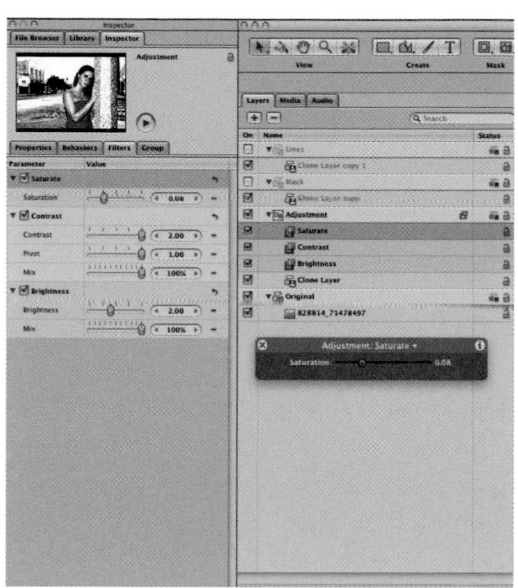

3 Click on the **Adjustment** group. **Add Filter/Color Correction/Brightness**. Set **Brightness** to **2.0**. **Add Filter/Color Correction/Contrast**. Set **Contrast** to **2.0**, **Pivot** to **1.0**. **Add Filter/Color Correction/Saturate**. Set **Saturation** to **.08**.

5 Enable the **Lines** group. **Add Filter/Stylize/Line Art**. Adjust as appropriate for your clip. Set **Paper Opacity** to 0.

6 For extra credit add a new clone layer (click on **Original**, press **K**). **Add Filter/Stylize/Halftone**. Set the **Blend Mode** of the new group to **Overlay**.

Pen and Ink

THIS PROJECT GIVES A PEN and Ink look. The fine, high-contrast lines you get with this effect mean it's best not to use it with an interlaced display.

Basically we're going to take the "Photocopy" effect from the earlier exercise and use the Indent filter to push everything into tight lines.

1 Start with a new project—Name the default group **Original**. Take an image or clip and place it on your canvas, in the **Original** group. Click on **Original** and press **K** to create a **Clone** group. Name the new group **DOG1**. Select **DOG1**. Press **⌘D** to duplicate it. Name the new group **DOG2**.

3 **⌘**-Select **DOG1** and **DOG2**. Press **⌘Shift G** to group them both. Name the new group **Pen and Ink**. Add **Filter/Stylize/Indent**. Set **Softness** to **0**, **Brightness** to **1**, **Ambient** to **.44**, and **Depth** to **20**.

IMAGE COURTESY SCOTT SNYDER

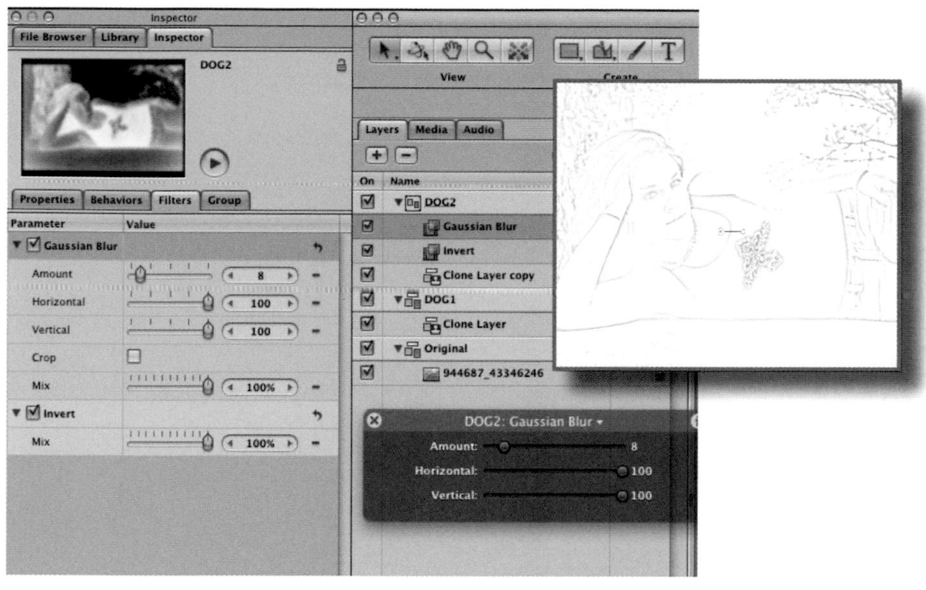

2 Select the **DOG2** group. **Add Filter/Color Correction/Invert**. **Add Filter/Blur/ Gaussian Blur**. Change the **Blend Mode** of **DOG2** to **Add**. If you've done everything right, you should see a white screen with a faint outline of your image. Adjust the **Gaussian Blur Amount** up to about **8**.

4 **Add Filter/Sharpen/Unsharp Mask**. Drag **Amount** to **2.0**.

HOT TIP

If your original material is noisy, you may run into problems with this effect. You can reduce the noise somewhat by applying a slight Gaussian Blur to your original footage.

4 Image Effects

Cartoonify

OR **ADVENTURES IN CEL SHADING.** To use this effect, you don't need to read the following—this is, after all, a cookbook. And a cook needn't understand the high temperature breakdown of sodium bicarbonate to bake cookies. So if you want, just jump right into the project.

The essence of Cel Shading is quantizing the colors—what does that mean? Quantization is breaking the image into discreet color regions. Sort of like the difference between a ramp and stairs. If you look at an animation cel, there are specific color paints for areas of the image and detail is provided by dark lines outlining features.

The question is how to do it to a video image? I settled on the idea that I didn't want to quantize the color information per se. I could simply quantize the luminance information and vectorize that, but how to add back the color?

Motion doesn't have a colorspace filter—no easy way to convert from RGB to YUV (Y being the luminance, and UV being the color information). However, the equations that define the conversion are as follows:

$$R = \mathrm{R} + 1.140(0.615R - 0.515G - 0.100B)$$

$$G = \mathrm{G} - 0.395(-0.147R - 0.289G + 0.436B) - 0.581(0.615R - 0.515G - 0.100B)$$

$$B = \mathrm{B} + 2.032(-0.147R - 0.289G + 0.436B)$$

Where *RGB* is the new image, RGB is the luma image, and RGB is the chroma image.

That looks complicated, but armed with some scratch paper, it simplifies to this:

$$R = \mathrm{R} + .700R - .587G - .114B$$

$$G = \mathrm{G} - .320R + .413G - .114B$$

$$B = \mathrm{B} - .289R - .587G + .885B$$

which I can re-arrange to be one add and two subtractions like this:

$$R = \mathrm{R} + .700R - .587G - .114B$$

$$G = \mathrm{G} + .413G - .114B - .320R$$

$$B = \mathrm{B} + .885B - .289R - .587G$$

This kind of math can be done with just Blend Modes, Color Solid generators, and a couple of Channel Swaps in Motion.

IMAGES COURTESY OCTAVIO ARIZALA AND MAREK BERNAT

1 Okay. Start with a new project. Name the default **Group Original**. Place the image you wish to cartoonify in that group

2 Select **Original**. Press K to create a clone layer. Name the new group **Luma**. Rename the **Clone Layer** to **Splitter**. **Add Filter/Color Correction/Desaturate**.

3 Click on **Splitter**. Press ⌘D to duplicate it. Name it **Lower**. Press ⌘D. Name the copy **Upper**.

4 Select **Splitter**. **Add Filter/Color Correction/Threshold**. Set **Smoothness** to 0. Select **Upper**. ⌘-Select **Lower**. Type ⌘Shift M to add **Image Mask** layers to each. Change the **Channel** in each to **Luminance**.

5 Drag the **Splitter** layer into the image well for **Upper's Image Mask**. Drag the **Splitter** layer into the image well for **Lower's Image Mask**. Click on the **Invert** mask button (only on **Lower's Image Mask**).

6 Click on **Lower**. **Add Filter/Stylize/Vectorize Color**. Change **First Color's** RGB to **.44**, **Second Color** to **.33**, **Third Color** to **.20**, and **Fourth Color** to **0**. Change **Resolution** to **4**, **Smoothness** to 0, and **Curvaceousness** to **.25**.

continued...

Cartoonify (continued)

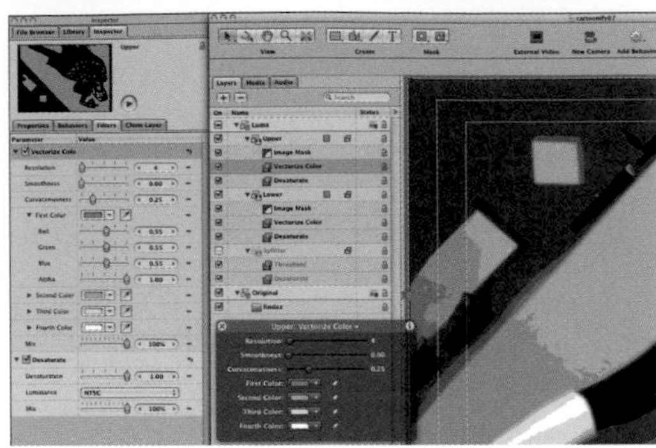

7 Click on **Upper**. Add **Filter/Stylize/Vectorize Color**. Change **First Color's** RGB to **.55. Second Color** to **.67, Third Color to .85**, and **Fourth Color** to **1.0**. Change **Resolution** to **4**, **Smoothness** to **0**, and **Curvaceousness** to **0.25**.

8 Collapse the **Luma** group. Click on **Original**. Press **K** to create a clone layer. Call the new group **Lines**. **Add Filter/Blur/Gaussian Blur**. Set the **Amount** to **1** (this is to reduce noise). **Add Filter/Stylize/Line Art**. Adjust to a pleasing level of detail. Set the **Paper Opacity** to **0**.

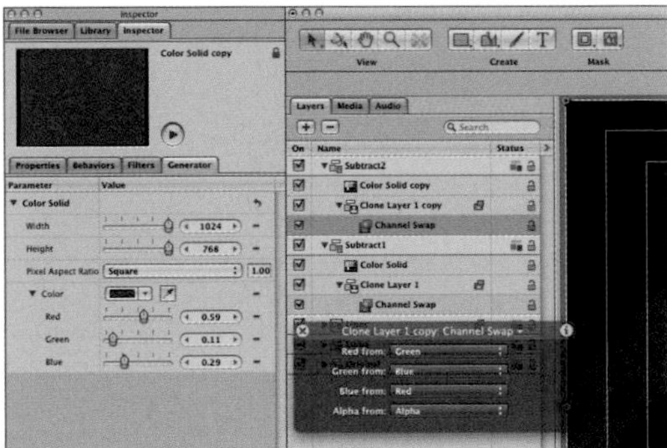

11 Click on **Subtract1**. Type **⌘D**. Name the duplicate **Subtract2**. Change the **Color Solid's** color to **.59, .11, .29**. Change the **Channel Swap** to **Red from Green, Green from Blue, Blue from Red**.

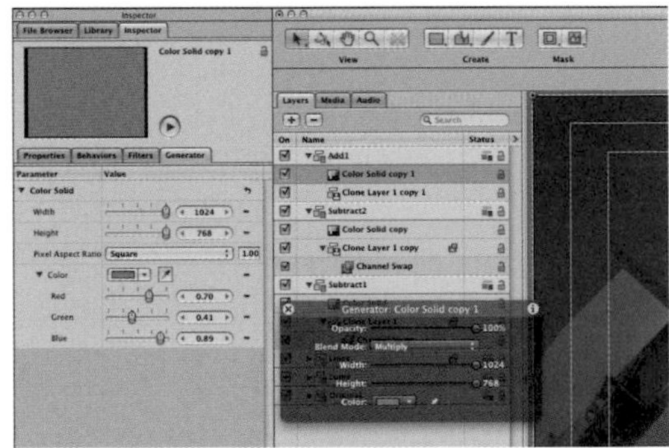

12 Select **Subtract2**. Press **⌘D**. Change the name to **Add1**. Change the **Color Solid copy 1** to **.70, .41, .89**. Delete the **Channel Swap** filter from **Clone Layer 1 copy 1**.

15 Some clips can benefit from a bit of black "overprinting."

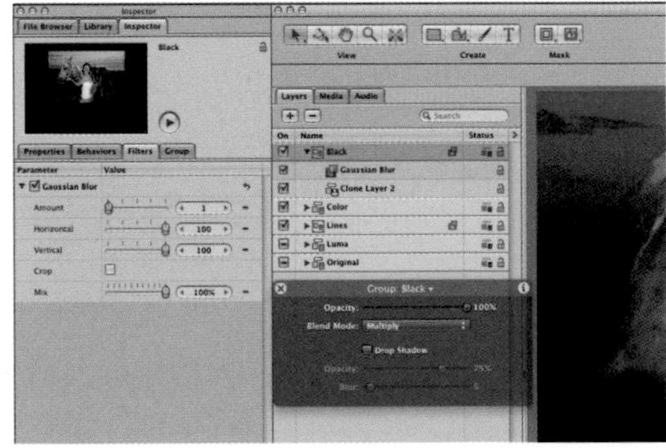

16 Select the **Original** group. Press **K**. Name the new group **Black**. Set its **Blend Mode** to **Multiply. Add Filter/Blur/Gaussian Blur**. Set **Amount** to **1** (this is to reduce noise).

9 Now that we've got our cartoonified grayscale version, let's add back the color. Collapse the **Lines** group. Select **Original**. Press K. Name the new group **Subtract1**. Go to the **Library** and grab a color solid generator and place it above the **Clone Layer 1**.

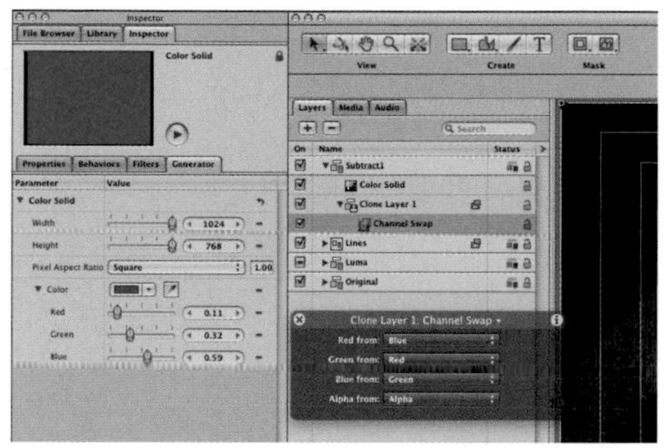

10 Set the **Blend Mode** of the **Color Solid** generator to **Multiply**. Set the color to **Red .11**, **Green .32**, **Blue .59** (from the math in the opening). Select the **Clone Layer 1**. **Add Filter/Color Correction/Channel Swap**. Set **Red from Blue**, **Green from Red**, **Blue from Green**.

HOT TIP

If you have trouble Shift-selecting a number of groups, collapse the groups first. Otherwise you'll have to hold down the ⌘ key and click on each group.

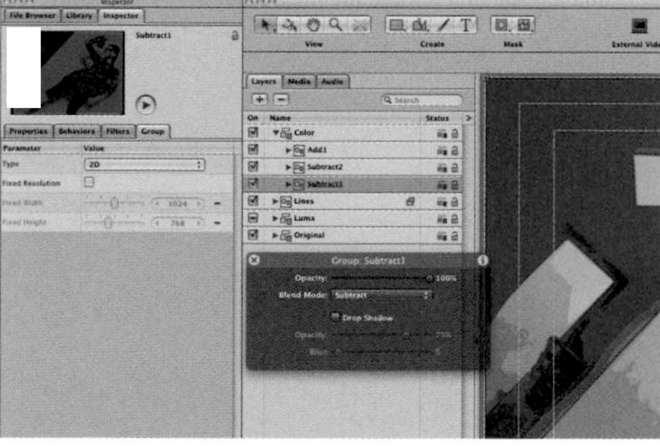

13 Almost there. Set the **Blend Mode** of **Subtract1** to **Subtract. Subtract 2 to Subtract. Add1** to **Add**. Shift select **Add1**, **Subtract2**, **Subtract1**. Type ⌘ Shift G. Name the new group **Color**.

14 If you prefer your details outlined in black, you can shift the **Lines** group to the top.

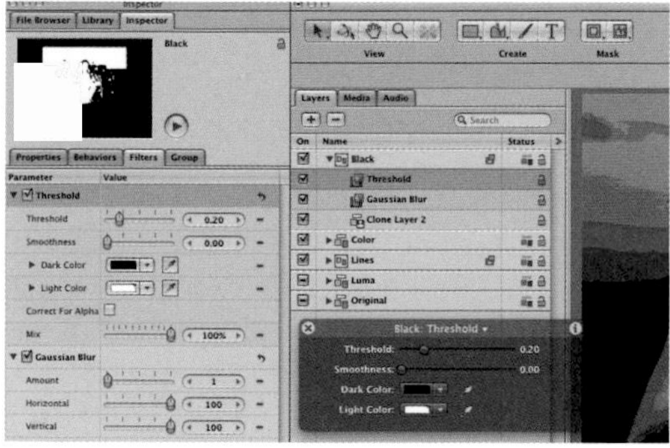

17 Select the **Black** group. **Add Filter/Color Correction/Threshold**. Set **Smoothness** to 0. Adjust **Threshold** for a good appearance.

18 Adding back some black really improves the image.

Comic Book

THIS PROJECT TURNS YOUR CLIP into a comic book. When you're done, use Motion to track in the word balloons.

We will use the Color Reduce filter to limit the color range to make the image more graphic and then add a Halftone filter for each of the Red, Green, and Blue channels. On top of that, we'll add a black overprinting layer and a modified DOG to provide the outlines.

1 Begin with a new project. I'm using **Presentation Large.** Name the default group **Original**. Place your clip there. Click on the **Original** group. Press **K** to create a clone layer. Name the new group **Red**.

4 Click on **Red**. **Add Filter/Stylize/Halftone**. Set the **Scale** to **4**. **Add Filter/Color Correction/Tint**. Set **Color** to **R 1, G 0, B 0**.

7 Click on **Original**. Press **K**. Name the new group **Black**. **Add Filter/Color Correction/Threshold**. Set **Threshold** to **0.14**. **Smoothness** to **0.02**. Set the **Blend Mode** to **Multiply**.

2 Click on the **Clone Layer**. Add **Filter/Color Correction/ Channel Swap**. Set **Green from** to **Red**. Set **Blue from** to **Red**.

3 Add **Filter/Color Correction/Color Reduce**. Set **Match Color 1** and its **Replace with** to **Black**. For **Match Color 2** and **Replace with**, set to **R .33**, **G .33**, **B .33**. Set the third pair's RGB to **.67**. Set the fourth's to white.

5 Click on **Red**. Press ⌘D. Name the duplicate group **Green**. Expand **Green** and **Clone Layer copy**. For **Channel Swap**, change **Red/Green/Blue froms** to **Green**. Click on **Green**. Change the **Halftone's Angle** to **15**. Change the **Tint's Color** to full green. Change the **Blend Mode** to **Add**.

6 Click on **Green**. Press ⌘D. Name the duplicate group **Blue**. Expand **Blue** and **Clone Layer copy 1**. For **Channel Swap** set **Red/Green/Blue froms** to **Blue**. Click on **Blue**. Change the **Halftone's Angle** to **45**. Change the **Tint's** color to full **Blue**.

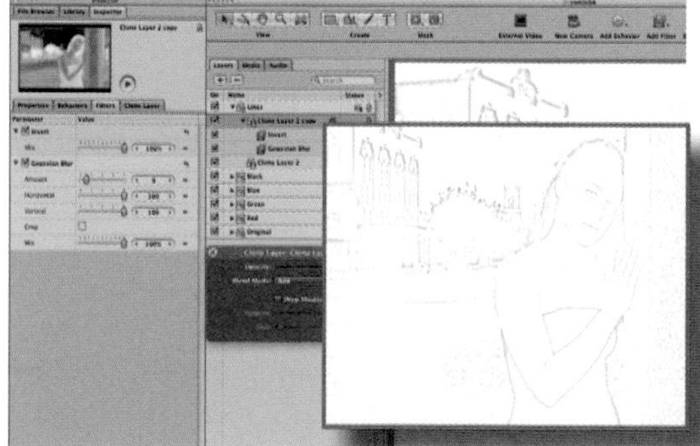

8 Click on **Original**. Press K. Name the new group **Lines**. Click on **Clone Layer 2**. Press ⌘D. Click on **Clone Layer 2 copy**. Add **Filter/Blur/Gaussian Blur**. Set **Amount** to **9**. Add **Filter/Color Correction/Invert**. Set the **Blend Mode** to **Add**.

9 Click on **Lines**. Add **Filter/Sharpen/Unsharp Mask**. Add **Filter/Color Correction/Equalize**. Set **White Point** to **0.92**. Set **Black Point** to **0.90**. Set **Blend Mode** to **Multiply**.

HOT TIP

If you want to make your clip seem more like a newspaper photo than a comic book, leave off the Color Reduce plugin and reduce the Opacity of the Lines group.

Pastel Drawing

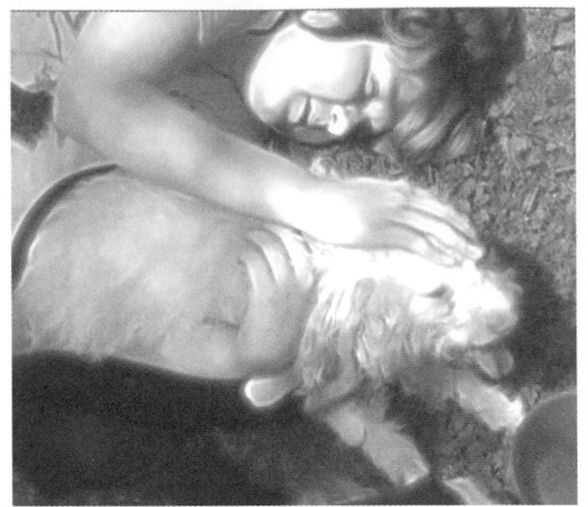

IMAGE COURTESY REILLY SHEFFIELD

IT WON'T WORK WITH all material, but this pastel look can add a nice romantic, painterly quality to an otherwise mundane clip.

The effect is created by preprocessing the clip with the Aura filter, using the Line Drawing filter, and then adding the inverse of the result to our original image.

1 Begin with a new project. Name the default group **Original**. Place your clip in the **Original** group.

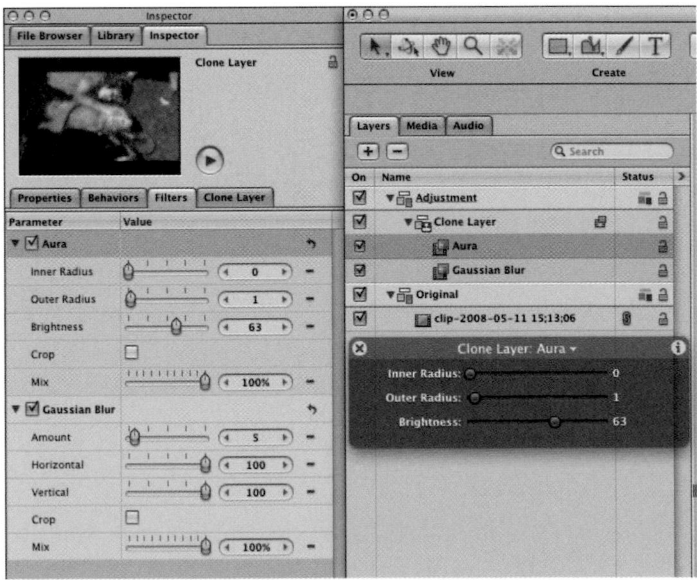

3 Select **Clone Layer**. Add **Filter/Blur/Gaussian Blur**. Set **Amount** to **5**. Add **Filter/Glow/Aura.** Set **Inner Radius** to **0**. Set **Outer Radius** to **1**. Set **Brightness** to **63**.

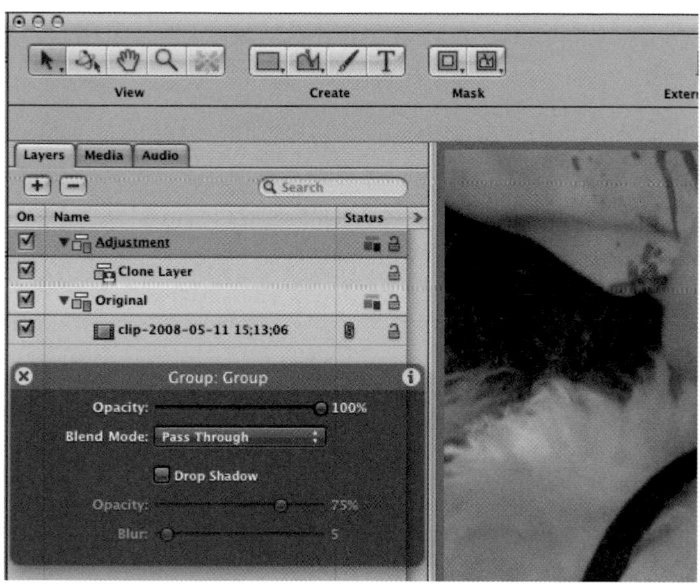

2 Select **Original** group. Press **K** to create a clone layer. Name the clone layer group **Adjustment**.

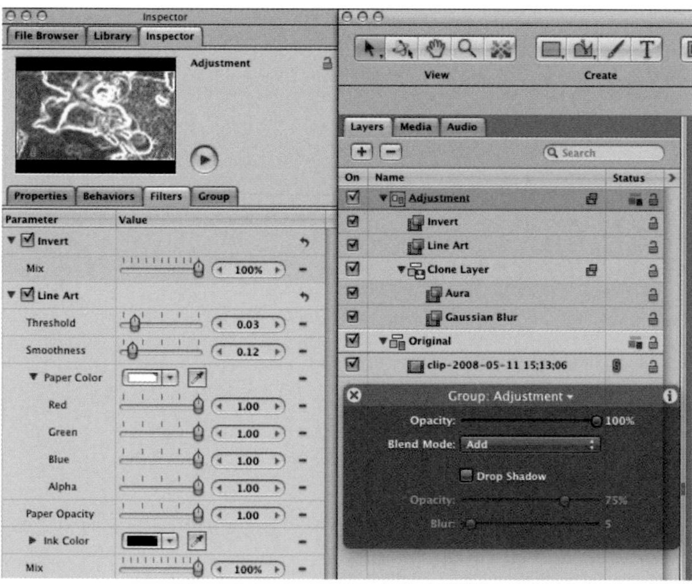

4 Click on **Adjustment**. Add **Filter/Stylize/Line Art**. Set **Threshold** to **0.03**. Set **Smoothness** to **0.12**. Set the **Paper Color** to pure white. **Add Filter/Color Correction/Invert**. Select the **Adjustment** group. Set **Blend Mode** to **Add**.

HOT TIP

Depending on your clip, you may need to do some color correction before this effect will work properly.

Poster Paint

POSTER PAINT IS A THICK, OPAQUE form of watercolor known in elementary schools as tempera, and in art circles as gouache.

As any schoolchild knows, it comes in bright, dense colors, and paintings made with poster paint often lack subtle shading.

We'll produce a similar effect using a heavily saturated Aura filter without the glow, coupled with a Line Art layer to add detail.

1 Start with a new project. Name the default group **Original**. Put your clip in it. Press K to create a clone layer. Click on the new group. Press ⌘D to duplicate it.

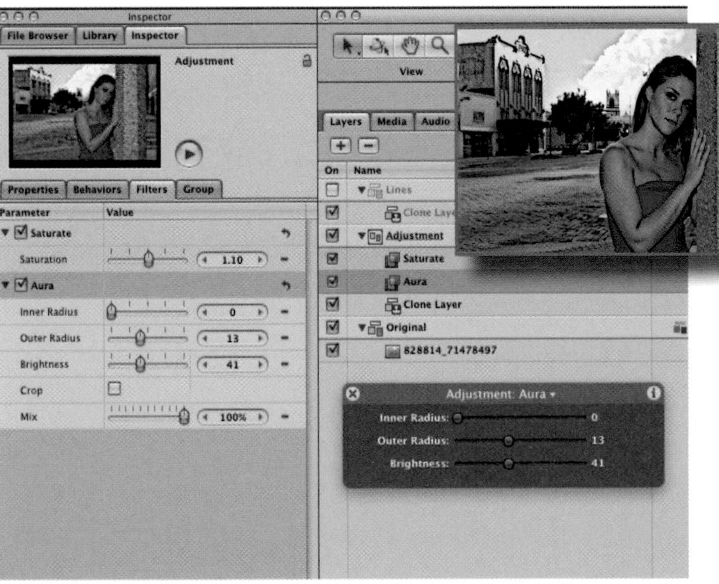

3 Click on the **Adjustment** group. **Add Filter/Glow/Aura**. Set **Inner Radius** to **0**. Set **Outer Radius** to **13**. Set **Brightness** to **42**. **Add Filter/Color Correction/ Saturate**. Set **Saturation** to **1.10**.

IMAGE COURTESY SCOTT SNYDER

2 Name the bottom **Clone Layer** group **Adjustment**. Name the top **Clone Layer copy** group **Lines**. Disable **Lines**.

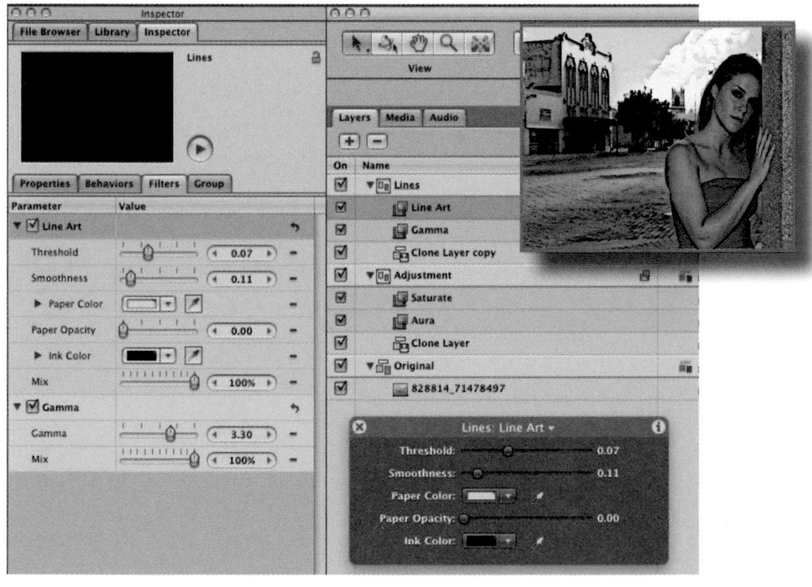

4 Enable the **Lines** group. **Add Filter/Color Correction/Gamma**. Set **Gamma** to **3.31**. **Add Filter/Stylize/Line Art**. Adjust as appropriate for your clip. Set **Paper Opacity** to 0.

HOT TIP

Another way of avoiding the outlining of highlights is using an "over layer" with a threshold filter like in the "Line Drawing" project.

Glazed Enamel

SAY YOU WANTED TO MAKE A talking piece of pottery. Or maybe you want to bring a glazed statue to life.

Using a similar technique to the Chrome and Golden text projects in the last chapter, we can create a simulated Glazed Enamel painting technique.

IMAGES COURTESY JYN MEYER

1 Start with a new project. Name the default group **Original**. Put your clip in it.

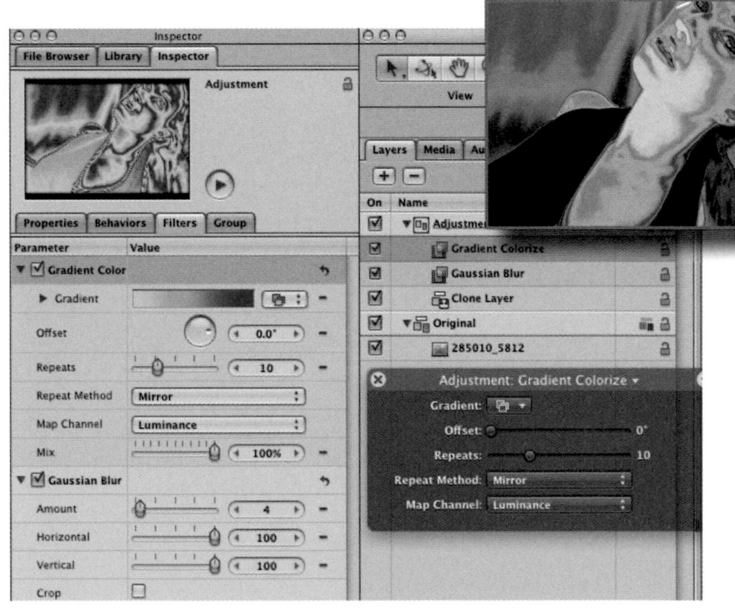

3 Add Filter/Blur/Gaussian Blur. Add Filter/Color Correction/Gradient Colorize. Set the **Gradient** to **Atlantic Blue**. Set the **Repeats** to 10.

2 Select the **Original** group. Press K to create a clone layer. Select **Group**. Name it **Adjustment**. Change the **Blend Mode** to **Soft Light**.

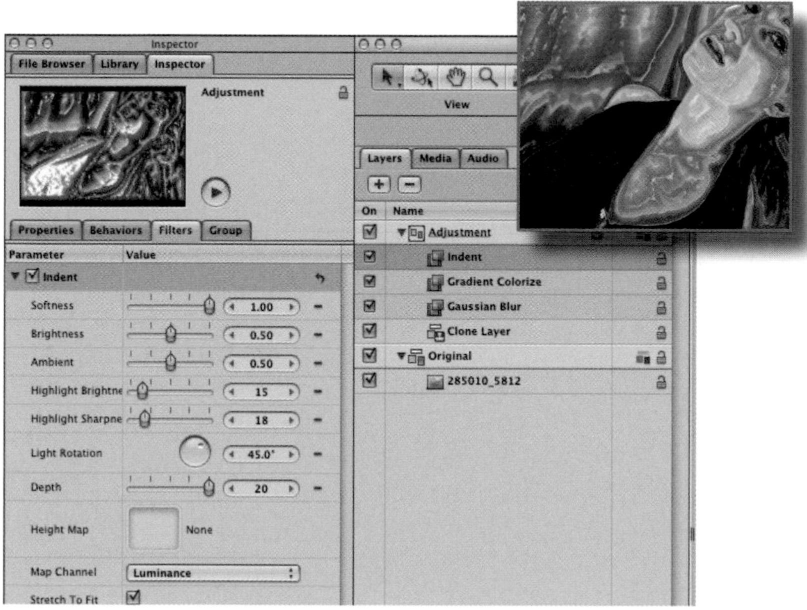

4 Add **Filter/Stylize/Indent**. Set **Softness** to **1.0**. Set **Highlight Brightness** to **15**, **Highlight Sharpness** to **18**, and **Depth** to **20**.

What went wrong

A case study in failure

WHILE IT'S ALWAYS GRATIFYING TO tell a story about one's success—you know, the warm fuzzy feeling you get for a job well done—I thought it might be more instructive to tell a little about a job that went awry.

I was working on a series of national commercials. This involved the editorial, effects, and finishing. The agency asked if we could do the motion graphics as well. They involved, I was informed, some titles swirling out of a glass of stirred up product. I did a quickie test and said, Sure, we can do that.

Because I was doing the editorial, I left the Motion graphics for later and concentrated on editing. Once the agency was happy with the edits, I came back to the graphics. I started by tweaking my quickie test and showed that to the agency.

Hmmmm..., they said. Not quite right.

At this point I should tell you something I've learned the hard way over my career. Just because a client can tell you they don't like something doesn't mean they can tell you what they don't like. This tidbit is often not known even to the clients themselves. In fact, they may tell you to change something completely unrelated to what's causing them to dislike an effect/edit/etc. You make the change, and they still don't like it, so they offer up another change, which you dutifully perform, but it's still not right. And so begins the cycle of frustration.

If you keep going down this path, your project becomes increasingly distorted and heading in the wrong direction. Something important to remember here: you are not the only one experiencing this frustration. So is your client.

Now back to this particular project. I listened the client's feedback and started increasingly elaborate tactics. I took the title, broke it up into little squares and had them come swirling up out of the spinning liquid. Hmmm..., not quite right. I changed the squares into little balls that unrolled into squares that then melded into the title. I colored the balls the same chocolaty color as the liquid, had them change to white as they unrolled into squares, and then formed the title. Hmmm..., not quite right.

I can't blame this all on client requests. They hadn't asked me to break the title into pieces. I'd recently become enamored of Motion's simulation behaviors and the organic patterns they could create. When you get a new hammer, every problem looks like a nail.

Then I learned that we were not going to use the "badge" title that I'd been working from, it was going to be simple text. (Changing specs like this in the middle of a project is not uncommon and just something you have to get used to.) So I abandoned my disassembled title squares and tried sparkles. Nope! Bubbles? Nooo.... I was flailing.

At this point, the agency art director took my executive producer aside and asked if we could go to an outside vendor–someone who specialized in Motion graphics. What could I say? With a healthy chunk of time already eaten up by my attempts and a deadline looming, I went back into editor mode to work on the change notes we'd received and prepare the effects, and the rest of the titles for the spots.

How do you combat this cycle of frustration? There is no prescribed answer, no certain step-by-step to ensure it doesn't happen to you. Part of the solution lies in how you phrase your questions.

Don't ask what the client would like changed. Try to get them to express what they don't like and, just as important, what they do like. Listen carefully. That simple advice is so important I should repeat it. Listen carefully. It's up to you to divine from their feedback just what changes you should be making. You're the expert. If your doctor says you need your appendix taken out, she doesn't ask you how she should perform the surgery.

This can require some diplomacy on your part. Often clients will offer changes for you to perform. Even if you are certain that it won't result in success, it doesn't mean you can ignore their request. You can't simply tell the client, "Well, that won't work." They usually need to see it. (And sometimes it *does* work.) If you think you have a better idea, do it as well as their request.

When the outside vendor delivered the final graphic, I couldn't believe it. Not only was it perfect for the spots, but it wasn't far from my original quickie test. It was simply more organically integrated into the swirling liquid so that it seemed to originate as a stream of lighter colored liquid spiraling out of the glass.

On the one hand, I was relieved that the final result wasn't some impossible-to-do effect. I could have done it. On the other hand, I had only myself to blame. I couldn't hide behind requirements beyond the capability of the equipment and software I possessed. If I'd been listening to the client's needs and been able to deliver the effect they wanted, thousands of dollars that went to an outside vendor would have instead stayed within our company.

Don't make the same mistake.

■ Motion doesn't come with plugins or filters or behaviors designed to break apart images. In this chapter, we'll learn how to use Motion's existing tools to explode people, slice and dice images, and perform other tasty mayhem.

5 Breaking Up

IMAGES FLYING APART and reassembling are a dynamic way to make transitions, focus attention, and add excitement to your Motion graphics projects.

In most other chapters in this book, the projects are "standalone"—that is, you can turn to any given project and follow it through without doing any of the other projects in that chapter.

However, because of the complexity of the techniques explained in this chapter, many of the projects build on the foundations laid down in earlier pages.

For that reason, it may be better to approach this chapter in a more linear fashion.

Dissolving People

I FIRST REMEMBER SEEING this effect in the early CGI movie, *The Lawnmower Man*. Now, you too can turn people (or text or graphics) into particles. Basically, anything with an alpha channel can be atomized.

We're going to take a foreground element that has an alpha channel to limit a **Random Filled** replicator. We'll take advantage of a little used mode called "Take Image Color," which allows the replicator elements or particles to take on the color of the image they're being limited by.

We'll use the Random Motion behavior to "kick" the replicator elements/particles free and gravity to pull them down.

Special thanks to Dustin Werstler and his lovely daughter Nicole for the photo used.

1 Start your project with three groups: **Particles, Foreground,** and **Background.** Your background can be whatever you want. I used a gradient filled rectangle.

4 Now, shorten your **Foreground** group to be **25 frames. Add Behavior/Basic Motion/Fade In/Fade Out.** Set the fade in to **0**, set the fade out to **7** frames. This will fade out our clear image as the particles take over.

7 Set the **Points** to a high enough number to fill the foreground layer (that's why you did fixed resolution in step 3 above). I set mine to **20000.** Set the **Color Mode** to **Take Image Color.** Drag the **Particulate** person until she exactly overlays the foreground image.

IMAGE COURTESY DUSTIN AND NICOLE WERSTLER

2 Your foreground can also be whatever you need as long as it has an alpha channel. I used a greenscreen photograph. Turn off the **Background** group and press Shift A to view your alpha channel. Press Shift C to bring back the color view. Don't forget to turn back on your **Background** group.

3 Crucial for best performance, set your **Foreground** group to fixed resolution and make sure it's ONLY big enough to contain your foreground image. That way the minimum number of particles will have to be generated to fill it.

5 Select the **Particles** layer, and then press C and draw a tiny circle to use as a particle. The smaller the circle, the greater detail you will see, but the more particles you will need to fill your image and the lower the performance.

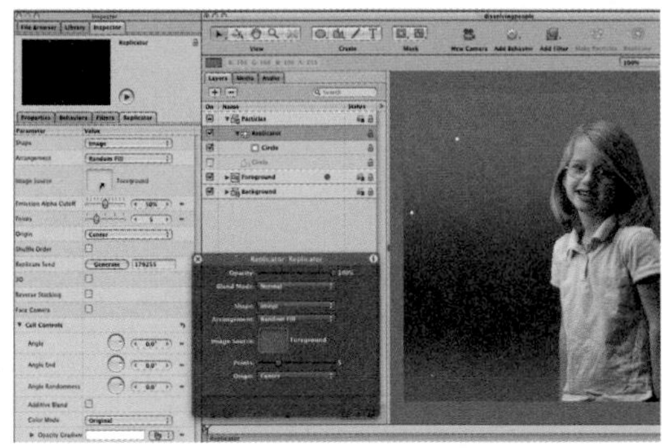

6 Press L or click on the **Replicate** button in the toolbar. Change the **Shape** to be **Image** and the **Arrangement** to be **Random Fill**. Now drag the **Foreground** group into the image well.

8 In the timeline, drag the start of the **Particles** group to frame 15. **Add Behavior/Simulations/Random Motion** to **Replicator**. Click the **Affect Subobjects** checkbox. Set the **Amount** to **44.** You can leave the rest of the settings at default.

9 **Add Behavior/Basic Motion/Fade In/Fade Out**. Set the **In** to **6**, the **Out** to **0**. **Add Behavior/Simulations/Gravity.** Click **Affect Subobjects**. You'll have to render this to see the effect. When you're moving around 20,000 particles, it can take a while.

HOT TIP

When Motion uses an Image to determine the shape of a replicator, it works within the space of the entire image that is being used to limit it, but uses the alpha channel to determine which replicator elements are visible.

This can require generating an absurd number of elements: 20,000 or more.

To keep the number of elements to the minimum required, use fixed resolution on the Foreground group and make it only big enough to hold the image.

Exploding People

WHEN I FIRST DID the Dissolving People project, I called it Exploding People. I showed it to someone who said, "That's not an Exploding Person, that's a Dissolving Person," and I had to agree. So, building on that project, I did some variation and came up with this Really Exploding Person.

Instead of using a circle, we draw a jagged shape to build our exploding person from. A Repel behavior causes the person to bulge ominously before a massive injection of Random Motion causes him or her to burst. To add to the mayhem, a Tint filter is used to bloody the whole effect up.

Rather than repeat verbatim the first four steps from the previous Dissolving People project, turn back a page and do those 4 steps first, and then continue with step 5 on this page.

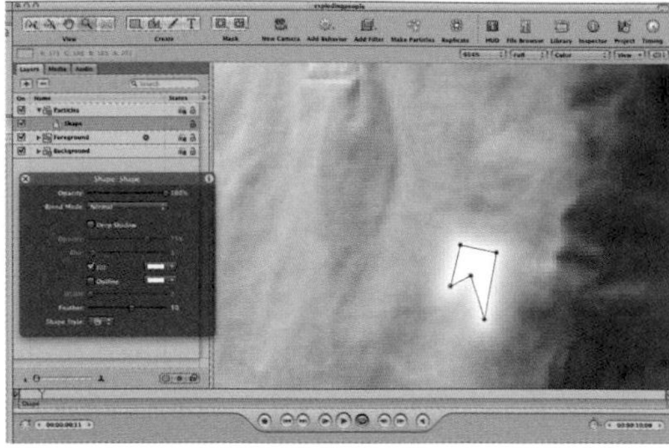

5 (continued from step 4 on previous page) Select the **Particles** group, then press **B** to activate the **Bezier** tool and draw a tiny jagged fragment to use as a particle. Set the **Feather** to 10.

8 In the timeline, drag the start of the **Particles** group to frame 15. **Add Behavior/Simulations/Repel** to the **Replicator**. Set **Strength** to **75.** With **Repel** selected, move forward 5 frames (to 19) and press **O** to set its duration.

11 Position to frame 23. Click on the **Shape**. In the **Shape** tab, under the **Inspector**, right/**ctrl**-click on **Feather** and select **Randomize**. With **Randomize** selected, press **I** to set the in point for the effect. Set the **Amount** to **10.** Set the **Frequency** to **0.50** and **Noisiness** to **0.12.**

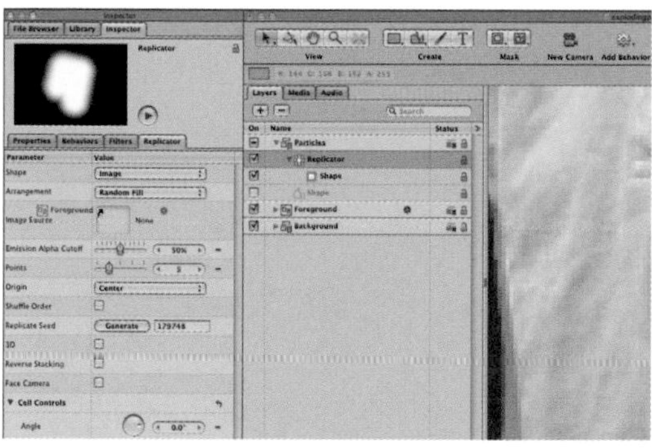

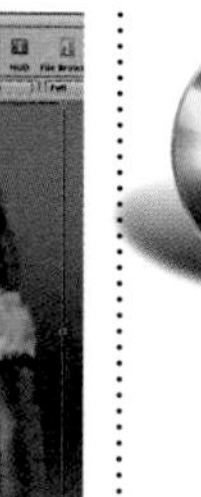

6 Press **L** or click on the **Replicate** button in the toolbar. Change the **Shape** to be **Image** and the **Arrangement** to be **Random Fill**. Now drag the **Foreground** group into the image well.

7 Set the **Points** to **20000.** Set Angle **Randomness** to **200.** Set the **Color Mode to Take Image Color.** Set the **Scale** to **50%**, the **Scale** randomness to **40%**. Drag the **Particulate** person until they exactly overlie the foreground image.

9 Move back one frame to 18. **Add Behavior/Simulations/ Random Motion** to the **Replicator**. Press **I** to set the in point. Click the **Affect Subobjects** checkbox. Set the **Amount** to **5000.** With **Random Motion** selected, move forward 8 frames (to 26) and press **O** to set its duration.

10 Click on the **Particles** group. Add **Behavior/Basic Motion/Fade In/Fade Out**—set the **Fade In Time** to **3**, the **Fade Out Time** to **0.** Add **Behavior/Simulations/ Gravity**. Click the **Affect Subobjects** checkbox.

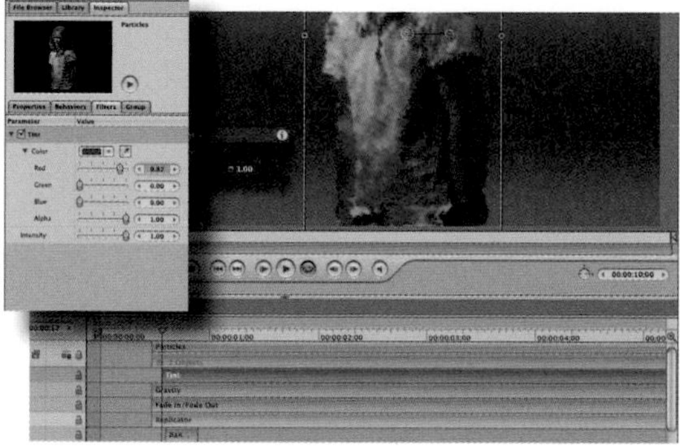

12 Finally, let's bloody things up a bit. Go to frame 17. Click on the **Particles** group. **Add Filter/Color Correction/Tint**. Press **I** to set the in point. Set the color to **Red** 0.87 and **Green** and **Blue** to 0.

13 Let's fade up to that. Right-click on the **Tint/Intensity** and select **Ramp.** Click on **Ramp** in the timeline. Press **I**. Set the **Start Value** to -1 and the **End Value to 0.** Position to frame 22. Press **O**. We're done!

Pointillism

MUCH LIKE THE POINTILLIST paintings of Georges Seurat, we will be creating an image with many tiny points or shapes.

IMAGE COURTESY PARKER SHEFFIELD

We will animate this as though a gust of wind blew the paint daubs right off the canvas.

Just like the Dissolving and Exploding People projects, a replicator with the Color Mode of Take Image Color will build our image. We will use a Tile Fill arrangement because Random Fill takes too many points to cover the frame without blank spots. To keep the image looking more like a painting and less like cross stitch, Angle Randomness will be used to introduce variation and make the image more organic looking.

In order to cut down on the work the computer has to do, the Edges filter will be used to isolate areas where smaller points can add greater resolution and use larger shapes to cover the rest of the image.

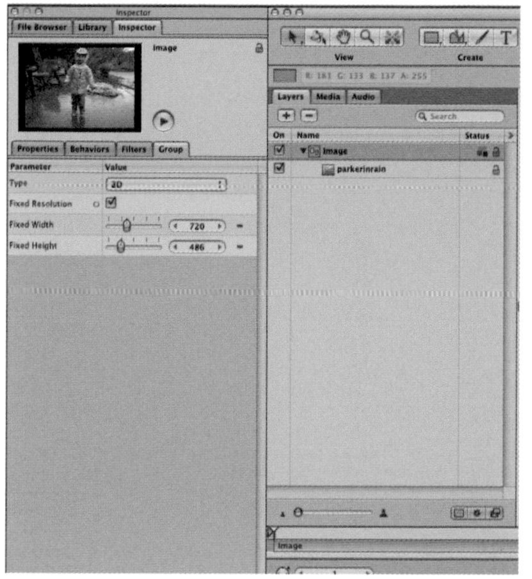

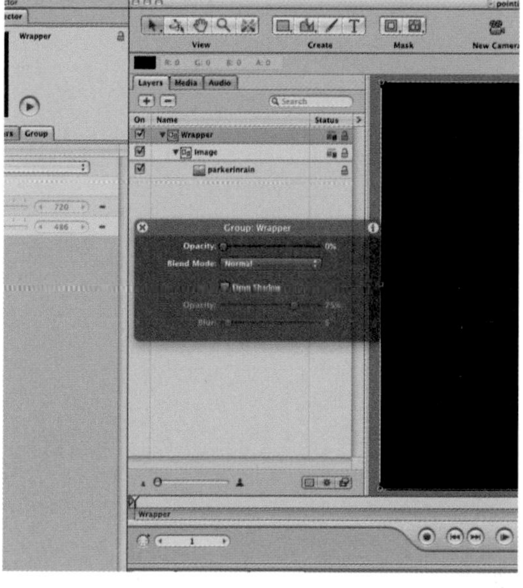

1 Start with a new project. Make it 90 frames (3 seconds) long. Place your picture in the first group, call the group **Image**, and set it as **Fixed Resolution**, the size of your project (720x486).

2 Because we'll need to hide the original image, we need to enclose it in a "wrapper." Select the **Image** group and press ⌘ Shift G. Name the enclosing group "Wrapper." Set its **Opacity** to 0.

HOT TIP

Surrounding an area with detail can be as effective at definition as including that area.

Too large an area given over to detail will defeat our purpose and cause excessive render times.

3 Create a new group called **Process**. Click on the **Image** group. Press K to create a clone. Name this clone layer **Detail Mask**. Click on the **Image** group again. Press K to create a clone. Name this clone layer **Detail**. Move **Detail Mask** and **Detail** to the **Process** group.

4 Click on the **Detail Mask** layer. **Add Filter/Stylize/Edge Work**. The white areas are where we will be seeing higher levels of detail. Adjust to suit your image. I set mine to **Radius 2, Blur 3.00, Amount 12, Smoothness 1.14.**

continued...

Pointillism (continued)

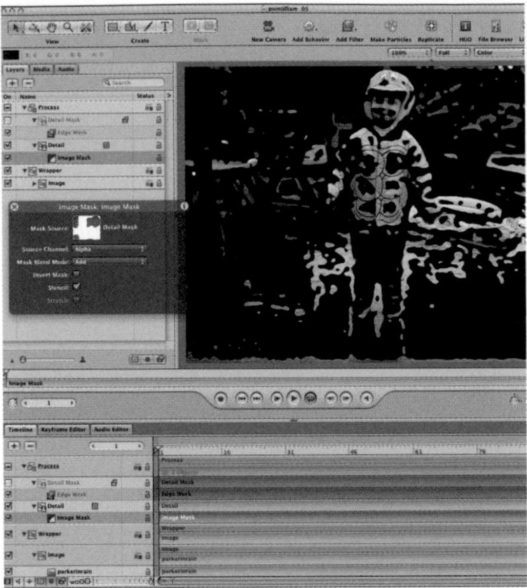

5 Click on the **Detail** layer. Type ⌘ Shift M to add an **Image Mask**. Drag the **Detail Mask Layer** onto the **Image Mask** and release.

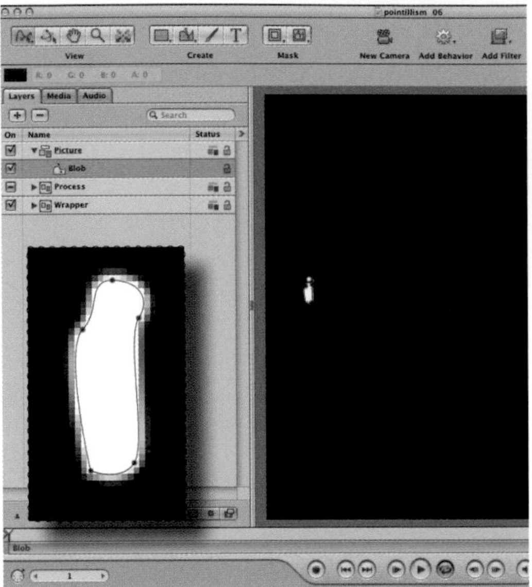

6 Click on the **Process** group. Set its **Opacity** to **0.** Add a new group and name it **Picture**. Press **B** to select the **Bezier** tool. Draw a small oblong shape. This will be used for the coarse paint daubs. Name it **Blob**.

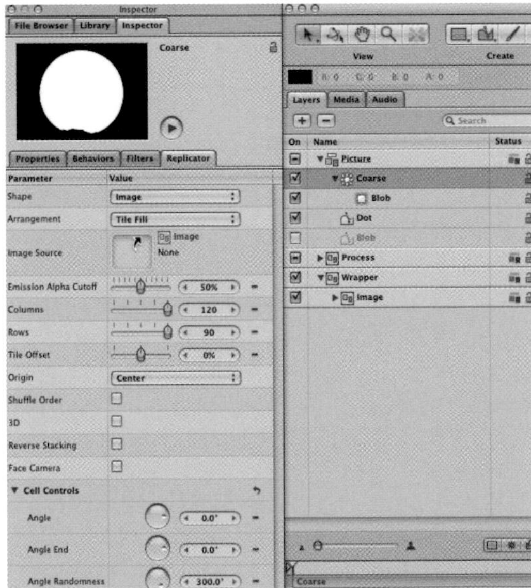

9 Select **Blob**. Press **L** or click on **Replicate** in the toolbar. Call the replicator **Coarse**. Set the **Shape** to **Image**. Set the **Columns** to **120, Rows** to **90**, and **Angle Randomness** to **300. Set Color Mode** to **Take Image Color**. Drag the **Image** group into the **Image Source** well.

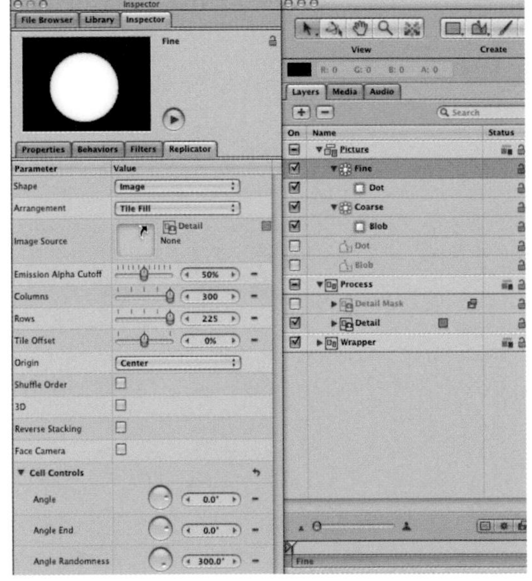

10 Select **Dot**. Press **L** or click on **Replicate** in the toolbar. Call the replicator **Fine**. Set the **Shape** to **Image**. Set the **Columns** to **300, Rows** to **225**, and **Angle Randomness** to **300. Set Color Mode** to **Take Image Color**. Drag the **Detail** group into the **Image Source** well.

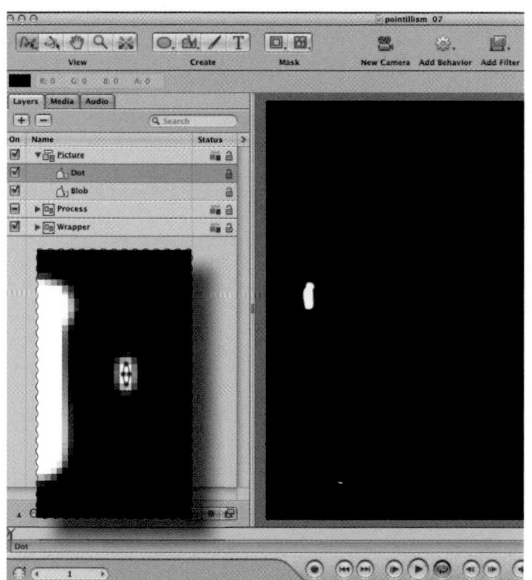

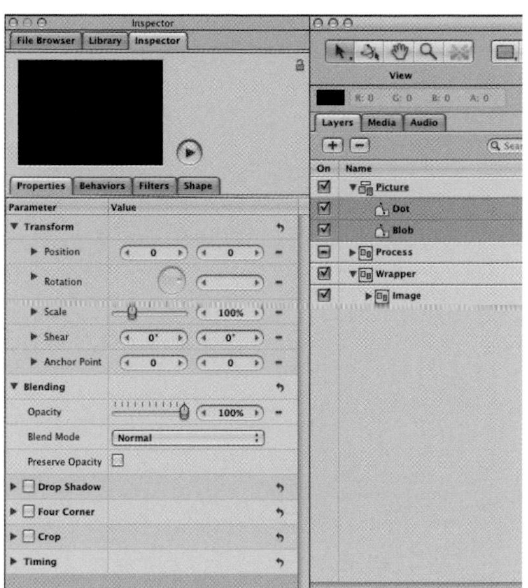

HOT TIP

Instead of a random shape you could get a nice stylized effect by using a defined shape like a leaf, etc.

7 Press the C key to select the **Circle** tool. Draw a small oval. This will be used for the fine detail. Call it **Dot**.

8 Click on **Dot** and **Blob**. In the **Properties** tab, set their **Position** to **0,0.**

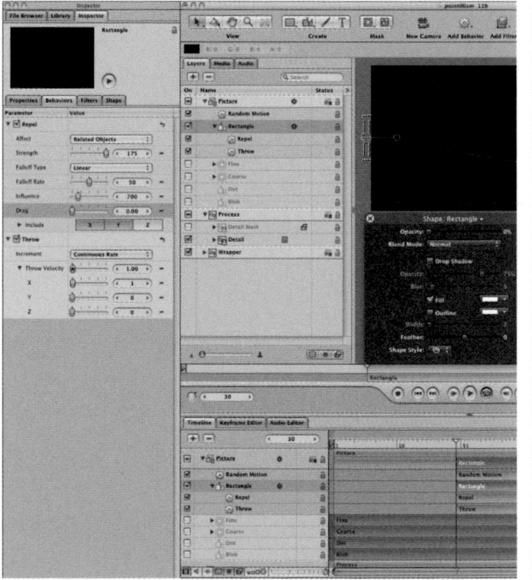

11 Now the picture is done– let's sweep it away. First, to speed interaction, temporarily turn off the **Fine** and **Coarse** replicators. Position to frame **30.** Click on the **Picture** group. **Add Behavior Simulations/Random Motion.** Press F. Click the **Affect Subobjects** checkbox. Set the **Drag** to **-5.**

12 Press R to activate the **Rectangle** tool. Draw a small rectangle just off screen. Set the rectangle's **Opacity** to 0. **Add Behavior/Basic Motion/Throw. Add Behavior/ Simulations/Repel.** Set **Strength** to **175, Falloff Rate** to **50** and **Influence** to **700.** Set **Throw Velocity X** to **1.** Turn back on the fine and coarse replicators and render your project.

Shattering Basic

ELSEWHERE IN THIS CHAPTER, I'll talk about how to break an image into little rectangles, but with this method, we can apparently break an image into more complex, even seemingly random shapes. I say apparently because we're not really "breaking" the image up; rather, we're taking a full frame and masking out all but a portion of it. We use a replicator to repeat the process on multiple copies of the image to create all the pieces. Here's a graphical representation of the process.

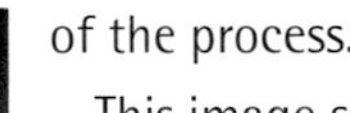

This image shows the full frame as the red-outlined rectangle and the blue triangle is a replicator mask that reveals only a portion of the full image. These are then stacked up like transparencies to re-assemble the full image.

This means that even though only a small sliver of the image is visible in any given "piece," the piece is actually the size of the full frame.

Because of the complexity of this project and the many ways it can be used, I'm going to start with one way to break up an image. After that we'll go on to variations of this technique and different ways of using the process.

IMAGE COURTESY OCTAVIO ARIZALA

1 Start with a new project. Name the first group **Image.** Place the picture you want to "shatter" in this group. Press B to activate the **Bezier** tool. Use it to draw a triangle between the center of the picture to the lower left-hand corner.

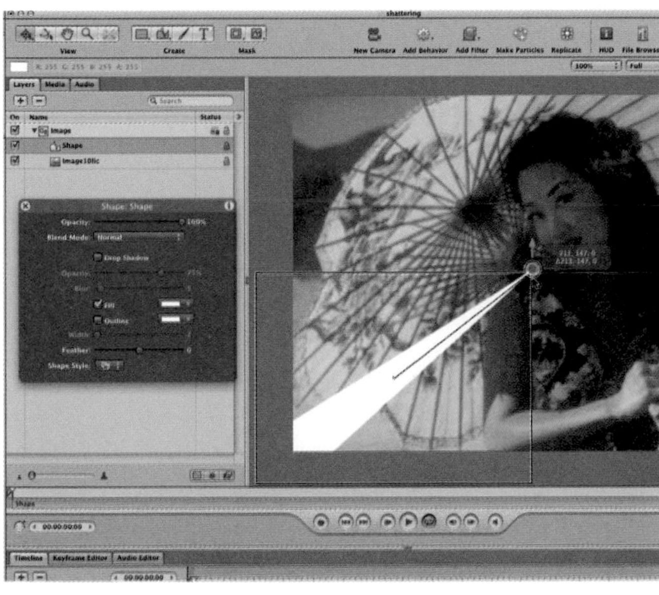

2 Press tab until the **Adjust Anchor Point** tool activates. Use it to move the triangle's **Anchor** point to its tip.

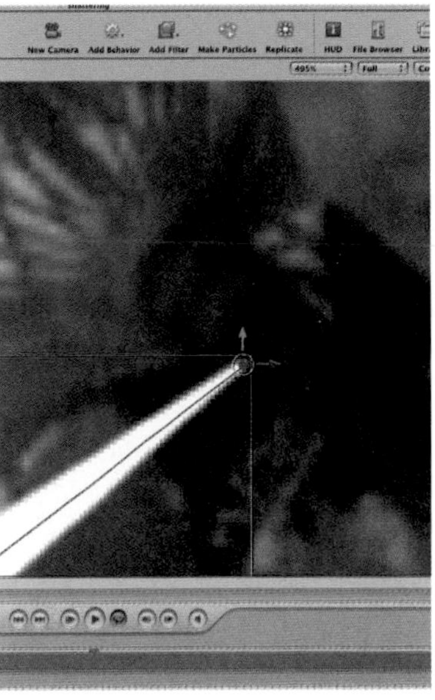

3 Zoom in for accurate placement.

continued...

Shattering Basic (continued)

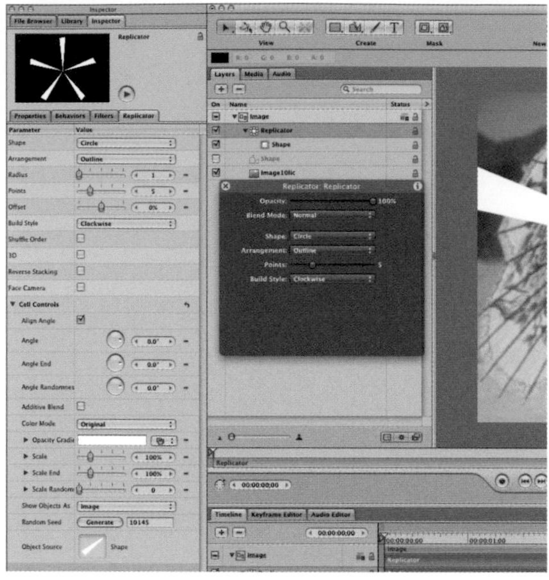

4 Click the **Replicate** button in the toolbar, or press **L**. Change the **Replicator Shape** to **Circle**. Change the **Arrangement** to **Outline**. The **Radius** to **1**. Click the **Align Angle** checkbox.

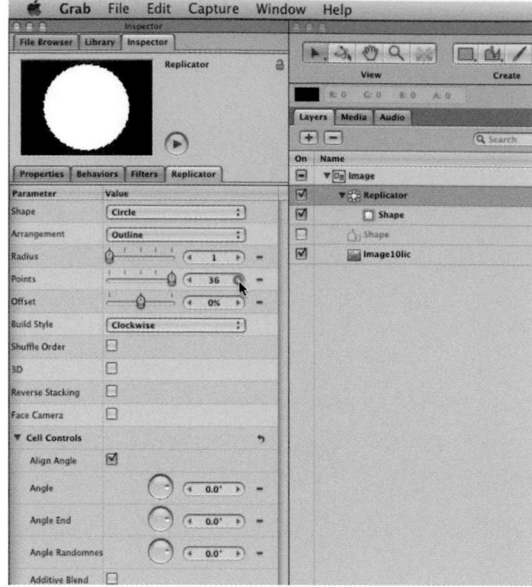

5 Up the number of points until the picture is just covered. *Remember this number.* In this case, it was **36**.

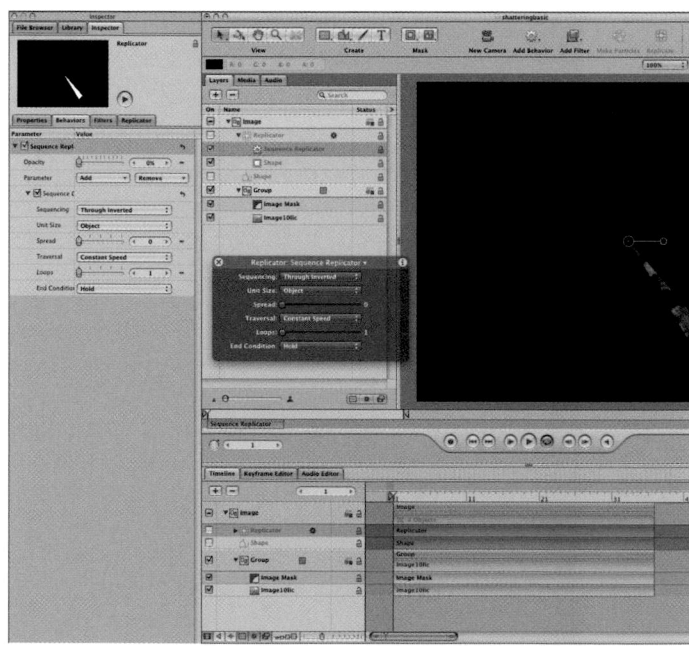

8 Click on the Replicator. **Add Behavior/Replicator/Sequence Replicator**. Set **Sequencing** to **Through Inverted** and the **Spread** to **0**. Then **Parameter Add Opacity** and set it to 0%. This will run through the elements of your Replicator, turning one on per frame.

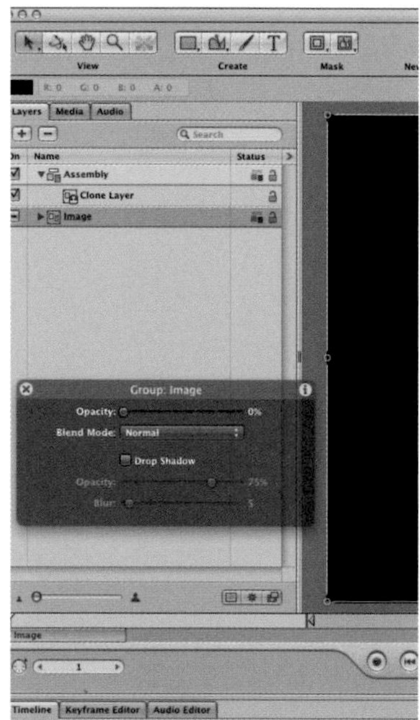

9 Now that we've broken our image into pieces, let's put it back together. Click on the **Image** group and press **K** to create a clone layer. Name the new group **Assembly**. Turn the **Image** group **Opacity** to 0%.

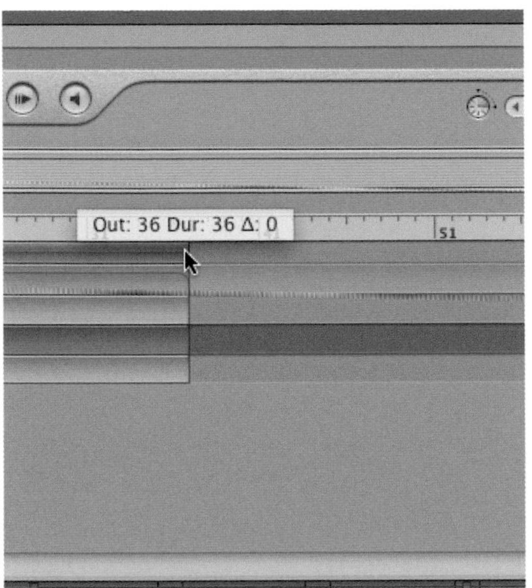

6 Drag the end of your Image group to be the same number of frames I told you to remember in the previous step **(36).**

7 Click on your image in the **Layers** tab. ⌘ *Shift* **G** to group it. ⌘ *Shift* **M** to add an **Image Mask.** Drag your Replicator into the image well.

HOT TIP

If you find very faint lines between your replicator mask pieces, instead of adding another segment, you can try adding width to the outline of the base shape. Feathering can also help.

10 Click on the **Clone Layer**. Press **Replicate** (**L**). Rename the Replicator **Pieces.** Change the **Shape** to **Circle** and **Arrangement** to **Outline.** Set the **Radius** to 0. *Do NOT click the* Align Angle *checkbox.* Set the **Points** to the number from Step 5 that I told you to remember. Turn off **Play Frames**. Set the **Source Frame Offset** to **1.** Bingo! there is your image re-assembled. Save this project as **ShatteringBasic** and use it as the basis for the next few exercises.

Into Pieces

LET'S SEND THE PIECES FLYING as though from impact.

Note that this effect is 2D and although we're simulating depth, we're actually only moving in two dimensions. Because of this, we won't pay the overhead of a 3D project.

Later in the chapter we'll go over how to build this into a template to be used as a transition in Final Cut Pro.

IMAGE COURTESY OCTAVIO ARIZALA

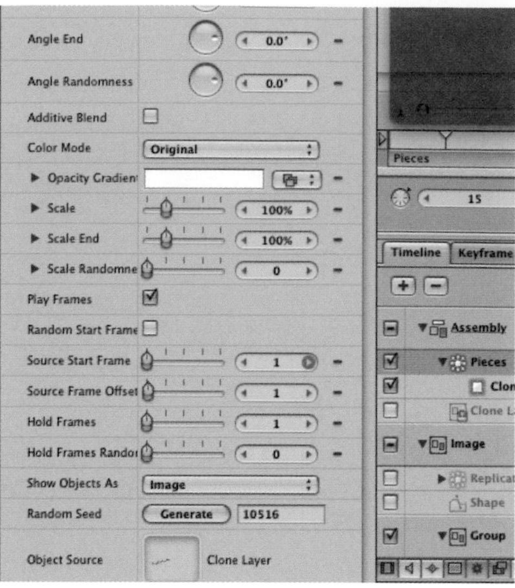

1 Start by loading your **ShatteringBasic** project (described earlier in the chapter). **Click** on the **Pieces** replicator in the **Assembly** group. Check the **Play Frames** checkbox In the **Inspector/Replicator** tab.

4 Before the image is broken up, you still see the extrusion. **Clone Layer** to the rescue.

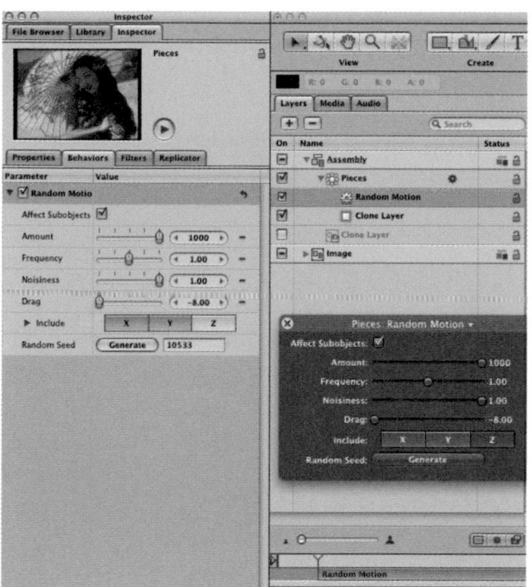

2 Position about 15 frames into your timeline and **Add Behavior/Simluations/Random Motion**. Press **I** to make the behavior start at the current position. Click the **Affect Subobjects** checkbox. Set the **Amount** to **1000**. Set the **Noisiness** to **1.0**. Set the **Drag** to **-8**. You'll have to type in these values as the sliders don't go far enough.

3 This is enough to do a basic shatter, but let's enhance it. First, let's give some depth to the pieces with an **Extrude** filter. Go to frame 20. Click on the **Clone Layer** (as above). **Add Filter/Stylize/Extrude**. Set the **Distance** to **10**. That looks good, but there's a problem.

HOT TIP

If you don't like the pattern the pieces are flying in, just go to the Random Motion Behavior and hit the Generate button next to Random Seed until you get a pattern you do like.

5 Go to frame 1. Open the **Image** group. Open the **Group** group. Click on your image. Press **K**. In the **Layers palette,** grab the new **Clone Layer** and drag it to the top of the **Assembly** group.

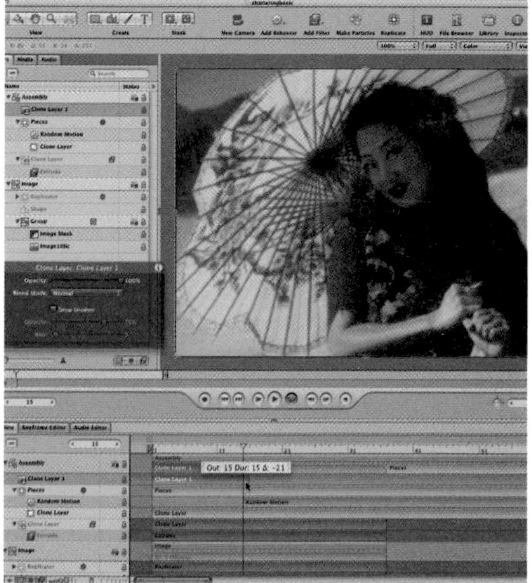

6 Now, in the **Timeline**, drag the end of the new **Clone Layer** until it ends just as the **Random Motion** effect begins (they overlap by one frame). This covers up the extrusion until the shatter begins.

Puzzling

THIS DEMONSTRATES USING A different kind of replicator to generate our matte. In this case, we'll be using puzzle pieces, but they could just as well be any shape.

IMAGE COURTESY OCTAVIO ARIZALA

1 Let's start with the **Shatter2pieces** project. First delete the **Image/Replicator** layer and the **Shape** that we were using. Select them both and press the Delete key or Right/ctrl-click on them and select **Delete.** Then turn off the **Assembly** group while we rebuild the **Image** group.

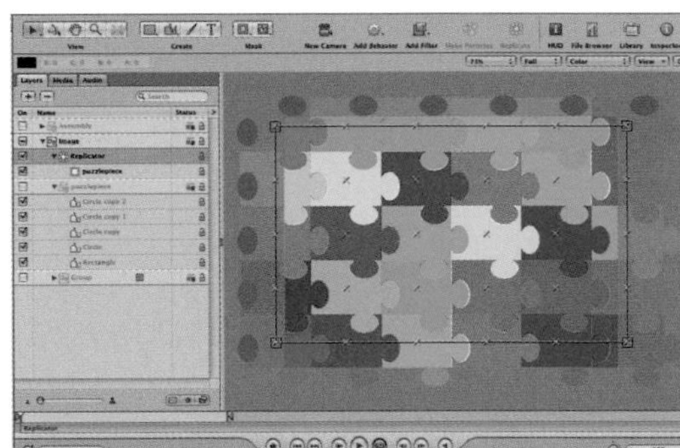

4 You may have to futz with the sizing, spacing, number of rows and columns, outline widths on shapes to make the pieces all interlock. I've colored the pieces a random color here and turned on the **View/Show Full View Area** to show the configuration. Make sure yours are just white.

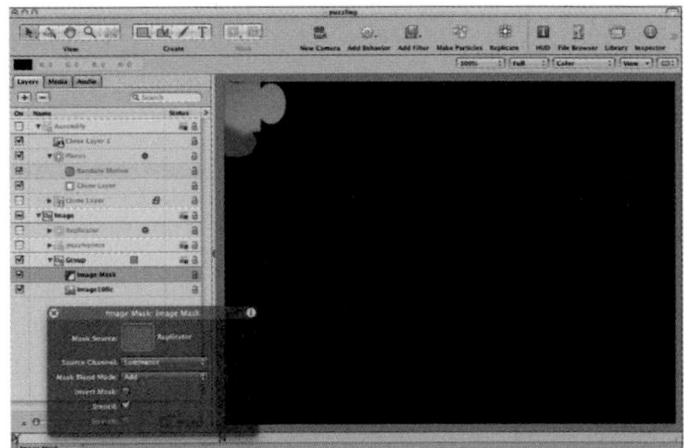

7 Turn back on the **Image/Group** group. Turn the disclosure triangle for the **Image/Group** group and click on its **Image Mask.** Change the **Source Channel** to **Luminance.** Drag the **Replicator** into the image well.

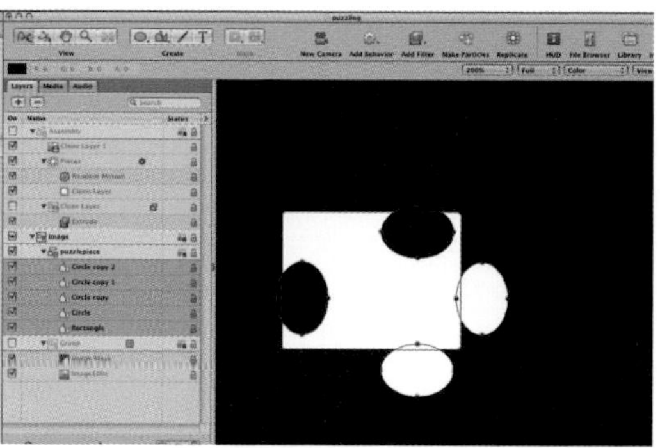

2 Turn up the **Opacity** of the **Image** group to **100%.** Turn off the **Image/Group** group. Add a group within the **Image** group, name it **puzzlepiece**, and then create a puzzle piece within it in the center of the screen. I used a rectangle and 4 ovals, two white and two black. See HOT TIP for more clues.

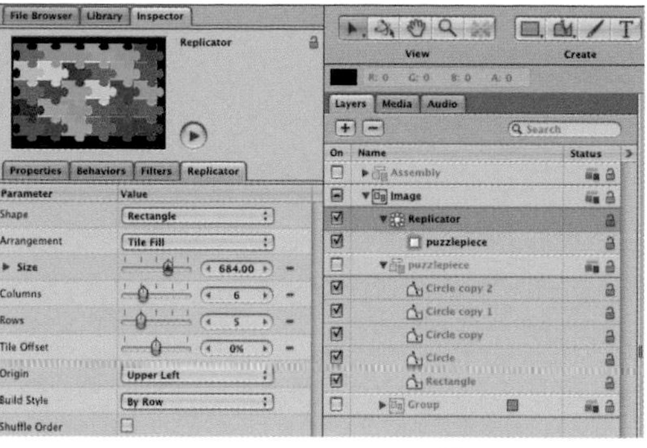

3 Select the **puzzlepiece** group and press **L** to replicate. Move the new **Replicator** to the **Image** group. Delete the empty **Group**. Click the **Additive Blend** checkbox. Change the **Origin** to **Upper Left** and the **Build Style** to **By Row**.

HOT TIP

The puzzle piece you create is critical to the success of this project. It must interlock with copies of itself to create a seamless blanket for the project to work.

For this reason, I used copies of the same oval to make both the white "tabs" and the black "slots" and aligned their centers exactly.

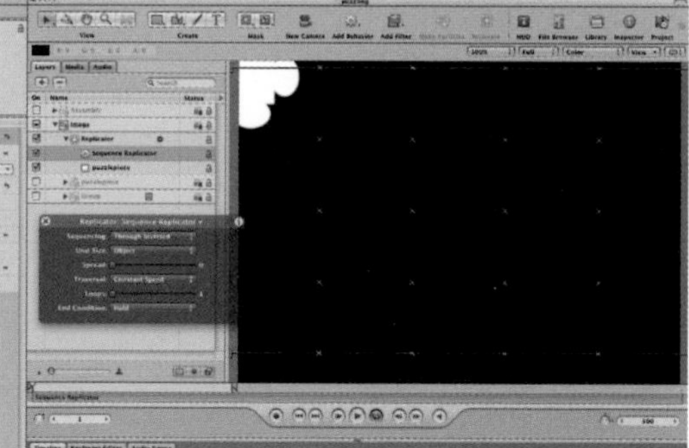

5 Click on the **Replicator. Add Behavior/Replicator/ Sequence Replicator.** Set **Sequencing** to **Through Inverted.** The **Spread** to **0.** Then **Parameter Add Opacity** and set it to **0%.** This will run through the elements of your replicator, turning one on per frame.

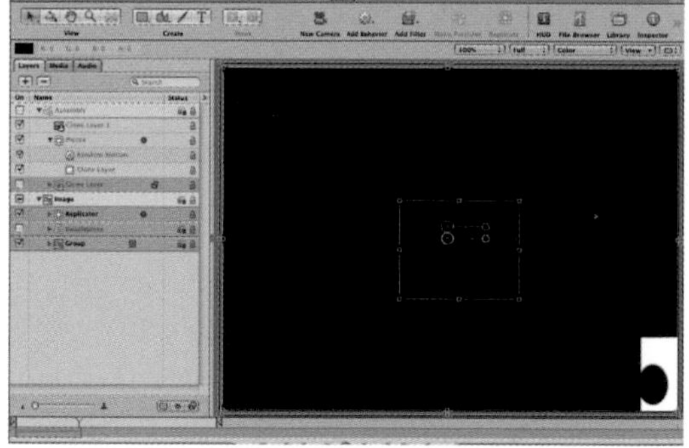

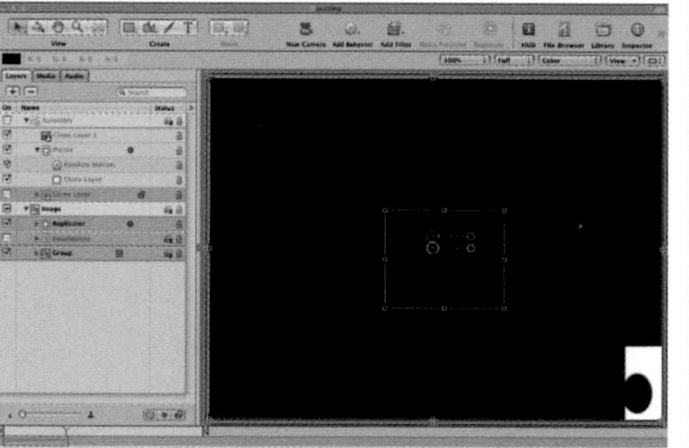

6 Now for a little math—multiply your replicator rows by columns to get the total number of pieces. In my case: 6 x 5 = 30. Now ⌘-click on all the layers in the **Image** group and the **Clone Layer** above them. Go to frame 30 (or the total number of your pieces). Press **O**.

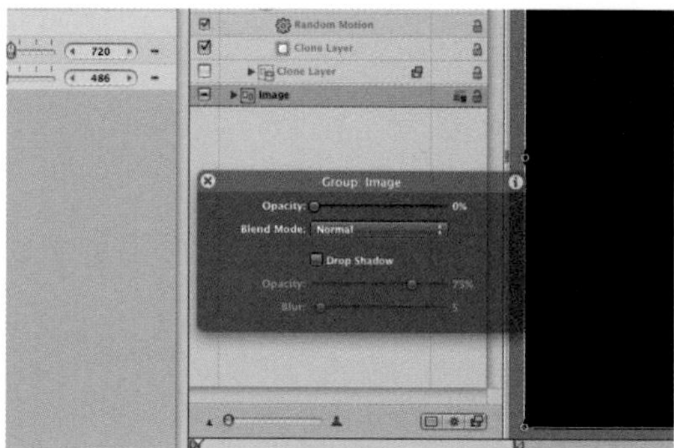

8 Turn the **Image** group's opacity to 0.

9 Turn back on the **Assembly** group. Click on the **Pieces** replicator. Turn OFF the **Play Frames** checkbox. Change the **Points** to **30** (or the total number of pieces). Click the **Shuffle Order** checkbox. Now when it's hit by the **Random Motion** behavior, your puzzle will go flying.

Sequencing Puzzling

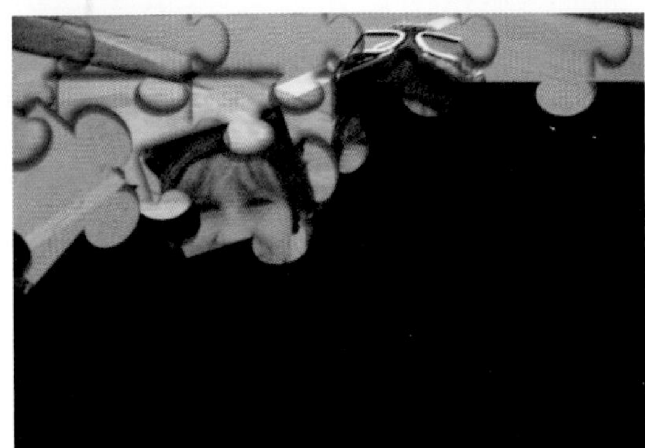

EVERYTHING DOESN'T HAVE to be about shattering and explosions—we can use the Sequence Replicator behavior to generate some choreographed motion and BUILD something.

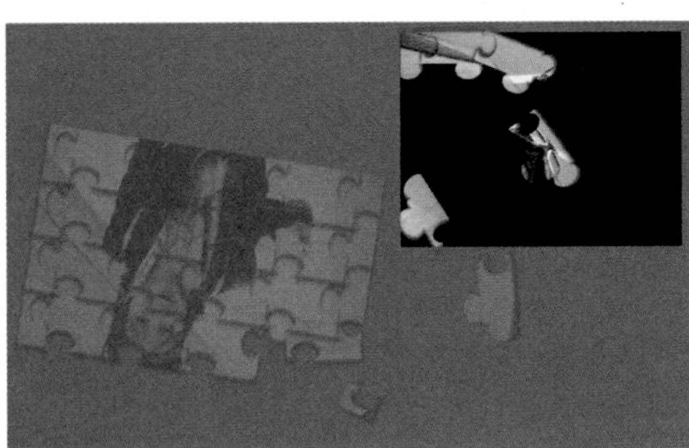

We'll start with our Puzzling project and add a Sequence Replicator behavior to move it piece by piece from off screen to assemble before our eyes.

1 Start with the **Puzzling** project from the previous exercise. Because I always say "Save Early, Save Often," save your project now as **PutTogether**. Select **Clone Layer1** and the **Random Motion** behavior and delete them.

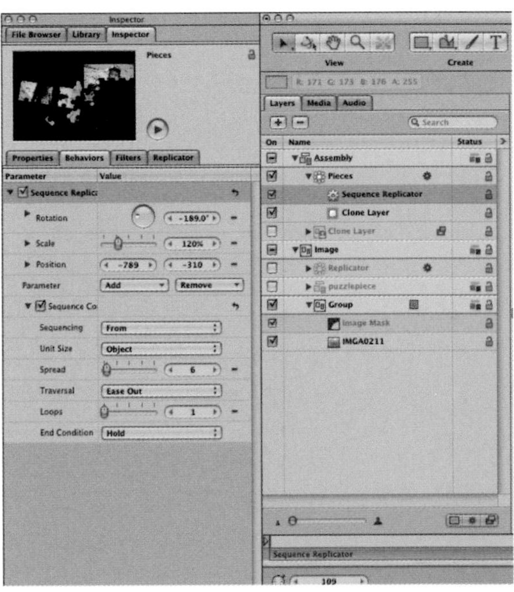

4 Set the **Rotation** to **-189. Scale** to **120%. Position X** to **-789. Position Y** to **-310.** Set the **Spread** to **6.** Change the **Traversal** to **Ease Out**.

IMAGE COURTESY PARKER SHEFFIELD

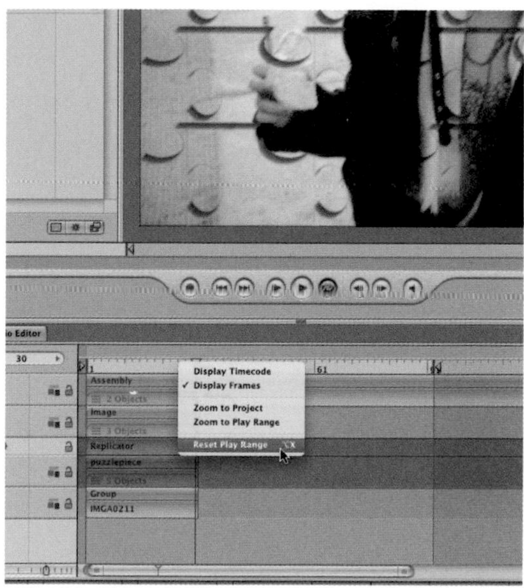

2 Type ⌥X or right/ctrl-click on the timeline and select **Reset Play Range.**

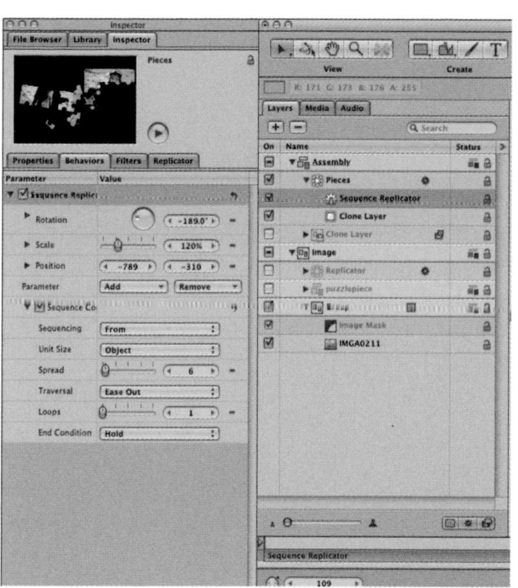

3 Click on the **Pieces** replicator and **Add Behavior/ Replicator/Sequence Replicator. Parameter Add Rotation, Scale, Position.** Change the **Sequencing** to **From.**

HOT TIP

As a "cleaner" variation on this project,

try disabling the Extrude from the Assembly/ Clone Layer.

You can also turn off its Drop Shadow as well.

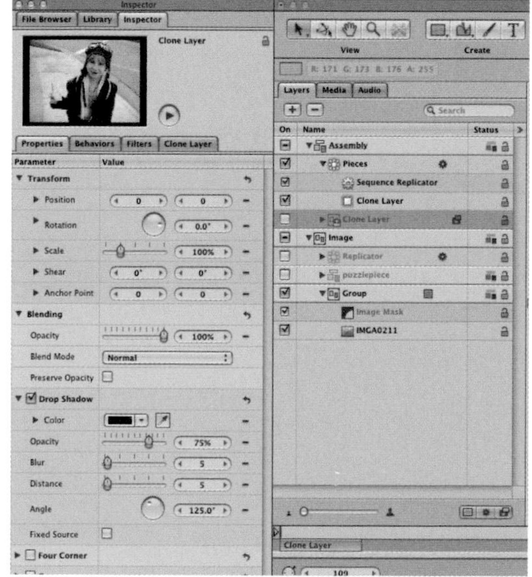

5 Click on the **Clone Layer** in the **Assembly** group. Turn on **Drop Shadow Checkbox.** Set the **Angle** to **125.**

6 If you want the pieces to come in faster, shorten the **Sequence Replicator** behavior in the timeline.

Random Destruction

TORN, IRREGULAR EDGES give this breakup a difference. Random sizing and rotation, coupled with an irregular shape give us the ability to break our image into varying shapes.

IMAGE COURTESY OCTAVIO ARIZALA

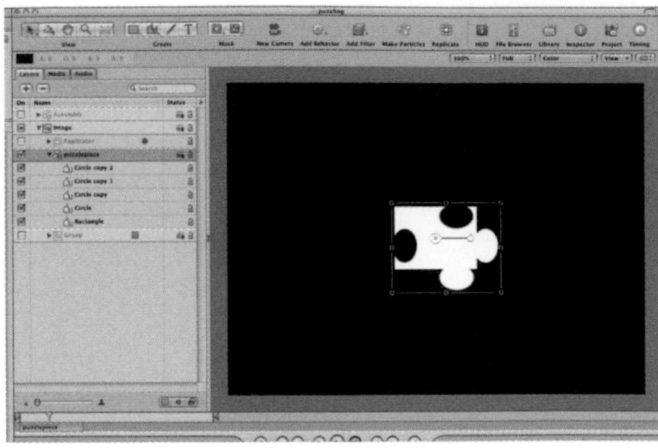

1 Start with your **Puzzle** project. Living by the dictum "Save Early, Save Often," save your project now as **RandomDestruction**. Turn off the **Assembly** group. Turn the **Opacity** of the **Image** group to **100%.** Turn off the **Image group/Replicator**. Turn on the **puzzlepiece** group.

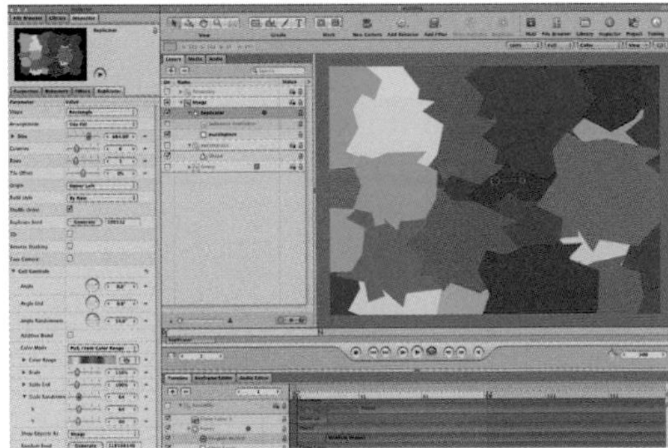

4 Click the **Shuffle Order** checkbox. Adjust the **Angle Randomness** as high as you can without seeing black holes in your "replicator quilt." Same for the **Scale Randomness.** The settings are interrelated, so you may have to do some back and forth fiddling. When you're done, change the **Color Mode** back to **Original.**

7 Select the **Pieces** replicator. Position a few frames past the point where you want the pieces to disappear. Drag the radius out until the pieces are off screen. In this case about **750.** Right/ctrl-click on the **Radius**. Select **Ramp**. Press O to make the **Ramp** end at this point.

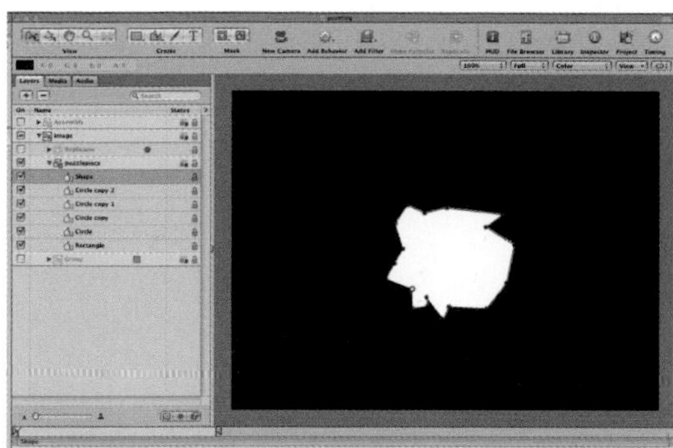

2 Now press **B** to activate the **Bezier** tool and draw a random shape over the top of the puzzle piece.

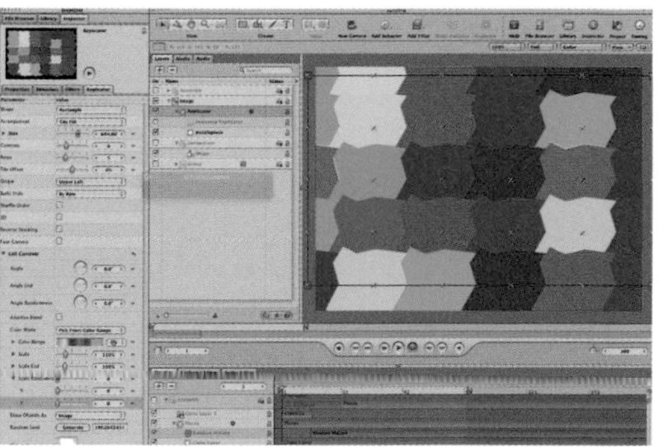

3 You can now delete the other parts of the **puzzlepiece**. Turn off the **puzzlepiece** group. Turn on the **Replicator** layer. Temporarily turn off the **Sequence Replicator** behavior. I've turned the **Color Mode** to **Pick From Color Range** and used a **Rainbow** gradient to show what's going on.

5 Turn back on on the **Sequence Replicator** behavior. Turn off the **Replicator**, and turn on the **Group**. Set the **Image** group's **Opacity** to **0.** And turn back on the **Assembly** group.

6 Prior to this, we'd been using the **Random Motion** behavior to shatter our image. Another way to blast the pieces apart is to simply change the **Radius** of the **Pieces** replicator. Delete the **Random Motion** behavior.

8 Position to the first frame where the image disappears (just after **Clone Layer1**). Press **I**. Drag the **Start Value** down until the pieces all come together. It will be the negative of the figure it took to make them all fly out from step 7 above. Drag the **Curvature** to **100%**.

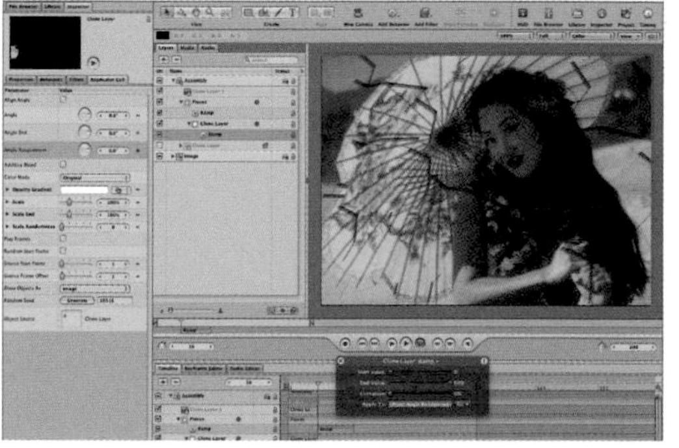

9 Let's make the pieces spin as they fly away. Select the **Pieces** replicator. Right/**ctrl**-click on the **Angle Randomness** and select **Ramp**. Make it the same duration as our last ramp. Set the **End** value to **600.** That's it!

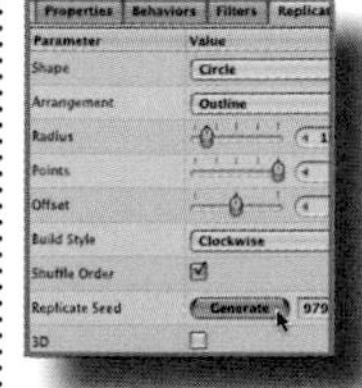

HOT TIP

If you don't like the pattern the pieces are flying off in, simply hit the Generate button on the Replicate Seed until you see something you like.

Sweeping Changes

BREAKING UP AN IMAGE and reassembling it into a new image is a dynamic way to make a transition.

What we're doing here is making a random stack of our image assembly and then using a "long lens" on our camera to flatten everything. As we rotate around to our incoming image, we widen our angle of view to make the pieces stand out, and then narrow it back down to flatten the incoming image.

While this can be used within Motion, we'll be building it as a template so it can be used as a transition from within Final Cut Pro.

1 Start with your **Puzzling** project. Open up the **Image Group/puzzlepiece**, the **Assembly/Pieces**, and **Assembly/Clone Layer**. ⌘-select the top **Clone Layer1**, the **Random Motion** behavior, the **Extrude** filter, and all the **Circles** (leave the **Rectangle**). Right/ctrl-click and select **Delete**.

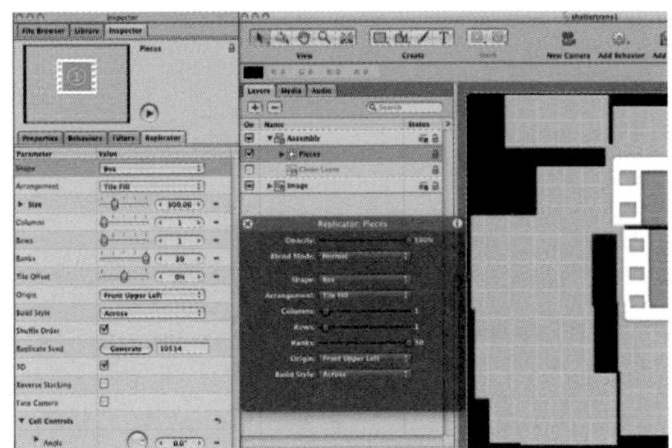

4 Now we're going 3D. Select the **Pieces** replicator and click the **3D** checkbox. Change the **Shape** to **Box**. Set the **Arrangement** to **Tile Fill. Columns** 1, **Rows** 1, **Ranks** = *the number of pieces in the project*—in this case **30.** Change the **Origin** to be **Front Upper Left**.

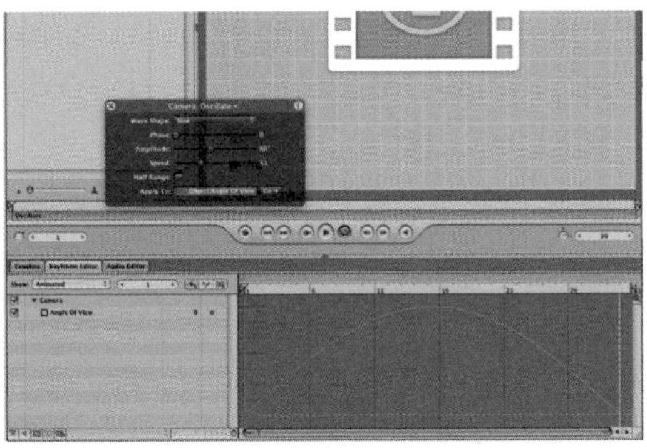

7 If you select the **Keyframe Editor** tab, you'll be able to see what's going on. Set the **Amplitude** to **80.** Set the **Speed** to **31.** You can see that our **Angle of View** will start out at 0, smoothly slide to **80,** and then back down.

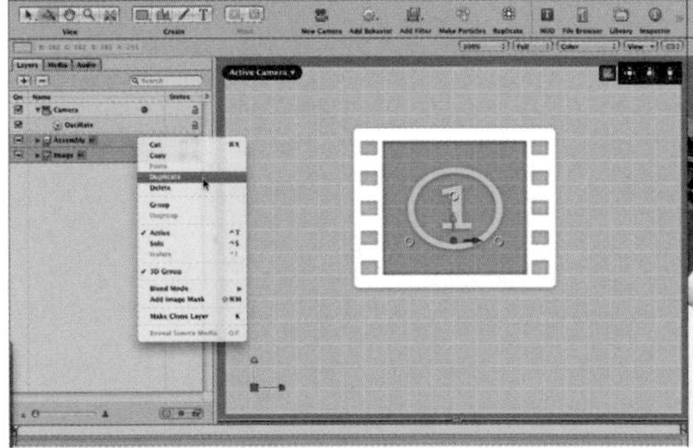

8 We're done with our "Outgoing" image, so now let's duplicate it for the "Incoming." Select both the **Assembly** and **Image** groups and right/ctrl-click and choose Duplicate or press ⌘D.

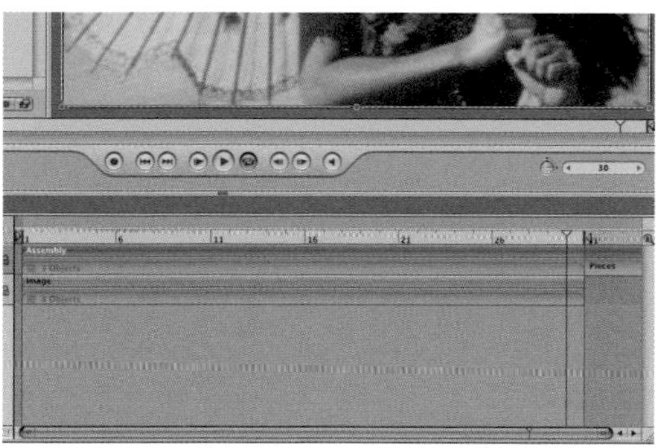

2 Click in the **Project Duration** field and set your duration to **30.** Then right/ctrl-click on the timeline and select **Reset Play Range**. Then select **Zoom to Play Range**.

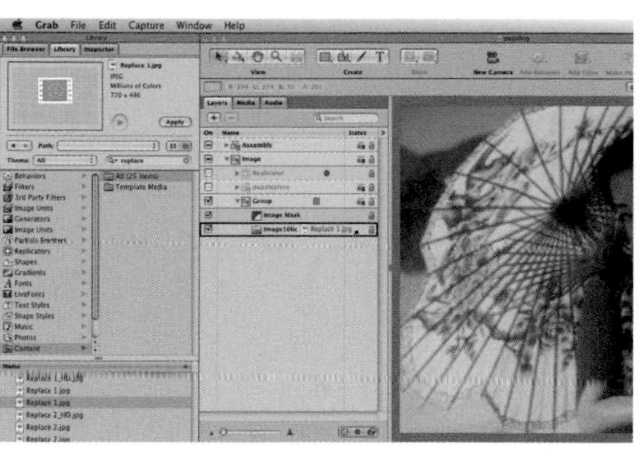

3 Since we're making a template, let's use a **Replace** graphic from **Library/Content**. Type **replace** into the search field to help you find it. We're building this template for standard def, so we'll use the 720x486 graphic. Grab it and drag it over the top of our image and when the pointer turns into a curved arrow, let go.

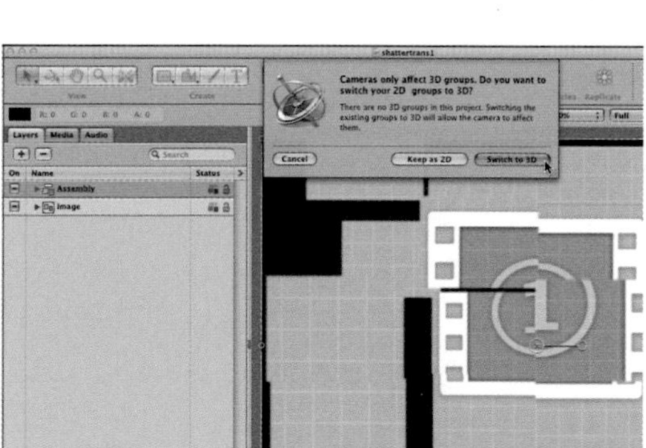

5 Click on the **New Camera** button in the toolbar. You'll get a requester about 3D groups. Select **Switch to 3D**.

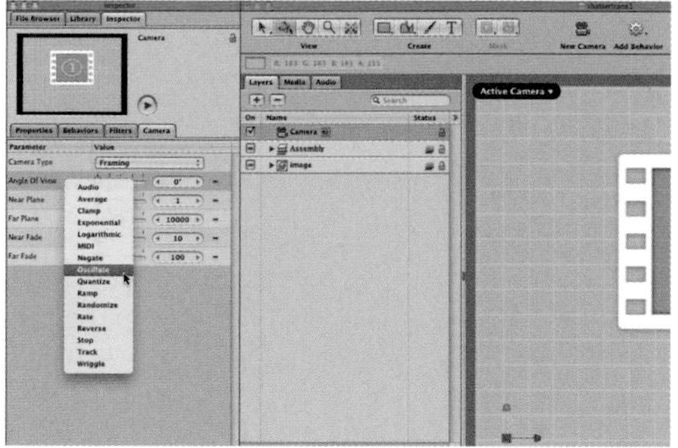

6 The reason our picture looks a bit shuffled is that the pieces are of varying Z-depths from our camera. We'll flatten it now. Change the **Angle of View** to **0.** Then, while on frame 1, right/ctrl-click on the **Angle of View** and select **Oscillate**.

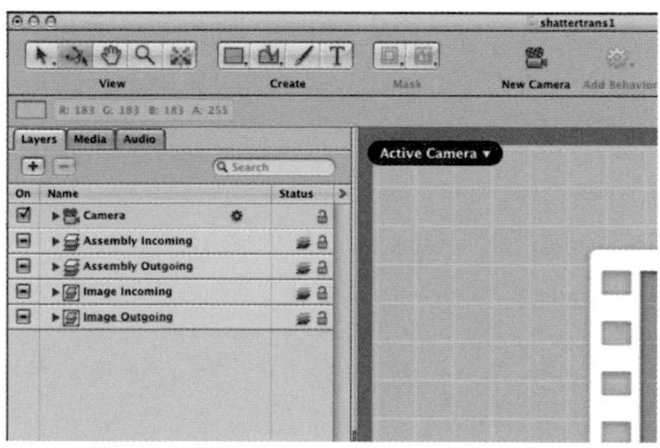

9 Rename the copies **Assembly Incoming** and **Image Incoming**. Name the originals **Assembly Outgoing** and **Image Outgoing**.

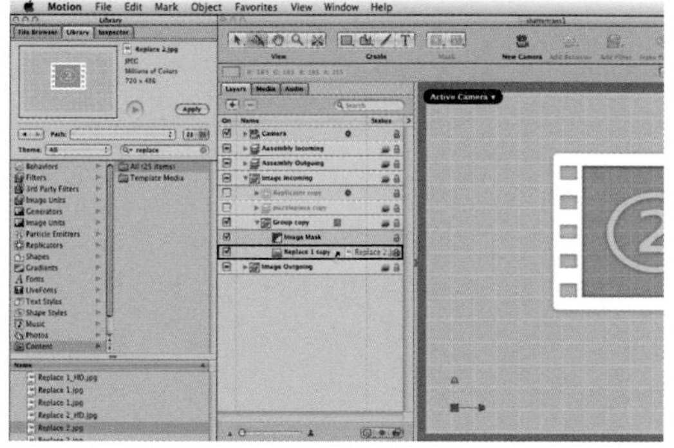

10 Open **Image Incoming/Group copy**—replace the **Replace 1 copy** image with a **Replace 2** image from our **Library/Content** as in Step 3 above. Rename the layer **Replace 2** if necessary.

continued...

Sweeping Changes (continued)

11 Click on the **Assembly Incoming** group. Under **Properties**, set the **Rotation Y** to **-90.** This places it at right angles to the camera.

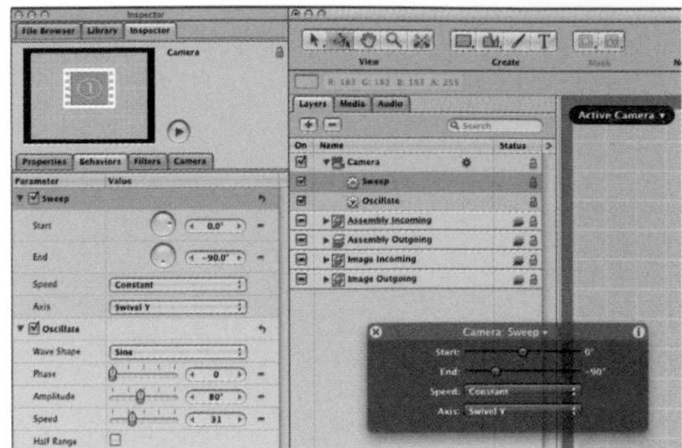

12 Select the **Camera**. **Add Behavior/Camera/Sweep.** Set the **End** to -90.

15 One last bit of cleanup—the **Image** wells show up in Final Cut Pro in the order they are found in the layers, so let's swap the **Image Incoming** and **Image Outgoing** groups. Don't worry about the **Assembly** groups.

16 Now select **Save as Template...** from the **File** menu. If you don't already have one, create a new theme with the **New Theme...** button. Call it **Transitions**. Let's name this template **Shatter Sweep1**.

18 While we're at it, let's modify this transition and make it pivot the sweep at the corner instead of the center of the images.

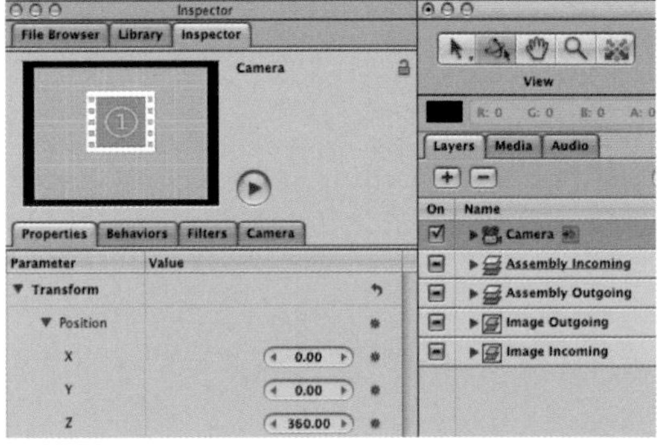

19 Start with the camera. Under **Properties**, change the **Z Position** to **360** (half our width of **720**). You won't notice any change yet.

IMAGES COURTESY TIKI BAR TV

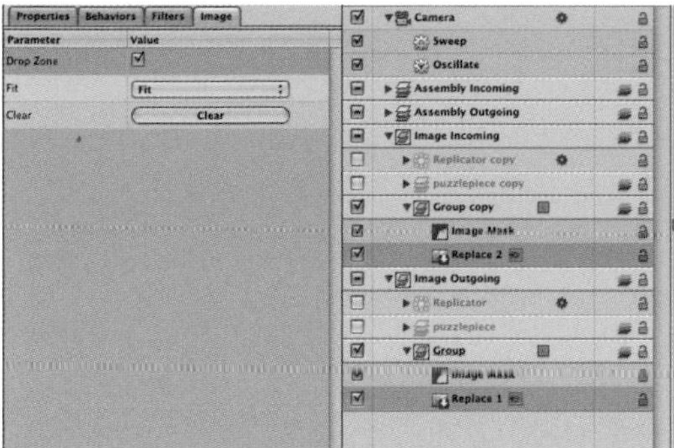

13 Let's save this as a Master Template for use in Final Cut Pro. ⌘-select both images and click the **Drop Zone** checkbox in the **Image** tab.

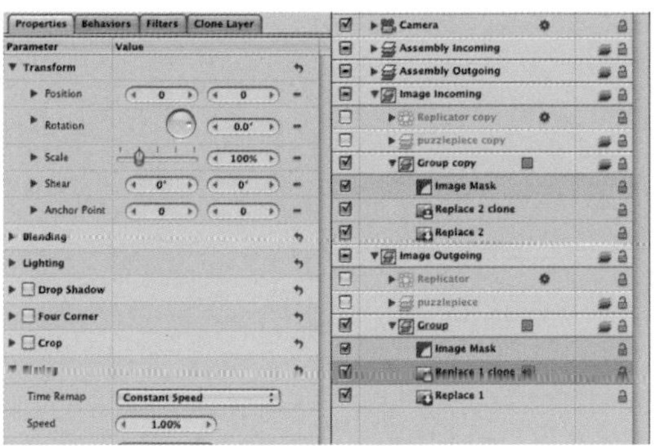

14 We need to freeze the incoming video or each box will come from a different frame. With the playhead parked on frame 1, select the **Replace2** layer. Press K to create a clone layer. Name it **Replace2 clone.** Go to the **Properties** tab and under **Timing**, set the **Speed** to 1%. Do the same for the **Replace1 layer.**

17 To use this template, in Final Cut Pro, cut the **Shatter Sweep1** Master **Template** between the clips you want to transition, and then double click on it in the timeline to throw it into the viewer and select the **Controls** tab.

18 Razor the clip one frame before the **Shatter Sweep1** template in your timeline. Drag it into the **Replace1** well. Drag the clip after the template into the **Replace2** well.

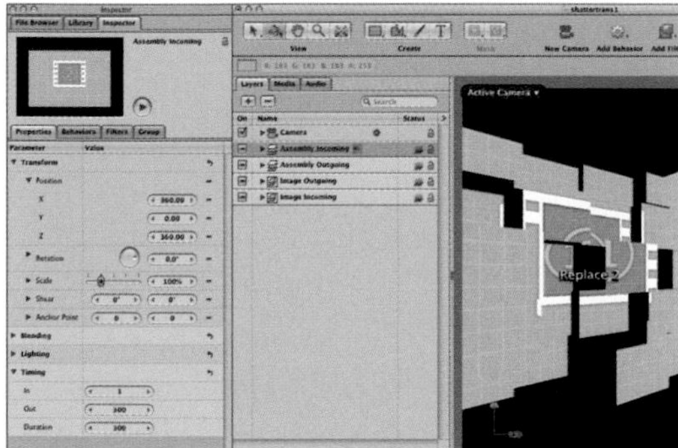

20 Now go to the **Assembly Incoming** group and in the **Properties** tab, change **Position X** to **360** and **Position Z** to **360.** This moves the incoming "wall" half a screen to our right and half a screen forward so the **Outgoing** and **Incoming** images meet in the corner. Positioning at frame 16 makes this easy to see.

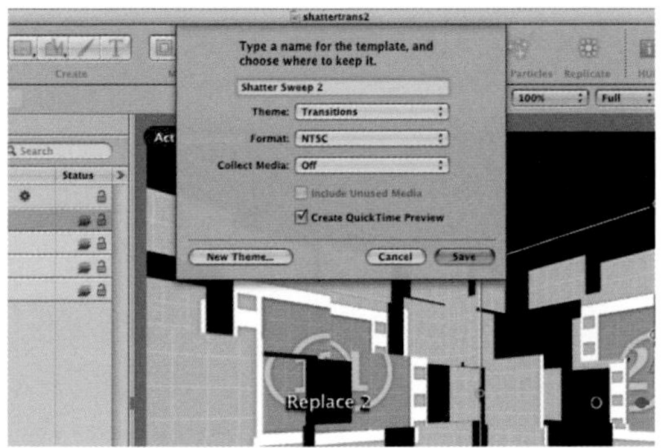

21 Save this template the same way as above, but call it **Shatter Sweep2.**

Iris and Other Transitions

MOST OF THE PROJECTS in this chapter cause the image to leave the screen in some dramatic way. This gives us the perfect opportunity to build them into a transition template for use in Final Cut Pro by placing our new image behind the first so that the first image, when exploded, shattered, etc., reveals the new image behind it.

IMAGES COURTESY REILLY AND PARKER SHEFFIELD

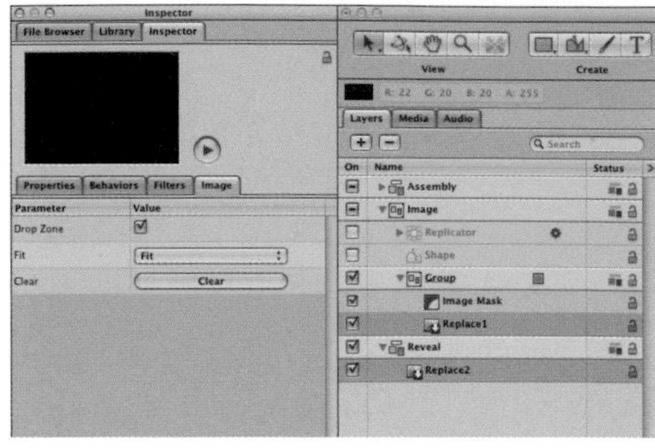

1 Begin with the **shatteringbasic** project. Name the base image **Replace1**. Add a new group and call it **Reveal**. Move it behind all the layers Add a new image to the **Reveal** group (your own or from the library). Call it **Replace2**. Click the **Drop Zone** button for both **Replace1** and **Replace2**.

4 Select the **Assembly/Pieces** replicator. Right/ctrl-click on the **Radius** and select **Ramp**.

7 To use this template in Final Cut Pro, place your playhead where you want the transition to occur. In the **Sequence** menu, select **Add Master Template**. Pick your transition, and then select **Insert.**

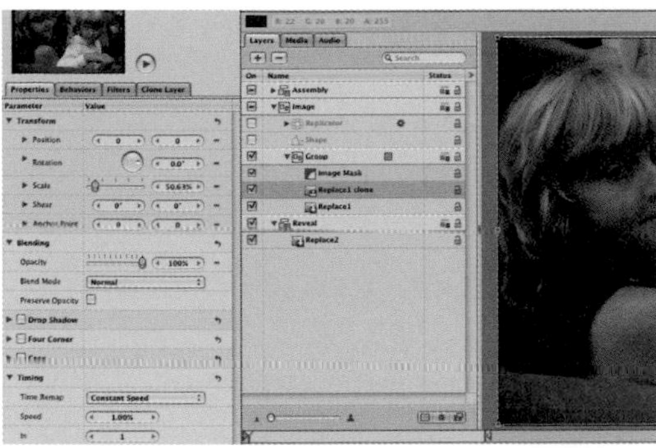

2 We need to freeze any moving video or each piece will come from a different frame. While on frame 1, select the **Replace1** still and press **K** to create a clone layer. Name it **Replace1 Clone**. In the **Properties** tab of **Replace1 Clone**, set the **Speed** to **1%**. Repeat cloning and freezing for the **Replace2** image.

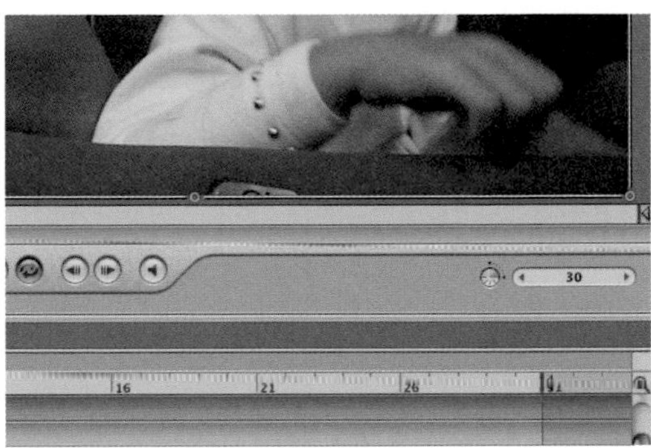

3 Set the project duration to 30 frames.

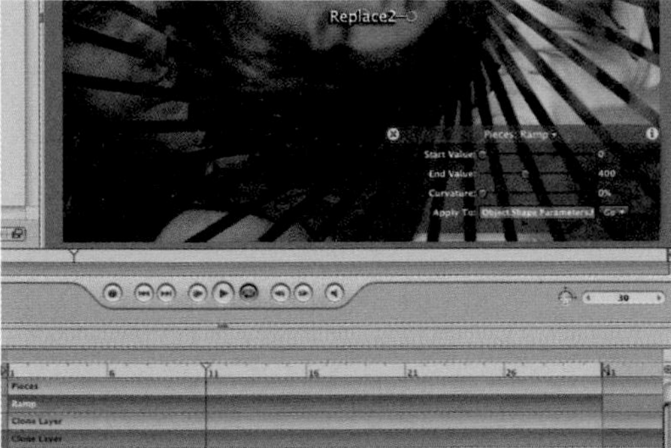

5 Set the **End Value** to **400.** Go to frame 30 and press **O** to truncate your ramp there. If there are still portions of your outgoing image visible, up the **End Value** of the **Ramp** until they are out of frame.

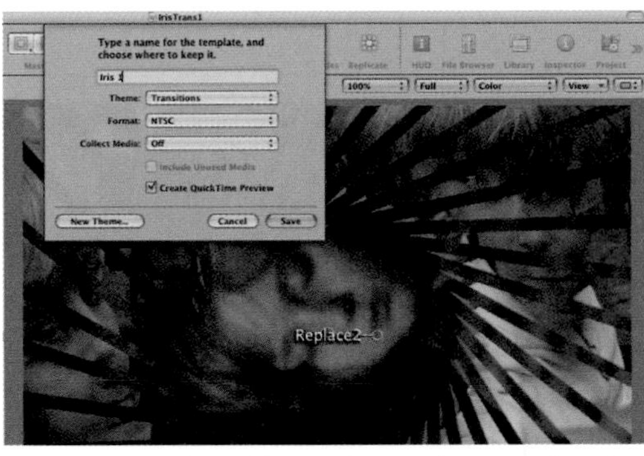

6 Save your project as **Iris1**, and then save it as a template. If you don't already have a **Transitions** theme, create one with the **New Theme...** button. Let's name this template **Iris1**.

HOT TIP

Because we're not breaking up the Replace2 image, you can decide not to freeze it and have the incoming video moving.

However, you will have to trim the clip following the transition by 31 frames AFTER you drag it into the Replace2 well. This is to make up for the 30 frames that will be playing during the transition.

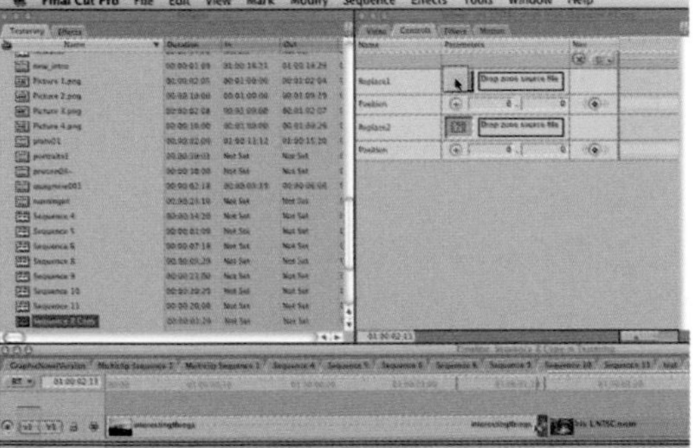

8 This places it in your timeline and your viewer. Razor the clip one frame in front of the newly added template and then drag that frame into the **Replace1** image well. Drag the clip after the transition into the **Replace2** image well. Render.

9 Use the same technique to turn other projects into transitions.

5 Breaking up Is Easy to Do

Power Strips

SLICING OUR IMAGE INTO STRIPS gives us the ability to do many things with it. This project shows you how to build a rotating transition.

We start a fixed resolution layer that is as wide and tall as we want our strips to be. Then with a ramp on the position, we slide our image up one "strip width" per frame, essentially creating a series of stills with a different strip of our image on each frame.

A clone layer allows a replicator to see this as a movie and we can re-assemble our image and play with it.

In this case, we're doing horizontal strips, but the same method can be used to produce verticalstrips as well. Later in the chapter we'll use a more sophisticated variation of the same technique to break our image into a grid of moveable pieces.

IMAGES COURTESY CHRIS AND PARKER SHEFFIELD

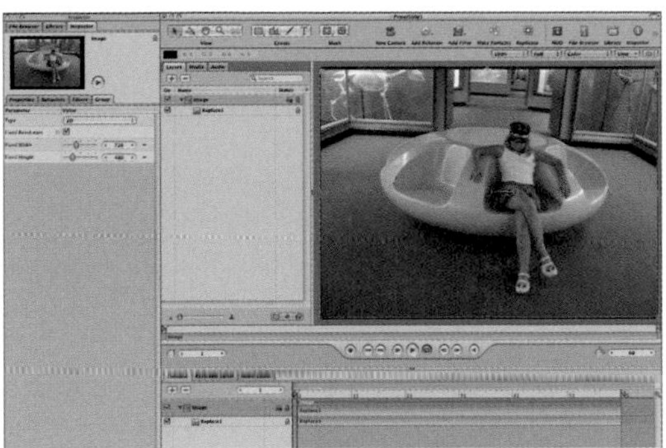

1 Start with a new project. Set its duration to 60 frames. You can use a replace graphic from the library, or a picture of your choice. If you use your own graphic, name the still **Replace1**. Name its group **Image1** and set it to be fixed resolution at 720x480 (or the size you're using).

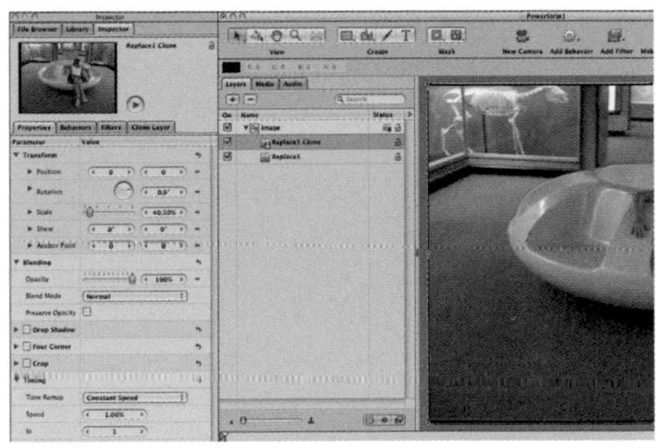

2 Because it's a transition, we need to freeze the incoming video for the slicing to work properly. While on frame 1, select the **Replace1** still and press K to create a clone layer. Name it **Replace1 Clone**. In the **Properties** tab of **Replace1 Clone**, set the **Speed** to 1%. Trim the **Image** group to project length.

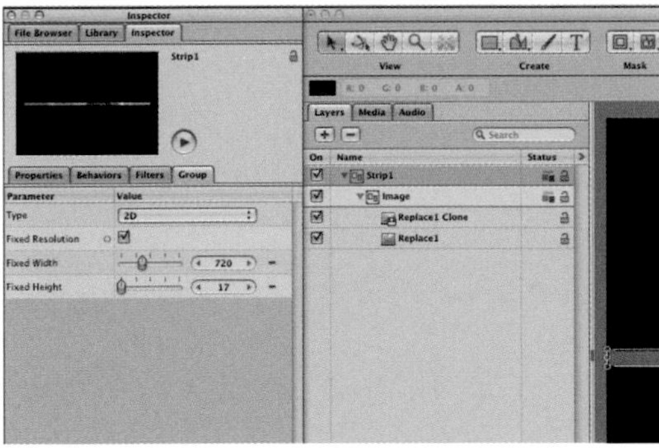

3 Select **Image** group. Press ⌘ Shift G. Name the new containing group **Strip1**. We're using 30 horizontal strips, so the width will be 720. The height is 480/30, or 16. For overlap, we add 1, so our total is 17. Height/number of strips + 1. Set the **Strip** group to **Fixed Resolution**: 720x17.

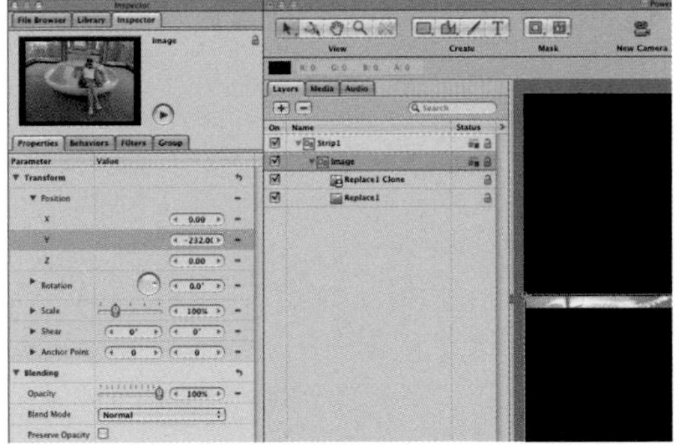

4 Now we have to move our image layer down so we're starting on the very top of our image. We need to set the **Y Position** to – **1/2** of the project height minus the strip height. (480 - 16)/2 = 232 Click on the **Image** group and set the **Y Position** to **-232.**

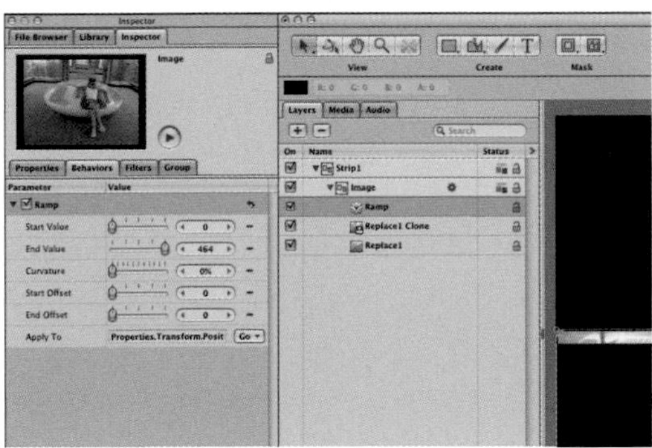

5 We need to add a ramp to move our **Image** group through the strip "window" the height of our project minus the height of one strip. 480 - 16 = 464. Right/ctrl-click on the **Image** group's **Y Position** (which we just set) and select **Ramp**. Set the end value to **464.**

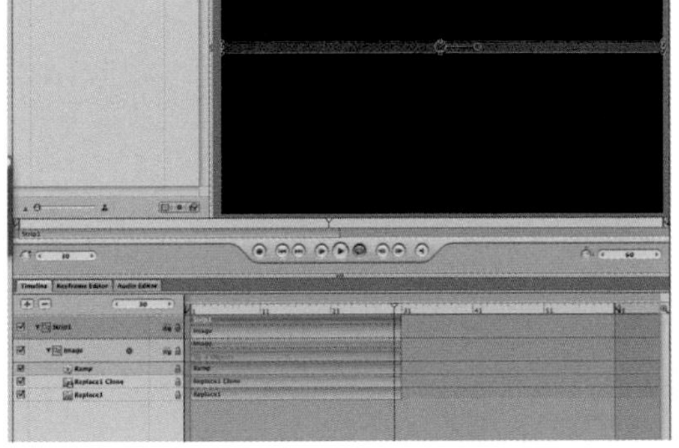

6 Our image moves through the **Strip** window, but too slowly. Because we want 30 strips, we need to do it in 30 frames. Select the **Strip1** group, position to frame 30, and press O. Now we have 30 frames, one for each strip.

continued...

Power Strips (continued)

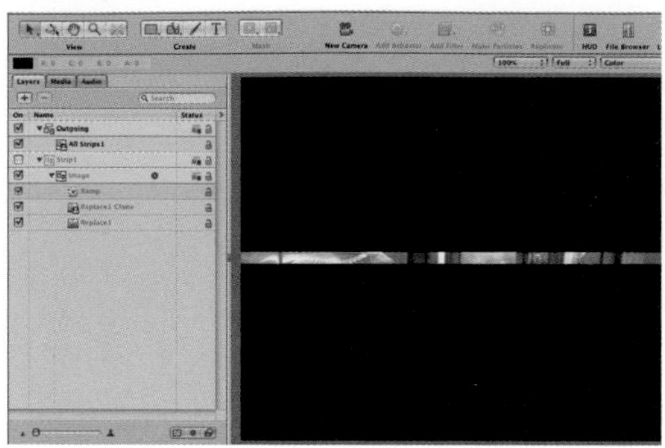

7 Position back to frame 1. With the **Strip1** group selected, press **K** to create a clone layer. This is to allow the replicator to deal with it as a movie. Name it **All Strips1**. Name its group **Outgoing**. Turn off the **Strip1** group.

8 Select **All Strips**. Press **L** to replicate. Change the **Shape** to **Line**. We calculated the **Y Position** in Step 4 above as **232.** Set the **Start Point** to **0, 232** and the **End Point** to **0, -232**. Set the **Points** to the number of strips (30). Click the **3D** checkbox. Turn off the **Play Frames**. Set the **Source Frame Offset** to **1.**

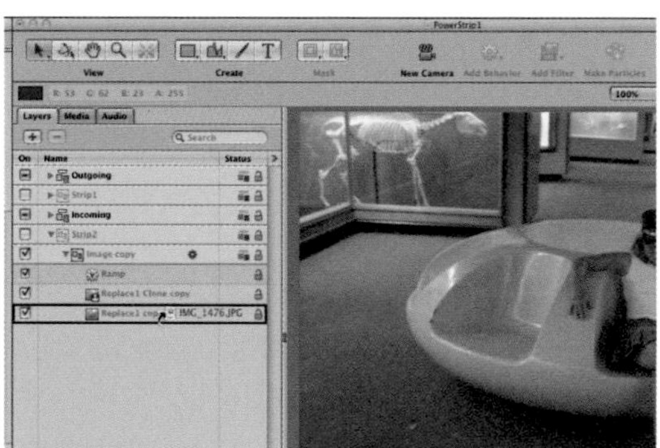

11 Expose **Strip2/Image Copy** and drag your incoming image over the **Replace1 Copy**. When the arrow is curved, let go. Rename **Replace1 Copy** to **Replace2**.

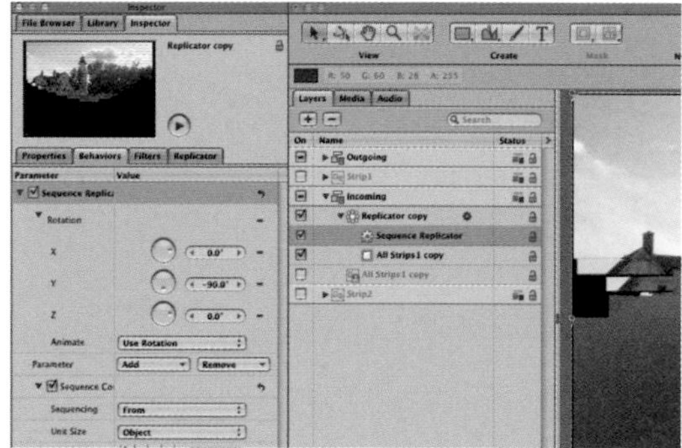

12 Select the **Incoming/Replicator Copy/Sequence Replicator** behavior. Change the **Y Rotation** value to **-90**. Change the **Sequencing** to **From**.

15 **Clone Layer** to the rescue! Position on frame 10. Click on the **Incoming** group. Press **K**. Move to frame 31. Press **I**. Perfect!

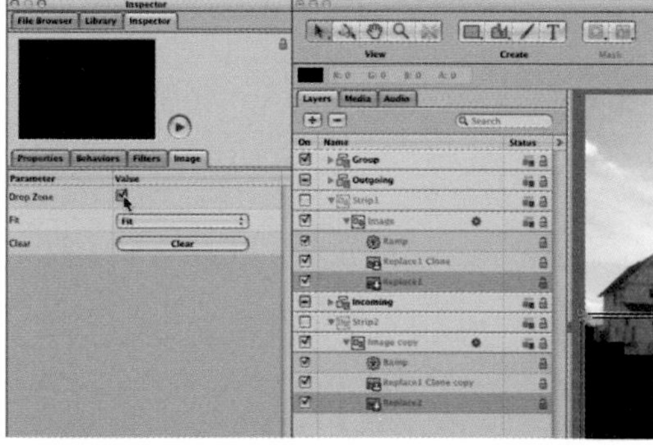

16 **⌘**-select **Replace1** and **Replace2**, and then click the **Drop Zone** checkbox. Save your project as PowerStrip1.

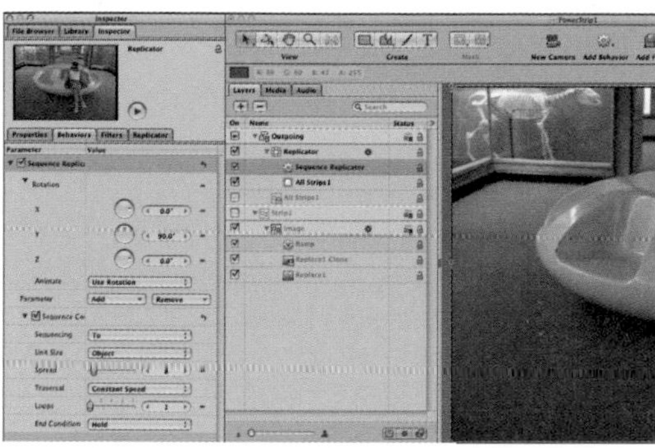

9 Select **Outgoing/Replicator**. Add **Behavior/Replicator/ Sequence Replicator**. Add **Parameter Rotation**. Set **Y** to **90** (leave **X** and **Z** alone). Set **Spread** to **8**.

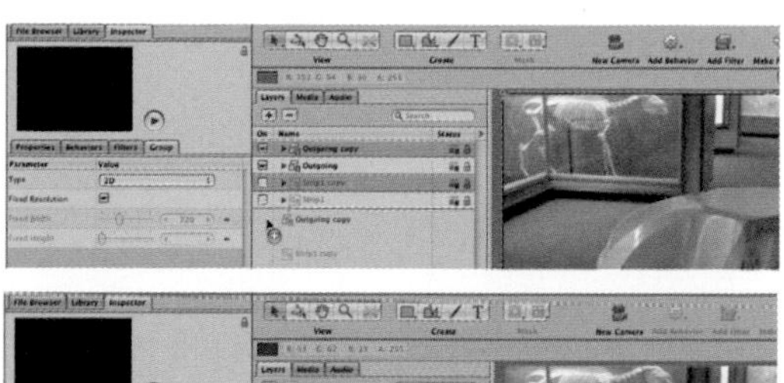

10 Now to add our incoming image. Select both the **Outgoing** and **Strip1** groups. Press ⌘D. While the copies are both still selected, drag them down and to the left until the pointer has a plus sign on it, and then let go. Rename **Outgoing Copy** to **Incoming** and **Strip1 Copy** to **Strip2**.

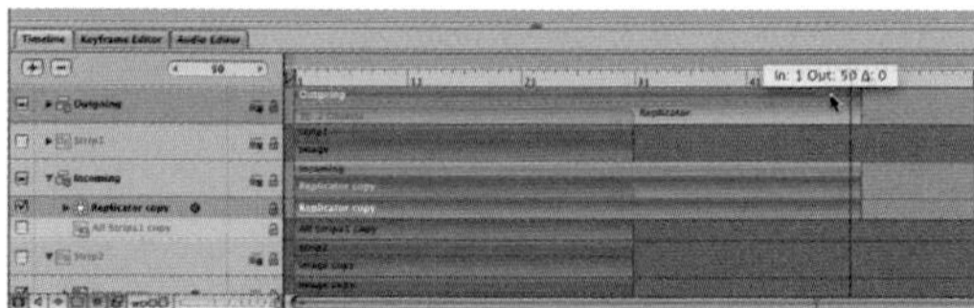

13 To fix the overlap, position to frame 50. Shift select the **Outgoing** and **Incoming** groups. Press O. Grab just the **Incoming** group in the timeline and slide it 10 frames to the right until it butts against the end of the project.

14 Now only one problem remains: The overlap between **Outgoing** and **Incoming** is good at the top, but as the rotation sequences to the bottom of the image, the **Outgoing** should be underneath the **Incoming.**

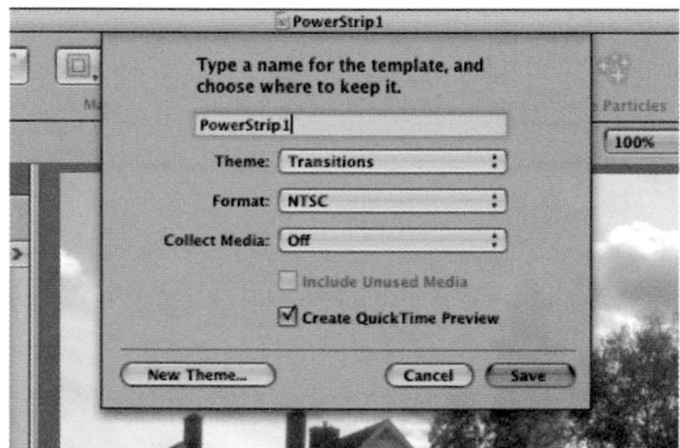

17 Then save it as a **Template** in **Theme Transitions.** Call it **PowerStrip1.** See Steps 17 and 18 of *Sweeping Changes* for how to use this transition in Final Cut Pro.

18 The ways this technique can be used are limited only by your imagination. Have fun!

HOT TIP

For this project to work properly, incoming and outgoing images should have the same dimensions.

Card Dance Basic

CARD DANCE IS A SOPHISTICATED plugin found in After Effects that can be used to achieve a number of elaborate and complicated effects. While Motion does not contain a the same ability, a variety of interesting effects can be achieved with this aproximation.

We're going to start with a basic project that will allow you to break an image into pieces, and we'll build on that basic project to create some elaborate effects.

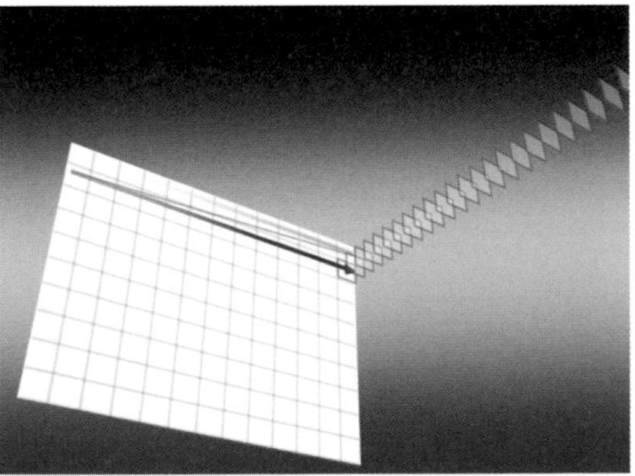

If you did the previous Power Strip project, you have some idea of what we'll be doing here. We're going to create a fixed resolution layer and slide our image past that window, one column at a time, and then move down one row and repeat.

We'll end up with a bunch of frames that are pieces of our image. We'll copy them into a clone layer that allows a replicator to see it as a movie and address individual frames.

The replicator lets us re-assemble our original image and some Random Motion behavior breaks them free. We'll save this project as CardBasic.

1 First, you need to decide how many pieces you want to break your image into. I chose 20 columns and 15 rows for a total of 300 pieces. To determine piece size, divide your project width by columns and height by rows. 720/20 = 36. 480/15 = 32. So our pieces will be 36x32—close to square.

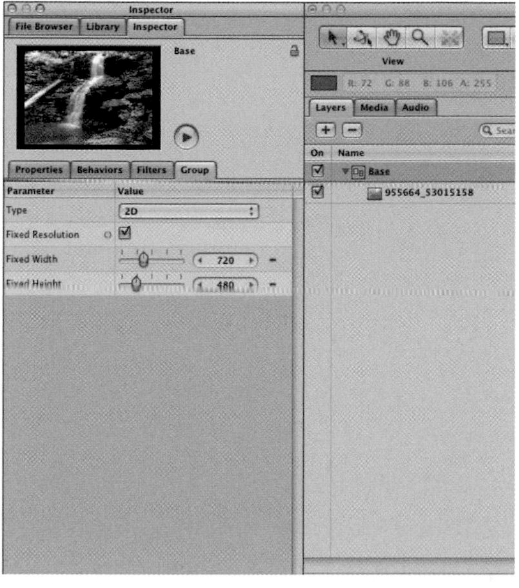

2 With that bit of math out of the way, time to create your project. It needs to be at least as long as the number of pieces you're going to have. In my case 300 frames. Name the default group **Base.** Set it to be fixed resolution 720x480. Add your image to the **Base** group.

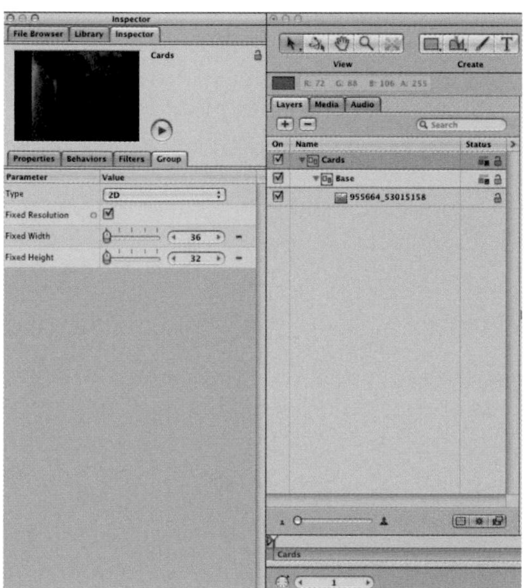

3 Select the **Base** group. Type ⌘ Shift G (or select **Menu/Object/Group**). Name the new enclosing group **Cards.** Set it to be fixed resolution and the size of our pieces we figured out in step 1 above—in this case, 36x32.

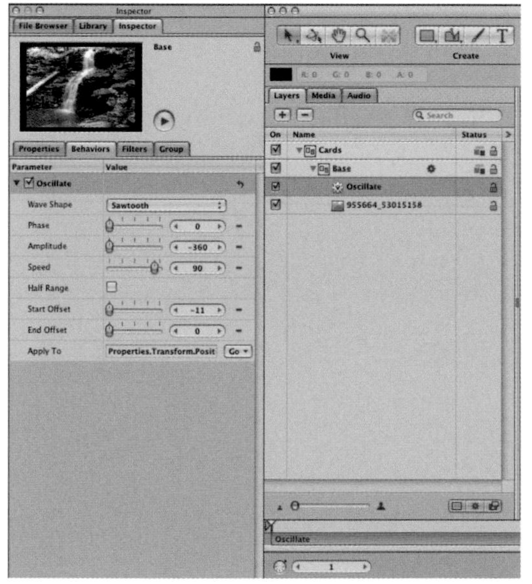

4 We will use the **Sawtooth Oscillator behavior** on the **X** Position to repeatedly scan our object left and right. Click on the **Base.** Right-click on the **X Position.** Select **Oscillate.** Change the **Wave Shape** to **Sawtooth, Amplitude** to **-360** (half our project width), and speed to **90.** Set offset to **-11.**

continued...

Card Dance Basic (continued)

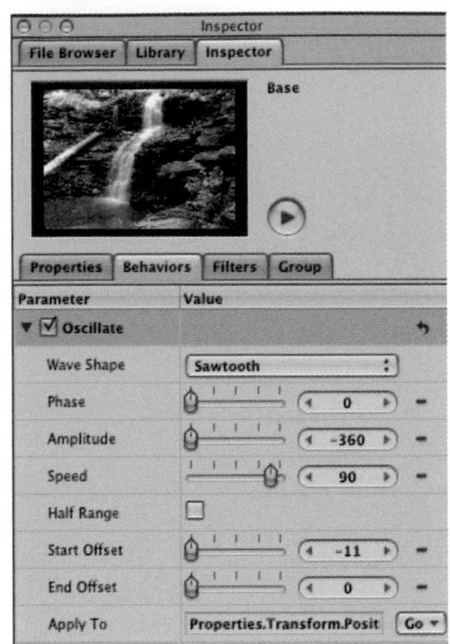

5 Now we need to move the **Base** so we can start the scan in the upper left-hand corner. The **Position** needs to be (project size - piece size) divided by 2. Or (720 - 36)/2 = 342 and negative (480 - 32)/2 = -224. Click on **Base** and set the **Position** to 342, -224.

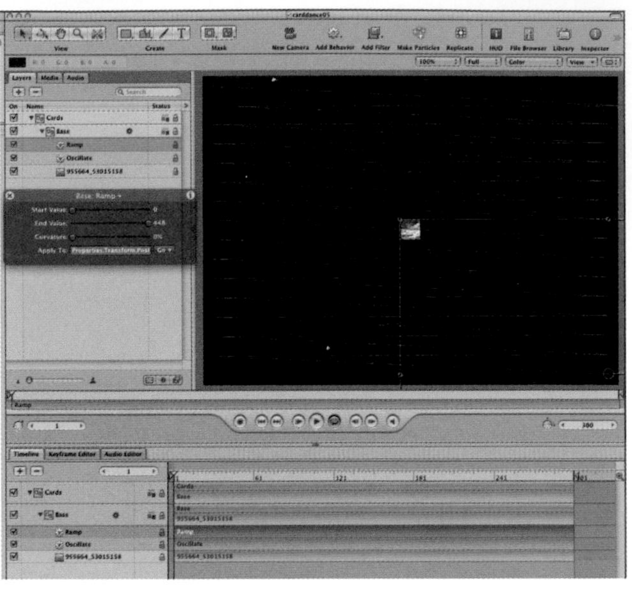

6 If you press **Play**, you'll see your image scan across every 20 frames. Now we need to move it up to grab rows. Select **Base.** Go back to frame 1. Right/ctrl-click on **Position Y.** Select **Ramp**. Set the **End** value to the height of the project or **480.**

8 Select the **Cards** group. While on frame 1, press K to create a clone layer. Name the new group **Assembly** and the clone layer **Cards Clone.** Select the **Cards** group again. Set the **Opacity** to **0.**

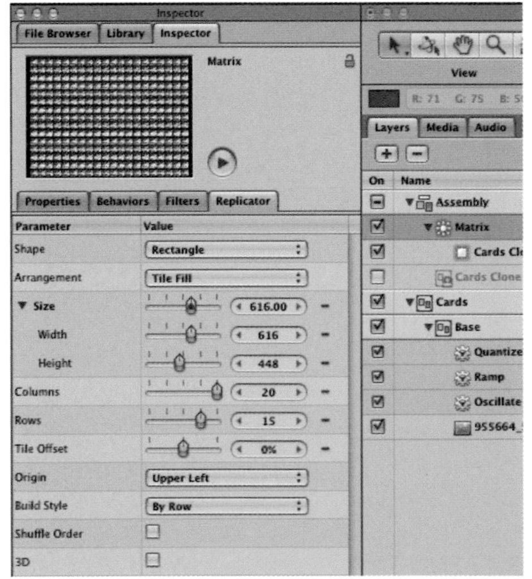

9 Click on the **Cards Clone** layer. Press L. Name the replicator **Matrix.** Set the **Size** to be **616x448.** Set the rows and columns to the dimensions you determined in Step 1 (20x15). **Set Origin to Upper Left** and **Build Style By Row.**

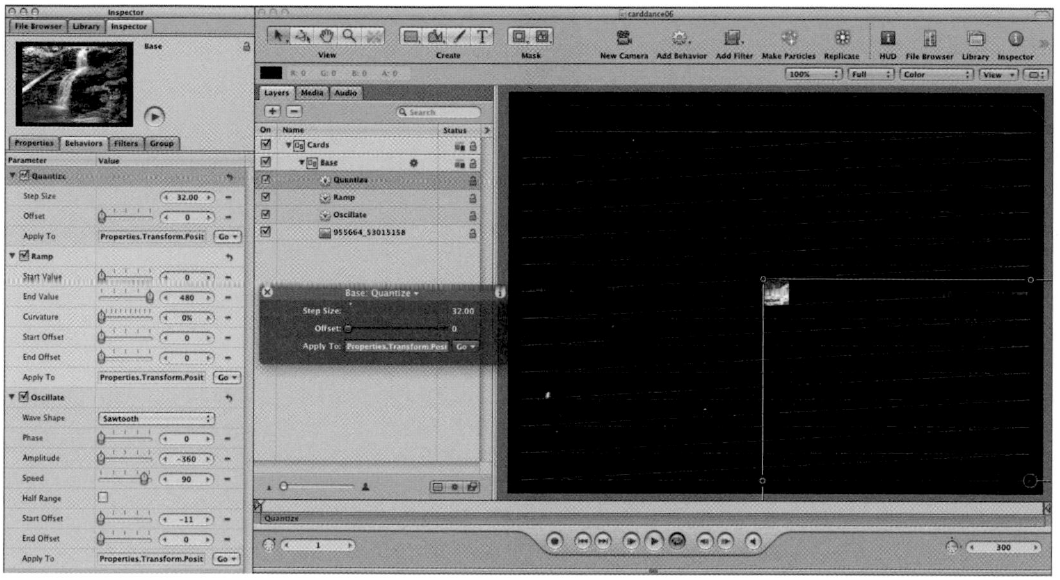

7 That works, but it's continuous. It is constantly moving down. We need it to hold still for each row. Select **Base**. Right/ctrl-click on **Position Y**. Select **Quantize**. Set the **Step Size** to the height of our pieces (32). There we go! Jumps down a row at a time.

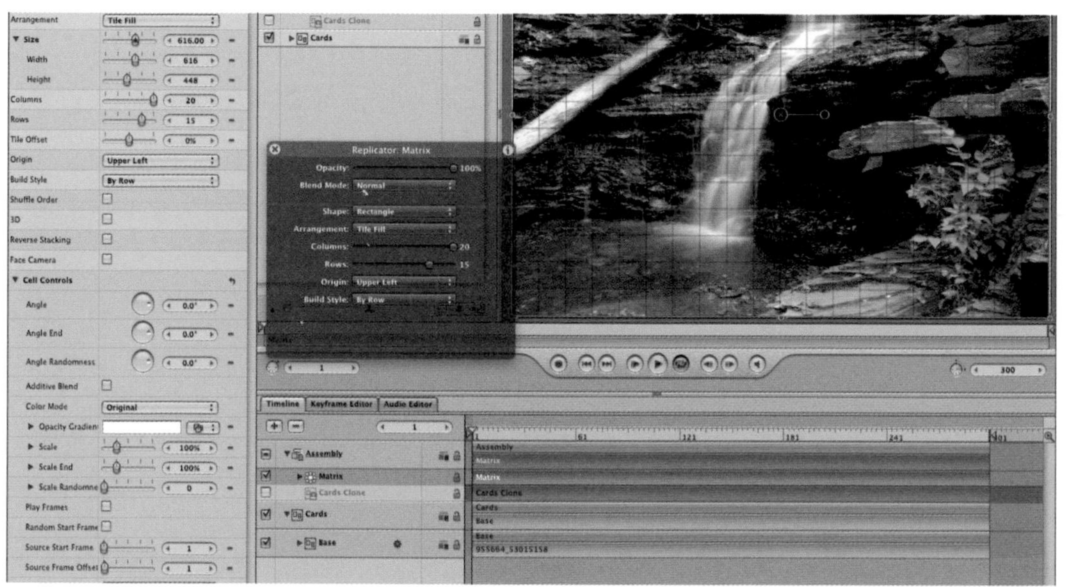

HOT TIP

Because of rounding errors, we lose the lower two right-hand pieces.

10 Turn off **Play Frames**. Set **Source Frame Offset** to **1**. BINGO! There's your image! Now save your project as **CardsBasic** and let's play.

2D Orbital

SPIRALING IN FROM A SEEMINGLY random sea of picture fragments the image assembles itself in an elegant and beautiful ballet.

We're still 2D here, so we get some very cool stuff without the overhead of moving into the 3D realm yet.

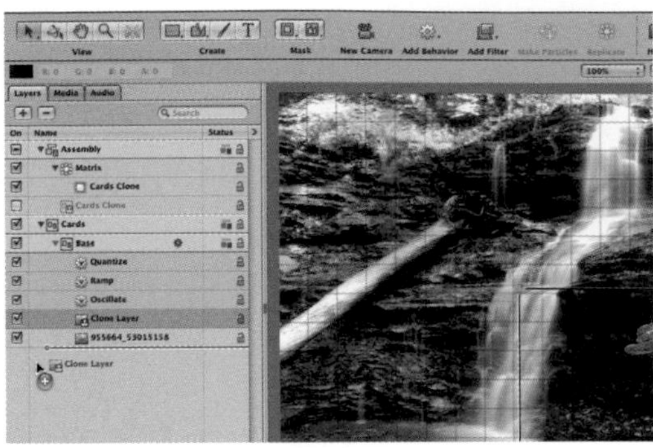

1 Start with the **CardBasic** project. You'll notice that you can see lines, so let's cover those over with a clone layer. While on frame 1, Open **Cards/Base** and select your image. Press **K** to create a clone layer. Now drag it to the bottom and left until you get the plus arrow, and let go.

4 While still on frame 15, click on the **Matrix** replicator. **Add Behavior/Simulations/Random Motion.** Press **I**. Click the **Affect Subobjects** checkbox. **Add Behavior/ Simulations/Orbit Around.** Press **I**. Click the **Affect Subobjects** checkbox. Set **Strength** to **96.** Set **Influence** to **1800.**

7 If you press **Play,** you'll see the image break up and orbit our invisible rectangle, but they stay oriented toward the top. Click on the **Matrix** replicator. **Add Behavior/ Simulations/Align to Motion.** Click the **Affect Subobjects** checkbox. That looks better!

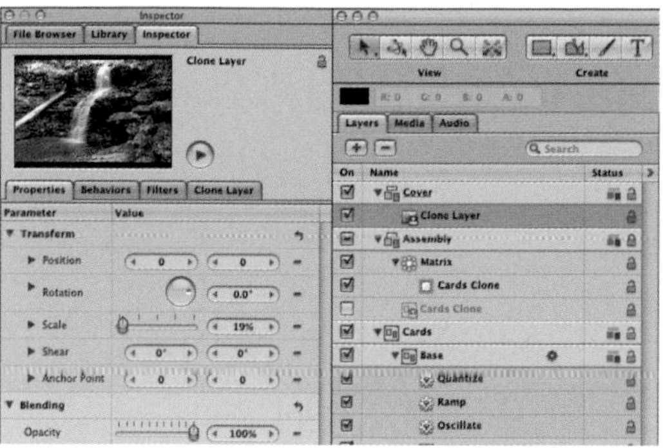

2 Name the new group **Cover**. Move it to the top of your layers. Click on the **Clone Layer**. Under the **Properties** tab, set the **Position** to **0,0.**

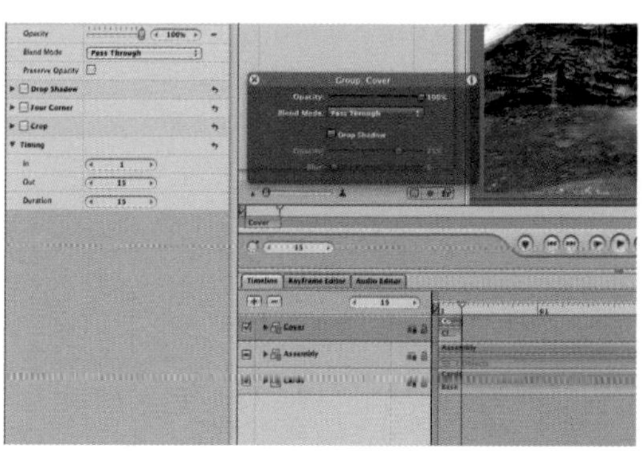

3 Select the **Cover** group. Position to frame 15. Press O to truncate the group there.

5 Press R, and then draw a small rectangle in the center of the screen. Set its **Opacity** to **0.**

6 Select the **Orbit Around** behavior. Drag the rectangle into the **Object** well.

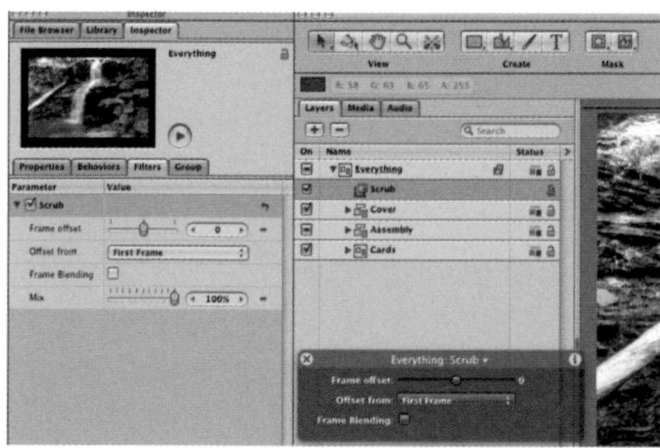

8 To make this more interesting, let's run it backward. Select all three groups (**Cover, Assembly,** and **Cards**). Press ⌘ Shift G. Call the new group **Everything. Add Filter/Time/Scrub.** Change the **Offset** to **First Frame.** Turn off **Frame Blending.**

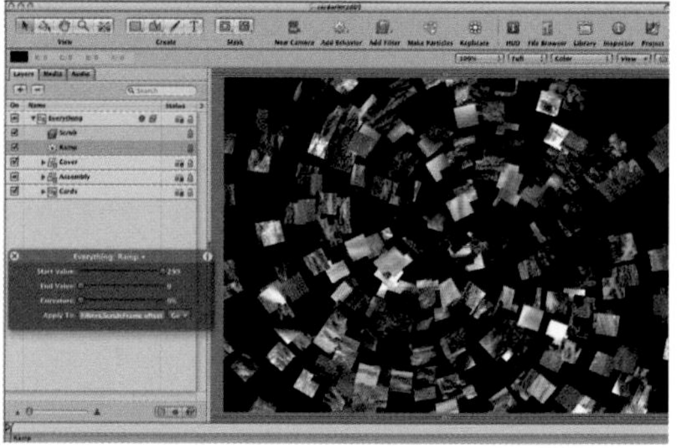

9 Right/ctrl-click on the **Frame Offset** and select **Ramp.** Set **Start Value** to **299.** Voilà! Instant reverse.

3D Card Dance Dazzle

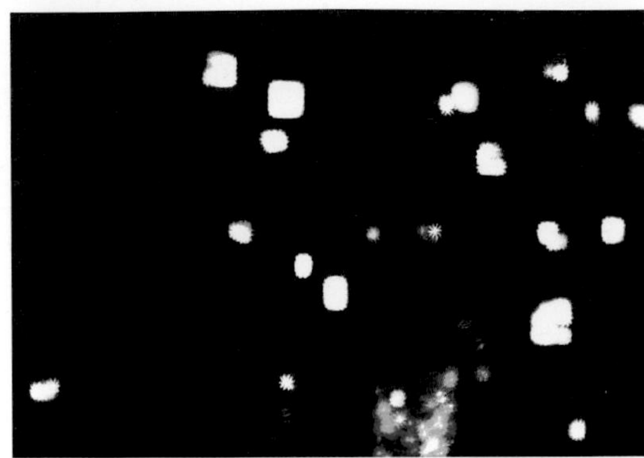

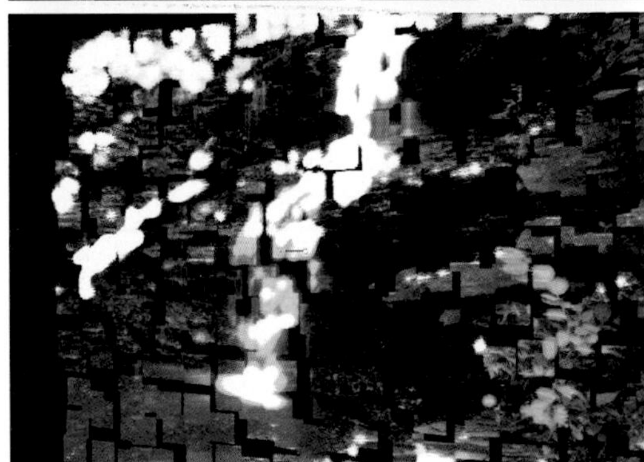

AT FIRST WE SEEM TO BE TRAVELING through a chaotic galaxy of variegated stars. Gradually their paths converge and surprisingly assemble into a complete image.

Now we've gone full 3D—there's overhead associated with it, but it's worth it.

1 Start with the **CardBasic** project. You'll notice that you can see lines. Let's cover those over with a clone layer. While on frame 1, open **Cards/Base** and select your image. Press K to create a clone layer. Now drag it to the bottom and left until you get the plus arrow, and then release it.

4 While still on frame 30, click on the **Matrix** replicator. **Add Behavior/Simulations/Random Motion**. Press I. Click the **Affect Subobjects** checkbox. Set the **Amount** to **1024** and **Noisiness** to **1.0.** Include **X, Y, Z.** Set **Position** to frame 60. Press O.

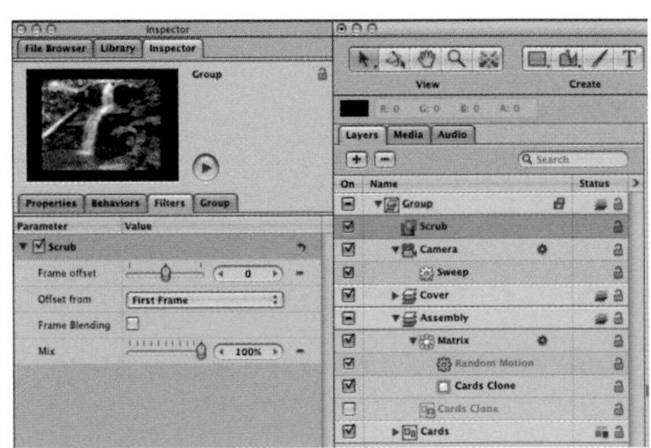

7 Select **Camera**, **Cover**, **Assembly**, and **Cards**. Press ⌘ Shift G to group them. Then **Add Filter/Time/Scrub**. Change **Offset from** to **First Frame**. Turn off **Frame Blending**.

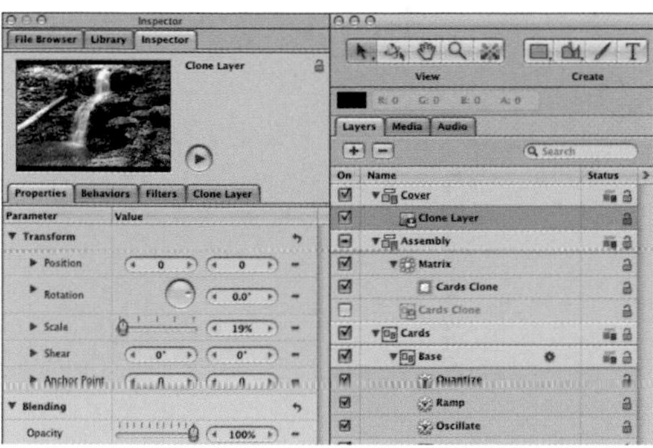

2 Name the new group **Cover**. Move it to the top of your layers. Click on the **Clone Layer**. Under the **Properties** tab, set the **Position** to **0,0**.

3 Select the **Cover** group. Position to frame 30. Press **O** to truncate the group there.

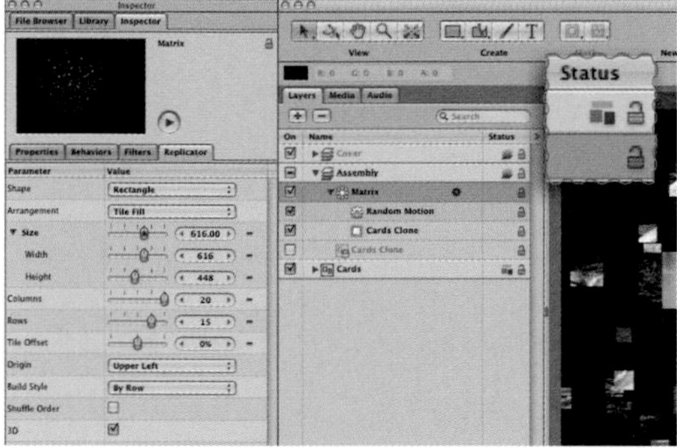

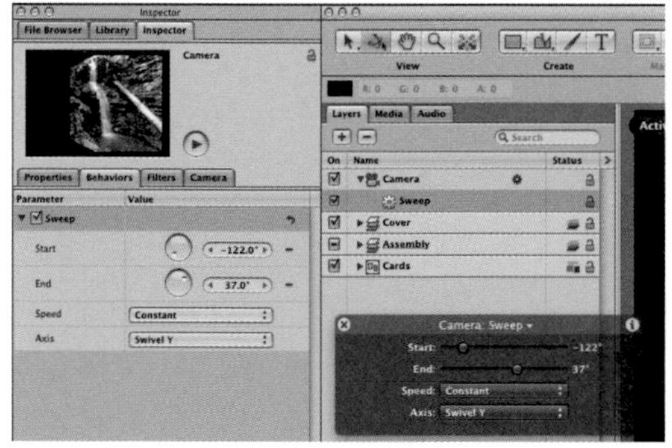

5 Now it's time to jump to 3D. Click on your **Matrix** replicator. Set the **3D** checkbox. Change the **Assembly** group and the **Cover** group to 3D. Note inset.

6 Position to frame 1. Click the **New Camera** button in the toolbar. **Add Behavior/Camera/Sweep**. Set the **Start** to -122 and the **End** to **37**.

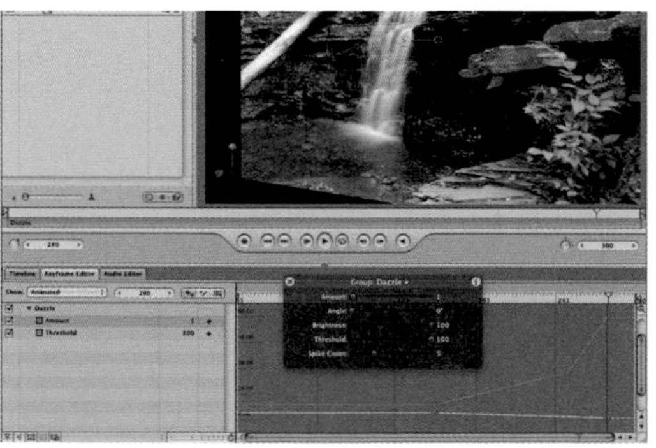

8 Press **A**, or the red **Record** button to the left of the transport controls. Set **Frame offset** to the duration of your project **(300)**. Position to the end of your project. Set **Frame offset** to **0**. Press **A** again to turn off **Record**.

9 Go back to frame 1. **Add Filter/Glow/Dazzle**. Set your **Spike Count** to **5**. Press **A** to begin recording. Set **Amount** to 4, **Threshold** to **15**. Go to frame 150. Set **Amount** to **4** and **Threshold** to **14**. On frame 250, set **Threshold** to **46**. On frame 280, set **Amount** to **1**. Set **Threshold** to **100**. Press **A** to stop recording.

How to make Motion faster

I LOVE THE REAL-TIME ASPECTS OF Motion. It really fosters a "play with it" approach and the ability to find interesting effects by simply trying new things. However unique its real-time capabilities are, it's easy to bog Motion down, if you're not paying attention. Here are some tips to keep Motion running as fast as possible.

There are two areas of performance I'd like to address. One is overall playback performance–that is, how to keep up your playback frame rate. And the other I like to call "Interactive" performance. That's how responsive Motion is as you work with it. First the overall performance.

In the online forums, I often hear the complaint that Motion is not taking advantage of a user's multiple CPUs. That's because Motion is almost entirely dependent on the GPU–that's GPU, not CPU. In other words, it relies on the Graphics Processing Unit–i.e., your graphics card. The CPU plays a role, calculating speed changes, particle positions, etc. But all of the heavy lifting is done by your graphics card.

Therefore, get the fastest one you can afford. But, at least at the present time, do not buy multiple cards. That doesn't spread the work; it just confuses Motion. And unless you're into the modding scene and are prepared to flash a PC card with Mac firmware, make sure you purchase a Mac-compatible card (if that sentence sounded like gobbledygook to you, you are NOT into the modding scene).

Next, RAM RAM RAM! Motion, because of its real-time architecture loads EVERYTHING into memory. Unlike Final Cut Pro, it doesn't stream from disk. All of your project is loaded into memory so it can flow to the graphics card as fast as possible. If you don't have enough physical RAM to hold your project, it'll be paged out to the virtual memory, which means it ends up on your hard disk and must be brought in piecemeal.

The corollary to this is keep your projects as short as you can. Don't load in more than 30 seconds if you can help it. If each standard definition frame takes up about a megabyte, 1 second is roughly 30 MB. Multiply that by 30 seconds and you're already getting close to a gigabyte of RAM, just for one video stream. Quadruple that for a 1080P HD stream and you can see how your performance would drop if your project is too long. If you do have a longer project, try limiting your play range to smaller sections as you work.

Often it's recommended to stick to one monitor, but I did some testing and I found little advantage to this. Yes, it splits your graphics card's video RAM, but with modern graphics cards sporting half a gig or more of VRAM, this is becoming less of a factor. For me, the increased productivity of two screens of work area more than outweighs any performance gain that might be had.

Get a modern Mac. Since everything must go into and out of the graphics card, the PCIe bus has much more bandwidth than the AGP graphics interface found in older G4/G5 PowerMacs (and Motion 4 doesn't run on PPC).

That's it for the brute force playback tips. Now to address things you can do to make Motion more responsive–something I like to call "Avoiding the spinning beachball."

Turn off thumbnail previews in both the timeline (setting in Preferences), and in the Layers palette (popup up menu in the corner of the Layers palette). Why, you might ask, would those little images slow Motion down? The answer is simple. Motion must build and scale each of those images individually each time you pause since they reflect the frame you're parked on. If one of your layers has hundreds of particles, it must be imaged *for that layer alone* and then resized for the thumbnail. If you have a lot of layers, it can really add up.

Thumbnails alone can cause a LONG wait as each layer is imaged, sized, and placed in the thumbnail every time you stop playback.

Similarly, don't have any layers selected when you begin playback. Motion will have to create a thumbnail for that layer in the Inspector pane when you pause playback. Also, with no layer selected, Motion won't have to draw outlines during playback.

If you're using RAM preview, clear it periodically. Motion hangs onto RAM previews for as long as it can, because an undo or parameter change can make it valid again and it won't need to re-render. This is very handy, but can start to clog up your system with RAM previews stacked up in memory.

Don't turn on motion blur while you build a project. Because motion blur is built by fading together several frames, each frame gets imaged multiple times, dramatically increasing render times.

Text is especially draining of resources in Motion 3. This is likely because Motion keeps it as a vector shape and must often rasterize each character on a frame-by-frame basis. Because of this, try to keep your Render Quality set to Normal or Draft. Just turn on High Quality render to visualize an individual frame or when exporting. Motion 4 is *considerably* faster in dealing with text and sports other render speedups as well.

Turn off layers you've finished building them to improve performance while you work in other areas. Or "bake" them by exporting that layer and bringing the Quicktime back into Motion to serve as a "precomp" of that layer. Export a Layer or Group by using Export Selection. In the Export dialog under the After Export pop-up menu, you have the option to automatically bring the exported Quicktime movie back into the project. Once you've done that, turn off the original group or layer. If you need to make changes later, remove the "precomp" Quicktime and re-export it the same way.

Keep your particle count to a minimum and, perhaps more important, keep particle life to a minimum. Adjust the life so that a particle will "die" after it's left the screen; otherwise; you're just imaging offscreen particles that contribute to the overhead but are never seen again. Fixed resolution can help with this–it can keep Motion from imaging particles once they've left the screen. Motion may still remember them, but it won't spend time rendering them.

Finally, if you're just playing around, keep the complexity down–smaller replicators, lower particle count, fewer blurs, etc.–once you figure out what you want to achieve, then you can up the complexity to suit your idea.

Putting water in a shower, birds in the sky, or rain in the air is an easy job for Motion.

6 Reality Enhancement

SIMPLY ADDING SMOKE TO A BATTLE scene can greatly improve the realism of the action. In this chapter, we'll use some of Motion's capabilities to add believable facsimilies of natural phenomena to still and moving images.

Wet Wet Wet

IN THIS PROJECT, WE'LL SIMULATE water running over an object. This can be used on a photo, as in this example, or over type, etc.

We'll use the indent filter to create a wet or "shrink-wrapped" version of our image, and then we'll use a modified Noise generator to make it seem to flow over our base image.

A note on the photo: Dr. Tiki and the gang at Tiki Bar TV played an elaborate and effective rickroll on the Tiki Bar TV cognoscenti by first seeding this photo around the Internet. Many thanks to LaLa for allowing its use here. (If that seems like gibberish to you, consult your favorite jargon translator, or ignore it—the project will still work) .

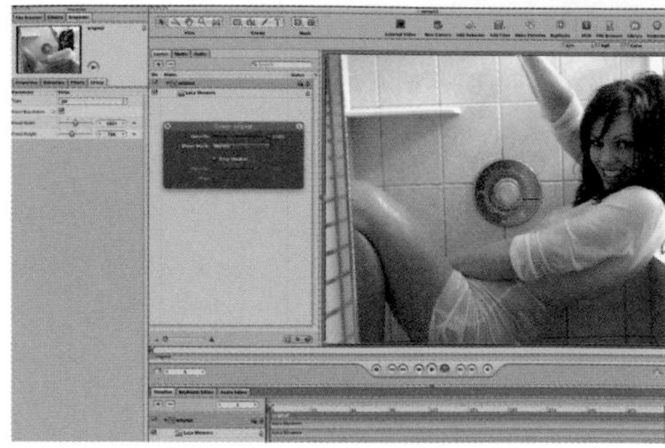

1 Start with a new project. Name the default **Group original**. Set it to **Fixed Resolution.** Place your image there.

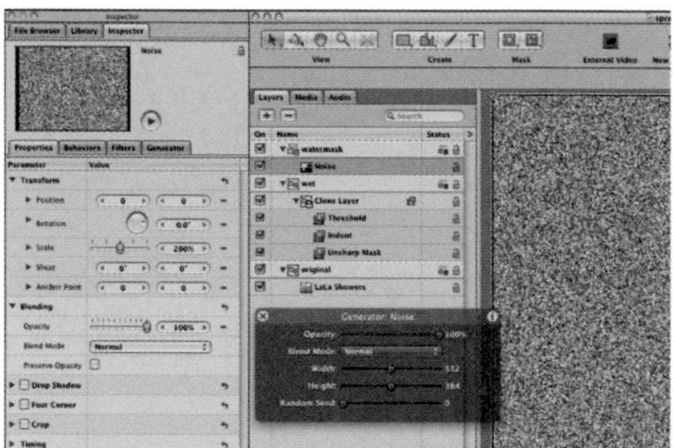

4 Add a new group on top of everything else. Call it **watermask**. Add a **Noise Generator** from the **Library** to it. We want it to be coarser than single pixels, so set the **Width** and **Height** to be half of that of your project. Then scale it to **200%**.

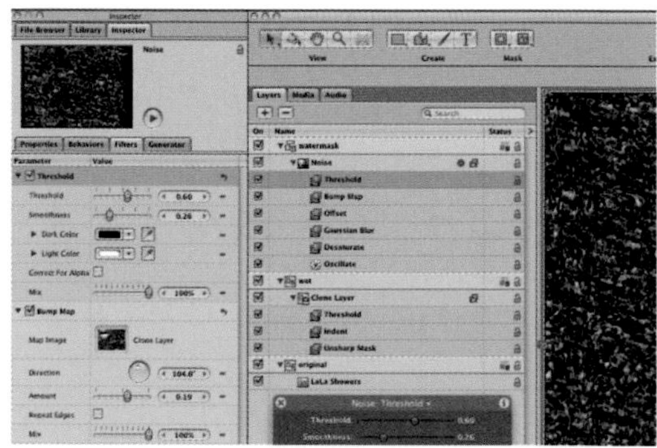

7 Add **Filter/Distortion/Bump Map**. Set **Direction** to **104°**. Set **Amount** to **0.19**. Drag the **Clone Layer** into the **Map Image** well. **Add Filter/Color Correction Threshold**. Set **Amount** to about **.6** and **Smoothness** to **.26**.

IMAGE COURTESY LARA DOUCETTE

2 With the **original** group selected, press **K** to create a clone layer. Name the new group **wet**. Set its **Blend Mode** to **Add**. Set **Opacity** to **68%**. Select the **Clone Layer**. **Add Filter/Sharpen/Unsharp Mask.**

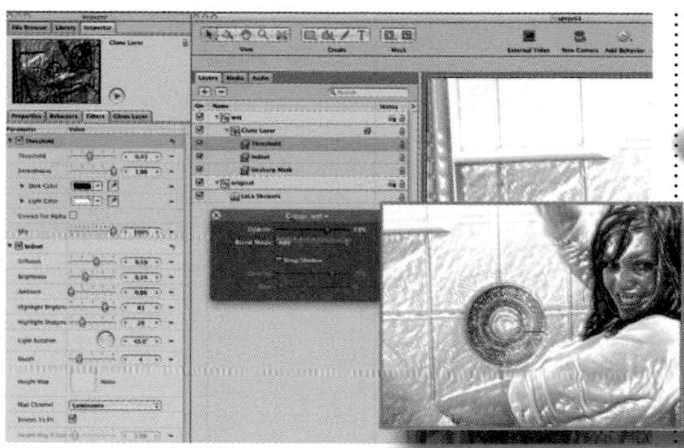

3 **Add Filter/Stylize/Indent.** Set **Softness** to **.59**, **Brightness** to **.34**, **Ambient** to **0**, **Highlight Brightness** to **81**, and **Highlight Sharpness** to **28**. **Add Filter/Color Correction/ Threshold.** Set **Threshold** to **.43** and **Smoothness** to **1.0**.

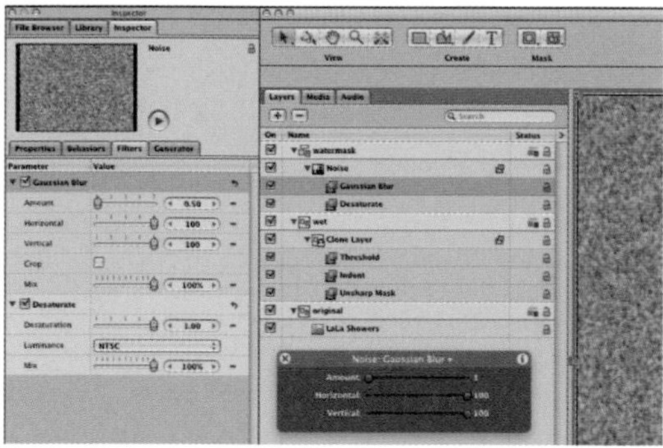

5 With the **Noise** generator selected, **Add Filter/Color Correction/Desaturate. Add Filter/Blur/Gaussian Blur.** Set **Amount** to **.5**.

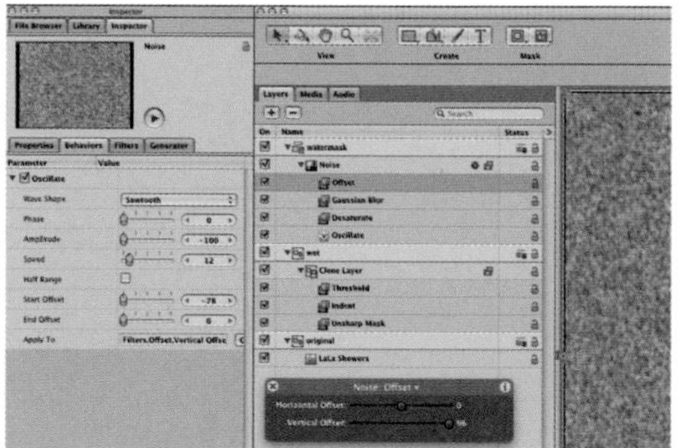

6 **Add Filter/Tiling/Offset.** Right/**ctrl**-click on **Vertical Offset**. Select **Oscillate**. Set the **Wave Shape** to **Sawtooth**, the **Amplitude** to **-100**, the **Speed** to **12**, and the **Start Offset** to **-78**.

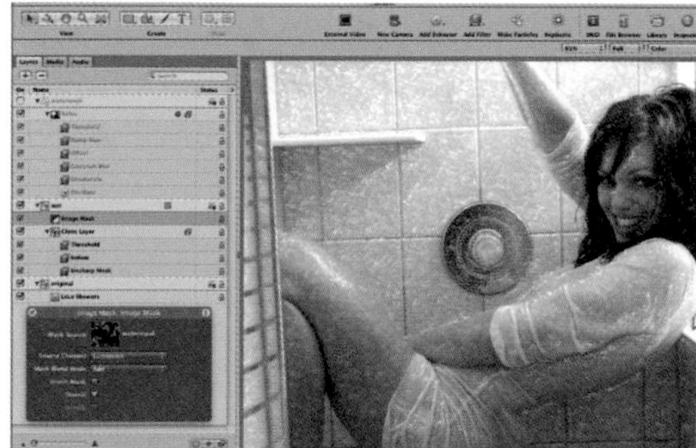

8 Select **wet**. Type **⌘ Shift M** to add an **Image Mask** to it. Set the **Source Channel** to **Luminance**. Drag the **watermask** group into the **Image Mask**'s image well.

9 Note most of these values may have to be altered to suit your image and needs.

Rainy Day Activity

RAIN IS A DIFFICULT thing to light and photograph. But it's a pretty easy effect to add to any still or moving video. This is one of the cases where "We'll fix it in post" can make a lot of sense.

1 Start with a new project. We're going to make this a template, so as a place holder, we'll add **Library/Content/Template Media/Seasons/Fall Background.mov** as a place holder. Go to the **Image** tab under **Inspector** and select the **Drop Zone** checkbox. Then name the drop zone **Background**.

4 Add **Filter/Color Correction/Threshold**. Set the **Threshold** value to **0.90** and the **Smoothness** to **0.00**. Add **Filter/Blur/Directional Blur**. Set the **Amount** to **6** and the **Angle** to **260**.

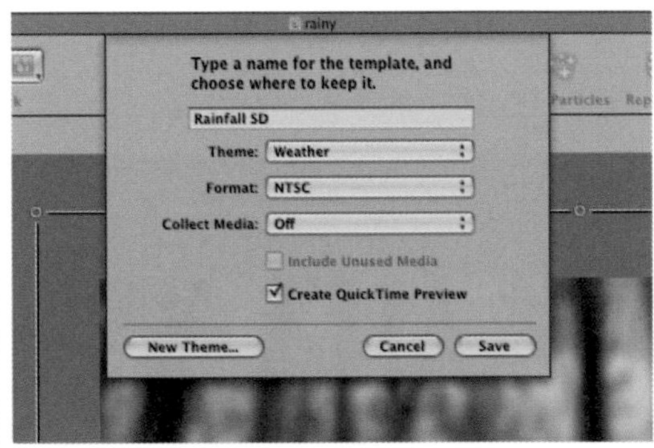

7 Save as a template. Let's call it **Rainfall SD** and put it in a New Theme—call it **Weather**.

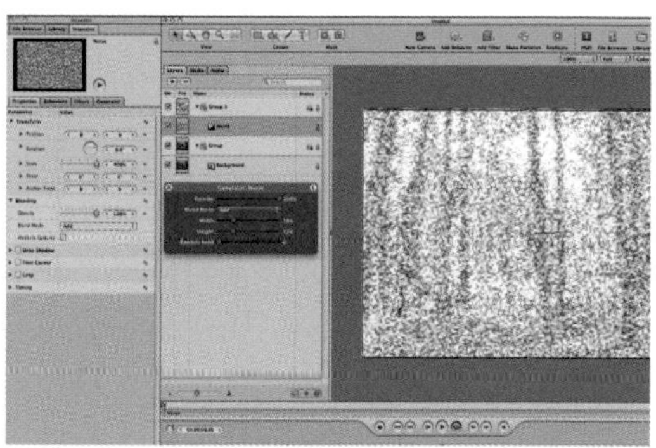

2 Use the **+** sign under the **Layers** tab to add a new group. Arrange it to be above the default **Group**. Grab **Library/ Generators/Noise** and put that into our new group, and then set the size to **180x120**. This is because we're going to want our rain to be larger than a single pixel.

3 Switch to the **Properties** tab of the **Noise** generator and set the **Scale** to **400%**. Set the **Blend Mode** to **Add**.

5 Now animate it. Right/ctrl-click on the **Angle** under **Directional Blur**. **Add Behavior/Wriggle**. Set the **Amount** to **2.00** and the **Apply Mode** to **Add and Subtract**.

6 Select the **Generator** tab, and then Right/ctrl-click on **Random Seed** and select **Randomize**. Press **Play** and watch the rain come down.

8 To access the template within Final Cut Pro, click on the generators dropdown in the viewer.

9 Then use the drop zone to put your clips out in the rain.

Flock of Birds

SOMETIMES ALL YOU HAVE OF A LOCATION IS a still. Adding some natural movement to it can really bring it to life.

This project is a bit complicated, but as my dad used to say, complexity is merely simplicity put together. First we'll construct a mock bird shape and animate it using oscillators. Then we'll build it into a flock using a particle emitter and send it across the screen. We'll be taking advantage of the distance to minimize the details.

IMAGE COURTESY MIKE MUNCHEL

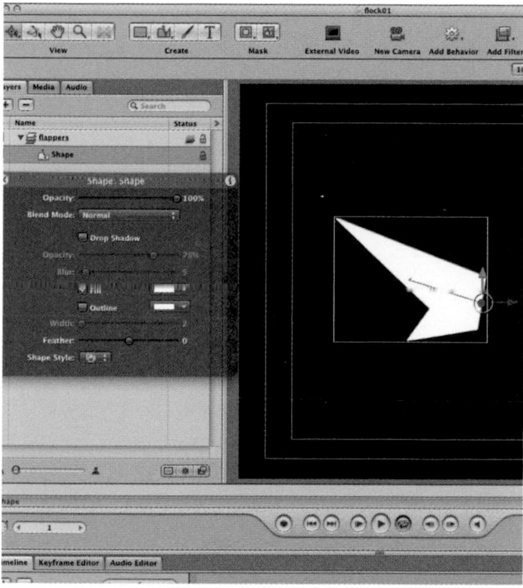

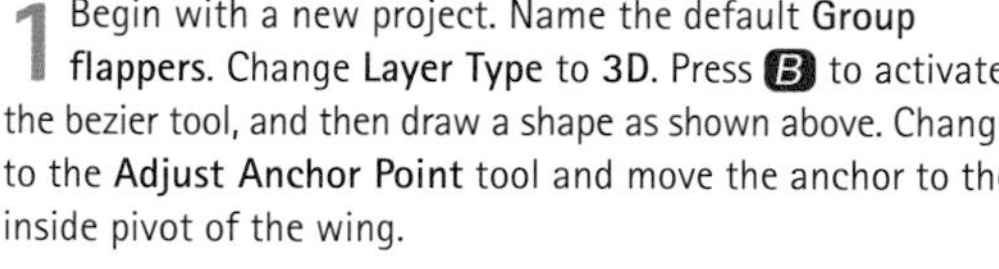

1 Begin with a new project. Name the default **Group flappers**. Change **Layer Type** to **3D**. Press **B** to activate the bezier tool, and then draw a shape as shown above. Change to the **Adjust Anchor Point** tool and move the anchor to the inside pivot of the wing.

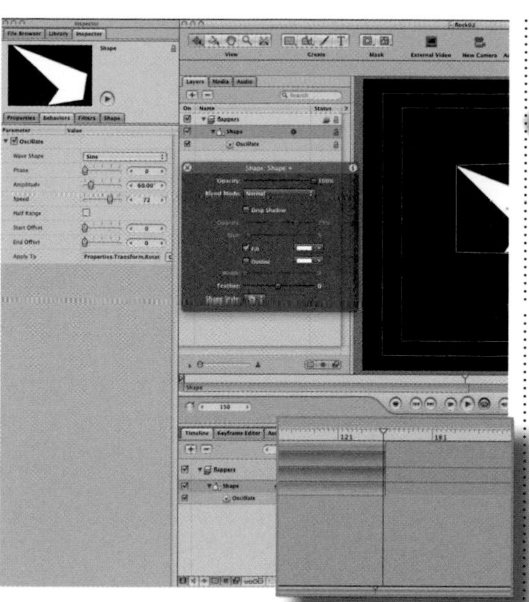

2 In the **Properties** tab, ensure the **Position** is **0,0**. Right/**ctrl**-click on the **Y Rotation**. Select **Oscillate**. Set the **Amplitude** to **60°**, the **Speed** to **72**. Go to frame 150. With **Shape** selected, press **O** to truncate it there.

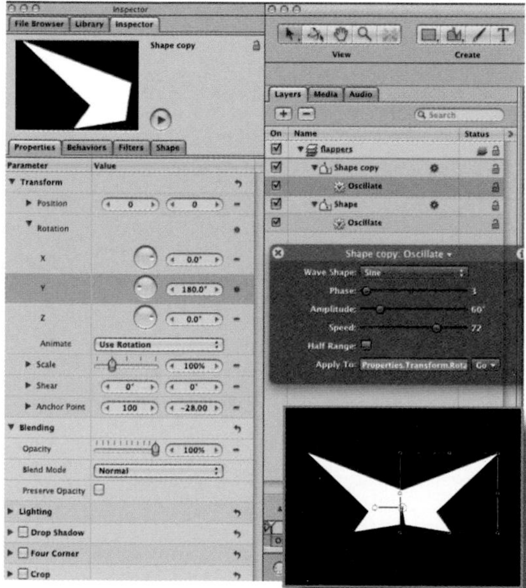

3 Go back to frame 1. Press **⌘D** to duplicate the **Shape.** In the **Properties** tab, change the **Y Rotation** to **180°**. Select **Oscillate**. Change the **Phase** to **3**.

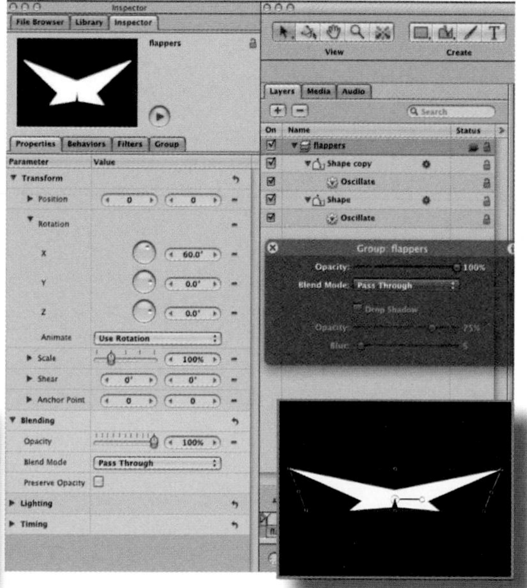

4 Select **flappers**. In the **Properties** tab, change the **X Rotation** to **60°**. Now you've got your basic bird.

continued...

Flock of Birds (continued)

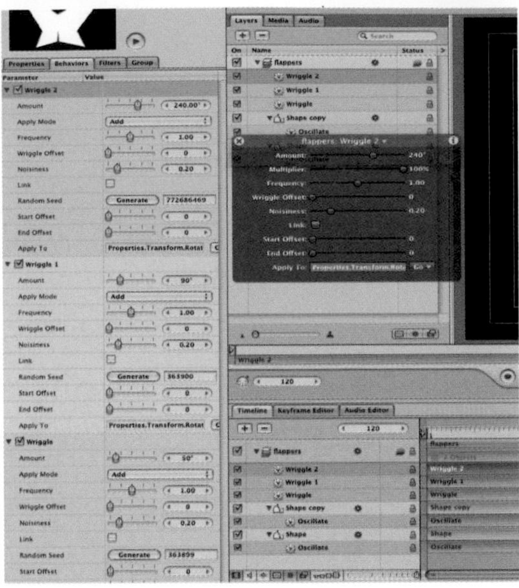

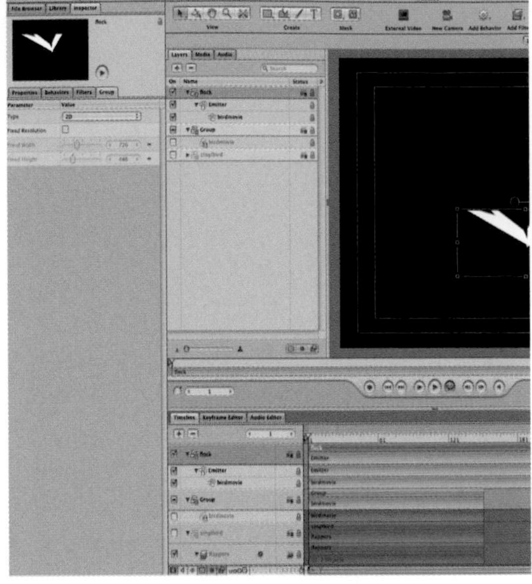

5 Right/ctrl-click on **X Rotation**. Select **Wriggle**. Change the **Amount** to **50°**. Change the **Noisiness** to **.2**. Back in the **Properties** tab, right/ctrl-click on **Y Rotation**. Select **Wriggle**. Set **Amount** to **90°** and **Noisiness** to **.2**. Do that once more for **Z**, but set **Amount 240°** and **Noisiness** to **2**.

6 With **flappers** selected, press ⌘Shift G. name the new group **singlebird**. Change it to **2D**. Press K. Name the clone layer **birdmovie**. Turn off **singlebird**. Select **birdmovie**. Press E, or click the **Make Particles** button in the toolbar. Move the **Emitter** to a new group. Call the new group **flock**.

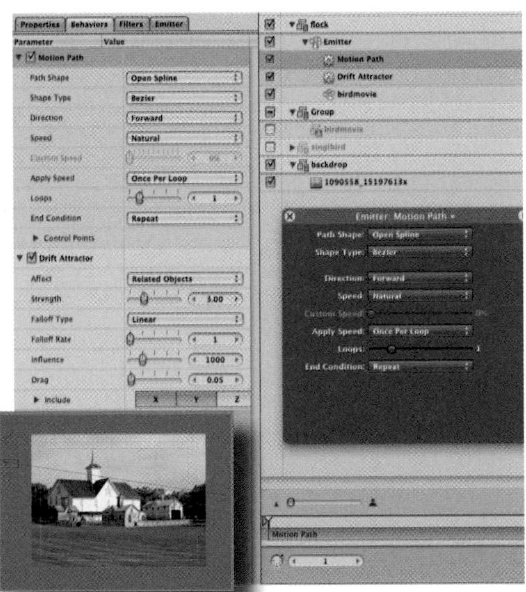

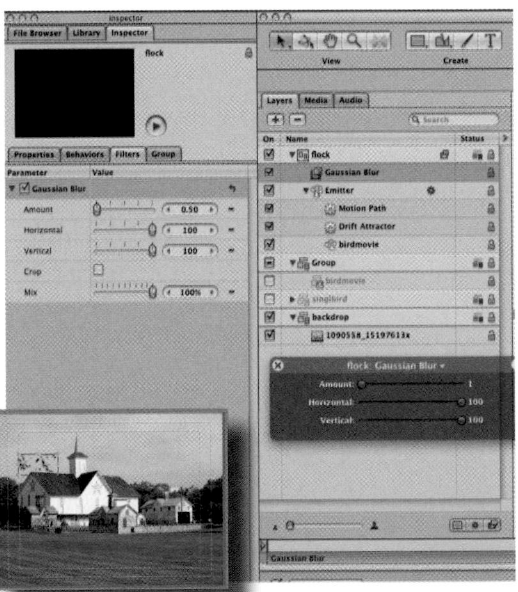

9 Add **Behavior/Simulations/Drift Attractor**. Change **Drag** to **0.05**. Add **Behavior/Basic Motion/Motion Path**. Set the **Speed** to **Natural**. Set the beginning point and ending point as appropriate for your image.

10 They're going to look a little sharp for their distance, so with **flock** selected, **Add Filter/Blur/Gaussian Blur**. Set **Amount** to **0.5** or **0.25**.

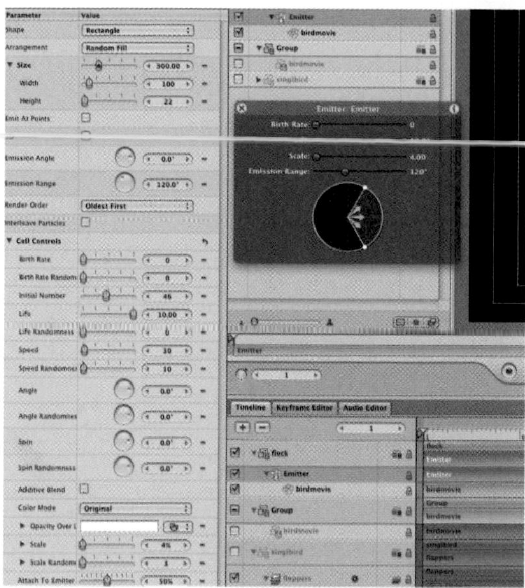

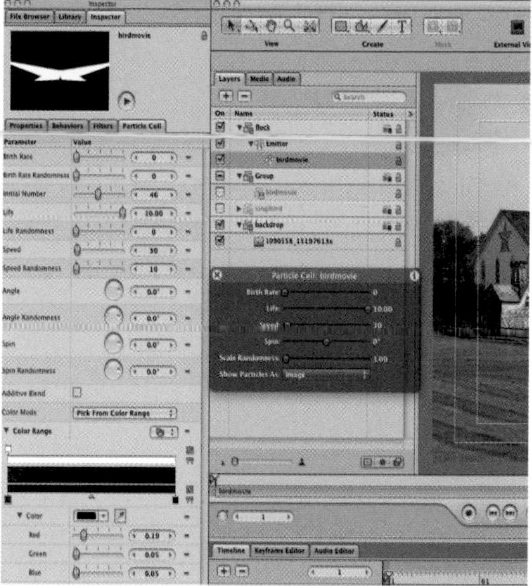

7 Set **Shape** to **Rectangle**, **Arrangement** to **Random Fill**, **Width** to **100**, **Height** to **22**, **Emission Range** to **120**, **Birth Rate** to **0**, **Initial Number** to **46**, **Life** to **10**, **Speed** to **30**, and **Speed Randomness** to **10**. **Scale** will depend somewhat on your initial size. I set mine to **4%**. Set **Scale Randomness** to **3** and **Attach to Emitter** to **50%**.

8 Create a new group named **backdrop**. Place it at the bottom of your stack. Put your still/clip there. Select **Emitter**. Change the **Color Mode** to **Pick From Color Range**. Set your **Color Range** gradient to a dark gray to a really dark gray, or make it a dark brown gradient.

11 You can put a little zoom on your new comp by selecting all the groups and pressing ⌘ Shift G. Name the new group **comp**. Add **Behavior/Basic Motion/Grow Shrink**. Adjust to taste.

Transient Display Glitch

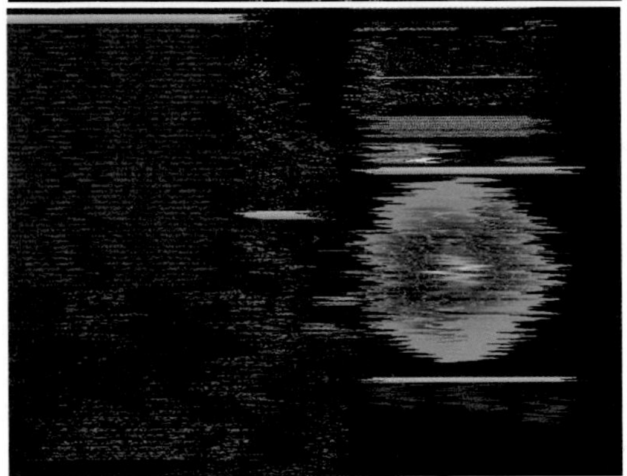

WE'VE ALL SEEN IT IN Hollywood movies. The evil sentient virus takes over your computer and the first sign is a transient glitch in the video display (usually accompanied by an appropriate ominous sound effect).

This is easy to produce in Motion (see a variation on this as a Glitch Transition in the Transitions chapter). We'll generate some grainy noise and use the stripes filter to turn it into horizontal lines that we'll use to drive a Displace filter. One interesting thing about this project is we'll use a Wriggle behavior to vary the amount of displacement, modulated with the Quantize behavior, so we only get the spikes.

1 Start with a new project. I'm using **Presentation Large** because I'm using a mock computer screen movie (you can find it on the disc). Rename the default group as **noisemaker**. In **Library/Generators**, select **Noise**, and press **Apply.**

3 Turn off **noisemaker**. Add a new group above **noisemaker**. Name it **image**. Drag your clip/image into the **image** group. **Add Filter/Distortion/Displace**. Drag the **noisemaker** group into the **Map Image** well. Set **Horizontal** and **Vertical Scale** to 0.

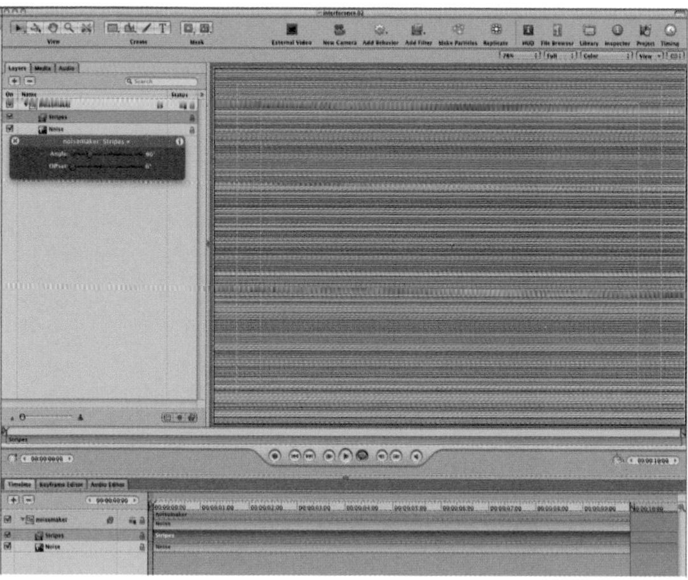

2 Select **noisemaker**. Add **Filter/Distortion/Stripes**. Change **Angle** to **90°**.

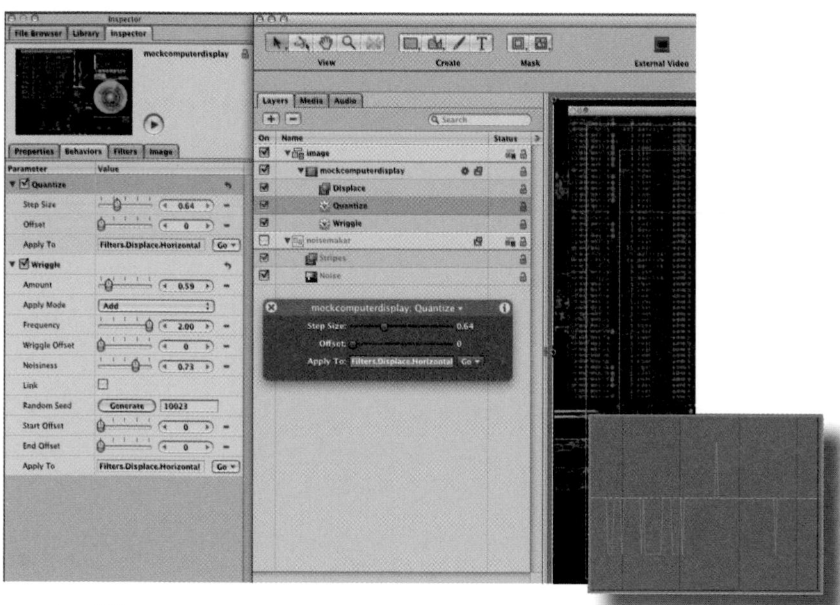

4 Right/ctrl-click on **Horizontal Scale**. Select **Wriggle**. Set the **Amount** to **0.59**, **Frequency** to **2.00**, and **Noisiness** to **0.73**. Back in the **Filters** tab, right/ctrl-click on **Horizontal Scale** and select **Quantize**. Set **Step Size** to **0.64**.

HOT TIP

You can make the interference lines thicker by pulling the same trick that we used in the Rainy Day Activity project: make the generator smaller and resize.

6 INTERLUDE

Getting work

WITH MOTION GRAPHICS, LIKE ANY CREATIVE field, you are hired based on your reputation. The client needs to believe you can deliver before you've created anything for them. Now, maybe you've done work for them before, so you have a proven track record, but what if you don't? How can they put this faith in you? One way is to have a killer reel, and here you run into the classic chicken/egg problem. To get work you need a reel, and to have something to put on your reel, you need work.

The first reservoir to draw on is personal projects, but they need to look like finished and complete pieces. Potential clients can be leery of material that is cute, complex, or innovative, but obviously non-professional. However, you do have an advantage here—your time is your own and you should use it to polish your pieces to a professional shine. Quality is vastly more important than quantity. Use your best work.

Don't be afraid of pro bono work—it can be a good way to sharpen your skills and fatten your reel. But pro bono is not a synonym for shoddy. If you agree to a job, do it to the best of your ability, no matter how much you're being paid. If you have to make time concessions due to overlap of paying jobs, make sure you work that out with your client, in advance. Just because they're getting something for free, doesn't mean they don't have deadlines too.

Spec spots are another way to get some practice in. However, they are a bit different from pro bono work. Whereas pro bono work is very likely to see distribution in some manner, spec spots rarely see anything other than life on a director's reel. In fact, in the 20 odd years I've been in this business, I've only ever done one spec spot that was actually picked up by the client and run on TV (and I got paid for my efforts). That was a commercial for Heineken. That doesn't mean you don't do them; in fact, they can be a great showcase for your graphics capabilities And they should have a more relaxed deadline as there isn't a client to satisfy. Furthermore, the better your piece looks, the better the director's reel looks, the more likely that director is to get work, the better your chances that the director will bring that work to you.

What should your reel look like? Starting with a "summary" montage is good. I usually edit mine to some appropriate music. What kind of music? Your choice will reflect on you. You want to use something entertaining and with character, but not too extreme in either direction–i.e., not elevator music and not speed metal. Your edit should pay attention to the music. In other words, this should be like a little music video with your graphics work as the raw footage. I try to avoid current popular music as this can make your montage seem dated too quickly.

How long for your montage? One minute is probably too short. Four minutes is too long. Ultimately, It should be long enough to keep the viewers entertained and short enough to leave them wanting more.

As well as your montage, you should include finished samples of your work. It is important to show potential clients your work in context. If it's a commercial, include the entire spot. Longer form material will require judicious editing to showcase your work properly.

I recommend creating a DVD of your reel. If you're not comfortable with DVD Studio Pro, iDVD has a lot of great templates that can be customized and put to use. However, you have a lot more latitude in DVDSP. Try to use the menu as another point to show off your motion graphics prowess.

Even though a DVD will show your work with better quality, if at all possible, get your reel online as well. While I still do send out reels of my work on DVD, more often these days, there is no patience for physical shipment. People want to see it now. Web hosting with virtually no limitation on storage or bandwidth is currently available for less than $99 a year. If you're unfamiliar with HTML, use an editor like Dreamweaver or iWeb or one of the Web-builder templates that are often part of those $99 Web-hosting packages.

Try to make the online versions of your montage/clips the best possible quality. I use Compressor with the H.264 LAN preset for most of my online clips. It's a good trade-off between size and quality. And don't put your stuff on YouTube for clients to see. That just screams unprofessional. As an aside, NEVER NEVER NEVER use YouTube for client approval postings. I personally know of instances where commercials were leaked because of this foolish practice.

Finally, get your client's approval before using their material in your reel. (Remember: as work for hire, they own your efforts.) Usually they will have no problem with your use. However, most often the caveat that comes with their approval will be that you can't display something until after their commercial is broadcast.

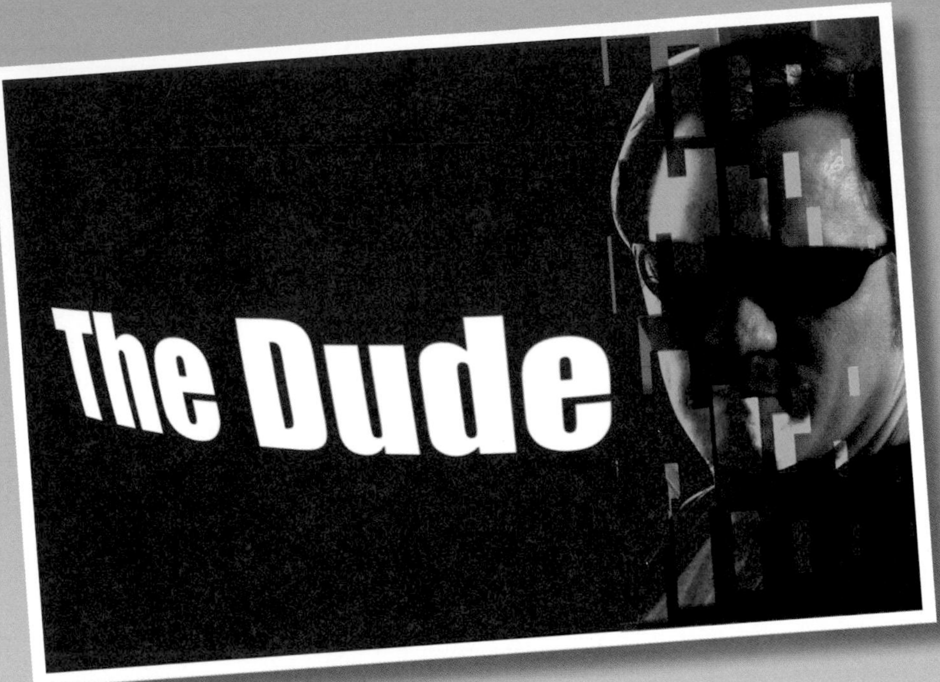

In many projects, the transition is king. Motion allows you to build an infinite library of transition templates and techniques that will keep your viewers bedazzled and awestruck. From line drawings to cartoons to comic books to complicated color effects, Motion can do amazing things to your still and moving images.

Motion

7 Transitions

OR HOW TO GET THERE FROM here. Motion can be used to build custom transitions, whether it's to bring up a new line of type or a new image. These transitions can be saved as templates and accessed from within Final Cut Studio. It's like an infinite expansion pack.

Page Peel

OKAY, IT'S ALWAYS BEEN A CHEESY effect, which is why I suspect the Motion designers never included it (they're probably members of the I.O.F.T.E.O.P.P.A.L.F. (Internat'l Organization For The Elimination Of Page Peels And Lens Flares)). However, in the interest of academic study, much as scientists kept a copy of the smallpox virus around for study, I present a Motion version of the classic Page Peel.

This project has two layers: a front and back and a masking layer. Adjusting the mask will take a few steps, and there is a kind of trick to the mask. In order to use the same mask for the front and back of the peel, we'll use inverted alpha for the front page mask and luminance for the back page matte.

IMAGE COURTESY PARKER SHEFFIELD

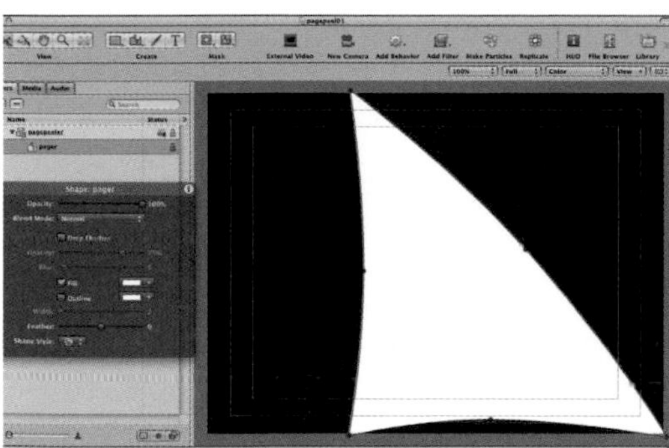

1 Start with a new project. Set your project duration to 90 frames. Rename the default group **pagepeeler**. Now, press **B** to activate the bezier tool. Draw a sort of curvy triangle as above. You can draw it as a triangle, and add points in the middle of each side to round it out. Name it **pager**.

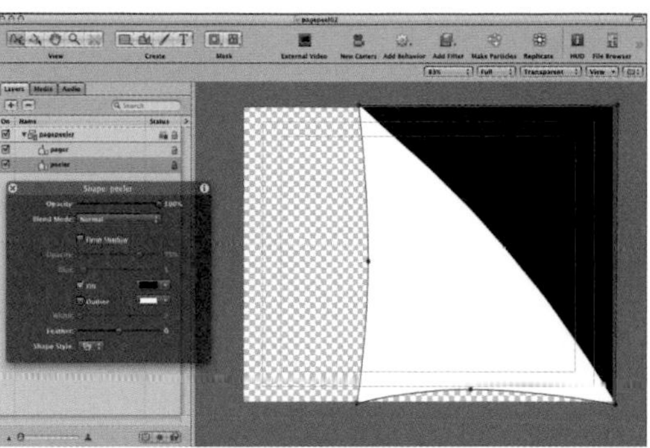

2 With **pager** selected, press **⌘D**. Name the copy **peeler**. Set its **Fill** color to **black**. Right/**ctrl**-click on the middle point in the hypotenuse and select linear. Pull it out to form a right angle as above. I've made the background transparent so you can better see what I'm doing. Drag **pager** above **peeler**.

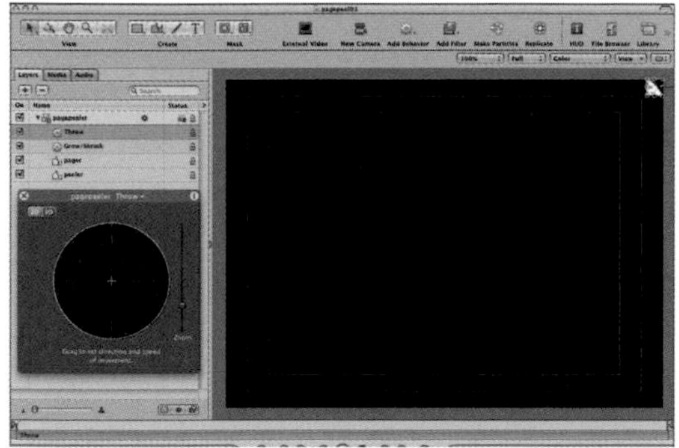

3 Select **pagepeeler**. In the **Properties** tab, set the **Scale** to **5%**. Drag the tiny black and white square over to the upper right-hand corner of your canvas. **Add Behavior/Basic Motion/Grow/Shrink. Add Behavior/Basic Motion/Throw.**

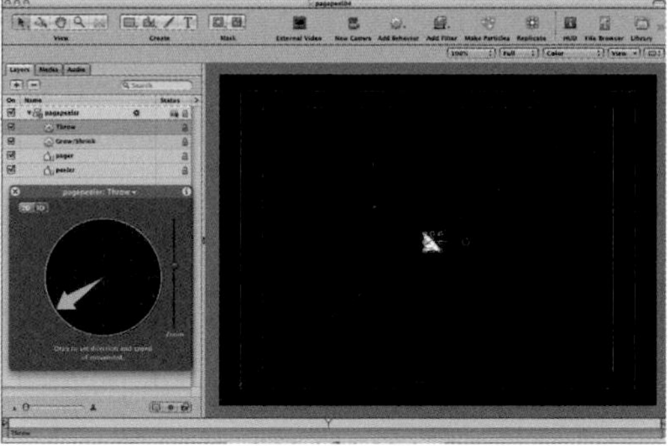

4 Position to the middle of your project (frame 45). Select **Throw**. Set **Increment** to **Ramp to Final Value**. Using the HUD, adjust the angle and distance until **pagepeeler** is in the center of the frame.

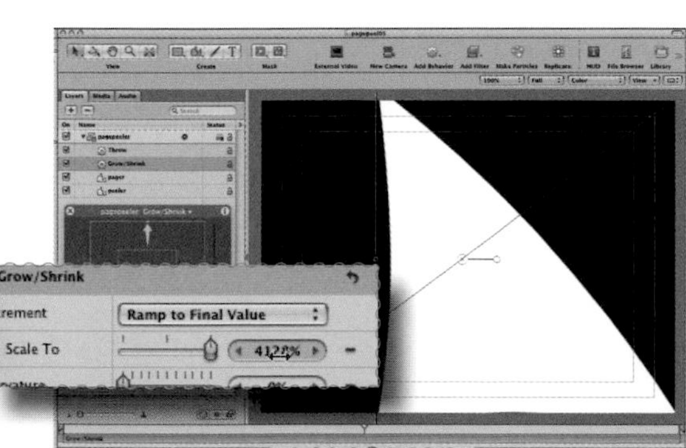

5 Now select **Grow/Shrink**. Set **Increment** to **Ramp to Final Value**. Adjust **Scale To** until the white triangle just goes over the height of the frame. You'll probably have to use the virtual slider in the **Inspector**.

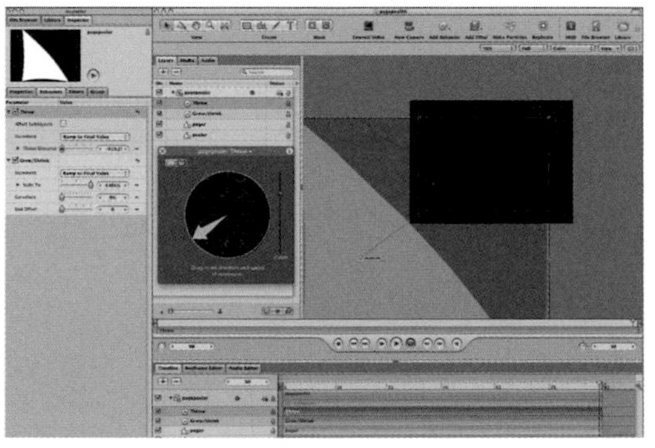

6 Now go to frame 90 and in the **Inspector**, use the virtual slider to adjust the **Throw Distance** until the white triangle just clears frame. **Shift V**. Using Show Full Viewing Area can help. **Shift V** again to turn off.

continued...

Page Peel (continued)

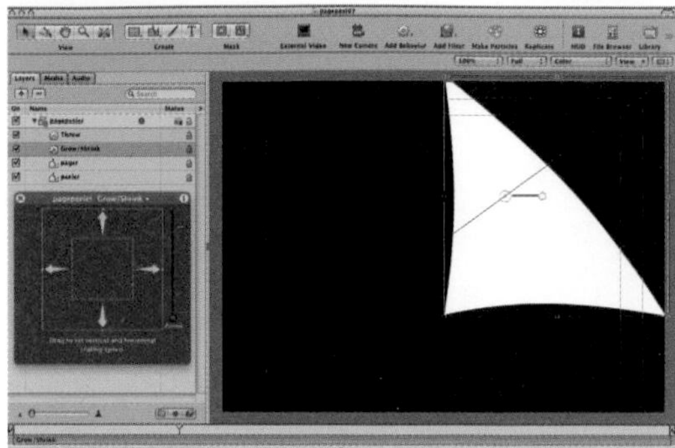

7 Finally, go to frame 24. Select **Grow/Shrink**. Adjust **Scale To** until the points of the triangle touch the edge of the frame. This will vary depending on the size of your original element. Mine was arount 5100%.

8 Go back to frame 1. Add a new group above **pagepeeler**. Name it **pagefront**. Place your clip/image in this group. Select **pagefront**. Type ⌘ Shift M to add a mask layer. Drag **pagepeeler** into the **Mask Source** well. Click the **Invert Alpha** box.

11 Select **backpage**. **Add Filter/Distortion/Flop**. In the **Properties** tab, set **Rotation** to **90°**. Increase **Scale** by 10%.

12 Move **backpage** until its (now) lower left corner is framed by the triangle in the upper right corner of your canvas. **Add Behavior/Basic Motion/Throw**.

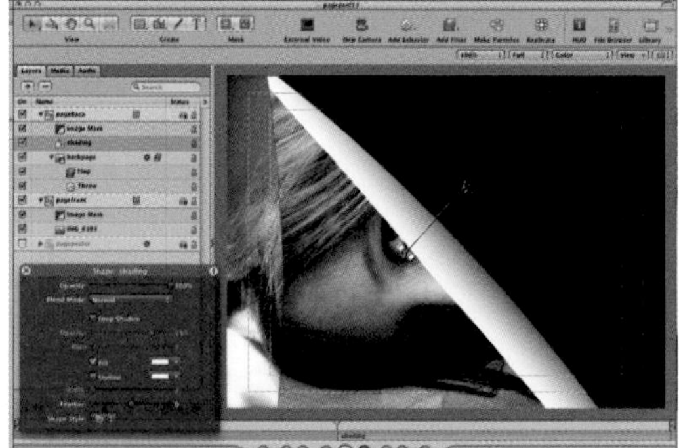

15 Name it **shading**. Set the **Fill Mode** to **Gradient**. Set **Gradient** to **Grayscale**. Adjust as above.

16 Go back to frame 1. Press **I**. Set the **Blend Mode** to **Multiply**. In the **Properties** tab, set the **Scale** to **5%**. Drag the tiny shape over to the upper right-hand corner of your canvas. Set **Opacity** to **75%**.

IMAGE COURTESY PARKER SHEFFIELD

9 Add a new group on top of everything. Call it **pageback**. Select your original Image. Press K to create a clone layer. Name it **backpage**. Drag it into the **pageback** group (or use a new image if you want the back different from the front).

10 Select **pageback**. Type ⌘ Shift M to add an image mask. Set the **Source Channel** to **Luminance**. Drag **pagepeeler** into the **Source Image** well.

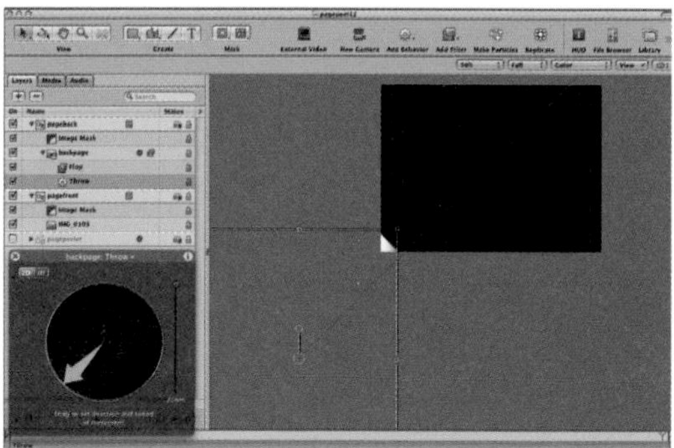

13 Set **Increment** to **Ramp to Final Value**. Go to the last frame of your project. Adjust the arrow in the HUD until the (now) upper right corner of **backpage** just clears the lower left corner of your canvas. You may also need to use the virtual slider to get it to move far enough.

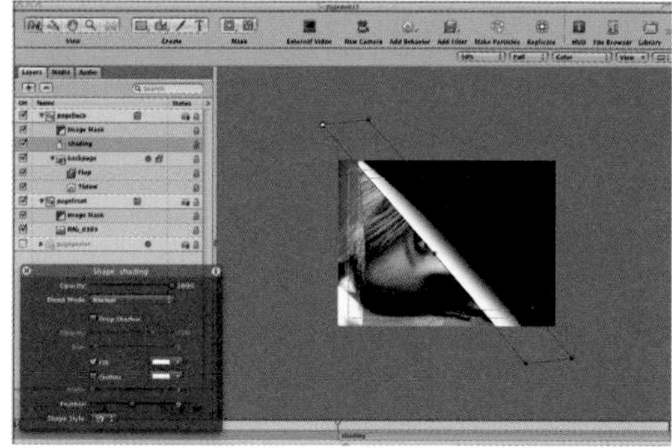

14 Position to frame 45. Press B to activate the **Bezier** tool. Draw a shape as seen above diagonally following the edge of the peel.

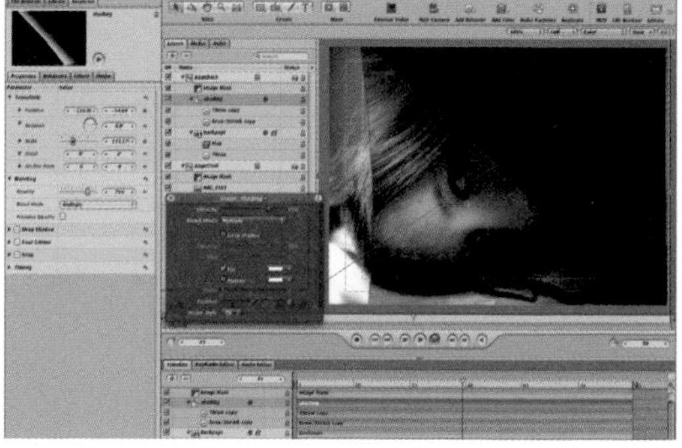

17 Now go back to the **pagepeel** group and Shift-select both **Throw** and **Grow/Shrink**. Hold down the ⌥ key and drag copies of them onto shading. Go to frame 45. Select **shading** and position it just over the peel as above.

18 Fine tune **Throw** to keep the shading in place over the peel if necessary. Finally, in the **Properties** tab of **pageback**, turn on **Drop Shadow**. Adjust to taste.

Free Wipes

FREE WIPES! NO, NOT THE KIND Mr. Monk uses. Motion comes with a huge variety of built-in transitional replicators in the Library (there are more than just wipes). And they're easy to use. This project shows you how to use just one, but the principles apply to all.

IMAGES COURTESY LARA DOUCETTE & JYN MEYER

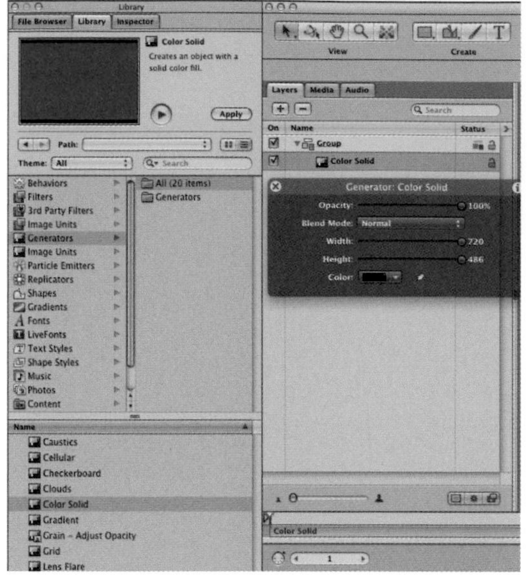

1 Start with a new project. Go to **Library/Generators** and select **Color Solid**. Press **Apply**. Change the **Color** to black.

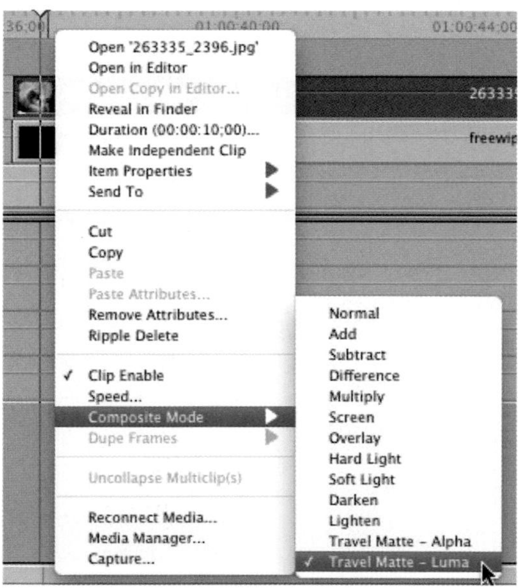

4 To use this as a transition in Final Cut Pro, place the outgoing clip on V1, this Motion project on V2, and the incoming clip on V3. Set the **Composite Mode** of the clip on V3 to be **Travel Matte-Luma**.

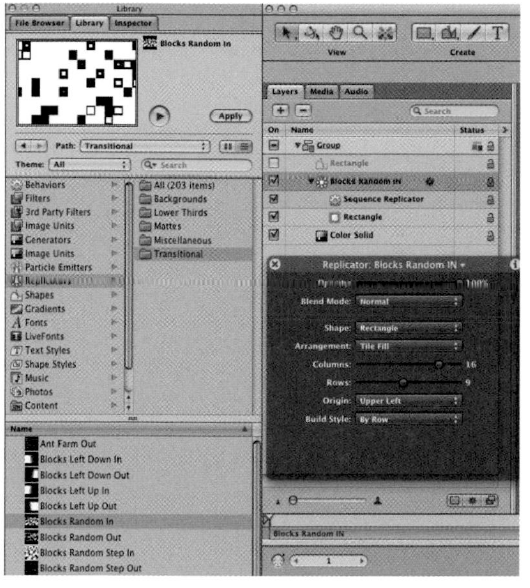

2 Now go to **Library/Replicators/Transitional**. Select one of the replicators and click **Apply**. For transitioning TO something, chose one that goes from black to white (away from something, chose one that goes from white to black). I chose **Blocks Random In**.

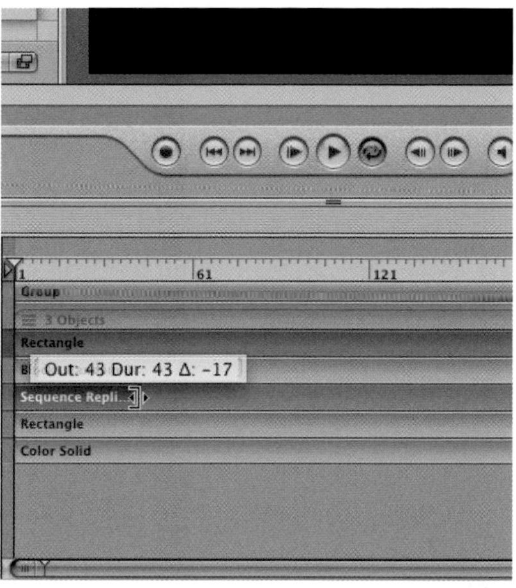

3 Depending on the transition chosen, you may be able to change the duration of the **Sequence Replicator** to govern how long the transition takes.

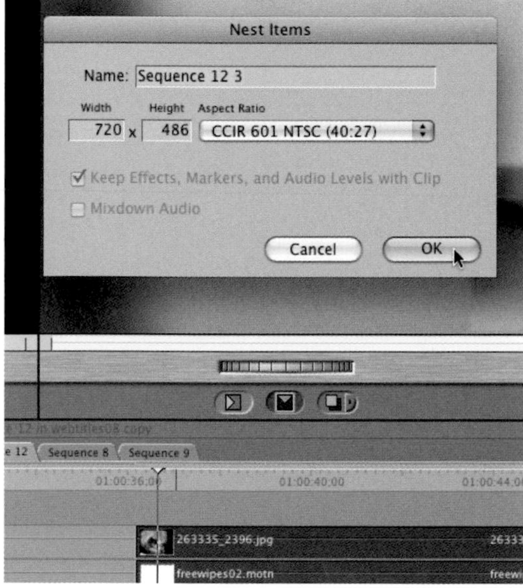

5 For a neat trick in Final Cut Pro, select the incoming image and the Motion project and type ⌥C to nest the two into one. Click Okay for the default.

6 Then hold the ⌥ key and double-click on the nest. In the Motion tab in Final Cut Pro, turn on **Drop Shadow** and adjust.

Glitch Transition

SOMETIMES WHEN YOU'RE CUTTING an interview you need to remove something—an "Ummm...," an "Ahhh...," a long thoughtful pause. And you don't have B-roll or a second camera. There's always a jump cut or a white flash. But here's an alternative that's a little less cliched—the video glitch, a little loss of sync or static.

Use sparingly—a few frames is all you need.

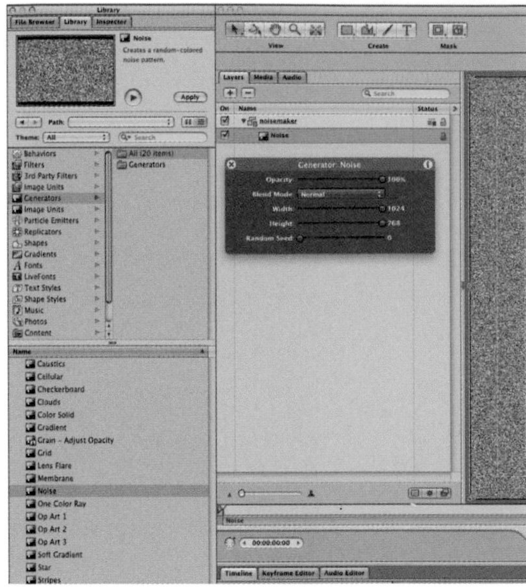

1 Start with a new project. Use a preset appropriate to your project. Rename the default group as **noisemaker**. In the **Library/Generators**, select the **Noise** generator, and press **Apply**.

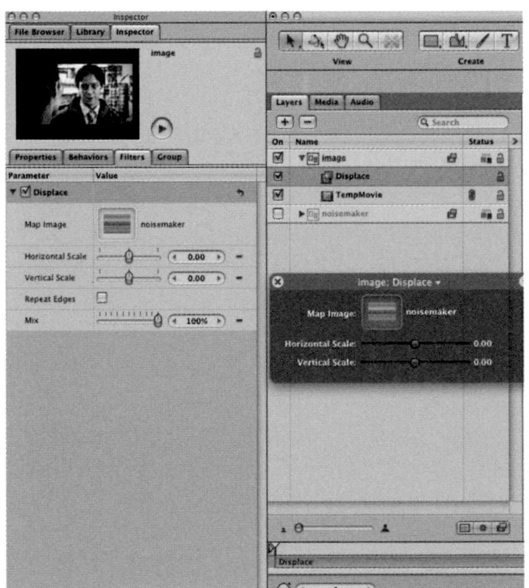

4 Select the **image** group. Add **Filter/Distortion/Displace**. Drag the **noisemaker** group into the **Map Image** well. Set **Horizontal** and **Vertical Scale** to 0.

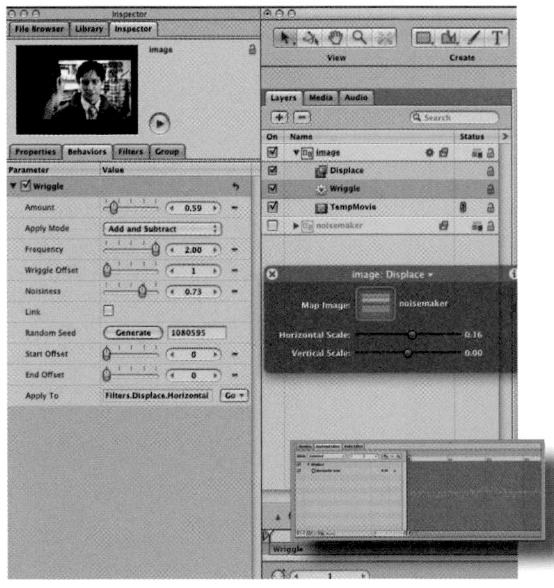

5 Right/ctrl-click on **Horizontal Scale**. Select **Wriggle**. Set the **Amount** to **0.59**, **Apply Mode** to **Add and Subtract**, **Frequency** to **2.00**, **Wriggle offset** to **1**, and **Noisiness** to **0.73**.

IMAGE COURTESY REILLY SHEFFIELD

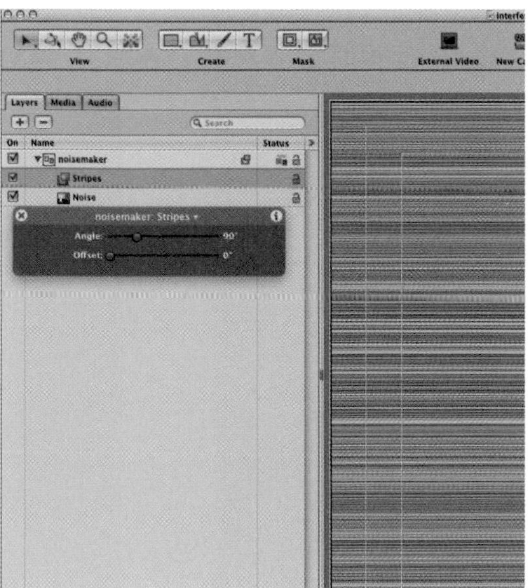

2 Select **noisemaker**. Add **Filter/Distortion/Stripes**. Change **Angle** to 90°.

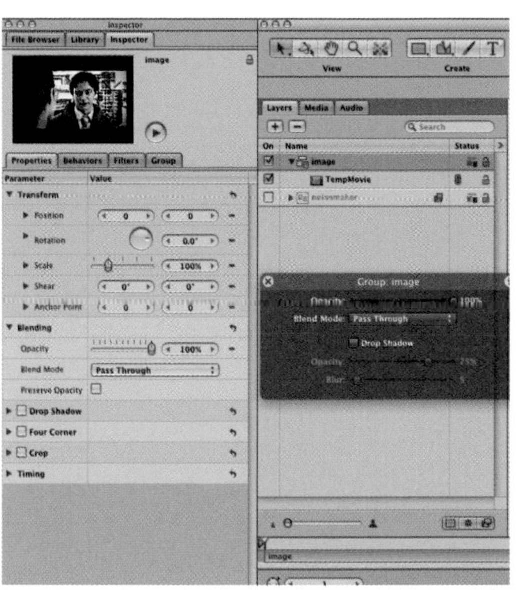

3 Turn off **noisemaker**. Add a new group above **noisemaker**. Name it **image**. Drag your clip/image into the **image** group. If you're preparing this for use as a template, choose a temporary image (perhaps from **Library/Content**).

HOT TIP

You can make the interference lines larger by pulling the same trick that we used in the Rainy Day Activity project: make the generator smaller and resize.

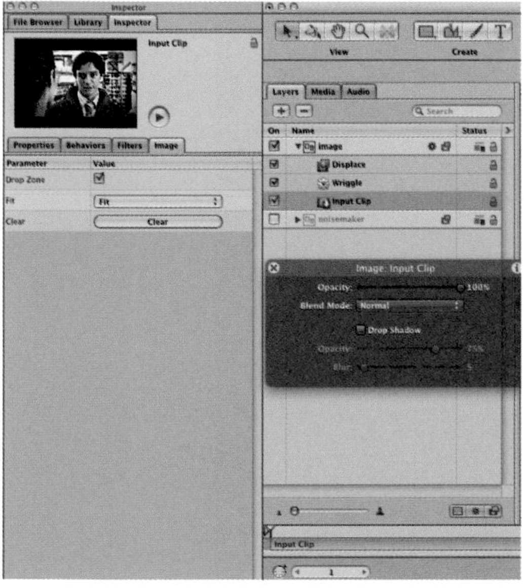

6 To prepare this for use in Final Cut Pro, rename your clip/image to **Input Clip**. In the Image tab, select **Drop Zone**. If you'd like your temp image to be used as the preview, *don't* click **Clear** yet.

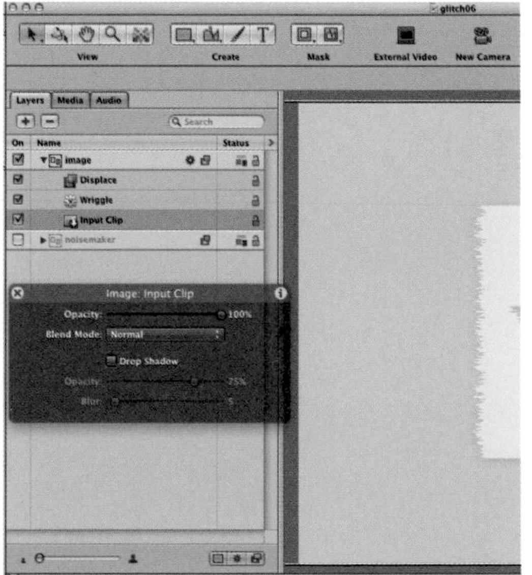

7 Select **Save as Template**. If you don't already have a theme called **Transitions**, add one. Name your template **Glitchy Transition**. Press **Save**. Now you can click **Clear** in the **Image** tab, and then **Save as Template** again. This time turn off **Create QuickTime Preview**.

Rounded Pixelate

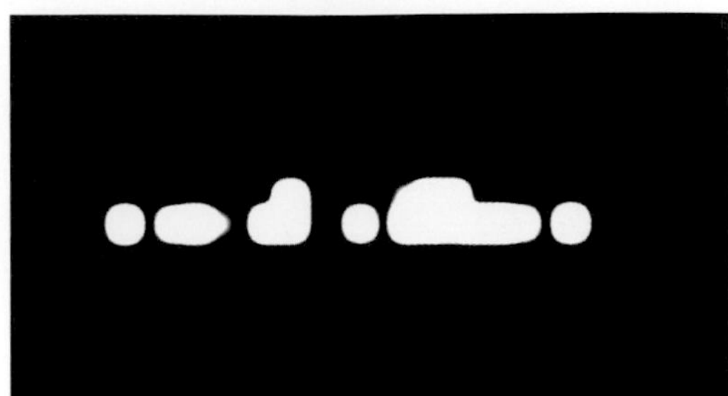

Rounded Pixelate

I HAD TO COME UP WITH AN interesting text effect for a mockup of a television show. That show never aired, so now the effect is yours—I call it rounded Pixelate.

What we do is to take our text, Pixelate it, and then blur and threshold the result. We can't do that to the text directly, because it has its own alpha channel, but we'll rasterize it by using it as a mask for a white rectangle over a black rectangle.

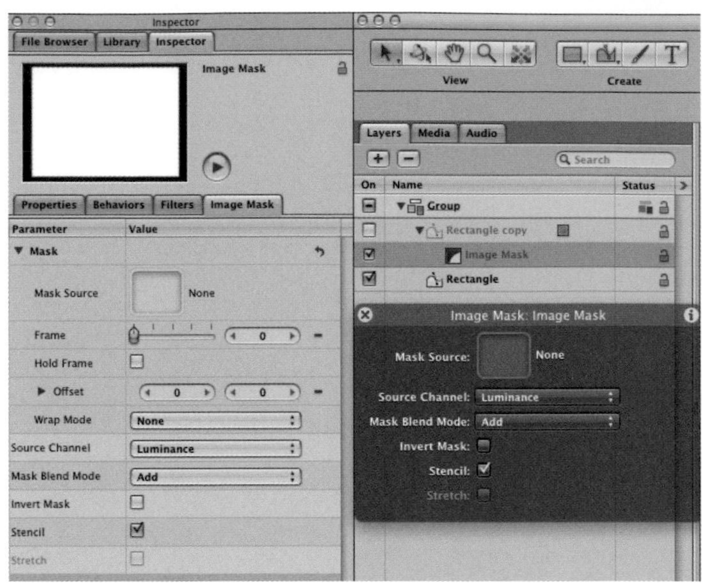

1 Start with a new project. Press R to activate the rectangle tool. Draw a black rectangle that fills the screen. Duplicate it and change the fill to white. Type ⌘ Shift M. Set the **Source Channel** to **Luminance**. Turn off **Rectangle copy** for now.

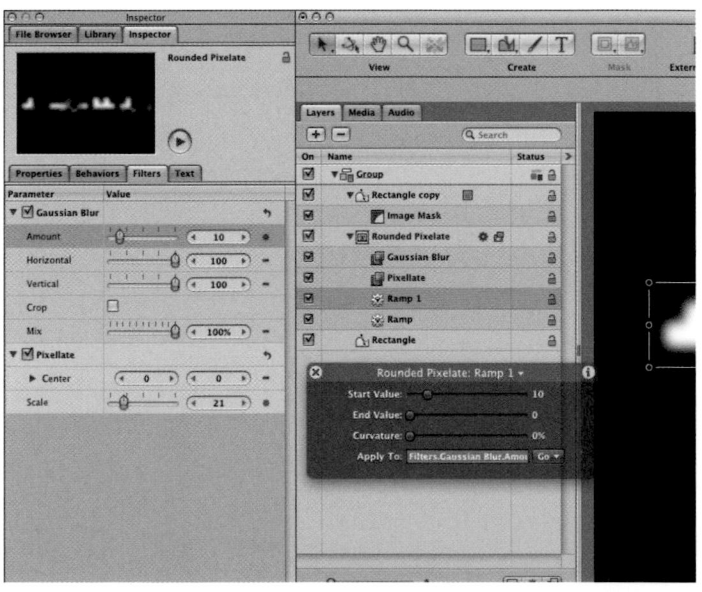

3 Turn your text layer back on. Select the Pixelate filter, right/ctrl-click on **Scale**. Select **Ramp**. Set **Start Value** to **20**. Back in the **Filters** tab, right/ctrl-click on the **Gaussian Blur Amount**. Select **Ramp**. Set the **Start Value** to **10**.

2 Activate the **Text** tool and type your text. Place it between the two rectangles. **Add Filter/Stylize/Pixelate**. Set **Scale** to 1. **Add Filter/Blur/Gaussian blur**. Set the **Gaussian Blur Amount** to 0. Drag your text layer into the **Image Mask**. Turn on the white **Rectangle copy**.

4 Select **Group**. **Add Filter/Color Correction/Threshold**. Set **Threshold** to **0.10**, and **Smoothness** to **0.05**. ⌘-select **Threshold**, **Rectangle copy**, **Gaussian Blur**, **Pixelate**, **Ramp 1**, and **Ramp**. Position to frame 15. Press O.

DV Dropout

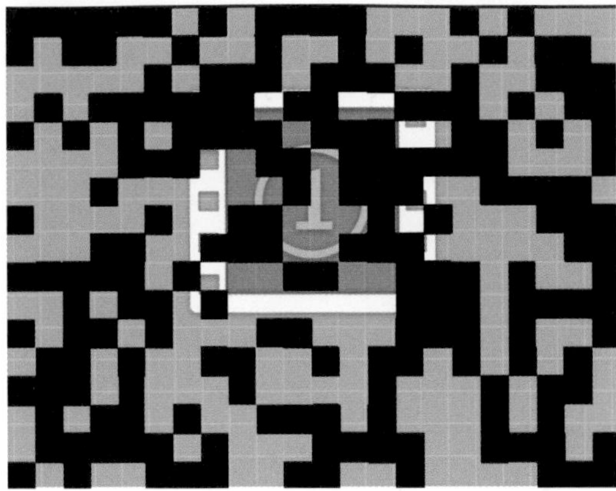

WHEN DIGITAL TAPE HAS dropouts, you get this characteristic pattern of squares that fill back in as the tape continues to play. Sometimes that glitch is just what you need to bridge some jump cuts while you're editing away on those single-camera interviews for the DVD extras.

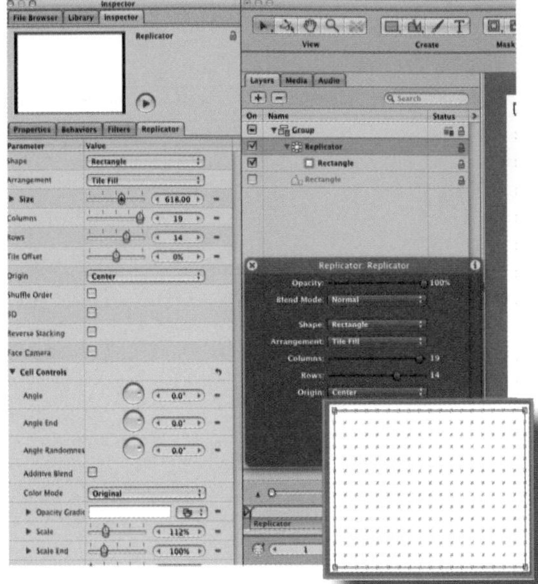

1 Start with a new project. Set the **Duration** to 10 frames. Draw a small square in the center of the screen. Press **L** or click the **Replicate** button in the toolbar. Drag the replicator out until it fills the screen. Up the **Columns** and **Rows** until the screen is just filled. If it's too close to add another row/column, tweak the **Scale**.

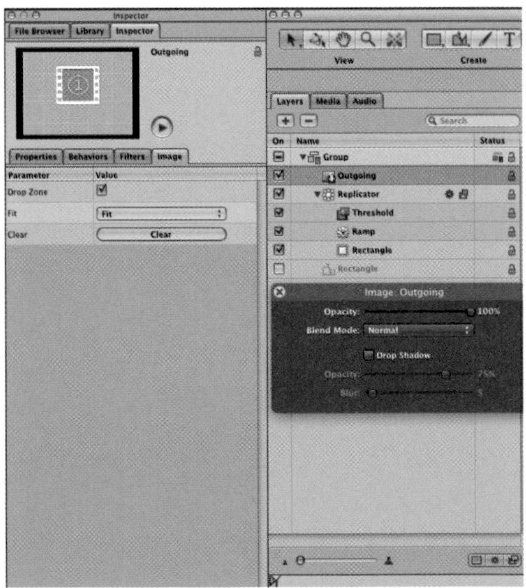

4 In **Library/Content**, select the **Replace1.jpg** that's appropriate to your project. Click **Apply**. Change its name to **Outgoing**. In the **Image** tab under **Inspector**, click **Drop Zone**.

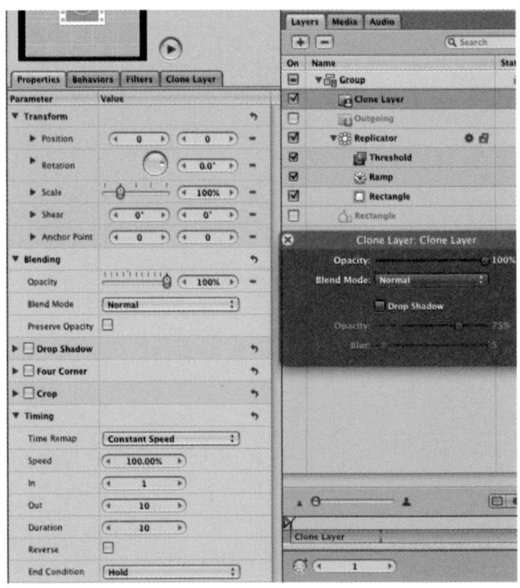

5 Press **K** to create a clone layer. In the **Properties** tab, under **Timing**, set the **Duration** to 1. Set **End Condition** to **Hold**. Now drag it back out to full length (this effectively freezes the clip). Turn off **Outgoing**.

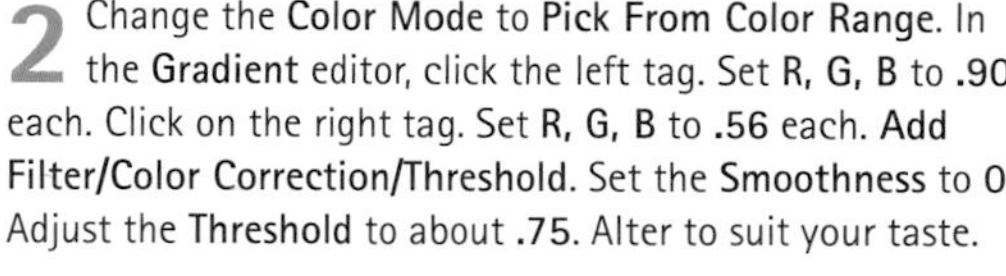

2 Change the **Color Mode** to **Pick From Color Range**. In the **Gradient** editor, click the left tag. Set **R, G, B** to **.90** each. Click on the right tag. Set **R, G, B** to **.56** each. **Add Filter/Color Correction/Threshold**. Set the **Smoothness** to 0. Adjust the **Threshold** to about **.75**. Alter to suit your taste.

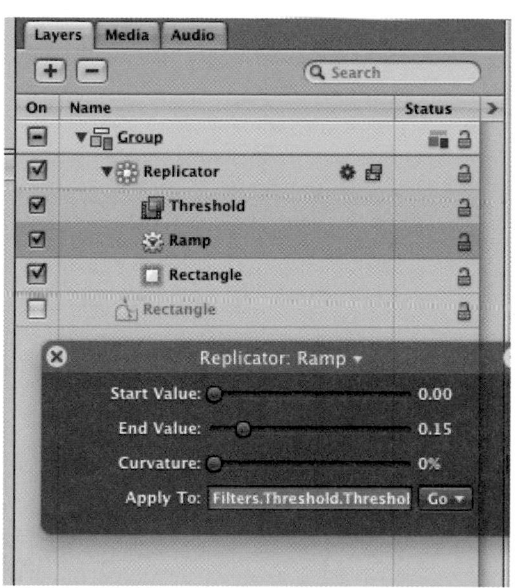

3 Right/ctrl-click on **Threshold** and select **Ramp**. Position to frame 10. Adjust **End Value** until you *just* lose all the squares. Then go back to frame 1.

6 Press ⌘ Shift M. Change the **Source Channel** to **Luminance**. Drag the **Replicator** into the **Image Mask** well.

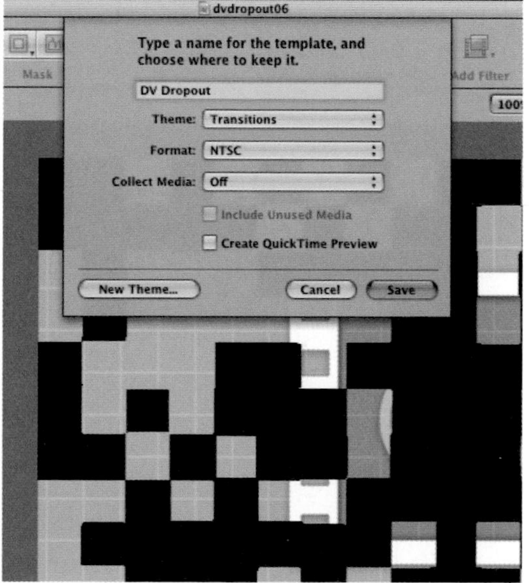

7 Save it as a **Template** (⌘ ⌥ S). If you don't already have a theme called **Transitions**, create one and place it there. To use this in Final Cut Pro, cut it onto a video layer over the incoming clip. Razor the last frame of your outgoing clip and place it in the **Outgoing** well.

Raindrops keep fallin'

THIS IS A TRANSITION THAT simulates seeing our image through a puddle of water that is disturbed by a rain shower that clears, revealing our new image.

As designed, this transition takes 7 seconds: 3 seconds for lead-in, 1 second for dissolve, and 3 seconds for lead-out.

1 Start in Final Cut Pro. Build your timeline with your outgoing clip on **V1** and your incoming clip on **V2**, with a 1-second overlap. Keyframe the **Opacity** of the incoming clip to go from **0** to **100%** in the 1-second overlap.

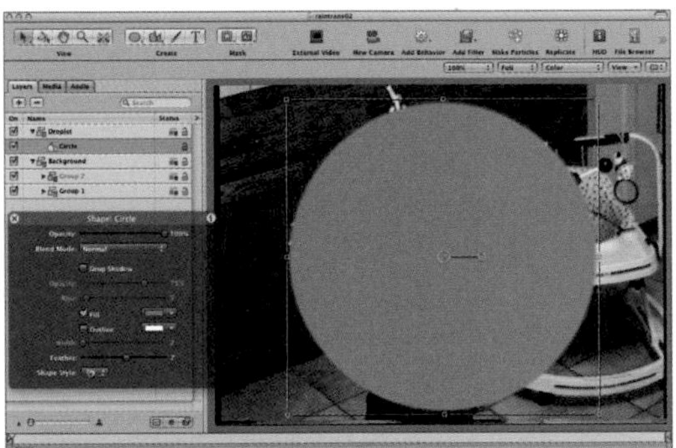

4 Press the C key to activate the **Circle Shape** tool. Hold down the Shift and ⌥ keys and click in the center of the screen. Draw out the circle until it nearly fills the screen top to bottom. Fill it with mid-gray, and set the **Feather** to **7**.

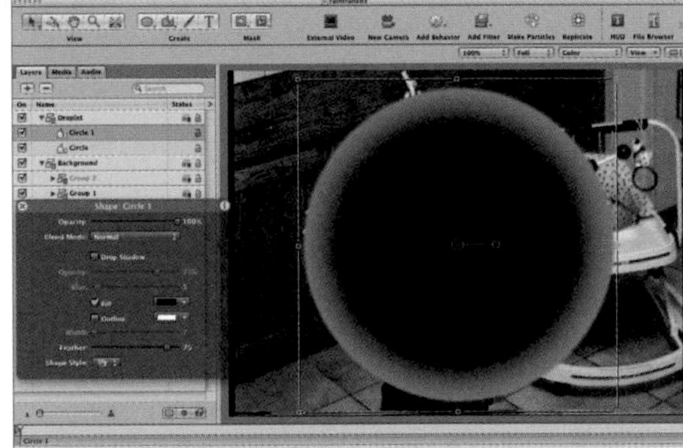

5 Create a smaller concentric circle over the first circle. Feather its edge to **75** and set its fill to **Black**.

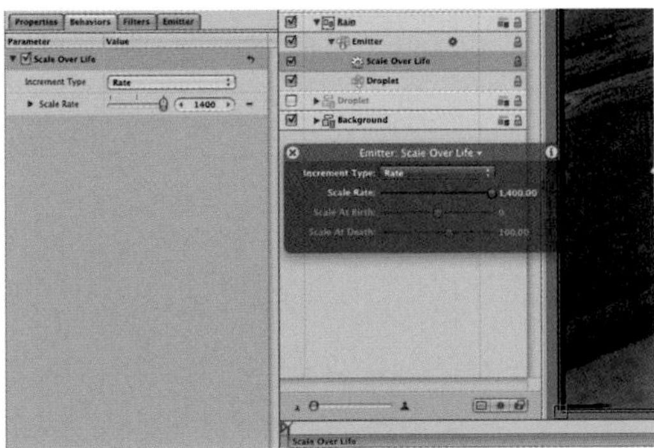

8 With **Emitter** selected, **Add Behavior/Particles/Scale Over Life**. Set the **Increment Type** to **Rate** and the **Rate** to about **1,400**.

9 Right/ctrl-click on the **Birth Rate** and select **Ramp**. Set the **Start Value** to **–45** and leave **End Value** at **0**. Make the ramp's **Duration** about **2 seconds.**

IMAGE COURTESY REILLY SHEFFIELD

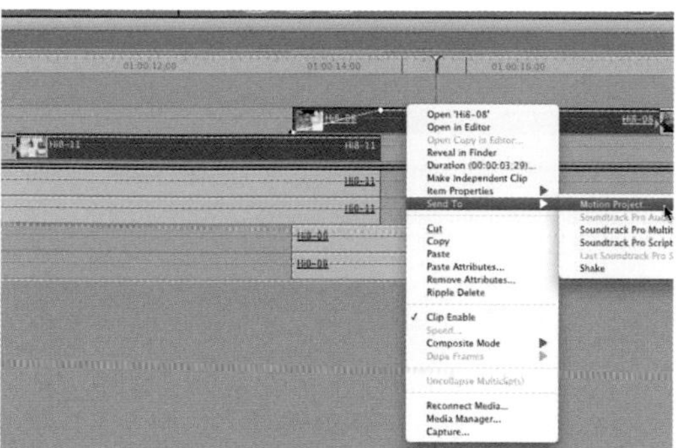

2 Use the razor blade to place an edit point 3 seconds before he overlap in the outgoing clip on **V1** and 3 seconds after the overlap in the incoming clip on **V2**. Select both, right/ctrl-click on the clips, and select **Send To Motion.**

3 Make sure all groups are collapsed. **Select All** (⌘A). ⌘Shift G. Name the new group **Background.** Add a new group above it and call it **Droplet** and that's where we'll create our raindrop.

6 Select **Droplet** and press E to create a particle emitter. Name the new group **Rain.** Set the **Blend Mode** to **Screen.** Set **Fixed Resolution.** Select **Emitter.** Set the **Shape** to **Rectangle** and **Arrangement** to **Random Fill.** Using the **Adjust Item** tool, drag the corners out to the corners of the frame. Set **Birth Rate** to **45, Life** to **3.3**, and **Speed** to **0.**

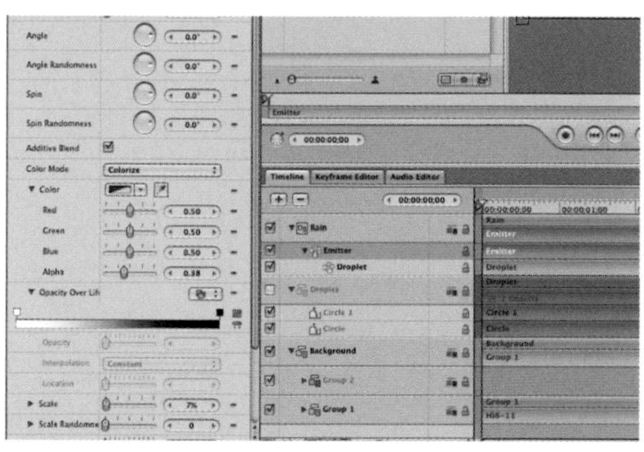

7 Click **Additive Blend.** Set **Color Mode** to **Colorize. R, G, B** to **0.50** each. Set **Alpha** to **0.38.** Set the right-hand tag of **Opacity Over Life** to **0%.** Set **Scale** to about **7%.**

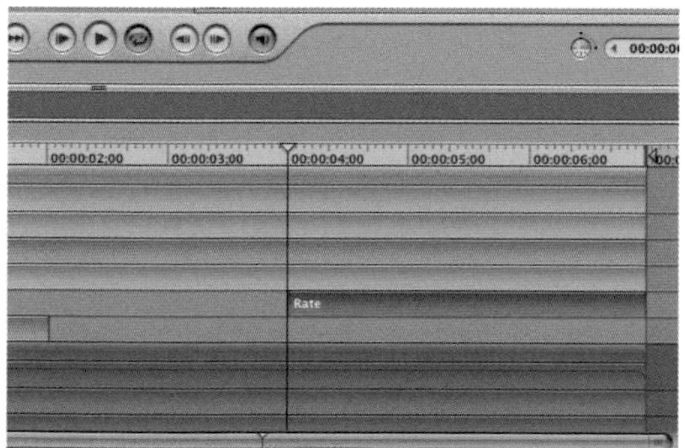

10 Right/ctrl-click on the **Birth Rate** again and add a **Rate** behavior. Set **Rate** to **-90** and make it start around 3 seconds from the end and last until the end.

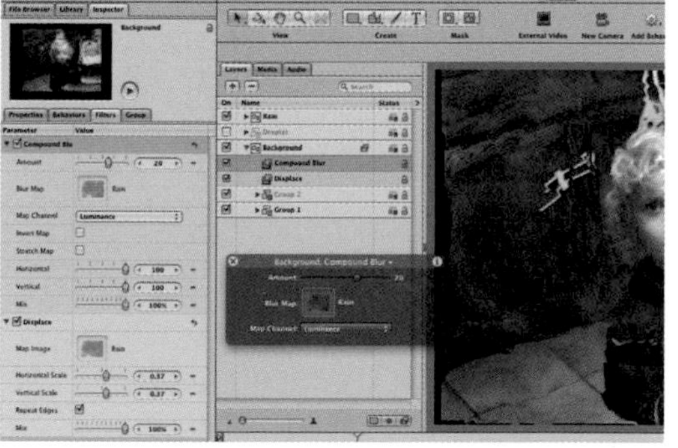

11 Select **Rain.** Set **Opacity** to **50%.** Select **Background. Add Filter/Distortion/Displace.** Drag the **Rain** group into the **Source Image** well, and then set the **Horizontal** and **Vertical** to **0.37.** Click **Repeat Edges. Add Filter/Blur/Compound Blur, Map Channel** set to **Luminance**, and the **Amount** to **20.**

Scanline Transition

THIS IS A SIMPLE transition that can be used as a mask in Motion or Final Cut Pro. It starts with a black screen and then randomly fills it with lines. The same technique could be used for a variety of shapes—circles, squares, etc.

So, along with the built-in Replicator-based transitions that come with Motion, you can construct an infinite variety of custom ones.

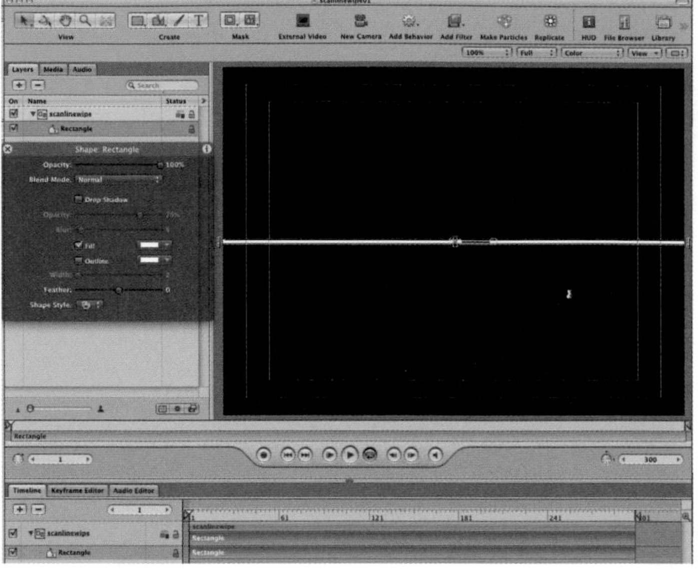

1 Begin with a new project. Rename the default **Group** to **scanlinewipe**. In the **Group** tab, set **Fixed Resolution**. Press **R** to activate the **Rectangle** tool. Use it to draw a thin white line horizontally across the middle of the screen.

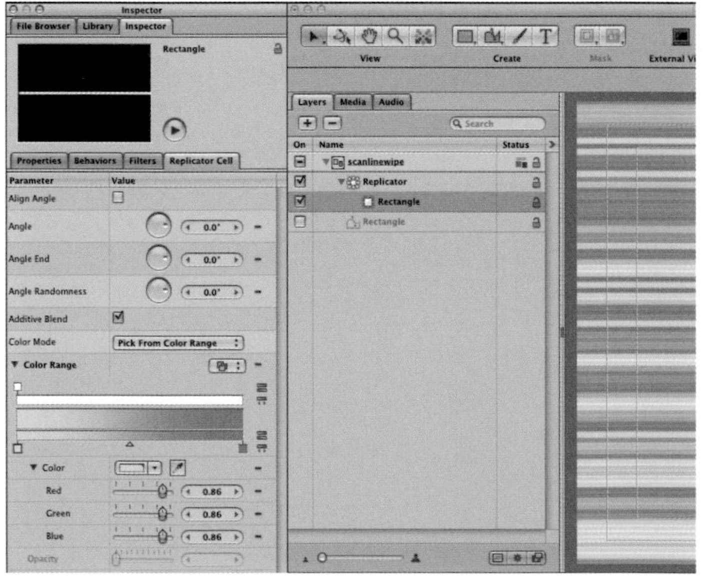

3 Select the **Rectangle** replicator cell. Set **Color Mode** to **Pick From Color Range**. Set the range to nearly white (**.86** for **R, G, B**) through mid-gray (**.50** for **R, G, B**).

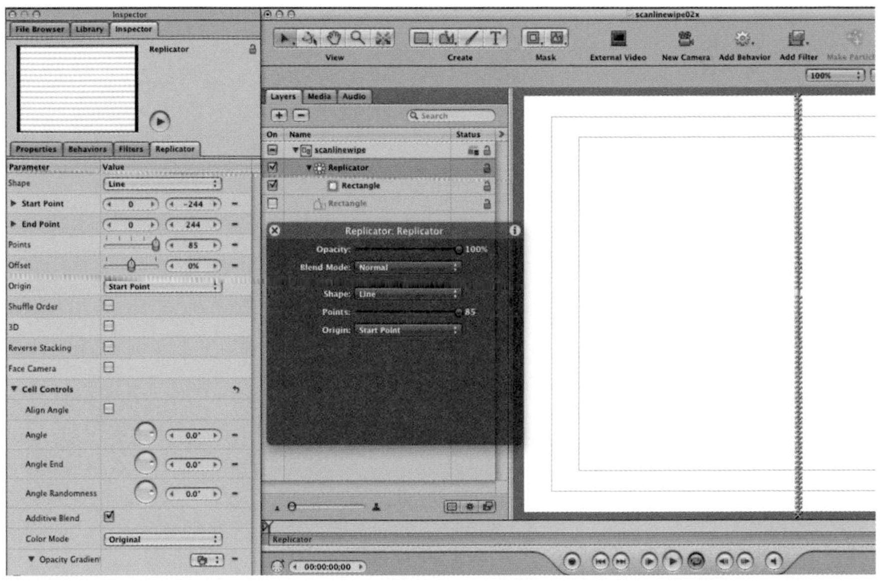

2 Press **L** or click the **Replicate** button in the toolbar. Change the **Shape** to **Line**. Drag the line from the top to the bottom of the screen vertically, or set the **Start Point** to 0, **-244** and **End Point** to 0, **244**. Increase the **Points** until the lines just fill the screen. Click **Additive Blend**.

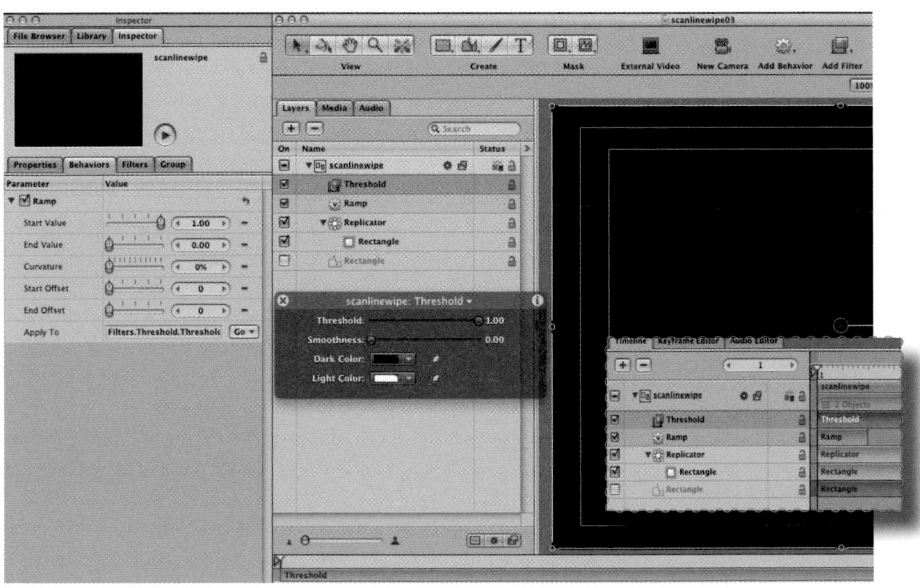

4 Select **scanlinewipe**. **Add Filter/Color Correction/Threshold**. Set **Threshold** to 0 and **Smoothness** to 0 and Right/**ctrl**-click on **Threshold**. Select **Ramp**. Set **Start Value to 1** and **End Value** to 0. Go to frame 30. Press **O** to truncate the ramp. Changing this length changes the transition duration. Use this project to create transitions in the same way as in the Free Wipes project earlier in this chapter.

HOT TIP

By changing the shape used and the Replicator parameters, an infinite variety of transitions can be built.

Animated Dissolve

IMAGES COURTESY OCTAVIO ARIZALA & JYN MEYER

I WAS WORKING ON A commercial that involved animating and transitioning between a series of stills.

I wanted the transitions to be more than simple dissolves, but in keeping with the subject matter of the still photographs, I wanted to maintain an "organic" quality to them. I modified the Light Dots2 particle emitter in Motion and added a fade to white to create a number of "transitional movies" that started in black, built to white, and then used them as mattes.

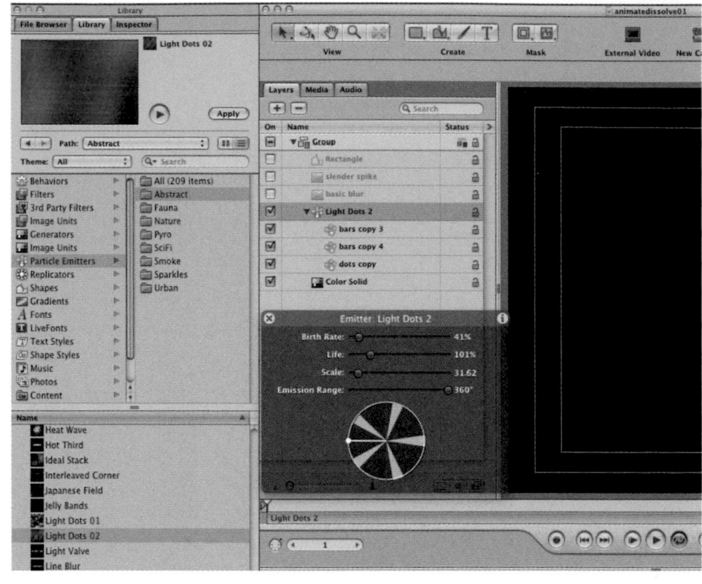

1 Start with a new project. First In **Library/Generators**, select **Color Solid** and press **Apply**. Set the **Color** to **Black**. Go to the **Library/Particle Emitters/ Abstract**. Grab **Light Dots 02** and place it in the center of your canvas.

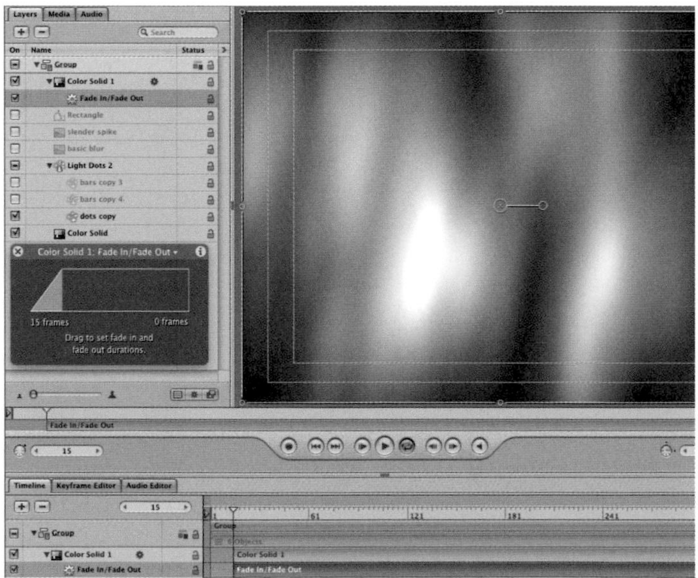

3 Position to frame 15. In **Library/Generators**, select **Color Solid** and press **Apply**. Set the **Color** to **White**. **Add Behavior/Basic Motion/Fade in/Fade out**. Set the **Fade In** time to **15**. Set **Fade Out** time to **0**.

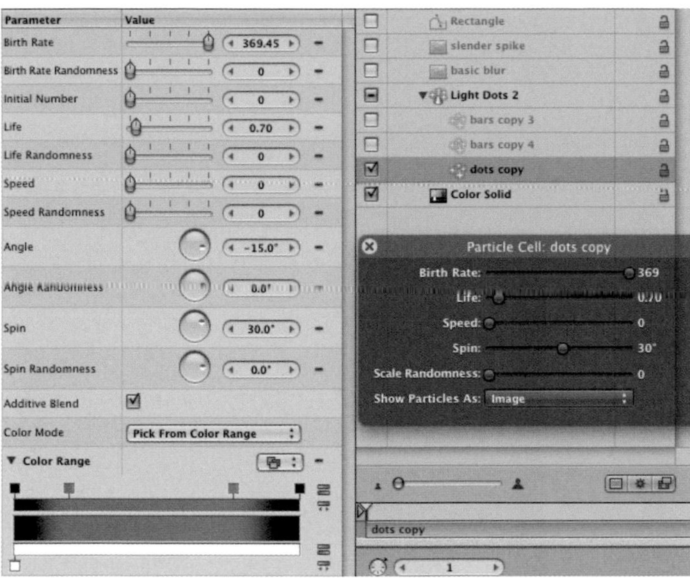

2 Disable both bars' particle cells. Select **dots copy**. Change the **Life** to .7 and **Spin** to 30. Change the base color in **Color Range** from purple to white.

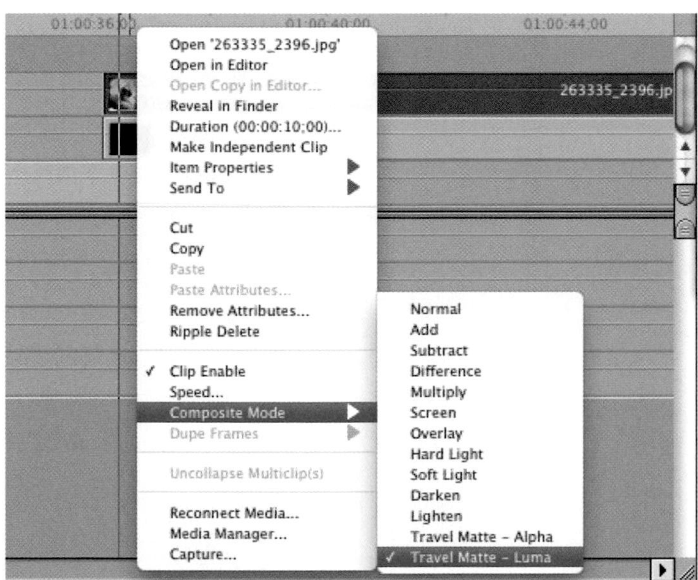

4 To use this as a transition in Final Cut Pro, Place the outgoing clip on **V1**, this Motion project on **V2**, and the incoming clip on **V3**. Set the **Composite Mode** of the clip on **V3** to be **Travel Matte-Luma.**

HOT TIP

To build variations on this transition, select the Dots Copy Particle cell and alter the Birth Rate, Speed, Angle, Spin, Scale, and/or hit the Generate button on the Random seed.

Clock Wipe

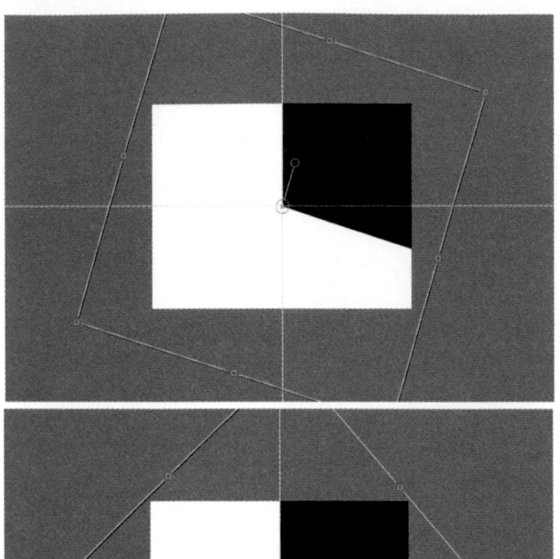

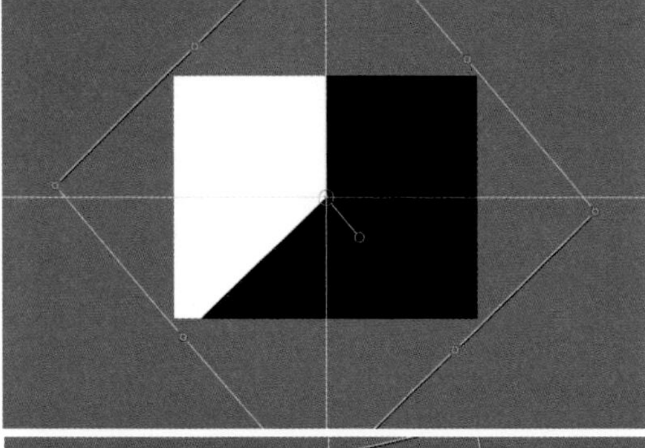

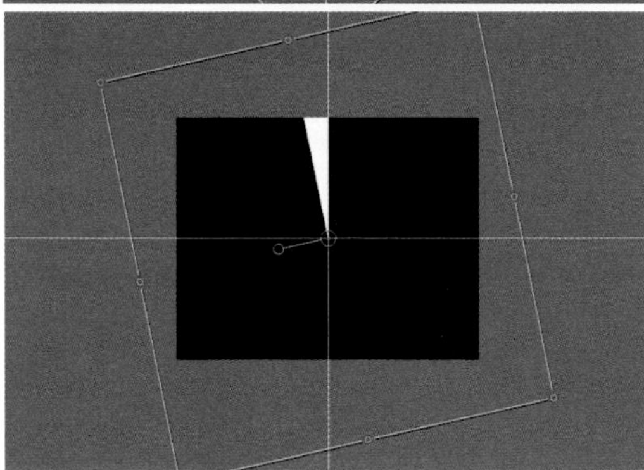

SURE IT'S CHEESEBALL, but sometimes cheeseball is just what is called for. Creating a clock wipe mask in Motion is not a one-click operation, but it's not too tough.

The interesting thing about the technique we'll be using here is that it automatically adjusts for whatever length you trim it to.

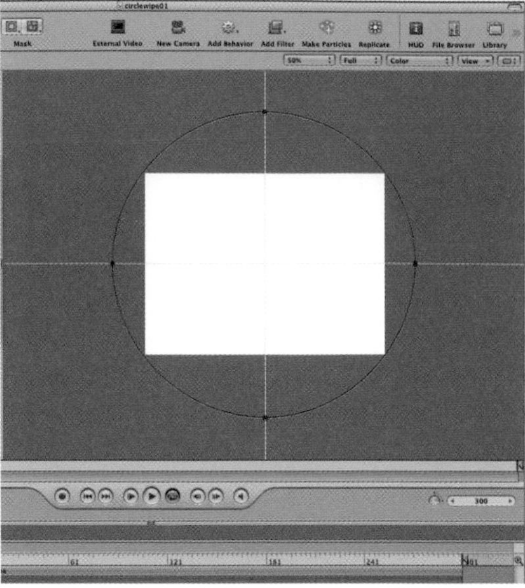

1 Start with a new project. Rename the default group to **clockwipe**. To help line everything up, go to the View menu and add a horizontal and a vertical guide. Press C. Place your cursor at the center of the screen. Holding down the ⌥ and *Shift* keys, pull out a circle that just fills the entire screen.

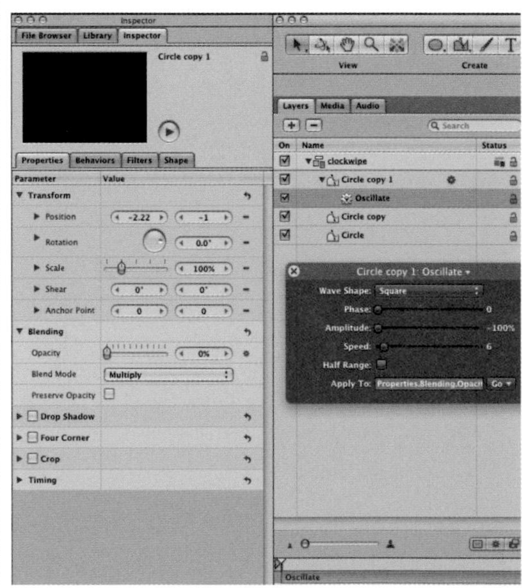

4 Select **Circle Copy 1**. In the **Properties** tab, set **Blend Mode** to **Multiply**. Right/*ctrl*-click on **Opacity**. Select **Oscillate**. Change the **Wave Shape** to **Square**, **Amplitude** to **-100%**, and **Speed** to **6**.

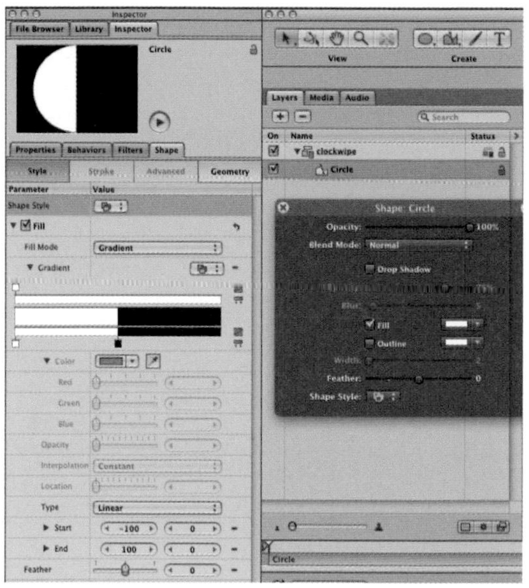

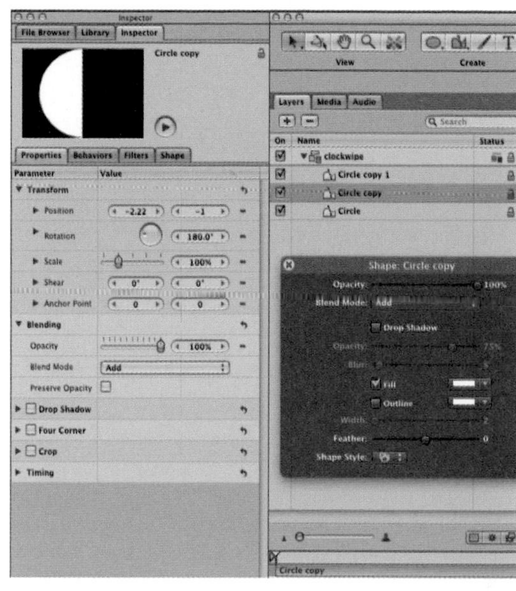

2 Change the **Fill Mode** to **Gradient**. Set the **Gradient** to **Grayscale**. Twirl down the **Gradient** section. Click on the **White** tag. Set **Interpolation** to **Constant**. Click on the **Black** tag. Set the **Location** to **50%**. Under **Type**, set **Start** to **-100, 0** and **End** to **100, 0**.

3 Press ⌘D twice. Select **Circle copy**. In the **Properties** tab, set **Rotation** to **180°**. Set **Blend Mode** to **Add**.

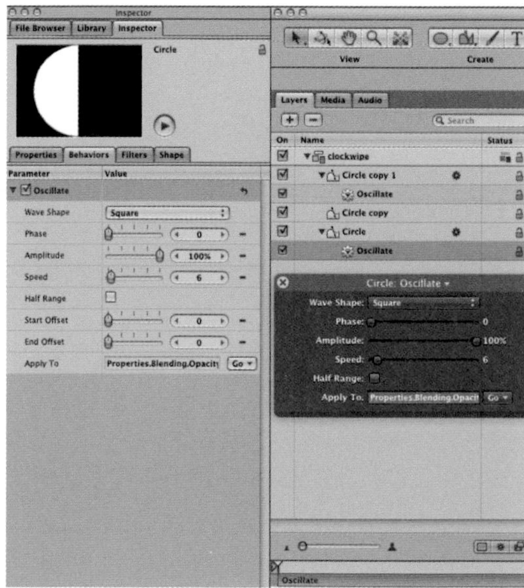

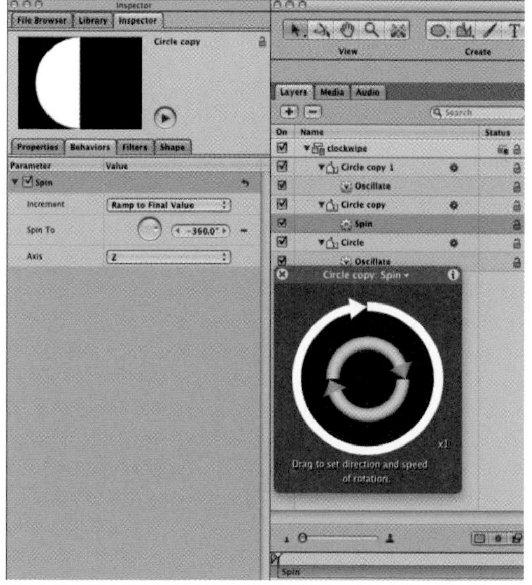

5 Select **Circle**. In the **Properties** tab, right/ctrl-click on **Opacity**. Select **Oscillate**. Change the **Wave Shape** to **Square**, and the **Speed** to **6**.

6 Finally, select **Circle copy**. Add **Behavior/Basic Motion/ Spin**. Change the **Increment** to **Ramp to Final Value**. Set **Spin To** to **-360**.

Advanced Clock Wipe

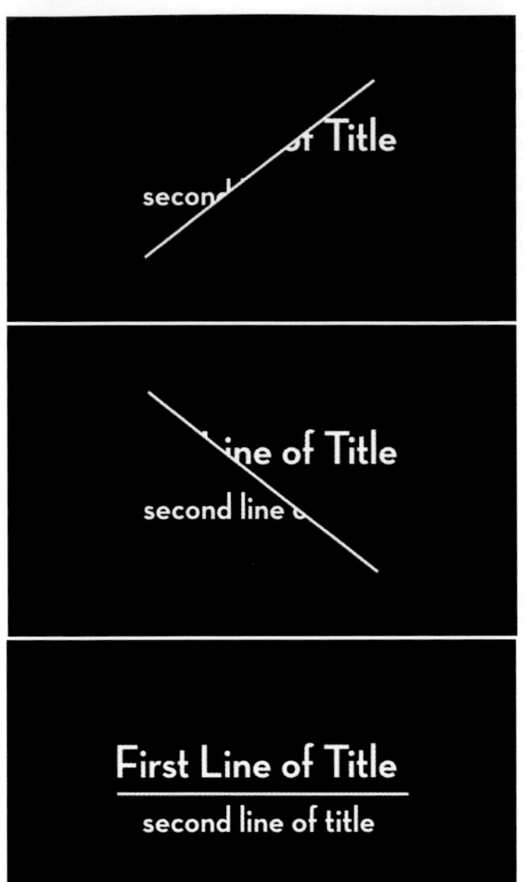

THIS TITLE REVEAL project has its roots in a clock wipe but is much more elegant. I've used it in a credit sequence for a short film and it was quite effective.

What it does is kind of tricky. The lower line of type is covered by a black rectangle that rotates to reveal it. The upper line of type has Preserve Opacity checked. This means that it will only be visible when there is something underneath it. So as the rectangle rotates to reveal the lower line of type, it slides under the the upper line of type, making it visible too.

1 Begin with a new project. Press T to activate the **Text** tool. Click in the middle of the frame, select your **Font**, **Size**, and **Color**. Set **Alignment** to **Center**. Type your first line. Press esc.

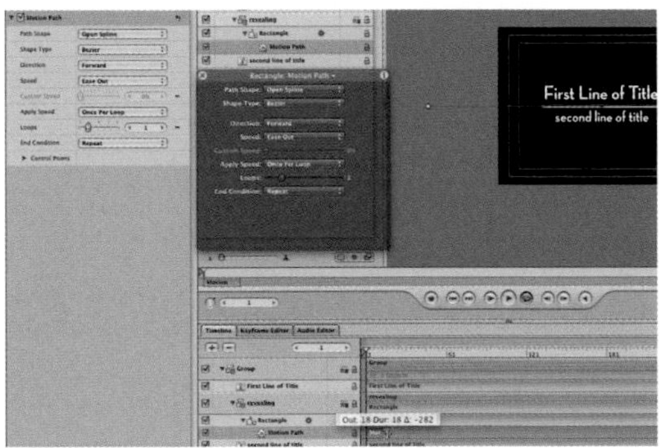

4 **Add Behavior/Basic Motion/Motion Path.** Adjust so the rectangle begins off screen (I chose it to come in from the left) and comes to rest back between the two lines of text. Set **Motion Path's** duration to about 18 frames and **Speed** to **Ease Out**.

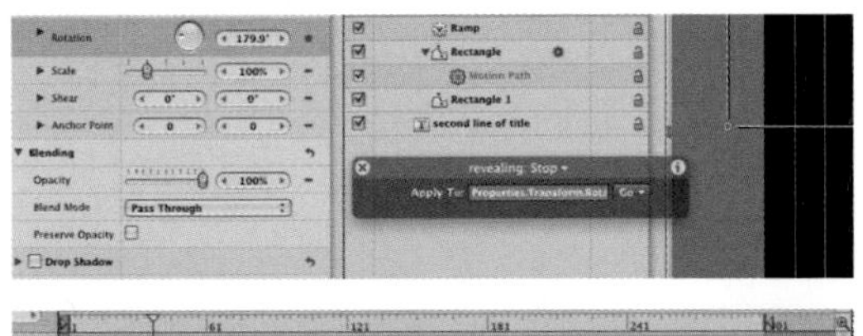

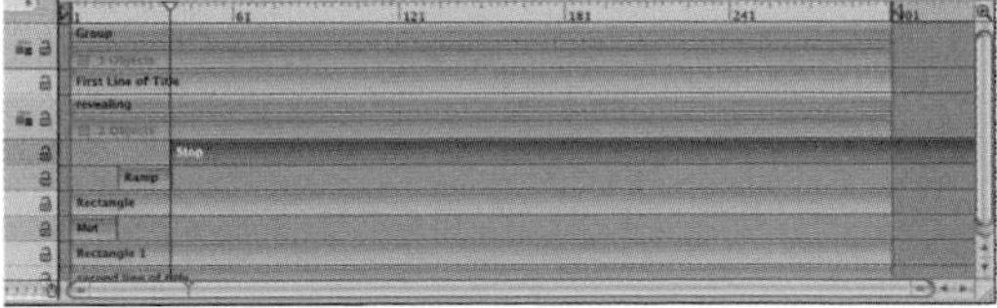

7 Position in the timeline to the last frame of **Ramp**. Right-click on **Rotation**. Select **Stop**.

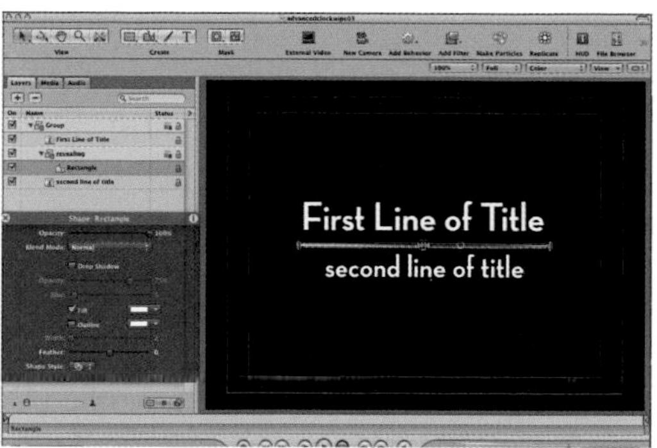

2 Click in the center of the screen below your first line, select your **Font**, **Size**, and **Color**. Set **Alignment** to **Center**. Type your second line. Press esc. Rearrange your layers if necessary so that your first line is above your second one in the **Layers** tab.

3 Add a new group between two text layers. Call it **revealing.** Press R to activate the **Rectangle** tool. Draw a thin white rectangle separating the two lines of text.

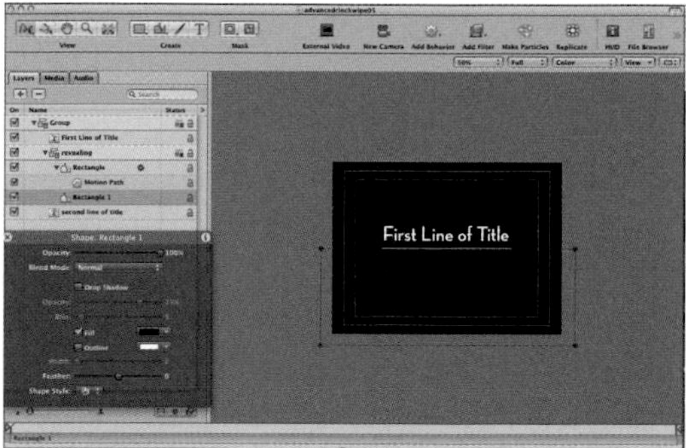

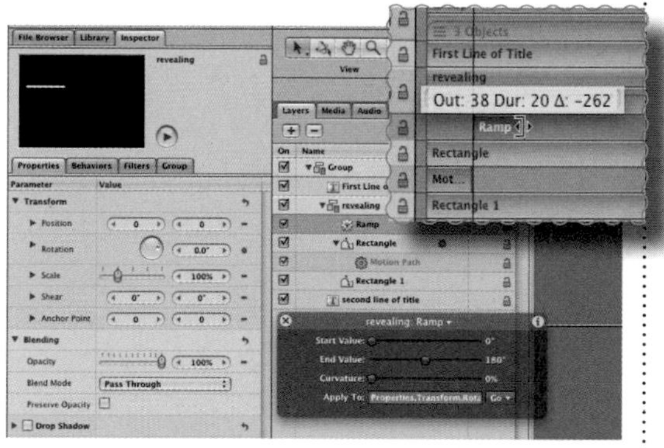

5 Again, activate the **Rectangle** tool. Draw a large black rectangle that extends off screen and lines up with the bottom of the thin white rectangle.

6 With the **revealing** group selected, in the **Properties** tab, right/ctrl-click on **Rotation**. Select **Ramp**. Set the **End Value** to **180**. Position 1 frame after the **Motion Path** behavior ends. Press I to start **Ramp** there. Set **Ramp's** duration to about **20**.

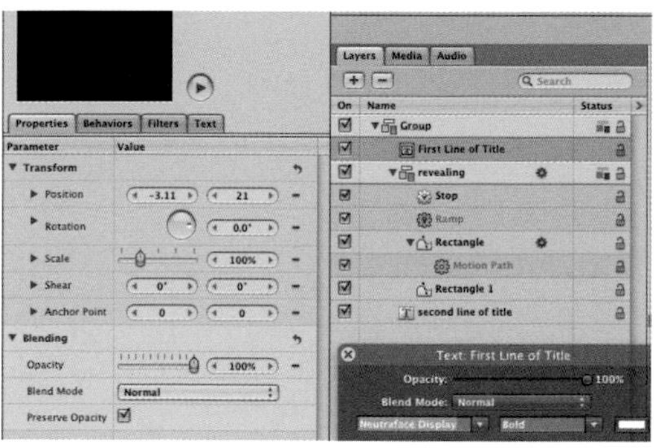

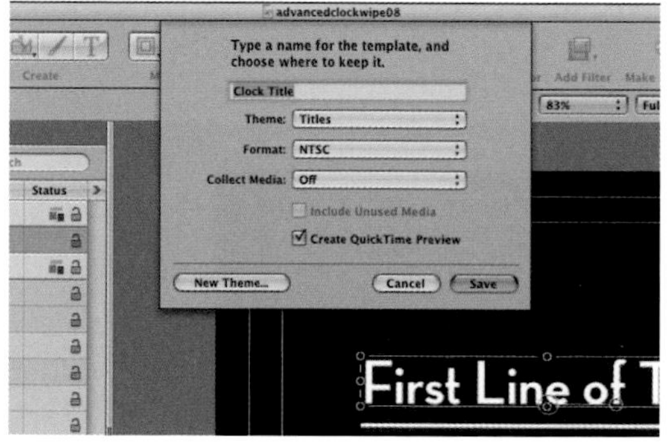

8 Select the first line of text. In the **Properties** tab, under **Blending**, click **Preserve Opacity**.

9 Now you save this as a template for use in Final Cut Pro.

Flashy Intro

As a closing exercise to this chapter, I decided to put together a flashy mock-title sequence or intro using a few of the tricks and techniques we've learned.

To build this, I took a random bit of footage I'd shot of my fellow editors, Nelson Brann (aka The Dude) and Camila Rhodes (aka The Beauty) on the patio outside Pistolera Post (where I work) and loaded it into Final Cut Pro.

I then poked around SoundDogs.com for a while and purchased some appropriate music for the intro—something with a spy flavor.

I took the clip, let it play while The Dude said a line, froze it for long enough to have a title come up on it, and then let it play til The Beauty said a line and froze it for her title.

Don't worry about having to recreate the Final Cut Pro project, I'm including the finished movie that I sent to Motion on the disc.

Owing to the complexity of this project, this one's more of a guide than a precision step by step.

IMAGES COURTESY NELSON BRANN & CAMILA RHODES

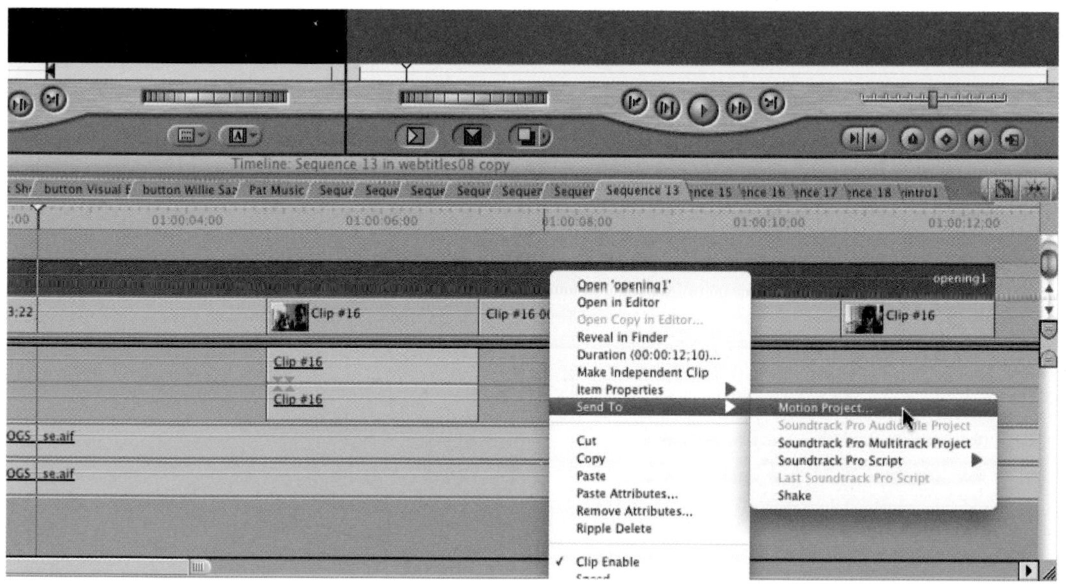

1 As I said in the intro, I started in Final Cut Pro to work out my timings, music, etc. Once I had those locked, I exported a Quicktime file, brought it back in, and cut it over the top of my original edit so that if I wanted to make changes later, I had easy access to the original edit. This also allowed me to "bake in" any filters like color correction, etc. I then sent the rendered clip to Motion.

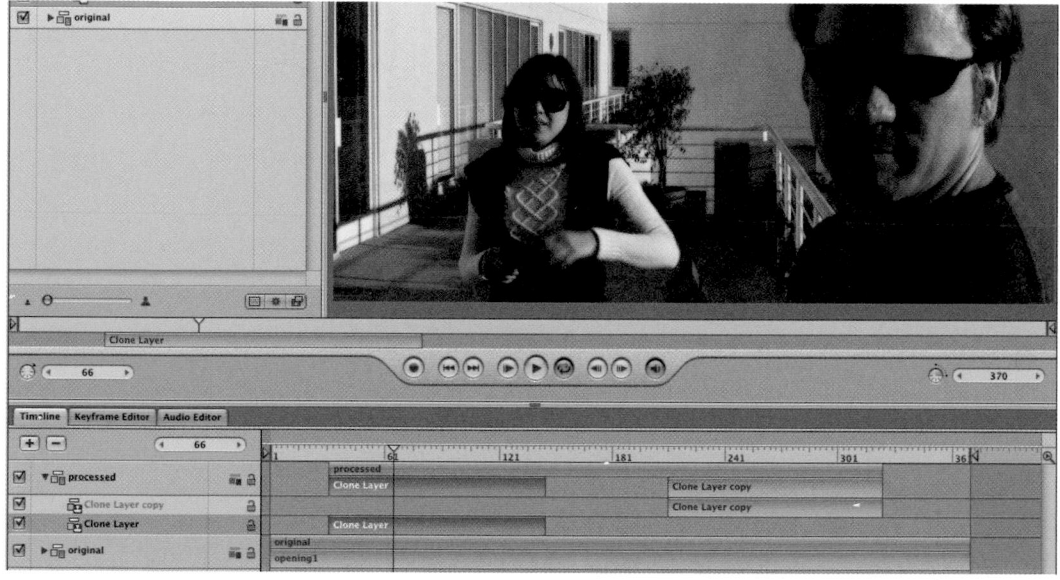

2 Once in Motion, I created two clone layers to do the processing on and trimmed them to cover the freeze areas of the sequence. I put them in a group called **Processed**.

HOT TIP

Final Cut Pro should always be treated as the hub of all things done with Final Cut Studio.

continued...

Flashy Intro (continued)

3 To effect the movie poster look, I used a **Threshold** filter and adjusted to taste and then a **Colorize** filter with two shades of blue.

5 I created a **title1** group to place my title in. I used a bold font (Impact) to type my title, and to give it a bit of dash, I added a **Sphere** filter and adjusted position and radius to suit.

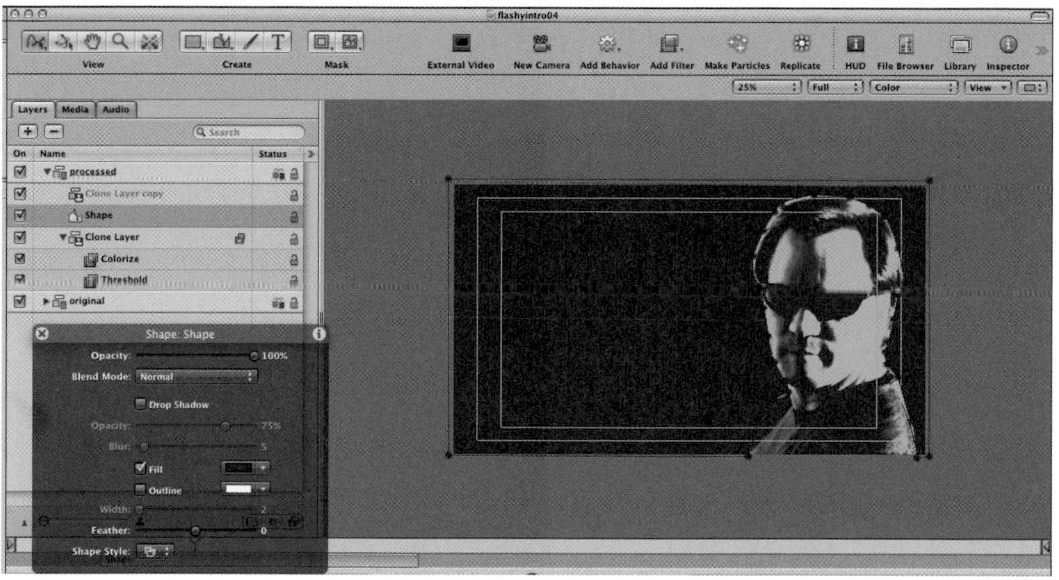

4 To complete the look, I used a shape colored the same as my dark blue from my **Colorize** filter, and I drew around my main character (a pen tablet really helps with the drawing).

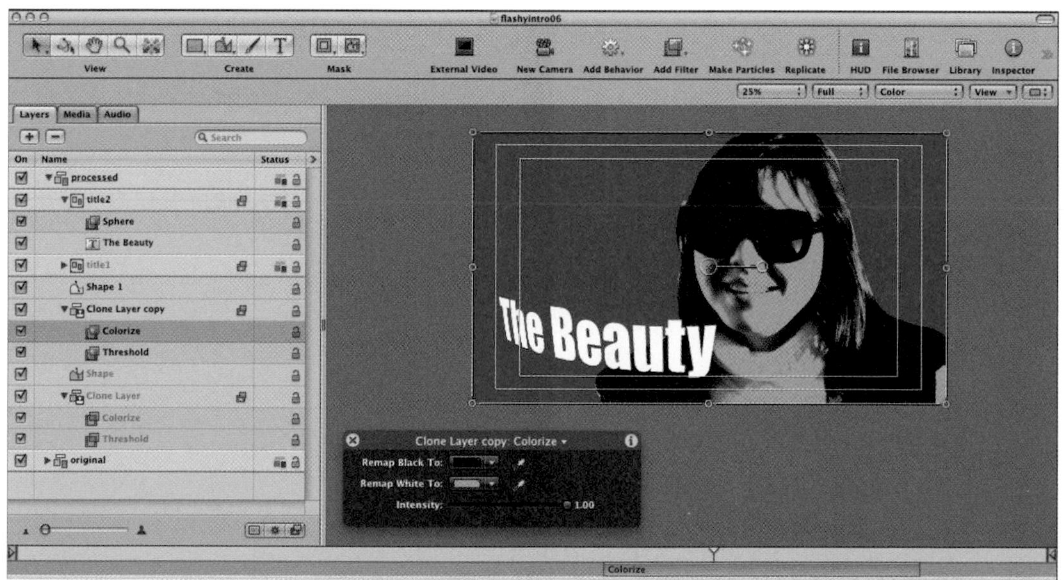

6 I did the same thing for my second character, only this time I used a pink and brown colorize and a red shape.

continued...

Flashy Intro (continued)

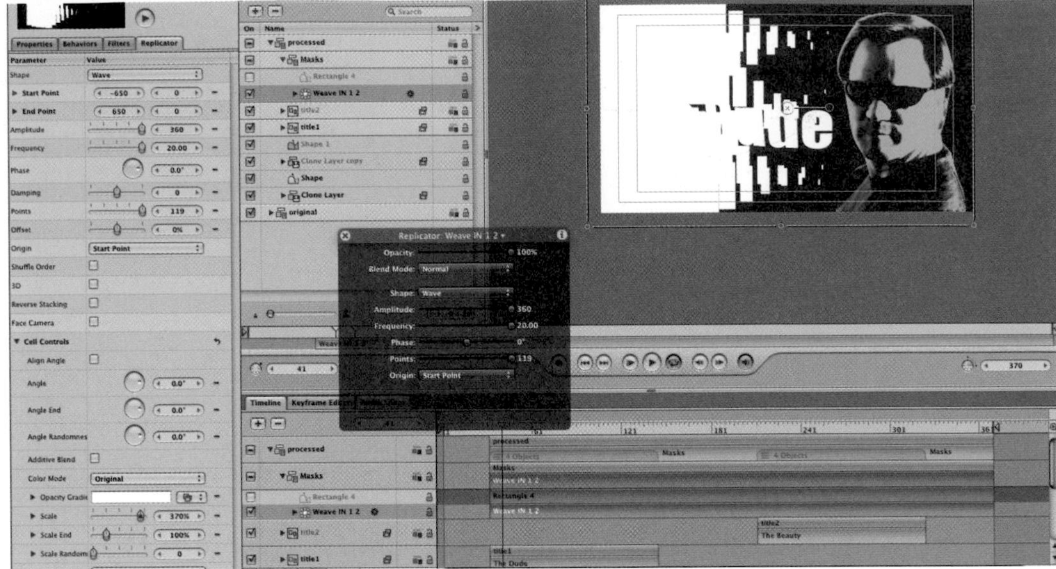

7 I didn't want the poster look to just pop on, so I created a **Masks** group and from the **Library/Replicators/Transitional**. I selected **Weave In 1** and pressed **Apply**. You'll want to size it so when it's done it fills the screen.

9 Once you've built with the **Masks** group, add an **Image Mask** to the **Processed** group, and then drag the **Masks** group into the **Source Image** well. And that's it, you're done!

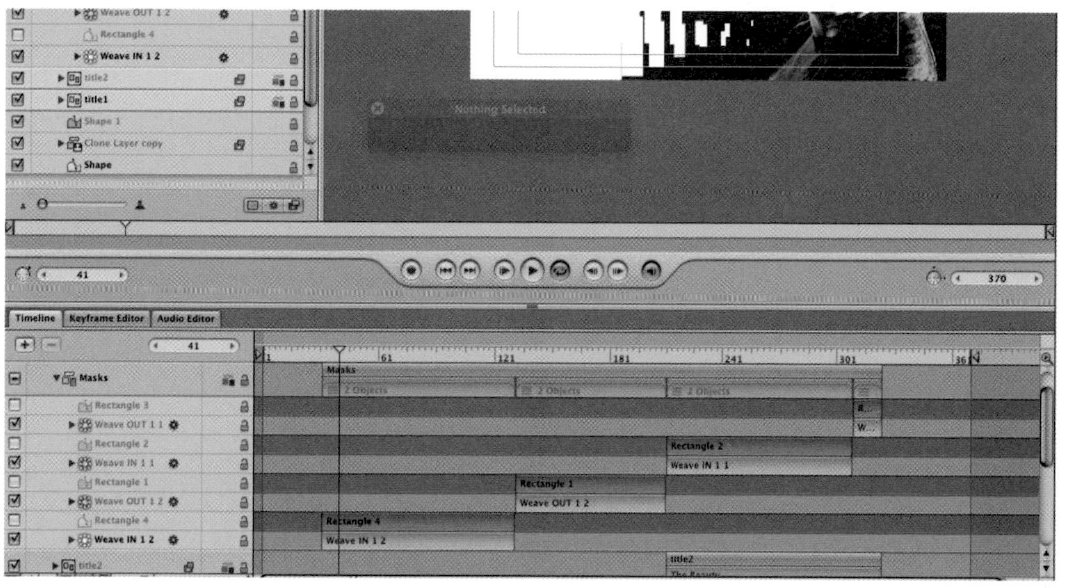

8 Backing up an appropriate amount of time, I added a **Weave Out 1** replicator and then sized and trimmed it. Repeat the procedure for the second character.

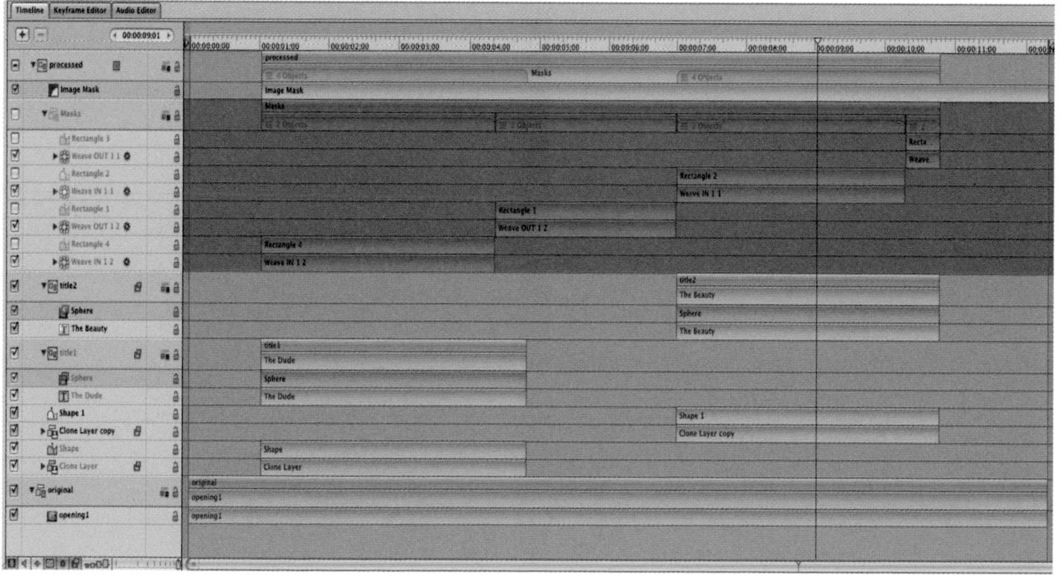

10 A look at the final timeline.

7 INTERLUDE

Technology vs. Magic

IT'S BEEN SAID THAT IF YOU understand something, that's technology, and if it's a mystery, it's magic. It's been my observation that people often approach complex things from those two perspectives–either it's **Technology** that they learn and understand so they can use it or it's **Magic** that they learn to use without understanding it. Either approach works and I've spoken to advocates from both camps.

To most people, automobiles and major appliances fall into the realm of Magic. Nevertheless, they are able to drive where they want to without having to take a course in auto mechanics and can use the microwave or dishwasher with impunity. I think it's the same with most complex software, Motion included.

Some folks don't want to understand it–they feel their creativity would be hampered if they became too "techie" and understood too much. To them, Creativity = Magic. I get that–it's related to "The Centipede's Dilemma":

> A centipede was happy quite,
> Until a frog in fun
> Said, "Pray, which leg comes after which?"
> This raised her mind to such a pitch,
> She lay distracted in the ditch
> Considering how to run.

The idea is that too closely examining something one does intuitively breaks the intuitive process. I understand that fear, but for me, two other principles override it. They are:

"Knowledge informs Creativity"
and
"Creativity expands Knowledge."

The more you use what you know, the more you learn, and the more you learn, the better you are at taking what's in your head and putting it up there on the screen. Knowing what you *can* do to create something is much more important than thinking of something wonderful you'd like to do, without having a clue of how to accomplish it.

In other words, what good is having a profound and guiding vision if you don't have the knowledge required to achieve it? (unless, of course, you're a director.)

Ultimately, the fears of Magicians are unfounded—I'm not talking about delving into the source of ideas or encouraging a forensic exam of the creative process. Rather it is the intimate knowledge of the tools required that will make you more productive and creative.

And I know, at least in the long run, that turning Magic into Technology doesn't stifle creative vision. I can say this because I have ideas all the time that I have yet to figure out how to achieve.

Special thanks to Spider Robinson, whose book **Variable Star** reminded me of the Centipede's Dilemma.

■ Motion's 3D capabilities are manifold. With just a few of them, your titling or graphic project can really stand out.

8 3D and Me

MOTION HAS HAD A FULL-FLEDGED 3D environment since revision 3, including cameras, lights, etc. The possibilities are astounding, but I have found in the two dimensional static medium of a book, it is difficult to show how to use them to their fullest extent.

This chapter will, instead, concentrate on clever and simple ways to use 3D and the appearance of 3D to enhance your projects.

The final two projects in this chapter, however, use full on 3D with lights, cameras, and action. You'll find them a bit longer and more complicated, but I think the effect is worth it.

Mock 3D

BEFORE MOTION HAD ADDED true 3D capability, I came up with this Mock 3D project. I thought it looked cool, but I still haven't found an effective use for it. Maybe you will.

I started with a replicator of rectangles, colored random shades of gray, and used the color cycling method to generate a panel of shifting gray shaded rectangles. I then fed that into the well for both Indent and Relief to get a series of growing/shrinking boxes.

IMAGE COURTESY PARKER SHEFFIELD

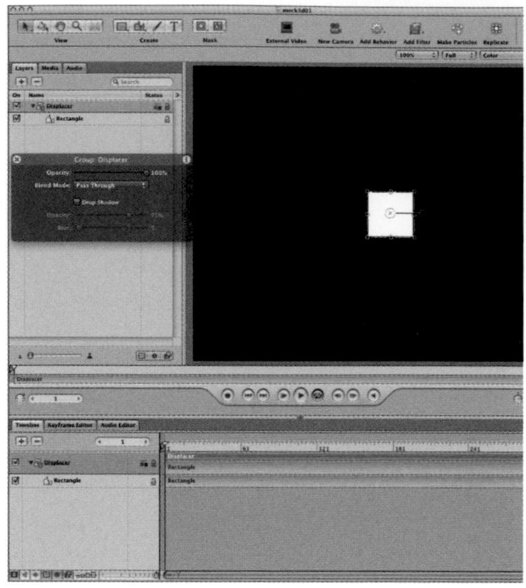

1 Start with a new project. Name the default group **Displacer**. Press **R** to activate the **Rectangle** tool. Hold down the **Shift** key and draw a square in the middle of the canvas.

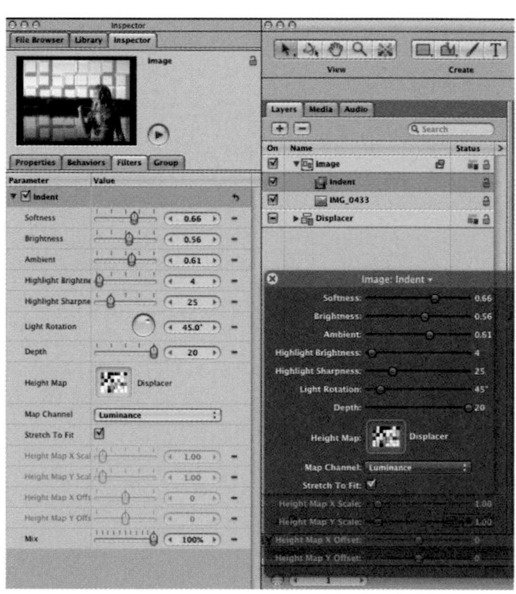

4 Add a new group on top named **Image**. Place your picture/clip in the **Image** group. With **Image** selected, **Add Filter/Stylize/Indent**. Set **Softness** to **.66**, **Brightness** to **.56**, **Ambient** to **.61**, **Highlight Brightness** to **4**, **Highlight Sharpness** to **25**, and **Depth** to **20**. Drag the **Displacer** group into the **Height Map** well.

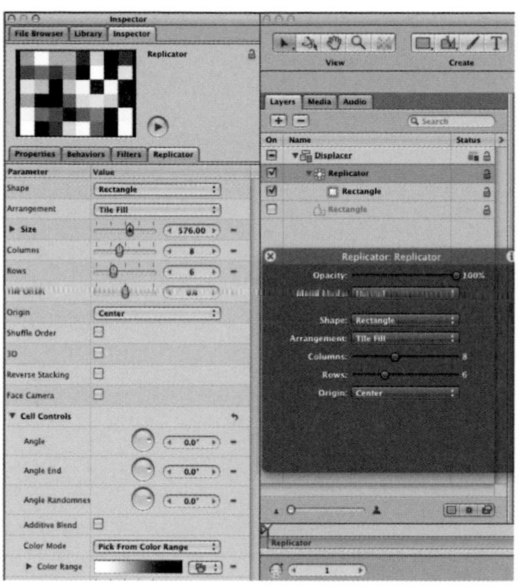

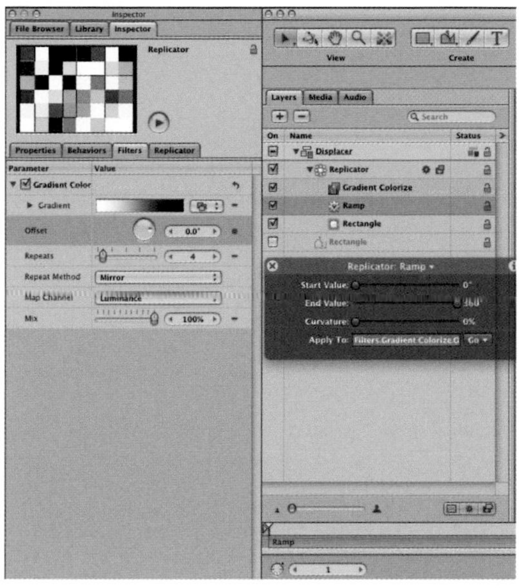

2 With the square selected, Press L or click on the **Replicate** button in the toolbar. Adjust the **Size** and **Rows** and **Columns** to create a grid of squares filling the screen. They should be touching each other but not overlapping. Set the **Color Mode** to **Pick From Color Range**. Set the **Color Range Gradient** to **Grayscale**.

3 Add **Filter/Color Correction/Gradient Colorize**. Set the **Repeats** to **4**. Right/ctrl-click on **Offset** and select **Ramp**. Set the **End Value** to **360**.

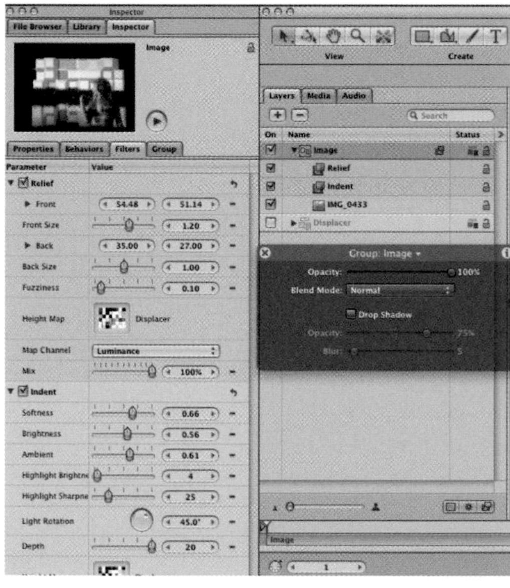

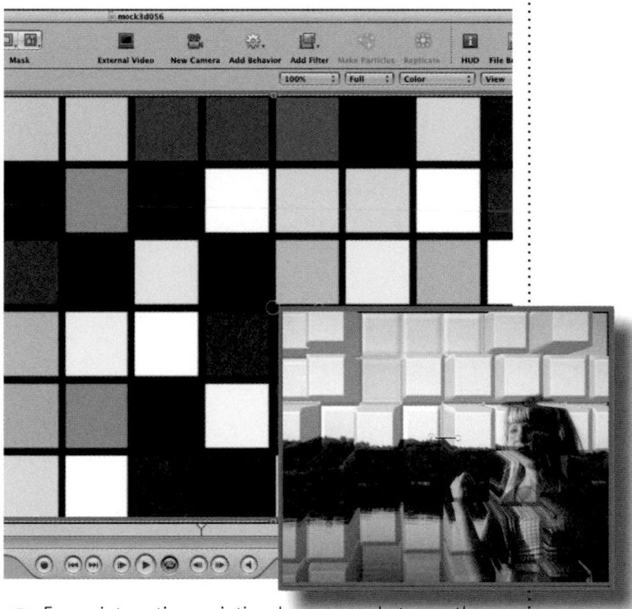

5 Add **Filter/Stylize/Relief**. Set the **Front** to 55, 52 and the **Front Size** to **1.2**. Set the **Back** to 35, 27 and **Back Size** to **1.0**. Drag the **Displacer** group into the **Height Map** well. Turn off the **Displacer** group. Then grab the entire **Image** group and recenter it.

6 For an interesting variation, leave space between the squares in the displacer.

Mirror Ball

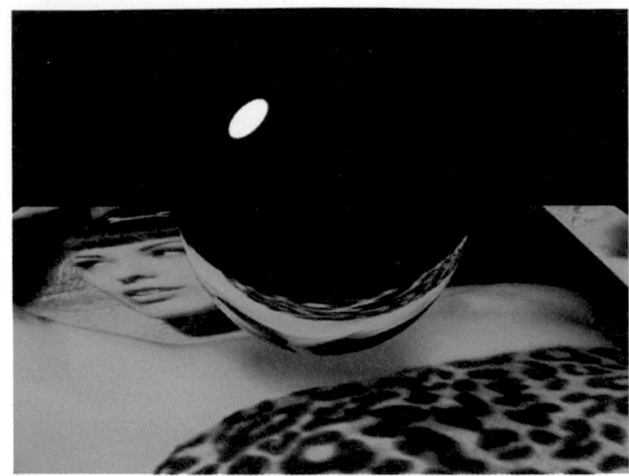

IMAGE COURTESY OCTAVIO ARIZALA

IN THIS PROJECT WE'RE GOING to construct a classic polished sphere that reflects its surroundings.

Now we could use the Sphere filter in Motion, but instead, let's use a Core Image filter—Motion has access to a raft of them. This one's called Glass Lozenge. We'll build a reflection map for it.

1 Start with a new project. Name the default group **original**. Place your image or clip in it. For the purposes of this project, we'll use a still and animate it with the **Offset** filter. Press K to create a clone layer. Name the new group **image**. Rename the **Clone Layer** to **original copy 1**. Turn off the **original** group.

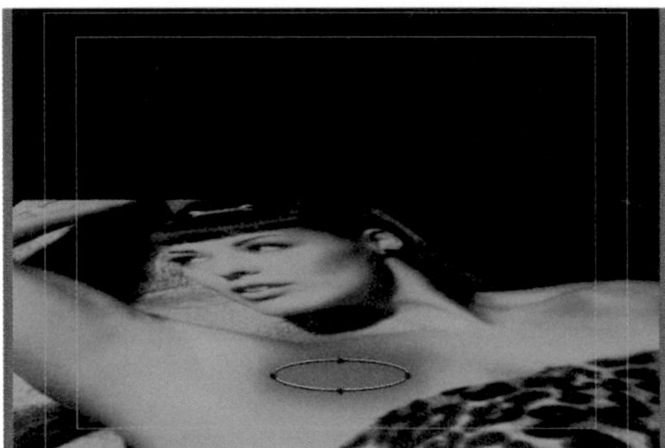

4 With **plane** selected, press C to activate the **Circle** tool. Draw a small black filled ellipse just below the center of the image. Set the **Feather** to about **80** and **Opacity** to **50%**. Name the circle **shadow**.

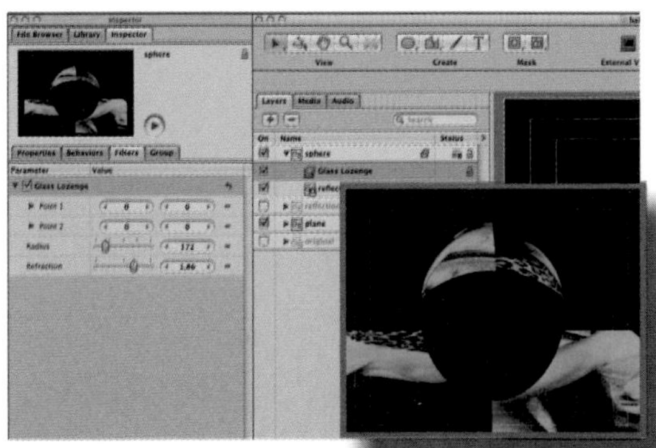

7 Select **sphere**. Go to **Library/Image Units/Distortion Effect**, and click on **Glass Lozenge**. Press **Apply**. Set **Point 1** and **Point 2** to **0, 0**. Set **Radius** to **172** and **Refraction** to **1.86**. Grab the **reflection** clone and adjust its vertical position until the "reflection" occupies an arc around the top of the "ball."

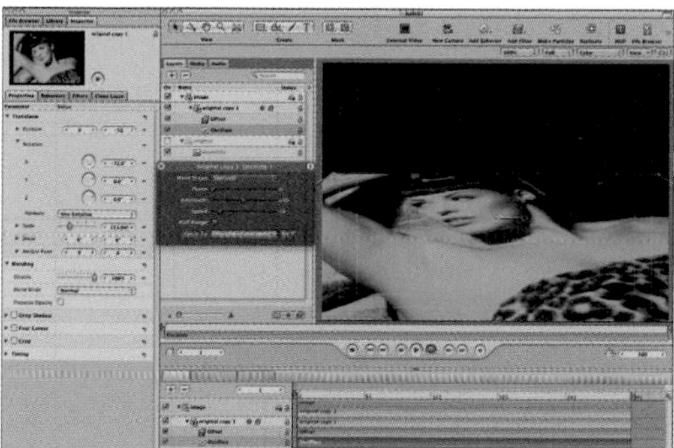

2 Select **original copy 1**. In the **Properties** tab, change **X Rotation** to **-72°**. Adjust **Position** and **Scale** until the image touches the bottom of the screen and is about full width at the top. Add **Filter/Tiling/Offset**. Right/ctrl-click on **Horizontal Offset**. Select **Oscillate**. Set the **Wave Shape** to **Sawtooth** and the **Speed** to **12**.

3 Select the **image** group. Press ⌘ Shift G. Name the new group **plane**. Set **Fixed Resolution**. Set **X** and **Y Position** to **0**. Reposition the **image** group if needed for good framing. Press R and draw a black filled rectangle that fills the screen. Place it below the **image** group.

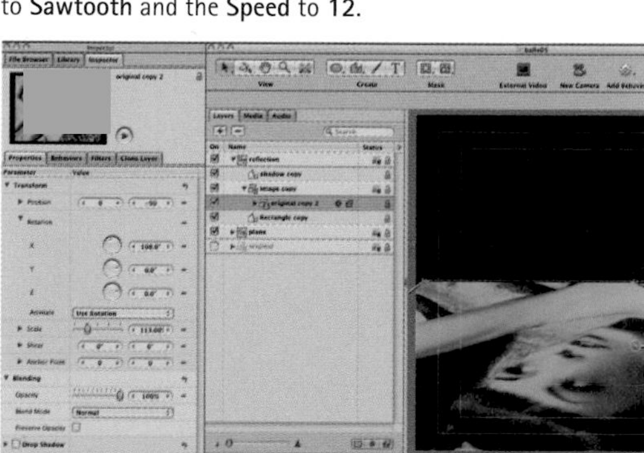

5 Now let's create the reflection map. With **plane** selected, press ⌘ D. Name the duplicate **reflection**. Select **original copy 2**. In the **Properties** tab, change the **X Rotation** to **108**. Set the **Y Position** about 40 lower, to about **-90**.

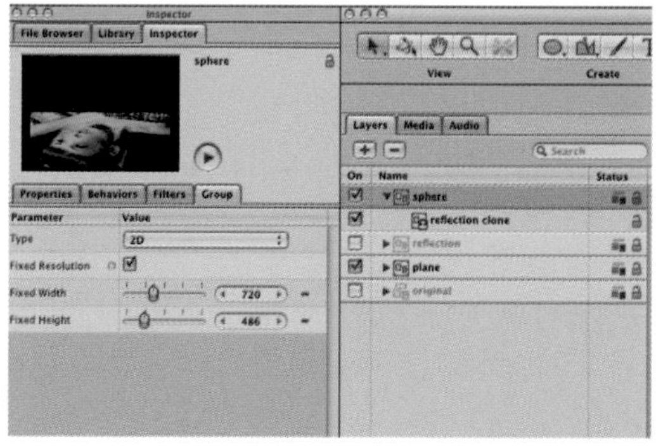

6 Now for the mirror ball. With **reflection** selected, press K to create a clone layer. Name the new group **sphere**. Select **Fixed Resolution**. Rename the **Clone Layer** to **reflection clone**. Turn off the **reflection** group.

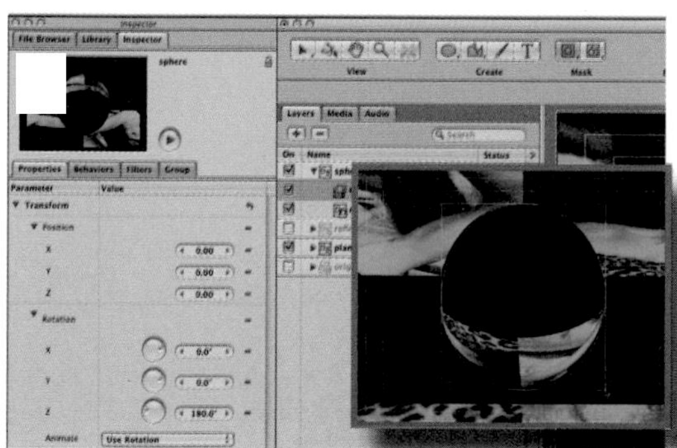

8 Select the **sphere** group. In the **Properties** tab, change the **Z Rotation** to **180°**. Select the **Circle Mask** tool (⌥ C). Hold down the ⌥ **(Option)** key, and click in the center of the sphere and drag the circle mask outward until it lines up with the edge of the ball.

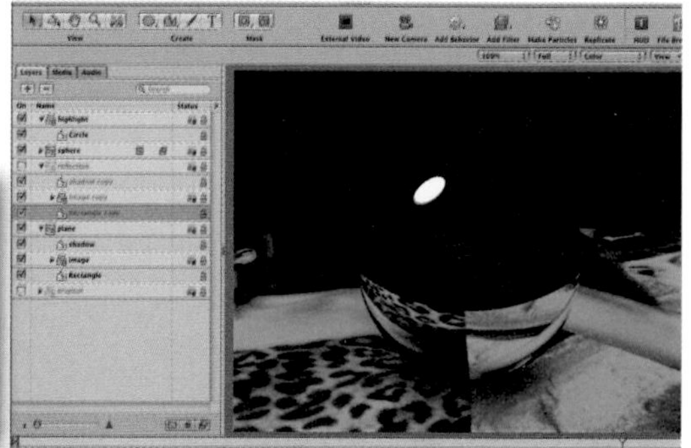

9 Finally, add a new layer over everything called **highlight**. Draw a small white ellipse. Rotate and position it as shown above. If needed, adjust the position of the **shadow** circle in the **plane** group. You can also adjust the fill of the **Rectangle** in the **reflection** group to make the sphere stand out against the black backdrop.

Crystal Ball

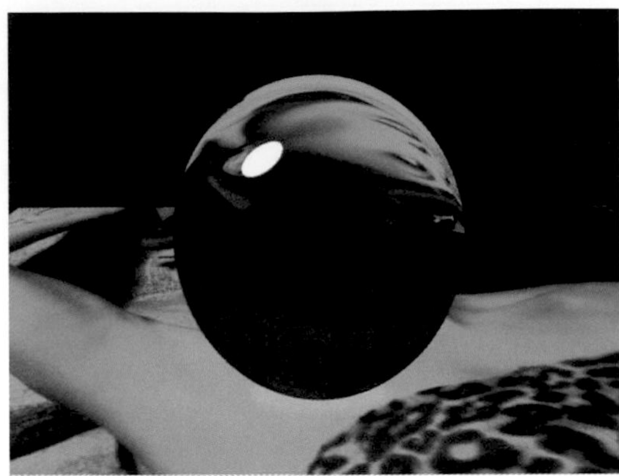

A CRYSTAL BALL COMBINES both reflection and refraction, so as well as our reflection map from the Mirror Ball project, we'll have to build a motion/position inverted *refraction map.* And since our crystal ball passes and focuses light, our shadow becomes a light.

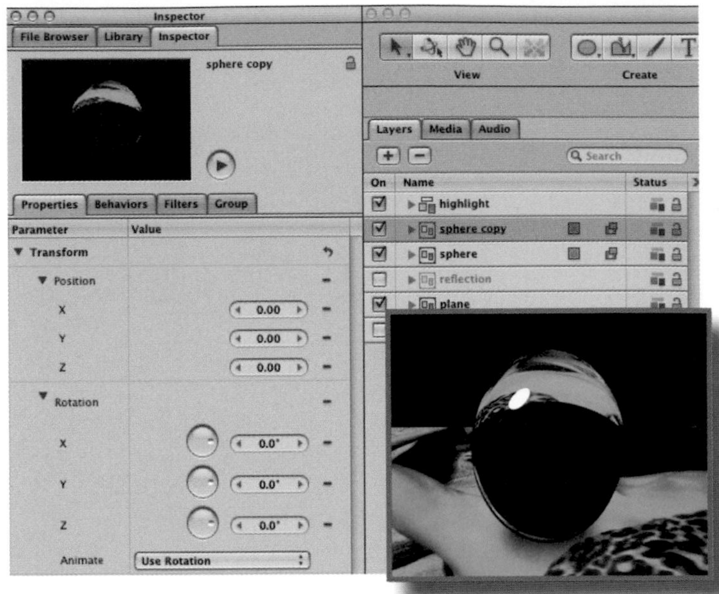

1 To build the Crystal Ball, begin with the completed Mirror Ball project from the previous page. While positioned on frame 1, select the **sphere** group. Press ⌘D. Select **sphere copy.** In the **Properties** tab, change the **Z Rotation to 0°.**

3 Select the **sphere** group. Move it above the **sphere copy** group. Change the **Blend Mode** to **Add.** Change the **Opacity** to **18%.** Ensure it lines up with the **sphere copy** group.

IMAGE COURTESY OCTAVIO ARIZALA

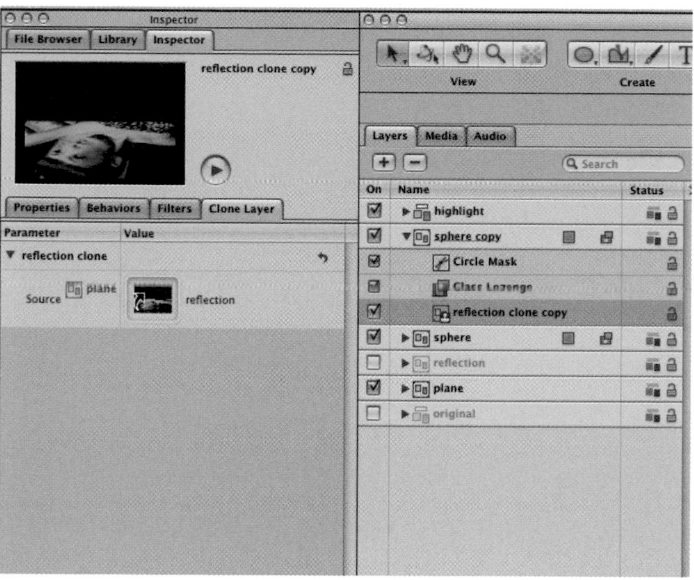

2 Select **reflection clone copy**. Drag the **plane** group into the source well.

4 Change the **Fill Color** of **shadow** to **White.** Change the **Feather** to **15**, the **Blend Mode** to **Overlay**, and the **Opacity** to **100%**. You can do the same to the **shadow copy** shape in the **reflection** group.

Big Blue Marble

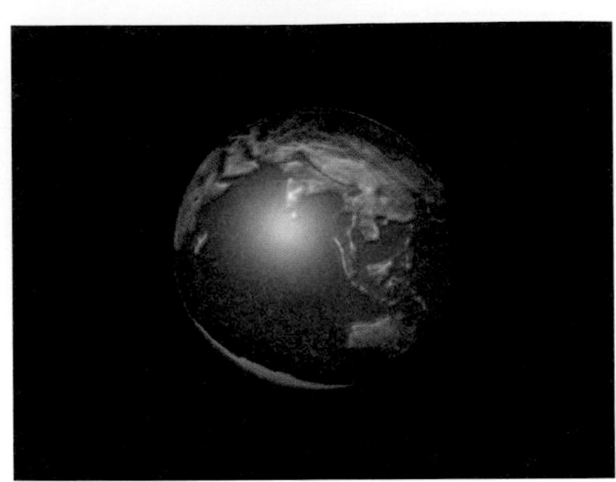

MAKING A SPINNING EARTH IS a classic. And in Motion, it's a pretty easy project, too.

Motion doesn't have 3D primitives like a sphere, so we'll use the Sphere filter instead. This is not a true sphere, which you'll see if you do the Text Around the World project, but it suits our purposes just fine. Combine it with the Starfield background for a real "space picture."

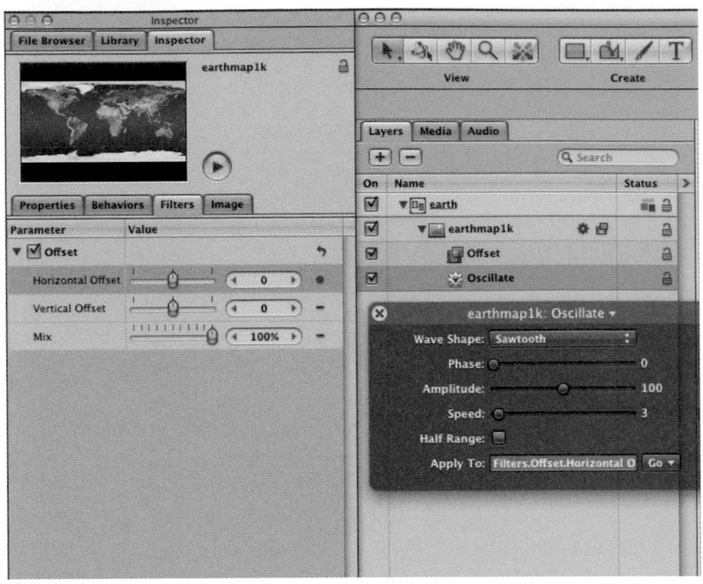

1 Start with a new project. Name the default group **earth**. Set **Fixed resolution**. Drag your earth map into it. **Add Filter/Tiling/Offset**. Right/ctrl-click on **Horizontal Offset**. Select **Oscillate**. Set the **Wave Shape** to **Sawtooth** and **Speed** to 3.

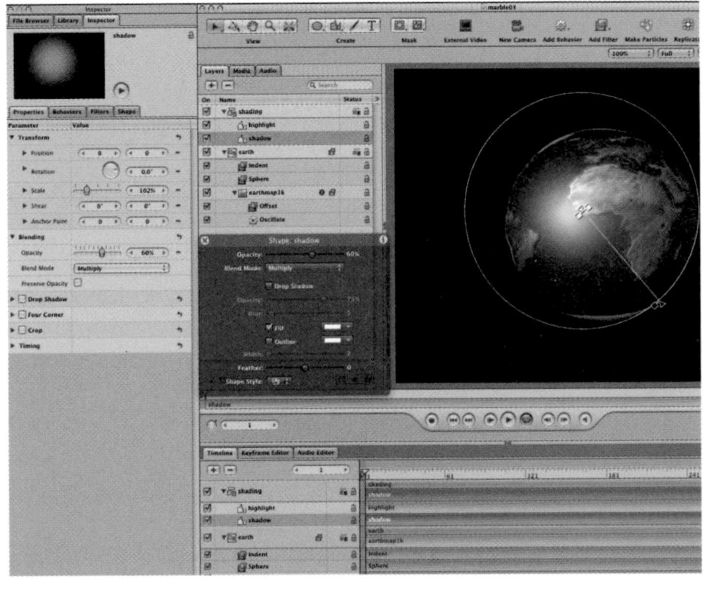

3 Select the **shading** group. Add a **Radial Gradient** filled circle the same size as your earth. Name it **shadow**. You can use **Grayscale** as the **Gradient**, and edit as above. Set the **Blend Mode** to **Multiply**. **Opacity** to 60%. Add a small white circle in the center of the sphere. Set the **Feather** to **85**, **Blend Mode** to **Add**, and **Opacity** to **60%**.

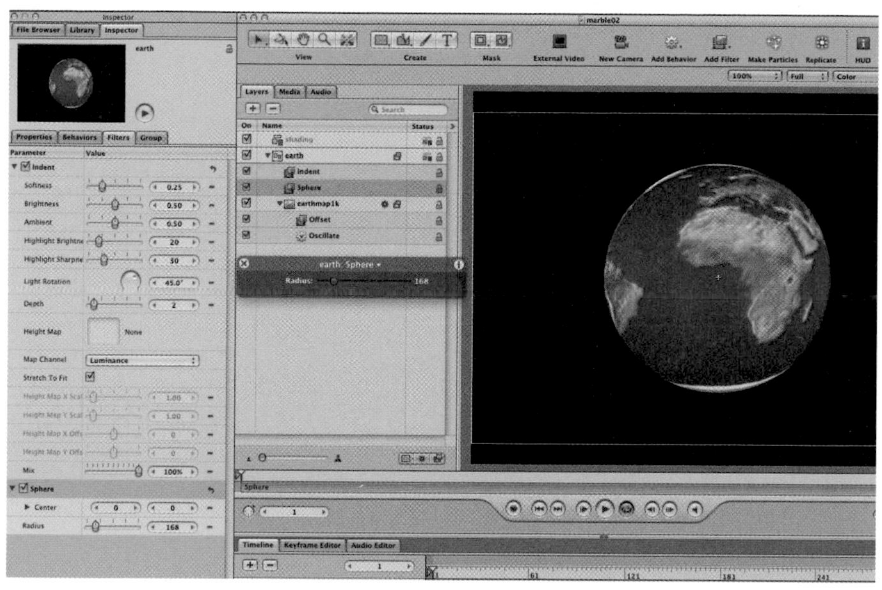

2 Select the **earth** group. **Add Filter/Distortion/Sphere**. Set the **Radius** to **168**. **Add Filter/Stylize/Indent**. Set the **Depth** to **2**. In the **Properties** tab, set the **Y Scale** to **89%**. Add a new group over the **earth** group. Name it **shading**.

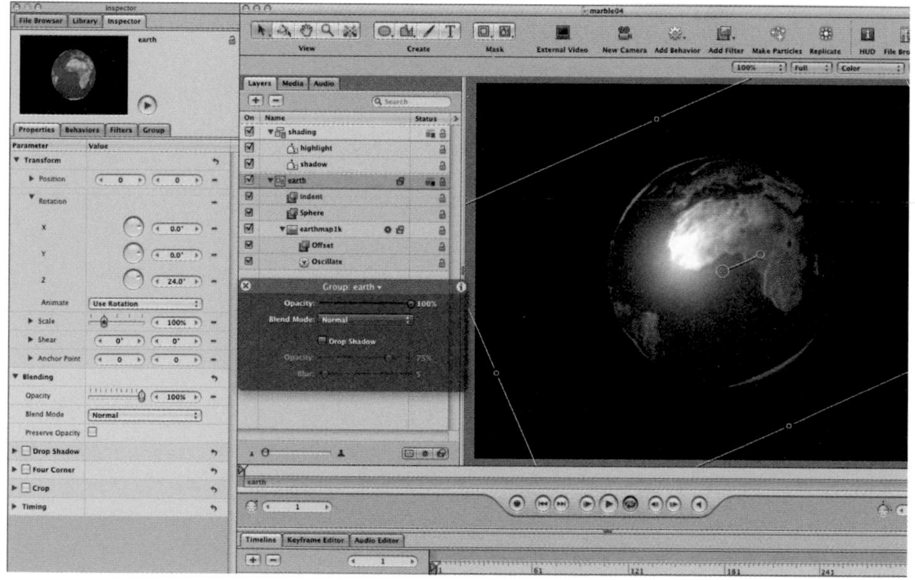

4 Finally, select the **earth** group. In the **Properties** tab, set the **Z Rotation** to **-24°**.

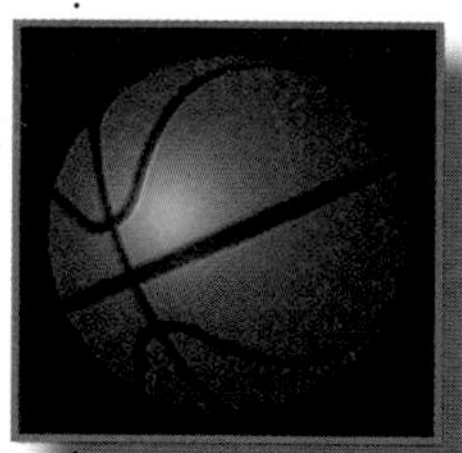

HOT TIP

It doesn't have to be a rotating Earth—there are texture maps out there used for 3D CG for any planet or ball you want.

Mock Shadows

WE DON'T NEED TO DIP into 3D and lighting to get shadows in Motion. We'll use the ever handy clone layer and a Gradient blur to help us out.

You may have noticed that we're halfway through the "3D and Me" chapter and still haven't used "real" 3D, just the *appearance* of it. We will use some of Motion's real 3D capabilities, including cameras and lights, later in this chapter, but as I mentioned in the chapter's intro, the 3D world is hard to convey in a 2D book.

The other advantage of keeping things 2D is you don't have the overhead that comes with Motion's 3D space.

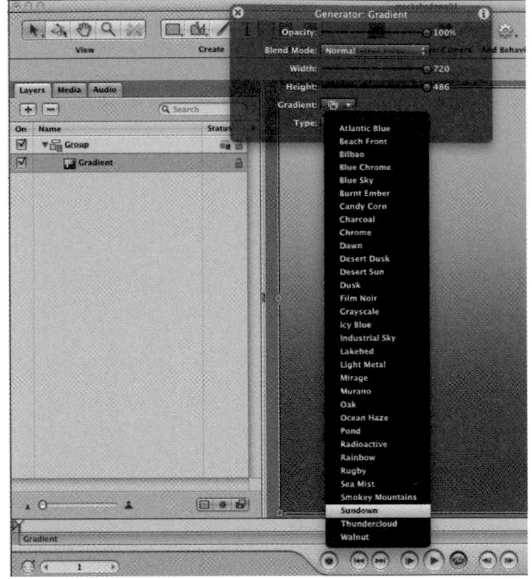

1 Start with a new project. From the **Library/Generators**, grab a **Gradient generator** and throw it on your canvas. Change the **Gradient** to **Sundown**.

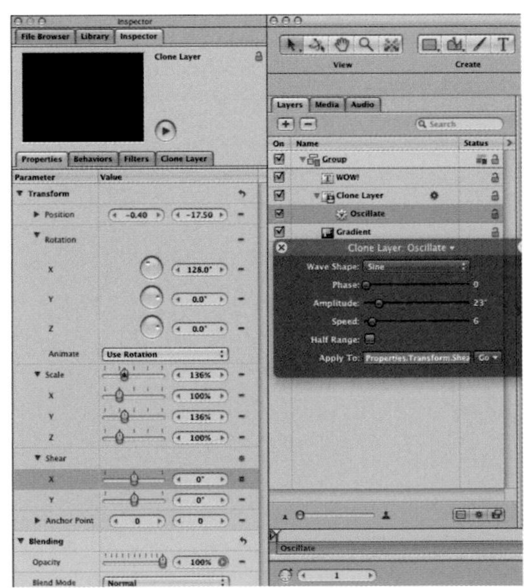

4 Right/ctrl-click on **X Shear** in the **Properties** tab. Select **Oscillate**. Set the **Amplitude** to **23**. Set the **Speed** to **6**.

2 Press **T** to activate the **Text** tool. Click on the center of the screen, set your **Font** to **Arial Black**, **Size** to **159** points, **Color** to dark brown, and **Alignment** to **Center**. Type the word **WOW!** Then press the **esc** key.

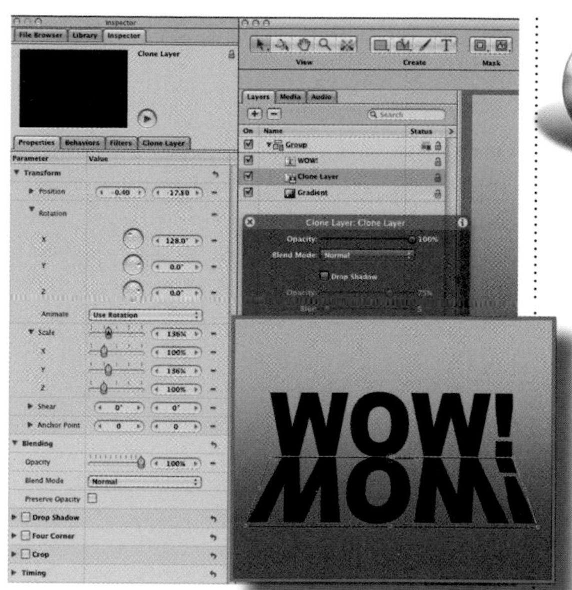

3 With the **WOW!** layer selected, press **K** to create a clone layer. Drag the clone layer below the **WOW!** layer on your stack. In the **Position** tab, set the **X Rotation** to **128°**. Line the clone shadow up just below your text. Set the **Y Scale** to **136**.

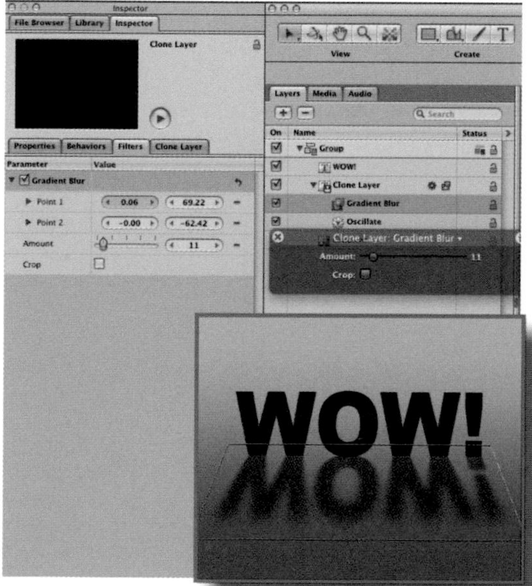

5 With **Clone Layer** still selected, set the **Blend Mode** to **Multiply. Opacity** to **60%**. **Add Filter/Blur/Gradient Blur**. Place **Point 1** at the top of your shadow and **Point 2** at the bottom. Set the **Amount** to **11**. Turn off **Crop**.

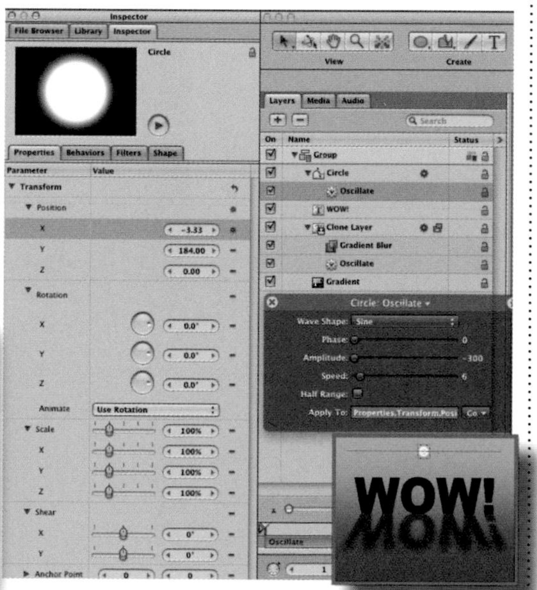

6 Draw a small circle in the "sky" above your word. Set the **Feather** to 7. In the **Position** tab, right/**ctrl**-click on the **X Position.** Select **Oscillate.** Set the **Amplitude** to **-300** and **Speed** to **6.**

Real Shadows

MOTION 4 GIVES US REAL 3D SHADOWS to play with, so let's re-create our Mock 3D "WOW!" shadow project from the previous exercise. Motion 4 also has improved performance when it comes to dealing with type and its 3D workspace, so this should run realtime for you.

In addition to 3D lighting and shadows, we'll use that ever handy Link behavior that came in Motion 4 too.

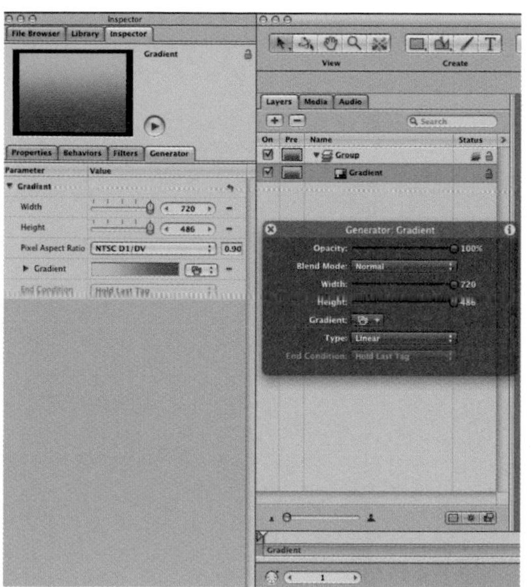

1 Start with a new project. Change the default group to **3D**. Go to **Library/Generators** and select **Gradient**. Click Apply. Change the **Gradient** to **Sundown**.

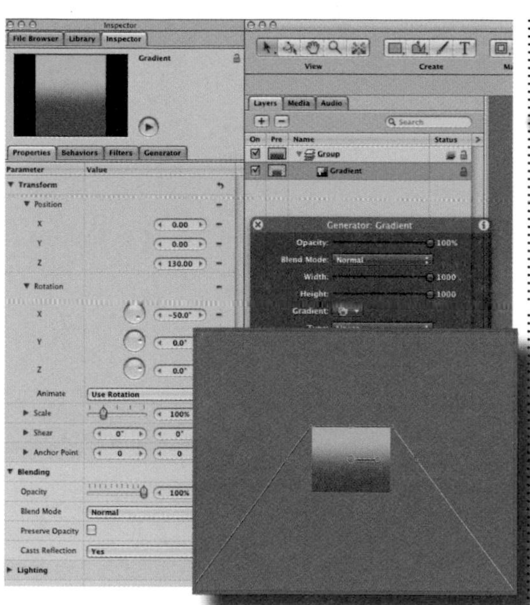

2 In the **gradient's Properties** tab, change the **Z Position** to **130**. Change the **X Rotation** to **-50**. Now we have black at the top. In the **Generator** tab, adjust the **Height** and **Width** until you've covered the black bits (about **1000x1000**).

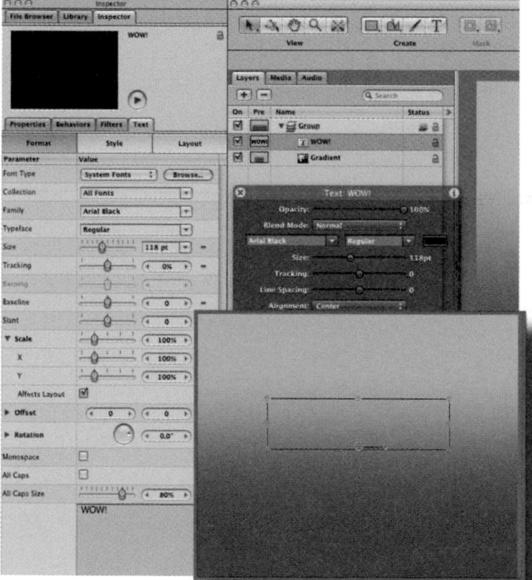

3 Press T, or activate the **Text** tool. Click in the center of the screen. Set your **Font** to **Arial Black**, **Color** to a deep warm brown (**R 0.23**, **G 0.02**, **B 0.0**), **Size 118 pt**, and **Alignment Centered**. Type **WOW!** Then press the esc key.

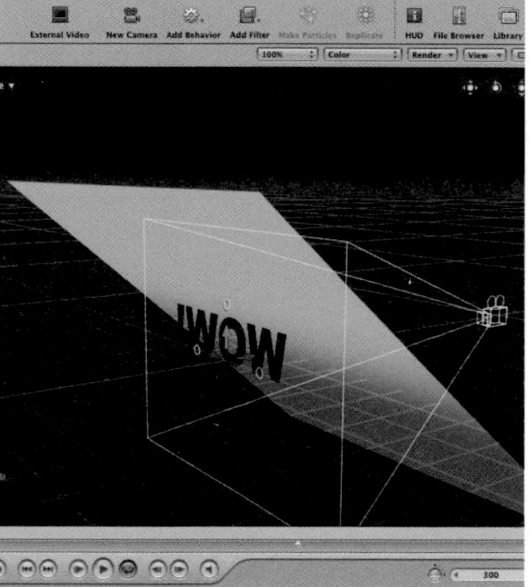

4 What happened? Where is our text? Although you don't need to for this project, clicking **New Camera** and looking from the side with **Perspective View** shows what's going on. Our text is hidden behind the angled gradient.

continued...

Real Shadows (continued)

5 If you did add a camera, switch back to the **Active Camera** view. Pull the **WOW!** text forward by altering its **Z Position** until the bottom of the letters just touches the gradient. For mine, **Z** is about **135**.

6 Now add a light: type ⌘ Shift L. Set the **Light Type** to Spot, **Intensity** to **270%**, **Cone Angle** to **82%**, and **Soft Edge** to **15°**. Set the **Shadows** checkbox. Set **Softness** to **9**.

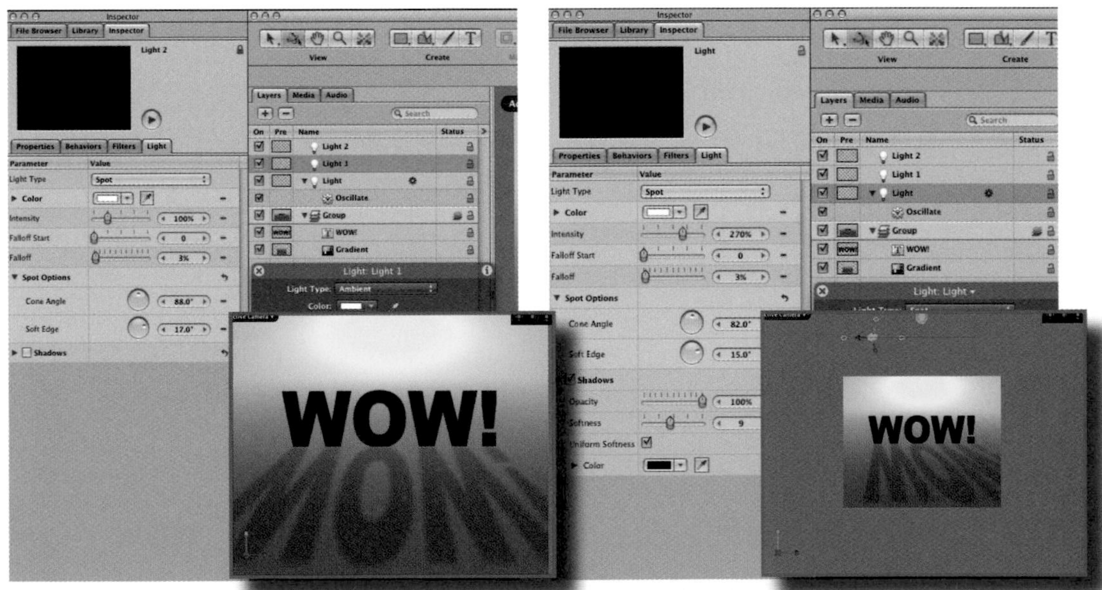

9 It's a little dark still. Add another light with ⌘ Shift L. Change **Light Type** to **Ambient**. Set the **Intensity** to **81%**. ⌘ Shift L to add another light. Set the **Light Type** to **Spot**. Set the **Cone Angle** to **88°** and **Soft Edge** to **17°**. Then go to the **Properties** tab and set **Y Position** to **465** and **Z Position** to **-8**.

10 If you press **Play** now, you'll see that the shadows generated by the spotlight track back and forth, but since lights themselves are invisible, there is no sun.

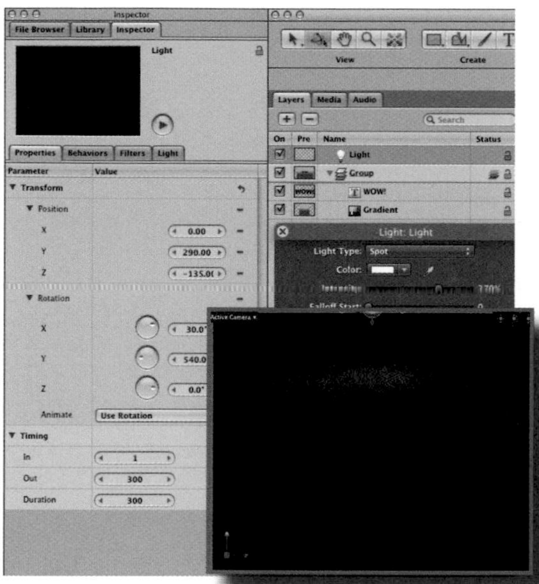

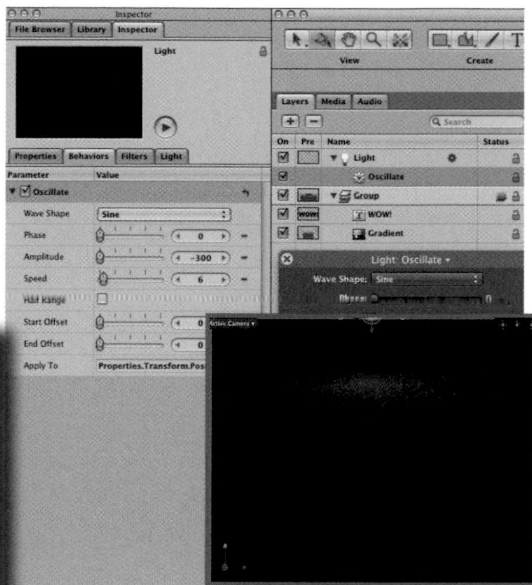

7 In the light's **Properties** tab, set **Y Position** to **450** and **Z** to **-135**. X Set **Rotation** to **30**, and **Y Rotation** to **540**.

8 Right/ctrl-click on **X Position**. Select **Oscillate**. Change the **Amplitude** to **300**. **Speed** to **6**.

11 Activate the **Circle** tool (C), and holding down the Shift and ⌥ keys, draw a small circle in the upper portion of the screen directly beneath the moving light. Set the **Feather** to 10. Change the **Blend Mode** to **Add**.

12 In the **Circle**'s **Properties** tab, turn off the **Cast Shadows**. Right/ctrl-click on the **X Position** and select **Link**. Drag the spot **Light** (the one with the **Oscillate** Behavior on it) into the **Source Object** well. Now we have a representation of the sun to follow our moving spot.

3D Orbital Text

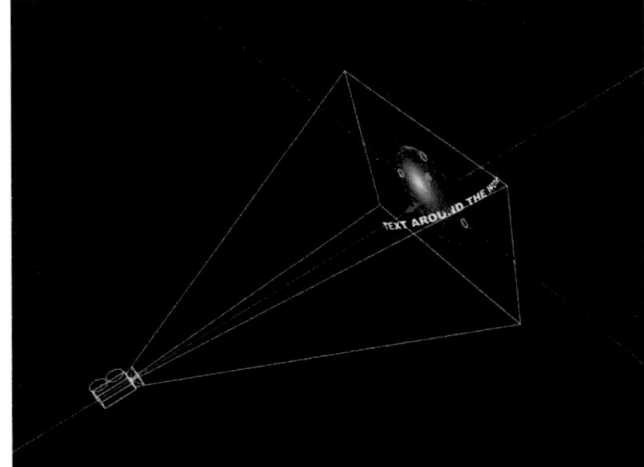

BECAUSE SOMETIMES YOU JUST need to orbit a message around the world.

This project brings to mind newsreel clips from the past century. As you can see above, in this case, we're faking the sphere. We'll use the Blue Marble project as a 2D prop in a 3D world.

And, just in case you're wondering, no—you can't put an extrude on the text. Nor can you have it leave a shadow across the surface of the Earth. Believe me, I tried. Most things just collapse the 3D and ruin the illusion.

1 Start with the results of the Blue Marble project. Select the **shading** and **earth** groups and press ⌘ Shift G. Change the **Group Type** to **3D**.

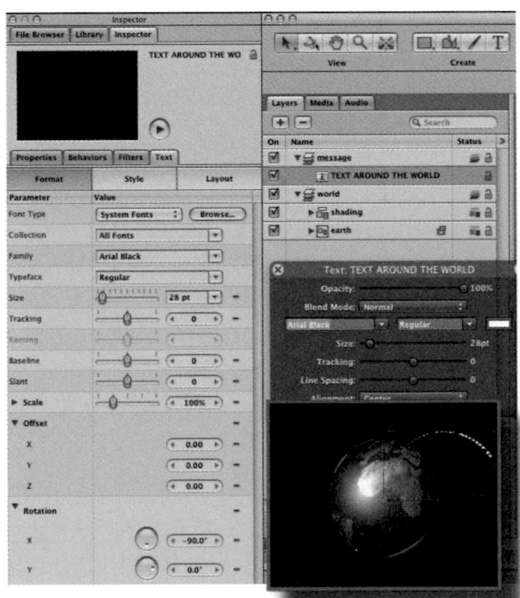

4 Now, in the **Text/Format** tab, set **X Rotation** to **-90°**. Don't worry if your text disappears.

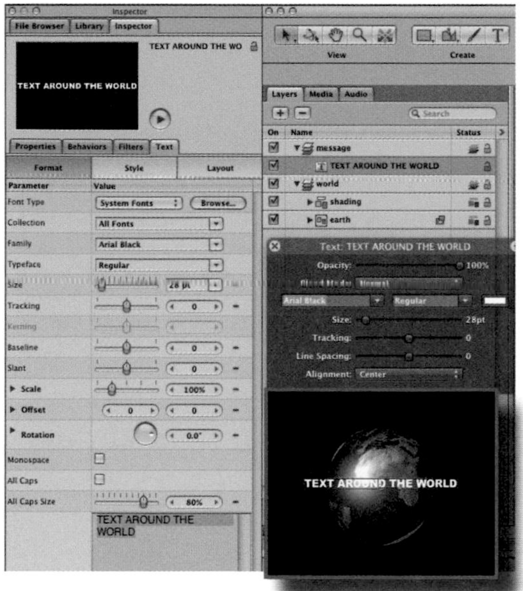

2 Add a new group. Name it **message**—it should also be **3D**. Press **T** to activate the **Text** tool. Click on the center of the screen. Set your **Font** to **Arial Black**, **Size** to **28 pt**, and **Alignment** to **Center**. Type your message, and then press the **esc** key.

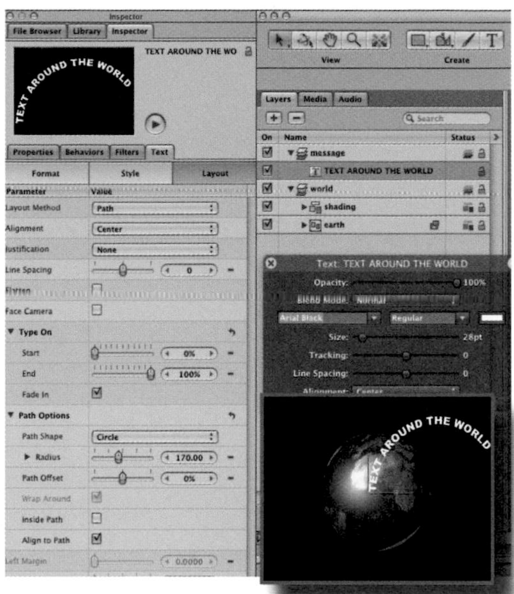

3 Then select the **Text/Layout** pane. Change the **Layout Method** to **Path**. Set the **Path Shape** to **Circle**. **Radius** to **170**.

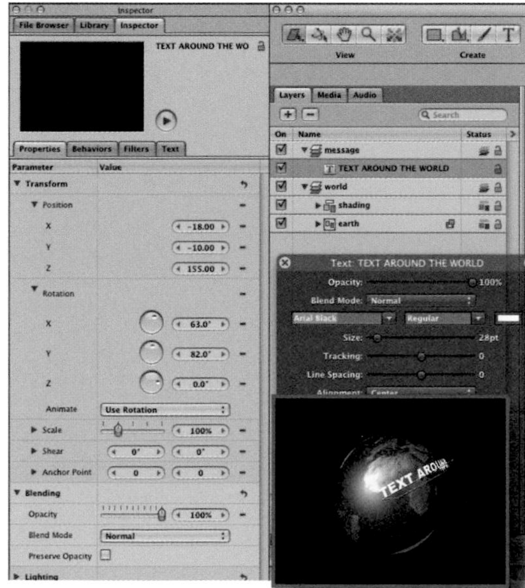

5 Go to the **Properties** tab. Set the **X Position** to **-18**, **Y** to **-10**, **Z** to **155**, **X Rotation** to **63°**, and **Y Rotation** to **82°**.

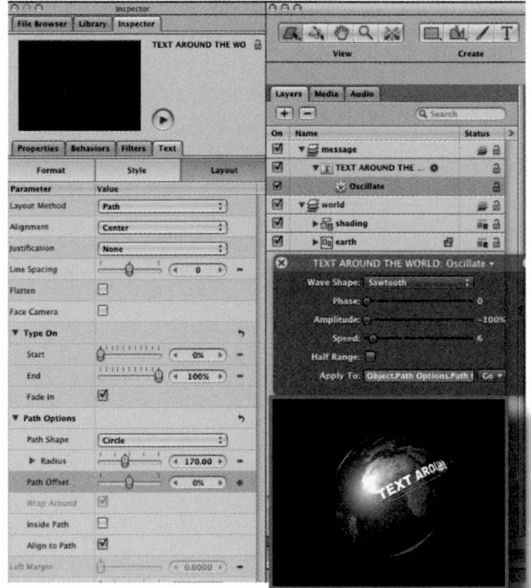

6 Finally, under **Text/Layout**, right/**ctrl**-click on **Path Offset**. Select **Oscillate**. Change the **Wave Shape** to **Sawtooth**. Change the **Amplitude** to **-100** and **Speed** to **6**.

Wordstorm

WHAT CAN YOU DO with this? I don't know, maybe float it next to your protagonist to show her confusion? Use it to build a random answer generator? It's up to you.

What I'm doing is similar to the LetterCube project. I created a group with single frames, each containing a word centered in the frame, I then did a Make Clone Layer. Motion treats a clone like a movie. So I replicated it and turned off the Play frames and turned on Random Start frame and got a replicator of random words.

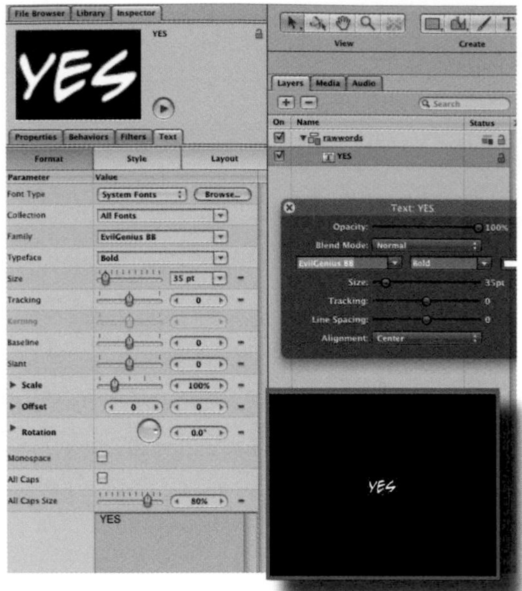

1 Start with a new project. Name the default group **rawwords**. Activate the **Text** tool. Click in the middle of the screen. Set **Font** to something you like (I chose Evil Genius). Set **Size** to **36** pt. and **Alignment** to **Center**. Make the **Color White**. Type the word **YES**. Press esc.

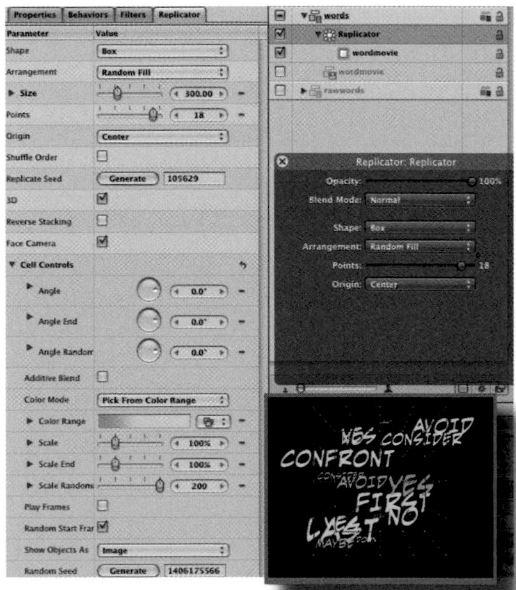

4 Select **wordmovie**. Press L. Click the **3D** checkbox. Change the **Shape** to **Box**, **Arrangement** to **Random Fill**, and **Points** to **18**. Click **Face Camera**. Set **Color Mode** to **Pick From Color Range** and **Color Range Gradient** to **Pond**. Set **Scale Randomness** to **200**. Unset **Play Frames**. Click **Random Start Frame**.

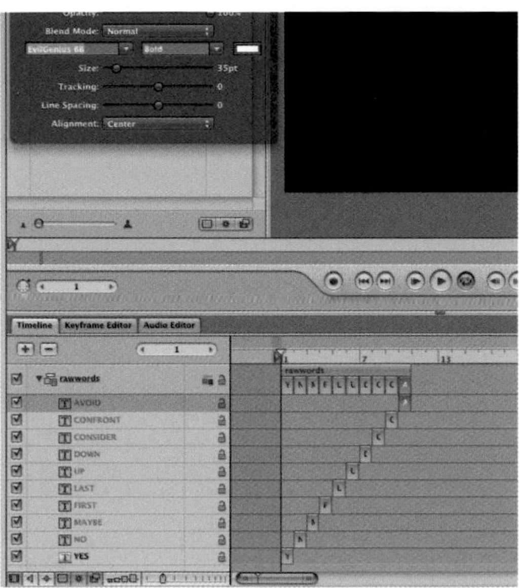

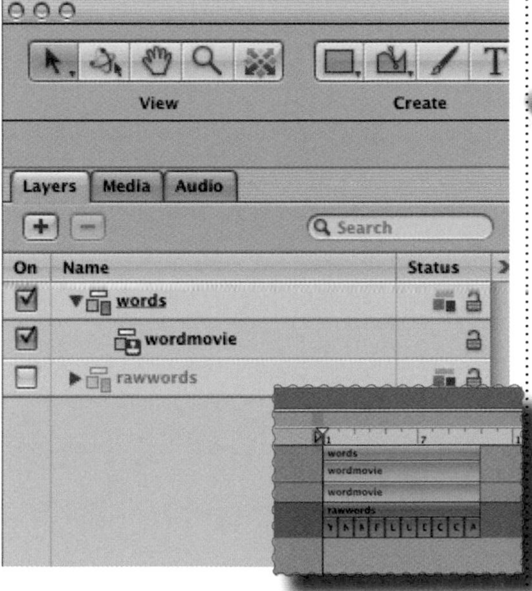

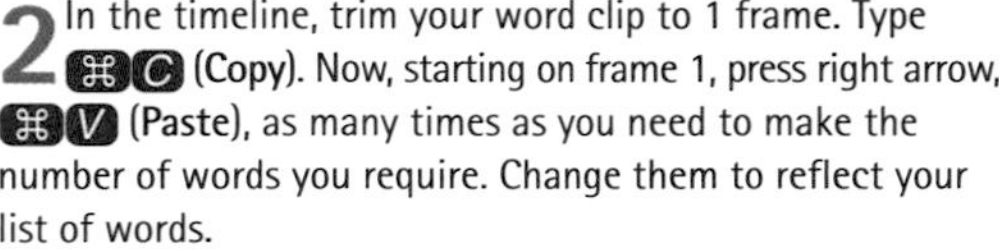

2 In the timeline, trim your word clip to 1 frame. Type ⌘C (Copy). Now, starting on frame 1, press right arrow, ⌘V (Paste), as many times as you need to make the number of words you require. Change them to reflect your list of words.

3 You should now have a segment that has all your words on separate frames. Position to frame 1. Select the **rawwords** group. Press K to create a clone layer. Name the **Clone Layer** group **words**. Name the **Clone Layer wordmovie**. Turn off **rawwords**.

5 In the **Properties** tab of the **Replicator**, ctrl/right-click on the **X Rotation**, and select **Wriggle**. Change the **Amount** to 190°. **Apply Mode** to **Add and Subtract**. Set **Noisiness** to **.11**. Back in the **Properties** tab, right/ctrl-click on **Z Rotation**. Select **Wriggle**. Change the **Amount** to 133°. **Noisiness** to **.15**.

Rolodex

THIS IS A SIMPLE FLIPPING Rolodex card simulation. You can, of course, choose to make it more elaborate by replacing the rectangle with a Rolodex card shape and, using the same techniques outlined in the Word Storm or Letter Cube projects, have different information on each card. Perhaps build it into a complex DVD menu.

What we're doing here is using a circle replicator on a rectangle along with lighting and a camera. It's animated by placing a ramp on the offset parameter in the replicator.

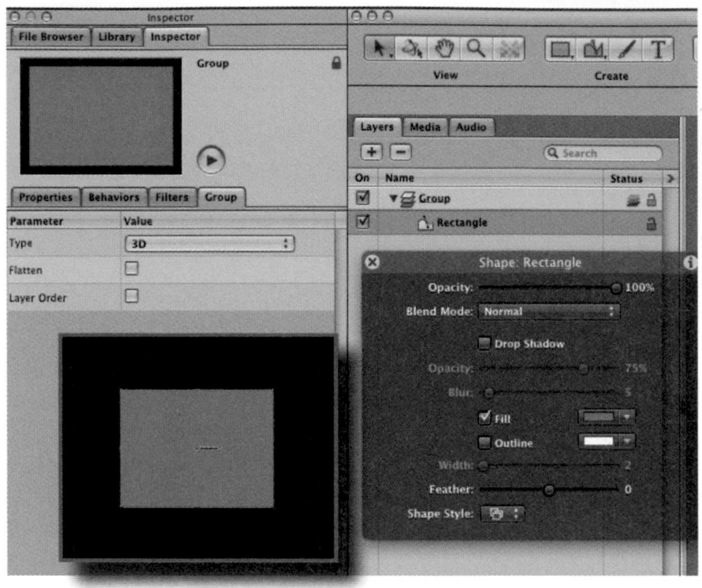

1 Begin with a new project. Set the default group's type to **3D**. Draw a colored rectangle in the center of the screen—I chose a nice lavender color.

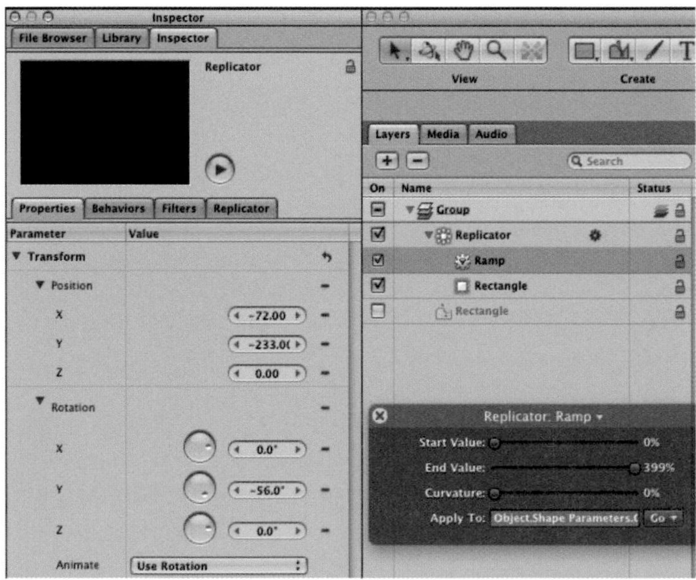

3 Right/ctrl-click on **Offset.** Select **Ramp.** Set **End Value** to **399.** In the **Properties** tab, change the **X Position** to **-72, Y** to **-172, Y Rotation** to **-56°.**

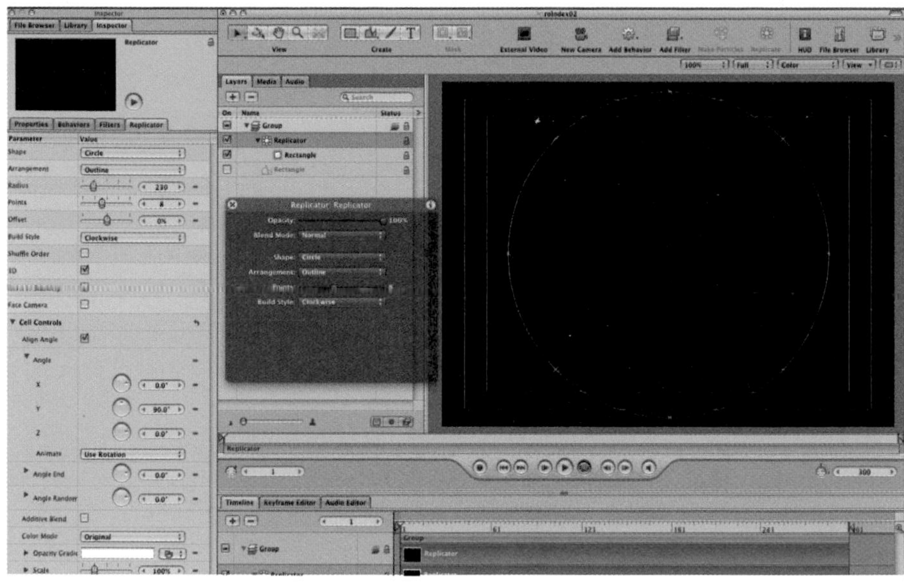

2 Press **L** or click the **Replicate** button in the toolbar. Change the **Shape** to **Circle**. Set **Radius** to **230**, **Arrangement** to **Outline**, and **Points** to **8**. Click **3D**. Click **Align Angle**. Change the **Y Angle** to **90°**. Your rectangles will disappear—don't worry.

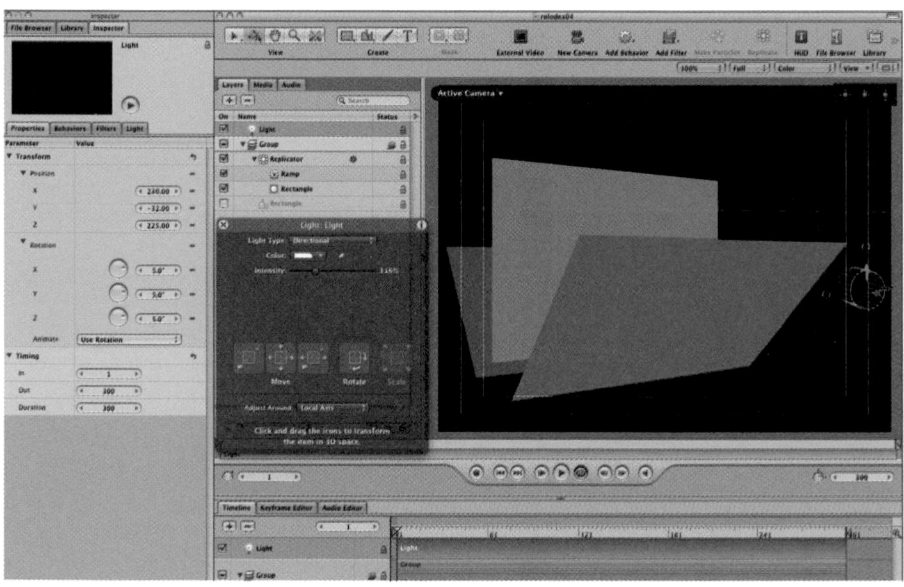

4 Press **Shift ⌘ L** to add a new light. Change the **Light Type** to **Directional**, and **Intensity** to **116%**. In the **Properties** tab, set the **X Position** to **230**, **Y** to **-32**, **Z** to **225**. Set the **X Rotation** to **5°**, **Y** to **5°**, **Z** to **5°**.

Super Easy Video Cube

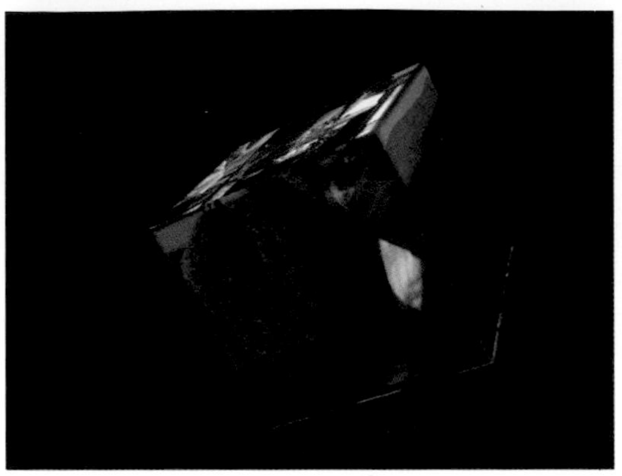

THIS PROJECT PAINTS six different sections of an input clip onto the sides of a cube, and then rotates the cube in all directions.

We'll use a couple of replicators, and the project needs to be longer than the active playing portion to make Motion load the whole clip.

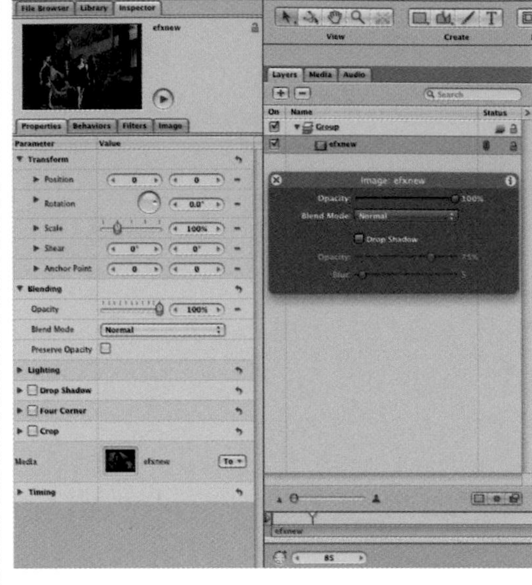

1 Start with a new project, I made it **1800** frames long, even though the active part is only **300** frames long. This is to allow a different section of the video clip to map to each of the six faces of the cube. Set the default group to **3D**. Add your video clip.

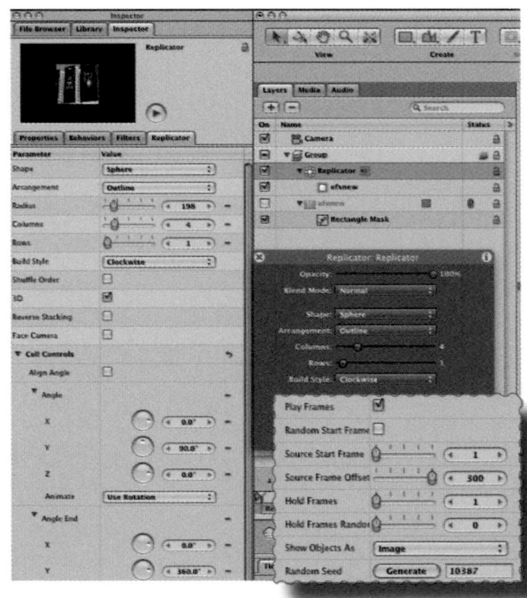

4 Select your clip. Press L or click the **Replicate** button in the toolbar. Click the **3D** button in the **Replicator** tab. Change **Shape** to **Sphere, Arrangement** to **Outline, Columns** to **4, Rows** to **1**. Change the **Y Angle** to **90° AND Y Angle** End to **360°**. Set **Source Frame Offset** to **300**.

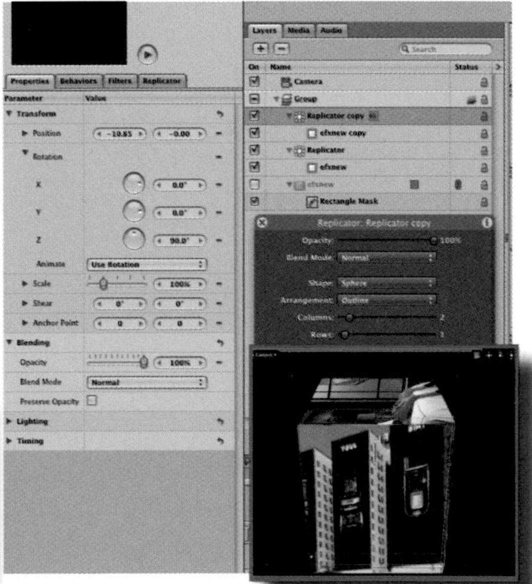

5 Adjust **Radius** until the edges of the video squares just meet. Press ⌘D to duplicate it. With **Replicator copy** selected, change the **Columns** to **2**. Change the **Source Start Frame** to **1200**. In the **Properties** tab, set **Z Rotation** to **90°**.

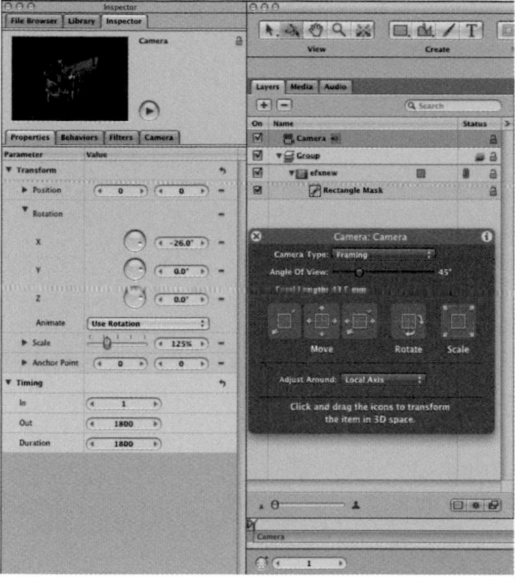

2 With your video clip selected, press ⌥R to activate the **Rectangle Mask** tool. Position the pointer to the center of your clip. Hold down the ⌥ and Shift keys and drag the rectangle mask out to nearly the top/bottom edge of your clip. This creates a square of video.

3 Click the **New Camera** button. Set the **X Rotation** to **-26**. Set the **Scale** to **125%**.

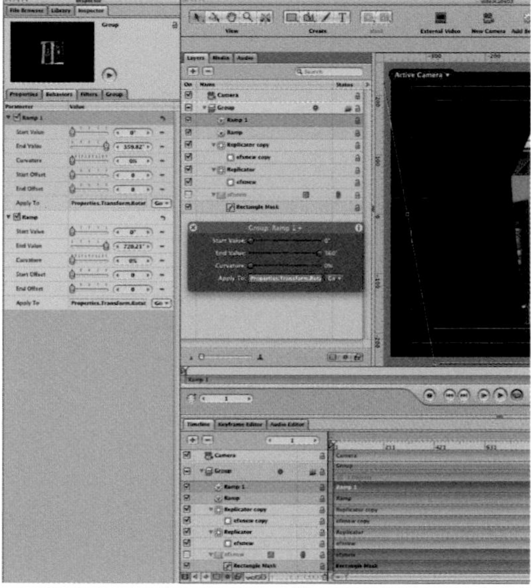

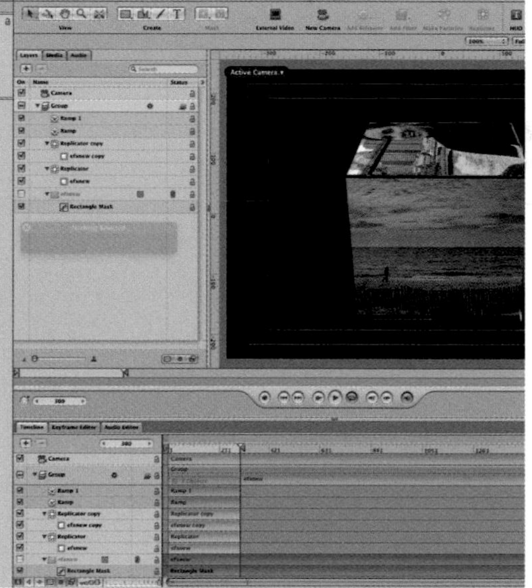

6 Select **Group**. In the **Properties** tab set **Scale** to **80%**. Right/ctrl-click on **X Rotation**. Select **Ramp**. Set the **End Value** to **720**. Back in the **Properties** tab, right/ctrl-click on **Y Rotation**. Select **Ramp**. Set the **End Value** to **360°**.

7 Position to frame 300. ⌘-Select **Replicator, Replicator copy, Ramp,** and **Ramp1**. Press O. Unselect everything, and press O again to set the play range. For a cool variation, click on the **Rectangle Mask**. Set the **Feather** to **51**.

Perspective Art Titles

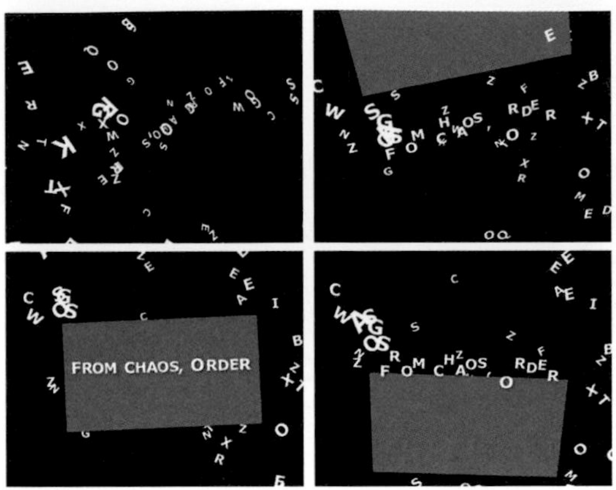

A FRIEND OF MINE, MIKE Mench, gave me this idea,—and another friend, Shane Ross, gave me the name Perspective Art. What we have here is a seemingly random cloud of letters that coalesce into a title. Just in time, a card flies in to highlight it and then flies out and the letters are again a jumble.

We create two bits. First our title: we select each character and give it a random Z offset and then use the X and Y offsets as well as the sizing to make it look right when faced straight on, but when viewed from any other angle, it looks a mess. The second bit is a letter cloud generated with a particle generator and the same letter movie technique we used in Matrix/Letter Cube/etc.

We then start the camera looking at a random thicket of letters and move the camera around until, facing from the proper direction, our title is revealed (aided by a well-timed fly-in of a card). Then after resting on the title for the requisite amount of time, we send the camera roving again.

We're only doing one title in this project, but I could well imagine hiding several in this letter cloud and sequentially moving the camera to each one Oh—one trick we'll use is a **Repel From** simulation behavior to keep the letter cloud from encroaching too close to our title.

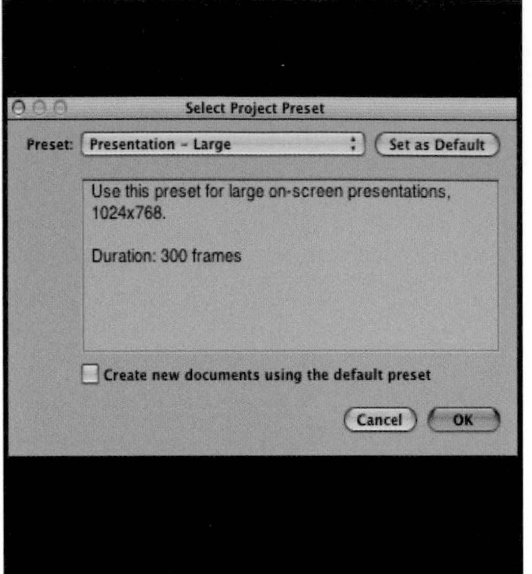

1 Start with a new project. To give myself more room I used **Presentation Large,** but you should use whatever is appropriate to your project, bearing in mind you may need to adjust some values to fit your needs.

4 Now, in the **Text/Format** tab, use the virtual slider on the **Z offset** to adjust the depth offset of the first letter to a random number between **100** and **-100.** If it gets too big or too small, adjust the **Scale** and **X** and **Y Offsets** to keep spacing and proportion.

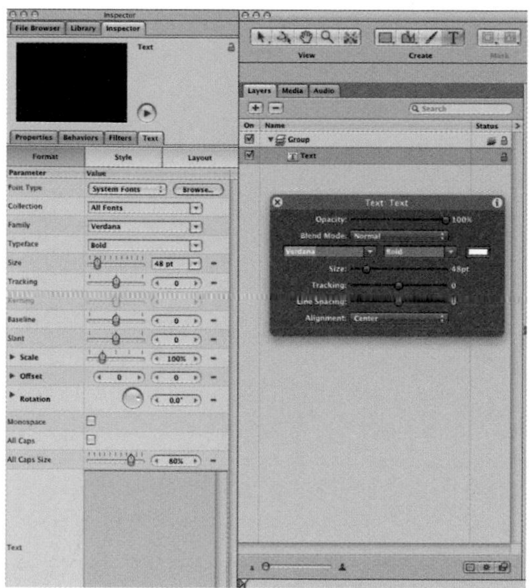

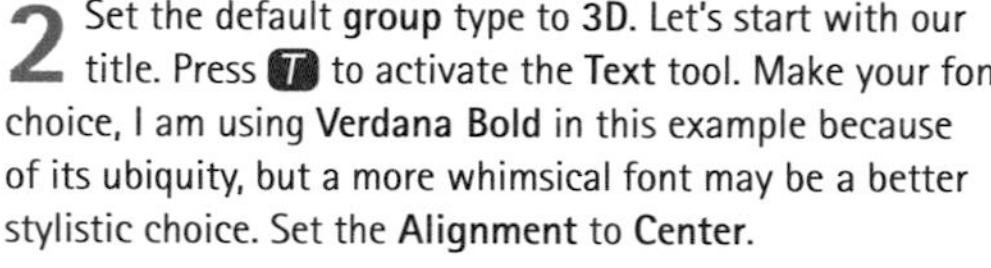

2 Set the default **group** type to **3D**. Let's start with our title. Press **T** to activate the **Text** tool. Make your font choice, I am using **Verdana Bold** in this example because of its ubiquity, but a more whimsical font may be a better stylistic choice. Set the **Alignment** to **Center**.

3 Type your message. I used FROM CHAOS, ORDER. After you've typed your message, don't press **esc**. Press left arrow to get to the beginning of your message. Now, hold down the **Shift** key and press right arrow once, selecting the first character of your message.

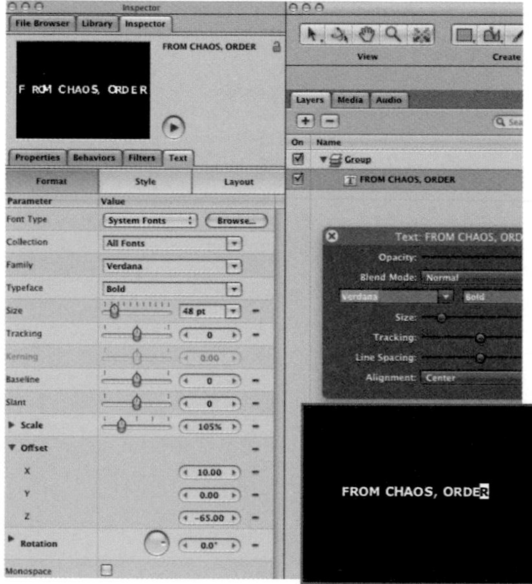

5 Press right arrow to unselect your first character. Then hold down the **Shift** key and press right arrow to select the second character and repeat the operation. Do this for each character; don't worry about the spaces. Try to be random in your offsets, and space out the characters.

6 Once you've finished, go to the **Properties** tab and drag the **X Rotation** to **45°** to see the results of your labor. If you don't feel it looks random enough, activate the **Text** tool, click on your message, select a character, and adjust.

continued...

Perspective Art (continued)

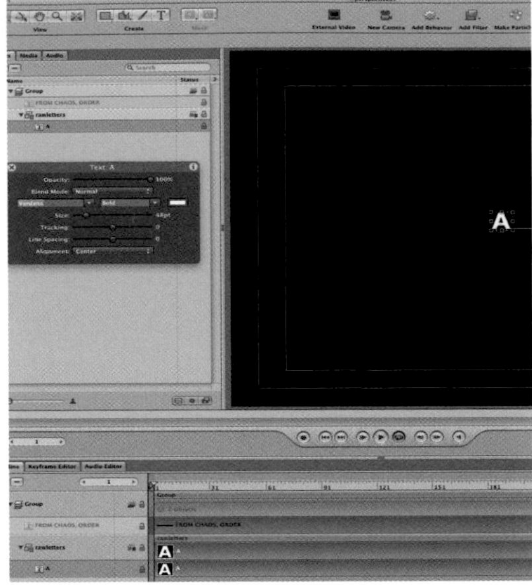

7 When you're happy, set the **X Rotation** back to **0**. Temporarily turn off your title. Add a new group at the bottom of your stack named **rawletters**. Make it 2D. Activate the **Text** tool. Click in the middle of the screen. Set **Alignment** to **Center**. Type the letter **A**.

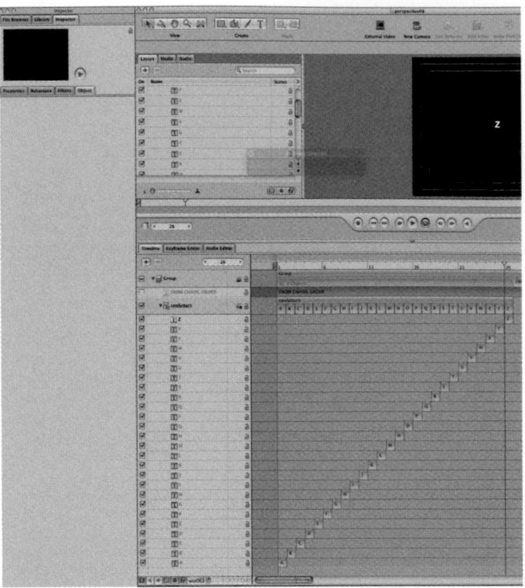

8 In the timeline, trim your letter a clip to 1 frame. Type ⌘**C** **(Copy)**. Now, starting on frame 1, press right arrow ⌘**V** (Paste) 25 times to make 25 copies of your single frame **A**. Change them to **B, C, D**... all the way to **Z.**

11 Now, let's protect our title from encroachment by the **lettercloud. Add Behavior/Simulations/Repel From** to **lettercloud**. Drag your title into the **Object** well. Set **Strength** to **100, Falloff Rate** to **36, Influence** to **380. Drag** to **1.0**.

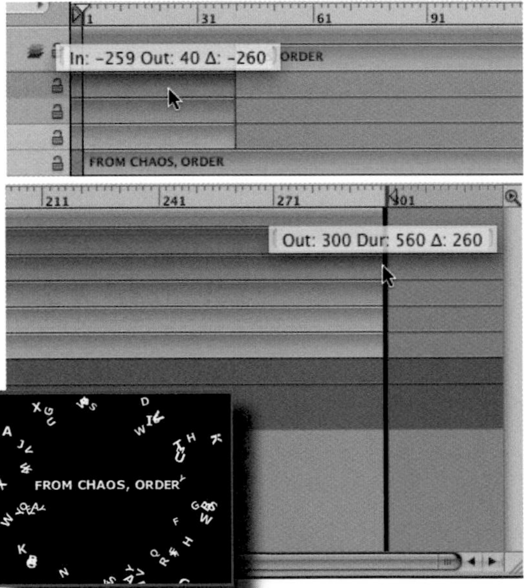

12 Grab **lettercloud** in the timeline and slide it to the left, toward the beginning of the timeline about **260** frames. This should allow time for the **lettercloud** elements to clear away from our title. Now trim the end of **lettercloud** until it reaches the end of the the timeline.

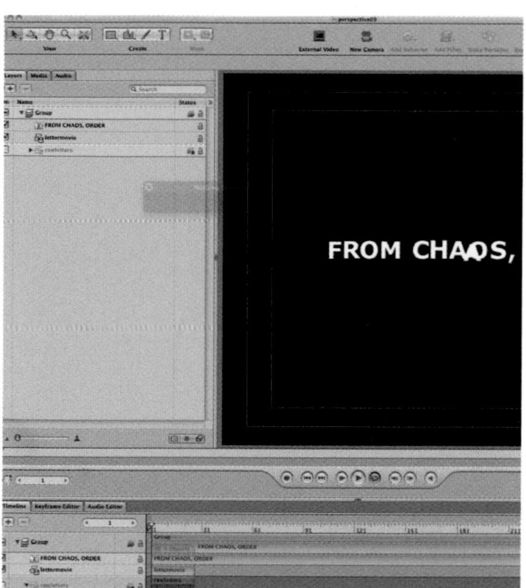

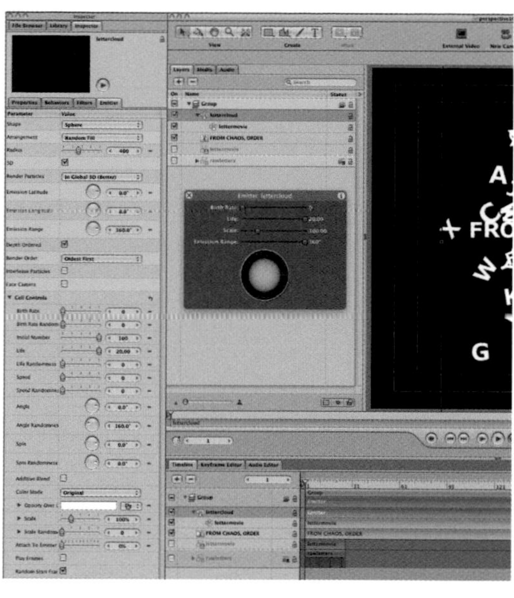

9 You should now have a 26-frame segment that has letters A through Z on separate frames. Position to frame 1. Select the **rawletters** group. Press K to create a clone layer. Rename the **Clone Layer** to **lettermovie.** Turn off **rawletters.** Turn back on your title.

10 Select **lettermovie** and press E. Name the new Emitter **lettercloud**. Click **3D**. Set the **Shape** to **Sphere, Arrangement** to **Random Fill. Radius** to **400. Render Particles In Global 3D**. Unset **Face Camera**. Set **Birth Rate** to **0. Initial Number** to **100, Life** to **20. Speed** to **0. Angle Randomness** to **160**. Unset **Play Frames**.

HOT TIP

If you don't like the arrangement of the letters, hit the Generate button on Random Seed until you get something you like.

13 Position to frame 1 and add a camera. **Add Behavior/Camera/Sweep**. Position to frame 125, and press O to truncate the **Sweep** behavior there. Set **Start** to **-141** and **Speed** to **Ease Both**. **Axis** will be **Swivel Y**.

14 Press ⌘D. Slide the duplicate behavior so it aligns with the end of the timeline. Set the **Start** to **0°** and the end to **141**.

HOT TIP

Hold down the Shift key to make it easier to line things up.

continued...

Perspective Art (continued)

15 **Add Behavior/Camera/Sweep.** Position to frame 135, and press O to truncate the **Sweep** behavior there. Set **Start** to **-150**, **End** to 0, **Speed** to **Ease Both**, and **Axis** to Tilt X.

16 Press ⌘D. Slide the duplicate behavior so it aligns with the end of the timeline. Set the **Start** to 0° and the **End** to 150.

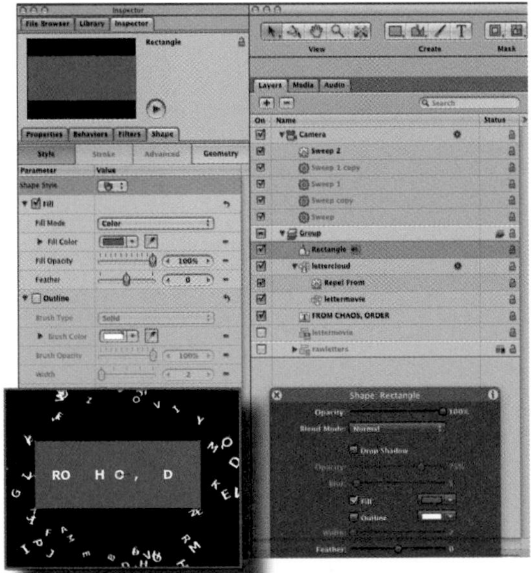

19 Now for the final bit, press R to activate the **Rectangle** tool. Draw a rectangle that will contain your title. If some or all of your title disappears behind the rectangle, don't worry—we'll fix that later. Make it a color you like so the white text stands out.

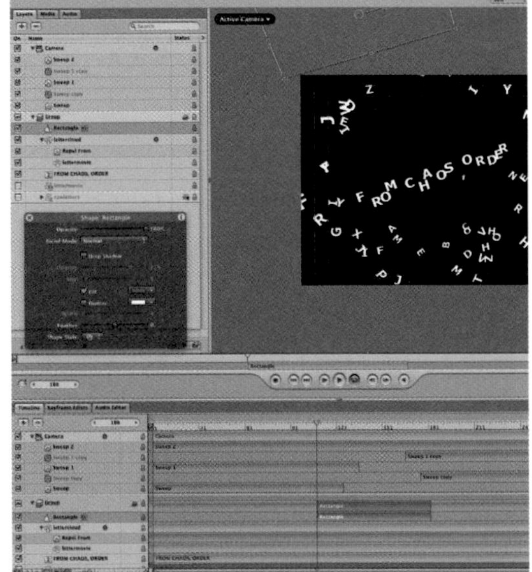

20 Now go to frame 182 and press O to end the rectangle there. Go to frame 108. Press I to start the rectangle there. Grab the rectangle and push it just off screen.

17 Add **Behavior/Camera/Sweep**. Set **Start** to **-40**, **End** to **40**, **Speed** to **Ease Both**, and **Axis** to **Roll Z**.

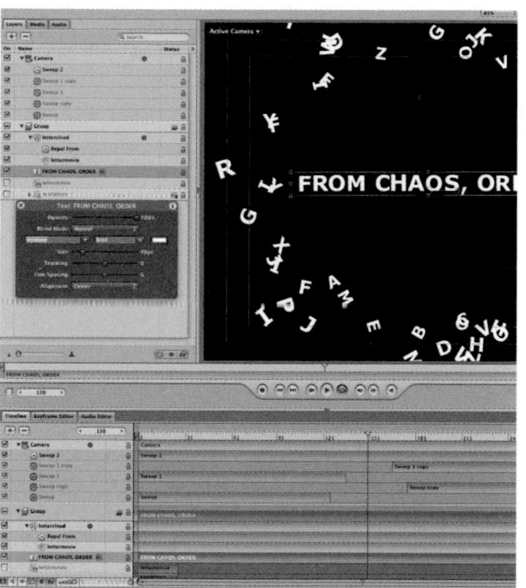

18 Position to frame 150. Check out your title—how does it look? If anything doesn't look right, activate the **Text** tool, click on your message, select a character, and adjust as in Step 6 above.

21 Add **Behavior/Basic Motion/Move**. Go to frame 128. Press O. Now go to frame 150. Adjust the **X**, **Y**, and **Z** so that the rectangle is centered behind your text. You'll probably have to set the **Z** to around **-100**. Set the **Speed** to **Ease Out**.

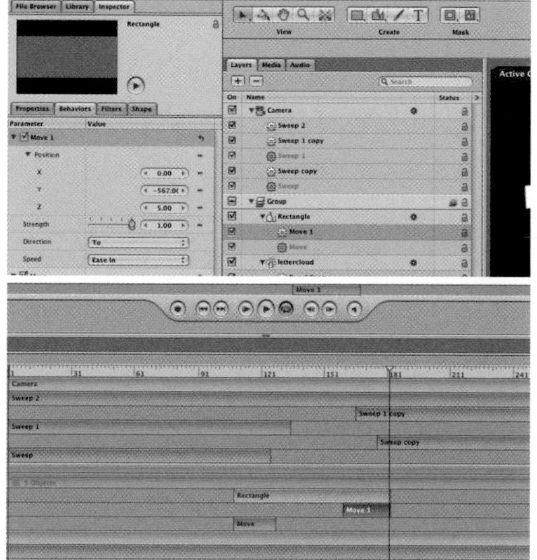

22 Add **Behavior/Basic Motion/Move**. Go to frame 160. Press I to start the move there. Go to frame 180. Adjust the **X**, **Y**, and **Z** so that the rectangle is now just offscreen. Set the **Speed** to **Ease In**.

3D Title Sequence

THIS TITLE SEQUENCE is designed to allow you to save it as a template and string multiple copies together.

It's a relatively big project, but not too tough—it's just hard to show 3D on a 2D page, so we take a lot of steps, but follow along and you'll be happy you did.

We'll be using the Framing behavior that is new in Motion 4. It makes it easy to aim your camera, even when you alter your project, as we'll see. We'll also take advantage of the new Depth of Field that's now available—these weren't around prior to Motion 4, so you'll have to alter the project if you're attempting this on an earlier version.

First, we'll create five titles. I'm using a font called Dirty Deco that's included on the disk. Then, once the titles have been created, we'll position them in 3Space, set up our camera dolly, add a light to illuminate our titles, and then add the framing behaviors. Finally, we'll add some atmosphere by positioning a 3D replicator in our title "corridor" and give the particles some random motion.

Ready? Let's get started.

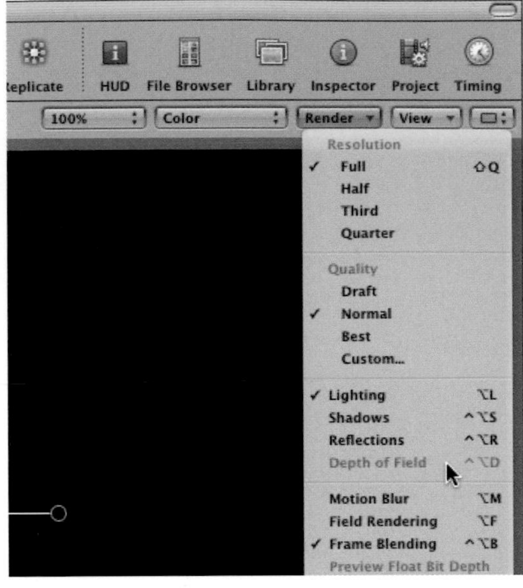

1 Start with a new project. Set the default group to be **3D**. For speed, go to the render pulldown (it gets its own menu in Motion 4) and turn off **Shadows** and **Reflections**. You can't turn off **Depth of Field** until we've added our camera.

4 With **First Title** selected, press ⌘D four times to make four copies. Turn them all off except **First Title copy**. Change its text to be **Second Title** and **Second Subtitle**. If you have trouble with the font size changing, put the cursor after the t in **First**, type **Second**, and delete the word **First**.

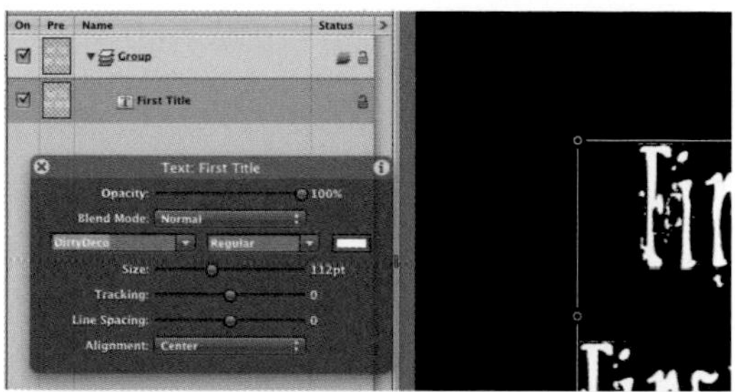

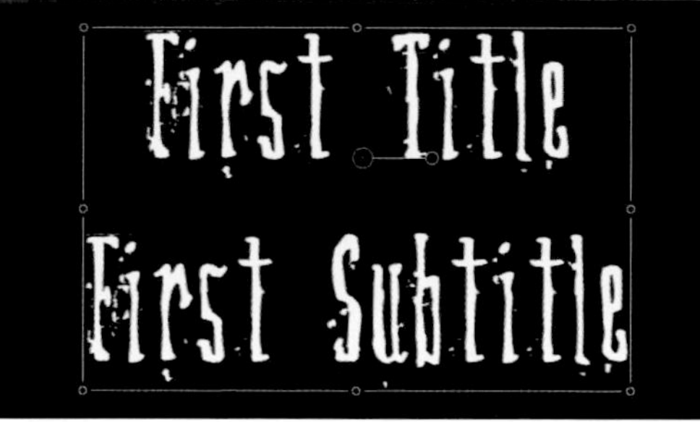

2 Press T to activate the **Title** tool. Click in the center of the page. Select your **Dirty Deco** font and set the size to about 112, **Alignment** to **Center**. Type **First Title**, press Return, then type **First Subtitle**, and press the esc key to exit the **Title** tool.

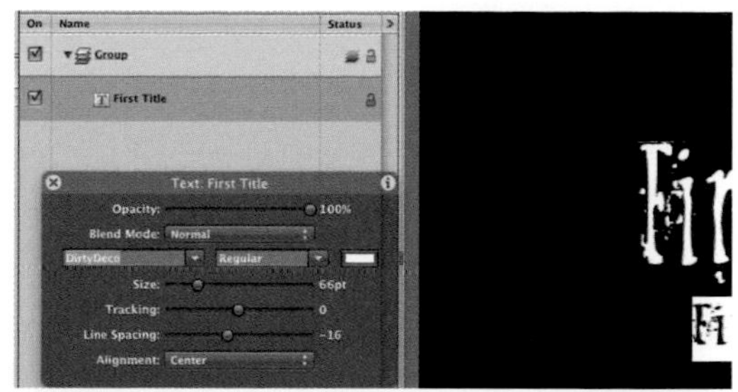

3 Now select the second line (**First Subtitle**) on screen, and dial down the **Size** to **66**. I also set my **Y Scale** to 56% to make the subtitle shorter. The lines are spaced a bit far apart, so set the **Line Spacing** to **-16**.

5 Repeat the process for **Third** and **Fourth**. Change the fifth copy to be **Final Title** and **Final Subtitle**. Turn all the titles back on now. In the next step we'll move into 3D mode and begin positioning everything.

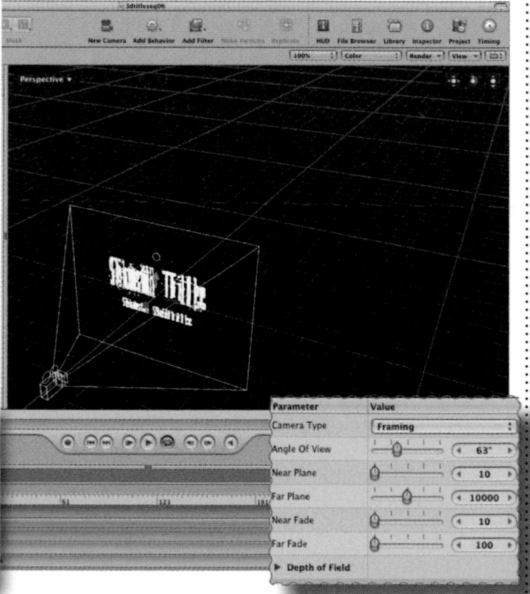

6 Add a camera. Change your view (upper left-hand corner of the screen) from **Active Camera** to **Perspective**. Use the movement tools (upper right-hand corner) to position your view as above. Set **Angle of View** to 63°. We'll deal with **Depth of Field** later.

continued...

3D Title Sequence (continued)

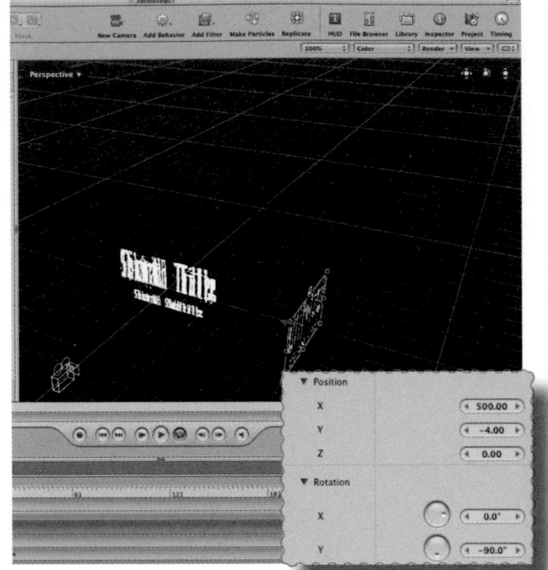

7 Select the **First Title**. In the **Properties** tab, twiddle down **Rotation** and change **Y** to **-90°**. Now set the **X Position** to about **500**. See how your title moved off to the right?

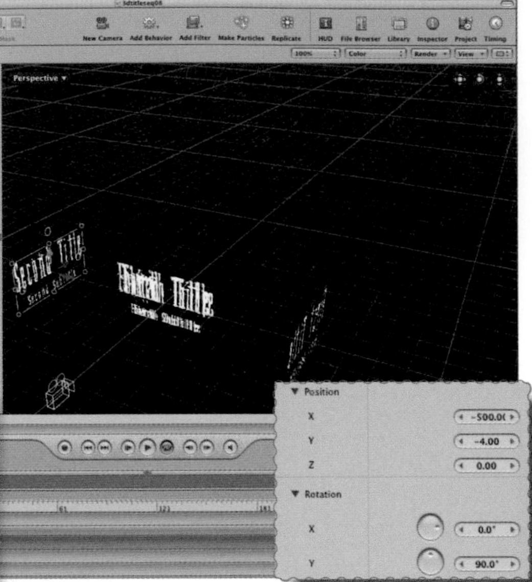

8 Select **Second Title**. Set its **Y Rotation** to **90°**. Set its **X Position** to about **-500**. Ah ha! It moved to the left.

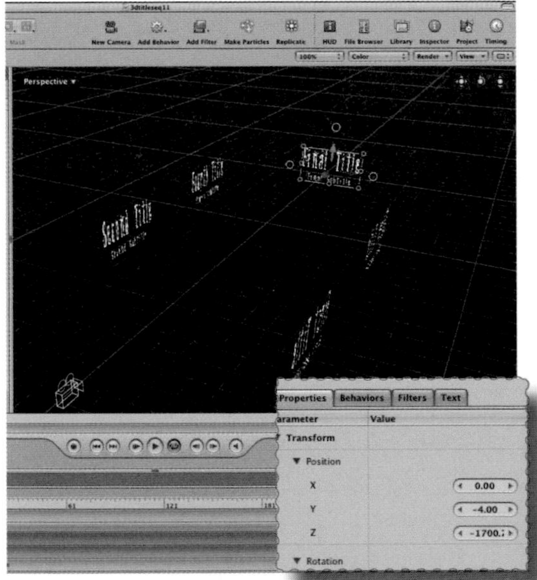

11 Grab the final title's blue arrow and slide it backward to cap our corridor. Yours may differ, but my final title ends at a **Z Position** of about -1700. Using the onscreen arrows it makes it easy to keep all our elements on the same plane (at least to start).

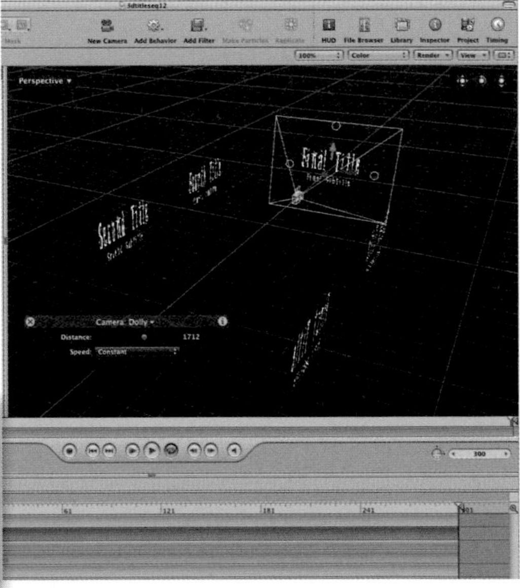

12 Select your **Camera**. **Add Behavior/Camera/Dolly.** Position to the end of your timeline. Adjust the **Distance** so that the camera's focal plane finishes just past Final Title.

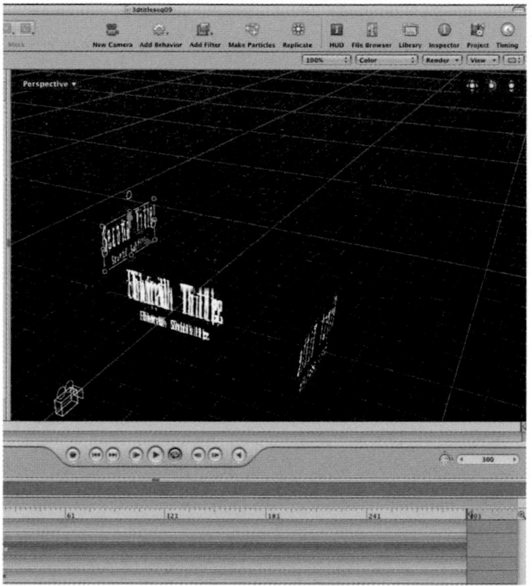

9 Now let's use some onscreen controls to help position our elements. Notice that our (still selected) **Second Title** has three arrows on it: green, blue, and red. Grab the red one and slide it farther away from us.

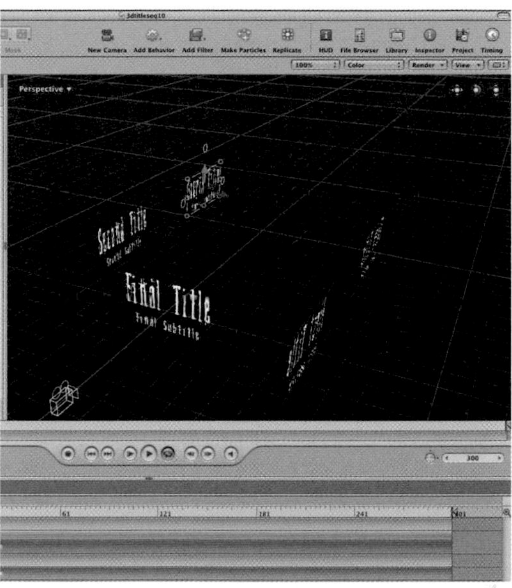

10 Repeat this process on the **Third** and **Fourth Titles**, using onscreen tools to move the elements around until you've built a kind of staggered "corridor" of titles.

HOT TIP

Use the Shift key to cause the angle of rotation to snap when using the onscreen controls.

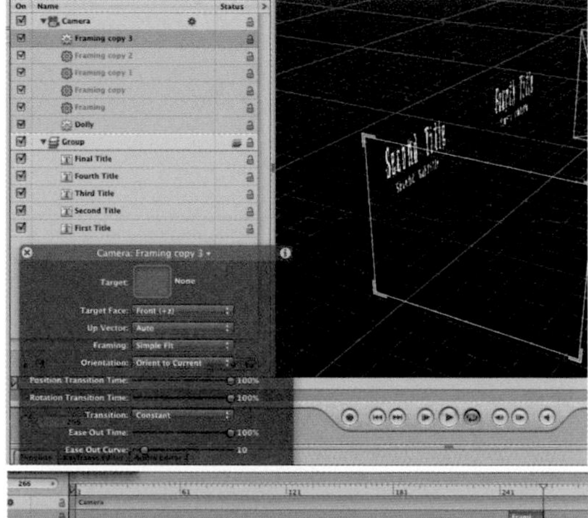

13 **Add Behavior/Camera/Framing**. Set **Framing** to **Simple Fit**. Change the **Position** and **Rotation Transition Times** to 100%. On frame 3 Press I. Move to frame 23. Press O. Press ⌘D four times to create four copies. Position them evenly along the timeline ending around frame 266.

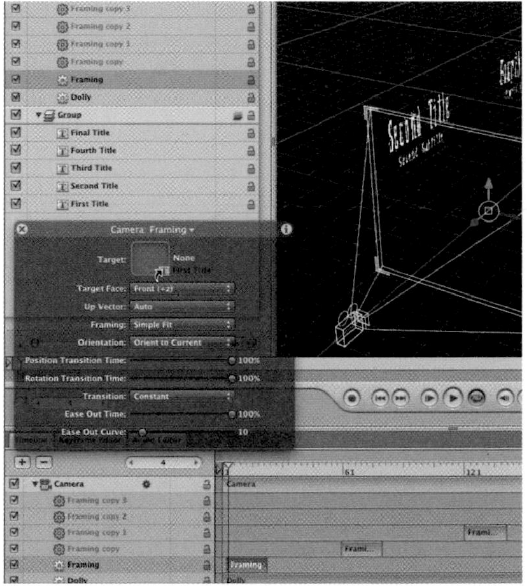

14 Select the first framing behavior. Grab **First Title** and drag it into the **Target** well. Click on the second framing behavior. Drag **Second Title** into its **Target** well. Repeat for all the **Framing/Title** pairs.

continued...

3D Title Sequence (continued)

15 Switch your view to **Active Camera** and press **Play**—NEATO! But, because our camera is moving and because framing places us in the center of the title, it feels like we're leaving our titles behind.

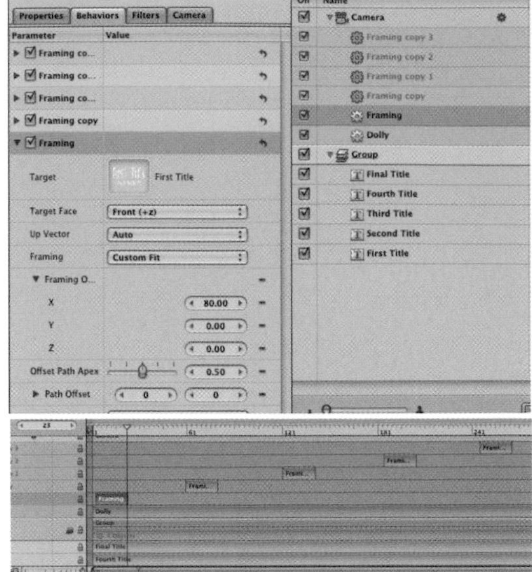

16 Select the first framing behavior and position just past the final frame of it. Change **Framing** from **Auto Fit** to **Custom Fit**. Now play with the **X** value so our camera arrives with the title a bit off center to the left, about **80**.

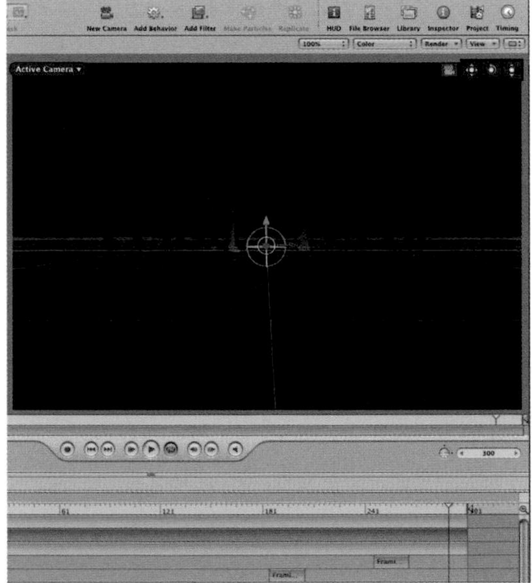

19 Still in **Active Camera** view. **Add Behavior/Basic Motion/Move.** Position to frame **290**. Adjust the **Z Position** of the **Move** behavior until the light just passes through the **Final Title**. It'll be a little farther than the Z **Position** of your **Final Title**. Mine was about **-1760**.

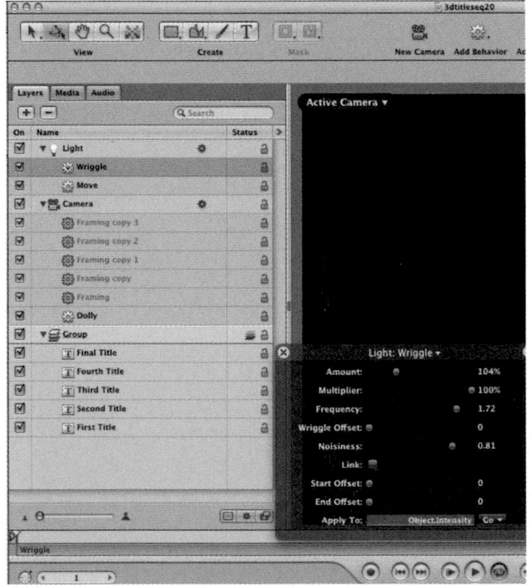

20 Position back to frame 1. Let's add a flicker to the light. Right/ctrl-click on **Intensity** and select **Wriggle**. Set **Amount** to **104%**, **Frequency** to **1.72**, and **Noisiness** to **0.81**.

17 Now when you play, our title slides past the screen. Adjust the other **Framing** behaviors the same way. The titles on the left (**Second** and **Fourth**) need a negative value in the **X** offset.

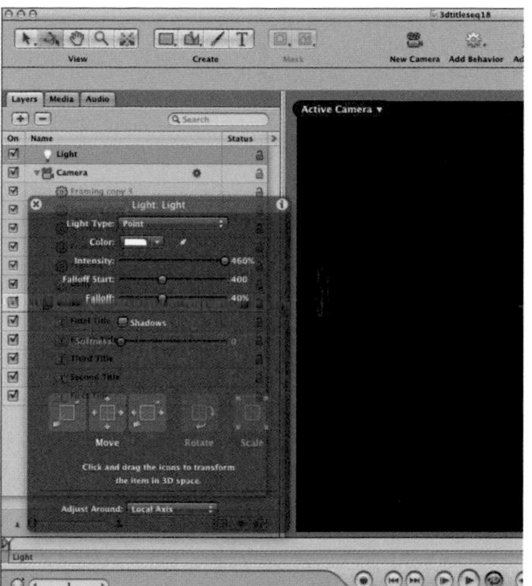

18 Onto Light! Back at frame 1, add a light. **Type** should be **Point**. Set **Falloff Start** to **400** and **Falloff** to 40%. Adjust the **Intensity** up until you can just see the edge of **Second Title**. Mine is about **460**.

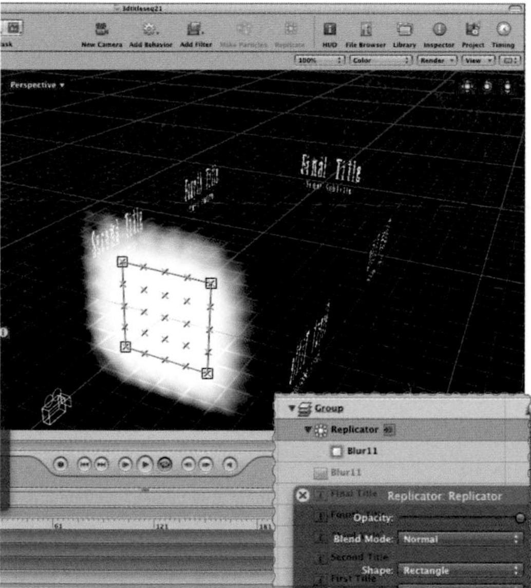

21 Now for the atmosphere. Turn off the light. Change to **Perspective View**. In **Library/Content/Particle Images**, select **Blur11**. Press **Apply.** Select **Blur11** in the **Layers** palette. Press **L** or click the **Replicate** button in the toolbar.

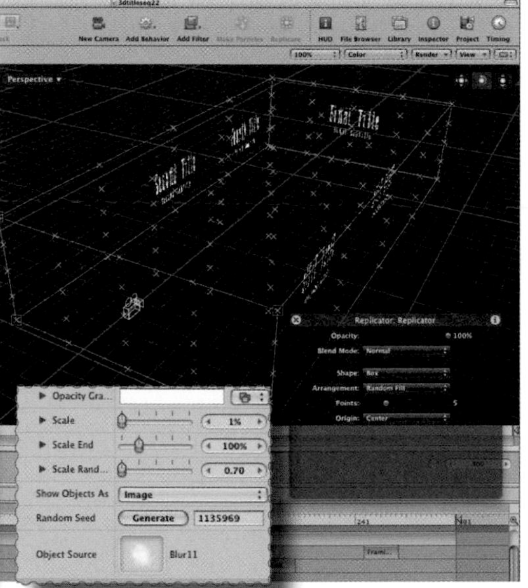

22 In the **Replicator** tab of the **Inspector**, click **3D**. Set **Shape** to **Box** and **Arrangement** to **Random Fill**. Click **Face Camera**. Set **Scale** to 1% and **Scale Random** to 0.70. Use the onscreen controls to size and position your **Replicator** box until it's a bit wider, deeper, and taller than your corridor.

continued...

3D Title Sequence (continued)

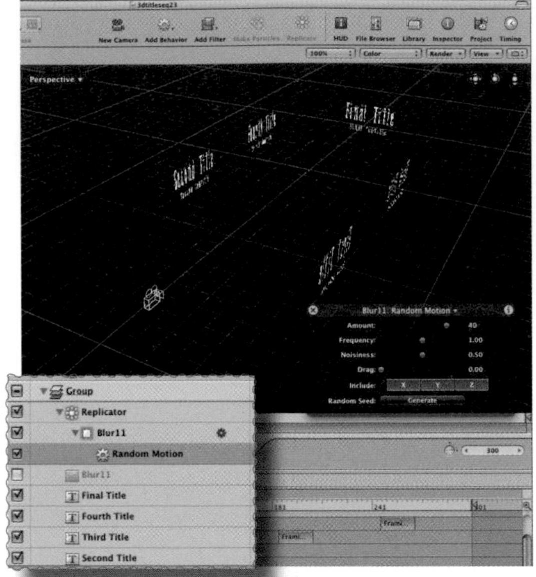

23 Change the **Points** to 700. In the **Replicator**, click on **Blur11**. **Add Behavior/Simulations/Random Motion**. Set **Amount** to 40. Click the **X**, **Y**, and **Z** buttons under **Include**.

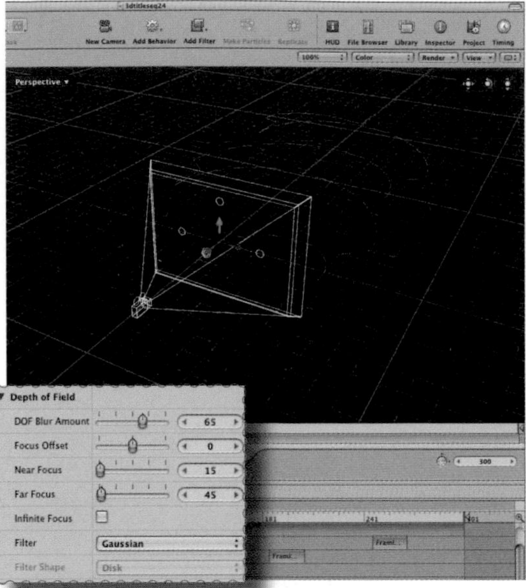

24 Turn back on the **Light**. Click on your camera. Twiddle down the **Depth of Field** disclosure triangle and change **DOF Blur Amount** to 65. Set **Near Focus** to 15 and **Far Focus** to 45.

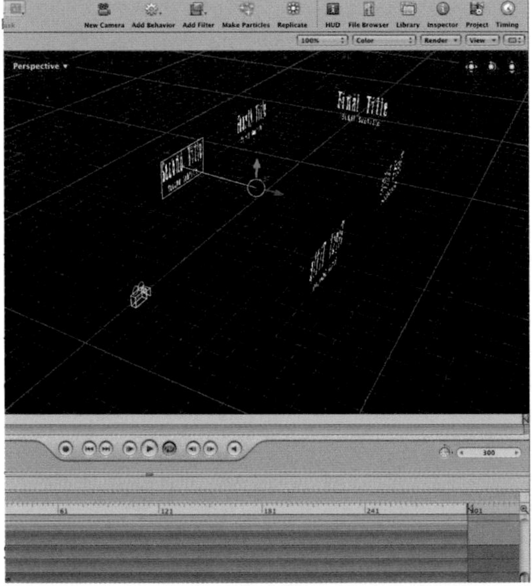

27 Change to **Perspective View**. Turn off the **Light** and the **Replicator** to speed interaction. Click on **Second Title**. Select the **Adjust Anchor Point** tool. Taking the blue arrow, drag the **Anchor Point** out to the centerline of the frame.

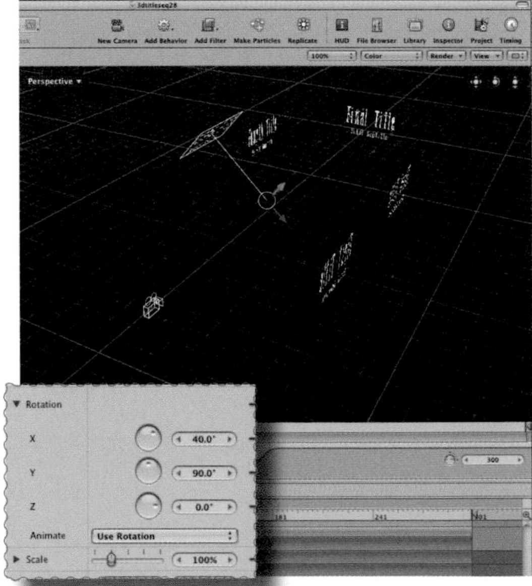

28 In its **Properties** tab, play with the **X Rotation**. Notice how the title moves around our centerline? Set the **X Rotation** to 40°.

25 Go back to your **Render** menu and turn on **Depth of Field.** Change view to **Active Camera**. Turn off the **Replicator** and do a RAM preview to check the motion and make adjustments if needed. In particular, you may need to set the **Z Framing Offset** for the final framing behavior to 70 or so.

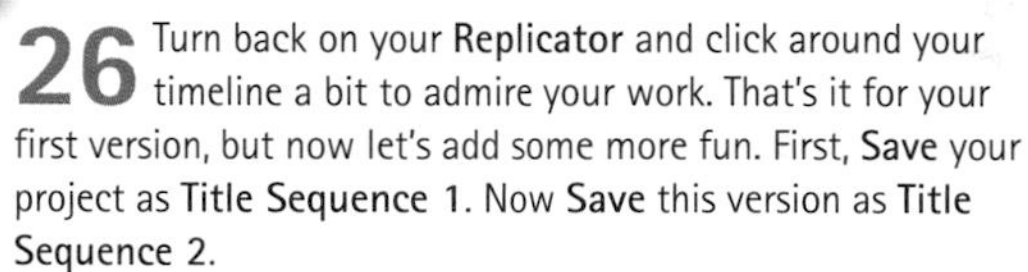

26 Turn back on your **Replicator** and click around your timeline a bit to admire your work. That's it for your first version, but now let's add some more fun. First, **Save** your project as **Title Sequence 1**. Now **Save** this version as **Title Sequence 2**.

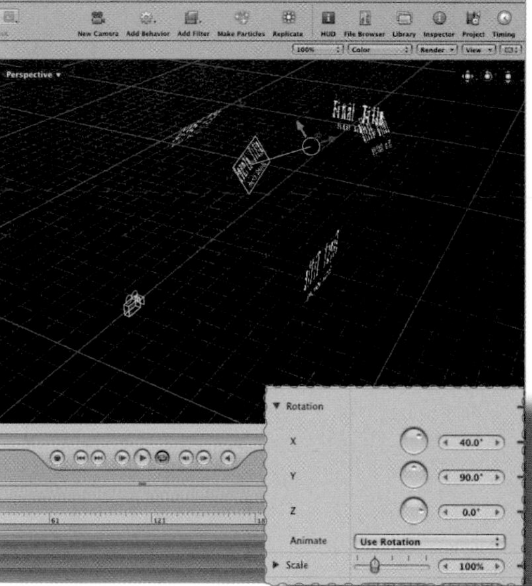

29 Move **Anchor Point** to the centerline for the **Third** and **Fourth** titles and change their **X Rotation**. Try some **Z Rotation** as well. You may have to adjust the **Height** of the **Replicator** if the cards have come out of the box (**Left** or **Right** view can help here).

30 Make sure your **Replicator** is turned back on. Now if you click on **Camera**, you'll see that the **Framing behaviors** have adjusted the camera's path to compensate for your repositioning. And when you play this, you'll see the camera move up and down as well. Save it, you're done.

8 INTERLUDE

Where do I get my ideas?

I'M OFTEN ASKED WHERE I GET my ideas. The easy answer is "they just come to me," which on one level is true. But that's only part of the answer. And not even a big part of it. Ideas don't generally form in a vacuum. There are always influences, and by placing yourself under those influences, you become more likely to think of something new.

One place I look for ideas is Photoshop tutorials. There are thousands of them out there. There are books upon books upon books. There are monthly magazines entirely devoted to techniques in Photoshop. There are Web-based tutorials. And while not all of the tutorials and techniques translate, many of them do.

Same goes for After Effects. Almost anything that can be done in After Effects you can do in Motion. Some of the projects in this very book are adaptations of After Effects tutorials.

Existing work. Watching television, movies, commercials, Web pages, etc.—We are bombarded with examples of motion graphics. Be aware and when you see something you like, imagine how it might be created in Motion. You might not achieve the exact same effect—it may be even better for having passed through your imagination.

Which brings me to my biggest source of inspiration. Playing. My teenage son has asked me why I don't play video games as much as I used to and part of my answer is Motion (I know—*what a geek!*).

Motion is my video game. I realize it can be hard after a day of working on the computer to find it in you, but sometimes it's good to just open up Motion and play. Fool around with no clear goal in mind. Try new things.

Not always, but often, after a bit of goofing around I'll come up with some interesting, weird, and at times completely useless effect. (My online friends usually indulge me when I IM them with "Wanna see something cool?" and send them my latest Motion project.)

No matter where they come from, the thing about good ideas is sooner or later, you will find a use for them.

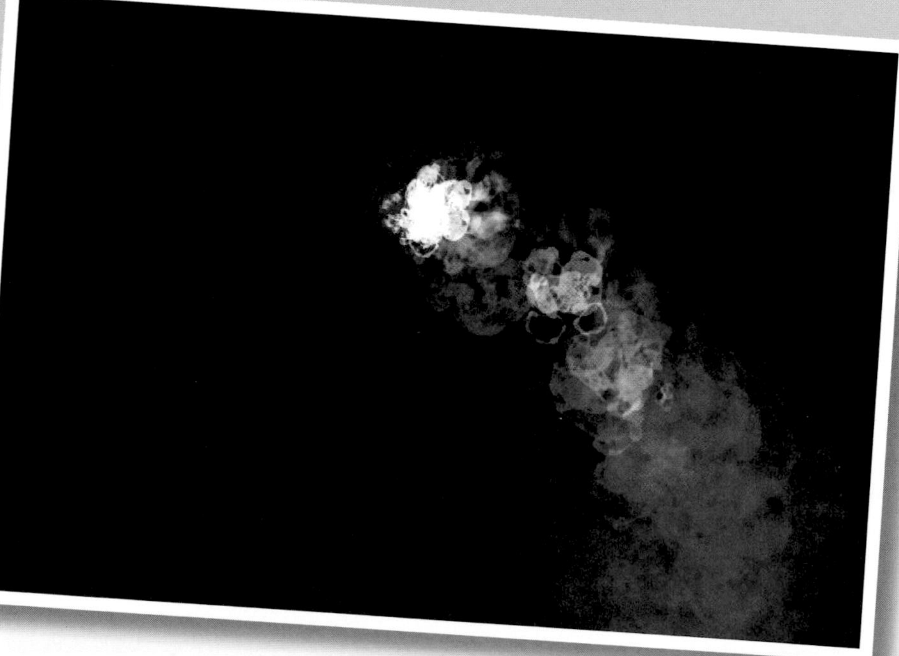

Singing happy faces and musically driven displays are just a couple of the audio effects you can achieve in Motion.

9 Audio Effects

MOTION IS THE ONLY TOOL IN THE Final Cut Studio suite that can take audio input and create visual effects with it.

Audio can add organic qualities to your projects like nothing else can. It's not entirely random and not completely regular.

I should note that some of the audio used in these exercises comes from the Additional Audio content that comes with Final Cut Studio. If you didn't install it, look for a copy on the included disc.

Shape Dance

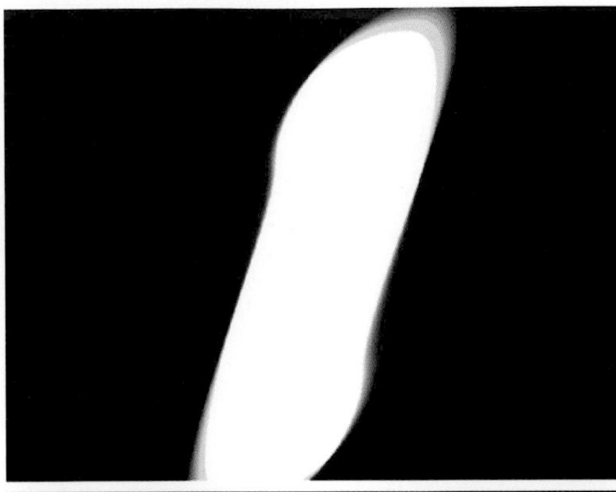

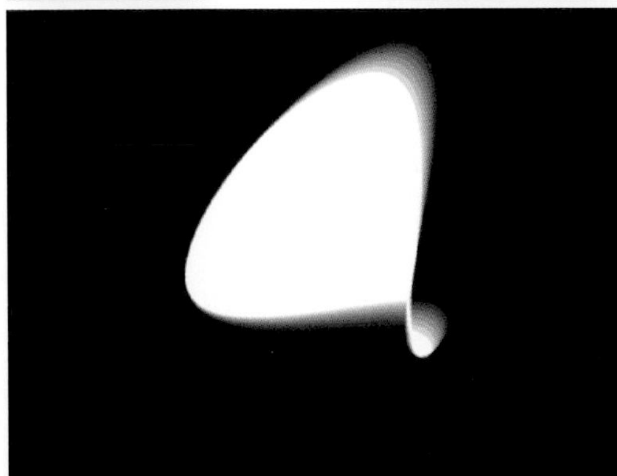

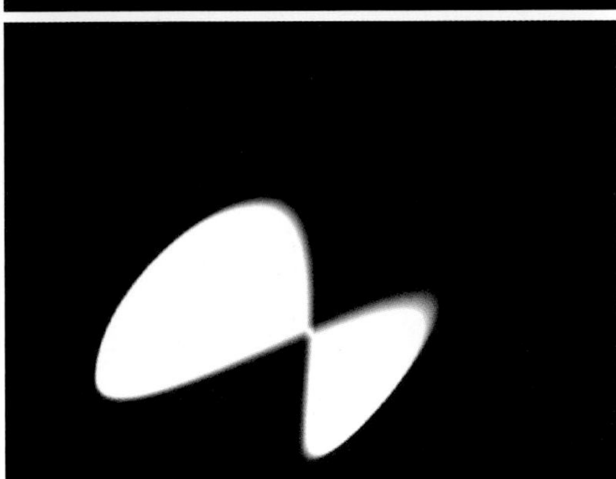

LET'S START BY BUILDING A simple shape distortion responding to a drum loop. We'll use one of the audio loops provided with Sound Track Pro to drive a Randomize Shape behavior.

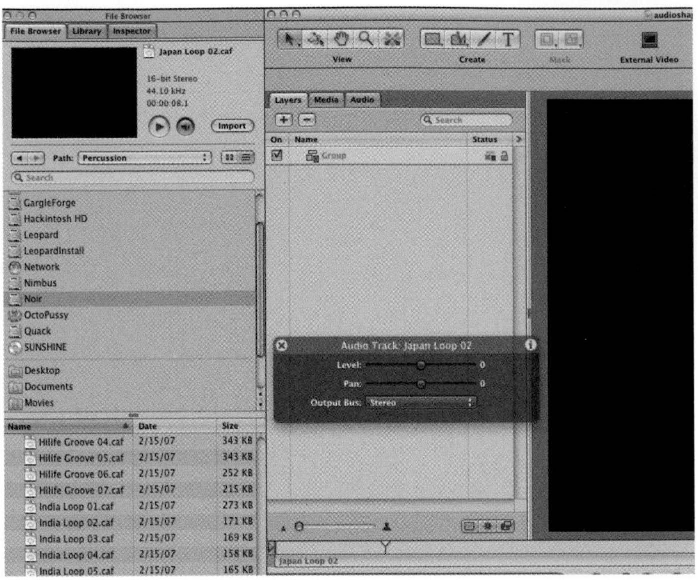

1 Start with a new project. Make it 8 seconds or 240 frames long (because this is the length of our audio loop). Go to **/Library/Audio/Apple Loops/Apple/Apple Loops for Soundtrack Pro/PowerFX Loops/Percussion/**, grab **Japan Loop 02.caf**, and throw it into your project.

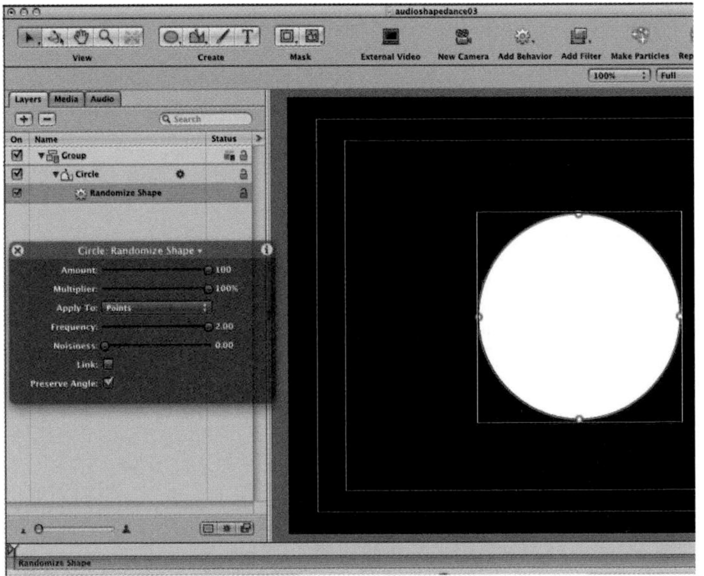

3 **Add Behavior/Shape/Randomize Shape**. Set **Amount** to **100**, **Apply Mode** to **Add and Subtract**, **Frequency** to **2.00**, and **Noisiness** to **0**.

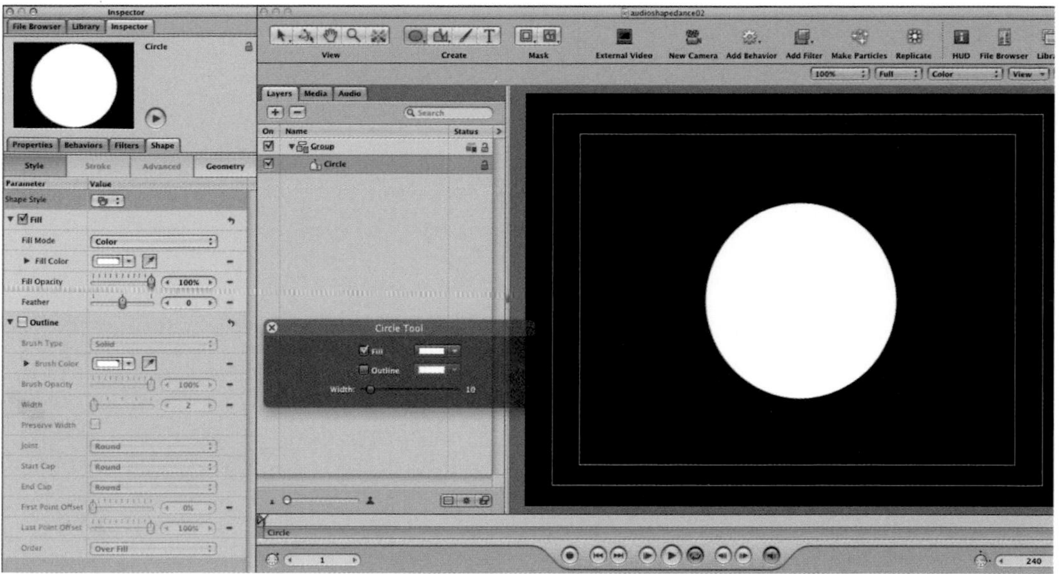

2 Press **C** to activate the **Circle** tool. Holding down the **Shift** and **⌥** keys, pull a medium circle out from the center of the screen.

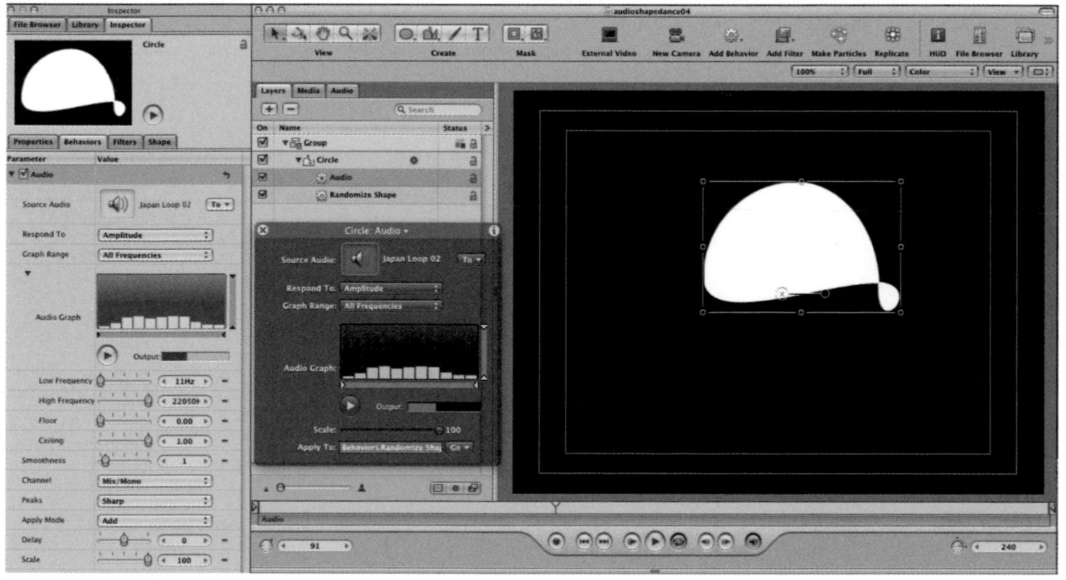

4 Right/**ctrl**-click on **Amount**. Select **Audio**. If you haven't already, click on the **Audio Disclosure** button on the bottom of the timeline, grab the **Japan Loop 02** clip, and drag it into the **Source Audio** well. Set **Scale** to **100**.

Text Dance

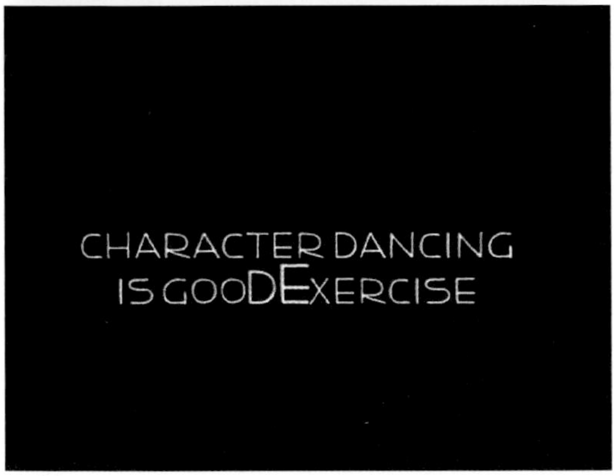

ANIMATING YOUR TEXT IN time with the music running under your titles would be next to impossible if you had to do it by hand. Motion makes it easy.

We'll use a Text Sequence behavior to run through each letter and drive its height based on the audio playing at that moment.

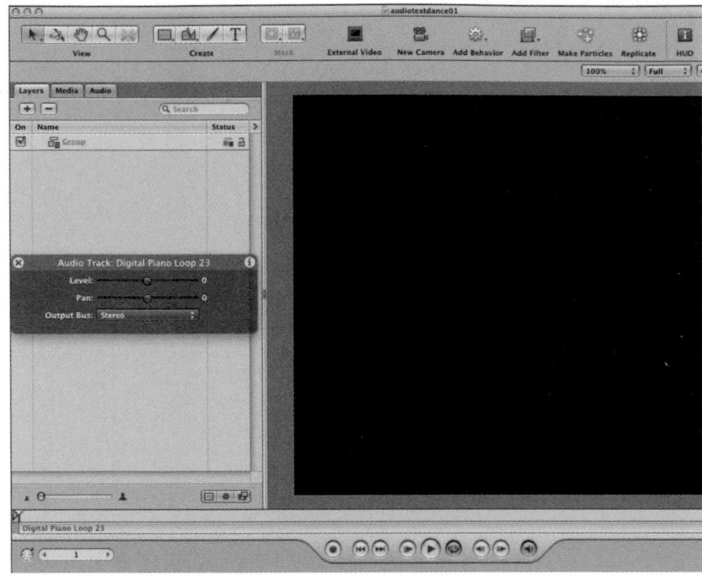

1 Start with a new project. Make it 5:20 seconds or 170 frames long (because this is the length of our audio loop). Go to **/Library/Audio/Apple Loops/Apple/Apple Loops for Soundtrack Pro/PowerFX Loops/Keyboards/Piano/Digital/**, grab **Digital Piano Loop 23.caf,** and throw it into your project.

3 Add Behavior/Text Animation/Sequence Text. Add Parameter/Format/Scale. Grab the **Sequence Text** behavior in the timeline and slide it **5** frames toward the head of the timeline.

2 Activate the **Text** tool. Click in the center of the screen. Choose your **Font** and **Size**. Set **Alignment** to **Center**. Type your message. I typed **CHARACTER DANCING IS GOOD EXERCISE**. Press **esc**.

4 Right/**ctrl**-click on **Scale** and select **Audio**. If you haven't already, click on the Audio disclosure button on the bottom of the timeline, grab the **Digital Piano Loop 23** clip, and drag it into the **Source Audio** well. Set **Delay** to **-1** and **Scale** to **1.20**.

Audio Meter

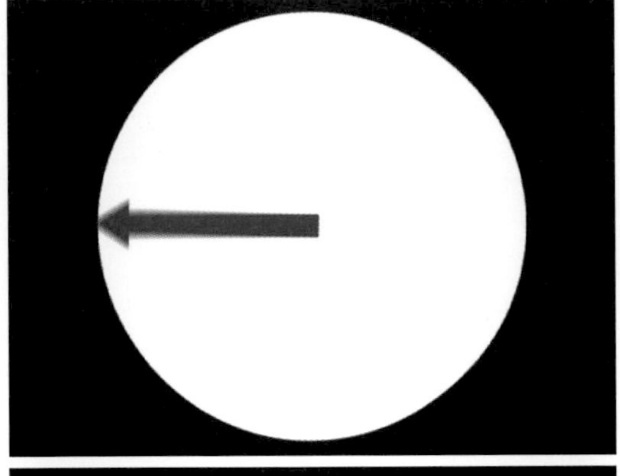

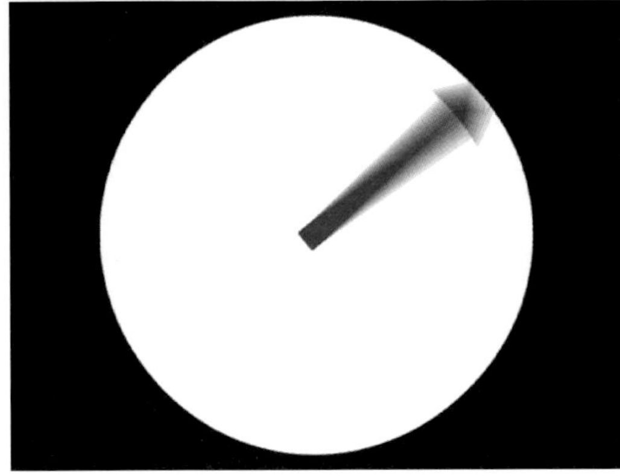

THIS IS A SIMPLE ANALOGUE-style meter responding to a drum loop. We'll use one of the audio loops provided with Sound Track Pro to drive a the rotation of a needle against a circle background.

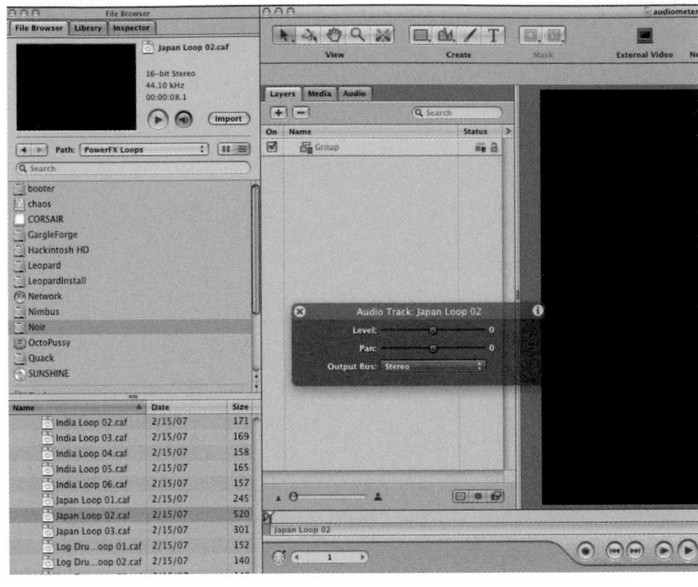

1 Start with a new project. Make it 8 seconds or 240 frames long (because this is the length of our audio loop). Go to **/Library/Audio/Apple Loops/Apple/ Apple Loops for Soundtrack Pro/PowerFX Loops/Percussion/**, grab **Japan Loop 02.caf**, and throw it into your project.

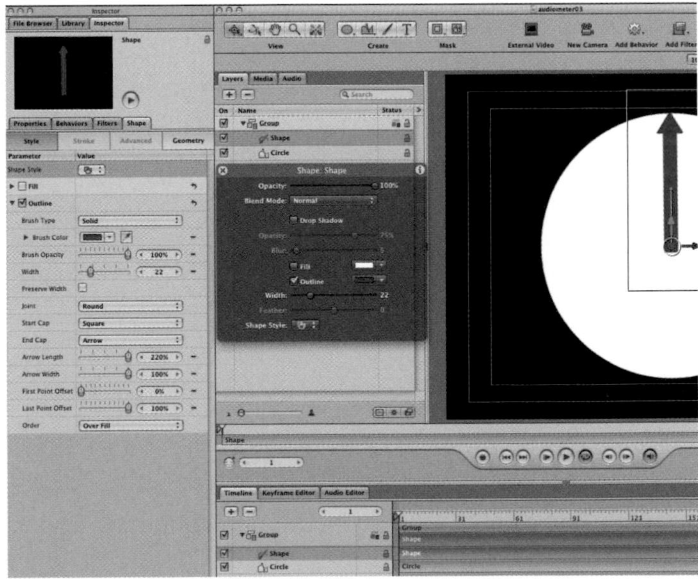

3 Press **B** to activate the **Bezier** tool. Draw a straight line by clicking first in the center of the circle and then near its outer edge. Press ⇥ to end the drawing. Turn off **Fill** and turn on **Outline**. Set **Width** to 22 and **Color** to **Red**. Set the **Start Cap** to **Square** and the **End Cap** to **Arrow**. Set **Arrow Length** to **220%**. Change to the **Adjust Anchor Point** tool and move the anchor point to the center of the **Start Cap**.

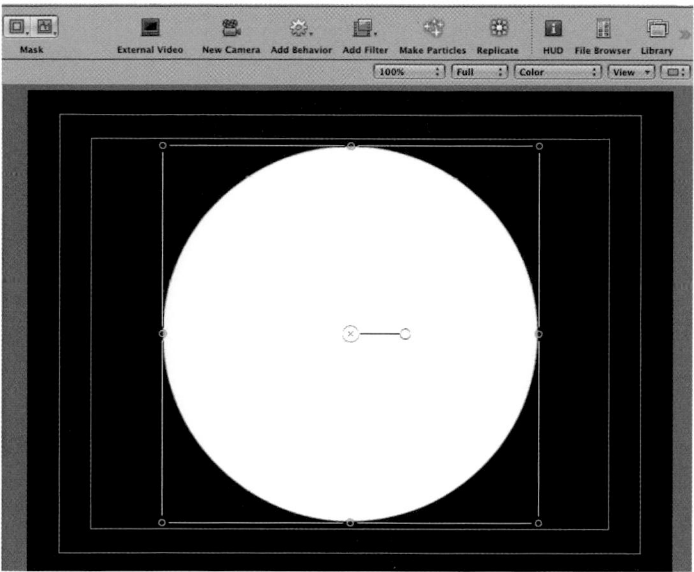

2 Press **C** to activate the **Circle** tool. Holding down **Shift** and **⌥** keys, pull a large circle out from the center of the screen.

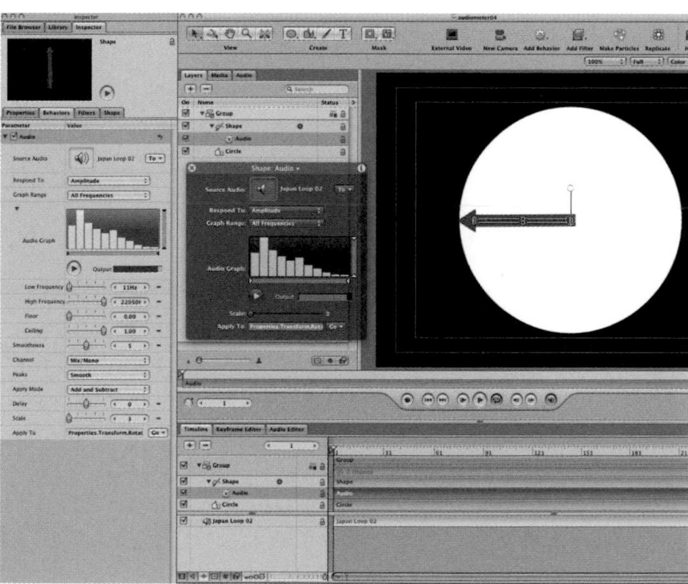

4 In the **Properties** tab, right/**ctrl**-click on **Rotation**. Select **Audio**. If you haven't already, click on the **Audio Disclosure** button on the bottom of the timeline, grab the **Japan Loop 02** clip, and drag it into the **Source Audio** well. Set **Smoothness** to 5, **Peaks** to **Smooth**, **Apply Mode** to **Add and Subtract**, and **Scale** to **3**. You can rotate the arrow to point to the left at the start.

Audio Oscilloscope

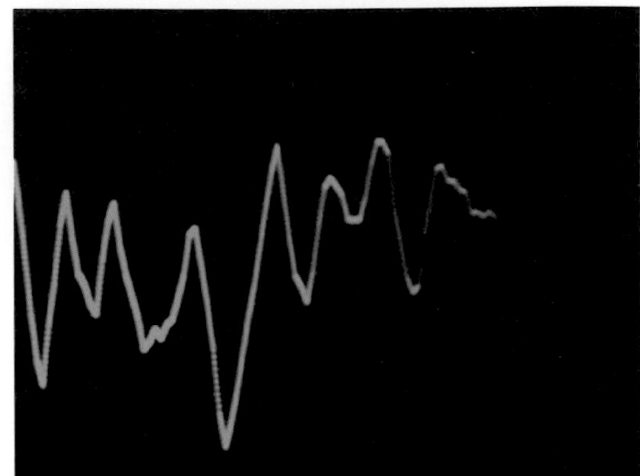

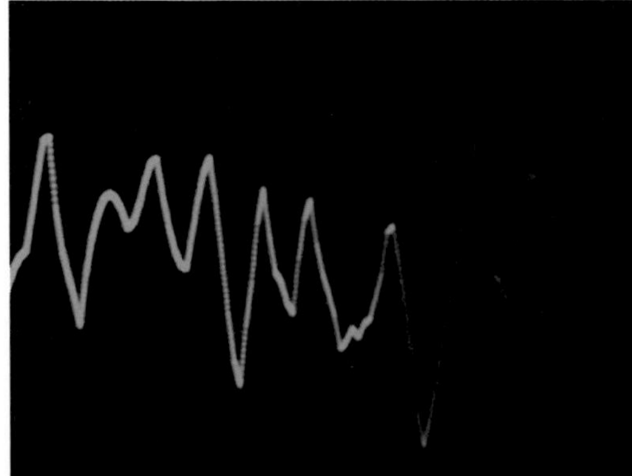

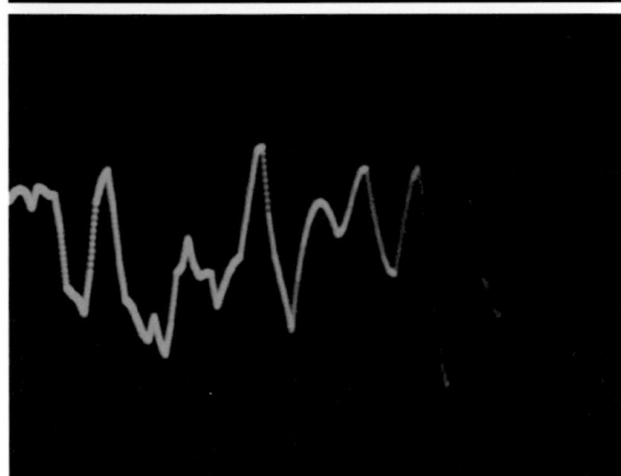

THIS IS NOT SHOWING A real audio waveform—it doesn't have that kind of resolution, but it does graph out the audio levels.

We'll use one of the audio loops provided with Sound Track Pro to drive the Y position of a particle generator.

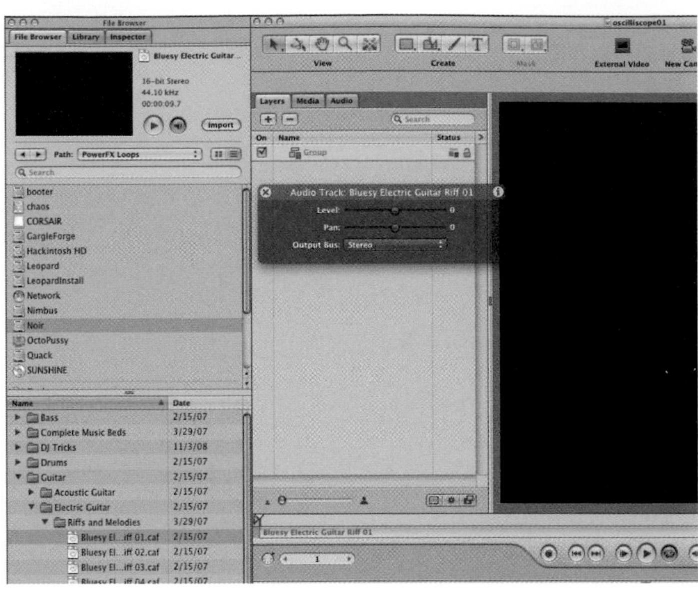

1 Start with a new project. Make it 9:18 seconds or 288 frames long (because this is the length of our audio loop). Go to **/Library/Audio/Apple Loops/Apple/Apple Loops for Soundtrack Pro/PowerFX Loops/Guitar/Electric Guitar/Riffs and Melodies/**, grab **Bluesy Electric Guitar Riff 01.caf**, and throw it into your project.

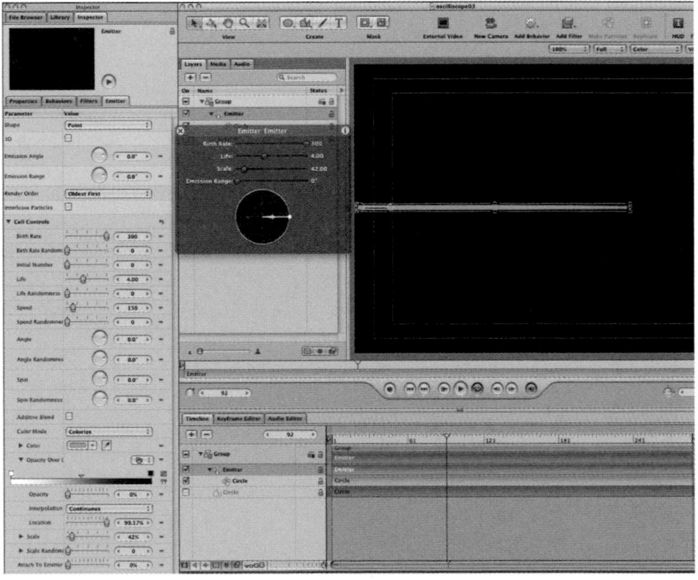

3 Press **E** or click the **Make Particles** button on the toolbar. Set **Emission Range** to **0**, **Birth Rate** to **300**, **Life** to **4.00**, **Speed** to **150**, **Color Mode** to **Colorize**, and **Color** to **Green**. Add a tag at the right of **Opacity Over Life** and set it to **0%**. Adjust **Scale** to suit the size of the circle you drew. Move the emitter to the left side of the screen.

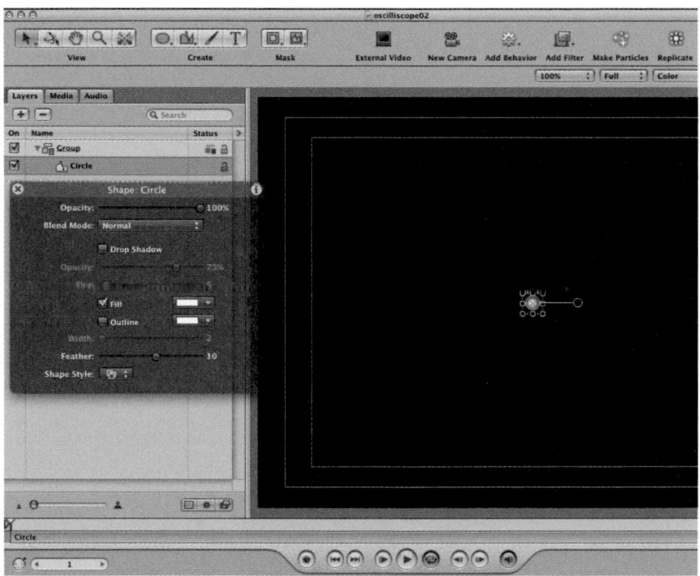

2 Press **C** to activate the **Circle** tool. Holding down the **Shift** and **⌥** keys, pull a small circle out from the center of the screen. Set **Feather** to about **10** or so.

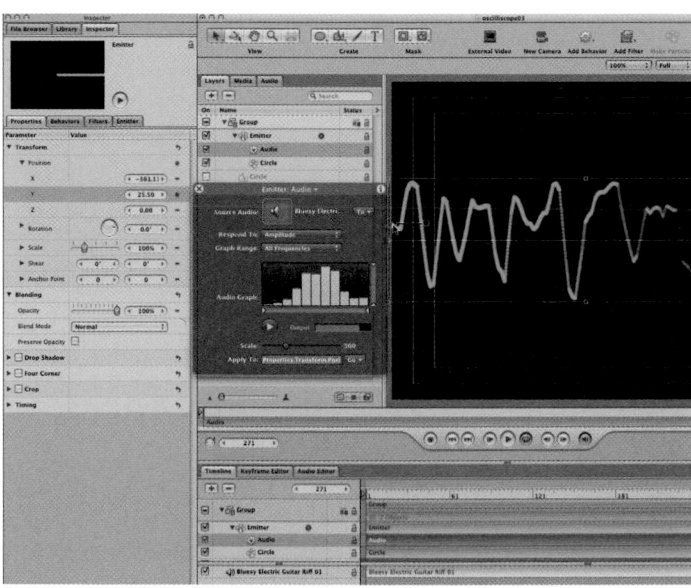

4 In the **Properties** tab, right/**ctrl**-click on **Y Position**. Select **Audio**. If you haven't already, click on the **Audio Disclosure** button on the bottom of the timeline, grab the **Bluesy Electric Guitar Riff 01** clip, and drag it into the **Source Audio** well. Set **Smoothness** to **2** and **Scale** to **300**. Position your playhead near the middle of the timeline, grab the whole emitter, and re-center.

Singing Mr. Happy

MOTION'S AUDIO TOOLS ARE not sophisticated enough to do syllable analysis and pick appropriate mouth shapes to match the sounds, but even without that level of sophistication you can have a surprisingly effective animation.

We're just going to use the audio behavior to drive the rotation of the mouth shape to change its profile. To aid the illusion, we'll add a blur and an indent filter for a fuller effect.

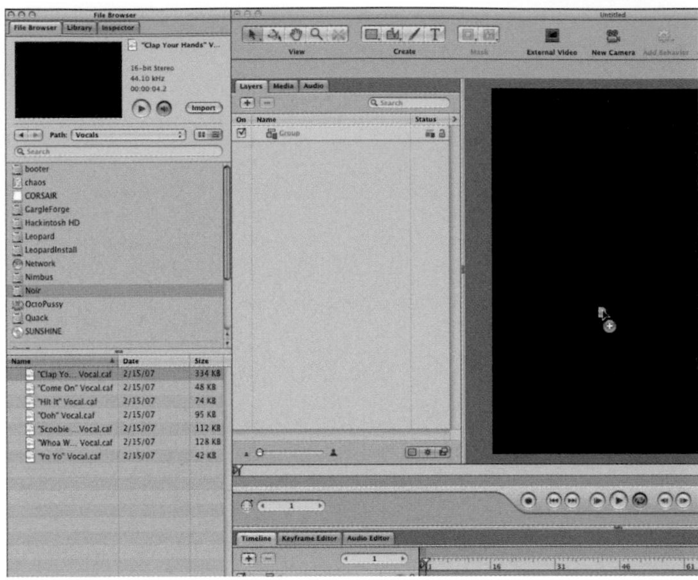

1 Start with a new project. Make it 4 seconds or 120 frames long (because this is the length of our audio loop). Go to **/Library/Audio/Apple Loops/Apple/ Apple Loops for Soundtrack Pro/PowerFX Loops/Vocals/**, grab **"Clap Your Hands" Vocal.caf**, and throw it into your project.

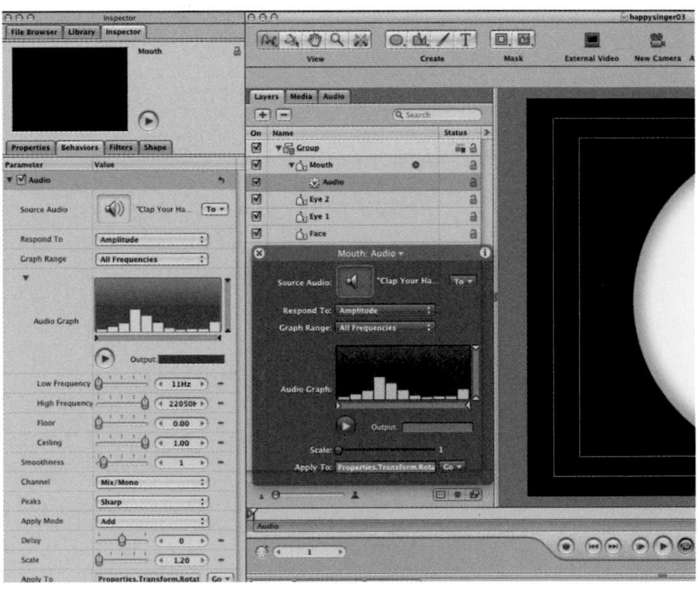

3 Select the mouth shape. In the **Properties** tab, right/ctrl-click on the **X Rotation**. Select **Audio**. If you haven't already, click on the **Audio Disclosure** button on the bottom of the timeline, grab the **"Clap Your Hands"** clip, and drag it into the **Source Audio** well. Set **Scale** to **1.20**.

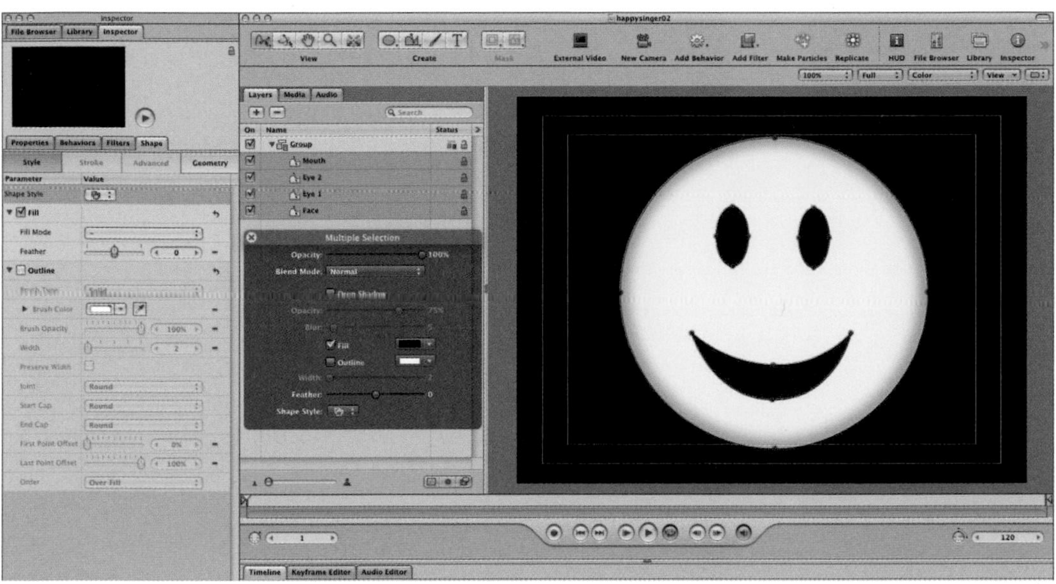

2 Draw a happy face using a yellow circle, two black ovals, and a bezier shape as above.

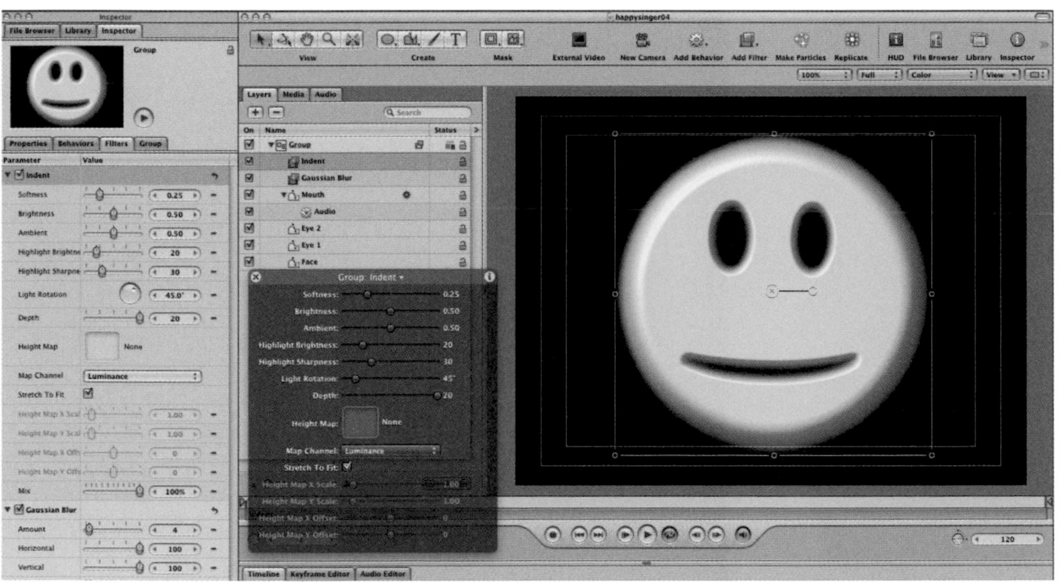

4 Select **Group**. **Add Filter/Blur/Gaussian Blur**. **Add Filter/Stylize/Indent**. Set **Depth** to **20**. Now press **Play** and watch your happy face sing.

Particle Dance

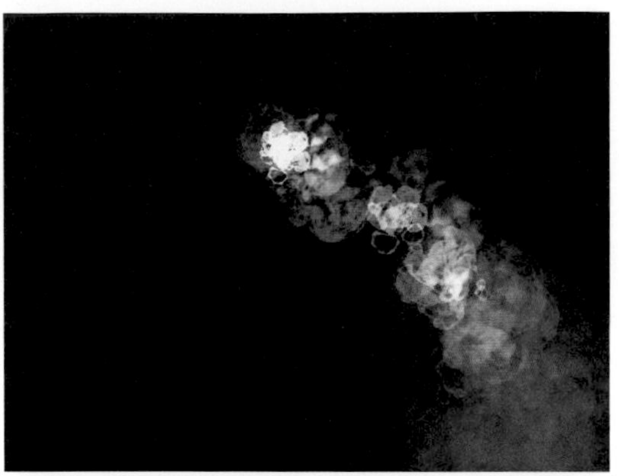

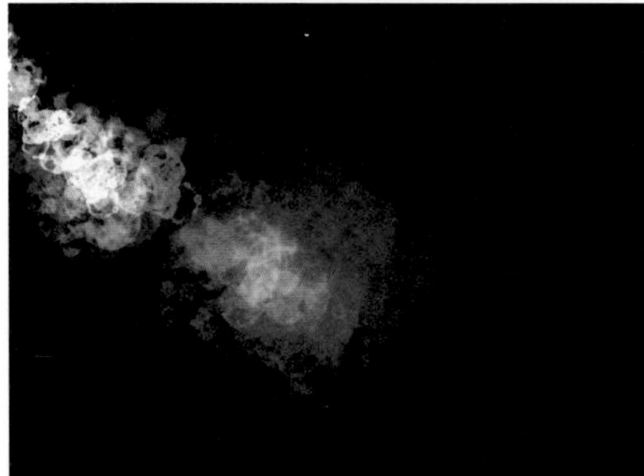

PARTICLE EMITTERS THAT LEAVE trails create an interesting display when you couple their movement with audio.

We'll create a particle emitter and adjust its wriggling around with an audio behavior. By setting a floor value, the movement will stop when the audio drops below the threshold.

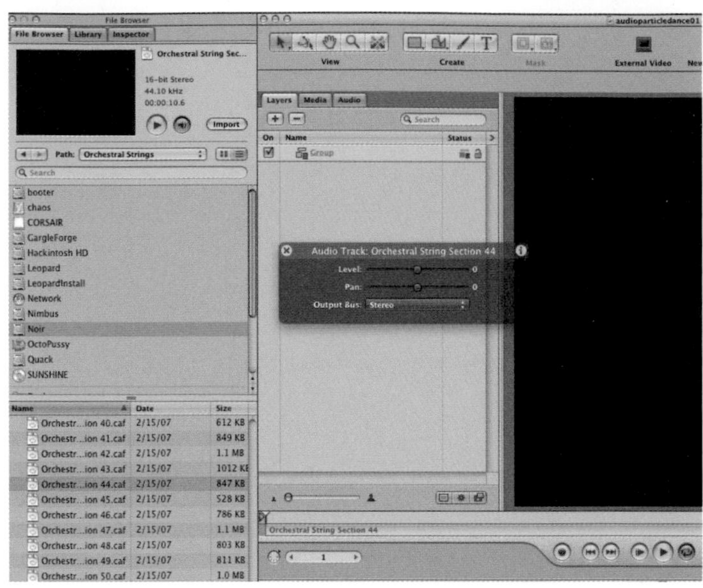

1 Start with a new project. Go to **/Library/Audio/Apple Loops/Apple/Apple Loops for Soundtrack Pro/PowerFX Loops/Strings/Orchestral Strings/**, grab **Orchestral String Section 44.caf**, and throw it into your project.

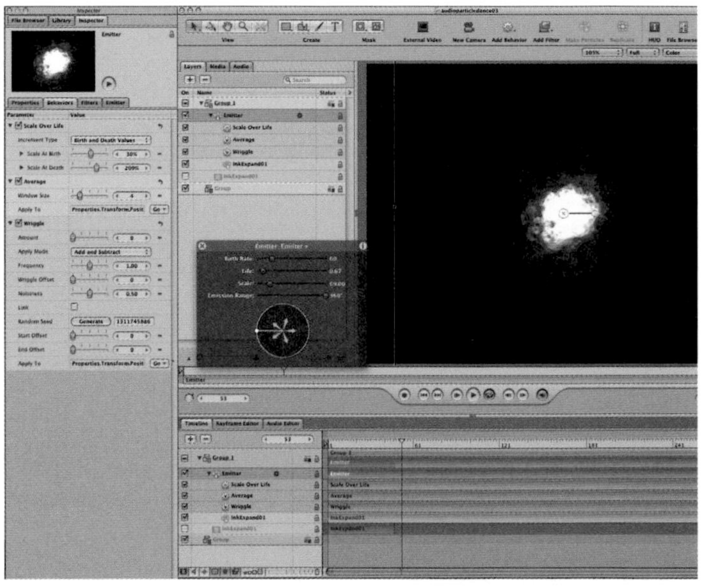

3 In the **Properties** tab, right/**ctrl**-click on **Position**. Select **Wriggle**. Set **Amount** to **0. Apply Mode** to **Add and Subtract**. Go back to the **Properties** tab. Right/**ctrl**-click on **Position**. Select **Average**. Set the **Window Size** to **4. Add Behavior/ Particles/Scale Over Life**. Set **Increment Type** to **Birth and Death Values**. Set **Scale at Birth** to **30%** and **Scale at Death** to **209%**.

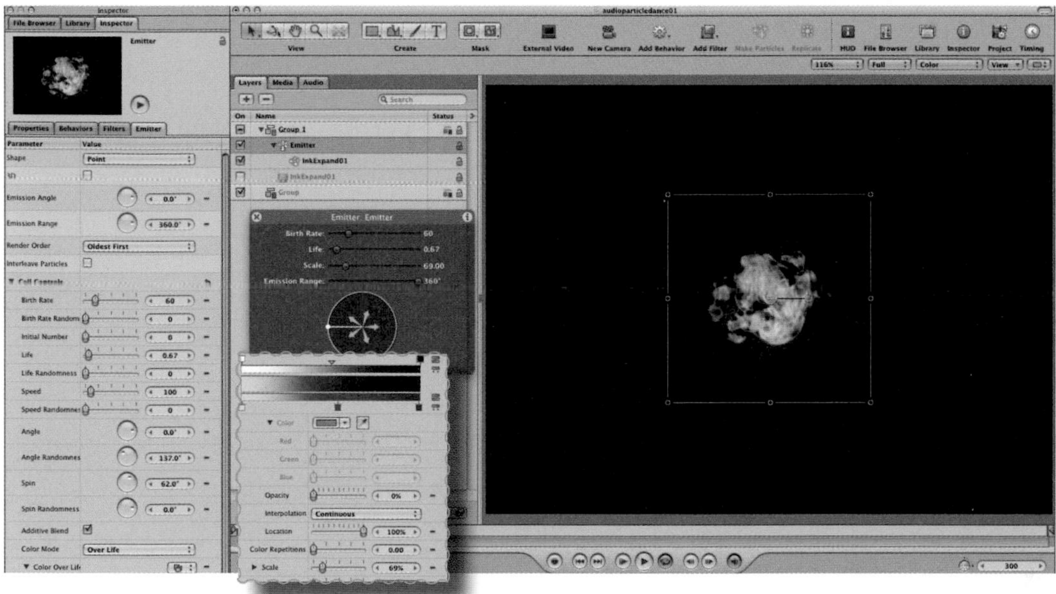

2 Now go to **Library/Content/Particle Images/**, click on **Ink Expand 01.mov**, and press **Apply**. Press **E** or click on the **Make Particles** button in the toolbar. Set **Birth Rate** to **60**, **Life** to **.67**, **Angle Randomness** to **137°**, and **Spin** to **62**. Click **Additive Blend**. Set **Color Mode** to **Color Over Life** and **Gradient** to **Icy Blue**. Add a tag to the right-hand **Opacity** gradient and set it to 0%. Set **Scale** to 69%.

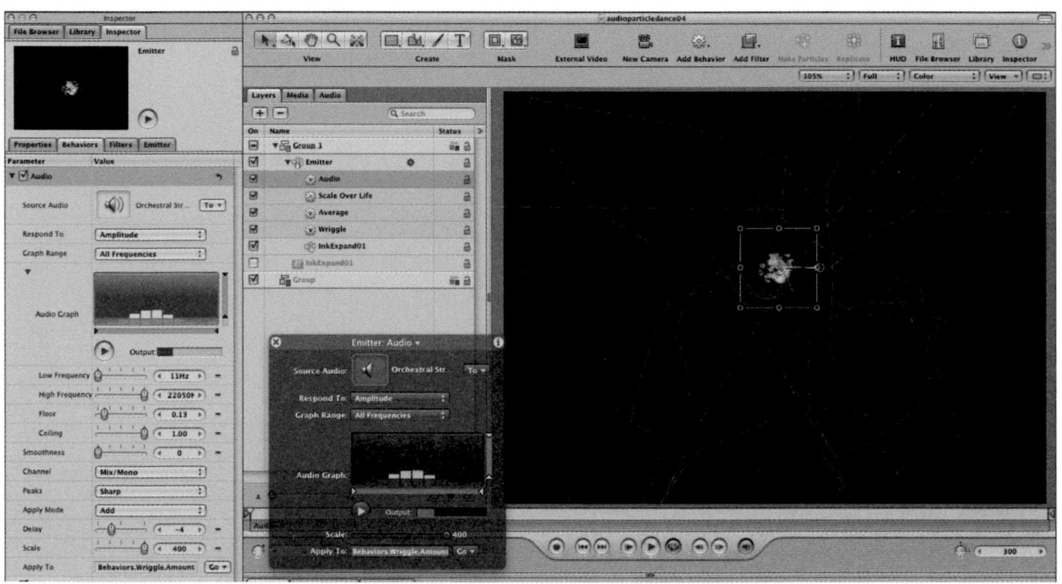

4 Right/**ctrl**-click on **Wriggle/Amount** and select **Audio**. If you haven't already, click on the **Audio Disclosure** button on the bottom of the timeline, grab the **Orchestral String Section 44** clip, and drag it into the **Source Audio** well. Set **Floor** to **.13**, **Delay** to **-4**, and **Scale** to **400**.

Tales of the velcro dog

And other helpful hints for the Motion graphics artist

I THOUGHT I'D INCLUDE AN ESSAY ON Things a Motion Graphics Artist Should Know. I wanted it to be larger than only my perspective, so I went to the Apple Motion forum (http://discussions.apple.com—look for Pro Applications: Video/Motion) and asked other motion graphics artists to contribute hints they found helpful. I took the provided hints, combined them with my own, reworded, etc. In no particular order.

One is a quasi-questionable practice I sometimes employed as an editor of music videos that I and other editors called "The Velcro Dog." It has other names too: "The Blue Duck," "The Purple Door knob," etc.

It goes back to the fact that you never wanted to turn in a "perfect" edit on the first pass. In fact, of the hundreds of music videos I've edited, I could count on one hand the number of times that I turned in an edit that the record label said "perfect, don't change a frame." Maybe it's a human need to justify their jobs, but inevitably, those in charge of approval would have to make some comment, request some change.

If your cut was perfect, these changes often would be for the worse, so sometimes it paid to add an obvious flaw to the edit that wasn't hard to change—thus the Velcro Dog, something bad that could be easily torn off. It might be as simple as a line that was out of sync or maybe a shot where the lead singer had his hair in his mouth or a story shot that was out of place. This gave those in charge something to focus on that you could fix without causing the cascading problems that more complex changes might require.

It was also something that you could change without problem if no one picked up on it.

But woe to you if someone in the chain of Artist, Video Commissioner, Management, A&R, Marketing, etc. decided he or she actually liked your little velcro dog. Then you had to live with seeing it on TV like that.

A Motion designer should be able to visualize his or her ideas before starting to do anything in any motion graphics application. Sketching, storyboarding, preparing sample stills in Photoshop—all that can save you a lot of time later. Applications like Motion or After Effects work best if everything is carefully planned. Doodling and improvising are not things you want to be doing when you are on a tight deadline. Think about your project like a movie set you have to prepare.

How to get paid. As much as everyone would love to concentrate on the artistic aspects of the work, it's still work and you have to pay the bills. This isn't as much of a problem when you're working for a company, but if you're freelance, Accounts Receivable is a function you have to make yourself familiar with

Every pixel counts.

How to balance a frame for full-frame graphics in much the same way that a photographer does.

Movement is relative to the size of the final product. Moving gfx elements projected onto large screens "appear" to move faster and can therefore be distracting instead of enhancing.

IMPORTANT: Must understand the video needs of the editor who is getting the gfx. That includes frame sizes, codecs, frame rates, etc.

When less is more.

Gfx artists need to know which way the Earth rotates. I can't tell you how often I see rotating Earth gfx spinning in a rotation so that the sun rises in the West and sets in the East.

We all want to "get the job," but agreeing to deliver a project with an unrealistically tight schedule is unwise on a number of levels. The quality suffers. There is less time to troubleshoot. Less time to love and finesse the work. When we do come through on schedule, dangerous precedents and expectations are set throughout the industry. Worst of all, we further the notion that "anything that's done on computers can be done quickly."

However, the reality of the marketplace dictates that a motion graphics artist needs to learn and employ time-saving tricks and skills, because the demands placed on you mean that while your first idea may not be your best idea, sometimes "good enough" is all you have time for.

Outflank your clients. Provide three choices for them and they'll almost always choose one.

If you present only one solution, they can either say yes or no. If you present multiple options, the answer will often be yes to one of them.

A motion graphics artist should know where to go to get answers to questions. In other words, a trusted, up-to-date resource list of good forums, books, websites, and even YouTube tutorials.

Recommended books:

The Animator's Survival Kit
Motion Graphic Design: Applied History and Aesthetics
Apple Pro Training Series: Motion Graphics and Effects in FCS2
Apple Pro Training Series: Motion 3
Apple Pro Training Series: Motion 4

Recommended DVDs:

Motion 3, Fast Forward
Motion 3, Deep Dive into 3D

Recommended sites:

discussions.apple.com–Pro Applications/Motion
applemotion.net
lynda.com
pixelcorps.tv
motionsmarts.com

Finally I'll leave you with this little diagram—created in Motion, of course. It's a Venn diagram of client options:

Thanks to: Pixel Ninja, Mark Spencer, 08malesh, Andy Neil, zoom00, ap_TonyTony, Adam Scoffield, Adam McCormick, specialcase, and Peter Wiggins for their contributions.

How to Cheat in

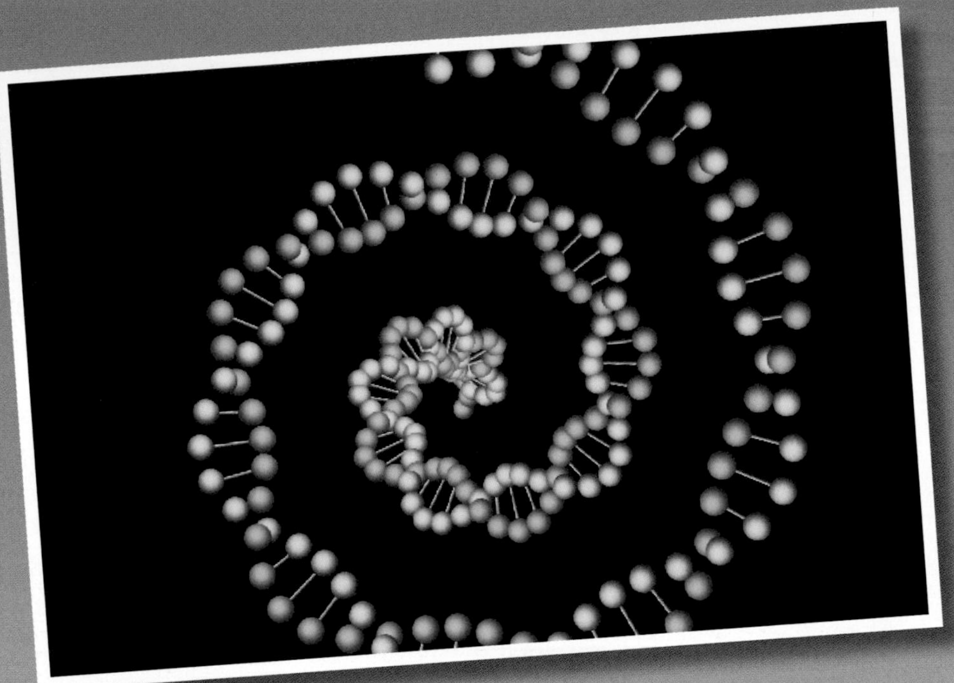

Whether you need to make some fake DNA, convert Motion into your desktop publishing solution, make some shiny plastic flowers, or build a porcupine, you can find out how in this chapter.

10 Grab Bag

HERE IS MY COLLECTION OF PROJECTS THAT just don't fit into the other chapters.

But, as the residents of the Island of Misfit Toys will tell you, there is a toy for every child and a child for every toy. I think you'll manage find something here that will be fun to play with.

Desktop Publishing

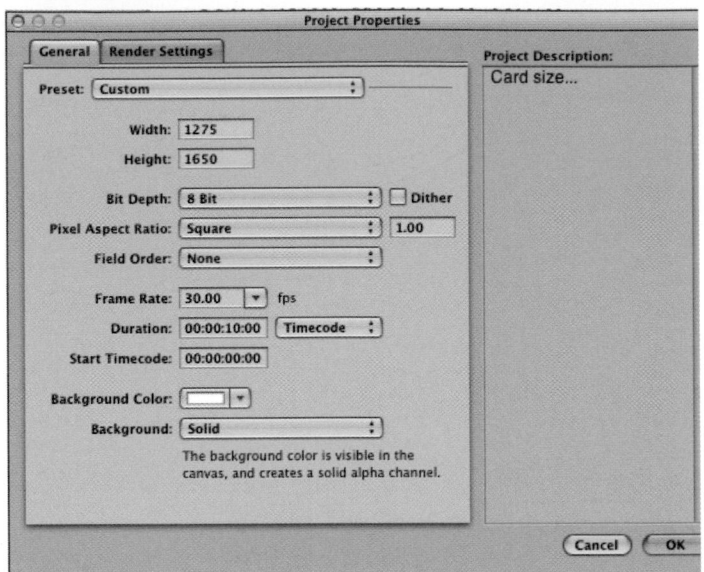

1 Start with a new project. Choose **Custom** and set its dimensions to 1275x1650. Make sure the **Pixel Aspect Ratio** is **Square** and **Field Order None**. Set the **Background Color** to **White**. Set **Background** to **Solid**.

CHARGED WITH MAKING my daughter's ideas for her birthday invitation concrete (or at least rendering them on paper), I reached for a tool I'm familiar with. Though Motion is not generally thought of as a desktop publishing tool, nonetheless, I pressed it into service.

At 150 dpi, 8.5x11 works out to be 1275x 1650, well within a 2048x2048 limit. So I did it up, used text effects not readily available in, say, Adobe InDesign. I used the Vector tools to draw my picture, the Replicator to do the eyelashes, etc. When I was finished, I just printed it from within Motion. Folded into quarters, it was exactly what she was looking for.

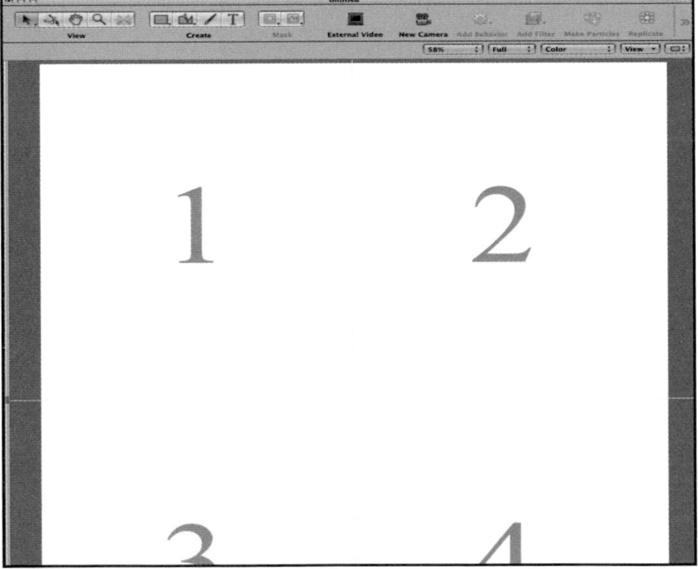

3 In Quadrant 1, place anything you want on the front of the card, and turn it upside down. Quadrant 2 gets anything for the back cover. Again, upside down. You can build it right side up on its own layer and then rotate it 180° and place it.

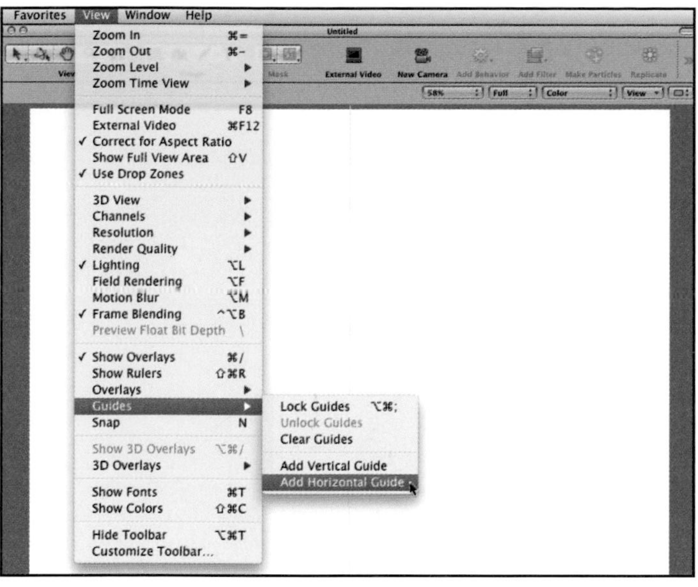

2 View/Guides/Add Horizontal. View/Guides/Add Vertical.

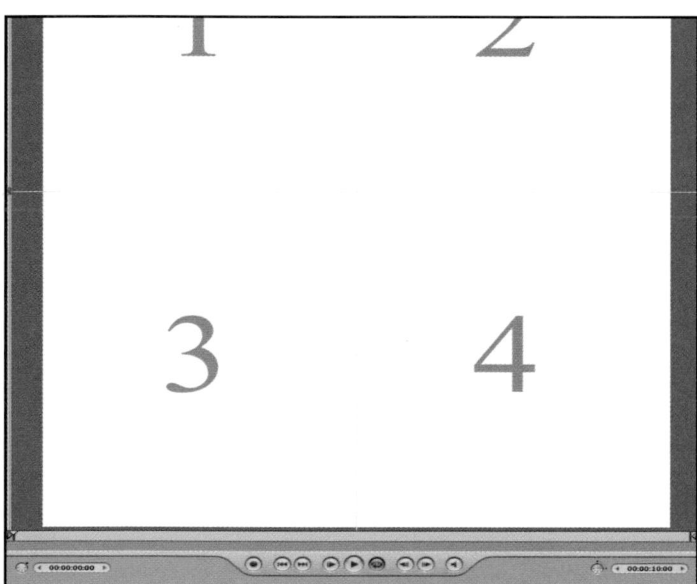

4 Quadrant 3 is left inside cover. Quadrant 4 is right inside. Now send it to the printer. Easy as pie!

Circular Swish

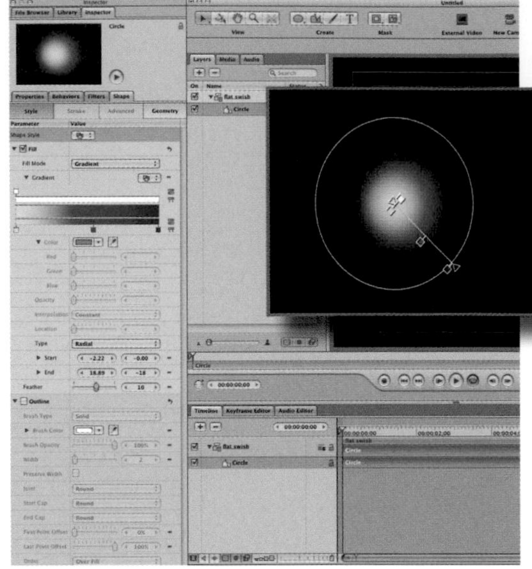

1 Start with a new project. Name the default group **flat swish**. Press **C** to activate the **Circle** tool. Draw a small circle. Change the **Fill Mode** to **Gradient**. Set the **Gradient** to **Icy Blue**, the **Gradient Type** to **Radial**, and **Feather** to **10**. Use the **Adjust Item** tool to edit the gradient as per the inset above.

THE ABC NETWORK USED to have this little wiggle thing going around their logo bug in the corner of the screen and I often wondered how to do it in Motion. I know they probably use 3D stroke in After Effects, but I'm not interested in becoming an AE guy, so I'd been trying to get the effect in Motion. Finally I had a breakthrough when I saw the trailer for *Who Killed the Electric Car*—which had a graphic probably also done in AE, but it made me think of using the ScanTunnel filter and I got a nice effect.

Please note: There are many variables to success here, you may need to play around a bit before you find a look that is satisfactory.

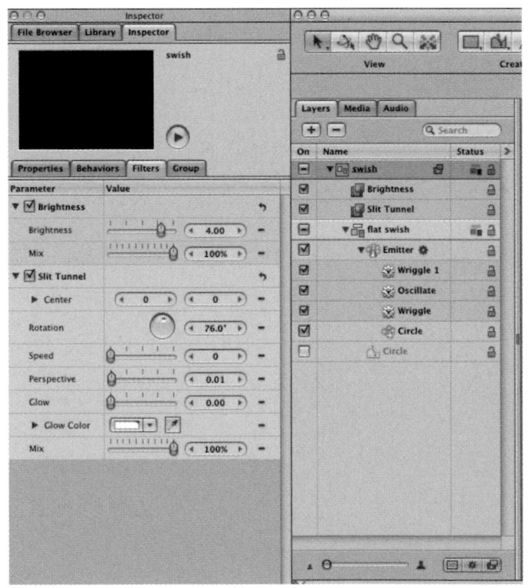

4 Select the **flat swish** group. Type **⌘ Shift G**. Name the new group **swish**. Click the **Fixed Resolution** checkbox. **Add Filter/Stylize/Slit Tunnel**. Set the **Rotation** to **76**, **Speed-to**, **Perspective to 0.01**, and **Glow to 0**. **Add Filter/Color Correction/Brightness**. Set **Brightness** to **4**.

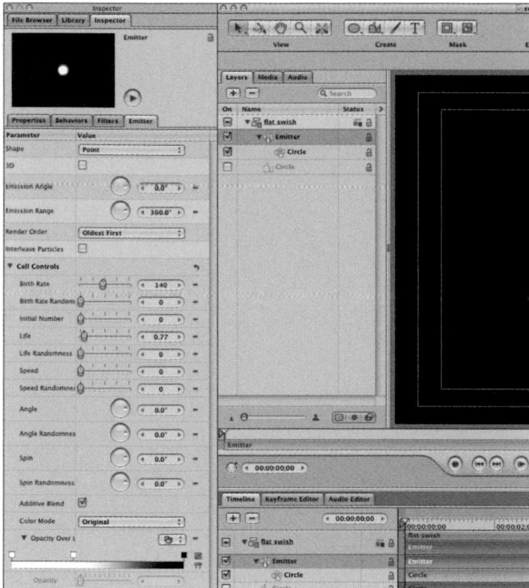

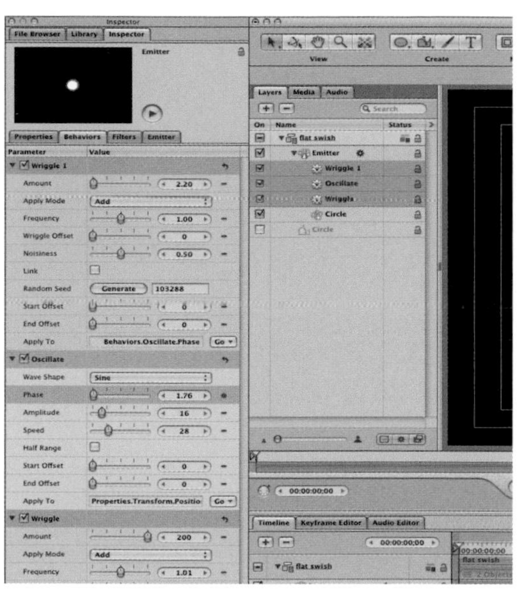

2 With **Circle** selected, press **E** or click the **Make Particles** button. Set the **Birth Rate** to **140**, **Life** to **.77**, **Speed** to **0**. Click the **Additive Blend** checkbox. In the **Opacity over Life** gradient, set a tag at **36** to **100%**. Set the tag at **100** to **0%**.

3 With the **Emitter** selected, in the **Properties** tab, right/**ctrl**-click on the **Y Position** and select **Wriggle**. Set **Amount** to **200**. Frequency to **1.01** and Noisiness to **0.13**. Back in the **Properties** tab, right/**ctrl**-click on the **X Position** and select **Oscillate**. Set **Phase** to **1.76**, **Amplitude** to **16**, and **Speed** to **28**. Right/**ctrl**-click on the **Oscillate Phase** and select **Wriggle**. Change **Amount** to **2.20**.

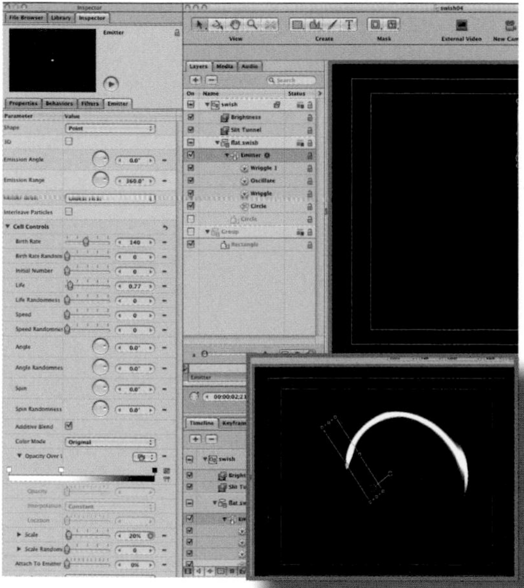

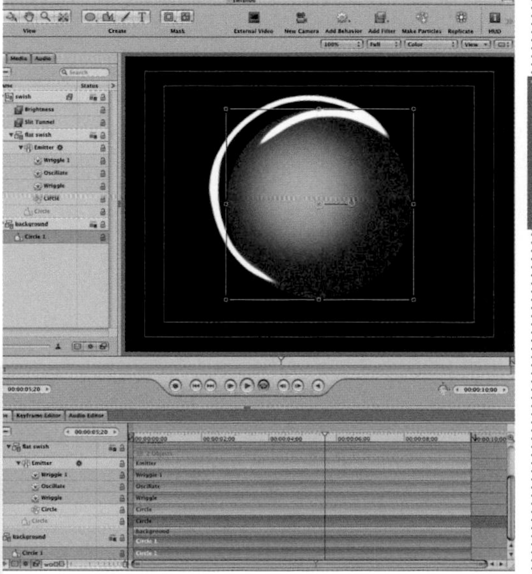

HOT TIP

If your swish looks something like this, you may have forgotten to set the Fixed Resolution checkbox on the Swish layer.

5 Now comes time to adjust. Select the **Emitter**, position to about 2 seconds, and set your scale to give the width of the swish you want. Then grab and rotate and position the **flat swish** group until you get the effect you're looking for. I like it somewhere around where it is in the inset.

6 Finally, add a new group. Name it **background** and place it below the **swish** group. Go back to frame 1 and add a gradient filled circle as above.

Dial Counter

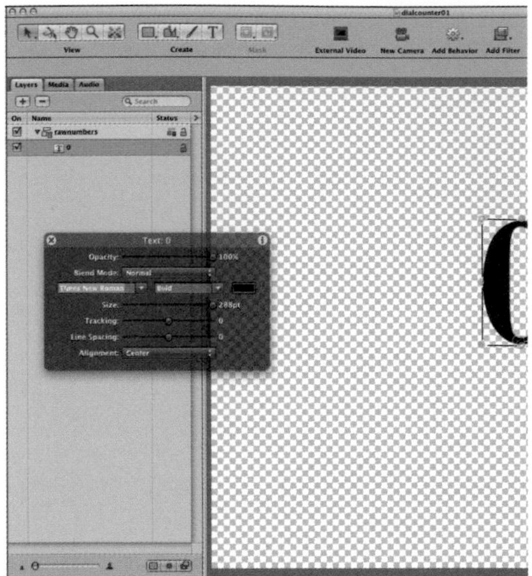

1 Start with a new project. Try **Presentation Large.** It will be hard to deal with a black background for a bit, so press **Shift T**. Name the default group **rawnumbers**. Activate the **Text** tool. Click in the middle of the screen. Set **Font** to **Times New Roman Bold, Size** to **288 pt**, and **Alignment** to **Center**. Make the color black. Type the number **0**. Press **esc**.

SOMETIMES THE WAY TO APPROACH a Motion project is to think of how something might be done in the real world and simulate it in Motion. That was the impetus behind this Dial Counter Motion project.

We'll use a couple of interesting techniques in this project: one is using a Replicator to build our dial, another is using an Oscillator to modify a behavior.

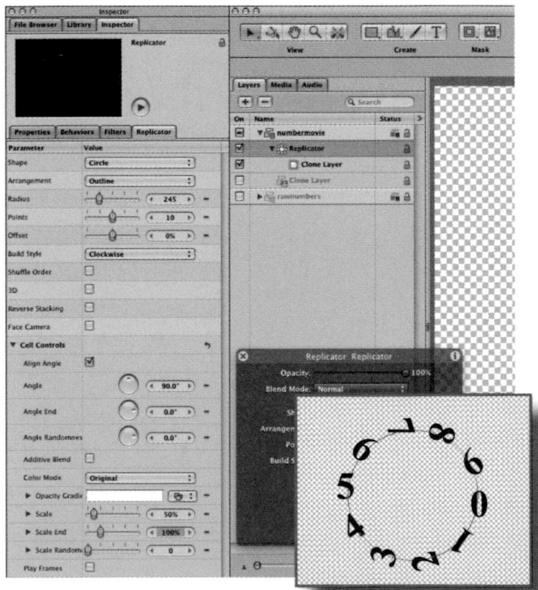

4 Select **Clone Layer**. Press **L**. Select the **Replicator**. Change the **Shape** to **Circle**, **Arrangement** to **Outline**, and **Radius** to **245** (note: if not using **Presentation Large**, this will be different). Set **Points** to **10**. Click the **Align Angle** checkbox. Set **Angle** to **90°** and **Scale** to **50%**. Unset **Play Frames**. Set **Source Frame Offset** to **1**.

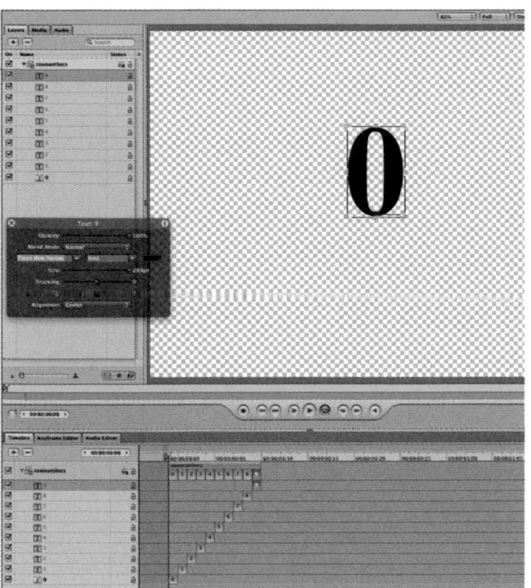

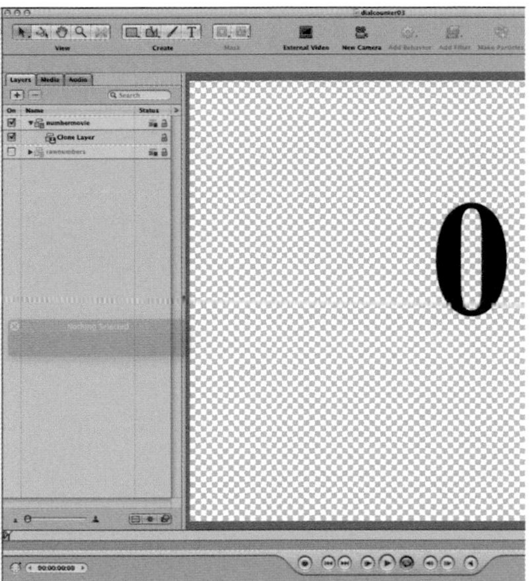

2 In the timeline, trim your number 0 clip to 1 frame. Type ⌘C **(Copy)**. Now, starting on frame 1, press right arrow, ⌘V **(Paste)** 9 times to make 9 copies of your single frame 0. Change their text to 1, 2, 3, ... all the way to 9.

3 You should now have a 10-frame segment that has numbers 0 through 9 on separate frames. Position to frame 1. Select the **rawnumbers** group. Press K to create a clone layer. Name the **Clone Layer** group **numbermovie**. Turn off **rawnumbers**.

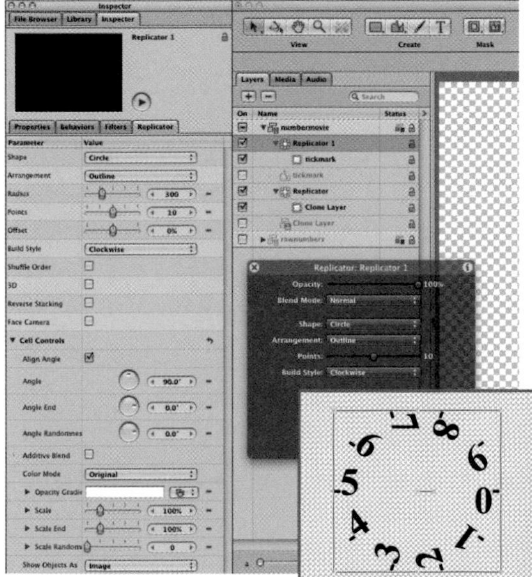

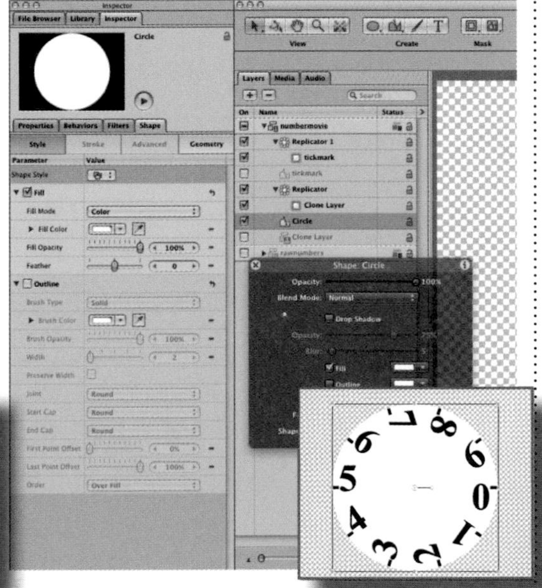

5 Activate the **Rectangle** tool. Draw a small black rectangle in the center of the screen. Call it **tickmark**. Press L. Change the **Shape** to **Circle**, **Arrangement** to **Outline**, **Radius** to 300, and **Points** to 10. Click the **Align Angle** checkbox and set **Angle** to 90°.

6 Press C to activate the **Circle** tool. Click in the center of the screen and hold down the Shift and ⌥ keys and pull outward until you have a circle as large as your replicator. Make it white. Place it behind **Replicator 1** and **Replicator**.

continued...

Dial Counter (continued)

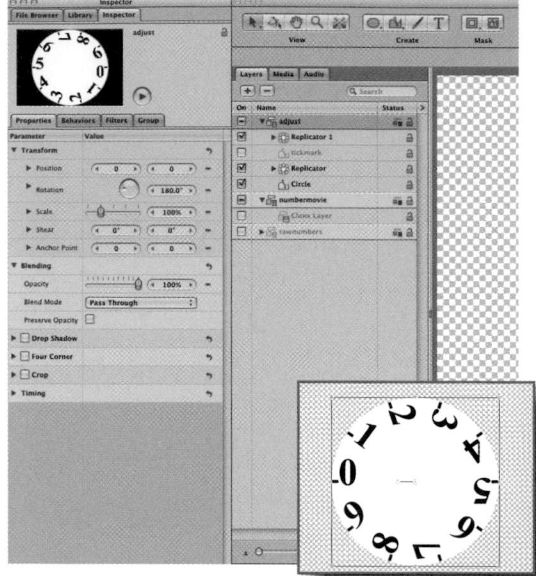

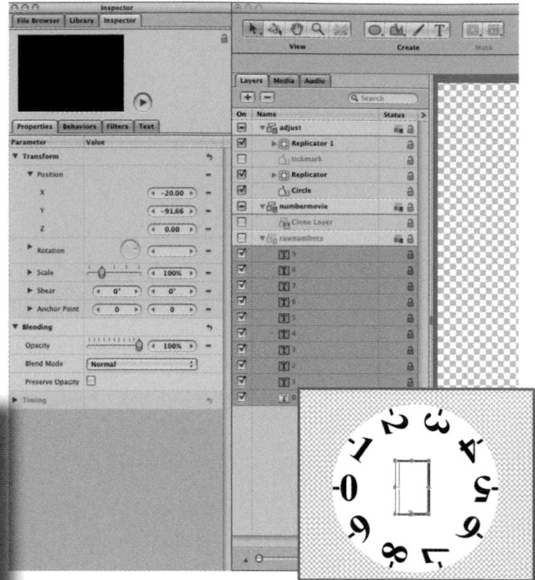

7 ⌘-select **Replicator 1**, **Replicator**, **Circle**, and **tickmark**. In the **Properties** tab, set **Position** to 0, 0. Press ⌘ Shift G. Name the new group **adjust**. Move it outside and above **numbermovie**. Rotate the **adjust** group until the numeral 0 is level on the left (180°).

8 The numbers probably don't line up—let's fix that. Open the **rawnumbers** group. Shift select layers **0–9**. In the **Properties** tab, adjust the **Y Position** until the numbers line up in the center of the tickmark. Adjust the **X Position** to alter the spacing from the tickmark.

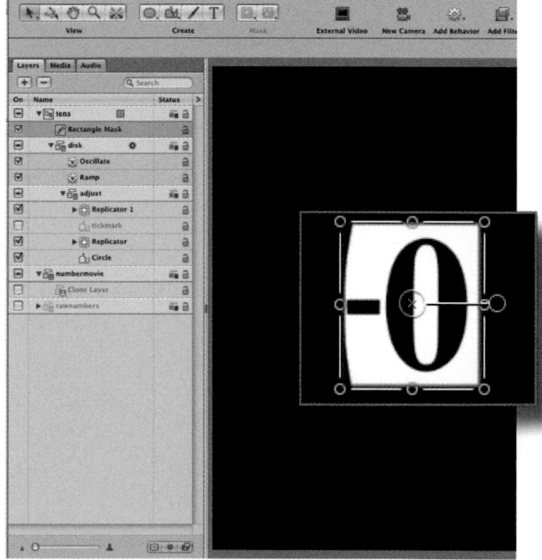

11 What's happening? The **Triangular Oscillation** is reinforcing the ramp half the time and countering it the other half, so the rotation pauses at each number.

12 Click on **disk**. Press ⌘ Shift G. Name the new group **tens**. Select the **Rectangular Mask** tool (⌥ R). Position to frame 1. Draw a mask that outlines the entire number, but not much more. Press Shift C to turn on the black background.

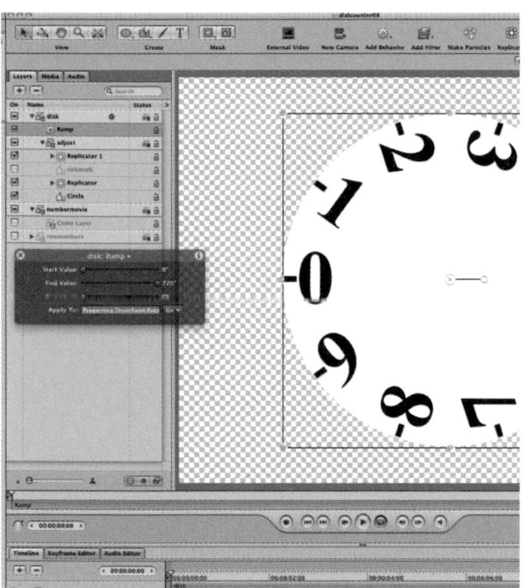

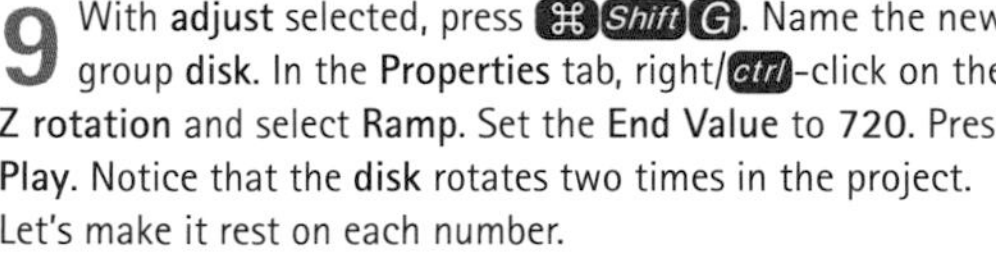

9 With **adjust** selected, press ⌘ Shift G. Name the new group **disk**. In the **Properties** tab, right/ctrl-click on the **Z rotation** and select **Ramp**. Set the **End Value** to 720. Press **Play**. Notice that the **disk** rotates two times in the project. Let's make it rest on each number.

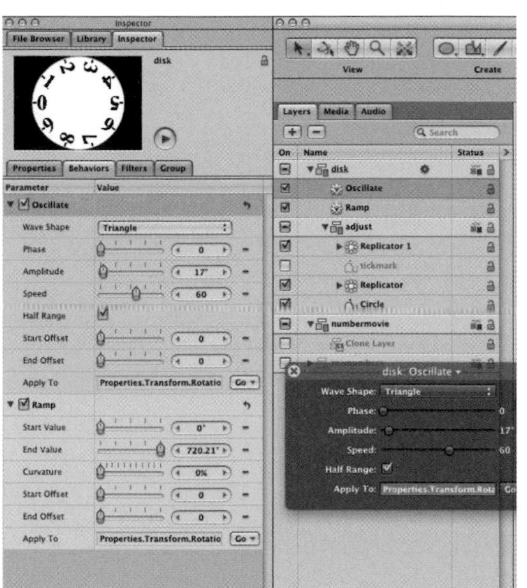

10 Go back to the **Properties** tab. Right/ctrl-click on the **Z rotation**. Select **Oscillate**. Set **Wave Shape** to **Triangle**. Set **Amplitude** to **17**. **Speed** to **60**. Click the **Half Range** checkbox. Now press **Play**. The disk should pause on each number.

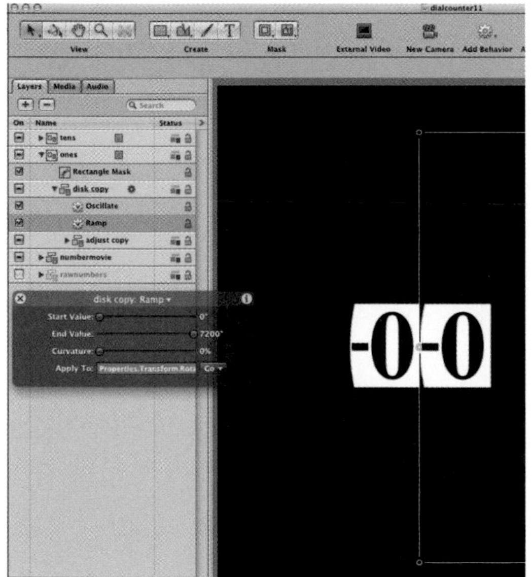

13 Select the **tens** group. Press ⌘ D to duplicate it. Name the copy **ones**. Change the **disk copy/Oscillate/ Speed** to **600**. Change the **Ramp End Value** to **7200**. This means it will run 10 times faster or 20 rotations in your project. Move the number to the right of the tens column.

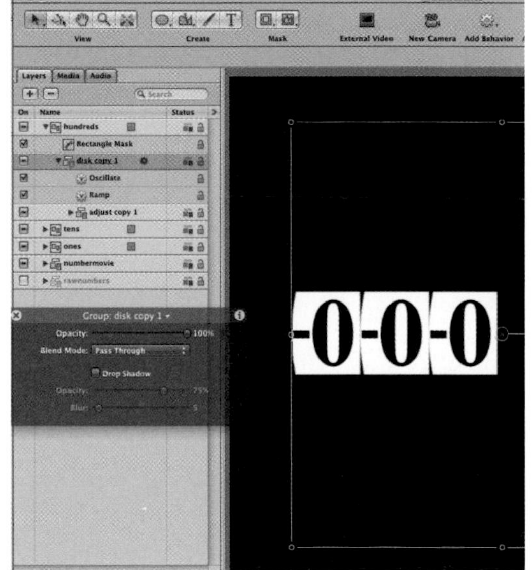

14 Select the **tens** group. Press ⌘ D to duplicate it. Rename it **hundreds**. Change the **disk copy 1/ Oscillate/Speed to 6**. Change the **Ramp End Value** to 72. This means it will run 10 times slower or .2 rotations in your project. Move the number to the left of the tens column.

Revolving Counter

THESE REVOLVING COUNTERS ARE like the mechanical counter on an old odometer or (for those old enough to remember them) gas pumps.

Much like the dial counters in the last exercise, we'll attempt to simulate the mechanical world with shifting bits and behaviors.

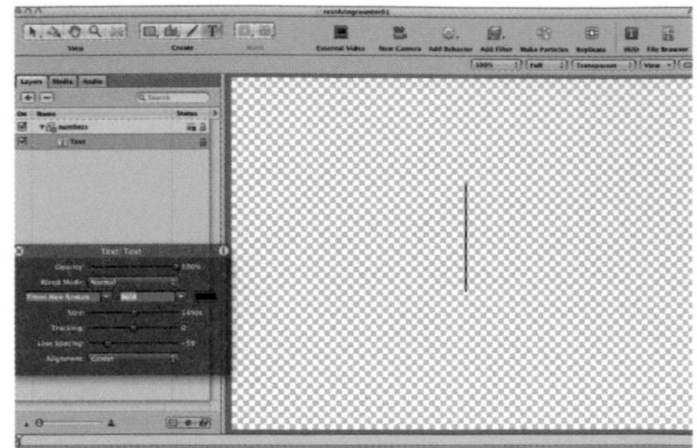

1 Start with a new project. Name the default group **numbers**. Press Shift T to turn on **Transparency**. Press T to activate the **Text** tool. Click in the middle of the screen. Set the **Font** to **Times New Roman Bold**, **Color** to black, **Size** to **149**, **Line Spacing** to **-59**, and **Alignment** to **Center.**

4 Select **Offset**. Right/ctrl-click on **Vertical Offset**. Select **Oscillate**. Change the **Wave Shape** to **Triangle**, **Amplitude to 4, and Speed** to **60**. Click the **Half Range** checkbox. Press **Play**. Now the numbers pause and advance.

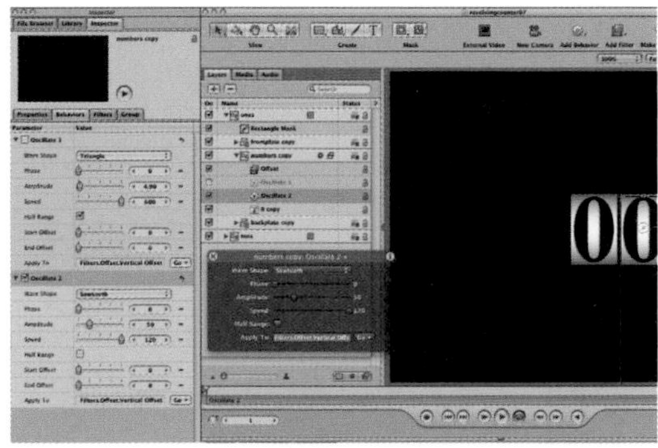

7 Select **tens**. Press ⌘D. Name the duplicate layer **ones**. Change its **Oscillate 2/Speed** to **120**. Disable **Oscillate 1** (it's moving so fast don't worry about pausing). Move the digit to the right of the tens digit.

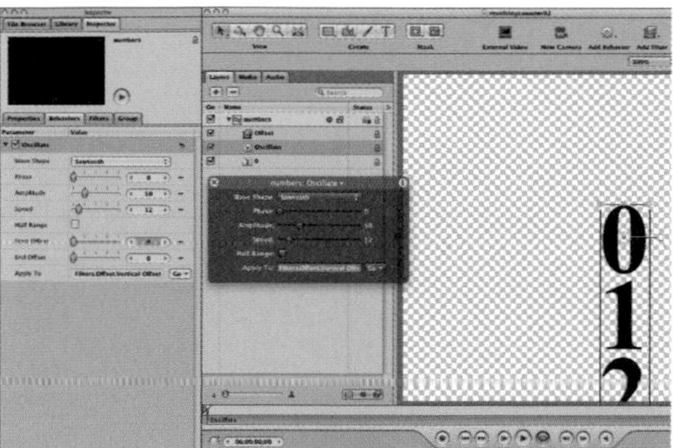

2 Type 0 Return 1 Return 2 Return etc. so you get a column of numbers from 0 to 9. Select the **numbers** group. **Add Filter/ Tiling/Offset**. right/ctrl-click on **Vertical Offset**. Select **Oscillate**. Set **Wave Shape** to **Sawtooth**, **Amplitude** to **50**, **Speed** to **12**. Press **Play**. The numbers should scroll by, twice for your project.

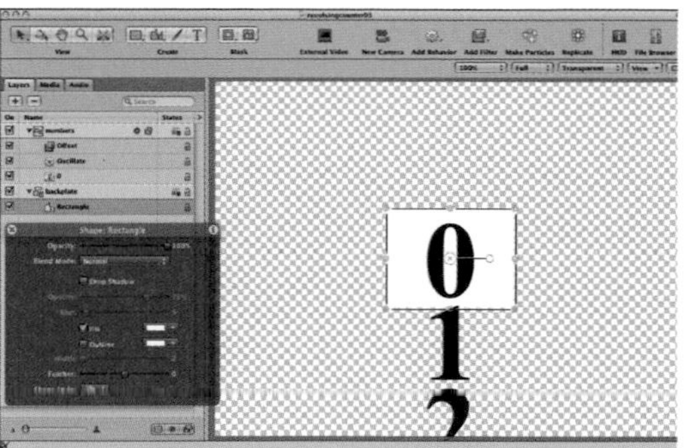

3 Go back to frame 1. Create a new layer below **numbers**. Name it **backplate**. Press R and create a white rectangle behind your numbers. Press Shift C. Now let's make it pause for each number.

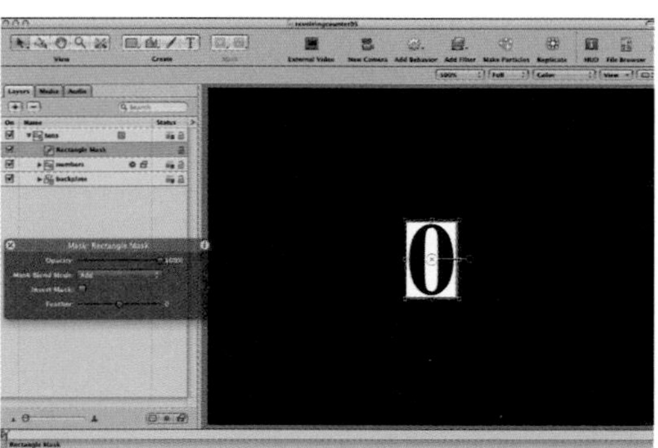

5 ⌘-select **numbers** and **backplate**. Press ⌘ Shift G. Name the new group **tens**. Press ⌥ R. Draw a mask around 0.

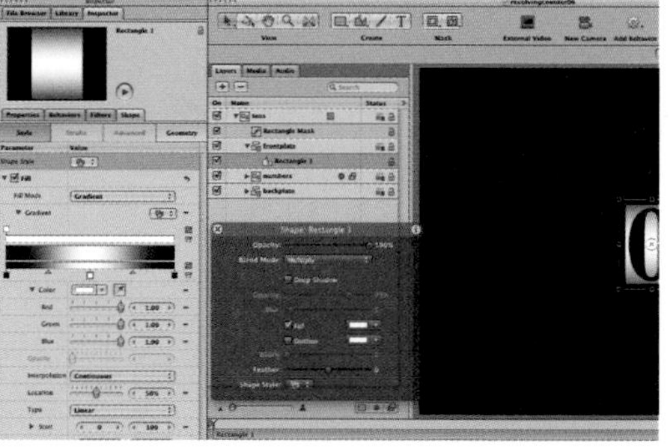

6 To add shading, add a new group on top of numbers and name it **frontplate**. Press R. Draw a rectangle over your number. Change the rectangle's **Fill Mode** to **Gradient**. Change the **Gradient** to have black on each end and white in the middle. Change its **Blend Mode** to **Multiply**.

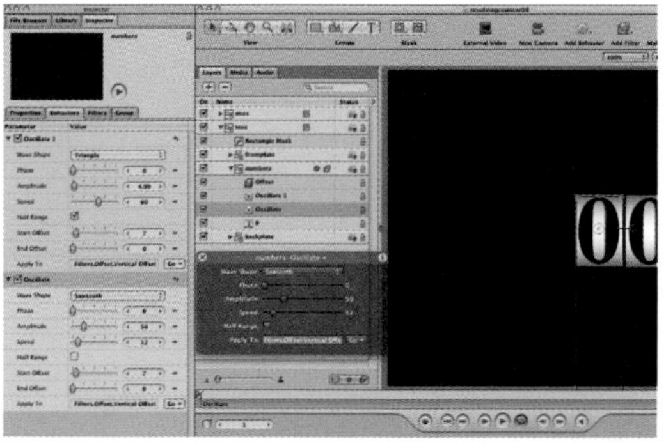

8 But the **tens** counter starts moving too soon! Open the **tens/numbers** and change **Oscillate 1** and **Oscillate's Start Offset** to **7**. That way it won't start advancing until the **ones** is up to about 7.

9 For enhanced realism, turn on **Motion Blur** *after* you've completed the project.

Parchment

EVER WANT TO CREATE A PIRATE treasure map? What should you put it on? Parchment, of course!

I was shown a Chris Zwar tutorial on how to make old-time paper (for backgrounds) in After Effects and I thought, Hey! We could do that in Motion. So, substituting the Cloud Generator for the After Effects Fractal Noise generator, off we go ... arrrgh!

1 Start with a new project. Go to your **Library/Generators** and select the **Clouds** generator. Press **Apply**. Set **Speed** to 0. Press ⌘D 4 times. Name the generators—from top down—**lines matte**, **stringy lines**, **chunky bits**, **splotches**, and **base layer**.

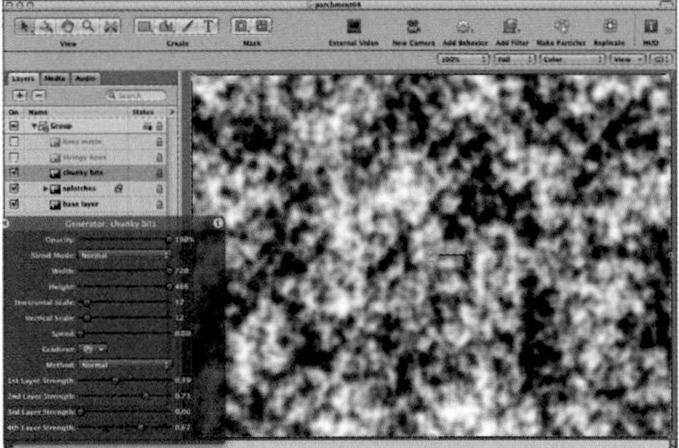

4 Turn on **chunky bits**. In the Generator tab, set **Horizontal** and **Vertical Scales** to 12. Set **1st Layer Strength** to .39, **2nd Layer Strength** to .73, **3rd Layer Strength** to 0, and **4th Layer Strength** to .67.

7 In the **Properties** tab, set **Y Scale** to 150%. Set **Opacity** to 10%. Set the **Blend Mode** to **Color Burn**. Type ⌘Shift M. Set the **Source Channel** to **Luminance**. Drag **lines matte** into the matte well.

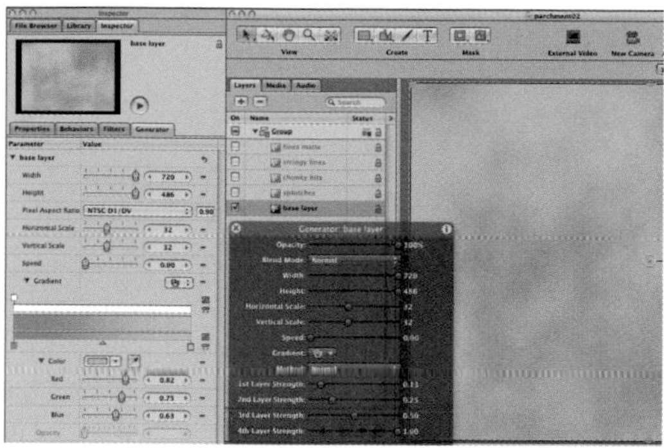

2 Turn off all but **base layer**. With **base layer** selected, in the **Generator** tab, set the **Gradient** left-hand color to **R .60**, **G .53**, **B .34**. Set the **Gradient** right-hand color to **R .82**, **G .75**, **B .63**.

3 Turn on **splotches**. Set **Horizontal** and **Vertical Scales** to **10**. In the **Generator** tab, move the **Gradient** left-hand color tab (black) to **20%**. Set the right-hand color tab to **R .76**, **G .71**, **B .59**, **Blend Mode** to **Multiply**, **Opacity** to **38%**, and **Add Filter/Color Correction/Channel Swap**. Set **Alpha** from **Red**.

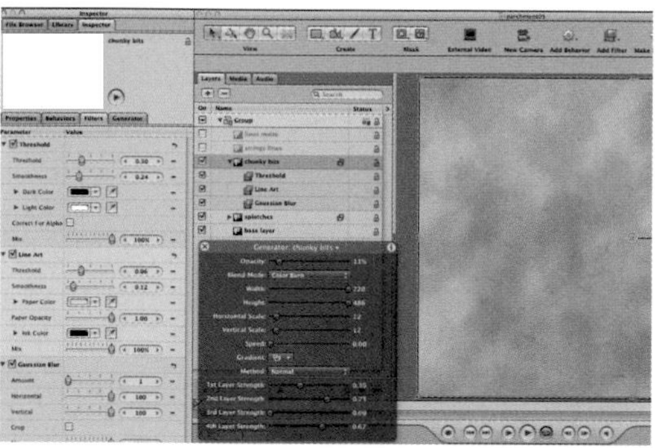

5 **Add Filter/Blur/Gaussian Blur**. Set **Amount** to **1**. **Add Filter/Stylize/Line Art**. Set **Threshold** to **.06**, **Smoothness** to **.12**. **Add Filter/Color Correction/Threshold**. Set **Threshold** to **.3** and **Smoothness** to **.24**. Set **Blend Mode** to **Color Burn** and **Opacity** to **11%**.

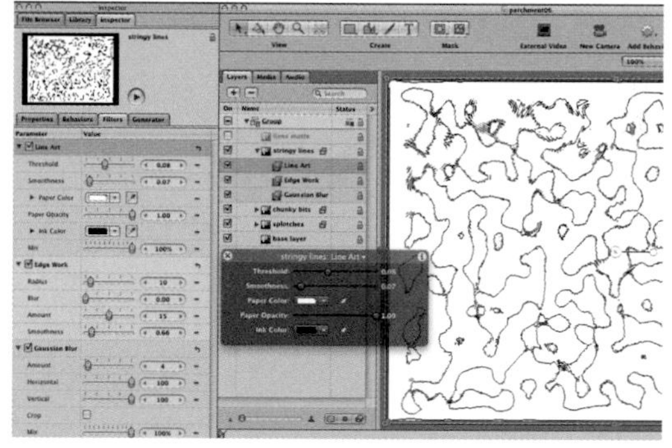

6 Turn on **stringy lines**. **Add Filter/Blur/Gaussian Blur**. **Add Filter/Stylize/Edge Work**. Set **Radius** to **10**, **Blur** to **0**, and **Smoothness** to **.66**. **Add Filter/Stylize/Line Art**. Set **Threshold** to **.08**, **Smoothness** to **.07**, **Paper color** to **White**.

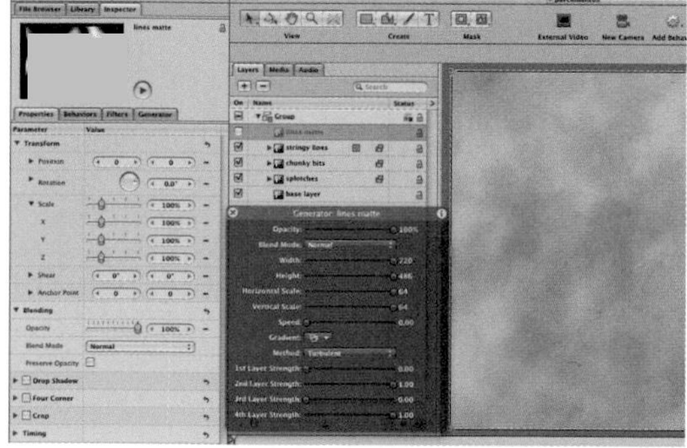

8 Select **lines matte**. Set **Horizontal** and **Vertical Scales** to **64**. Set **Method** to **Turbulent**. Set **1st Layer Strength** to **0**, **2nd Layer Strength** to **1.0**, and **3rd Layer Strength** to **0**.

9 Select **group**. In the **Group** tab, click the **Fixed Resolution** checkbox. **Add Filter/Stylize/Vignette**. Set **Size** to **.77** and **Darken** to **.16**. That's it!

Letter Cube

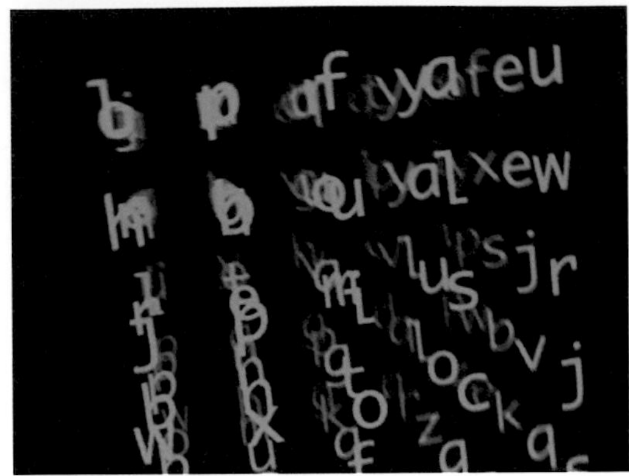

THIS PROJECT CREATES A ROTATING cube built of random letters. You could use this to create planes of letter textures that cameras can fly through, etc. And there's no reason to limit it to single letters—they could just as well be single frame images.

What I did was create a group with 26 single frames, each containing a single letter centered in the frame. I then did a Make Clone Layer. This creates a new instance of that layer that will reflect any changes you make to the original.

The neat thing about it is that Motion treats the new clone like a movie. So I replicated it and turned off the Play frames and turned on Random Start frame and got a 5 × 5 square of random characters.

I then clicked on the 3D checkbox in the Replicator inspector and changed the type to Box and voilà! instant cube filled with random characters. I applied a ramp to the Y rotation to show it off.

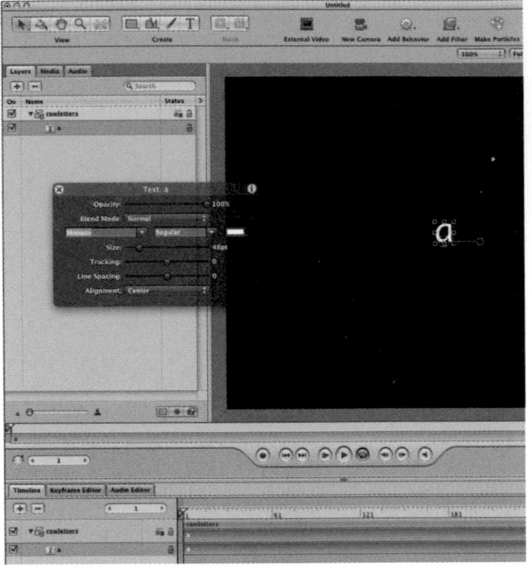

1 Start with a new project. Name the default group **rawletters**. Activate the **Text** tool. Click in the middle of the screen. Set **Font** to **Monaco** (or choose something you like). Set **Size** to **48** pt and **Alignment** to **Center**. Make the **Color White**. Type the letter **a**.

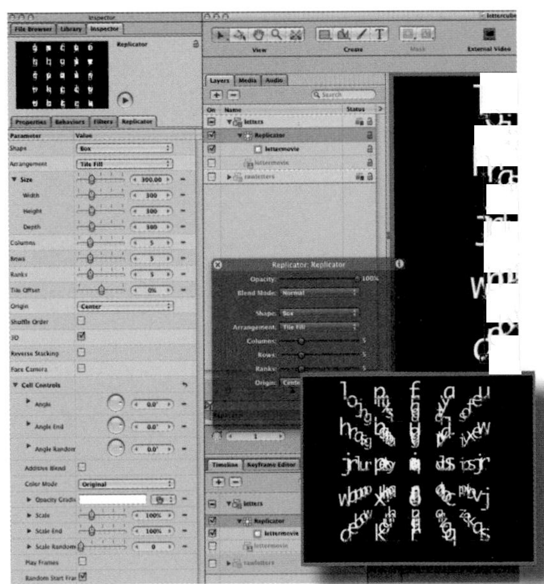

4 Select **lettermovie**. Press **L**. Select the **Replicator**. Click the **3D** checkbox. Change the **Shape** to **Box**. **Width, Height,** and **Depth** default to **300**. Unset **Play Frames**. Click **Random Start Frame**.

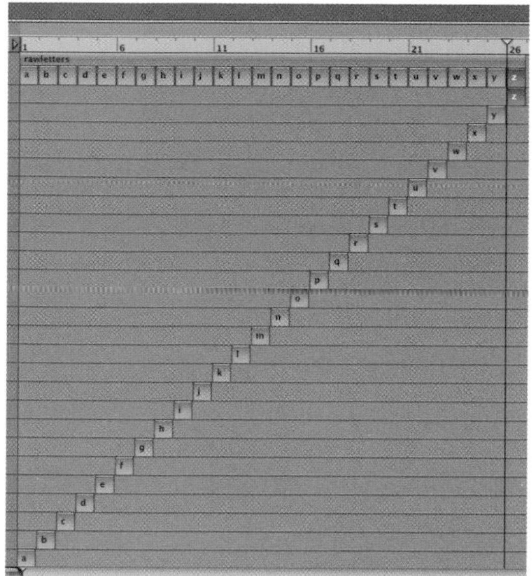

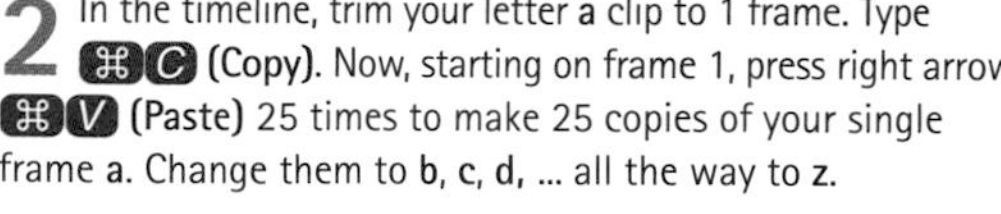

2 In the timeline, trim your letter **a** clip to 1 frame. Type ⌘C (Copy). Now, starting on frame 1, press right arrow ⌘V (Paste) 25 times to make 25 copies of your single frame **a**. Change them to **b**, **c**, **d**, ... all the way to **z**.

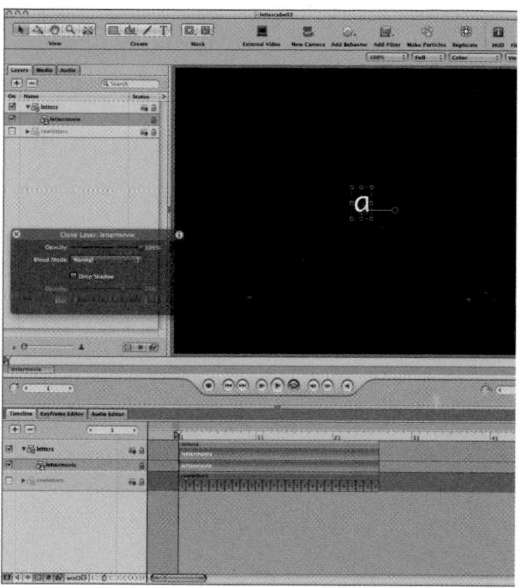

3 You should now have a 26-frame segment that has letters a through z on separate frames. Position to frame 1. Select the **rawletters** group. Press K to create a clone layer. Name the **Clone Layer** group **letters**. Name the clone Layer **lettermovie**. Turn off **rawletters**.

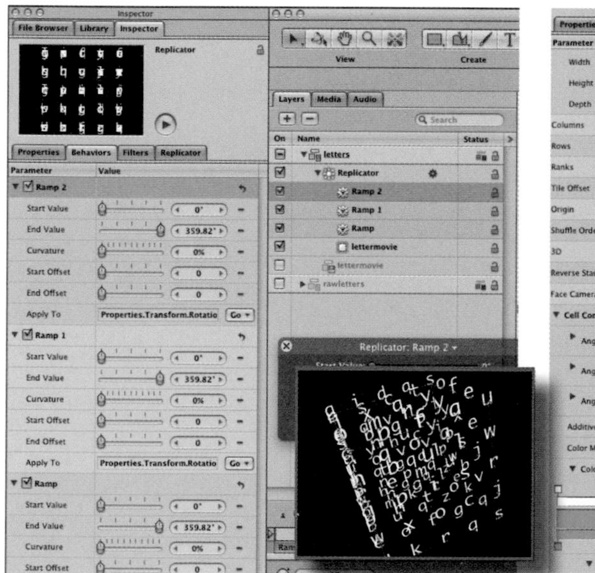

5 That's your basic cube. Let's rotate it to show it off. In the **Properties** tab of the **Replicator**, right/ctrl-click on the **X Rotation**, and select **Ramp**. Set the **End Value** to **360°**. Repeat for **Y** and **Z** rotations. If you want to fake depth of field, go on to Step 6, but the trick only works as a still.

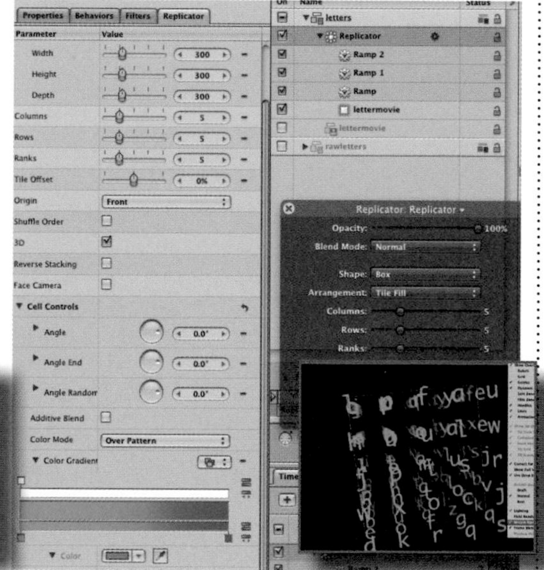

6 Select **Replicator**. Change **Origin** to **Front**. Change **Color Mode** to **Over Pattern**. Set the gradient to a bright green on the left and darker on the right. Use the **Adjust Anchor Point** tool to move the anchor point to the front of the cube (grab the blue arrow and move it forward.) Then turn on Motion Blur.

Green Rain

THIS IS NOT REALLY THE SAME as the green "code" rain from the *Matrix* movies title sequence, but it does recall them enough that you can use it in your own *Matrix* mockup movie.

Much the same as the Letter Cube project, we create a random character generator. Then we replicate it into strip of random characters, which we scroll through using the Offset filter. Then we use a particle emitter on a clone of the strip (so we can get random variations in the strip by starting on different frames), and we'll also throw on extra random letters and some color cycling animation to get more variation.

We can then bring up the title as we drop off the birth rate and use the Stripes filter to add interest to it.

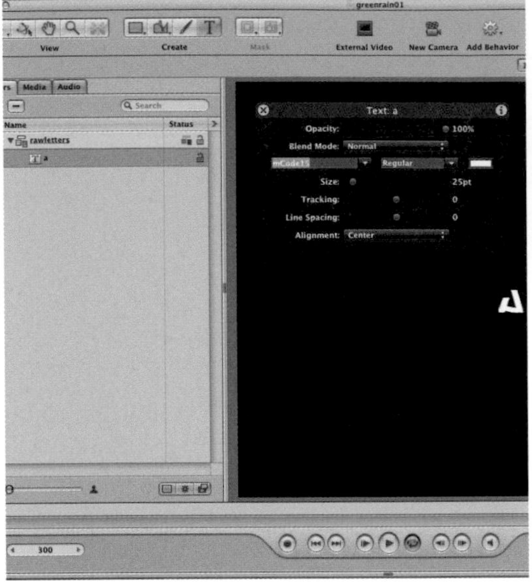

1 Start with a new project. Name the default group **rawletters**. Activate the **Text** tool. Click in the middle of the screen. Set **Font** to **mCode15** (included on the disc), or choose something you like. Set **Size** to **25 pt** and **Alignment** to **Center**. Make the **Color White**. Type the letter **a**.

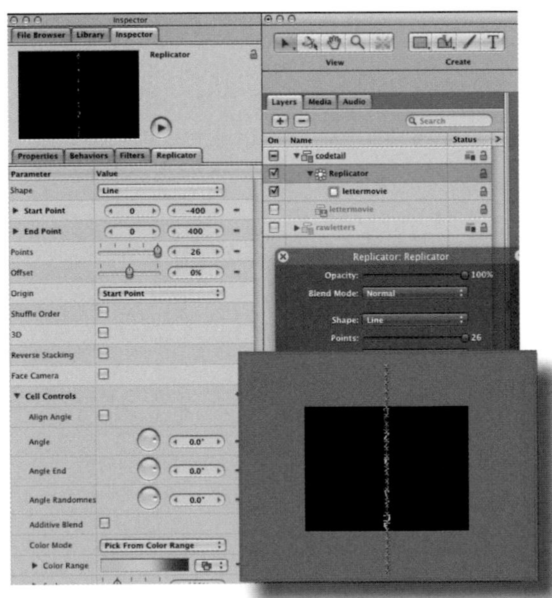

4 Select **lettermovie**. Press **L**. Change the **Shape** to **Line**. Set **Start Point** to **0, -400** and **End Point** to **0, 400** (this may vary depending on your project). Set **Points** to **26**. Set **Color Mode** to **Pick From Color Range**. Set the **Color Range Gradient** to **Thundercloud**. Unset **Play Frames**. Click **Random Start Frame**.

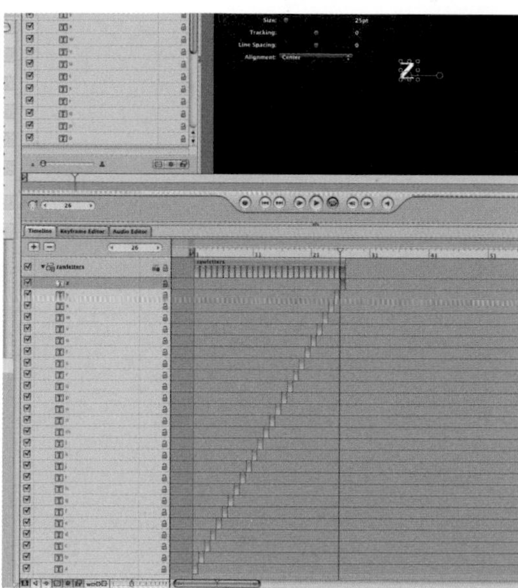

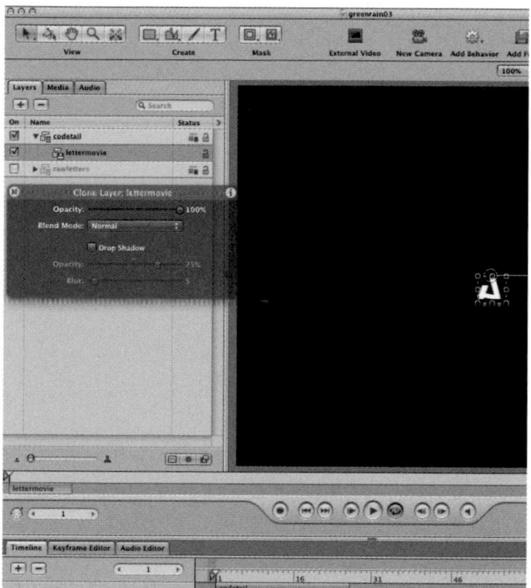

2 In the timeline, trim your letter **a** clip to 1 frame. Type **⌘C (Copy)**. Now, starting on frame 1, press right arrow, **⌘V (Paste)** 25 times to make 25 copies of your single frame a. Change their text to b, c, d, ... all the way to z.

3 You should now have a 26-frame segment that has letters a through z on separate frames. Position to frame 1. Select the **rawletters** group. Press **K** to create a clone layer. Name the **Clone Layer** group **codetail**. Name the **Clone Layer lettermovie**. Turn off **rawletters**.

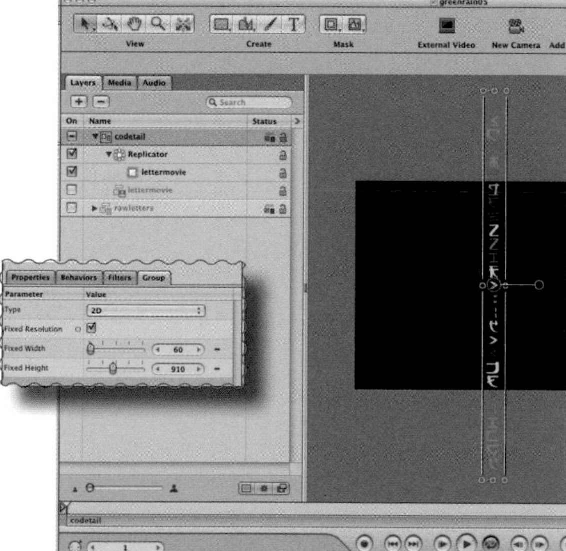

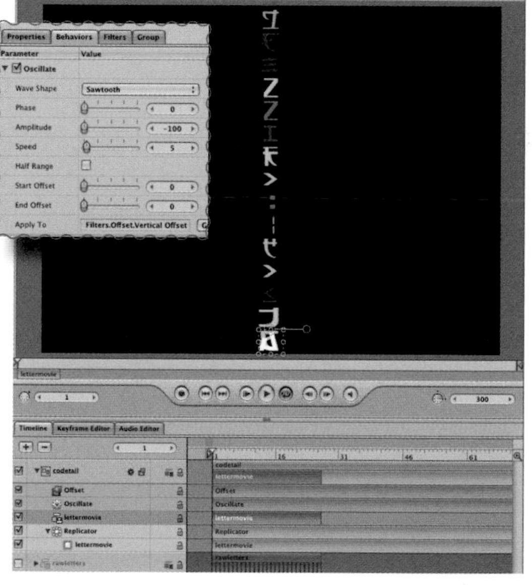

5 Press **Shift V** to see things offscreen. You should see the characters of the replicator poking out above and below the screen. Select **codetail**. Change it to **fixed resolution**. Set the dimensions to wide enough and tall enough to accommodate your replicator. In my case it was **60x910**.

6 **Add Filter/Tiling/Offset.** Right/**ctrl**-click on **Vertical Offset**. Select **Oscillate**. Change **Wave Shape** to **Sawtooth**. Set **Amplitude** to **-100**, and **Speed** to **5**. Turn on **lettermovie**, and move it to the bottom of the screen, just over the lowest letter.

continued...

Green Rain (continued)

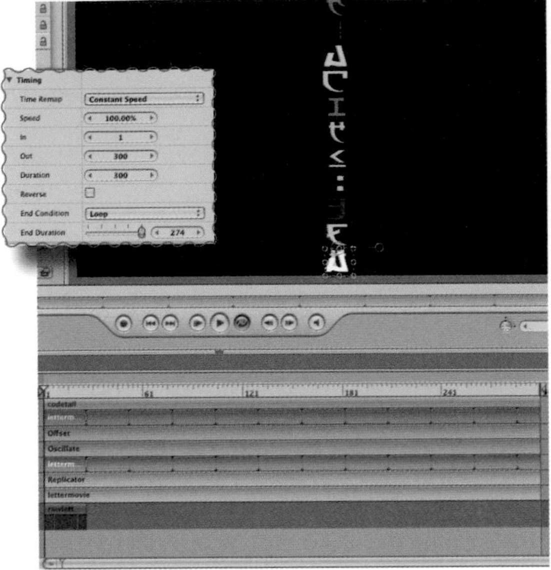

7 Select **lettermovie**. In the **Properties** tab, under **Timing**, set the **End Condition** to **Loop**. Drag the duration of **lettermovie** to the full length of the project.

8 Select **codetail**. Press **K** to create a clone layer. Turn off **codetail**. Name the new group **rain**. Name the **Clone Layer codemovie**. Select **codemovie**. Use the **Adjust Anchor** tool to move the anchor point to the bottom of the frame.

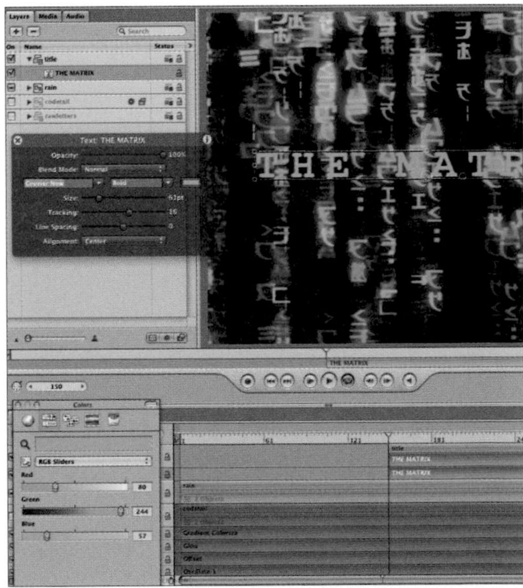

11 That's your basic **Code Rain** backdrop. To add a title, create new group over everything. Call it **title**. Set **Fixed Resolution**. Position to frame 150. Activate the **Text** tool. Set **Font** to **Courier New/Bold**, **Color** to Bright Green **Size** to **61**, **Tracking** to **16**, and **Alignment** to **Center**. Type your title. Press **esc** when done.

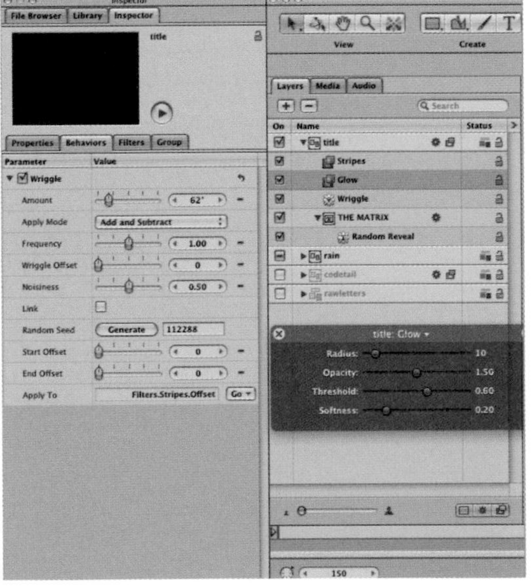

12 Add **Behavior/Text Basic/Random Reveal**. Select **title**. Add **Filter/Glow/Glow**. Set **Threshold** to **0.6**. Add **Filter/Distortion/Stripes**. Set **Mix** to **16%**. Right/**ctrl**-click on **Offset**. Select **Wriggle**. Set **Amount** to **62**. Set **Apply Mode** to **Add and Subtract**.

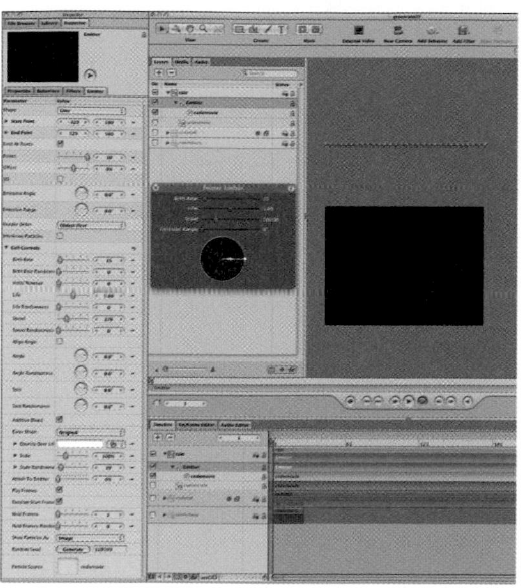

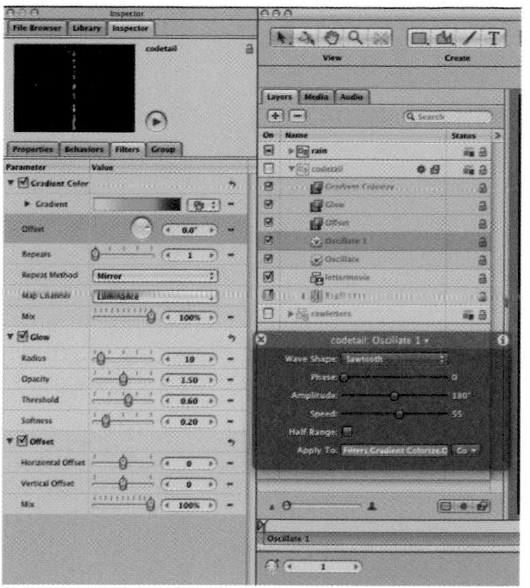

9 Press **E** or click on the **Make Particles** button in the toolbar. Change the **Shape** to **Line**. Set **Start Point** to **-329 and 735** and **End Point** to **329, 735**. Select **Emit At Points**. Set **Points** to **30**, **Emission Range** to **0**, **Birth Rate** to **15**, and **Speed** to **276**. Click **Additive Blend**. Add a right-hand tag in **Opacity Over Life**. Set it to **0%**. Set **Scale Randomness** to **19**.

10 Select **codetail**. Add **Filter/Glow/Glow**. Set **Threshold** to **0.6**. Add **Filter/Color Correction/Gradient Colorize**. Set the **Gradient** to **Radioactive**. Set **Offset** to **180°**. Right/**ctrl**-click on **Offset**. Select **Oscillate**. Set **Wave Shape** to **Sawtooth**, **Amplitude** to **180°**, and **Speed** to **55**.

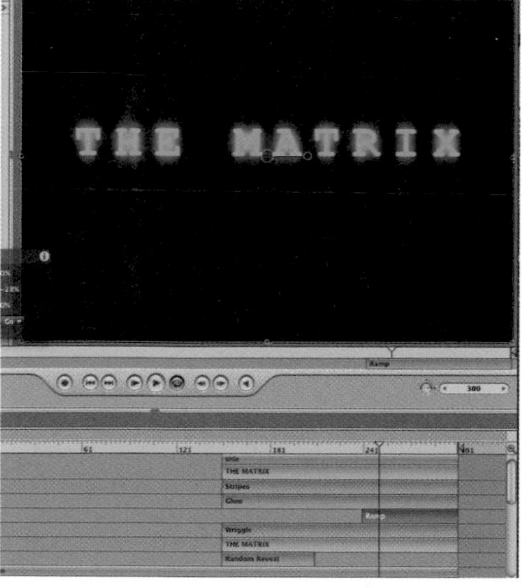

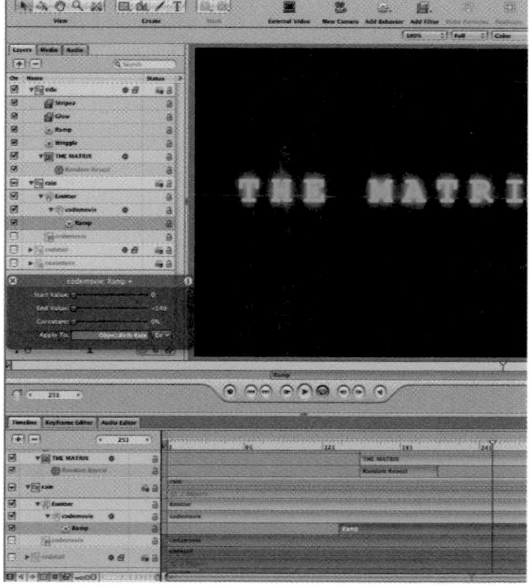

13 Position to frame 240. Select **Stripes**. Right/**ctrl**-click on **Mix**. Select **Ramp**. Press **I**. Set **End Value** to **-28**.

14 Select the **Emitter**. Position to frame 134. Right/**ctrl**-click on **Birthrate**. Select **Ramp**. Press **I**. Set **End Value** to **-140**.

Digitize Me

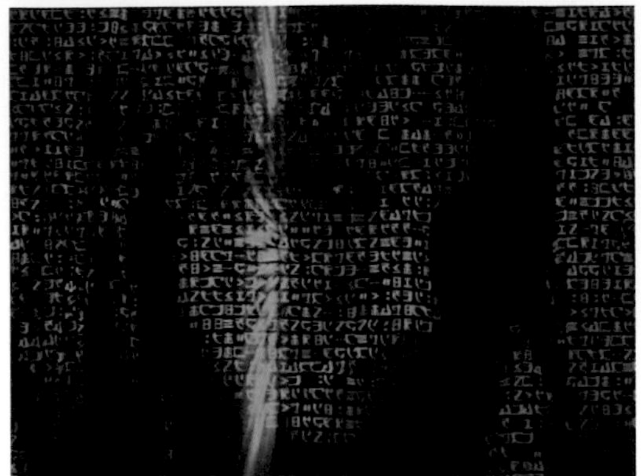

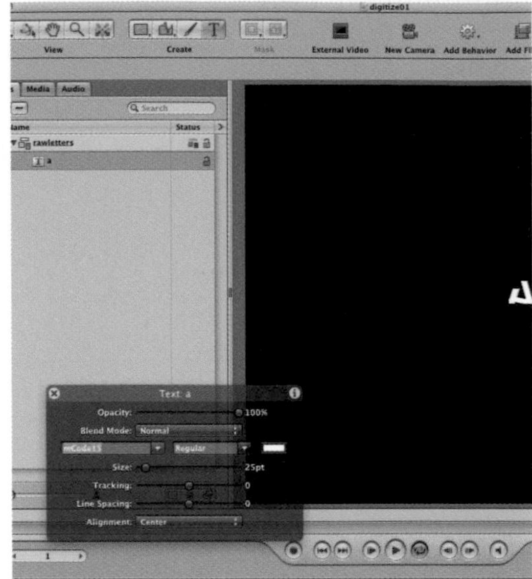

1 Start with a new project. Name the default group **rawletters**. Activate the **Text** tool. Click in the middle of the screen. Set **Font** to **mCode15** (included on the disc), or choose something you like. Set **Size** to **25** pt and **Alignment** to **Center**. Make the **Color White**. Type the letter **a**.

WHILE WE'RE IN THE MATRIX mode, let's create a "digital" portrait" out of "matrix code."

Just like Letter Cube and Green Rain, we create a random character generator (if that step is unclear because of the abbreviated explanation, visit Steps 2 and 3 in the Green Rain project). We replicate that and use a colorized version of our image as the shape for the replicator, which allows us to use the "Take Image Color" effect to give us our shading.

Once we've finished the basic replicator, we duplicate it to create our "scanning field." Then we add a bump map to distort our letters based on the contours of our original image. Finally we use our replicator copy with a Sequence Replicator behavior and the Light Rays filter to create a scanning effect.

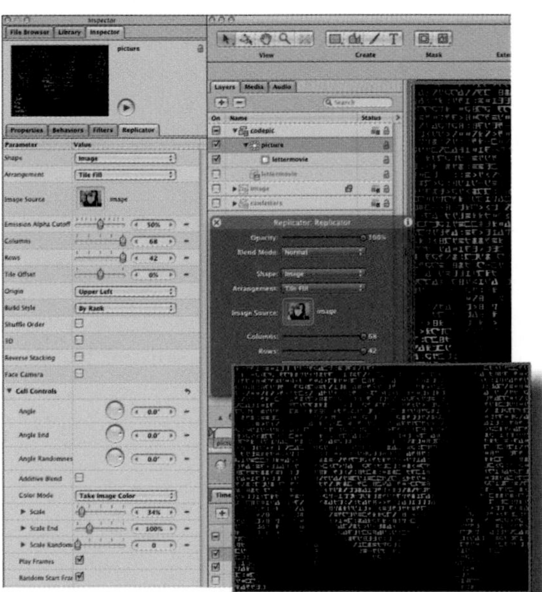

4 Select **lettermovie**. Press **L**. Rename the **Replicator** to **picture**. Change the **Shape** to **Image**. Drag your **image** group to the **Image Source** well. Set **Columns** to **68** and **Rows** to **42**. Set the **Origin** to **Upper Left**, the **Build Style** to **By Rank**, and the **Color Mode** to **Take Image Color**. Click **Random Start Frame**. Adjust the **Scale** so the letters fill the screen but are not touching.

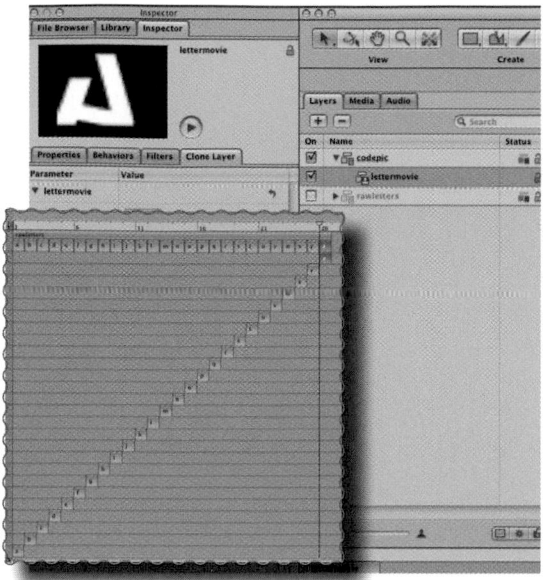

2 Trim your letter **a** clip to 1 frame. Type **⌘C (Copy)**. Starting on frame 1, press right arrow, **⌘V (Paste)** 25 times to make 25 copies of your single frame a. Change their text to b, c, d, ... up to z. Go to frame 1. Select **rawletters**. Press **K** to create a clone layer. Name the **Clone Layer** group **codepic**. Name the clone layer **lettermovie**. Turn off **rawletters**.

3 Create a new group. Call it **image**. Place your clip/picture in it. With **image** selected, **Add Filter/Color Correction/Colorize**. Change the **White** color to **Bright Green**. Turn off the **image** group.

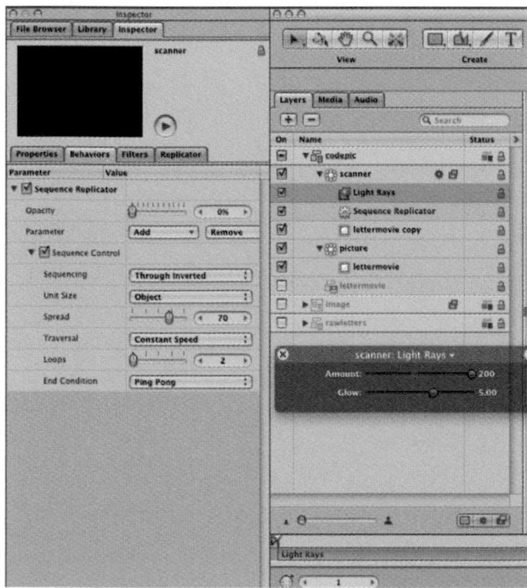

5 Press **⌘D**. Rename the **Replicator copy** to **scanner**. **Add Behavior/Replicator/Sequence Replicator**. **Add Parameter Opacity**. Change **Opacity** to 0%, **Sequencing** to **Through Inverted**, **Spread** to 70, Loops **2**, and **End Condition Ping Pong**. **Add Filter/Glow/Light Rays**. Set **Glow** to 5.

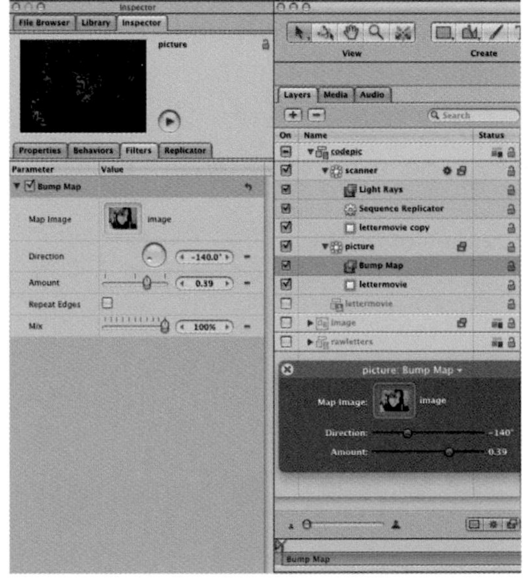

6 Finally, go back to the **picture** replicator. **Add Filter/Distortion/Bump Map**. Drag the **image** group to the **Map Image** well. Set **Direction** to –140° and **Amount** to 0.39.

Porcupine

I CALLED THIS PROJECT PORCUPINE because it looks like a ball of floppy spikes. It's one of those projects that I'm not sure what to do with, but I present it here as something interesting to learn from.

We'll use a wriggle of the phase of the oscillation of the postion of the the emitter. The Light Rays filter, because the rectangle is moving, causes the "spines" to flop up and down.

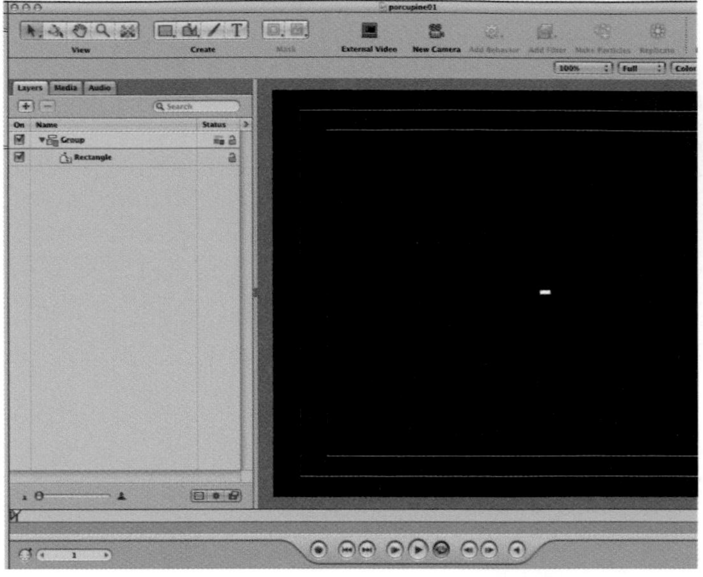

1 Start with a new project. Press R to activate the **Rectangle** tool. Draw a small rectangle in the center of the screen.

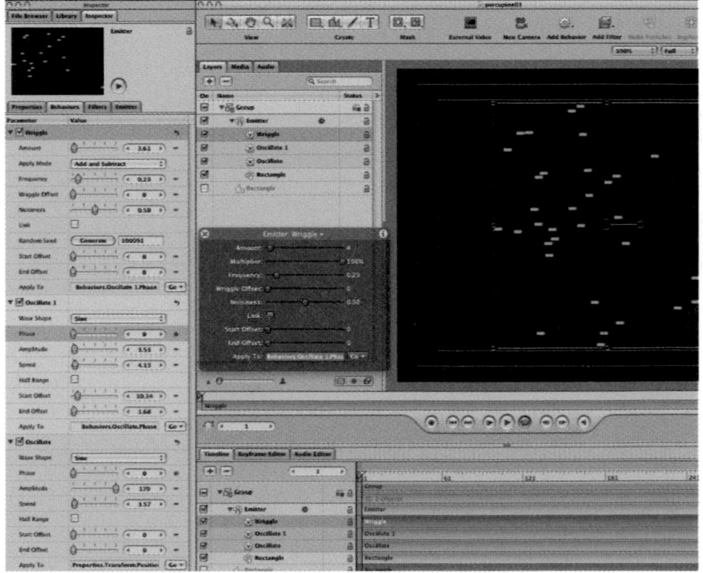

3 In the **Properties** tab, Right/ctrl-click on the **Y Position**. Select **Oscillate**. Set **Amplitude** to **170**. **Speed** to **3.57**. Right/ctrl-click on **Phase** and select **Oscillate**. Set **Amplitude** to **5.53**, **Speed** to **4.13**, **Start Offset** to **10.34**, and **End Offset** to **1.68**. Right/ctrl-click on **Phase** and select **Wriggle**. Set **Amount** to **3.61**, **Apply Mode** to **Add and Subtract**, and **Frequency** to **0.23**.

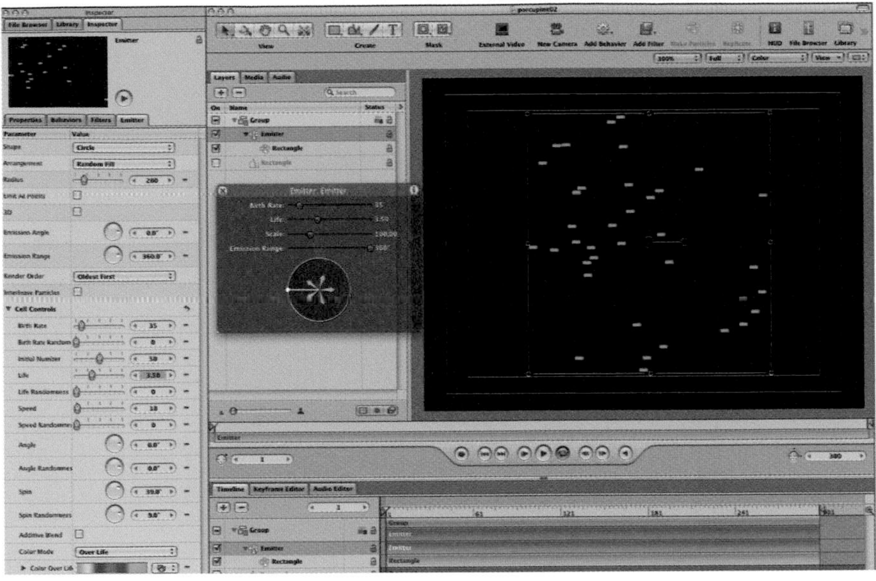

2 Press **E** or click on the **Make Particles** button in the toolbar. Set **Shape** to **Circle. Arrangement** to **Random Fill**. Set **Birth Rate** to **35, Initial Number** to **50, Life** to **3.5, Speed** to **18, Spin** to **39**, and **Spin Randomness** to **9**. Set the **Color Mode** to **Over Life**. Set the **Color Over Life Gradient** to **Rainbow**.

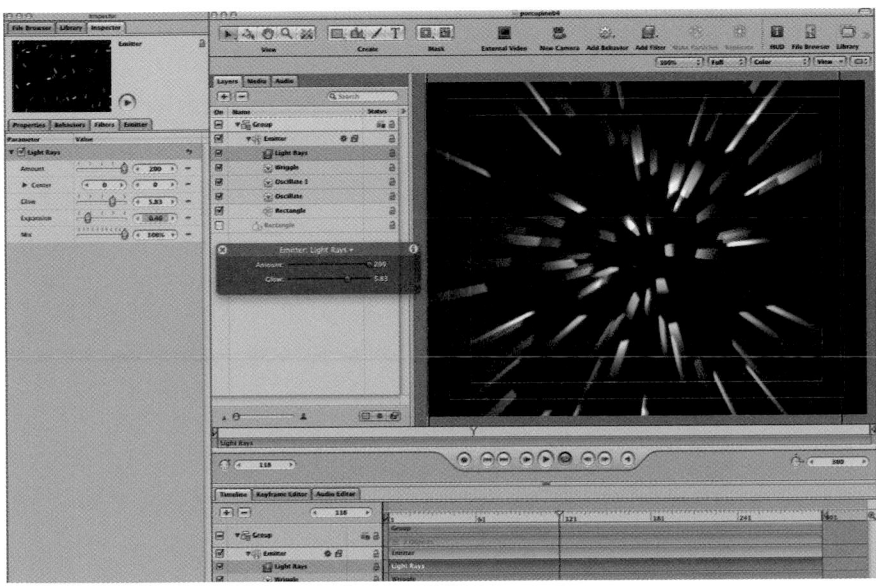

4 Finally, **Add Filter/Glow/Light Rays**. Set **Glow** to **5.83**. That's it!

Triangles

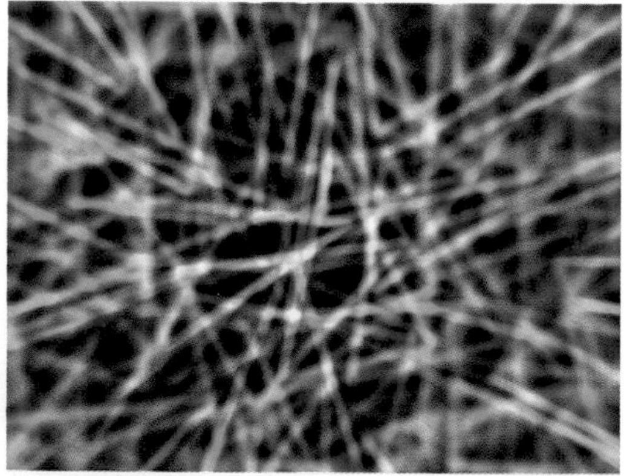

ALTHOUGH IT'S PROBABLY TOO busy to be a background, this project illustrates what you can do with a single graphic element and the Replicator. I used the Light Rays filter without a glow to give it a soft focus edge. Maybe it will inspire someone.

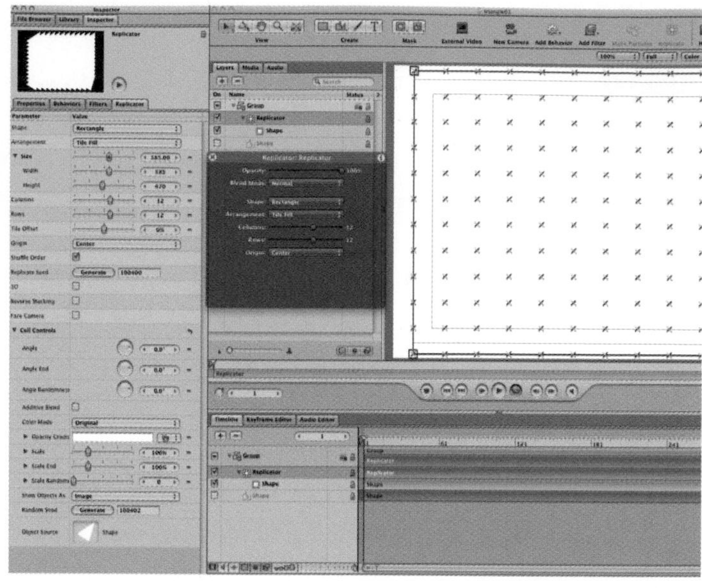

1 Start with a new project. Press B to activate the **Bezier** tool. Draw a mid-size triangle. Press L or click the **Replicate** button in the toolbar. Set the **Size** to be about **585 × 470** (this will vary depending on your project size). Make it about **12** rows by **12** columns. Click **Shuffle Order**.

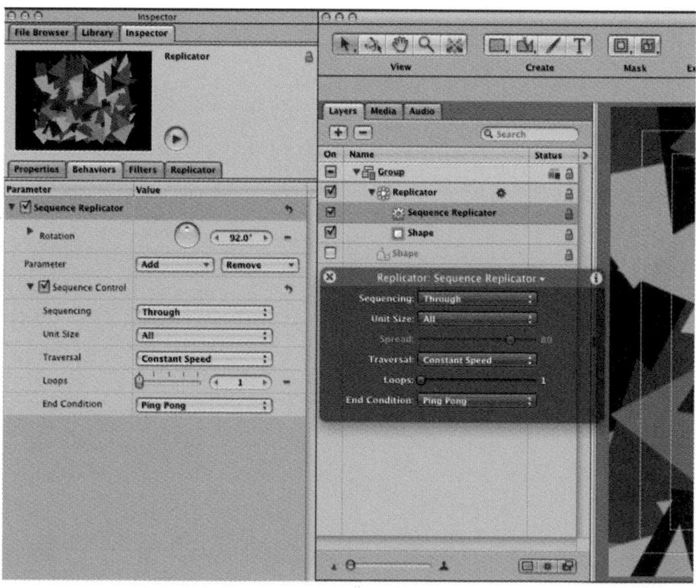

3 **Add Behavior/Replicator/Sequence Replicator. Add Parameter Rotation.** Set **Rotation** to **92**, **Sequencing** to **Through**, and **Spread** to **80**. Change **Unit Size** to **All**. Set **End Condition** to **Ping Pong**. Now your animation will cycle (see Hot Tip at the right if you have problems setting **Spread**).

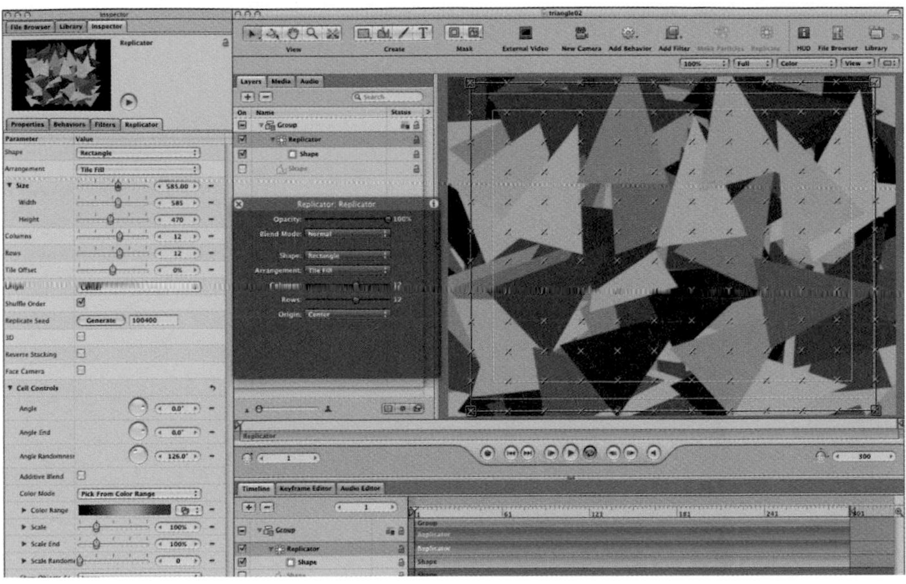

2 Set **Angle Randomness** to **126**. Set **Color Mode** to **Pick From Color Range**. Set the **Color Range Gradient** to your choice—I chose **Charcoal** for that camouflage effect. Try them all; see what you like.

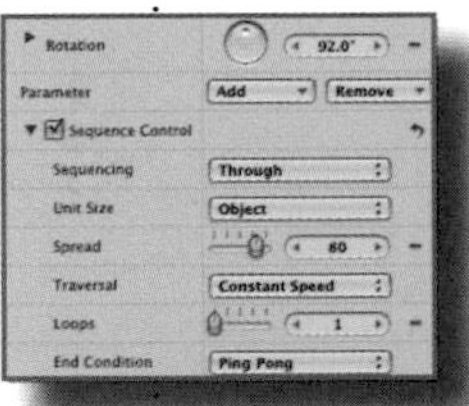

HOT TIP

In the Sequence Replicator behavior, you can't change the Spread when the Unit Size is set to All, so be sure to change it when the Unit Size is Object.

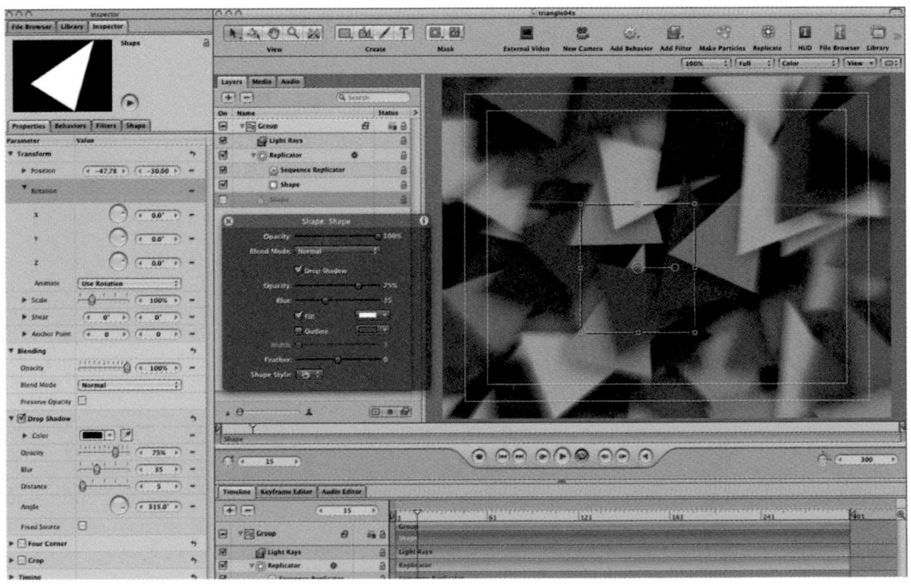

4 Click on **Group**. **Add Filter/Glow/Light Rays.** Set **Amount** to **56** and **Glow** to **1.00**. For interesting variations, try adding an **Outline** to the triangle, turning on its **Drop Shadow,** or selecting **Additive Blend** in the **Replicator.**

Plastic Flowers

1 Begin with a new project. Press **C** to activate the **Circle** tool. Draw a medium circle in the center of your screen. Set the **Fill Mode** to be **Gradient**. Change the gradient to **Grayscale**. If it doesn't look like the screen shot, change to the **Adjust Item** tool and edit the **Gradient** as seen above.

A FRIEND, RICHARD WAGNER, **longstrider** on the Apple Forums, posted this project as "Fun with Plastic Flowers." I'm presenting it here, largely unaltered, with just a slight variation for interest (I added the spin). This is what he said about it:

"It's a complex image, but it's simple at heart. The replicator cell is a circle with random scale and an Over Pattern color mode. A Sequence Replicator behavior has been tossed on to fade bits in and out. An Indent filter gives things their liquid/plastic look, and a Kaleidoscope filter lends the petals to the image."

Kaleidoscope is a great filter to muck around with—tweaking the segment angle and/or offset angle delivers loads of odd things.

You can get even more variations (shown above) by adding a Kaleidotile filter to the mix.

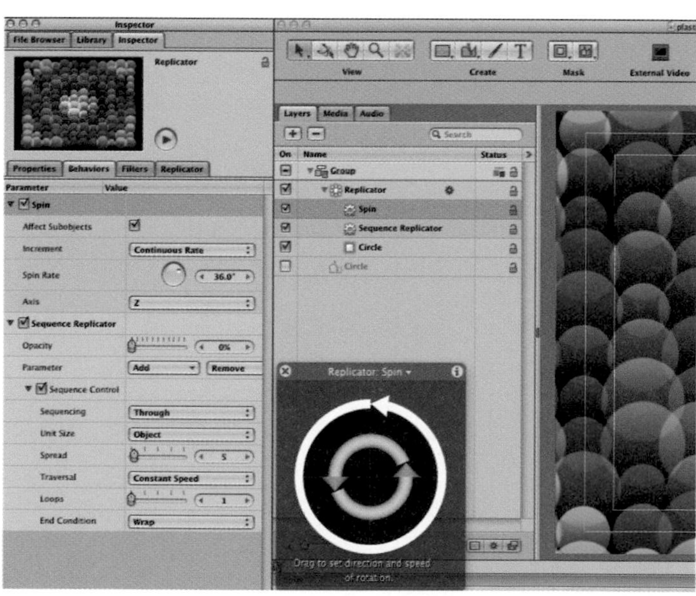

3 With the **Replicator** selected, **Add Behavior/Replicator/Sequence Replicator. Add Parameter Opacity.** Set **Opacity** to **0. Sequencing** to **Through, Spread** to **5, End Condition** to **Wrap. Add Behavior/Basic Motion/Spin.** Click **Affect Subobjects.** Set the **Spin Rate** to **36°**.

2 With the circle selected, press **L** or click on the **Replicate** button in the toolbar. Set **Size** to **720, 540**. Set **Rows** and **Columns** to **12**. Click **Shuffle Order**. Click **Additive Blend**. Set **Color Mode** to **Over Pattern**. Set **Color Gradient** to **Rainbow**. Set **Scale Randomness** to **61**.

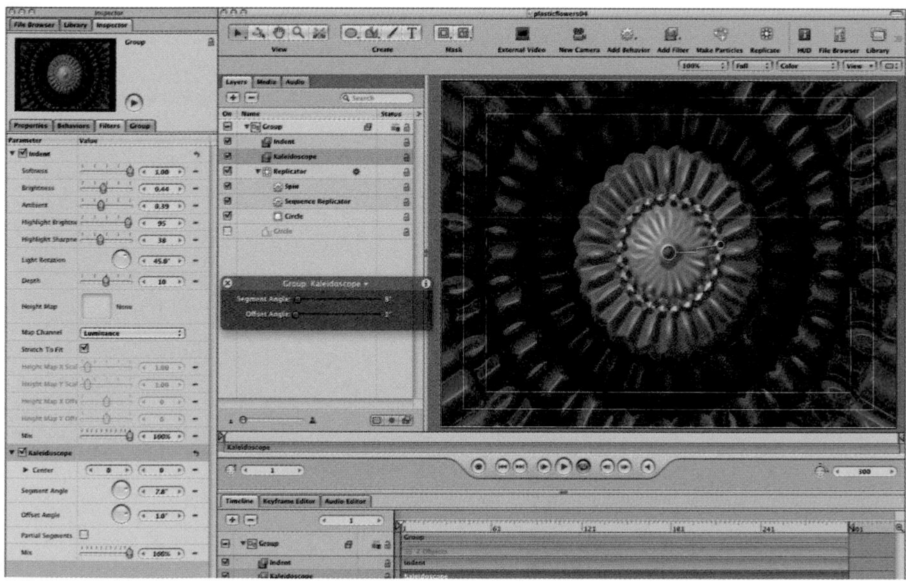

4 With **Group** selected, set **Fixed Resolution**. Add **Filter/Tiling/Kaleidoscope**. Set **Segment Angle** to **7.8** and **Offset Angle** to **1.0**. Add **Filter/Stylize/Indent**. Set **Softness** to **1.0**, **Brightness** to **.44**, **Ambient** to **.39**, **Highlight Brightness** to **95**, and **Highlight Sharpness** to **38**.

DNA

NOW, I'LL BE THE FIRST TO admit that this doesn't look anything like REAL DNA, but in graphical terms, it is an adequate representation.

We'll first create a little "dumbbell" that looks like a green ball and a blue ball spinning on a stick.

Then, using the clone layer technique, we'll replicate the dumbbell and have each copy offset by one frame. That way they'll appear to spiral around each other.

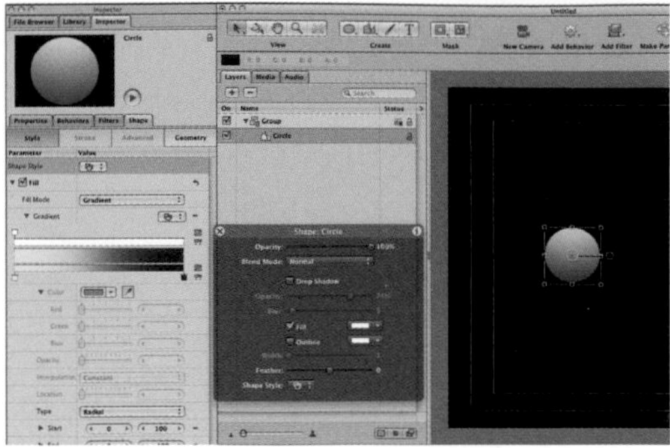

1 Start with a new project. Press C to activate the Circle tool and holding down the Shift key draw a small circle. Change the **Fill Mode** to **Gradient**. Change the **Gradient** from **Linear** to **Radial**. Set the **Gradient** to **Grayscale**, and change the **White** to a **Pastel Green** and the **Black** to a **Dark Green**.

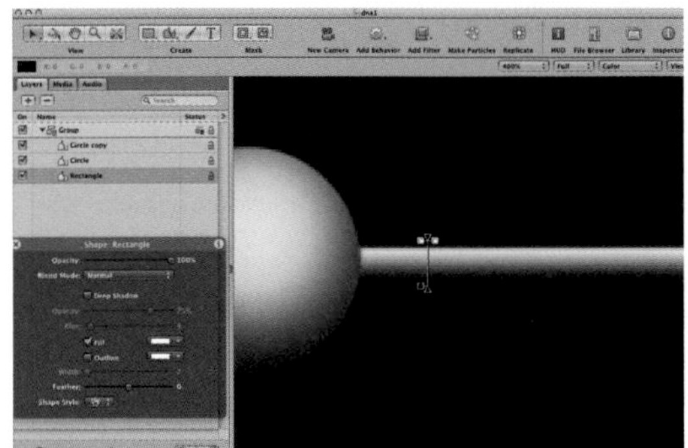

4 Press R to activate the **Rectangle** tool and draw a thin rectangle between them. Make sure it's below the two balls. in the layer palette. Make it a **Linear** gradient fill with a Gray Scale gradient and adjust so it looks like a metallic bar between the balls.

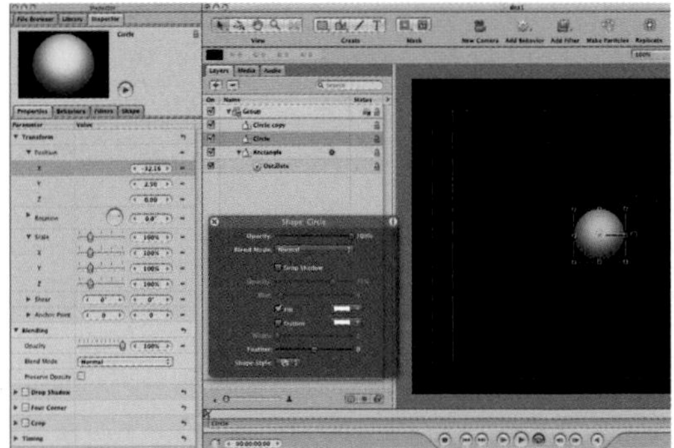

7 Then click on each circle and slide its **X Position** until they are both sitting directly over the compressed bar.

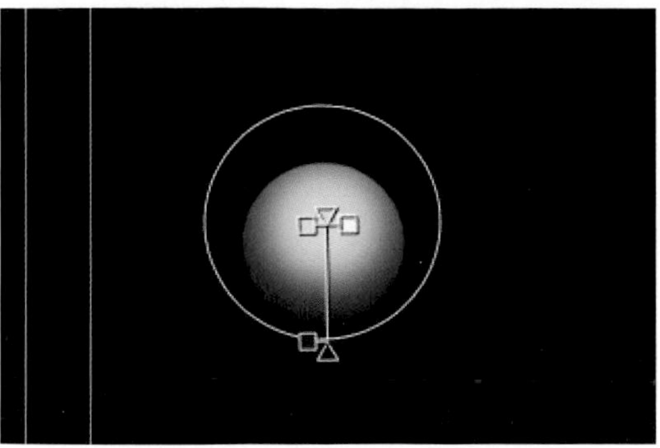

2 Now select the **Adjust Item** tool to bring up the **Gradient** tool and adjust to make the circle look like a ball.

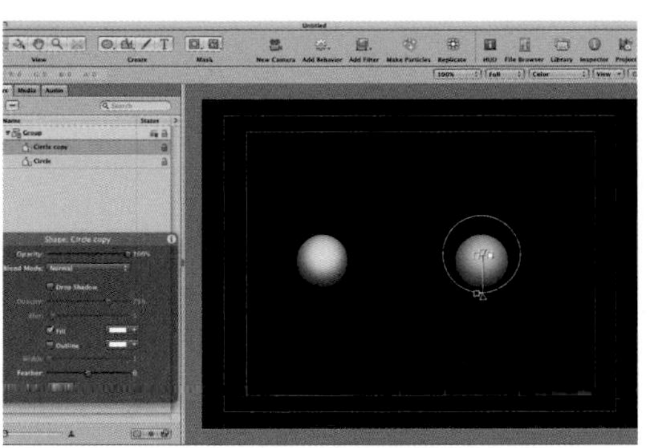

3 Duplicate your green ball and adjust the gradient colors to make it into a blue ball.

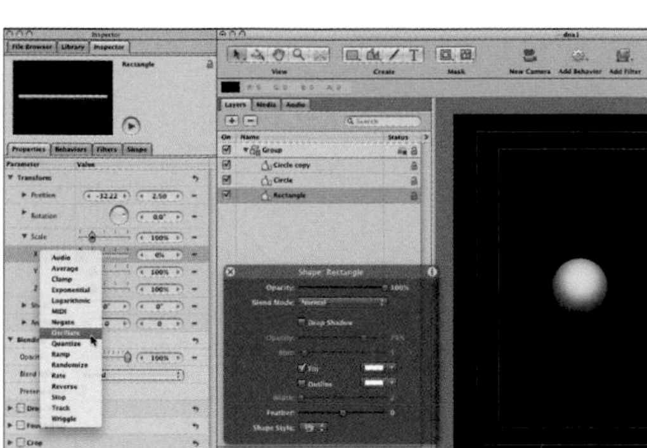

5 Once you've created the dumbbell click on the rectangle. In the **Properties**, set the **X Scale** to 0. Right/ctrl click on the **X Scale** and select the **Oscillate** behavior.

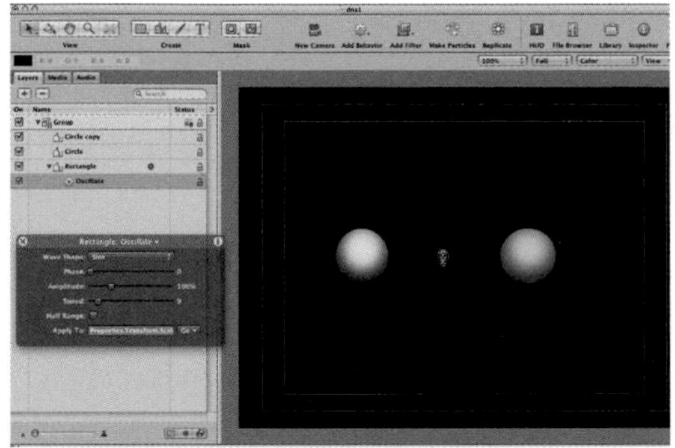

6 Set the **Oscillate Speed** to 9.

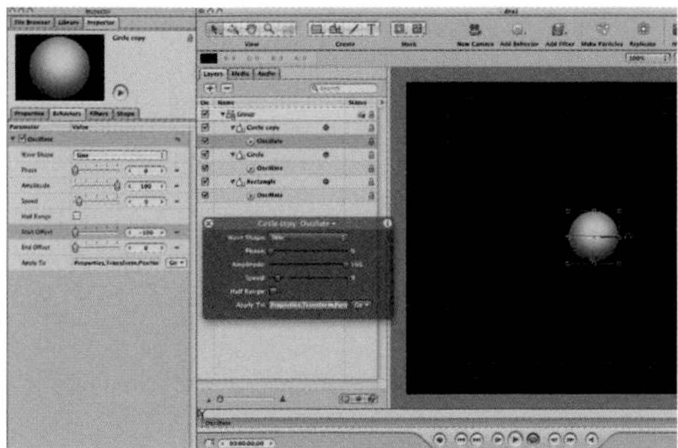

8 Now select the green circle and place an **Oscillate** behavior on the **X Position**. Set its **speed** to 9. Do the same for the blue circle, but set its **Start Offset** to -100. This will put it out of phase with the green circle by one cycle.

9 With one of the circles still selected, click on the keyframe editor and you'll see the sine wave graphed out. Move the playhead until it is at the point where the second cycle is about to begin. That is 6:19 or 200 frames.

continued...

DNA (continued)

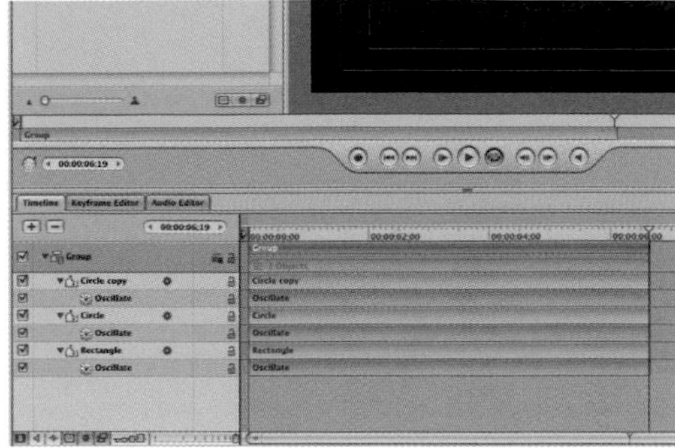

10 Now click on the timeline tab (without moving the playhead). Select the **Group** and press **O**. That will truncate our group.

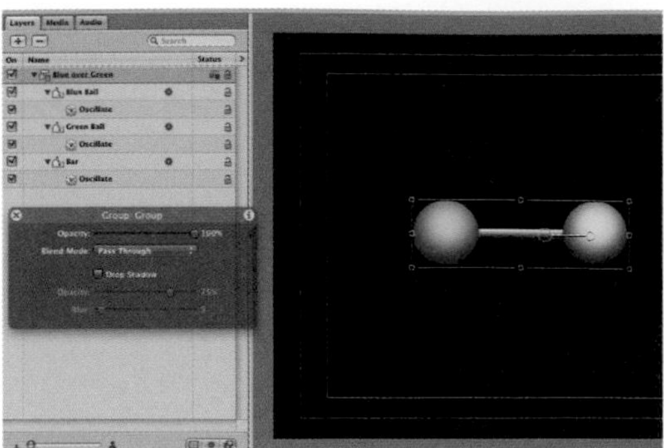

11 Things are going to start to get complicated, so let's name all our elements. Let's call them **Blue Ball**, **Green Ball**, **Bar**, and our **Group**, **Blue over Green**.

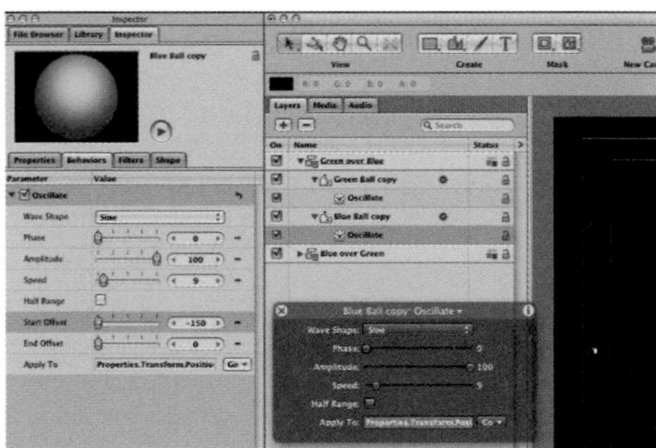

14 Click on the **Blue Ball Copy**. Change the **Oscillate Start Offset** from **-100** to **-150**. Click on the **Green Ball Copy**. Change its **Start Offset** to **-50**.

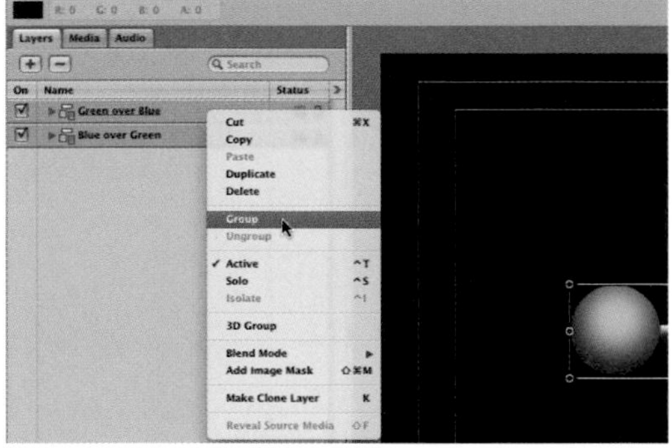

15 Collapse both layers and select them. Right/**ctrl**-click on them and select **Group**. Call the new group **Dumbbell**. Set the project duration to 6:20 or 200 frames. Press **Play** and watch the dumbbell appear to rotate. Press **Stop**.

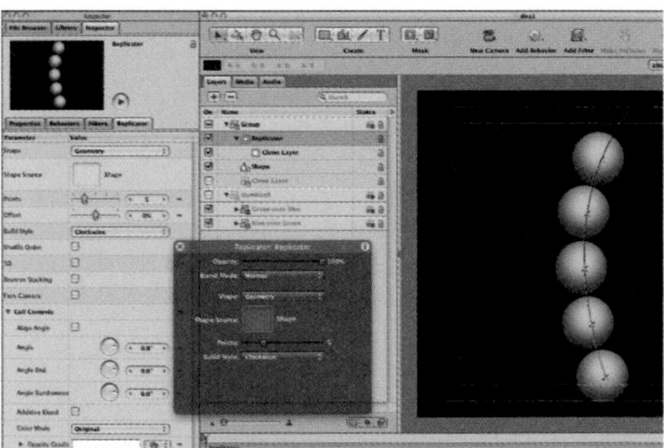

18 Click on the **Clone Layer** and press **L** or click the **Replicate** button in the toolbar. Change the **Type** from **Rectangle** to **Geometry**, and drag your newly drawn shape into the image well.

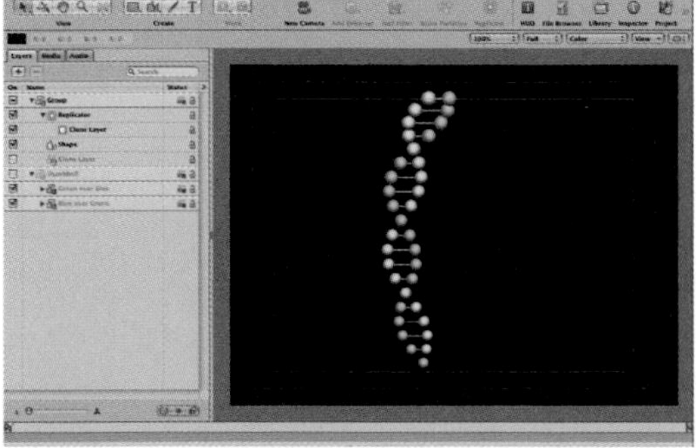

19 Set the **Points** to **20**, **Scale** to **20%**, **Scale End** to **140%**, and **Source Frame Offset** to **20**. Now press **Play** and watch your DNA rotate.

12 Collapse the **Blue over Green** group, then duplicate it (⌘D). Name the copy **Green over Blue**, and expand it. Reorder the layers so that the **Green Ball copy** is over the **Blue Ball copy**. Delete the **Bar copy**.

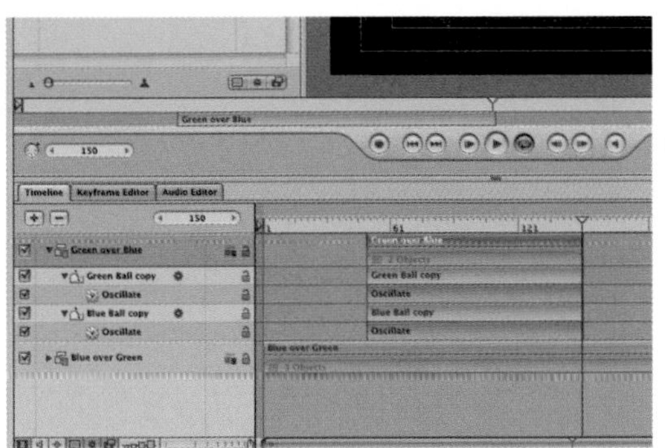

13 With the **Green over Blue** group selected, put the playhead at 1:19 (50 frames). Press I. Put the playhead at 4:29 (150 frames). Press O.

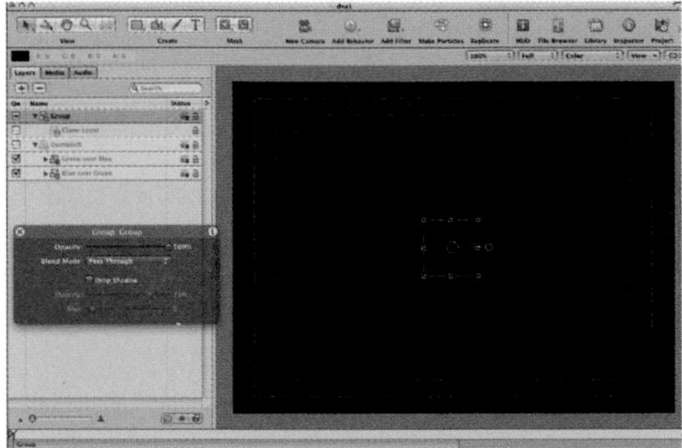

16 Okay. The difficult part is over. Position the playhead back to the beginning of the timeline. Click on the **Dumbbell** group and press K to make a clone layer. Turn off the **Dumbbell** group and the **Clone Layer**.

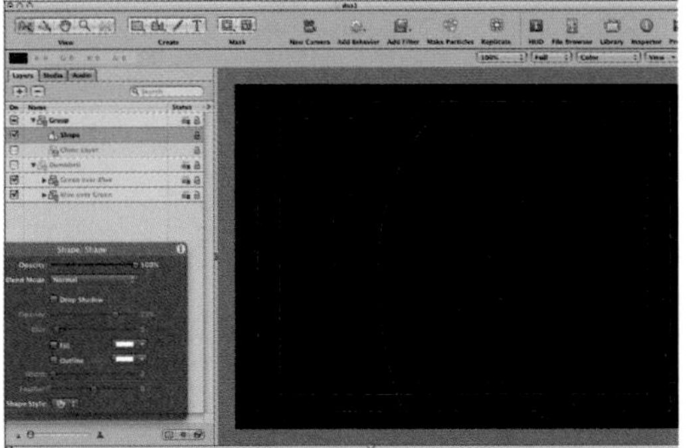

17 Press B to select the **Bezier** tool and draw a 3-point open shape. Press ⇥ to end the drawing.

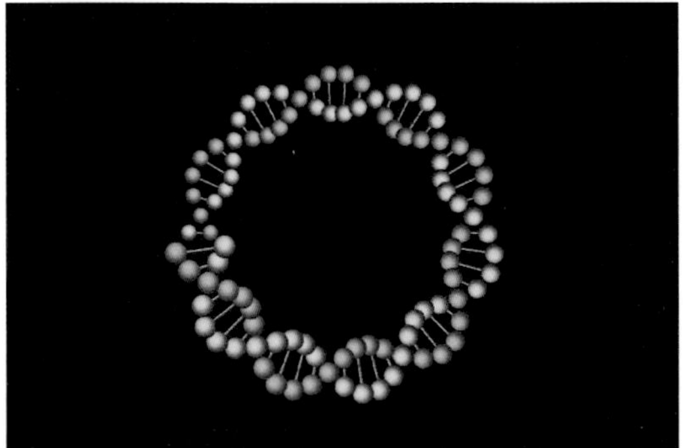

20 If you change your **Replicator** to **Circle**, switch arrangement to **Outline**, up the number of points, select **Align Angle**, adjust **Size**, and set the **Angle** to 90°, you'll get this plasmid effect.

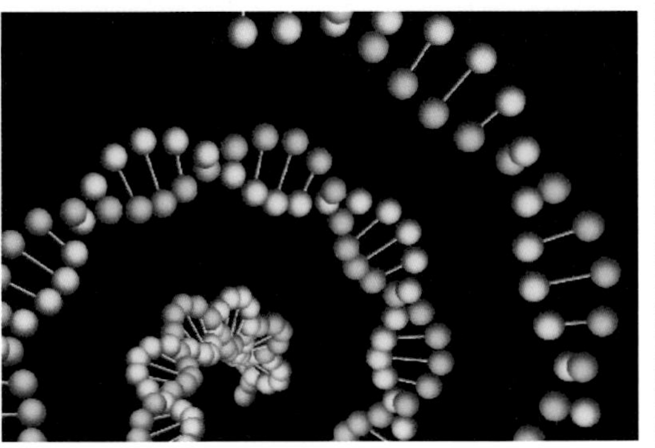

21 And here we have a single arm spiral...

Mock Hockney

IMAGES COURTESY BARIS WANSCHERS, NELSON BRANN & CAMILA RHODES, AND OCTAVIO ARIZALA

DAVID HOCKNEY IS A BRITISH artist, often associated with the photo collage style in which a number of quick snapshots are assembled into a large picture.

In this exercise we'll explore a quick and simple way of simulating that in Motion. It works with still or moving images.

1 Begin with a new project. Rename the default **Group** to **hockney**, add another group inside it, and call it **original**. Place your image/clip in this group. Now select **hockney**. Press R to activate the **Rectangle** tool. Draw a medium-sized rectangle in the center of the screen.

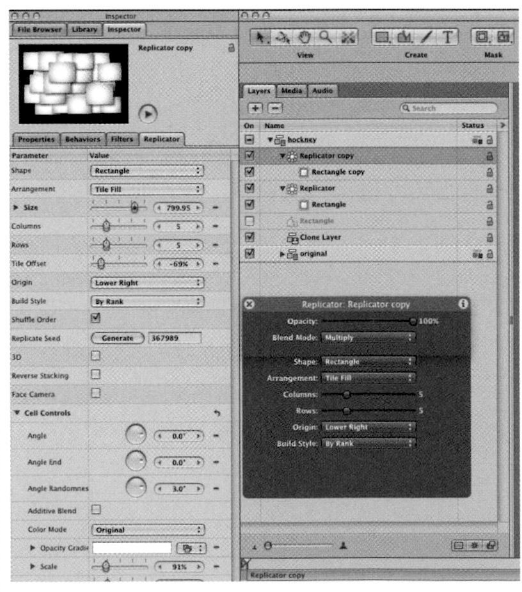

4 Suddenly, your image appears to be made up of snapshots, but the illusion rapidly dissipates as none of the "snapshots" is displaced. We'll add another layer of snapshots to fix that. Select **original** and press K to create a clone layer. Select **Replicator**. Press ⌘D to duplicate it.

2 Change the fill mode to **Gradient**. Change the **Gradient** to **Grayscale** and the **Type** to **Radial**. Using the **Adjust Item** tool, adjust your gradient to create shadows in the corners of your **Rectangle**. In the **Properties** tab, activate and adjust the **Drop Shadow** to suit your image.

3 Press **L** to replicate the **Rectangle**. Drag the size out to full screen. Set **Tile Offset** to **-69%**. Set **Origin** to **Lower Right** and **Build Style** to **By Rank**. Click **Shuffle Order**. Set **Angle Randomness** to **3.0°**. Set **Scale Randomness** to **30** or so. Set the **Blend Mode** to **Multiply**.

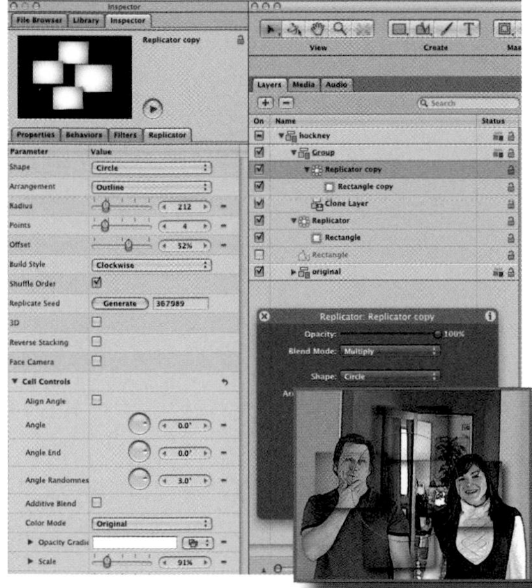

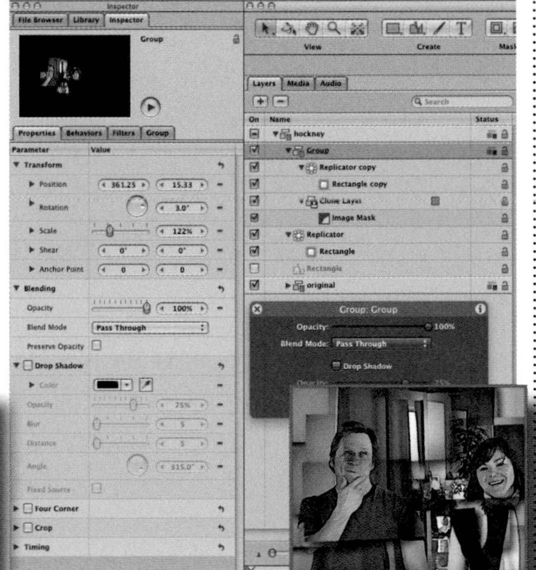

HOT TIP

For darker images, try inverting the gradient on your Rectangle and changing both Replicators' blend modes to Overlay.

5 Arrange the **Clone Layer** just below the **Replicator copy**. Select both the **Replicator** and the **Clone Layer**. Type **⌘ Shift G** to group them. With the **Replicator copy** selected, change the **Shape** to **Circle**, the **Arrangement** to **Outline**, and the **Points** to 4. Play with the **Offset** to get a good dispersed spacing.

6 Select the **Clone Layer**. Type **⌘ Shift M** to add an **Image Mask**. Drag **Replicator copy** into the **Mask Source** well. Turn the **Replicator copy** back on. Select **Group**. Set the **Scale** to about **125%** and the **Rotation** to about **3°**. Move the **Position** to suit your image.

Template Expansion

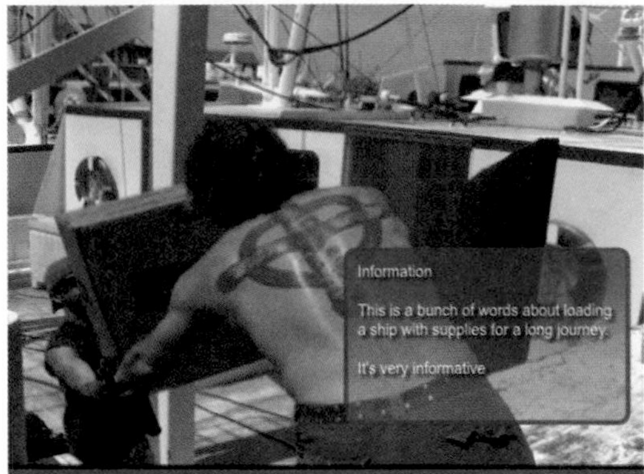

IMAGE COURTESY ART ALDRICH

THE NEW LINK BEHAVIOR in Motion 4 is very handy. In addition to allowing complex animations to be built from a single parameter change, it can be used to expand the functionality of Motion templates built for use in Final Cut Pro.

In Motion templates for Final Cut Pro, you can send and position images/clips via a Drop Zone, send text and specify the size and tracking for that text, and that's it.

Now with the Link behavior, you can change other parameters in your template as well. This will require some experimentation as not all parameters will translate between them and the ranges can require scaling. In this project, we'll construct a little "Info Box" that can be positioned wherever you need it in Final Cut Pro. The opacity of the backing box can be altered as well.

You could build an elaborate animated build-up of the Info Box in Motion, but for this project we'll go for simple.

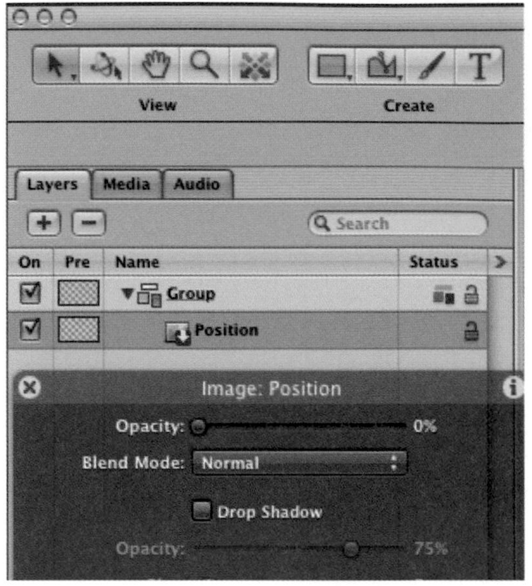

1 Start with a new project. Type ⌘ Shift D or select **Add New Drop Zone** under the **Object** menu. Name it **Position**. Set its **Opacity** to 0%.

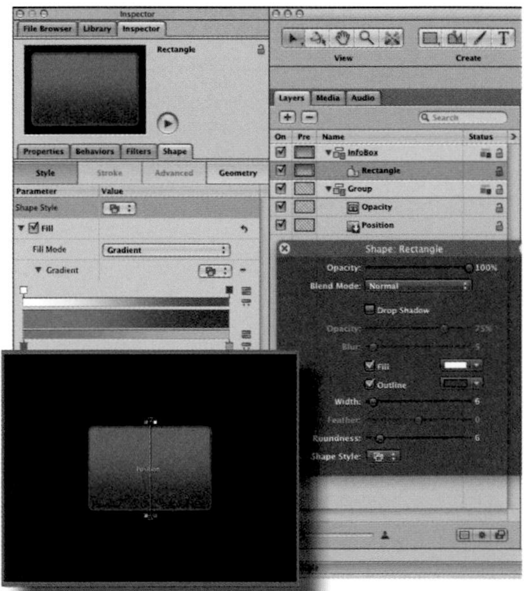

4 Set its color as you please. Perhaps with a gradient. Give it an outline of a slightly darker color. Give it a bit of **Roundness**. You could also add a title bar at the top. We're going for simple here, so we'll leave that out for now.

2 Press T to activate the **Text** tool. Click in the middle of the screen. Set the **Size** to **150**. Type a—and then press the esc key. Name that text layer **Opacity**. Then set its **Opacity** to 0%.

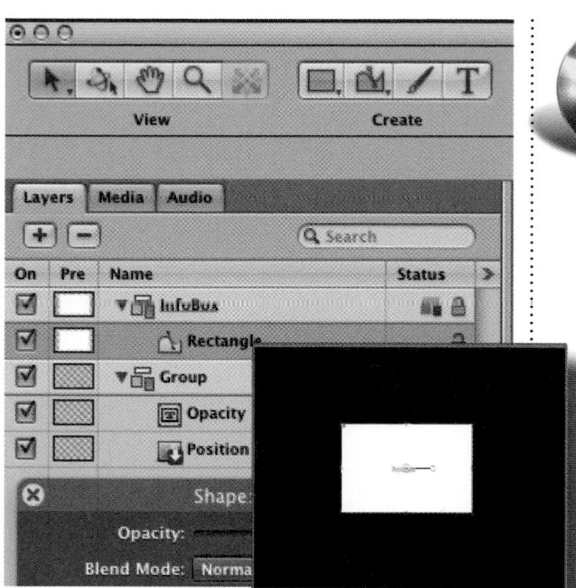

3 Add a new group. Name it **InfoBox**. Press R to activate the **Rectangle** tool. Click in the center of the screen and holding the ⌥ key, draw out a medium-sized box that will hold your information.

5 Press T to activate the Text tool, and click just inside the upper left corner of the rectangle. Then, still holding down the mouse button, draw a text box to fill the rectangle.

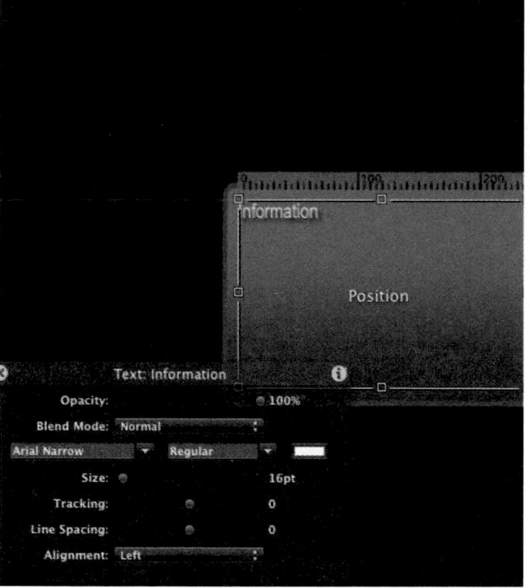

6 Set the **Font, Size, and Style (drop shadow?)** as you see fit. Type the word **Information** in it. Ensure that the layer is named **Information**. Now on to the **Links**.

continued...

Template Expansion (continued)

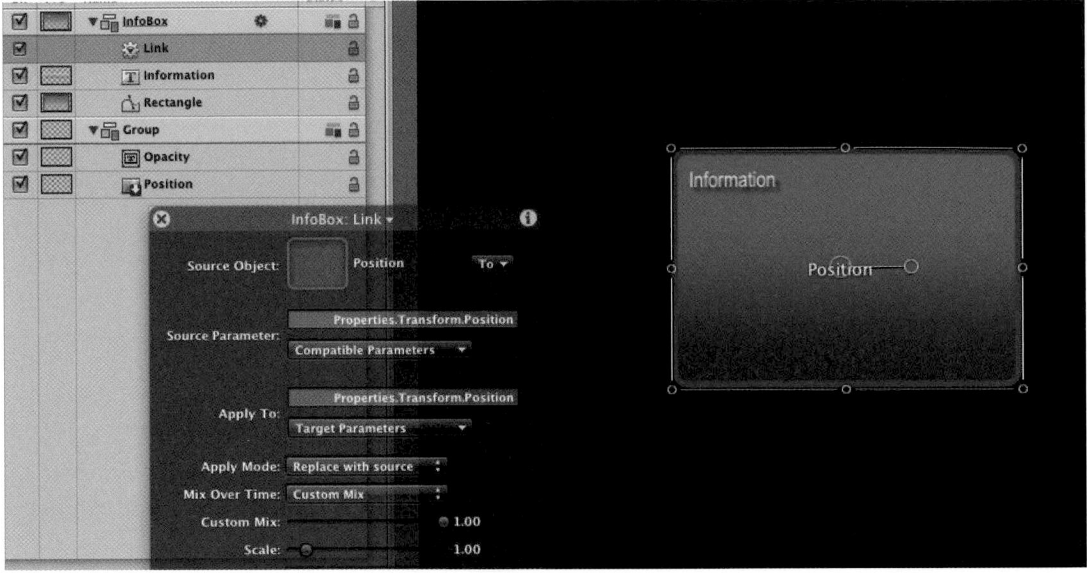

7 Select the **InfoBox** group. In its **Properties** tab, right/ctrl-click on the **Position**. Select **Link**. Drag the **Position drop zone** into the **Source Object** well. It should automatically select the **Position** drop zone's **Position** as the **Source Parameter**.

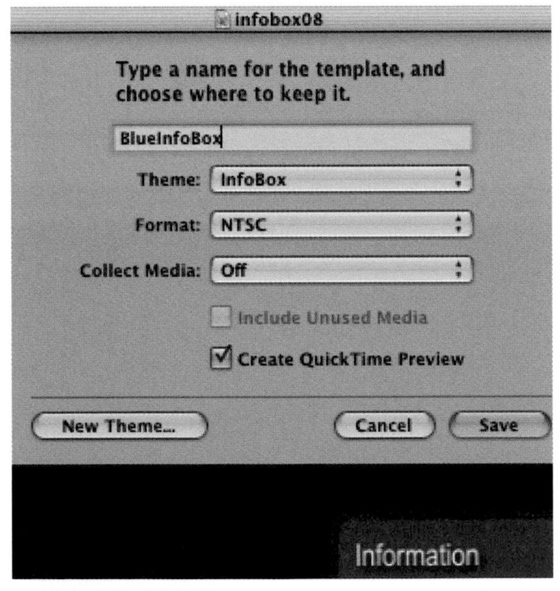

10 From the **File** menu, select **Save As Template**. Create a **New Theme** called **InfoBox**. Name the template **(perhaps -color-InfoBox).**

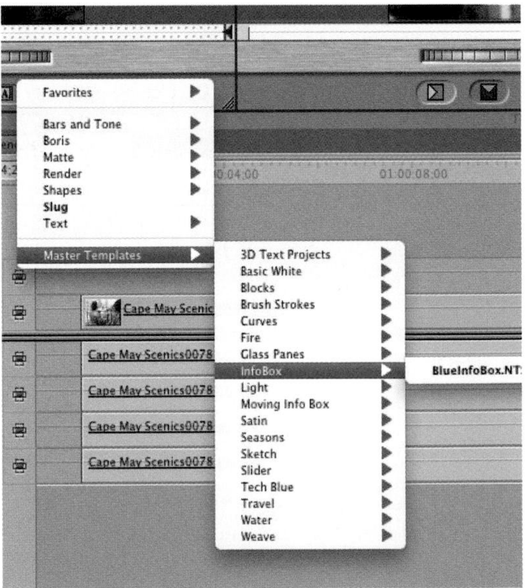

11 Quit Motion and go into Final Cut Pro. From the **Generator** menu (lower right-hand corner of your **Canvas**), select **Master Templates/InfoBox/BlueInfoBox** (or whatever you saved it as).

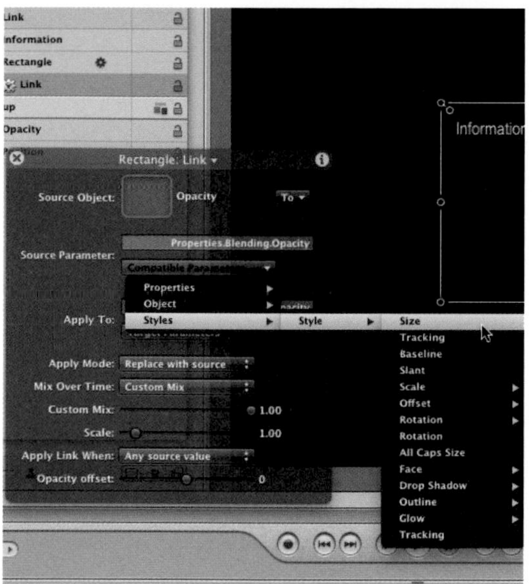

8 Now select the **Rectangle**. In the **Properties** tab, right/**ctrl**-click on **Opacity**. Select **Link**. Drag the **Opacity** type layer into the **Source Object** well. Under **Compatible Parameters**, select **Styles/Style/Size**.

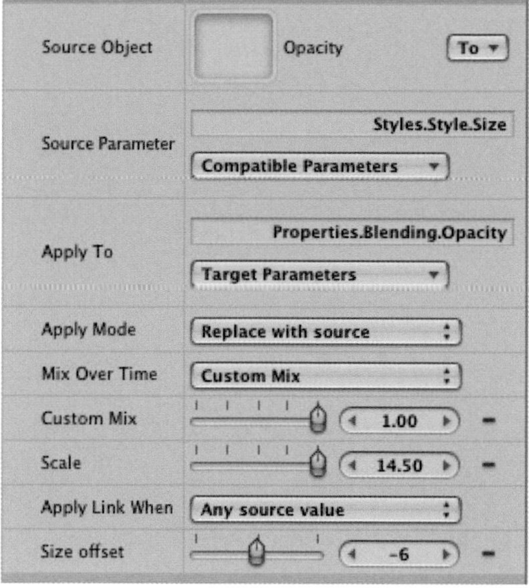

9 Set the **Scale** to **14.5** and the **Size offset** to **-6**. The **Scale** value was arrived at by experimentation and the **Size** offset because the smallest font size selectable is **6**.

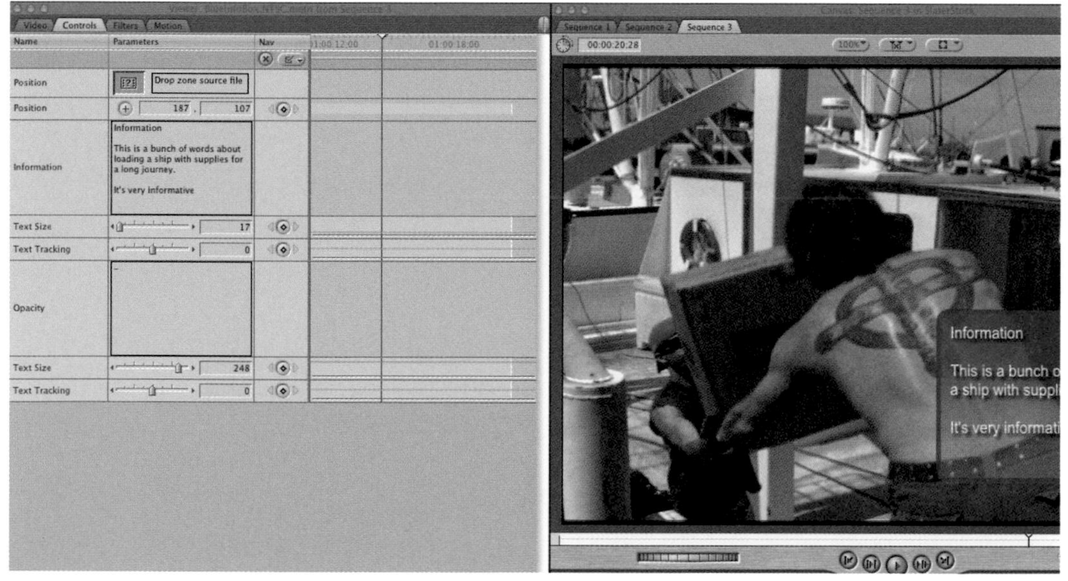

12 Cut it onto **V2** over your clip. Double-click on the template and go to the **Controls** tab in the **Viewer**. The **Position** dropbox can be used to place the **InfoBox** wherever you want onscreen. The **Text Size** of the **Opacity** text controls the opacity of the **InfoBox**. Turn it all the way down to **6** to make it transparent or up to **288** to make it opaque.

Index

D

E

F

G

H

N

O

P

S

T